Ascending *the* Mountain *of the* Lord

Ascending the Mountain of the Lord

Temple, Praise, and Worship
in the Old Testament

*edited by David R. Seely,
Jeffrey R. Chadwick,
and Matthew J. Grey*

THE 42ND ANNUAL
BRIGHAM YOUNG UNIVERSITY
SIDNEY B. SPERRY SYMPOSIUM

The Sperry Symposium is sponsored annually by Brigham Young University and the Church Educational System in honor of Sidney B. Sperry. In the course of his forty-five-year career as a religious educator, Dr. Sperry earned a reputation for outstanding teaching and scholarship. The symposium seeks to perpetuate his memory by fostering continuing research on gospel topics.

Copublished by the Religious Studies Center, Brigham Young University, Provo, Utah, and Deseret Book Company, Salt Lake City, Utah.

© 2013 Brigham Young University
All rights reserved.

Any uses of this material beyond those allowed by the exemptions in U.S. copyright law, such as section 107, "Fair Use," and section 108, "Library Copying," require the written permission of the publisher, Religious Studies Center, 167 HGB, Brigham Young University, Provo, Utah 84602. The views expressed herein are the responsibility of the authors and do not necessarily represent the position of Brigham Young University or the Religious Studies Center.

DESERET BOOK is a registered trademark of Deseret Book Company.

Visit us at DeseretBook.com

Library of Congress Cataloging-in-Publication Data
Sperry Symposium (42nd : 2013 : Brigham Young University), author.
    Ascending the mountain of the Lord : temple, praise, and worship in the Old Testament / David R. Seely, Jeffrey R. Chadwick, and Matthew J. Grey, editors.
        pages cm
    Includes bibliographical references and index.
    ISBN 978-1-60907-581-1 (hardbound : alk. paper) 1. Bible. Old Testament—Congresses. 2. Temples—Congresses. 3. Temple work (Mormon Church)—Congresses. 4. The Church of Jesus Christ of Latter-day Saints—Doctrines. I. Seely, David Rolph, editor of compilation. II. Chadwick, Jeffrey R., editor of compilation. III. Grey, Matthew J., editor of compilation. IV. Title.
    BX8628.S72 2013
    221.6—dc23   2013023292

Printed in the United States of America
Publishers Printing, Salt Lake City, UT
10 9 8 7 6 5 4 3 2

Contents

Preface... ix

1. The Old Testament and Easter
   Kent P. Jackson 1

Sacred Space, Ritual, and the Old Testament Temple

2. "That I May Dwell among Them": Liminality and Ritual in the Tabernacle
   Daniel L. Belnap 12

3. The Garden of Eden, the Ancient Temple, and Receiving a New Name
   Alex Douglas 36

4. The Tree of Knowledge as the Veil of the Sanctuary
   Jeffrey M. Bradshaw 49

5. "Come Near unto Me": Guarded Space and Its Mediators in the Jerusalem Temple
   Avram R. Shannon 66

6. Clothed in Holy Garments: Apparel of the Temple Officiants of Ancient Israel
   Alonzo L. Gaskill 85

7. Gestures of Praise: Lifting and Spreading the Hands in Biblical Prayer
   David M. Calabro 105

8. Worship: Bowing Down and Serving the Lord
   Jennifer C. Lane 122

9. "I Will Bless the Lord at All Times": Blessing God in the Old Testament
   Dana M. Pike 136

10. The Context of Temple Worship: Early Ancient Egyptian Rites
    John S. Thompson 156

11. The Rejection and Rehabilitation of Worship in the Old Testament
    Jared M. Halverson 184

12. Approaching Holiness: Sacred Space in Ezekiel's Temple Vision
    Jacob Rennaker 202

Sacred Encounters in the Old Testament

13. Theophany on Sinai
    Amy B. Hardison 218

14. Darkness, Light, and the Lord: Elements of Israelite Theophanies
    Kerry Muhlestein 232

15. "The Lord . . . Bringeth Low, and Lifteth Up": Hannah, Eli, and the Temple
    Julie M. Smith 255

Psalms and Praise in the Old Testament

16. Seeing God in His Temple: A Significant Theme in Israel's Psalms
    Andrew C. Skinner 270

17. Old Testament Psalms in the Book of Mormon
    John Hilton III 291

18. Parallels between Psalms 25–31 and the Psalm of Nephi
    Kenneth L. Alford and D. Bryce Baker 312

19. The Psalms Sung: The Power of Music in Sacred Worship
    Shon D. Hopkin and J. Arden Hopkin 329

20. "Give Me Right Word, O Lord": The JST Changes in the Psalms
   David A. LeFevre 349

The Old Testament Temple and the Latter Days

21. The Great Jerusalem Temple Prophecy: Latter-day Context and Likening unto Us
   Jeffrey R. Chadwick 367
22. What Old Testament Temples Can Teach Us about Our Own Temple Activity
   Richard O. Cowan 384

Index 403

Preface

"Let them make me a sanctuary; that I may dwell among them" (Exodus 25:8). With this statement, the Lord defined for ancient Israel the primary meaning of the tabernacle and later the temple. The presence of God in their midst at the temple provided a focal point for Israelite worship and represented the link between heaven and earth. The temple was the center of priesthood service, sacrifice, and prayer. Three times a year, Israelite families made pilgrimage up to the temple in Jerusalem to ritually enter into the presence of the Lord and worship him there. A temple psalm illustrates this pilgrimage: "Who shall ascend into the hill of the Lord?" (Psalm 24:3). Based on this passage, the theme of the 2013 Sperry Symposium is "Ascending the Mountain of the Lord: Temple, Praise, and Worship in the Old Testament."

Likewise, in the Restoration the Lord commanded Joseph Smith and the Saints to build a temple: "And with iron, with copper, and with brass, and with zinc, and with all your precious things of the earth; and build a house to my name, for the Most High to dwell therein" (D&C 124:27). Just as in ancient times, the temple was a place for the Lord God of Israel to dwell in the midst of his covenant people.

From the beginning, Joseph Smith and the Latter-day Saints have understood latter-day temple worship as a continuation of the tradition of temple building and worship in the Old Testament. The plans of the temple were received by revelation just as in the Old Testament. Joseph Smith modeled the dedication of the Kirtland Temple (D&C 109) on Solomon's dedicatory prayer of the ancient Israelite temple (1 Kings 8), and the pulpits there combined the Aaronic Priesthood, known from the Old Testament with the newly restored Melchizedek Priesthood. The Nauvoo Temple bore the inscriptions "House of the Lord" and "Holiness to the Lord," which were associated with the ancient temple, and the early Utah temples, like the temple in Jerusalem, were oriented facing east.

Thus, from the Prophet Joseph Smith to the present, gospel scholars have sought to study the Old Testament and understand the temple with the hope that such study will enhance our modern appreciation and understanding of the temple. Scholars like James E. Talmage, Sidney B. Sperry, and especially Hugh Nibley produced studies of biblical temples. This year's Sperry Symposium is a continuation of Latter-day Saint scholars studying the Old Testament Temple.

Modern Latter-day Saints studying the accounts of the Old Testament temples often find similarities with ancient temples that resonate with their own temple experiences, yet often biblical accounts of the Old Testament temple and temple worship seem strange and incomprehensible. Historians remind us that there are significant differences between the present and the past: that "the past is a foreign country, they do things differently there."[1] To properly understand the Old Testament temple, it must be studied in its own historical, cultural, and spiritual context. The study of biblical temples has been enhanced in our day by an added understanding of the biblical text, from a burgeoning corpus of archaeological data about ancient sacred places and worship, and from a growing body of cross-cultural studies. Thus the Latter-day Saint scholars in the 2013 Sperry Symposium bring to the biblical text their training and expertise to explore and elucidate the biblical temple and temple worship in its ancient setting.

This year's Sperry Symposium theme attempts to encompass the various areas of temple study. This volume begins with the keynote address by Professor Kent P. Jackson on three messianic events prophesied in the Old Testament, and the papers thereafter are organized topically for the readers' convenience. The first section contains papers about sacred space and ritual in the tabernacle, Solomon's Temple, and Ezekiel's vision of a future temple. These studies include examinations of sacred space and ritual, the Garden of Eden and the temple, holy garments, gestures of praise, worship, blessing, Egyptian temple sacrifice, and the sacred space in Ezekiel's temple. The second section contains studies on theophany in the scriptures: occasions when God reveals himself to humans—including God's appearance at

Sinai and Hannah's encounter with the Lord at Shiloh. The third section includes studies on the Psalms related to ancient Israelite temple worship, comparisons between biblical and Book of Mormon psalms, and a review of the JST changes in the Psalms. Finally, the last section containing two studies dealing with the Old Testament Temple and the Restoration.

Many have given of their time and energy in the conception, organization and presentation of the Sperry Symposium. As the Sperry Committee for 2013, we first express our gratitude to the authors and presenters of the symposium who have brought intellect, energy, and the Spirit to these fine studies. Next we thank the reviewers who carefully read the manuscripts and offered valuable suggestions to the authors. We would also like to thank the editors and designers at Brigham Young University's Religious Studies Center and at Deseret Book Company who refined and designed this volume. And finally, we thank Patty Smith and her assistants. Patty brings a wealth of experience to the task of organizing the annual Sperry Symposium. She has worked countless hours throughout this year for this volume—and she has already started on the Sperry Symposium for next year!

David Rolph Seely
Jeffrey R. Chadwick
Matthew J. Grey
Patty A. Smith

Sperry Symposium Committee

Note

1. This is a quote from L. P. Hartley in his novel *The Go-Between*, and the title of an important book studying this phenomenon: *The Past Is a Foreign Country*, by David Lowenthal (Cambridge University Press, 1985), which explores how the present and the past share similarities and differences.

1

The Old Testament and Easter

Kent P. Jackson

This is not an academic paper; it is more like a homily. We normally don't use the word *homily* in Latter-day Saint circles, but we actually do homilize frequently. A homily is a sermon, one that is often based on, or follows, the reading of a scriptural text. This sermon meets that definition. Some homilies are associated with special events in the Christian calendar, as is this one. And many, like this, have been the means of expressing thanks and joy for the goodness of God, in keeping with our themes of temple, praise, and worship. My homily is titled "The Old Testament and Easter." It is based on the truth that Jesus is Jehovah, the God of the Old Testament, and that "all things which have been given of God from the beginning of the world, unto man, are the typifying of him" (2 Nephi 11:4). I will focus on three Easter events: Palm Sunday, Jesus' suffering in Gethsemane, and Jesus' Resurrection. In important ways, all three are Old Testament events, although they are recorded in the New Testament. If you do not know the connection between Easter and the Old Testament, this homily is for you.

Kent P. Jackson is a professor of ancient scripture at Brigham Young University.

Triumphal Entry

Our first Old Testament event in the New Testament is the Triumphal Entry, perhaps the New Testament's ultimate example of praise and worship.

Every spring on the Sunday before Easter, Christians around the world commemorate Jesus' Triumphal Entry into Jerusalem that is recounted in the Gospels of Matthew, Mark, Luke, and John. The day is called Palm Sunday, and it begins the Holy Week that culminates in the celebration of Jesus' Resurrection. In Jerusalem, this commemoration takes on special meaning, because a procession follows a route very close to that followed by Jesus in the original event. On Palm Sunday in the Latin (Western European) calendar, pilgrims from around the world join local Arab Catholics in a service at the little church at Bethphage that marks the beginning of Jesus' entry into Jerusalem on that day. Crusaders in the twelfth century identified what they believed was the very rock from which Jesus mounted the young donkey; it is still on display in the church today.

To begin the annual commemoration, bishops, priests, and believers meet in the courtyard behind the church for a joyful remembrance of Jesus' saving work. The Latin Patriarch of Jerusalem, the Catholic Church's highest authority in the Holy Land, pronounces a blessing on the annual event. Palestinian Catholic scout troops carrying banners lead the way of the procession. Following them are thousands of worshippers holding palm branches, joyously re-creating Jesus' entrance into the Holy City. They walk from east to west—up over the Mount of Olives, down the Qidron Valley, past the traditional location of the Garden of Gethsemane, up the other side of the Qidron, through St. Stephen's Gate, into Jerusalem's Old City, and into the nine-hundred-year-old St. Anne's Church, where in joyous ceremony the Palm Sunday celebration is concluded.

The biblical story thus commemorated gives us every reason to rejoice. It is one of the rare events in Jesus' ministry that is recounted in all four of the Gospels, showing its importance.

In Luke, we read that as Jesus ascended the Mount of Olives from Jericho on his final journey to Jerusalem, approaching Bethany and Bethphage, he sent two disciples ahead to procure a young donkey on which he could ride. They brought it to Jesus, "cast their garments upon the colt, and they set Jesus thereon. And as he went, they spread their clothes in the way. And when he was come nigh, even now at the descent of the mount of Olives, the whole multitude of the disciples began to rejoice and praise God with a loud voice for all the mighty works that they had seen; saying, Blessed be the King that cometh in the name of the Lord: peace in heaven, and glory in the highest" (Luke 19:35–38).

Luke does not include the information that Mark provides that people "spread their garments in the way: and others cut down branches off the trees, and [spread them out] in the way" (Mark 11:8). They did this to create for Jesus a carpeted path, signifying great honor and reverence. Matthew tells us that the people shouted, "Hosanna to the Son of David: Blessed is he that cometh in the name of the Lord; Hosanna in the highest" (Matthew 21:9). John adds, "Blessed is the King of Israel that cometh in the name of the Lord" (John 12:13).

"Hosanna," "King," "Son of David," "King of Israel, that cometh in the name of the Lord"—this language is carefully chosen and very meaningful. It is true that the people in the multitude knew they were not welcoming just any Galilean rabbi to Jerusalem. But there is much more than that to the words they chose. The texts of all four Gospels show that the people in the crowd, and the Gospel writers themselves, knew they were experiencing a *biblical event*—an Old Testament event.

How do we know this? All of the words and phrases spoken by the multitude in response to Jesus' presence come from the Old Testament. *King*, *Son of David*, and *King of Israel* are obvious allusions to Israel's kingship in the Old Testament, established with David and to be continued through his descendants (see 2 Chronicles 13:5; 21:7; Psalm 89:3–4). Titles like these were not chosen lightly by Jews in Jesus' time but were reserved to identify messianic hopes. It was not a new kingdom that Jews desired but the restoration of that of the Old Testament, and the people recognized it in the person of Jesus of Nazareth. His coming "in the name of the Lord" highlights the multitude's level of praise and worship. The Psalms tie praise and worship to God's name: "O Lord our Lord, how excellent is thy name in all the earth!" (Psalms 8:9); "All nations whom thou hast made shall come and worship before thee, O Lord; and shall glorify thy name" (Psalm 86:9); "I will praise thee, O Lord my God, with all my heart: and I will glorify thy name for evermore" (Psalm 86:12).

To strengthen the connection with the Old Testament, Matthew and John saw in the Palm Sunday event the fulfillment of an ancient prophecy. "All this was done," Matthew reports, "that it might be fulfilled which was spoken by the prophet" (Matthew 21:4). He then quotes Zechariah 9:9 (see Matthew 21:5), as does John (see John 12:15), which is rendered as follows in the King James translation: "Rejoice greatly, O daughter of Zion; shout, O daughter of Jerusalem: behold, thy King cometh unto thee: he is just, and having salvation; lowly, and riding upon an ass, and upon a colt the foal of an ass."

The setting in Zechariah's prophecy is clearly millennial. With images familiar from other Old Testament prophecies, it points to a day in which the Lord will establish peace throughout the earth. Zechariah tells us that God will destroy the military armaments of men—characterized by *chariot*, *horse*, and *battle bow*. He will rule over all the world, and in that day, those who are in prison will be freed through the blood of the covenant (see Zechariah 9:11). The fulfillment of the prophecy will thus be in a context associated with Jesus' Second Coming, not his First.

So how is the Triumphal Entry a fulfillment of a millennial prophecy? When the Savior entered Jerusalem, he rode over the Mount of Olives and into the city in careful reflection of the events foretold in the prophecy. It is obvious from the record that all things transpired as they were intended as a means of identifying his actions with the foretold events of the distant future. The purpose of the Triumphal Entry was to proclaim who Jesus was, to identify the man Jesus of Nazareth with the holy Messiah who would come at the end of time. Thus his earthly life and ministry were themselves both prophecies and signs of his millennial reign. He rode a donkey rather than a horse (as we might expect) because in biblical times, a horse was primarily military equipment, and he was coming as the Prince of Peace. Matthew knew the connection with the prophecy when he wrote his account, and John tells us that it was only after Jesus' ascension—after the Apostles had received the Holy Ghost—that they understood fully what had happened (see John 12:16).

In the Palm Sunday event, the connection between the Old Testament and Easter starts to become clear. Jehovah, the God of ancient Israel, would triumph over Israel's foes and reign over all the world as King of Kings. Jesus' messianic triumph over death and sin would show him to be not only Israel's promised Messiah but also Israel's God.

Gethsemane

Our next Old Testament event recorded in the New Testament is Jesus' experience in the Garden of Gethsemane.

Each year on the night of Holy Thursday in the Latin calendar, three days before Easter Sunday, a most moving service takes place in Jerusalem's Roman Catholic Basilica of the Agony. Sometimes called the Church of All Nations, this twentieth-century church stands on the location of earlier churches built by the Byzantines and later the Crusaders. Near the base of the Mount of Olives and opposite the Holy City, the place has been revered from early Christian times to the present because it is considered to be where Gethsemane was located in the days of Jesus.

The annual service takes place late in the evening, well after dark, to reproduce the environment of the night Jesus spent there with his disciples before his arrest and crucifixion. Even in daytime, the church represents night, its windows in darkened glass and its ceiling in dark blue studded with stars. Beneath and in front of the altar, an extensive slab of bedrock is believed to be where Jesus "fell on his face, and prayed, saying, O my Father, if it be possible, let this cup pass from me: nevertheless not as I will, but as thou wilt" (Matthew 26:39). Those words capture much of the mood of the Holy Thursday service that commemorates Jesus' last earthly night.

The service includes singing by a choir, singing by the congregation, and spoken parts—prayers and scripture readings—in Latin, Arabic, English, Spanish, German, French, Italian, Hebrew, and Polish. Among the readings are the accounts from the Synoptic Gospels that tell of Jesus' experience in Gethsemane. Following the service, a candlelight procession takes the worshippers across the Qidron Valley and up to the west, ending at the Church of St. Peter in Gallicantu, which commemorates Caiaphas's palace to which Jesus was taken after his arrest in Gethsemane.

Matthew, Mark, and Luke give accounts of Jesus' experience in the garden. Mark relates the events in their simplest form:

> And they came to a place which was named Gethsemane: and he saith to his disciples, Sit ye here, while I shall pray.
>
> And he taketh with him Peter and James and John, and began to be sore amazed, and to be very heavy;
>
> And saith unto them, My soul is exceeding sorrowful unto death: tarry ye here, and watch.
>
> And he went forward a little, and fell on the ground, and prayed that, if it were possible, the hour might pass from him.

And he said, Abba, Father, all things are possible unto thee; take away this cup from me: nevertheless not what I will, but what thou wilt. (Mark 14:32–36)

Jesus was alone through much of the ordeal because his disciples slept. Only Luke adds that "there appeared an angel unto him from heaven, strengthening him" (Luke 22:43). Matthew's description that Jesus "fell on his face" (Matthew 26:39) seems to reflect the essence of Christ's suffering, but only Luke tells us that "being in an agony he prayed more earnestly: and his sweat was as it were great drops of blood falling down to the ground" (Luke 22:44). Likely, none of the accounts can come close to describing what really happened that night, and John's silence on the whole experience continues to puzzle thoughtful readers.

Was this an Old Testament event? The Gospel writers thought so. Each account includes references to events of that night fulfilling Old Testament prophecy. Matthew and Mark record Jesus quoting a passage to say that the disciples would abandon him and flee (see Zechariah 13:7; Matthew 26:31; Mark 14:27). In Luke, Jesus states, "For I say unto you, that this that is written must yet be accomplished in me" (Luke 22:37), then quoting Isaiah 53:12. Matthew was more explicit that the events of the evening were in fulfillment of prophecy. Were things not to proceed as intended, "how then shall the scriptures be fulfilled . . . ?" (Matthew 26:54). In the end, "all this was done, that the scriptures of the prophets might be fulfilled" (Matthew 26:56).

Light of Life

Our final Old Testament event written in the New Testament is the Resurrection of Jesus Christ, characterized by the light of new life that he brings. Jesus said, "I am the true light that lighteth every man that cometh into the world." He is "the light and the Redeemer of the world; the Spirit of truth, who came into the world, . . . and in him was the life of men and the light of men" (D&C 93:2, 9).

Christians of many persuasions use light in their worship services. Often this is in the form of candles, whose flames can represent the light of Christ. Following the practice of lighting oil lamps in ancient Israel's temple, many Christians light candles with ascending flames representing prayers going up from the worshipper to heaven. Darkness represents the absence of divine presence, as light represents God's nearness.

Perhaps the most remarkable use of flame in Christian worship is found in the celebration of the Miracle of the Holy Fire in Jerusalem each year. On Holy Saturday in the Orthodox Christian calendar, the day before Orthodox Easter, worshippers gather in Jerusalem to participate in this extraordinary celebration of the Resurrection that has been going on for over a thousand years. The ritual is not found in Western—that is, Catholic and Protestant—churches. The celebration of the Holy Fire takes place only in Jerusalem, yet it is loved throughout all of Eastern Christianity and is even broadcast live in some Orthodox countries.

Thousands of worshippers flock to the Holy City on that day. Many are local Palestinian Christians, but pilgrims from Russia, Greece, and other Orthodox lands come to participate in this event. They enter Jerusalem's Church of the Resurrection (called by Catholics and Protestants the Church of the Holy Sepulcher) with a bundle of candles in hand. The bundles contain thirty-three thin candles, one for each year of the Savior's life. Thousands of worshippers fill the massive church, and many others line the surrounding streets of the Old City in all directions. All come with their candles unlit and approach the building in a spirit of praise and worship. This is one of the most glorious celebrations in their religious calendar.

Orthodox Christianity's highest authority in the Holy Land, the Greek Orthodox Patriarch of Jerusalem, presides over the ceremony. He is assisted by bishops of the Armenian and Syriac Orthodox Churches and others. In the church, the traditional site of Jesus' crucifixion, burial, and resurrection, the annual celebration renews the power and message of Jesus' life. Inside the church is a structure identified as the tomb of Jesus. It contains two rooms, the outer representing the place where angels announced the Resurrection, and the inner representing the Savior's burial place. The Patriarch enters alone into the tomb, his own bundle of candles unlit, as others wait in anticipation of his return. Soon fire is seen from within the structure, and the Patriarch emerges, holding his bundle of burning candles. The tradition is that the starting of the Holy Fire on his candles is a miracle unaided by matches or other incendiaries.

The bells of the great church start to peal as the Patriarch's lighted candles are seen. He extends his candles to those nearest him to ignite theirs. Those in turn are touched to others, and thus the flame spreads rapidly to the candles in the hands of all the worshippers within the church. From there, the flame spreads outside the building to thousands more along the streets, and within mere minutes of hearing the church bells sound, worshippers hundreds of meters from the church receive the flame from others ahead of them. Many take their lighted candles to their homes to keep the flame alive. The fire is even transported to other lands as the celebration continues abroad, and so the light that comes from the place of Jesus' triumph over darkness spreads all over the world.

In the Old Testament's praise and worship, God is associated strongly with light. He is its source and provides its sustaining power (see Genesis 1:3; Psalm 74:16). When the tabernacle was built, there was great emphasis on the means of illumination within it (see Exodus 25:31–37; 40:24–25; Numbers 8:1–4). We read in the Psalms, "The Lord is my light and my salvation" (Psalm 27:1). Worshippers pray, "Lord, lift thou up the light of thy countenance upon us" (Psalm 4:6); "For thou wilt light my candle: the Lord my God will enlighten my darkness" (Psalm 18:28); "For with thee is the fountain of life: in thy light shall we see light" (Psalm 36:9). We read that those who will be blessed will be those who walk "in the light of [God's] countenance" (Psalm 89:15).

The association of God with light also plays a role in prophecies of the future. Isaiah writes that "the light of Israel shall be for a fire, and his Holy One for a flame" (Isaiah 10:17); "Then shall thy light break forth as the morning" (Isaiah 58:8); "Arise, shine; for thy light is come, and the glory of the Lord is risen upon thee. For, behold, the darkness shall cover the earth, and gross darkness the people: but the Lord shall arise upon thee, and his glory shall be seen upon thee. And the Gentiles shall come to thy light, and kings to the brightness of thy rising" (Isaiah 60:1–3).

In Jesus' own words and in those of the Evangelists, the New Testament connects directly with our Savior these Old Testament images of God as Israel's light. Jesus was the light that "shineth in darkness; and the darkness comprehended it not." He is "the true Light, which lighteth every man that cometh into the world" (John 1:5, 9). The Savior himself taught, "I am the light of the world: he that followeth me shall not walk in darkness, but shall have the light of life" (John 8:12); "As long as I am in the world, I am the light of the world" (John 9:5); and "I am come a light into the world, that whosoever believeth on me should not abide in darkness" (John 12:46).

In making statements like these, Jesus was asserting his identity as Jehovah, God of the Old Testament.

The Easter Message of the Old Testament

In their narratives and letters, the writers of the New Testament sometimes made connections and comparisons with the Old Testament that seem to modern readers to discard the intent of the original authors. Some Old Testament passages cited in the New Testament do not seem to actually mean what the New Testament writers took them to mean. I do not know if Matthew, to mention one author, believed that all the Old Testament passages he related to Jesus' life truly referred to Jesus when the Old Testament authors wrote them. But his use of those passages and his application of them to Jesus shows that he understood well a fundamental principle of the Bible: Jesus' life, suffering, death, and Resurrection are the very message of the Old Testament. How could it be otherwise, for Jesus' life, suffering, death, and Resurrection are at the heart of all truth.

Believers in New Testament times had the same Old Testament text that we have today. Through images, types, and shadows, it teaches us fundamental truth, but few of its passages are overtly centered on Jesus Christ. One that certainly qualifies is Isaiah's Suffering Servant prophecy (Isaiah 53), which is very hard to explain as anything but a prophecy of Jesus. When the disciple Philip encountered a man from Ethiopia reading from that text, Philip asked, "Understandest thou what thou readest? And he said, How can I, except some man should guide me? . . . The place of the scripture which he read was this, He was led as a sheep to the slaughter; and like a lamb dumb before his shearer, so opened he not his mouth." The Ethiopian asked, "Of whom speaketh the prophet this? of himself, or of some other man? Then Philip opened his mouth, and began at the same scripture, and preached unto him Jesus" (Acts 8:30–32, 34–35). Abinadi read the same Isaiah text to hostile listeners who could not see Jesus in the Old Testament. After reading it, he concluded, "God himself shall come down among the children of men, and shall redeem his people" (Mosiah 15:1).

After his Resurrection, Jesus met two disciples on the road to Emmaus. They were troubled over the recent events of Jesus' death and rumored Resurrection. Jesus said to them, "O fools, and slow of heart to believe all that the prophets have spoken: ought not Christ to have suffered these things, and to enter into his glory? And beginning at Moses and all the prophets, he expounded unto them in all the scriptures the things concerning himself. . . . And they said one to another, Did not our heart burn within us, while he talked with us by the way, and while he opened to us the scriptures?" (Luke 24:25–27, 32). Clearly, Jesus was able to open the Old Testament to see in it, and teach from it, truths that were not visible to ancient readers and remain not visible to modern readers unaided by his revelation.

The message of Christ is indeed not absent from the Old Testament. In this great book of scripture, faith and repentance are fundamental to the person and character of Israel's God. His capacity to save is one of the hallmarks of his personality, and faith in his ability to deliver his people from every enemy teaches faith in his capacity to save from the greatest enemies—sin and death. Jehovah's longsuffering and willingness to receive repentant sinners characterizes his nature. Repentance was possible because his arm of mercy was ever extended to those who forsook their sins and came to him. Thus sincere Israelite worshippers who knew nothing of Jesus Christ understood both faith and repentance and saw them as the foundations of their relationship with a merciful God—even if they did not know the full details of their salvation.

Israel's temple worship taught the Christian gospel, because vicarious atonement and subsequent forgiveness are at the very heart of the temple sacrifices. Faithful ancient Israelites knew that they could not save themselves from sin but needed to rely on the intervention of God to deliver them spiritually. Jesus, his Book of Mormon prophets, and the writers of the New Testament revealed that Christ himself was to be God's sacrificial lamb, but the fundamental principles had already been made known in the Mosaic law. And Israel's Messiah was Jehovah himself, something not always clear in the Old Testament but understood by Jesus' followers in the Book of Mormon and the New Testament. Honorable people who looked forward to a saving Messiah were looking forward to the coming of Jesus, and many recognized him when he came.

By teaching Jehovah's love and mercy and bearing testimony of him, all of the Old Testament prophets were testifying of Christ, as the Book of Mormon says they did (see Jacob 4:4–5; 7:11). Those who could see with an eye of faith saw Jehovah as the center of all their righteous desires and devotions. Those who were taught, as was the man from Ethiopia, or whose eyes were opened, like the disciples on the road to Emmaus, were enabled then to perceive rightly that Jesus of Nazareth was their Messiah and God's unblemished offering in their behalf. One such disciple, John the Baptist, was able to testify when he saw Jesus, "Behold the Lamb of God, which taketh away the sin of the world" (John 1:29).

Christian writers from Paul to the present have seen in the message of Easter the purpose and fulfillment of the Law and the Prophets. Easter, indeed, is the culmination of the Old Testament, the reason for its covenant, the message of its Mosaic law, the objective of its temple, and the fulfillment of all the hopes and aspirations of its worshippers. Israel's temple, praise, and worship had their ultimate aim in the Easter mission of the Old Testament's saving Messiah, Jesus Christ.

2

"That I May Dwell among Them": Liminality and Ritual in the Tabernacle

Daniel L. Belnap

For many, it can be difficult to discern the spiritual value of the rituals described within the Old Testament. This is certainly understandable, since the culture that performed these acts is separated from us by some three thousand years. Yet throughout the scriptures we are told that the Lord speaks to his children in their language and in their tongue, "that they might come to understanding" (D&C 1:24). Though the symbolism and imagery may be unfamiliar to us, we can trust that the symbols used and the rites performed by ancient Israel were meant to teach us familiar gospel principles and that Israel worshipped in Old Testament times as sincerely as we do today.

The term *worship* stems from the English word *worth*, suggesting that worship is the process by which we recognize the worth of God and in return receive revelation concerning God's appreciation of our worth.[1] Just as we gain an understanding of these truths through our worship at the temple, so too ancient Israel understood the true natures of man and God, and the manner of the relationship they could have with God by their experiences in the temple and tabernacle. Though sometimes difficult to perceive, these truths lay at the heart

---

Daniel L. Belnap is an assistant professor of ancient scripture at Brigham Young University.

of the tabernacle and the rites performed therein, and when we recognize that, it increases our own appreciation of their sublime nature.

"And I Shall Dwell among My People"

Like the temple ordinances today, the significance of ancient Israel's religious practice was enhanced by the symbolism incorporated into the spaces of their worship. For ancient Israel, this space was primarily the temple or the tabernacle.[2] As Latter-day Saints, we often consider the tabernacle and the temple as one and the same, differentiating them only by the mobility of the former. While it is true that the rites performed in both sacred edifices were apparently the same,[3] there were distinctive differences in the places themselves that may have taught Israel unique lessons as to whom and what they worshipped. Perhaps the first noticeable difference, besides the permanence of the temple versus the mobility of the tabernacle, was the scale, both in terms of architecture and furniture. The temple was noted for its grandiose, majestic nature. The building itself was approximately forty-five feet high.[4] Many of the temple items and furniture, such as the brazen sea, the altar, and the movable stands, were also striking because of their oversized dimensions.[5] Everything about the temple was oversized, making it difficult to imagine how the objects associated with it were used. A central purpose of the magnitude, however, seems to have been to serve as a reminder of God's might and grandeur as creator and sustainer of the universe.[6] Certainly, recognition of God's supernal nature was a necessary part of an Israelite's spiritual understanding. The scriptures are filled with exhortations to remember the true splendor of God in order to instill a requisite humility. President Brigham Young reiterated the significance of understanding this splendor when describing how he would pray until he recognized the exact, awe-inspiring nature of the being who received his prayer.[7]

Yet if that was the purpose behind the sacred structures, then how does that explain the much more modest scale of the tabernacle? Unlike the temple, those entering the tabernacle did not encounter a roof that soared above them forty feet, but found instead a ceiling that stood only fifteen feet high and items and furniture that were much more life-sized.[8] The tabernacle was a much smaller, more intimate edifice, and this aspect would have highlighted a different dynamic in the relationship between the worshipper and God—a dynamic that emphasized the similarities between God and man. This is not to say that the tabernacle lacked cosmic symbolism. Like the temple, the tabernacle represented the divine realm, and in fact it appears that the writers of Exodus deliberately invoked the Creation to describe the building of the tabernacle.[9] But where the temple accentuated the majestic and awesome nature of God, the tabernacle's more intimate setting accentuated the liminality of these sacred spaces; they were truly places where both God and man could come and interact.

The function of the tabernacle appears to be straightforward. In Exodus 25:8, God simply states, "And let them make me a sanctuary [literally, "a holiness"]; that I may dwell among them." Though the English translation suggests that the edifice was meant to be the actual dwelling place of God, the Hebrew term *shakan*, translated as "dwell," implies a nonpermanent residence.[10] In other words, while the verb can signify a long stay, it does not necessarily suggest an indefinite stay. In light of this, it may be more accurate to view the tabernacle as more of a meeting place rather than as a permanent dwelling place of God.[11]

Recognizing the tabernacle as a meeting place suggests that the purpose of the tabernacle was to facilitate the interaction between the visiting parties, God and man, rather than as the permanent home of God. In this, then, the tabernacle space represented a place that was neither in the mortal world nor in the divine world but was specifically designed for interaction by parties from both worlds. Such spaces, neither fully in one state nor another but straddling both, are known as liminalities, or liminal spaces, so named from the Latin *limen*, meaning "doorway" or "threshold."[12] Significantly, these spaces are not meant to be permanent but are merely transition points where individuals can interact in ways not possible in "regular" space because of physical or social limitations, or prepare one to move from one social state to another.[13] Though the term *liminality* may be new to readers, if they are temple-attending Latter-day Saints they are quite familiar with the concept. When a Saint speaks of attending the temple as leaving the world temporarily in order to commune with God, and reemerging stronger and more powerful than before, such language reflects the liminal nature of the temple, both in practice and in space.

Just as with today's temples, many aspects of the tabernacle, both functional and symbolic, highlighted its liminal nature, though not always in an obvious way. For instance, all of the entrances associated with the tabernacle, such as the gate, the entrance into the tabernacle proper, and the veil separating the Holy Place from the Holy of Holies, were distinguished from the surrounding cloth by their coloration, having been dyed in blue, scarlet, and purple. Any explicit meaning behind this selection of colors is unknown since the text gives no indication of their significance, but they clearly distinguished these spaces from other spaces in the tabernacle.[14] Besides the colors, these spaces also shared a similar function—to mark where one could enter and leave. This unique function (as opposed to other spaces) is the very definition of liminality. The color pattern set these spaces apart and highlighted their unique function. Blue, scarlet, and purple were also dominant in the clothing worn by the priest. The association of the priest with these colors suggests that the priest was a liminal figure, or one who moved between the different states and whose purpose was to facilitate such movement, which in fact, is exactly what the priest did.[15]

The same colors also appeared as part of the "roof" of the tabernacle, which actually surrounded the tabernacle. Made up of four layers of cloth, the innermost layer was fine linen colored in scarlet, blue, and purple and embroidered with gold filament in the image of cherubim (see Exodus 26:31). The presence of the same color scheme that was, as previously shown, associated with liminality, suggests that the rooms surrounded by this material were liminal spaces that differed from the "reality" that existed outside of the tent—spaces specifically dedicated to direct interaction between God and mortals.

Besides the color scheme, the types and functions of items found within the sanctuary may also have emphasized the liminal nature of the tabernacle proper. The sanctuary itself was divided into two rooms by the veil, of which the larger of the two possessed only three items: the menorah, the table of the bread of the presence, and the altar of incense, all three either made of pure gold or covered in gold (see Exodus 26:33–35);[16] and while all three may have had cosmic significance it is also noteworthy that each served a mundane, domestic function. Thus, while the menorah may have represented the cosmic tree, functionally its purpose was to provide light within the room like any other lamp.[17] Similarly, the table of the presence, so named for the bread that was placed on the table and replaced every Sabbath, was, functionally, simply a table with food on it. Even the incense altar appears to have had a domestic analogue, as both texts and archaeological evidence suggest that private households used incense.[18] Another thing these items have in common is their association with rites of hospitality.[19] The concept of hospitality had an important social and cultural function in the ancient world, but since hospitality dealt with the relationship between the host and the guest, the guest being by definition an impermanent member of the household, its association with the tabernacle specifically highlighted the temporary, liminal nature of the tabernacle.[20]

The implication of liminality continued as one moved beyond the Holy Place to the veil, which separated the Holy Place from the Holy of Holies. The veil was similar to the other cloth items, being made of fine linen embroidered with purple, scarlet, and blue thread. Yet, unlike the other cloth items associated with ingress and egress (the other "doors"), the veil also included images of cherubim similar to those on the innermost roof covering. Thus, when in the holy room, cherubim images could be seen on the ceiling and on the eastern "walls," the western walls incorporating the same colors but lacking the cherubim design, while the Holy of Holies was completely surrounded by the non-cherubim–embroidered cloth and its symbolism.

While we are not told specifically why the cherubim were to be incorporated into these demarcations of space, cherubim are found elsewhere in the Old Testament, and their functions within these other texts may provide insight into their presence in the tabernacle. Their first function is to guard selected space. In Genesis, following the exile of Adam and Eve, cherubim are placed before the tree of life which itself appears to be in the most easterly portion of the garden. Thus the presence of the cherubim demarcates the garden into at least two sections: the most easterly, which possesses the tree of the life, and the rest of the garden. In essence, the cherubim are acting like the veil in the temple, separating the holy garden from its Holy of Holies equivalent, the tree of life.[21] Yet their function is not only to keep things out, but to allow them in as well. Similarly, the veil was not a one-way entry—it marked both ingress and egress.

Another function associated with the cherubim is that of movement. First Samuel 4:4 is the first reference to speak of God as sitting between cherubim, a concept repeated a number of times in the Old Testament, culminating in the writings of Ezekiel, where the cherubim are depicted not only as beings that surround God but also as those that bear him from place to place.[22] Not only did the cherubim serve to mark the space in which one could interact with God, but their presence also signified that the space was not permanent, thus the embroidered cherubim images on the veil would have indicated that liminal nature of the veil.

The verb used to describe the function of the veil itself, *hibdil*, appears to be a specialized term used almost exclusively in the "priestly" literature to describe the separating or the ordering of the different elements of the creation: light from dark, upper waters from lower waters, day from night—which in turn reflected the creation of the social cosmos (the separation of man and woman, the separation of child from parent, the establishment of marriage, and the ability to discern or categorize between good and evil).[23] Each of these further advanced the cosmos, or the ordered state, from the chaotic state that existed prior.

The use of the verb suggests that the veil may have also represented the ongoing nature of the creation, as well as the distinction between mortal and divine spheres. Elsewhere in the scriptures, God's heavenly abode is described as a tent, with the "curtains stretched out still" suggesting that the cosmos was architecturally represented by the tabernacle (see Moses 7:30; also Psalm 104:2–3; Isaiah 40:22, 42:5; Jeremiah 10:12). Yet the irony of this "separation" is that as the cosmos was divided it became more and more possible for man and God to interact more fully. Thus the separation of the Holy Place and the Holy of Holies by the veil, a representation of the order and organization of the cosmos, also represents the coming together of the divine and mortal worlds.

The final element associated with liminality was the Holy of Holies itself. As in the Holy Place, the roof, which draped over the northern, southern, and western sides, was made of blue, scarlet, and purple cloth with cherubim embroidery, as was the eastern wall, or veil. Thus the Holy of Holies was completely surrounded by cloth marked with liminal symbolism, suggesting that the space within, the room itself, was wholly liminal space. In terms of furniture, the room possessed only the ark of the covenant, also known as the ark of the testimony, and the lid for the ark, or the mercy seat. The ark was a wooden box encased in gold, about two and a half feet in length and one and a half feet in both width and height. It contained the two tablets of stone upon which was written the law of God by God himself as well as a pot of manna.[24] The mercy seat consisted of two cherubim with wings that touched each other, thus creating an open-air enclosure on top of the ark.

As mentioned, one of the designations for the ark is the ark of the testimony. The Hebrew term translated as "testimony" in this case indicates the establishment of a relationship between two parties.[25] The two items placed in the ark emphasize this function in that they represent two items that God himself provided to facilitate the relationship between God and Israel. The tablets of stone contained the moral/ethical precepts by which Israel could be made holy and therefore enter into his presence, while the manna represented the means by which God interacted directly in the livelihood of Israel.

The presence of the manna and the stone tablets—representing God's contribution to the God-Israel relationship—coupled with the presence of the cherubim—representing the liminal nature of the space in the tabernacle—lead us to the supernal reason given as to why the Israelites should have a tabernacle: "that I may dwell among them." God's express desire to be in the midst of or "among" his people demonstrates a mortal-divine relationship not existing in other religions of the ancient Near East.[26] There, in the ultimate liminal space of the Holy of Holies, one confronted tangible symbols of God's effort and desire to be among his people. The entire tabernacle structure and attendant items culminated in the revelation that God himself desired interaction with them, while the emphasis on liminality highlighted the reality of mortal-divine relationships, which in turn elucidated the true worth of God and humans.

"To Make Atonement"

As important as the tabernacle symbolism is to our discussion on worship, we must still address the idea of worship as an action that one performs. For ancient Israel, worship involved the acts of sacrifice and initiation, rituals of the law of Moses. The instructions and descriptions of these rites make up sizeable portions of Exodus, Leviticus, and Numbers, and for many are difficult to follow and appreciate. More often than not, the practice of these rites is associated with the phrase "letter of the law," which refers to a state of worship where the enactment of these rites is emphasized, in contrast with the focus on intent (over action) that is present in the supposedly higher "spirit of the law." Yet, for Latter-day Saints, a significant part of the Restoration of the gospel was the reinstitution of rituals that emphasized the relationship of mortals and deity and the performance of which spoke directly to what we could accomplish here and become eternally. The significance of these rites to our worship and to our understanding cannot be overstated. And just as we recognize the value of our own rites, we can recognize that the rites described in Old Testament texts were of great value to the ancient Israelites as well.

Ritual is, at the core, a social event; one that seeks to include, maintain, or exclude an individual or individuals from a given community. When looked at from this perspective, the rituals established in the law of Moses either initiated individuals or items into the community of God and Israel, or reconciled and restored an individual to that relationship. Both functions stress the worth of God and humans; the worth of God in that these rituals teach us the value of God in their salvation, and the worth of mortals in that the performance of these rituals allows us to enter into the presence of God.

Our discussion of specific rituals will begin with those rites encompassing the second ritual function, reconciliation or restoration—the sacrificial offering system outlined in the first eight chapters of Leviticus. The first of the three offerings associated with reconciliation is the burnt offering, or the *olah* offering (derived from the Hebrew '*alah*, meaning "to ascend"); the Hebrew designation reflecting the nature by which this offering ascends into the divine realm, and the English reflecting that the entire animal or offering is burnt.

The instructions concerning the performance of the burnt offering in Leviticus 1 began with the requirements for the offering itself. The ideal offering was a male bovine, without blemish.[27] The offering had to be offered voluntarily, meaning the offerer willingly chose to be a part of the ritual process and was not forced to participate. That the offerer was a willing participant in the ritual process is significant and suggests that the efficacy of the rite was tied to the willingness of all participants.

Upon presentation at the tabernacle, the offerer placed a hand on the head of the animal, an act repeated in each ritual offering, at which point the reader was told: "and it shall be accepted for him to make atonement for him" (Leviticus 1:4). Some have suggested that the placing of the hand indicated that a substitution was to take place, the animal now representing the offerer; others believe that it simply indicated ownership.[28] The performance of this act recorded in Numbers 8:6–19 may give some insight into the act's significance.

This particular section of scripture is about the Levites who were to work in the tabernacle precincts. Though Aaron and his children came from the Levitical tribe, the selection of the tribe as a whole was meant to represent the firstborn of all the tribes:

> Thou shalt bring the Levites before the tabernacle of the congregation: and thou shalt gather the whole assembly of the children of Israel together:
> And thou shalt bring the Levites before the Lord: and the children of Israel shall put their hands upon the Levites:
> And Aaron shall offer the Levites before the Lord for an offering of the children of Israel, that they may execute the service of the Lord. . . .

> For they are wholly given unto me from among the children of Israel; instead of such as open every womb, even instead of the firstborn of all the children of Israel, have I taken them unto me.
>
> For all the firstborn of the children of Israel are mine, ...
>
> And I have taken the Levites for all the firstborn of the children of Israel.
>
> And I have given the Levites as a gift to Aaron and to his sons from among the children of Israel, to do the service of the children of Israel in the tabernacle of the congregation, and to make an atonement for the children of Israel: that there be no plague among the children of Israel, when the children of Israel come nigh unto the sanctuary. (Numbers 8:9–11, 16–19)

As the text makes clear, following the placement of Jacob's, or Israel's, hands on the heads of the Levites, this tribe was to "do the service of the children of Israel in the tabernacle ... and to make an atonement for the children of Israel: that there be no plague among the children of Israel," when Israel approached the sanctuary. Thus it would appear that the laying of hands on another was a tangible transfer of representation. In other words, the Levites now represented the firstborn of Israel, who were chosen initially to serve on the behalf of all Israel. The service they were to perform being "to make an atonement."

So what does it mean to make an atonement? The term *atonement* was first used in a theological sense by William Tyndale.[29] Literally meaning "at one with," the term was used to describe the reconciliation between God and humans. In the Old Testament, to make an atonement is the translation of the verb *kpr*, a term that is difficult to translate correctly. Noting the similarities between this verb and the Akkadian verb *kuppuru*, which means to cleanse by wiping off, many have suggested that the verb is expiatory in meaning.[30] This does appear to be the case when the term is associated with the sin offering, which is offered when offense or uncleanliness has been experienced. Yet "to make atonement" is also one of the purposes behind the burnt offering, which is not offered as a direct result of sin or wrongdoing. In connection with sin offerings, the Hebrew *kpr* term is either preceded or followed by the explicit mention that the sin of offense is forgiven. Thus two types of atonement appear to be associated with the sacrificial rituals: (1) the atonement that is associated with the forgiveness of sins, reflected in the sin offering, and (2) the <u>atonement enacted not for sin or wrongdoing at all, such as in the case of the burnt offering</u>.

One element that appears to have played a crucial role in the act of making atonement was the manipulation of blood; indeed, blood played a fundamental role throughout the sacrificial system. In Leviticus 17:10–14, we are told:

> And whatsoever man there be of the house of Israel, or of the strangers that sojourn among you, that eateth any manner of blood; I will even set my face against that soul that eateth blood, and will cut him off from among his people.
>
> For the life of the flesh is in the blood: and I have given it to you upon the altar to make an atonement for your souls: for it is the blood that maketh an atonement for the soul.
>
> Therefore I said unto the children of Israel, No soul of you shall eat blood, neither shall any stranger that sojourneth among you eat blood....
>
> For the life of all flesh is the blood thereof.[31]

As the verses above indicate, blood represented the concept of life—the dynamic element that made living things alive—and was, by virtue of that significance, a divine possession utilized by God to effect atonement. For example, in the burnt offering, following the placement of the hand, the animal's blood could be used to make an atonement. The animal was slaughtered and divided into sections, and some parts were immediately put on the altar (the head and the fat), while others were first washed. The blood was collected and splashed on the sides of the altar, presumably effecting atonement.

Blood also played an important role in the rite of the sin offering. As in the burnt offering, following the placement of the hand and the slaughter of the animal, the priest gathered the blood. But instead of splashing it against the sides of the altar, in the sin offering the priest took the blood and daubed it on certain items throughout the tabernacle precinct. When performing this rite on behalf of the whole Israelite congregation, the priest splashed the blood seven times before the veil separating the Holy Place from the inner Holy of Holies. The priest then took the blood and smeared it on the horns or corners of the altar of incense in the Holy Place that stood before the veil, pouring the remaining blood at the base of the altar of burnt offerings outside.

The placing of the hand on the forehead, similar to the placing of the hand on the Levites as recorded in Numbers 8, would suggest that the animal was not a substitute but represented the individual, and thus its blood could be used to affect what atonement was necessary in a positive manner for the participant. If we consider the holy anointing oil to be representative of God, then the pouring of the life-representing blood onto items already anointed by the anointing oil was suggestive of contact made between God and the mortal. Furthermore, as the blood of the representative interacted with the oil on the surface of this most holy altar, it too became holy; thus the individual represented became holy as well—able to interact with God himself.

The term *holy* is actually translated from two related Hebrew terms: *qodesh* and *qadosh*. Unlike Indo-European languages, Hebrew does not have vowel letters, but derivations of the root, with subsequent nuances to the general meaning of the term, are demonstrated through the use of prefixes, suffixes and vowel sounds. So even though *qodesh* and *qadosh* stem from the same root, *qdsh*, the different vowel sounds suggest nuances between the two.[32]

Of the two, *qodesh* is much more common, used 468 times in the Hebrew Bible. It is used to describe a number of things, such as the clothing of the priests, the animals offered for sacrifice, and the instruments in the tabernacle. The term *qadosh*, on the other hand, is only used 106 times, and the items considered *qadosh* are much more limited. Chief among them is God, the holy one (*ha-qadosh*). Certain locations where God may be present are also *qadosh*, though the sanctuary itself is *qodesh*. But second to God, *qadosh* is most commonly used in exhortations that man should become *qadosh* as God is *qadosh*.

Though both terms stem from the same root, for the most part there is no overlap in usage. Instead, those things that are considered *qadosh* are differentiated from those that are *qodesh* in that *qadosh* items possess a unique dynamic quality: the "ability to move things (or people) into, or at least toward, the realm of the divine."[33] It is for this reason that God is *qadosh*. As Moses clarifies elsewhere, God's primary responsibility is to "bring to pass the immortality and eternal life of man" (Moses 1:39), a process of moving individuals from a lesser state into the ultimate divine state. This dynamic quality lies at the heart of the term *qadosh* in the law of Moses; throughout Leviticus, precepts are established with the injunction that Israel be holy (*qadosh*), for, as the Lord says, "I the Lord your God am holy," or *qadosh*.[34] In following the command to become *qadosh*, individuals in Israel were expected to move others towards the divine state, like God himself did. The ordinances performed were not simply busy work given because the people were wicked, but were in fact meant to transform the people of Israel into "partakers of the divine nature."

As significant as the use of blood on the altar appears to have been in atonement rituals, in some cases, it was not essential. In Numbers 16:46–47, Aaron made atonement between God and Israel by burning incense, while in Numbers 25, the priest Phinehas made an atonement for the children of Israel by killing (not upon the altar) an Israelite man and a Midianitish woman who profaned the sanctuary. Similarly, in Numbers 31, following a conquest against the Midianites, the military leadership of Israel brought gold and other war booty to the tabernacle "to make an atonement for [their] souls before the Lord" (Numbers 31:50). Unlike in the rituals of animal sacrifices, blood played no role whatsoever in the atonement process of these narratives, yet atonement was still achieved. Moreover, the act that replaced the function of the blood was different in each of these instances suggesting that there were at least four recognized ways of enacting atonement: the offering of blood sacrifice upon the altar, the use of incense, the killing of those who profaned sacred space, and the presentation of gold.

What are we to make of these four disparate ways of enacting atonement? First, the acts presuppose an already existing relationship between Israel and God. In other words, these acts do not highlight the entering into of a relationship with God; instead their purpose was to reconcile or renew an already existing relationship. Second, as those that required an item coming into contact with the altar demonstrated, we see the primary purpose of atonement was to make one holy and therefore like God. Third, in all cases the atoning acts were performed by mortals to bring themselves into a state where they could interact with God and receive his beneficence. This last point cannot be stressed enough. From the biblical texts, it appears that atonement required the actions of two parties, God and mortal, in which the latter was responsible to create a situation that allowed God to engage with him or her. Thus, in the liminal space of the tabernacle, acts of atonement made it possible for human and God, each one willing and desirous to engage with the other, to in fact interact directly.[35]

It is not hard to see the Christological symbolism inherent within each of these sacrificial acts. The Book of Mormon makes it quite clear that recognizing

Christ's supernal act of atonement was an essential part of the rituals of the law of Moses. In his discourse to the priests, the prophet Abinadi declared that the purpose of the law and rituals were to facilitate Israel's remembrance of God and their duty to him: "Therefore there was a law given them, yea, a law of performances and of ordinances, a law which they were to observe strictly from day to day, to keep them in remembrance of God and their duty towards him" (Mosiah 13:30). Earlier, Nephi made clear that the law directed one towards Christ (2 Nephi 25:23–30). Nephi's father, Lehi, explained in particular the relationship between the atonement and the rituals of Moses, calling Christ's act a "sacrifice for sin," or in other words, a sin offering. Christ's sacrifice is certainly reflected in the sin offering, the explicit purpose of which is to bring on forgiveness through the individual's offering. Just as the blood of the sin offering covers certain items of the tabernacle, thereby reconciling to God the individual represented by the offering, Christ's blood covers us, reconciling us to his Father. Similarly, the burnt offering represents all that he offered in order to bring about reconciliation as well as what we are expected to offer for this reconciliation.[36]

But perhaps most importantly, Christ and the agency he expressed in performing the atoning sacrifice is an example to us that we too can have a direct relationship with the Father. Just as he offered up a sacrifice of a broken heart and a contrite spirit, so he has encouraged us to do the same, showing us that it is possible for us to achieve our ultimate goal of oneness with the Father.

Through their performance, Israel expressed their desire to be reconciled in their covenant relationship with God; a relationship that emphasized their divine nature and potential to become holy, just as God himself was; a relationship that is the very essence of worship.[37]

"For the Anointing of the Lord Is upon You"

As important as the atonement rites were to Israel's worship, there was another category of rites that may have been equally as important—those performed when making the relationships in the first place. Such was the purpose of the rite described in Exodus 24, the anointing of the tabernacle and the priests as described in Exodus 40 and Leviticus 8, and the reintroduction of the leper described in Leviticus 14. Like the rites of reconciliation, while each rite of induction or inclusion differed from one another at points, there does seem to have been a common element that defined these rites as part of their own classification, that element being the placement of blood, water, or oil on the individual being introduced or reintroduced into the society.

The first such ritual is described in Exodus 24 following Moses' reception of the law as written on the first sets of stone tablets. The occasion, as verse three suggests, is Israel's acceptance of the law: "And Moses came and told the people all the words of the Lord, and all the judgments: and all the people answered with one voice, and said, All the words which the Lord hath said will we do." According to the text, Moses then copied the law down onto another medium, rose up the next morning, built an altar, and erected twelve pillars representing the twelve tribes of Israel. Since priests had not been ordained yet, he had young men of Israel, perhaps firstborn youth, offer both burnt and peace offerings, both of which included the splashing of blood against the sides of the altar.

But unlike in later burnt and peace offerings, in this account only half of the blood was used against the sides of the altar. The other half was splashed on the people following the reading of the law and the people's declaration that they would obey the precepts within:

> And he [Moses] took the book of the covenant, and read in the audience of the people: and they said, All that the Lord hath said will we do, and be obedient.
>
> And Moses took the blood, and sprinkled it on the people, and said, Behold the blood of the covenant, which the Lord hath made with you concerning all these words. (Exodus 24:7–8)

In this case, the blood became the tangible symbol of the covenant made between God and Israel, and the splashing of blood upon the altar perhaps suggested that the altar stood as a symbol for God.[38] In other words, blood was splashed on the altar, which represented God, just as blood was splashed on the people—both parties were bound by blood and partook of the covenant experience.

Other inclusion rites incorporate the same symbolic system. In Exodus 40, following the instructions concerning the building of the tabernacle, instructions are given concerning the sanctification of the tabernacle and Aaron and his sons as priests. The setting up of the tabernacle began from the inside—starting in the Holy of Holies and moving in a clockwise fashion, from the setting up of the table of the bread of the presence, to the menorah, to the altar of incense. It then moved to the outside and the setting up of the altar, followed, finally, by the placing of the laver. These items were then anointed with the holy anointing oil. Unlike other oil, the anointing oil was a scented oil, made according to a specific formula, to be used solely to sanctify the items within the tabernacle:

> And thou shalt anoint the tabernacle of the congregation therewith, and the ark of the testimony,
>
> And the table and all his vessels, and the candlestick and his vessels, and the altar of incense,
>
> And the altar of burnt offering with all his vessels, and the laver and his foot.
>
> And thou shalt sanctify them, that they may be most holy: whatsoever toucheth them shall be holy.
>
> And thou shalt anoint Aaron and his sons, and consecrate them, that they may minister unto me in the priest's office. (Exodus 30:26–30)[39]

It was with this oil that the tabernacle and the items were anointed, presumably following the same pattern as the setting up of the tabernacle: beginning in the Holy of Holies and moving outward until finished at the wash laver. Leviticus 8 tells us that the altar of burnt offering was splashed seven times as well as anointed, meaning that not only was the oil poured over the top of the altar, but it was also splashed on the sides. After that, Aaron and his sons were brought forward and washed. Moses then clothed Aaron and anointed him by pouring the oil over his head, which also sanctified him, meaning he was made into one who could minister. At that point, an ox was offered up for a sin offering, presumably on behalf of Aaron and his sons, the blood being daubed on the horns of the altar, as one would expect. This was followed by another sacrifice of two rams. The first of the rams was treated as a burnt offering, with the blood splashed on the sides of the altar. The second was slaughtered, but instead of splashing all of the blood on the sides of the altar, some of it was daubed on the right earlobe, the right thumb, and the right big toe of Aaron and his sons. The final rite of the sanctification process was to take the blood on the altar, which had mingled with the anointing oil, and splash it onto Aaron, and his sons, rendering him "hallowed, and his garments, and his sons, and his sons' garments" (Exodus 29:21). As with the splashing of the blood onto the whole of

> Maybe this is where sprinkling came from.

Israel in Exodus 40, the splashing of the blood and oil onto Aaron effected the establishment of the relationship between Aaron and God.

Unlike the atonement rites, the induction rites used to establish the initial relationship with God were not repeated. In other words, whereas all the atoning rituals were repeated often, the act of being anointed or splashed with the blood or oil, once done, was never performed again. Moreover, in the case of the tabernacle's dedication, the process of anointing began from the inside out, from the Holy of Holies to the laver outside. The direction from which the anointing began, with the oil specifically designated as God's own, and the single performance of the act, all suggest that the act was to be understood as if God himself were doing it. Just as individuals prepared themselves to enter into the presence of God, the anointing process seems to have suggested that God did not just wait but prepared the space and items so that such interaction was possible. In other words, just as mortals sanctified themselves and the space around them to reconcile themselves with God, so God participated in preparing the space and the individual so that reconciliation could happen. Unlike the acts of the mortal, however, which had to be repeated often, God's anointing act only needed to be done once to transform the individual or item into a state of holiness.[40]

This transformation by God is expressed throughout Leviticus. Leviticus 21:10–12 reveals that the high priest is not allowed to act like the rest of society during the mourning process because "the crown of the anointing oil of his God is upon him." The same concept can be found earlier in chapter 10, where, following the deaths of Nadab and Abihu, Aaron and the remaining sons are told to "not let the hair of your heads hang loose, and do not tear your clothes, lest you die, and wrath come upon all the congregation . . . and do not go outside the entrance of the tent of meeting, lest you die; for the anointing oil of the Lord is upon you" (English Standard Version, Leviticus 10:6–7).

As the two passages suggest, the oil belonged to God himself, transforming that which touched it and making those items representative of him or able to interact with him. Aaron, having been anointed, is not allowed to engage in normal, profane behavior. The anointing allows Aaron to interact with the divine. In this case, though, the liminality is created by God himself. In other words, the anointing is a divine act, creating an environment that allows mortal acts to have efficacy. In essence, the anointing is the divine reaching out to mortals.

28   Daniel L. Belnap

[handwritten: As are all ordinances.]

Thus the anointing rite is significant in that it is a divine action, a ritual enacted by God himself to enact the transformation of others into a divine state, even if the rite is performed through a mortal representative. His divine rite using his oil appears to be the allusion in Psalm 45:7, which describes the election of the righteous by God: "Thou lovest righteousness, and hatest wickedness: therefore God, thy God, hath anointed thee with the oil of gladness above thy fellows." This in turn leads to Isaiah 61:1, 3 where the transforming nature of the anointing again comes to the fore as the anointed is empowered with the ability to change the environment of others, anointing them with the oil of joy, thus transforming them and allowing them to be become part of the divine realm (v. 3):

> The Spirit of the Lord God is upon me; because the Lord hath anointed me to preach good tidings unto the meek; he hath sent me to bind up the brokenhearted, to proclaim liberty to the captives, and the opening of the prison to them that are bound. . . .
>
> To appoint unto them that mourn in Zion, to give unto them beauty for ashes, the oil of joy for mourning, the garment of praise for the spirit of heaviness; that they might be called trees of righteousness, the planting of the Lord that he might be glorified.

What is particularly pleasing about this rite of induction is that in many ways it is the complement to the atonement rites. Both sets of rituals present the performer, either divine or mortal, as one who wants to have a relationship with the other. In the case of the atonement rites, they emphasize an individual's right to have a relationship with God, even the inherent right to become like God, while the initiation rites demonstrate God's continuing work to bring that result about. And it is these truths that lie at the heart of true worship, for one cannot truly worship God without knowing both one's own worth and the inestimable worth of God and that God knows these truths also, two principles taught richly and beautifully in the tabernacle and its rites.

Conclusion

Though it is difficult for those of us living in today's modern worldview to recognize the supernal truths of the gospel in what appear to be archaic and antiquated practices of ancient Israel, that does not mean the gospel is not there. The Apostle Paul compared the law and its attendant tabernacle and ordinances to a schoolmaster. In truth, when one does begin to understand the rich symbolism and meaning, we can begin to see the value of those texts that describe in detail the tabernacle's liminal architecture and the rites performed within. Not only do they reveal the manner by which ancient Israel demonstrated their devotion to God, but they also provide us the opportunity to understand more deeply the power of our own worship. Certainly we learn that the universal hope of exaltation, the end result of all true worship, was as real to them as it is for us.

Notes

1. *Oxford English Dictionary*, "worship." Old English *weorðscipe*, later *wurð-*, *wyrð-*, northern *worðscipe* , < *weorð* worth adj. + *-scipe* -ship suffix. The formation is peculiar to English.

2. There is some indications in the Bible that there were other forms of sacred space (certain "high places") that were viewed as legitimate sacred spaces, but these are few and far between. More common in both the prophetic writings and in the Deuteronomistic writings, only worship performed at the temple or the tabernacle was legitimate.

3. This assumption arises from the fact that certain offerings, such as the burnt offering and the peace offerings, are explicitly mentioned as being performed in both places. For other rites, such as the placing of the bread on the table of the bread of the presence or the daily lighting of the menorah, this is less clear, since no explicit mention is made of their performance. Yet the similarities in basic architecture and furniture suggest that these rites too were performed in both places.

4. First Kings 6 gives us the measurements of the temple, while Exodus 25–26 gives us the measurements for the tabernacle. The actual measurements described in the Old Testament utilize the cubit. The exact length of the cubit is complicated by the fact that there were a number of different "cubits" in the ancient Near East, and it is unclear as to which one meant when the authors of these texts used the term. In this paper, the author has used the cubit measurement provided in the Bible Dictionary, or a cubit as 17.5 inches. It is possible that the cubit actually used was the royal cubit, used in Egypt and elsewhere, in which case the dimensions provided would have been even larger.

5. The brazen sea that rested upon the backs of twelve bronze oxen, was between 7 to 9 feet deep, which, when coupled with the oxen, meant the entire structure stood at least 10 to 12 feet high. Carts and other moveable stands supposedly used for preparation stood at least 6 feet high. The altar was massive, measuring approximately 30 feet by 20 feet and 15 feet high. In the Holy of Holies the cherubim covering the ark were immense and awe-inspiring, measuring 15 feet in height with a wing span of 15 feet each (7.5 feet each wing). For more on the significance of these scales, see Elizabeth Bloch-Smith, who discusses the significance of these grand scales in her study "Solomon's Temple: The Politics of Ritual Space," in *Sacred Time, Sacred Space: Archeology and the Religion of Israel*, ed. Barry M. Gittlen (Winona Lake, IN: Eisenbrauns, 2002), 83–94.

6. Bloch-Smith, "Solomon's Temple," 84–85: "Accordingly, the exaggerated size of the structures in the Solomonic Temple courtyard would suggest that they were not intended for human use but belonged to the realm of the divine. Lacking archeological remains of the bronze Molten Sea and stands or corroborating evidence of their size, one can only determine by faith whether or not they were cast to the biblical specifications. Superhuman-sized objects likely stood in the courtyard, conveying to ancient Israelites that they served a divine function. . . . Thus the courtyard objects conveyed Yahweh's enthronement in the royal chapel with the attendant empowerment of the king and divine blessings for all of Israel." Israel was not the only nation to use the temple architecture and structure to emphasize this nature of God. One particular site, the Ain Dara temple in Syria, possesses flagstones in which footprints were engraved. The footprints alternate so that it appears that they are the prints left by one walking into the temple. The footprints themselves measure three feet in length, suggesting that they represented the footprint of something or someone approximately sixty-five feet tall.

7. Brigham Young, in *Journal of Discourses* (London: Latter-day Saints' Book Depot, 1854–86), 16:28: "If I did not feel like praying, and asking my Father in heaven to give me a morning blessing, and to preserve me and my family and the good upon the earth through the day, I should say, 'Brigham, get down here, on your knees, bow your body down before the throne of Him who rules in the heavens, and stay there until you can feel to supplicate at that throne of grace erected for sinners.'"

8. The altar of the tabernacle was about 7.5 feet by 7.5 and 4.5 feet high, and the only cherubim found in the Holy of Holies were those on the lid of the ark, which itself was the same length and width of the ark itself, approximately 3.5 by 2 by2 feet.

9. Two recent studies have emphasized this relationship. See John H. Walton, *Genesis 1 as Ancient Cosmology* (Winona Lake: Eisenbrauns, 2011) and L. Michael Morales, *The Tabernacle Prefigured*, Biblical Tools and Studies 15 (Walpole, MA: Peeters, 2012).

10. *Theological Dictionary of the Old Testament* 14 (Grand Rapids, MI: Eerdmans, 2005), šākan, 692–702.

11. One of the terms for the tent itself, the *ohel moed*, or tent of meeting, emphasizes this function of the tabernacle.

12. Anthropologist Arnold Van Gennep was the first to coin this term in regard to ritual and ritual space in his seminal study *Les Rites de Passage* (1939). But it was Victor Turner in his seminal work *The Ritual Process: Structure and Anti-Structure* (Ithaca: Cornell University Press, 1969) who suggested that liminal space created what he called "communitas," or the ability to engage in social relationships in a liminal space that would otherwise not be able to happen.

13. Thus rites of passage, marriage, puberty, birth, manhood, and womanhood, are performed in liminal spaces created for just that purpose.

14. While there is no explicit explanation to these colors provided in the text, they do appear elsewhere in the Bible. All three are noted as colors associated with clothing worn by well-to-do individuals, including royalty. They are also incorporated in cloth assigned to cover the items of the tabernacle when the camp of Israel was moving. According to Numbers 4, the ark was to be covered by the veil, then a layer of badger skin, then a cloth of blue; the table of shewbread was covered in blue, then scarlet cloth, then badger

skin. The menorah, the altar of incense, and the other items used in the sanctuary itself were covered in blue cloth, followed by a layer of badger cloth. The altar of burnt offering was to be covered in purple cloth then badger skin. Unfortunately, while it is clear what Israel was expected to do, why they were to do it in this manner or what the symbolism was in doing it this way it is not clear. It is intriguing that of the colors themselves, two of them, the red and the blue are primary colors, while the purple is a blend of both, but while it is fun to speculate on the theological nature of this relationship, to do so would simply be surmise.

15. According to the text, the priest was meant to act as the go-between for God and mortals, fulfilling a function like liminal space.

16. Philip Peter Jenson, *Graded Holiness: A Key to the Priestly Conception of the World*, Journal for the Study of the Old Testament Supplement Series 106 (Sheffield, England: Sheffield Academic Press, 1992), 103: "The predominance of gold in the Tabernacle can be related to its valued physical properties and great social significance. This is the basis for the analogies which are made between the human and divine spheres, and a close connection between gold, divinity, and holiness is evident throughout the ancient Near East. God is rare, desirable, and very costly, and fittingly represents the dignity and power of those who are able to possess it, to a pre-eminent degree, God."

17. Carol L. Meyers, *The Tabernacle Menorah: A Synthetic Study of a Symbol from the Biblical Cult*, ASOR dissertation series 2 (Missoula, MT: Scholars Press, 1976), explores both the symbolic and functional aspects of the menorah.

18. Whether the burning of incense in the home had religious meaning is unclear, though it does appear that at least in the sixth century BC some were burning incense to other deities in their houses. Yet other texts suggest that burning incense was not necessarily a religious act, but simply made the home a more pleasing place to be. See Seymour Gitin, "The Four-Horned Altar and Sacred Space: An Archaeological Perspective," in *Sacred Time, Sacred Space*, 95–123, 108 specifically. Also, C. Houtman, "On the Function of the Holy Incense (Exodus XXX 34–8) and the Sacred Anointing Oil (Exodus XXX 22–33), in *Vetus Testamentum* 42, no. 4 (1992): 458–65: "As incense was burnt in the houses of the well-to-do to create a pleasant atmosphere, and as the purity of the aromatics and the exquisite character of the fragrance indicated the status of their residents, so the incense of the sanctuary also was a symbol of status" (463).

19. Hospitality rites included the preparation and presentation of food, the offering of shelter and rest, the washing of feet, and the offering of incense, all of which are also associated with the temple and its rites. For more on the role of incense in hospitality, see Béatrice Caseau, *Eudoia: The Use and Meaning of Fragrances in the Ancient World and Their Christianization (100–900 AD)* (PhD diss., Princeton University, 1994), 150–51: "Perfumes and incense were therefore on the shopping list of all respectable hosts. A shopping list preserved on a damaged third century papyrus is revealing on this aspect: 'you know what hospitality requires, so get a little . . . from the priests and buy some incense.' Nicostratus cited by Athenaeus, makes a list of what is necessary to insure a successful party: sweetmeats, perfume, wreaths, frankincense, and a flute girl. These traditions of offering perfumes and incense with giving a banquet were not a Greco-Roman innovation. Examples of similar practices can be gathered from ancient Egyptian or Mesopotamian

iconography. A Megiddo ivory dating from the twelfth century depicts a festive scene. Behind the king seated on a throne come two servants, one with a bowl, probably filled with wine, the other with a vessel filled with perfume, since he brings it to his nose. This ancient piece of art testifies on the perduration of the use of perfumes in festive traditions. This was a common regional characteristic. A relief from the palace in Nineveh represents the king of Assyria feasting with his queen and surrounded by censers. The prophet Amos mentions the anointing of the guests during a banquet. These traditions were kept in Jewish houses, where incense and spices were burnt at the end of the meal, while perfumes were used to cleanse one's hands."

20. Ancient hospitality from an ancient Near Eastern perspective differs from our modern understanding of hospitality. While we tend to associate hospitality with service, or selfless acts by one party, rendered because of the individual's moral or ethical stance, ancient hospitality required reciprocity between the two parties to transform the unknown and therefore dangerous into a recognizable and therefore controllable state. In other words, hospitality was not expected to be a selfless act on the part of the host, but a ritualized process by which the guest was introduced into the family structure and rendered harmless, subjugated to the authority of the host, see T. R. Hobbs, "Hospitality in the First Testament and the 'Teleological Fallacy,'" in *Journal for the Study of the Old Testament* 95 (2001): 3–30: "As a guest, a stranger is in a liminal phase, and may infringe upon the guest/host relationship: by insulting the host through hostility or rivalry; by usurping the role of the host; by refusing what is offered. On the other hand, the host may infringe: by insulting the guest through hostility or rivalry; by neglecting to protect the guest and his/her honor; by failing to attend to one's guests, to grant precedence, to show concern" (11). See also Robert Ignatius Letellier, *Day in Mamre, Night in Sodom: Abraham and Lot in Genesis 18 and 19*, Biblical Interpretation Series 10 (Leiden: E. J. Brill, 1995), 155: "In nomadic societies of the ancient Middle East hospitality to a stranger was a sacred obligation, a manifestation of social graciousness that touches the deepest values. . . . The guest is sacred and it is an honour to provide for him." For more on ancient Near Eastern hospitality, see Andrew Arterbury, *Entertaining Angels: Early Christian Hospitality in its Mediterranean Setting* (Sheffield, UK: Sheffield Phoenix Press, 2005); Jean-Jacques Glassner, "L'hospitalité en Mésopotamie ancienne: aspect de la question de l'étranger," in *Zeitschrift für Assyriologie und vorderasiatische Archologie* 80, no. 1 (1990): 60–75; Michael Herzfeld, "'As in Your Own House': Hospitality, Ethnography, and the Stereotype of Mediterranean Society," in *Honor and Shame and the Unity of the Mediterranean*, ed. David D. Gilmore (Washington DC: American Anthropological Association, 1987), 75–89; Scott Morschauser, "'Hospitality,' Hostiles and Hostages: On the Legal Background to Genesis 19.1–9," in *Journal for the Study of the Old Testament* 27, no. 4 (2003): 461–85; Robert C. Stallman, "Divine Hospitality in the Pentateuch: A Metaphorical Perspective on God as Host" (PhD diss., Westminster Theological Seminary, 1999).

21. The verb used to describe the cherubims' function in the Garden of Eden is *shakan*, the root from which *tabernacle* is translated.

22. See all of Ezekiel 10. For more on the function of the cherubim, see T. N. D. Mettinger, "cherubim," in *Dictionary of Deities and Demons in the Bible*, ed. Karel Van

Der Toorn, Bob Becking, and Pieter W. Van Der Horst (Leiden: Eerdmans, 1999), 189–192.

23. *Theological Dictionary of the Old Testament* 2, "*bdl*," 1–3: "*bdl* is used in a typical way in the Priestly account of creation (Gen. 1:4, 6, 7, 14, 18): the individual phases in creation are depicted as a separation of the different elements form one another.... The author uses the word *bdl* in order to emphasize a major idea in the Priestly account of creation, viz., that the creator-God is a God of order rather than a mythological procreator" (2).

24. Numbers 17:10–11 notes that Aaron's blossoming rod, the indicator of his chosen status as high priest, was also placed in the ark. The rod is also mentioned in Hebrews 9:4, along with the tablets and a pot of manna.

25. *Theological Dictionary of the Old Testament* 6, *yā'ad*, 135–44. This is also the root for *mo'ed*, the term translated as tent of "meeting", one of the designations for the tabernacle which highlights the function of the tabernacle as a meeting place rather than a dwelling place.

26. For the Mesopotamian perspective, see Jean Bottéro, *Religion in Ancient Mesopotamia*, trans. Teresa Lavender Fagan (Chicago: University of Chicago Press, 2001): "The divinity was never the object of an anxious, enthusiastic pursuit; "to seek out (*šē'û*) a god," as was sometimes said, was out of a need for his protection, his assistance. It was not inspired by a desire to be close to him, to be in his presence, to have the peace or happiness of finding oneself in his company. Hymns professing a bottomless desire for a god's presence indicate admiration (as in the case of the moon god, the splendid lamp of the night) and not an impatience to get closer to him.... One submitted to them, one feared them, one bowed down and trembled before them: one did not 'love' or 'like' them.... [Temples] were not only to shelter them but to isolate them in peace and allow them to lead, separately and among themselves, a peaceful and refined existence in a magnificent solemn place where their subjects knew they could be found and admire them, take care of them, and request their benevolent aid" (37, 115). For the Egyptian perspective see Erik Hornung, *Conceptions of God in Ancient Egypt: The One and the Many*, trans. John Bains (Ithaca, NY: Cornell University Press, 1982): "The first emotion that grips an Egyptian who encounters a deity or the image of a god is fear, mixed with wonder and exultation.... The gods created the world and ensure that not only mankind but all beings can live and grow in it. But to what end? What made the creator god call the world and all its creatures into being and keep them in being? No Egyptian text is known which gives direct, unambiguous answers to questions of this sort: the Egyptians evidently did not consider these to be serious issues.... The Egyptians believed that by performing the cult and presenting themselves before the god they were at least increasing his existence and presence, while also keeping his negative, dangerous side at a distance. Cult actions do not coerce but they do encourage the gods to show their gracious side—for the converse of a god's love on mankind his violent aspect, which is always present beneath the surface and must be assuaged by means of appropriate cult services.... The Egyptians evidently never experience a longing for union with the deity. They keep their distance from the gods, whom no one can approach too closely without being punished" (197–8, 205, 207).

27. This applies only to the burnt offering. In the case of the sin offering, a goat was often used. But whatever animal was used, the unblemished nature of it was essential.

28. See Jacob Milgrom in *Leviticus 1–16: A New Translation with Introduction and Commentary*, Anchor Bible 3 (New York: Doubleday, 1991), 149–53, who discusses each approach and then presents his own.

29. See David Rolph Seely, "William Tyndale and the Language of At-one-ment," in *The King James Bible and the Restoration*, ed. Kent P. Jackson (Provo, UT: Religious Studies Center, Brigham Young University: Salt Lake City: Deseret Book, 2011), 25–42.

30. *Theological Dictionary of the Old Testament* 7, kipper; kappōreṯ, kōper, kippurîm, 290.

31. In Leviticus 3:16–17 we learn that both fat and blood are considered the Lord's.

32. *Theological Dictionary of the Old Testament* 12, qdš, 521–545.

33. E. Jan Wilson, *"Holiness" and "Purity" in Mesopotamia*, Alter Orient und Altes Testament 237 (Kevelaer: Butzon & Bercker; Neukirchen-Vluyn; Neukirchener, 1994), 87–88. For more discussion on the distinction of these terms, see Gaye Strathearn, "'Holiness to the Lord' and Personal Temple Worship," in *The Gospel of Jesus Christ in the Old Testament*, ed. D. Kelly Ogden, Jared W. Ludlow, and Kerry Muhlestein (Provo, UT: Religious Studies Center, Brigham Young University; Salt Lake City: Deseret Book, 2009), 219–32.

34. Leviticus 19:2. This exhortation is found throughout Leviticus (see also 11:44–45, 20:7, 21:8, speaking of the priests), as well as Deuteronomy (see Deuteronomy 7:6; 14:2, 28:9).

35. Though one often recognizes only the role of the priest in the actualization of these acts, the instructions found in Leviticus highlight the role of the "average" Israelite in the initiation and preparation elements of the ritual as well.

36. Interestingly, "to make atonement" is not mentioned as a function of the third form of animal sacrifice, the "peace offering." This may be because the peace offering is not offered to overcome a deficit or division between God and man, but instead to commemorate the fulfillment of a vow, or other blessed event, in which God's hand is recognized. In other words, there is no need for atonement to be made because the peace offering recognizes that atonement, or reconciliation, is already present.

37. Biblical scholar Jonathan Klawans considers this in his article "Pure Violence: Sacrifice and Defilement in Ancient Israel," in *Harvard Theological Review* 94, no. 2 (2001): 135–57: "Jon D. Levenson... has argued that the biblical narrative of tabernacle (and temple) construction take on a cosmic significance.... In so doing, Levenson demonstrates that the priestly traditions understand tabernacle and temple construction as an act of *imitatio Dei*. If the building of the temple can be understood as an act of *imitatio Dei*, and if the process of preparation for the rituals that will take place there can be understood likewise, can this concept help us to better understand at least some aspects of ancient Israelite animal sacrifice?" (p. 145).

38. The concept of inanimate objects representing God is found elsewhere in the Old Testament. For instance, the ark of the covenant represented God when taken into battle against the Philistines. Likewise, both the Book of Mormon and New Testament Saints understood that the bronze serpent represented Christ.

39. We are told that Aaron was to cleanse, or make atonement, or make the tabernacle useful for reconciliation, followed by anointing it seven times in seven days and which point it is now most holy space, and whatsoever touches it will also be holy. What *holy* means will be discussed later. For now it is enough to recognize that the process is done, like a creation, for seven days so that atonement can be made there from then on.

40. That Moses is performing the rite instead of God is not a hindrance since he is more than a priest; he acts in the stead of God. For more on the association of Moses with God, see W. A. Meeks, "Moses as God and King," in *Religions in Antiquity: Essays in Memory of Erwin Ramsdell Goodenough*, ed. J. Neusner, Numen Supplemental 14 (Leiden: E. J. Brill, 1968), 353–59; also Crispin Fletcher-Louis, "4Q374: A Discourse on the Sinai Tradition: The Deification of Moses and Early Christology," in *Dead Sea Discoveries* 3, no. 3 (Leiden: E. J. Brill, 1996): 236–52. This principle is of course found in Restoration scripture: "And I will lay my hand upon you by the hand of my servant Sidney Rigdon" (D&C 36:2).

3

The Garden of Eden, the Ancient Temple, and Receiving a New Name

Alex Douglas

The concept of ritual renaming holds special significance within Latter-day Saint theology; Church authorities, including Joseph Smith, have taught that worthy individuals are given a new name in the presence of God and that this name is sacred.[1] As Latter-day Saints looking back at ancient history, we understand the Old Testament and its temple ordinances according to these teachings, yet when we examine the scriptures, the record is practically silent regarding temple renaming.[2] In taking together the teachings of Latter-day Saint leaders and the lack of strong biblical witnesses, we are faced with two possibilities. First, perhaps ritual renaming did take place in the temple and knowledge of this practice was lost over time. As is discussed below, there is still much that scholars do not know about the temple, and we would not be the first to attempt to reconstruct ancient practice from subtle references in the Bible. The second possibility is that ritual renaming never took place in Old Testament times. From a theological standpoint, little is lost by such an admission; after all, Joseph Smith often claimed to reveal doctrine that had never before been known.

Alex Douglas is a PhD student in Hebrew Bible/Old Testament at Harvard University.

This paper is not an attempt to prove that ritual renaming took place in the ancient world. Rather, it is an exploration of the biblical witnesses from a Latter-day Saint point of view. It examines indications within the Bible itself that ritual renaming could have been performed, and it imagines how such a ritual might look and how it fits into what we know of ancient temple practice. In both areas, modern revelation invites us to make connections and see beyond a minimalist approach to the text, while sound methodology prevents us from drawing definite conclusions beyond what is attested in the sources. Our reconstruction of these rituals must be hypothetical, but hypothetical reconstructions can still be informative as we view latter-day ideas through the lens of early scripture. Occasional allusion is made in the Old Testament to receiving a new name in connection with the temple. Furthermore, details from the temple's construction, later extrabiblical interpretation, and parallel ancient Near Eastern sources show how the temple was patterned after the Creation and the Garden of Eden; using this connection—and through a close examination of the Creation story—we can see more clearly how ritual renaming might have functioned in the Old Testament temple, if indeed it was performed at all.

Understanding the Ancient Temple

Before we begin, let us first consider what we know of the ancient temple, as well as what constitutes valid evidence in reconstructing what we do not know. In some areas our knowledge is extensive, particularly where the Pentateuch specifies how an ordinance should be performed. Yet it is equally clear that the early temple descriptions leave out many details; for example, while we know that Israelites gathered at the temple for major festivals, scholars still know relatively little of how people participated in these festivals in the preexilic period.

To flesh out this picture, scholars turn to a number of sources. First, they turn to indirect evidence within the Bible, such as psalms that seem to have been used in temple ritual.[3] Books such as Samuel and Ezekiel describe events that take place in the temple, and later pseudepigraphic writers—often writing in the centuries around Christ—provide another view. Finally, rabbinic evidence such as the Mishnah can also be used. Each of these sources must be used with caution. Many authors wrote well after the Second Temple was destroyed, and many may have shaped their descriptions to fit their own views. Allusions within the Bible are equally problematic, for if we use allusion to reconstruct temple ritual, we are liable to overread our sources and find evidence for ritual that may not have existed. All of the sources mentioned above can be helpful, however, in identifying ancient attitudes toward the temple, and when used carefully, they can help us understand aspects of temple worship that might otherwise be obscure in the biblical text. With these limitations in mind, let us now turn to the evidence for ritual renaming.

Allusions to Ritual Renaming

One of the first references in the Old Testament to ritual renaming comes in Isaiah 56:5. In this passage, the Lord speaks of foreigners and eunuchs—people who were typically excluded from temple service—and he says that in the last days, "unto them will I give in mine house and within my walls a place and a name better than of sons and of daughters: I will give them an everlasting name, that shall not be cut off." True to Isaiah's style, almost everything in this passage could be interpreted in multiple ways,[4] but it is interesting to note the imagery by which the people's reversal of fortune is conveyed. Not only will the Lord give them "an everlasting name," but he explicitly says that he will do so in the temple.

Six chapters later, the prophet turns his attention to Jerusalem. During the Babylonian captivity, the land of Israel was humiliated, suffering a similar fate to the foreigners and eunuchs, and according to Isaiah 62:4, Jerusalem was called Forsaken (ʿăzûbâ) and Desolate (šəmāmâ). When the Lord restores his people, he tells Jerusalem, "thou shalt be called by a new name, which the mouth of the Lord shall name" (Isaiah 62:2). In this restoration, the holy city is given the name Married (bəʿûlâ) and My Delight is in Her (ḥepṣî-bāh). Like the eunuchs, Jerusalem experiences a reversal of fortune, and along with this new reality the city is given a new name that embodies these hopes and expectations. In the ancient world, the giving of new names in such situations was not uncommon; in fact, according to John McKenzie, a new life situation "*demanded* a new name in order that it be recognized as new."[5] At the end of Isaiah this theme appears again when the prophet says that the Lord will destroy the wicked but will "call his servants by another name" (Isaiah 65:15).

In Numbers 6:27 the Lord tells the priests how they are to bless the Israelites, and after revealing the blessing, the Lord says, "And they shall put my name upon the children of Israel." Here the Lord puts his own name upon the Israelites rather than an individual name, but the underlying concept of bestowing a name

The Garden of Eden, the Ancient Temple, and Receiving a New Name

upon the worshipper is similar. Further, the bestowal of a new name is here tied to the priests, unlike in the Isaiah passages. If this did take place at the temple, it also serves as a striking parallel to King Benjamin, who gathered the people to the temple to bestow the name of Christ on them (see Mosiah 5:6–11).

While these verses are certainly suggestive from a Latter-day Saint point of view, it bears repeating that they are merely allusions, and they are imperfect parallels to the idea of individual renaming outlined by Joseph Smith. In both Numbers and Isaiah, names are conferred upon a city and upon the larger Israelite community, but nothing is said of individuals. Further, it is unclear how literally these names were understood—after all, today we do not call Jerusalem "My Delight is in Her." What then can these verses tell us? The references above show that Isaiah could draw upon imagery of the Lord, granting new names to individuals within the temple, whether or not such temple renaming actually took place. The passage from Numbers shows that the idea of priests putting a name ("the Lord") on the Israelites was not a foreign concept, even though it tells us nothing of how or why this was carried out. In short, these passages are suggestive, but on their own they offer only loose support for the Latter-day Saint concept of ritual renaming. To better understand temple renaming, we must turn to other sources from the Bible.

The Temple and the Garden of Eden

The stories of the Creation and the Garden of Eden are some of the best sources we have for understanding the ancient temple.[6] The temple was viewed as a model of the cosmos,[7] and we can clearly see both Eden's paradisiacal state and the creation of the world reflected in its construction. In fact, much in the temple was designed to emulate and recreate the Garden of Eden for Israelite worshippers. For example, the interior of the temple was made entirely of cedar, and as Solomon decorated the walls, the Bible tells us that "he carved all the walls of the house round about with carved figures of cherubims and palm trees and open flowers, within and without" (1 Kings 6:29). The palm trees and flowers alone would conjure images of Eden, but the cherubim make the reference certain; in fact, outside of the temple and God's throne, Eden is the only other place in the Bible where cherubim appear.

The items within the temple were also decorated to represent a garden. The two great pillars leading to the inner court were adorned with lilies, and they were decorated as two large trees, being covered with two-hundred pomegranates each (see 1 Kings 7:19–20). Just as the pillars, the golden menorah in the sanctuary was envisioned as a tree, and in its description we hear that it had "branches," "flowers," and "bowls made like unto almonds" (Exodus 25:31–33). Ten similar lampstands lined the sides of the inner sanctuary (see 1 Kings 7:49), and with each modeled as a tree, the effect must have been similar to walking into a forest.[8]

The ancient Israelites were well aware that the temple appeared as a garden. According to one legend, the prophet Zechariah had a vision where he saw a man "standing among the trees of the tabernacle,"[9] an image no doubt conjured by the pillars and lampstands of the main hall. Similarly the psalmist says of the righteous: "like the palm tree . . . they are planted in the house of the Lord" (Psalm 92:12–13). Further reinforcing the impression of a garden scene were the animals depicted throughout the sanctuary. Washbasins covered with "lions, oxen, and cherubims" (1 Kings 7:29) could be found within the temple, and the great bronze laver stood on twelve oxen and was decorated "with flowers of lilies" (1 Kings 7:25–26).

The temple was not modeled after just any garden; it was meant to represent Eden, and many of the characters from the Eden story appear in Solomon's temple. In Eden, cherubim were placed to guard the way to the tree of life, and in the temple, two giant cherubim—each fifteen feet tall—guarded the entrance to the Holy of Holies (see 1 Kings 6:23–28). The priest in the temple represented Adam (see below), and even the serpent makes an appearance. In 2 Kings 18:4 we learn that the bronze serpent made by Moses in the wilderness had been incorporated into Israelite worship (though the righteous king Hezekiah opposed this practice).[10]

Further tying the temple to the Creation story is the way the temple's construction is narrated. When the tabernacle is built under Moses, the narrative shows many verbal parallels to the Genesis account of the Creation. Mention of the "spirit of God" (*rûaḥ ʾĕlōhîm*) begins the creation of the world and the tabernacle; Moses and God "see all the work" done; and after they "complete the work," they provide a blessing (compare Genesis 1:2; 1:31; 2:2; 2:3 with Exodus 31:3; 39:43; 40:33; 39:43, respectively).[11] In imitation of the seven-day division of creation, Moses enters God's presence on the seventh day of being on Sinai, he is given seven sets of instructions on the tabernacle, and the construction narrative is divided by seven refrains of "as the Lord commanded Moses" (see

Exodus 24:16; 25:1; 30:11–24; 31:1, 12; 40:19–32).[12] Construction of Solomon's Temple follows a similar pattern. It was created in seven years, its dedication took place at a seven-day festival in the seventh month, and Solomon's dedicatory prayer centered around seven major petitions (see 1 Kings 6:38; 8:2, 31–53).[13] In short, the temple was a microcosm in the truest sense of the word, and the biblical author went to great lengths to show the thematic ties linking the temple back to the stories in Genesis 1–3.

The connection between Eden and the temple, while striking when we look at the temple decorations, also runs much deeper. For example, the temple is frequently described as being on top of a mountain. It is called "mount Zion" (Isaiah 8:18), "the mountain of the Lord's house" (Isaiah 2:2), or "the mountain of [the Lord's] inheritance" (Exodus 15:17).[14] The image of a mountain conveyed proximity to God, and "In cultures which have a heaven, earth, and hell, the mountain 'center' is the axis along which these three cosmic areas are connected and *where communion between them becomes possible.*"[15] Mountains and temples were so closely intertwined that the line between them often blurred,[16] and it is thus telling that when Ezekiel describes the Garden of Eden, he places it on a mountain, just as the temple. According to Ezekiel 28:13–14, "Eden the garden of God" is located "upon the holy mountain of God." Eden was a temple where the presence of God dwelled.

Consistent with the mountain imagery associated with Eden and the temple, both are also the source of rivers that flow out and provide life to the surrounding area. Eden's river divided into four heads: the Tigris, Euphrates, Pison, and Gihon. As for the temple, its source of water was the Gihon, a spring that shared the name of the river mentioned in Eden (see 1 Kings 1:43–46), and the restored millennial temple is also pictured with a river flowing out from its base to water the earth (see Ezekiel 47:1–12; Zechariah 14:3–8; Joel 3:16–18).

Adam as a Priest

Eden was symbolically recreated in the temple's creation, in its position as a sanctuary, and even in its decorations. As mentioned above, many of the characters from the Eden story were also represented in the temple, and Adam was represented by the priest. This can be seen in the role both play in their respective sanctuaries, their clothing, and the activities they performed.

In the temple, priests performed a double role as mediators between God and humans. First they represented the people before God. In everything from individual offerings to national catastrophes, the priest stood before God in place of the individuals to make intercession on their behalf. On the other hand, priests also represented God before the people. When an individual needed to go before the Lord, it was the priest who stood in the Lord's place and delivered his messages, as can be seen in Deuteronomy 19:17 or 1 Samuel 1:17.

In the Garden of Eden, Adam is likewise depicted as a representative of both God and man. He is the quintessential man, as implied by his name, 'ādām ('man' in Hebrew). His role in the Eden story is an embodiment of the human race, and his journey from innocence to transgression can be seen in all of our lives. Yet while Adam is clearly a symbol of humanity, he is just as clearly depicted as a symbol of God. He is the image and likeness of his creator, and like God, he is charged to "have dominion . . . over all the earth" (Genesis 1:26). In the broader Near Eastern context, his very presence in the garden was a further reminder of his role as God's representative: "Ancient kings would set up images of themselves in distant lands over which they ruled in order to represent their sovereign presence . . . Likewise, Adam was created as the image of the divine king to indicate that earth was ruled over by Yahweh."[17]

In ancient sources outside of Genesis, Adam is also depicted wearing priestly garments. In prophesying of the downfall of the king of Tyre, Ezekiel compares this king to an Adam figure who has been cast out of Eden. He says, "Thou hast been in Eden the garden of God; *every precious stone was thy covering*, the sardius, topaz, and the diamond, the beryl, the onyx, and the jasper, the sapphire, the emerald, and the carbuncle, and gold" (Ezekiel 28:13; emphasis added). This is no mere list of precious stones; each one of the stones mentioned is also found on the high priest's breastplate (see Exodus 28:17–20).[18] A less overt comparison can be seen in *Genesis Rabbah*, a collection of ancient rabbinic commentary. Here it is stated that Adam was clothed in garments of light "which were like a torch [shedding radiance.]"[19] This is reminiscent of the holiness ascribed to the priests' clothing, and later biblical authors likewise describe priests as "clothed with salvation" (2 Chronicles 6:41) and "clothed with righteousness" (Psalm 132:9). Extrabiblical accounts also speak of priests clothed in "a holy and glorious vestment."[20]

Even the language used to describe Adam's work in the Garden of Eden is the same language used of priests for their service in the temple. Priests are charged primarily with guarding and keeping the sanctuary, as in Numbers 3:7, where the priests are to guard (*šmr*) the charge of the sanctuary and keep (*'bd*) its service. When Adam is put in Eden, his primary responsibility is likewise to guard (*šmr*) and keep (*'bd*) it, as Genesis 2:15 tells us. With only a few exceptions, these two Hebrew roots are used together exclusively in reference to Adam and the priests in their duties to their respective sanctuaries.[21]

In accounts of Adam and Eve that occur outside the Bible, other authors also made the connection between Adam and priest. In the pseudepigraphic work *Life of Adam and Eve*, Adam is shown collecting incense to burn as an offering to God (an activity that was strictly reserved for priests),[22] and in the Book of Moses he is shown performing sacrifice (see Moses 5:5–6).[23] Rabbinic tradition holds that the dust used to create Adam was taken from the site of the future temple,[24] and in the *Life of Adam and Eve*, the author claims that Solomon built the temple on the site where Adam used to pray.[25]

Both within and without the Bible, Eden is presented as a type of temple where God's presence dwells, and in this temple Adam is depicted as a priest. But given the intimate connection between these two spheres, it would be insufficient to say that the temple was a "representation" of Eden, or even that it was a "recreation" of it. In the ancient mind, the temple *was* the Garden of Eden, and Eden was the world's first temple. In Jerusalem, the temple served as "a survival of the primal paradise lost to the profane world ... It connects the protological and the eschatological, the primal and the final, *preserving Eden* and providing a taste of the life of intimacy with God."[26] Having established the connection between Eden and temple, as well as between Adam and priest, we can now look at how naming is used in the creation stories to understand how ritual renaming might have functioned in the ancient temple.

Naming in the Creation Accounts

Naming plays a central role in both the initial account of the Creation and the story of the Garden of Eden. In Genesis 1, God's creative actions are recounted in extremely minimalistic fashion, and his works are described in a matter-of-fact tone. In the entire chapter there are only eight verbs used in connection with him: he creates (*br'*), sees (*r'h*), forms (*'šh*), sets (*ntn*), speaks (*'mr*), blesses (*brk*), and divides (*bdl*), and within this sparse description, he names (*qr'*) a total of five times. It is not enough for God to create the light or the firmament; he must name them for his creation to be considered complete.

This conferral of names is no trivial matter, nor is it simply an afterthought to the Creation story. As Porter and Ricks show, "In the cultures of the ancient

Near East, existence was thought to be dependent upon an identifying word, that word being a 'name.' The name of someone (or something) was perceived not as a mere abstraction, but as a real entity, 'the audible and spoken image of the person . . . his spiritual essence.'"[27] Names were thought to be a central part of existence,[28] and thus it comes as no surprise that naming plays a major role in Genesis 1.

In Genesis 2, Adam continues God's work by naming the animals. Aside from the well-known commandment about the tree of knowledge of good and evil, Adam's responsibilities in Eden were twofold: he was to guard and keep the garden (just as the priests do for the temple) and give names to the animals. In both of these tasks Adam stands in God's place as his representative, doing the work that God would otherwise do. Adam was created in the image of God, and just as God confers names, so Adam does as well in a type of *imitatio dei*.

There are three scenes in the Eden story that are particularly suggestive in regard to temple naming. The first is when God "formed every beast of the field . . . and brought them unto Adam to see what he would call them: and whatsoever Adam called every living creature, that was the name thereof" (Genesis 2:19). In this verse, Adam does not move about the garden; rather, God brings each creature and presents it before Adam, and he has given Adam the authority to declare what the creature's name should be. This type of presentation before God's representative lies at the heart of temple worship,[29] and in fact all the Israelites were commanded to "come to appear before the Lord . . . in the place which he shall choose [i.e., the temple]" at the end of every seven years (Deuteronomy 31:10–11).[30] The parallel of the animals appearing before Adam at the end of the seven-day creation is striking.[31]

In the next scene, woman is created, and just as the animals are brought, so the Lord "brought her before the man" (Genesis 2:22). To read the Eden story as a temple account, the woman is here presented before the priest. When Adam confers a name upon her, we learn that this name is highly significant, and by playing on the Hebrew root, it indicates both the woman's origin and her destiny: "This is now bone of my bones, and flesh of my flesh: she shall be called Woman (*'iššā*), because she was taken out of Man (*'iš*). Therefore shall a man leave his father and his mother, and shall cleave unto his wife (*'ištô*): and they shall be one flesh" (Genesis 2:23–24).

After the man and woman partook of the forbidden fruit, they were cast out of the garden. God pronounced curses upon them both, and included in the statement of the woman's curse was the promise that she would bear children (see Genesis 3:16). Expulsion from Eden and childbirth marked a new beginning in woman's life, and along with this change she received a new name. Like the first name, this name was also given by Adam, and the name was meaningful to her new situation. Genesis 3:20 reads, "And Adam called his wife's name Eve (ḥawwā); because she was the mother of all living (ḥāy)."[32]

What This Means for the Temple

As we have seen, there are numerous connections between the temple and the Garden of Eden, and there are many ways we can interpret these parallels. It is clear that the temple was meant to recreate Eden within Israel. Garden imagery abounded in the temple: palm trees, lilies, pomegranates, flowers, lions, and oxen were represented everywhere, and the branches of the golden lampstands would have created a virtual forest within the hêkāl ("the Holy Place"). The bronze serpent could be seen within the temple precincts, and the Holy of Holies—the ultimate source of life—was guarded by two giant cherubim. In this garden temple would have stood the priest, representing both God and man as Adam does in Eden.

What is less clear, however, is how naming functioned within this temple. If the Genesis account is indicative of temple practice, then perhaps we might imagine a worshipper symbolically approaching Eden by coming to the temple. It is possible that the Lord's command to the priests to "put my name upon the children of Israel" (Numbers 6:27) corresponds to Adam's conferring a name upon the animals and upon Eve. In this case, rather than an individual name, here the worshipper would symbolically take upon himself the name of the Lord. If such a ritual did take place in the temple, it would be fitting for Isaiah to draw upon this imagery in telling the people that the Lord would give them "in mine house and within my walls a place and . . . an everlasting name" (Isaiah 56:5), and that they would "be called by a new name, which the mouth of the Lord shall name" (Isaiah 62:2).

On the other hand, it is possible that the Eden account is not a description of temple ordinances. Reconstructing ancient temple practice is a tenuous endeavor, and it is made all the more so by the nature of the sources available. The Bible is a complex work, and much of the evidence presented here has been circumstantial. But when we approach the evidence with these limitations in mind, we can at least speak of possibilities.

The evidence of Genesis 1–3, taken together with the references to renaming found elsewhere in the Old Testament, does leave open the possibility that such a ritual took place. Ritual renaming would fit nicely with what we know of the ancient temple. Names held great significance in antiquity; a name was thought to embody who a person was and what the future might hold. If such renaming did take place in the ancient world, it should come as no surprise that this work be carried out by God's representatives and in his house.

Notes

1. See, for example, Kent P. Jackson, comp., *Joseph Smith's Commentary on the Bible* (Salt Lake City: Deseret Book, 1994), 219, and Victor Ludlow, "John: The Once and Future Witness," *Ensign*, December 1991, 55.

2. In this paper, I describe the conferral of a new name as "ritual renaming." Although there are problems with equating these two ideas (discussed below), this paper uses "ritual renaming" rather than using a qualified expression. Although mention will be made of the tabernacle and the Second Temple, this paper focuses on Solomon's Temple as the locus for renaming.

3. For example, see Sigmund Mowinckel, *The Psalms in Israel's Worship* (Dearborn, MI: Dove, 2004). Mowinckel is perhaps most famous for using Psalms to reconstruct a Festival of Yahweh's Enthronement.

4. For example, the word translated as 'place' ($yād$) is also the word for 'hand'; alternatively, it could refer to a commemorative monument, as in 2 Samuel 18:18. The word 'name' ($šēm$) can also refer to testimony or even seed (see Isaiah 55:13 and 66:22), thus in another interpretation the Lord here refers to setting up a commemorative monument in the temple for these people.

5. John L. McKenzie, *Second Isaiah* (Garden City, NY: Doubleday, 1968), 178; emphasis added.

6. For a discussion of ties between Eden and the temple found in the Book of Mormon, see Kevin Christensen, "The Temple, the Monarchy, and Wisdom: Lehi's World and the Scholarship of Margaret Barker," in *Glimpses of Lehi's Jerusalem*, ed. John W. Welch, David Rolph Seely, and Jo Ann H. Seely (Provo, UT: FARMS, 2004), 449–522.

7. Such a conception appears, for example, in Isaiah 6. The prophet sees the symbol of God's glory fill the temple (verse 1), after which the seraphim cry, "the whole earth is full of his glory" (verse 3). See Jon D. Levenson, "The Temple and the World," *Journal of Religion* 64, no. 3 (July 1984): 286, 289–90.

8. For a discussion of Edenic imagery in the temple, see Jon D. Levenson, *Sinai and Zion: An Entry into the Jewish Bible* (New York: HarperCollins, 1985), 111–45, and G. K.

Beale, *The Temple and the Church's Mission: A Biblical Theology of the Dwelling Place of God* (Downers Grove, IL: InterVarsity Press), 50–80.

9. *Testament of Adam* 4:7, trans. S. Robinson, in *The Old Testament Pseudepigrapha*, ed. James Charlesworth (New Haven: Yale University Press, 2009), 1:995.

10. Although the biblical narrative does not specify where the serpent was located, it likely would have been in the temple, as many scholars hold; see Lowell K. Handy, "Serpent, Bronze," in *The Anchor Bible Dictionary*, ed. David Noel Freedman (New York: Doubleday, 1992), 5:1117. Both New Testament and Book of Mormon authors connect Moses' lifting up the serpent to Christ, but the serpent had many meanings in the ancient world. Given the abundant Eden imagery in the temple, as well as the ability of symbols to convey multiple meanings, it seems likely that the serpent would have been interpreted in connection with the Eden narrative as well.

11. See Michael A. Fishbane, *Biblical Text and Texture: A Literary Reading of Selected Texts* (Oxford: Oneworld Publications, 1998), 12.

12. See Gary A. Anderson, "Biblical Origins and the Problem of the Fall," *Pro Ecclesia* 10, no. 1 (Winter 2001), 20–21. Both Fishbane and Anderson also note the strong emphasis on Sabbath rest in the tabernacle account, just as in Genesis.

13. See also Levenson, *Sinai and Zion*, 143–44.

14. Ezekiel even names the temple altar *har'ēl* (Ezekiel 43:15), which was apparently understood as "the mountain of God." See Levenson, *Sinai and Zion*, 139.

15. Richard Clifford, *The Cosmic Mountain in Canaan and the Old Testament* (Cambridge: Harvard University Press, 1972), 6; emphasis added.

16. Take for example the Cylinder of Gudea, which describes the temple thus:
The house, mooring stake of the country,
grown up 'twixt heaven and earth . . .
As the great mountain that it was,
the house abutted heaven,
shone, a very sun, in heaven's midst.
"The Cylinders of Gudea," B.i.1–2, 6–7, in *The Harps That Once . . . Sumerian Poetry in Translation*, trans. Thorkild Jacobsen (New Haven: Yale University Press, 1987), 425.

17. Beale, *The Temple and the Church's Mission*, 82.

18. For a discussion of the imagery used in Ezekiel and its connection to Adam, see Beale, *Temple and the Church's Mission*, 75.

19. H. Freedman and Maurice Simon, eds., *Midrash Rabbah* (New York: Soncino, 1983), 1:171; bracketed information in original. See also 1:130, where Adam is depicted offering sacrifice in Eden.

20. *Testament of Levi* 8:5, trans. H. Kee, in *Old Testament Pseudepigrapha*, 1:791.

21. The only other occurrences of *šmr* and *'bd* together are in commands to the Israelites to guard and keep the commandments (about ten times). See Beale, *Temple and the Church's Mission*, 67.

22. *Life of Adam and Eve* 29:1–5, trans. M. D. Johnson, *Old Testament Pseudepigrapha*, 2:285.

23. See also *Midrash Rabbah* 1:130, as pointed out above.

24. *Midrash Rabbah* 1:115. Targum Pseudo-Jonathan, an expansionistic Aramaic

translation of the Pentateuch, states that God "brought dust from the place of the sanctuary, and from the four winds of the earth, and a mixture of all the waters of the earth" to form Adam (Genesis 3:7; my translation). Adam is also led into Eden "from the mountain of worship, the place from whence he had been created" (Genesis 2:15; my translation).

25. *Life of Adam and Eve* 51:6–7 states that an angel appeared to Solomon and told him "where the place of prayer was where Adam and Eve used to worship the Lord God. And it is fitting for you to build the temple of the Lord, the house of prayer, at that place."

26. Jon Levenson and Kevin Madigan, *Resurrection: The Power of God for Christians and Jews* (New Haven, CT: Yale University Press, 2008), 89; emphasis added.

27. Bruce H. Porter and Stephen D. Ricks, "Names in Antiquity: Old, New, and Hidden," in *By Study and Also by Faith*, ed. John M. Lundquist and Stephen D. Ricks (Salt Lake City: Deseret Book, 1990), 1:501.

28. See, for example, the beginning of the Babylonian creation myth *Enuma Elish*, which describes the world before creation thus:

> When skies above were not yet named
> Nor earth below pronounced by name . . .
> When yet no gods were manifest,
> Nor names pronounced, nor destinies decreed.

The Epic of Creation 1.1–8, in *Myths from Mesopotamia: Creation, The Flood, Gilgamesh, and Others*, ed. and trans. Stephanie Dalley (Oxford: Oxford University Press, 1989).

29. Aside from the examples already cited of the priest delivering oracles on God's behalf, presentation before the priest as a representative of God can also be seen in cases of judgment where the parties are to appear "before the Lord, before the priests" (Deuteronomy 19:17).

30. Of course, all Israelite *men* were commanded to appear before the Lord three times a year, but it is only in this passage that explicit mention is made of everyone being present: "men, and women, and children, and thy stranger that is within thy gates" (Deuteronomy 31:12).

31. The exact chronology of Eden is unclear. If we follow Joseph Smith and read Genesis 1 as spiritual creation and Genesis 2–3 as physical, then Adam's naming of the animals would take place after day seven, as suggested above. If we follow those scholars who would attribute Genesis 1–2:4a and 2:4b–3:24 to two separate sources, then the relation of Eden to the seven creative days becomes much more problematic.

32. ḥawwā and ḥāy are associated with the root ḥyh "to live," though not necessarily by derivation.

4

The Tree of Knowledge as the Veil of the Sanctuary

Jeffrey M. Bradshaw

One thing that has always perplexed readers of Genesis is the location of the two special trees within the Garden of Eden. Although scripture initially applies the phrase "in the midst" only to the tree of life (Genesis 2:9), the tree of knowledge is later said by Eve to be located there too (see Genesis 3:3).[1] In the context of these verses, the Hebrew phrase corresponding to "in the midst" literally means "in the center."[2] How can *both* trees be in the center?

Elaborate explanations have been attempted to describe how both the tree of life and the tree of knowledge could share the center of the Garden of Eden.[3] For example, it has been suggested that these two trees were in reality different aspects of a single tree, that they shared a common trunk, or that they were somehow intertwined, as shown in figure 1.

Fig. 1. Intertwined Tree of Life and Tree of Knowledge in the Center of a Mountainous Garden of Eden Setting. From Lutwin, *How the Devil Deceived Eve* (detail), early fourteenth century.

Jeffrey M. Bradshaw, PhD, is a senior research scientist at the Florida Institute for Human and Machine Cognition (IHMC) in Pensacola, Florida (http://www.ihmc.us/groups/jbradshaw ; http://www.templethemes.net).

As we consider the story more carefully as a whole, it will become apparent why the confusion about the location of the two trees in the Genesis account may well be intentional. First, however, a brief review of the symbolism of the "sacred center" in ancient thought will help clarify the important roles that the tree of life and the tree of knowledge played "in the midst" of the Garden of Eden. One must consider the entire layout of the Garden of Eden as a sanctuary in order to make sense of the concept of the tree of knowledge as the *veil* of the sanctuary.

The Symbolism of the "Sacred Center"

Michael A. Fishbane describes the Garden of Eden as "an *axis mundi*. From it radiate primal streams to the four quarters.... It is the navel or *omphalos*," and the tree of life stands at "the center of this center."[4] Explaining the choice of a tree to represent the concepts of life, earth, and heaven in ancient cultures, Terje Stordalen writes, "Every green tree would symbolize life, and a large tree—rooted in deep soil and stretching towards the sky—potentially makes a cosmic symbol.[5] "In both cases it becomes a 'symbol of the centre.'"[6]

Ezekiel 28:13 places Eden on the mountain of God.[7] "Eden, as a luxuriant cosmic mountain becomes an archetype or symbol for the earthly temple."[8] Described by Isaiah as "the mountain of the Lord's house" (Isaiah 2:2), the Jerusalem temple can be identified—like Eden—as a symbol of the center.[9] Israelite traditions asserted that the foundation stone in front of the ark within the Holy of Holies of the temple at Jerusalem "was the first solid material to emerge from the waters of creation [see Psalm 104:7–9], and it was upon this stone that the Deity effected creation."[10] As a famous passage in the *Midrash Tanhuma* states:

> Just as a navel is set in the middle of a person, so the land of Israel is the navel of the world [cf. Ezekiel 38:12; see also Ezekiel 5:5].... The land of Israel sits at the center of the world; Jerusalem is in the center of the land of Israel; the sanctuary is in the center of Jerusalem; the Temple building is in the center of the sanctuary; the ark is in the center of the Temple building; and the foundation stone, out of which the world was founded, is before the Temple building.[11]

In such traditions, the center is typically depicted as the *most* holy place, and the degree of holiness decreases in proportion to the distance from that center. For instance, we can see this phenomenon in examples where the Lord himself is portrayed as standing in the center of sacred space. S. Kent Brown observes how at his first appearance to the Nephites Jesus "stood in the midst of them" (3 Nephi 11:8). Brown cites other Book of Mormon passages associating the presence of the Lord "in the midst" to the placement of the temple and its altar.[12] He also noted a similar configuration when Jesus blessed the Nephite children (fig. 2):

> As the most Holy One, [the Savior] was standing "in the midst," at the sacred center (3 Nephi 17:12–13). The children sat "upon the ground round about him" (3 Nephi 17:12). When the angels "came down," they "encircled those little ones about." In their place next to the children, the angels themselves "were encircled about with fire" (3 Nephi 17:24). On the edge stood the adults. And beyond them was . . . profane space which stretched away from this holy scene.[13]

Jesus' placement of the children so that they immediately surrounded him—their proximity exceeding even that of the encircling angels and accompanying fire—conveyed a powerful visual message about their holiness—namely, that "whosoever . . . shall humble himself as this little child, the same is greatest in the kingdom of heaven" (Matthew 18:4). Hence, Jesus' instructions to them: "Behold your little ones" (3 Nephi 17:23).

Moses' vision of the burning bush brings together three prominent symbols of the sacred center discussed above: the tree, the mountain, and the Lord himself (fig. 3). Directly tying this symbolism to the Jerusalem Temple, Nicolas Wyatt concludes, "The Menorah is probably what Moses is understood to have seen as the burning bush

Fig. 2. David Lindsley, *Behold Your Little Ones*, 1983.

in Exodus 3."¹⁴ Thus <u>we might see Jehovah as being represented to Moses as one who dwells on</u> a <u>holy mountain in the midst of the burning glory of the tree of life</u>.

The Tree of Knowledge as the Veil of the Sanctuary

Having explored the concept of the sacred center, we return to the question of how both the tree of life and the tree of knowledge could have shared the center of the Garden of Eden. Jewish commentary provides additional intriguing clues.

After describing how the Tree of Life was planted "precisely in the middle of the garden,"¹⁵ *The Zohar* goes on to assert that the tree of knowledge of good and evil was "not precisely in the middle."¹⁶ Clarifying what this might mean, an interesting Jewish tradition about the placement of the two trees is the idea that the foliage of the tree of knowledge hid the tree of life from direct view and that "God did not specifically prohibit eating from the tree of life because the tree of knowledge formed a hedge around it; only after one had partaken of the latter and cleared a path for himself could one come close to the Tree of Life."¹⁷ In other words,

Fig. 3. Dixie L. Majers, *Lit Menorah with Tree of Life*, 1985.

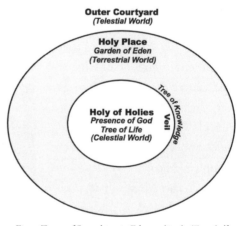

Fig. 4. Zones of Sacredness in Eden and in the Temple.¹⁸

although both trees were located, relatively speaking, in the central portion of Eden, one had to "pass through" the tree of knowledge that was "not precisely in the middle" before one could see and gain access to the tree of life that was "precisely in the middle of the garden."

Consistent with this Jewish tradition about the placement of the trees and with scholarship that sees the Garden of Eden as a temple prototype,[19] Ephrem the Syrian, a fourth-century Christian, called the tree of knowledge "the veil for the sanctuary."[20] He pictured Paradise as a great mountain, with the tree of knowledge providing a permeable boundary partway up the slopes (figure 4). The tree of knowledge, Ephrem concluded, "acts as a sanctuary curtain [i.e., veil] hiding the Holy of Holies, which is the Tree of Life higher up."[21] In addition to this inner boundary, Jewish, Christian, and Muslim sources sometimes speak of a "wall" surrounding the whole of the garden, separating it from the "outer courtyard" of the mortal world.[22]

Temple	Eden	Ark	Sinai
Holy of Holies	Summit/Heights ♦ God, Tree of Life ♦ The Victorious	Upper Deck ♦ Deity ♦ Noah	Summit/Heights ♦ The Glorious One
Veil	Tree of Knowledge		
Holy Place	Slopes ♦ Adam and Eve ♦ The Righteous	Middle Part ♦ Birds	Halfway Up ♦ Aaron Round About ♦ Priests
Outer Courtyard	Lower Slopes ♦ Animals ♦ Penitent Sinners	Lower Part ♦ Animals	Below ♦ People

Fig. 5. Ephrem the Syrian's Conception of Eden, the Ark, and Sinai.

In explaining his conception of Eden, Ephrem cited parallels with the division of the animals on Noah's ark and the demarcations on Sinai separating Moses, Aaron, the priests, and the people, as shown in figure 5.[23] According to this way of thinking, movement inward toward the sacred center was symbolically equivalent to moving upward toward the top of the sacred mountain.

Recall that on Sinai, Israel was gathered in three groups: "the masses at the foot of the mountain, where they viewed God's 'Presence' from afar; the Seventy part way up; and Moses at the very top, where he entered directly into God's Presence."[24] Likewise, Ephrem described the "lower, second, and third stories"[25] of the temple-like ark (see Genesis 6:16) so as to highlight the righteousness of Noah and to distinguish him from the animals and the birds.[26] Finally, as explained previously, Ephrem pictured Eden as a great mountain, with the tree of knowledge providing a boundary partway up the slopes.

Careful analysis of the narrative features of the Genesis account provides support for these perspectives about the nature of Adam and Eve's actions. Notice that the dramatic irony of the story is heightened by the fact that while the reader is informed about both trees (see Moses 3:9), Adam and Eve are only specifically told about the tree of knowledge (see Moses 3:16–17). As we will see below, the subtle conflation of the location of two trees in the sacred center of the Garden of Eden prepares readers for the confusion that later ensues in the dialogue with the serpent, and sets the stage for the transgression of Adam and Eve. Given his knowledge of both trees, Satan is enabled to exploit their ignorance to his advantage.

Fig. 6. Giuliano Bugiardini: *Adam, Eve* (detail), ca. 1510.

A "Temple" Setting for the Transgression of Adam and Eve

At the moment of temptation, Satan deliberately tries to confuse Eve. The devil knows that there are two trees in the midst of the garden, but only the tree of knowledge is visible to Eve (see Moses 4:9) since, according to Ephrem, the tree of life is hidden behind it.²⁷ To add to the confusion, Satan "made the two trees seem identical: the Tree of the Knowledge of Good and Evil would open her eyes, and she would be like God, knowing both good and evil. Almost the same was true of the tree of life, for Wisdom opened the eyes of those who ate her fruit, and as they became wise, they became divine."²⁸

Another theme of confusion stems from Satan's efforts to mask his identity. The painting shown in figure 6 portrays the tempter in the dual guise of a serpent and a woman whose hair and facial features exactly mirror those of Eve. This common form of medieval portrayal was not intended to assert that the woman was devilish, but rather to depict the devil as trying to allay Eve's fears, deceptively appealing to her by appearing in a form that resembled her own.²⁹ Though Satan is not said in scripture to have appeared to Eve as a woman, he did try to deceive her when he represented himself as a serpent, as will be explained below.

Of great importance in understanding the story of the transgression of Adam and Eve is the fact that the serpent is a frequently used representation of the Messiah and his life-giving power, as shown, for example, in this depiction of Moses holding up the brazen serpent (fig. 7).³⁰ Moreover, with specific relevance to the symbolism of the sacred location where he appeared to Eve in the Garden of Eden, evidence suggests that the form of the seraphim, whose function it was to guard the divine throne at the sacred center of the heavenly temple, was that of a fiery winged serpent.³¹ This idea gives new meaning to the statement of Nephi that the "being who beguiled our first parents . . . transformeth himself nigh unto an angel of light" (2 Nephi 9:9).

In the context of the temptation of Eve, Richard D. Draper, S. Kent Brown, and Michael D. Rhodes conclude that Satan "has effectively come as the Messiah, offering a promise that only the Messiah can offer, for it is the Messiah who will control the powers of life and death and can promise life, not Satan."³² Not only has the devil come in guise of the Holy One, he seems to have deliberately appeared, without authorization, at

Fig. 7. *Moses and the Brazen Serpent* (detail), ca. 1866.

a particularly sacred place in the garden.³³ If it is true, as Ephrem the Syrian believed, that the tree of knowledge was a figure for "the veil for the sanctuary,"³⁴ then Satan positioned himself, in the extreme of sacrilegious effrontery, as the very "keeper of the gate" (2 Nephi 9:41). Thus, in the apt words of Catherine Thomas, Eve was induced to take the fruit "from the wrong hand, having listened to the wrong voice."³⁵

This raises a question: since the knowledge imparted by the transgression of Adam and Eve was good, helping them become more like God (see Moses 4:28), why did Satan encourage—rather than prevent—their eating of the fruit of the tree of knowledge? Surprisingly, the scriptural story makes it evident that their transgression must have been as much an important part of the devil's strategy as it was a central feature of the Father's plan. In this one respect, the programs of God and Satan seem to have had something in common.

However, the difference in intention between God and Satan became apparent when it was time for Adam and Eve to take the *next* step.³⁶ In this regard, the scriptures seem to suggest that the adversary wanted Adam and Eve to eat of the fruit of the tree of life *directly after* they partook of the tree of knowledge—a danger that moved God to take immediate preventive action by the placement of the cherubim and the flaming sword to guard "the way of the tree of life" (see Moses 4:28–31; Alma 12:23, 42:2–3). For had Adam and Eve eaten of the fruit of the tree of life at that time, "there would have been no death" and no "space granted unto man in which he might repent"—in other words, no "probationary state" to prepare for a final judgment and resurrection (see Alma 12:23–24).

The Father did intend—eventually—for Adam and Eve to partake of the tree of life, but not until they had learned through mortal experience to distinguish good from evil.³⁷

The Forbidden Fruit as a Form of Knowledge

Whether speaking of the heavenly temple or of its earthly models, the theme of access to revealed knowledge is inseparably connected with the passage through the veil. Such knowledge includes the restoration of things from the former world that must be brought to "remembrance" (John 14:26) because they have been forgotten on earth.

With respect to the heavenly temple, scripture and tradition amply attest of how a knowledge of eternity is available to those who are permitted to enter within the divine veil.[38] For example, Jewish and Christian accounts speak of a blueprint of eternity that is worked out in advance and shown on the inside of that veil to prophetic figures as part of their heavenly ascent.[39] In a similar vein, Islamic tradition speaks of a "white cloth from Paradise" upon which Adam saw the fate of his posterity.[40] Nibley gives the "great round" of the hypocephalus as an Egyptian attempt to capture the essence of such pictures of eternity and shows how similar concepts have appeared in the literature of other ancient cultures.[41]

On the other hand, with respect to *earthly* temples, a conventional answer to the question of what kind of knowledge the tree of knowledge provided is supplied by Psalm 19:8. There, in similar terms to the description of the forbidden fruit in Genesis 3:6 ("pleasant to the sight, good for food and to be desired to make one wise"), God's law is described as "making wise the simple, rejoicing the heart and enlightening the eyes."[42] Gordon J. Wenham observes, "The law was of course kept in the Holy of Holies [of the temple]: the decalogue inside the ark and the book of the law beside it (see Exodus 25:16, Deuteronomy 31:26). Furthermore, Israel knew that touching the ark or even seeing it uncovered brought death, just as eating from the tree of knowledge did (see Numbers 4:20, 2 Samuel 6:7)."[43]

However, given explicit admissions in Jewish tradition about elements of the first temple that were later lost, plausibly including things that were once contained in the temple ark, it is not impossible that the knowledge in question may have included something more than the Ten Commandments and the Torah as we now know them.[44] Having carefully scrutinized the evidence, Margaret Barker concluded that the lost items were "all associated with the high priesthood."[45] Also probing the significance of the lost furniture "list of the schoolmen," Nibley, like Barker, specifically connected the missing "five things" to lost ordinances of the high priesthood.[46] By piecing together the ancient sources, it may be surmised that the knowledge revealed to those made wise through entering in to the innermost sanctuary of the Temple of Solomon included an understanding of premortal life, the order of creation, and the eternal covenant[47] and that it "provided a clue to the pattern and future destiny of the universe"[48] that "gave power over creation" when used in righteousness.[49] Thus the rending of the veil at the death of Christ symbolized not only renewed access to the divine presence in heaven but also the knowledge revealed in earthly temples that makes such access possible (fig. 8).⁵⁰

Consistent with this general idea about the nature of the forbidden fruit, Islamic traditions insist that the reason Satan was condemned after the Fall was because he had claimed that he would reveal a knowledge of certain things to Adam and Eve. In deceptive counterpoint to God's authentic teachings to Adam about a series of sacred names that he was to use to prove his worthiness before the angels,⁵¹ Satan is portrayed in one Islamic account as recruiting his accomplice, the "fair and prudent" serpent, by promising that he would reveal to it "three mysterious words" which would "preserve [it] from sickness, age, and death."⁵² Having by this means won over the serpent, Satan then directly equates the effect of knowing these words with the eating of the forbidden fruit by promising the same protection from death to Eve if she will but partake.⁵³

Fig. 8. William Bell Scott, 1811–90: *The Rending of the Veil*, 1867–68.

The fifteenth-century *Adamgirkʻ* asks, "If a good secret [or mystery⁵⁴] was in [the evil fruit], why did [God] say not to draw near?"⁵⁵ and then answers its own question implicitly. Simply put, the gift by which Adam and Eve would "become divine,"⁵⁶ and for which the tree of knowledge constituted a part of the approach, was, as yet, "an unattainable thing [t]hat was *not in its time.*"⁵⁷ Though God intended Adam and Eve to advance in knowledge, it seems that the condemnation of Satan came because he had acted deceptively and without authorization, in the realization that introducing the fruit of the tree of knowledge to Adam and Eve under circumstances of disobedience and unpreparedness would bring the consequences of the Fall upon them, putting them in a position of mortal danger.⁵⁸ Moreover, as was mentioned previously, it is clear that if Satan could have also induced Adam and Eve to partake of the tree of life at that time, there would have been even more serious consequences.

There is no question that the knowledge itself was good. However, some kinds of knowledge are reserved to be revealed by the Father himself "in his own time, and in his own way, and according to his own will" (D&C 88:68). As the Prophet Joseph Smith taught:

> That which is wrong under one circumstance, may be, and often is, right under another. . . .
>
> A parent may whip a child, and justly, too, because he stole an apple; whereas if the child had asked for the apple, and the parent had given it, the child would have eaten it with a better appetite; there would have been no stripes; all the pleasure of the apple would have been secured, all the misery of stealing lost.
>
> This principle will justly apply to all of God's dealings with His children. Everything that God gives us is lawful and right; and it is proper that we should enjoy His gifts and blessings whenever and wherever He is disposed to bestow; but if we should seize upon those same blessings and enjoyments without law, without revelation, without commandment, those blessings and enjoyments would prove cursings and vexations.[59]

By way of analogy to the situation of Adam and Eve and its setting in the temple-like layout of the Garden of Eden, recall that service in Israelite temples under conditions of worthiness was intended to sanctify the participants. However, as taught in Levitical laws of purity, doing the same "while defiled by sin, was to court unnecessary danger, perhaps even death."[60]

Hugh Nibley succinctly summed up the situation: "Satan disobeyed orders when he revealed certain secrets to Adam and Eve, not because they were not known and done in other worlds, but because he was not authorized in that time and place to convey them."[61] Although Satan had "given the fruit to Adam and Eve, it was not his prerogative to do so—regardless of what had been done in other worlds. (When the time comes for such fruit, it will be given us legitimately.)"[62]

Concluding Thoughts

Jewish and Christian teachings that the tree of knowledge symbolized the veil of the Garden of Eden sanctuary not only provide a coherent explanation for some puzzling aspects of the story of Adam and Eve, but are also consistent with an interpretive approach that attempts to comprehend how its story plot fits within larger metaplots throughout the Pentateuch—and sometimes even further afield. For example, we have already discussed how Ephrem related the three divisions of the templelike layout of the Garden of Eden to the three levels of Noah's ark and the three groups of Israelites at Mount Sinai. Recurring throughout the Old Testament and ancient Near East traditions are allusions to the layout of sacred spaces—as well as accounts of serious consequences for those who attempt unauthorized entry through the veil into the innermost sanctuary.[63]

This general thesis is useful as far as it goes. For example, in the stories of the transgressions of Adam and Eve, of the "sons of God" who married the "daughters of men," and of the builders of the Tower of Babel, we cannot fail to observe the common story thread concerning a God who places strict boundaries between the human and the divine. However, we must not forget a significant and opposite theme in Genesis 1–11—namely, that within some of these same chapters God is also portrayed as having sought to *erase* the divine-human boundary for a righteous few, drawing them into his very presence.[64] The prime examples of this motif are, of course, Enoch and Noah, of whom it was explicitly said that they "walked with God."[65] Happily, Latter-day Saints know that they can add the names of Adam and Eve to the exceptional list containing these two shining examples of righteousness. The Book of Moses avers that our first parents eventually had "all things . . . confirmed unto [them] by an holy ordinance" (Moses 5:59). From the story of Adam and Eve and their family found in modern revelation and latter-day temples, we know that the story of the Fall "is not an account of sin alone but the beginning of a drama about becoming a being who fully reflects God's very own image. *Genesis is not only about the origins of sin; it is also about the foundations of human perfection.* The work that God has begun in creation he will bring to completion."[66]

Notes

✦ Portions of this article were adapted from Jeffrey M. Bradshaw, *Temple Themes in the Book of Moses* (Salt Lake City: Eborn, 2010), 69–70, 74–76, 84, 96–103. See www.templethemes.net.

1. For a brief survey on the question of one or two trees, and related textual irregularities that point to a theme of deliberate confusion consistent with the thesis of this chapter, see Tryggve N. D. Mettinger, *The Eden Narrative: A Literary and Religiohistorical Study of Genesis 2–3* (Winona Lake, IN: Eisenbrauns, 2007), 5–11.

2. See, e.g., Meir Zlotowitz and Nosson Scherman, *Bereishis / Genesis: A New Translation with a Commentary Anthologized from Talmudic, Midrashic and Rabbinic Sources* (Brooklyn: Mesorah, 1986), 96, #398; Daniel C. Matt, *The Zohar, Pritzker Edition* (Stanford: Stanford University, 2004), Be-Reshit 1:35a, 220. The *Zohar* asserts, "The tree of life is precisely in the middle of the garden, conveying all waters of creation, branching below . . . by paths in every direction."

3. See diverse examples in Zlotowitz and Scherman, *Bereishis*, 96.

4. Michael A. Fishbane, "The Sacred Center," in *Texts and Responses: Studies Presented to Nahum H. Glatzer on the Occasion of His Seventieth Birthday by His Students*, ed. Michael A. Fishbane and P. R. Flohr (Leiden, Netherlands: Brill, 1975), 9.

5. Often symbolized as a cosmic tree, the temple also "originates in the underworld, stands on the earth as a 'meeting place,' and yet towers (architecturally) into the heavens and gives access to the heavens through its ritual." John M. Lundquist, "Fundamentals of Temple Ideology from Eastern Traditions," in *Reason, Revelation, and Faith: Essays in Honor of Truman G. Madsen*, ed. Donald W. Parry, Daniel C. Peterson, and Stephen D. Ricks (Provo, UT: FARMS, 2002), 675.

6. Terje Stordalen, *Echoes of Eden: Genesis 2–3 and the Symbolism of the Eden Garden in Biblical Hebrew Literature* (Leuven, Belgium: Peeters, 2000), 288–89.

7. Some readers object to the idea of Eden being located on a cosmic mountain, since this aspect is not mentioned explicitly in Genesis 2–3. See Gary A. Anderson, "The Cosmic Mountain: Eden and Its Early Interpreters in Syriac Christianity," in *Genesis 1–3 in the History of Exegesis: Intrigue in the Garden*, ed. G. A. Robins (Lewiston/Queenston: Edwin Mellen Press, 1988), 192–99 for careful readings that argue for just such a setting.

8. Anderson, "The Cosmic Mountain," 199.

9. "The three most important cosmic mountains in the Bible are Eden, Sinai and Zion." Anderson, "The Cosmic Mountain," 192. "The identification of the temple in Jerusalem with Eden is as old as the Bible itself." Anderson, "The Cosmic Mountain," 203.

10. John M. Lundquist, *The Temple: Meeting Place of Heaven and Earth* (London, England: Thames and Hudson, 1993), 7.

11. John T. Townsend, ed., *Midrash Tanhuma*, 3 vols. (Hoboken, NJ: Ktav, 1989–2003), Qedoshim 7:10, Leviticus 19:23ff., part 1, 2:309–10.

12. E.g., 2 Nephi 22:6; 3 Nephi 11:8, 21:17–18; cf. Isaiah 12:6; Jeremiah 14:9; Hosea 11:9; Joel 2:27; Micah 5:13–14; Moses 7:69; Zechariah 3:5, 15, 17. S. Kent Brown, *Voices from the Dust: Book of Mormon Insights* (American Fork, UT: Covenant Communications, 2004), 150–51.

13. Brown, *Voices from the Dust*, 147–48.

14. Nicolas Wyatt, *Space and Time in the Religious Life of the Near East* (Sheffield, England: Sheffield Academic Press, 2001), 169. Some might question this symbolism because the Menorah did not stand in the sacred center of the second temple. However, Margaret Barker argues that "there is reason to believe that the Menorah . . . originally

stood [in the Holy of Holies], and not in the great hall of the temple." *The Hidden Tradition of the Kingdom of God* (London, England: SPCK, 2007), 6. For more on this topic see Jeffrey M. Bradshaw, *In God's Image and Likeness 1: Ancient and Modern Perspectives on the Book of Moses* (Salt Lake City: Eborn, 2010), 755nE-212.

15. Matt, *Zohar*, Be-Reshit 1:35a, 220.

16. Matt, *Zohar*, Be-Reshit 1:35a, 220n921. Matt's note is a clarification of the meaning of the phrase in context. His translation of the text itself simply says "It is not in the middle."

17. Zlotowitz and Scherman, *Bereishis*, 101, cf. 96; see also Louis Ginzberg, ed., *The Legends of the Jews*, 7 vols. (Philadelphia, PA: The Jewish Publication Society of America, 1909–38; Baltimore, MD: Johns Hopkins University Press, 1998), 1:70, 5:91n50.

18. Compare Gary A. Anderson, *The Genesis of Perfection: Adam and Eve in Jewish and Christian Imagination* (Louisville, KY: Westminster John Knox Press, 2001), 57, fig. 5.

19. See, e.g., Gordon J. Wenham, "Sanctuary Symbolism in the Garden of Eden Story," in *I Studied Inscriptions from before the Flood: Ancient Near Eastern, Literary, and Linguistic Approaches to Genesis 1–11*, ed. Richard S. Hess and David Toshio Tsumura (Winona Lake, IN: Eisenbrauns, 1994), 399; Bradshaw, *In God's Image 1*, 146–49.

20. Ephrem the Syrian, "The Hymns on Paradise," in *Hymns on Paradise*, ed. Sebastian Brock (Crestwood, NY: St. Vladimir's Seminary Press, 1990), 3:5, 92. Note that the phrase "in the midst" was also used to describe the location of the heavenly veil (translated in the KJV as "firmament") in the Creation account (Genesis 1:6). See Ginzberg, *Legends*, 1:51–52: "On the second day [of Creation], I shall put a division between the terrestrial waters and the heavenly waters; so will he [Moses] hang up a veil in the Tabernacle to divide the Holy Place and the Most Holy."

21. Brock in Ephrem the Syrian, "Paradise," 52. See Jeffrey M. Bradshaw and Ronan J. Head, "The Investiture Panel at Mari and Rituals of Divine Kingship in the Ancient Near East," *Studies in the Bible and Antiquity* 4 (2012): 23–25, for examples of how treelike posts or columns holding up woven screens or partitions performed a similar function in ancient temples.

22. E.g., Gary A. Anderson and Michael Stone, eds., *A Synopsis of the Books of Adam and Eve*, 2nd ed. (Atlanta, GA: Scholars Press, 1999), 19:1a–19:1d, 56E–57E.

23. See Ephrem the Syrian, "Paradise," 2:9–13, 88–89, 3:1–5, 90–92.

24. John Eugene Seaich, *Ancient Texts and Mormonism: Discovering the Roots of the Eternal Gospel in Ancient Israel and the Primitive Church*, 2nd ed. (Salt Lake City: n.p., 1995), 660, see also 568–77, 661, 807–9.

25. For more on the symbolism of the temple in the ark, see Jeffrey M. Bradshaw, "The Ark and the Tent: Temple Symbolism in the Story of Noah" (paper presented at the Proceedings of the Symposium on "The Temple on Mount Zion," Provo, UT, September 22, 2012), to appear in David R. Seely and William J. Hamblin, *The Temple in Mount Zion* (American Fork, UT: Covenant Communications; Provo, UT: The Interpreter Foundation, forthcoming).

26. As an analogue to this idea, consider that the *Animal Apocalypse* in 1 Enoch 85–89 was written in a code that represents key individuals (and their righteous and wicked descendants) as "animals" of different colors. George W. E. Nickelsburg, ed.,

1 Enoch 1: A Commentary on the Book of 1 Enoch, Chapters 1–36; 81–108, Hermeneia: A Critical and Historical Commentary on the Bible (Minneapolis, MN: Fortress Press, 2001), 85–89, 364–67. Some "animals" (notably Noah and Moses) are eventually transformed into "men," which, according to Barker, *Hidden Tradition*, 45, represents the acquiring of angelic status after having been taught a "mystery" (see 1 Enoch 89:1). With regard to birds, note that the angel Yahoel is described as both man and bird in, e.g., the *Apocalypse of Abraham*. Andrei A. Orlov, "The Pteromorphic Angelology of the *Apocalypse of Abraham*," in *Divine Manifestations in the Slavonic Pseudepigrapha*, ed. Andrei A. Orlov, *Orientalia Judaica Christiana* (Pisacataway, NJ: Gorgias Press, 2009).

27. Mettinger, *Eden*, 34–41.

28. Margaret Barker, "Wisdom and the Stewardship of Knowledge" (Bishop's Lecture, Lincoln Cathedral Lectures, March 2004), 3, http://www.margaretbarker.com/Papers/WisdomAndTheStewardshipOfKnowledge.pdf.

29. Jennifer O'Reilly, "The Trees of Eden in Mediaeval Iconography," in *A Walk in the Garden: Biblical, Iconographical and Literary Images of Eden*, ed. Paul Morris and Deborah Sawyer, Journal for the Study of the Old Testament Supplement Series 136 (Sheffield, England: JSOT Press, 1992), 168.

30. Numbers 21:8–9; John 3:14–15; 2 Nephi 25:20; Alma 33:19; Helaman 8:14–15. See also Bradshaw, *In God's Image 1*, 247–48. Consistent with the idea of serpents as Seraphim guarding the celestial throne is the fact that the serpent was "put . . . upon a pole." This imagery evokes the function of guardians positioned at temple gateposts in ancient Mesopotamia who were responsible for the introduction of worshippers to the presence of the god. Bradshaw, *Investiture Panel*, 20–25.

31. James H. Charlesworth, *The Good and Evil Serpent: How a Universal Symbol Became Christianized* (New Haven: Yale, 2010), 444–45, see also 30, 87, 220, 258, 332, 426. See especially K. Joines, "Winged serpents in Isaiah's inaugural vision." *Journal of Biblical Literature* 86, no. 4 (1967): 410–15, cited in Charlesworth, *Good and Evil Serpent*, 444.

32. Richard D. Draper, S. Kent Brown, and Michael D. Rhodes, *The Pearl of Great Price: A Verse-by-Verse Commentary* (Salt Lake City: Deseret Book, 2005), 43; see John 5:25–26; 2 Nephi 9:3–26.

33. Draper, Brown, and Rhodes, 42, 150–51.

34. Ephrem the Syrian, "Paradise," 3:5, 92.

35. M. Catherine Thomas, "Women, Priesthood, and the At-One-Ment," in *Spiritual Lightening: How the Power of the Gospel Can Enlighten Minds and Lighten Burdens*, ed. M. Catherine Thomas (Salt Lake City: Deseret Book, 1996), 53.

36. Cf. Stordalen, *Echoes*, 231.

37. Bruce C. Hafen, *The Broken Heart: Applying the Atonement to Life's Experiences* (Salt Lake City: Deseret Book, 1989), 30.

38. See, e.g., Hugh W. Nibley, *Teachings of the Pearl of Great Price* (Provo, UT: FARMS, Brigham Young University, 2004), 10, 117.

39. For various examples, see Bradshaw, *In God's Image 1*, Moses 1:27-b, 62–63.

40. Muhammad ibn Abd Allah al-Kisa'i, *Tales of the Prophets (Qisas al-anbiya)*, ed. Seyyed Hossein Nasr, trans. Wheeler M. Thackston Jr. (Chicago: KAZI Publications, 1997), 82.

41. See Hugh W. Nibley and Michael D. Rhodes, *One Eternal Round*, vol. 19 of the Collected Works of Hugh Nibley (Salt Lake City: Deseret Book, 2010), 188–585.

42. Wenham's translation, as given in Wenham, "Sanctuary Symbolism," 403.

43. Wenham, "Sanctuary Symbolism," 403.

44. See, e.g., Bradshaw, *In God's Image 1*, 516–18, 658–60, 665–69, 679–81; Jeffrey M. Bradshaw, "The Ezekiel Mural at Dura Europos: A Tangible Witness of Philo's Jewish Mysteries?," *BYU Studies* 49, no. 1 (2010): 5–49.

45. Barker, *Hidden Tradition*, 6–7.

46. Hugh W. Nibley, "Return to the Temple," in *Temple and Cosmos: Beyond This Ignorant Present*, ed. Don E. Norton, vol. 12 of the Collected Works of Hugh Nibley (Salt Lake City: Deseret Book, 1992), 54; see D&C 84:19–26; JST, Exodus 34:1–2.

47. Margaret Barker, *The Older Testament: The Survival of Themes from the Ancient Royal Cult in Sectarian Judaism and Early Christianity* (London: SPCK, 1987), 82.

48. A. E. Harvey, *The New English Bible Companion to the New Testament*, 2nd ed. (Cambridge: Cambridge University Press, 2004), 533.

49. Barker, *Older*, 82; cf. JST, Genesis 14:30–31.

50. Matthew 27:51; Mark 15:38. In this connection, Nibley writes: "The *Gospel of Philip* depicts the rending of the veil not as the abolition of the temple ordinances, as the church fathers fondly supposed, but of the opening of those ordinances to all the righteous of Israel, 'in order that we might enter into . . . the truth of it.' 'The priesthood can still go within the veil with the high priest (i.e., the Lord).' We are allowed to see what is behind the veil, and 'we enter into it in our weakness, through signs and tokens which the world despises." See Wesley W. Isenberg, "The Gospel of Philip (II, 3)," in *The Nag Hammadi Library*, ed. James M. Robinson (San Francisco: HarperSanFrancisco, 1990), 85:1–20, 159. Hugh W. Nibley, *The Message of the Joseph Smith Papyri: An Egyptian Endowment*, 2nd ed. (Salt Lake City: Deseret Book, 2005), 444.

51. See Bradshaw, *In God's Image 1*, 177–79n3:19b.

52. G. Weil, ed., *The Bible, the Koran, and the Talmud; or, Biblical Legends of the Mussulmans, Compiled from Arabic Sources, and Compared with Jewish Traditions, Translated from the German* (New York City: Harper and Brothers, 1863; repr., Kila, MT: Kessinger Publishing, 2006), 26.

53. Weil, *The Bible, the Koran, and the Talmud*, 30.

54. Michael E. Stone, ed., *Adamgirk': The Adam Book of Arak'el of Siwnik'* (Oxford: Oxford University Press, 2007), 3.2.5, 53n108 and 1.3.70, 101.

55. Stone, *Adamgirk'*, 3.2.5, 53.

56. Stone, *Adamgirk'*, 1.3.71, 101. Note, however, that, according to the conception of this incident described in this chapter, this promise actually would reach its complete fulfillment through taking of the tree of life, not merely of the tree of knowledge alone as deceptively asserted here by Satan.

57. Stone, *Adamgirk'*, 1.3.27, 96; emphasis added.

58. See Jeffrey M. Bradshaw and Ronan J. Head, "Mormonism's Satan and the Tree of Life" (longer version of an invited presentation originally given at the 2009 Conference of the European Mormon Studies Association, Turin, Italy, July 30–31, 2009), *Element: Journal of the Society for Mormon Philosophy and Theology* 4, no. 2 (2010): 20–21.

59. Joseph Smith, *History of the Church of Jesus Christ of Latter-day Saints*, 7 vols. (Salt Lake City: Deseret Book, 1978), April 11, 1842, 5:135. Though Satan seems to have been aware of what had been done in *other* worlds, Moses 4:6 states that he "knew not the mind of God" with respect to *this* one. For more on this topic, see Bradshaw and Head, *Mormonism's Satan*, 44–45n89.

60. Anderson, *Perfection*, 129.

61. Nibley, "Return to the Temple," 63.

62. Hugh W. Nibley, "Gifts," in *Approaching Zion*, ed. Don E. Norton, vol. 9 of the Collected Works of Hugh Nibley (Salt Lake City: Deseret Book, 1989), 92.

63. See examples in Bradshaw, *Moses Temple Themes*, 123.

64. For a discussion of how the theme of the "two ways" structures chapters 5–8 of the Book of Moses, see Bradshaw, *In God's Image 1*, 342–51.

65. See Genesis 5:24; 6:9. For more on this topic, see Jeffrey M. Bradshaw and David J. Larsen, *In God's Image and Likeness 2: Enoch, Noah, and the Tower of Babel* (Provo, UT: The Interpreter Foundation, forthcoming).

66. Anderson, *Perfection*, 8; emphasis in original; see also Moses 1:39.

5

"Come Near unto Me": Guarded Space and Its Mediators in the Jerusalem Temple

Avram R. Shannon

To the Israelites, the temple represented God's presence on the earth and so stood as a singular symbol of his relationship with them. Therefore, the temple was one of the foundational institutions defining and establishing ancient Israelite culture and religion. Like most temples in the ancient world, the Israelite temple contained sacred space which was controlled and protected through the architectural features and arrangement of the temple, including the creation of borders. These borders clearly demarcated sacred from profane space, and passage through them was strictly controlled so that only those who were authorized could be admitted into God's presence.[1] The control of the sacred space demonstrated to the ancient worshippers at the temple that it was God's house, and those who entered did so at his sufferance.[2]

Many of the specific aspects of the ritual system associated with the ancient temple remain obscure and arcane to us. This is to be expected, since those rituals, like temple rituals throughout time, are sacred and have their sacredness protected by a veil of secrecy. Much that went on in the temple was simply not recorded.[3] Thus the actual ritual practices of the temple were hidden behind

---

Avram R. Shannon is a PhD candidate in the Department of Near Eastern Languages and Cultures at The Ohio State University.

both a metaphorical veil as well as literal veils (see Exodus 26:31–32). In spite of this secrecy, the Old Testament is very concerned with the temple and speaks of it and its officers often. This allows us to peer a little bit into the ritual system which it describes in order to better understand the how and the why of its operations, as in the case of the division of sacred space and the admittance of only select, authorized individuals.

The division of sacred space within the temple was supplemented and controlled by guardians, who protected and stood over the passages between different parts of the temple. Some of these guardians, such as the cherubim, were part of the iconography of the temple, and the Old Testament presents them using symbolic language of composite animal figures (Ezekiel 1:4–14). Other guardians were part of the personnel of the physical temple on the earth. Both types of guardians—along with the architectural divisions—reinforced the notion that temple space was not ordinary space but belonged to God. Because God dwelt in the temple, those who would gain access to the sacred precincts had to be properly purified and able to prove themselves to the guardians of sacred space. The Lord does not create borders and guardians in order to merely keep people out—rather, the gatekeepers are there to mediate who may and may not enter into God's presence. In this system, the unauthorized and the unprepared are kept from sacred things, while those who are able to prove their credentials are admitted through the various levels of holy space in order to experience the presence of God.

Architecture of the Temple

In order to understand the movement and the mediators between sacred spaces, it is first necessary to establish how space was organized in the house of the Lord in the Old Testament. The biblical record describes three different primary shrines[4] dedicated to the God of Israel in addition to other altars and high places, variously conceived.[5] These shrines are the tabernacle, described as being built by the children of Israel during the Exodus (Exodus 25–27); the Temple of Solomon, built by Solomon with materials assembled by his father, David (1 Kings 5–8); and the Second Temple, or Temple of Zerubbabel, which was built by the exiles returning from Babylon (Ezra 1, 3, 6).[6] All of these temples were places of animal sacrifice under the law of Moses, which was the primary ritual activity practiced at temples in ancient Israel.[7]

The existence of these three discrete shrines presents a difficulty to the modern reader looking back at the various temples; this difficulty derives from the long life of the several shrines which existed in Jerusalem. These shrines differed from one another in various respects, such as the size and shape of the main building in the temple complex and the placement of the altar. Not only did the Second Temple (Ezra 1:1–4) differ from the temple which had been destroyed by the Neo-Babylonian king Nebuchadnezzar (2 Kings 25:8–9), but even the destroyed First Temple had undergone structural changes which could have affected the rituals performed therein since Solomon had commissioned it four hundred years earlier (1 Kings 7).[8] One example of this difference occurs in 2 Kings 16:10–16; the Judahite king Ahaz replaced the sacrificial altar which was in the temple with one that he had seen while in the Aramean city of Damascus. Ahaz was not the only king who instituted changes to the temple, and these changes can sometimes obscure the data about temple rituals.[9]

In spite of these concerns, one can discern in the Bible a relatively constant conception of the physical division of sacred space. Although they differed in size and accoutrements, the Bible records a fair amount of continuity between the various shrines, since each one appears to be modeled on earlier ones.[10] One should be careful about reading too much across the temporal divide of the Old Testament, but these continuities provide clues about what was important in the ideology and symbolism of the Israelite and Jewish temples. The wilderness tabernacle provides the most detailed description of its physical dimensions and accoutrements in Exodus 25–30, followed by Solomon's Temple described in 1 Kings 6 and 7, with the Second Temple having the least discussion of these physical elements.[11]

Scholars have attempted to reconstruct the specifics of the architecture of the temple beyond what is found in the scriptures, with mixed results.[12] Use of the scriptures does allow for discussion on the basic outlines of the architecture of all the temples, which was the same for all three shrines. A temple consisted of a courtyard (Exodus 27:9–11; 1 Kings 6:3) surrounding a rectangular building (Exodus 26; 1 Kings 6:2–3; Ezra 6:3). The building was divided into two sections by a veil (Exodus 26:31; 1 Kings 6:21). The larger section was called "the Holy Place," while the other was "the Most Holy Place," or the "Holy of Holies." The Holy Place had within it the table for the shewbread (Exodus 25:23–30; 1 Kings 7:48), or bread of the presence; a seven-branched oil lamp (Exodus 25:31–40; 1 Kings 7:49); and the altar of incense (Exodus 30:1–8; 1 Kings 7:48). Beyond the veil, in the Most Holy Place, was the ark of the covenant, with the mercy seat situated on top (1 Kings 6:20). The ark was not present in the Second Temple.

The Division of Sacred Space

As the separation of the Holy Place from the Most Holy Place makes clear, the temple was divided into areas with different levels of holiness. The concern with the clear division between holy and non-holy derives in part from the requirement on Israel to be holy, after the example of the Lord (Leviticus 11:44). Dividing up the different levels of holiness into walls, partitions, and veils allowed the priests to control the sacred space. In fact, the idea of division and the subsequent order which it represents are central to the symbolic conception of the temple as the cosmic center. Division is represented in Hebrew by the word *hibdil*, which means "to separate," and it is often associated in the Old Testament with temples and priestly concerns. This word is given cosmological significance in the creation account of Genesis 1, where God separated many things, including light from darkness (Genesis 1:4). These acts of division established the cosmic order and placed everything into their proper sphere so they could interact "after their kind" (Genesis 1:21, 25).[13] The connection between the temple and cosmic order is not an accidental one, for the earthly temple represents the heavenly order brought to earth.[14]

As discussed above, the Israelite temples were divided by means of walls and veils, with the center part of the temple being the holiest space, separated even from the rest of the temple by means of a curtain, veiling the presence of God. In order to move towards the Holy of Holies, which was the physical and metaphorical center of the temple, a priest or worshipper had to pass through various courtyards, gates, and curtains, all of which divided and subdivided the sacred space in the holy precinct. It should be noted that an everyday Israelite worshipper did not have access to most parts of the temple, unlike modern temples in The Church of Jesus Christ of Latter-day Saints. The Old Testament explicitly limits access to the Holy Place to priests, and the Holy of Holies to the Aaronic high priest, and then only once a year on the Day of Atonement (Leviticus 16:2–14). In spite of the limits, however, the Holy of Holies was the sacred center of the temple, and so all movement from the profane world to the sacred world was towards that center. The physical divisions gave expression to the cosmic truth of the sacred, set-apart nature of the Lord and his house.[15]

The example of the Day of Atonement shows that unauthorized individuals were forbidden from entering certain areas, a division which served two purposes. The division of space both protected the space from defiling influences and protected the people from the dangers of entering holy space unprepared, especially those who were not authorized and ritually clean.[16] That God's immediate presence could be dangerous to the unprepared may be seen in Exodus 19:7–13, in which all of Mount Sinai is cordoned off as holy space and the penalty for violating the space is death (see also D&C 84:19–24). This cordon for the protection of the people parallels the walls and curtains of the various shrines in Israel and Jerusalem. That the boundary between profane and sacred space could be transcended is also seen from the Sinai example, as Moses, Aaron, and the elders of Israel all go into the mountain and see the Lord after being suitably prepared (Exodus 24:9–10). According to Doctrine and Covenants 84:23–25, the Lord wanted all of Israel to prepare to come into his presence at Sinai, but the people "hardened their hearts" (D&C 84:24) and were unable to do so. God wants all of his people to come back to him, and the divisions and the blocks on movement toward the Holy Place where he dwells are for protection rather than arbitrary rejection.

The movement between levels of holiness was facilitated by protective guards who watched over the way from one area to another and kept out the unauthorized. This idea of movement relates to the concept of liminality. Liminality was first suggested by anthropologists Arnold van Gennep and Victor Turner in their work on ritual and initiation.[17] They applied the idea primarily to rituals, such as the marriage rite, which mediates between the unmarried and the married state.[18] The word liminal derives from *limin*, which is a Latin word meaning "threshold," and so fits well in the current discussion. Movement between the various levels of holiness is accompanied by a corresponding liminal state, where there is danger. The guardians are mediators between the levels of holiness, mitigating the danger of the mingling of the profane and sacred world by controlling access to it. Once again, it should be noted that the guardians' job is not primarily to keep people out, but to admit the authorized. An examination of these guardians will illustrate more clearly how they controlled and mediated the space.

Cherubim

We begin with the mysterious guardians associated with every stage and version of the temple, which the Old Testament calls cherubim. The word *cherub* in its various forms occurs ninety-one times in the Old Testament, and in most of those references they are associated with the temple.[19] While many etymologies have been suggested for the word *cherub*, there is no consensus, although a derivation similar to Akkadian *kūribu*, associated with certain kinds of protective spirits in Mesopotamian thought, is possible.[20] The role of the cherubim as guardians is made explicit by their appearance in Genesis 3:24, where God places the cherubim "to keep the way to the tree of life." Another way of translating the Hebrew root *shamar*, rendered as "keep" in this verse, is to "guard" the way of the tree of life.

The guardianship of the cherubim was addressed by Antionah of Ammonihah, in the Book of Mormon, who asks Alma how Adam and Eve could live forever with the cherubim blocking the way to the fruit of the tree of life (Alma 12:20–21). For the apostate Antionah, the presence of the cherubim blocking the way meant that Adam and Eve—and by extension, the rest of humanity—could not pass them and that "there was no possible chance that they [humanity] should live forever" (Alma 12:21). Alma, responding to Antionah, stated that fallen humanity was prevented from eating from the tree of life so that they would not live forever in their misery (Alma 12:26). He then goes on to explain that because of the Atonement, humanity is able to return to God's presence through repentance, essentially passing by the cherubim to partake of the tree of life (see 1 Nephi 11:25). Alma's interpretation of the Garden of Eden and the cherubim has direct bearing on the sacred space in the temple and the mediators thereof. It has long been noted, by both Latter-day Saint and non–Latter-day Saint scholars, that the Eden story has temple significance, and, in fact, that the furniture and layout of the temples described in the Old Testament also relate to the Garden of Eden and the narrative of our first parents (Genesis 2–3).[21] Thus the presence of the cherubim in the Eden account fits into their guardianship of sacred space and their blocking of the unauthorized from God's presence, as signified by their association with the temple.

Images of cherubim also appear as part of the furnishings of the main temples in Israelite history. In the description of Solomon's Temple, such images bore up the washbasins, along with figures of lions and bulls (1 Kings 7:29).

These images were particularly associated with borders, where they symbolically controlled access from one point to another. For example, in the commands given to Moses to construct the tabernacle or tent shrine, the curtains which surround the temple were to be embroidered with cherubim (Exodus 26:1). Likewise, in the description of Solomon's temple, the walls were inscribed with images of cherubim (1 Kings 6:29). In addition, in both descriptions, the veil which separated the Holy Place from the Most Holy Place was embroidered with cherubim (Exodus 26:31, 1 Kings 6:32). In the Most Holy Place, Solomon placed large images of cherubim, whose wings shadowed over the ark of the covenant (1 Kings 6:23–28). The ark itself is described as having cherubim connected with it (1 Kings 6:23–25). The biblical text describes cherubim in both the Tabernacle and Solomon's Temple, and they were placed such that they guard and protect the borders between places, especially between the Holy Place and the Most Holy Place, as their presence on the veil indicates. The cherubim symbolically and iconographically guard the way back into God's presence.

The responsibility of the cherubim to guard the way to the Lord is shown by the iconography of the ark of the covenant. According to the biblical account, the ark was a gilded box which had a special covering placed upon it called the mercy seat in the King James Version of the Bible, although in Hebrew the word *kapporet* simply means "covering." The Old Testament records the command to make this covering in the following manner:

> And thou shalt make a mercy seat of pure gold: two cubits and half shall be the length thereof, and a cubit and a half the breadth thereof.
>
> And thou shalt make two cherubims[22] of gold, of beaten work shalt thou make them, in the two ends of the mercy seat.
>
> And make one cherub on the one end, and the other cherub on the other end: even of the mercy seat shall ye make the cherubims on the two ends thereof.
>
> And the cherubims shall stretch forth their wings on high, covering the mercy seat with their wings, and their faces shall look on to another; toward the mercy seat shall faces of the mercy seat be. (Exodus 25:17–20)

The presence of the cherubim on the mercy seat actually indicated the full name of the ark, which is the "Ark of the Covenant of the Lord of Hosts, who sits [or dwells] between the cherubim" (1 Samuel 4:4, author's own translation). The cherubim here protected the final access to God, who was often described, as in the verse from 1 Samuel quoted above, as sitting between the cherubim on the mercy seat.[23] They functioned as the primary symbolic guardians of the space which God inhabited. Their description in Ezekiel 1 as fantastic beasts with the faces of bulls, eagles, lions, and men gives them a fearsome appearance, enhancing their presentation as beings responsible for guarding the way to sacred and holy space.

The cherubim in Ezekiel 1 seem on the surface to be different from the other examples we have looked at, since they do not initially appear to have a temple context. In fact, they appear in vision to Ezekiel on the banks of the river Chebar in Mesopotamia, far away from Jerusalem. Their connection to the temple and their guardianship of the way to God becomes increasingly clear, however, as the book of Ezekiel progresses. In Ezekiel 10:18, because of the wickedness of the inhabitants of Jerusalem and their disregard for the sanctity of the temple (see Ezekiel 8) the glory of God—a phrase in the scriptures used to indicate God's presence—leaves the temple. As it does so, it is carried on the backs of the cherubim away from the temple in Jerusalem, representing the Lord's rejection of the Jerusalem temple as his house.[24] The cherubim's support of God's throne is one more example of their position as guardians of the sacred.

Human Guardians

The symbolic guarding role of the cherubim was supplemented in the earthly temple by human officers, whose responsibility it was to protect the space within the temple by controlling who could be admitted. As with many aspects of the ancient temple, the Old Testament is very terse on this topic, but it is possible to construct some idea of the personnel associated with the Jerusalem temple, especially as described in 1 Chronicles. The book of 1 Chronicles describes in some length the various personnel who worked within the temple, that is to say, the various courses of priests, musicians, and others who were responsible for maintaining the day-to-day operation of temple service.[25] One of the types of personnel mentioned particularly in 1 Chronicles chapters 9 and 26 is the *shoʻar*, which is translated in the King James Version as "porters."[26] The New Revised Standard Version has "gatekeepers," a translation which better represents in Modern English the sense of the Hebrew word, which shares the same root as the Hebrew word for "gate," *shaʿar*.[27] These officers were therefore responsible for maintaining the boundaries within the temple by controlling access to the temple through the gates.[28]

According to 1 Chronicles 9:19, the gatekeepers were descended from the family of Korah and so were part of the Levites, charged with nonsacrificial responsibilities in the temple (see also Exodus 6:24).[29] Their responsibilities are divided in this section into the "keepers of the gate of the tabernacle" and the "keepers of the entry." The phrase "keepers of the gate of the tabernacle" has a number of intriguing features. The Hebrew root translated here as "keepers" (*shamar*) is the same as that used of the cherubim in Genesis 3, which, as we have already seen, indicates guarding or protecting in addition to being responsible for something. The word "tabernacle" may be explained by the fact that the setting for 1 Chronicles 9 is during David's reign before the establishment of the First Temple under David's son Solomon.[30] The word *saf*, which is translated as "gate" in the King James Version of 1 Chronicles 9:19, is better signified by "thresholds." Realizing that these gatekeepers were the "guards of the threshold" helps to illustrate the liminal nature of the division of the sacred space that these officers were over. These keepers had important administrative functions within the temple, as well as having both military and royal functions. They served, for example, as kind of a police force for the temple.[31] They also oversaw physical aspects of the day-to-day running of the temple, as may be seen by their appearance in 2 Kings 22:4, where they are entrusted with temple funds that Josiah uses to repair the temple (see also 1 Chronicles 9:26–27).

Against this portrayal of the relative importance of the gatekeepers is Psalm 84:10, which discusses gatekeepers in a way that at first glance seems to imply that they were some of the lowest personnel in the temple. This verse has traditionally been translated as "I had rather be a doorkeeper in the house of my God, than to dwell in the tents of wickedness."[32] Taken like this, this verse suggests that being a doorkeeper is a fairly unimportant job in the temple. Some of this difficulty may be resolved by looking at the translation. The word translated in Psalm 84:10 as "doorkeeper" (*histofef*) is different from the word for gatekeeper (*shoʿar*), found in 1 Chronicles, which suggests that it points to something different from the office of gatekeeper. The word in Psalm 84 does come from the same Hebrew root as that for "threshold" (*saf*), which is where the traditional interpretation derives from. On the other hand, the Septuagint, the Greek translation of the Old Testament, has "I chose to be cast aside in the house of God, than to live in the coverts of sinners" (LXX Psalm 83 (84):10, New English Translation of the Septuagint). This is a reading which suggests being on the threshold, rather than some kind of officer. Ultimately, the Septuagint's reading seems to better fit the sense of the verse and the psalm and is to be preferred over that of doorkeeper, although the core message of contrast between the relative values of the temple and the world remains with both readings.[33] The difference in vocabulary, however, suggests that this verse does not refer to the specific office of gatekeepers in the temple, for that office served an important role in the practice and ritual of the Israelite temple.

Just as the temple brings together the cosmic and the earthly realms, so too do the human gatekeepers have cosmic and ritual functions. According to 1 Chronicles 9:24, the gatekeepers were stationed "in four quarters," which is to say on all four sides of the temple. This is described in further detail in 1 Chronicles 26:13–19, where several gatekeepers are set in the various directions. This fourfold division corresponds nicely to the four directions which the cherubim faced in Ezekiel 1, which in turn relates to other examples of Near Eastern temples.[34] As mentioned previously, one of the important points about the temple and its officers was that it was a symbolic representation on earth of the heavenly order. Thus, having gatekeepers stationed at each of the "four quarters," representing the four cardinal directions, creates a powerful symbol of the ordered cosmos and places the temple at the center of that cosmos. From the temple, the central place, one is able to travel in any of the four directions; and conversely, no matter what direction one approaches the presence of the Lord, one is met by a gatekeeper, for the only way to symbolically come toward the divine presence was through a gate mediated by a gatekeeper.

Ritual Entry and Credentials

In discussing the cosmic placing of the temple and the gatekeepers' role in it, we move from both the symbolic ideas of the cherubim and the pragmatic staffing of the temple concerns found in Chronicles towards a suggestion of the ritual practice associated with gatekeeping in the Jerusalem temple. This allows us to ask the question about how this concept was deployed and enacted in the ancient temple. As noted above, these rituals were secret and not recorded, but the Old Testament contains elements of liturgies or ceremonies associated with entrance into the temple and coming into the presence of the Lord. The gatekeepers were there not only to keep people out but also to allow the authorized to enter into sacred space. The question becomes what credentials indicated the ancient worshipper was, in fact, authorized to enter the house of the Lord.

In a paper discussing the idea of the credentials in two bodies of literature temporally situated on either side of the biblical narrative, John Gee examined the connections between a late antique branch of Jewish mystical literature, known as hekhalot or merkavah mysticism (circa third to fifth centuries AD), and the ancient Egyptian Pyramid Texts (circa 2520–2180 BC), in particular their ideas of gatekeepers, and the credentials needed to pass by them.[35] In the Jewish hekhalot literature, the gatekeepers are angelic beings to whom the merkavah mystic must give certain magical names in order to pass and view the chariot throne of God, which is considered to be in the center of the heavenly temple.[36] Likewise in the Egyptian funerary literature, the deceased must pass by certain gatekeepers, which could only be done with the knowledge of certain names. Both the Egyptian and the late antique Jewish examples derive from texts with a plausible ritual background, although that remains problematic for both corpora of texts. In both cases, the blocked entry is bypassed when the supplicant is able to provide the proper credentials. These two examples of ritual mediation and checking of credentials provide a framework against which we can discuss the ritual of the Israelite temple, especially the mediation of sacred space by gatekeepers. The book of Psalms represents the clearest place where answers to this question are found.

Gates in the Psalms

It has long been suggested that many of the Psalms have their foundation and basis within the ritual and liturgy of the Jerusalem temple.[37] One such psalm is Psalm 24, which contains a question and answer sequence about entrance to the temple, called here, as in other places, the hill or mountain of the Lord (Psalm 24:3).[38] This question and response give the psalm a strong liturgical aspect. Psalm 24:3 asks the question, "Who shall ascend into the hill of the Lord? or who shall stand in his holy place?" The answer to the question shows that the person who desires entrance to God's house and mountain must be clean: "He that hath clean hands, and a pure heart; who hath not lifted up his soul unto vanity, nor sworn deceitfully" (Psalm 24:4). Note the emphasis on truth-telling and purity in this passage. It is quite possible that this question and response were part of a ritual in order to be admitted to the temple, although it is also possible that the psalm is constructing this purely as a literary device. The question-and-answer form suggests a ritual, antiphonal performance, where one person or group speaks one part and another group or person responds. John Day calls both Psalm 24 and the very similar Psalm 15 "entrance liturgies," suggesting that they were part of a ritual to enter the temple.[39] There may have been other credentials required, but at the very least the worshipper was required to be trustworthy before passing by the guardians. Donald W. Parry has compared this process to a modern temple recommend interview, although he suggests that it was "self-administered."[40] Whether as a ritual model or only a symbolic hymn, the ability to go up and enter into the temple and to "stand in [God's] holy place" (Psalm 24:3) is based on the petitioners' ability to assert their cleanness and purity to the keeper who is mediating the space. Only those who are able to do so are permitted to enter into the presence of the Lord. Thus, the one who desires to come into the temple is required to provide credentials, which in this psalm are purity and honesty.

This same sort of interaction is also present within Psalm 15, which contains a longer interrogative section which closely parallels that found in Psalm 24.[41] In Psalm 15, entrance to the sacred precincts is even more clearly based upon ethical questions, although ritual purity would have been as much a concern here as elsewhere in the book of Psalms and the Old Testament. Where Psalm 24:4 has "clean hands, and a pure heart; who hath not lifted up his soul unto vanity, nor sworn deceitfully," Psalm 15 has a longer and more specific ethical injunction: "He that walketh uprightly, and worketh righteousness, and speaketh truth in his heart. He that backbiteth not with his tongue, nor doeth evil to his neighbour, nor taketh up a reproach against his neighbour. In whose eyes a vile person is contemned; but he honoureth them that fear the Lord. He that sweareth to his own hurt, and changeth not. He that putteth not out his money to usury, nor taketh reward from the innocent" (2–5). In both cases, entrance to the temple is dependent on the supplicant's purity and honesty.

The previous psalms may also be compared with Psalm 118:19–20, where the Psalmist instructs an unspecified gatekeeper, "Open to me the gates of righteousness: I will go into them, and I will praise the Lord: This gate of the

Lord, into which the righteous shall enter." The phrase "this gate" in verse 20 is suggestive of a ritual situation where the worshipper announces his or her presence and asks to be allowed to enter into the temple through the "gate of the Lord." The worshipper enters at the sufferance of the gatekeeper, signifying the sufferance of the Lord, and is only able to do so after offering up his or her credentials. This ritual of questioning and answering shows one way in which sacred space was controlled and mediated through the gates and gatekeepers of the temple. Worshippers are permitted to enter into holy places, but access to the temple is limited. The sacred precincts are only open to those who are able to prove their credentials of keeping the laws of ritual and ethical purity to the wardens, who are responsible for verifying that those laws are being kept.

Psalm 24 contains another element besides the "entrance liturgy" for the worshipper. After the section already quoted, the Psalms turns from the human worshipper to a direct address to the gates and to the everlasting doors: "Lift up your heads, O ye gates; be ye lift up, ye everlasting doors, and the King of glory shall come in" (Psalm 24:7). After this direct address, the question is asked, "Who is this King of glory? The Lord strong and mighty, the Lord mighty in battle" (Psalm 24:8). The command to the gates is then repeated, along with the question, to which the response is "the Lord of hosts, he is the King of glory" (Psalm 24:10). Like the first part of this psalm, the question and answer here suggests an antiphonal ritual performance. This part differs from the previous part, however, in that instead of the worshipper entering in through these gates, it is instead the Lord himself who is to be admitted. Because of this shift in address, biblical scholars have long debated whether Psalm 24 in its current state represents the conflation of two or more previous hymns on a similar theme—in this case admission to sacred guarded space.[42] These two sections of this psalm originally represented two separate compositions which have been placed together in a single psalm in order to illustrate part of the ritual conception within the temple at Jerusalem. Thus, Psalm 24 in its current state represents two snippets of a liturgy of protection and guardians in the Jerusalem temple.

The key difference between the two ritual liturgies is contained in God's authority, the totality of which is introduced in 24:1–2. The mortal worshippers in Psalms 24:3–6, Psalm 15, and Psalm 118:19–20 are required to declare their credentials—their purity, their freedom from deceit, and their righteousness.

On the other hand, when God comes to his own house, the only key necessary in order to get past the gatekeepers, represented by the gates in verses 7 and 10, is his own name. The question is not one of whether or not God is worthy enough to get past the gatekeepers—they merely ask who he is, and he tells them his name, allowing him to pass. The gatekeepers are there to guard thresholds between levels of holiness, to keep out the unauthorized, and let in the authorized. When God comes to the temple, he is admitted on the strength of his own name, for he is the only one authorized without qualification to enter his own house. All others the gatekeepers admit only at his sufferance.

Conclusion

One of the productive aspects of looking at ancient ritual, through however dark a glass (see 1 Corinthians 13:12), is that it helps us to better understand the conceptions which the ritual reinforced for the ancient worshippers at the Jerusalem temple. The temple, whether ancient or modern, is a physical and ritual expression of doctrine. The worshippers in the temple are living out the sacred story through the ordinances of the temple. This is one of the ways in which the Lord has taught his saints in all generations. For example, the animal sacrifices, which were such an important part of Israel's relationship to God in Old Testament times, taught lessons about life and death, giving things to God, and ultimately about the great and last sacrifice God himself would make (see Alma 34:10, Hebrews 9:11–15). The division and management of sacred space in the temple also taught symbolic lessons. It belonged to and was controlled by God. Movement to and through the temple is controlled, for the house of God is a house of order (see D&C 132:8), in much the same way that the universe is ordered.

The physical division of sacred space, with its cosmic significance, leads naturally to the symbolic guardians, represented most clearly by the cherubim, those beings in the scriptures who support and protect the way to God's throne. These beings perform functions on a symbolic and iconographic level identical or similar to those performed by the human wardens mentioned in descriptions of the temple cult. Their job, like that of the gatekeepers, was to guard or keep the way to God and to the tree of life. Only those who were authorized would be able to transcend their protection and enter into the presence of God.

Thus, the gatekeeper served as a physical actor showing that "no unclean thing" came into the presence of God within the temple (see 1 Nephi 10:21). He was a physical officer protecting both sacred space from interlopers and at the same time protecting interlopers from the divine wrath which came from penetrating into unauthorized space. Most importantly he allowed those who could prove their authorization into holy space to come into the presence of the Lord. All those who entered the temple did so at the Lord's suffrage, and were required to prove their worthiness to the gatekeeper, as evinced by ritual purity and truth-telling, in order to enter.

Modern temples in The Church of Jesus Christ of Latter-day Saints have similar concepts of gatekeepers who check the credentials to ensure that only the authorized enter. In order to enter the temple, modern worshippers must first prove their ethical worthiness by presenting a document from their ecclesiastical authorities, recommending they be allowed to enter. This is the functional equivalent of the original response in Psalm 24. This equivalency is a powerful example of theological continuity from the ideas which we have seen presented in the ancient temple at Jerusalem to the modern temples. In addition to the functional parallels, there are also symbolic parallels. Brigham Young famously observed at the ceremony for the laying of the cornerstones of the Salt Lake Temple: "Your endowment is, to receive all those ordinances in the house of the Lord, which are necessary for you, after you have departed this life, to enable you to walk back to the presence of the Father, passing the angels who stand as sentinels, being enabled to give them the key words, the signs and tokens, pertaining to the holy Priesthood, and gain your eternal exaltation in spite of earth and hell."[43] President Young's use of the word "sentinels" speaks of angelic guards, like the cherubim, blocking the way of all except the faithful. The endowment, as given in modern temples, ritually enables the faithful to symbolically prove their credentials and "pass" these angels.

Ultimately, all of these gatekeepers serve as representatives of the final gatekeeper, whom Jacob identifies as the Lord of Hosts himself. At that final gate there will be neither human officer nor cherub to bar our way, but only God himself, for "he employeth no servant there" (2 Nephi 9:41). In the end, only Jesus Christ is able to fully mediate for us and bring us finally into the presence of God.

Notes

I wish to thank my anonymous readers and especially my wife Thora Shannon, whose helpful comments helped me immensely with this paper.

1. Donald W. Parry follows Mircea Eliade in speaking about the absolute division between sacred and profane space in "Demarcation between Sacred and Profane Space: The Temple of Herod Model," in *Temples of the Ancient World*, ed. Donald W. Parry (Salt Lake City: Deseret Book; Provo, UT: FARMS, 1994), 413–39.

2. The idea of division and guarding of sacred space is, of course, not unique to either ancient Jewish temples or modern Latter-day Saint ones. Marcus von Wellnitz describes the entrance in medieval churches as having sculptural guardians who reminded worshippers of the need "to be clean in action and thought before presenting himself to deity and participating in sacred ordinances." Marcus von Wellnitz, "The Catholic Liturgy and the Mormon Temple," *BYU Studies* 21, no. 1 (1981): 2–35, 15.

3. John M. Lundquist, "What Is a Temple? A Preliminary Typology," in *Temples of the Ancient World*, 83–117, 109–11.

4. I use the word "shrine" here in order to highlight the fact that the Tabernacle was not a building as such and so differed in key respects from the other temples to God.

5. According to 2 Nephi 5:16, Nephi also a built a temple, but he gives us no information about its structure, cult, or personnel other than to tell us that it was "after the manner of the temple of Solomon." In addition to this, the archaeological record contains evidence of other important shrines to the Lord during the period of both the united and divided monarchies, which are not necessarily represented in the biblical text. Ziony Zevit, *The Religions of Ancient Israel: A Synthesis of Parallactic Approaches* (New York: Continuum, 2001), 247–66, contains a useful and detailed description of these elements. The prophet Ezekiel also describes at some length a vision which he received of a temple which was never built (Ezekiel 40–44).

6. After the period described within the Old Testament, this temple was expanded and improved upon by King Herod. This was the temple which stood during New Testament times and was destroyed by Rome during the Jewish Revolt in AD 70.

7. Lundquist, "What is a Temple?," 108. There is a very accessible discussion of the Israelite sacrificial system in Richard Neitzel Holzapfel, Dana M. Pike, and David Rolph Seely, *Jehovah and the World of the Old Testament* (Salt Lake City: Deseret Book, 2009), 113–15.

8. Carol L. Meyers, "The Elusive Temple," *Biblical Archaeologist* 45 (1982):, 33–44, 33.

9. The centralization of sacrifice under Hezekiah (2 Kings 18:4) and Josiah (2 Kings 22:3–7) are other examples of reforms made to the temple system, including possible ritual changes.

10. Frank More Cross, Jr., "The Priestly Tabernacle in Light of Recent Research," in *The Temple in Antiquity: Ancient Records and Modern Perspectives*, ed. Truman G. Madsen (Provo, UT: Religious Studies Center, Brigham Young University, 1984), 91–104.

11. Richard Neitzel Holzapfel and David Rolph Seely, *My Father's House* (Salt Lake City: Bookcraft, 1994), 39. The lack of information on the Second Temple is only in regard to the biblical text. Sources after the biblical period, such as Josephus and in particular the rabbinic Mishnah, have lengthy and very specific discussions about the Second Temple. See Jacob Neusner's "Map Without Territory: Mishnah's System of Sacrifice and Sanctuary," *History of Religions* 19 (1979): 103–27, especially 106.

12. See G. Earnest Wright, "Solomon's Temple Resurrected," *Biblical Archaeologist* 4 (1941): 17, 19–31; Paul Leslie Garber, "Reconstructing Solomon's Temple," *The Biblical Archaeologist* 14 (1951): 1–24; Leroy Waterman, "The Damaged 'Blueprints' of Solomon's Temple," *Journal of Near Eastern Studies* 2 (1943): 284–94; D. W. Gooding, "Temple Specifications: A Dispute in the Logical Arrangement between the MT and the LXX," *Vetus Testamentum* 17 (1967): 143–172; Leen Ritmeyer, "Envisioning the Sanctuaries of Israel—The Academic and Creative Process of Archaeological Model Making," *The Temple of Jerusalem: From Moses to Messiah*, ed. Steven Fine (Leiden: Brill, 2011), 91–104.

13. Mark S. Smith, *The Priestly Vision of Genesis 1* (Minneapolis: Fortress, 2010), 90–91. The anthropologist Mary Douglas argues that this concept of division, set in place during the Creation, serves as the background for the dietary laws found in Leviticus 11: "Holiness requires that individuals shall conform to the class to which they belong. And holiness requires that different class of things shall not be confused." *Purity and Danger* (New York: Routledge, 2002), 67.

14. Hugh Nibley's seminal work *Temple and the Cosmos* (Provo, UT: FARMS, 1992) is centered on this concept of the cosmological significance of the temple. See especially the chapters "The Meaning of the Temple" and "The Circle and the Square," http://maxwellinstitute.byu.edu/publications/books/?bookid=103.

15. Although it comes from an inscription relating to the Second Temple period, later than the biblical period, there is a Greek inscription which threatens death to Gentiles who cross the threshold into those parts of the holy precinct which were closed to them. *Corpus Inscriptum Judaicorum* 2, 1400. There is a line drawing and translation in Lundquist, "What is a Temple?," 109, figure 22.

16. A similar concept may be the idea behind Jacob's assertion that "no unclean thing can dwell with God" (1 Nephi 10:21).

17. See the discussion in Edith Turner, "Liminality," in *The Encyclopedia of Religion*, ed. Lindsay Jones, 2nd ed. (Detroit: Macmillan Reference USA, 2005), 8:5460–63. See also Victor Turner, *The Ritual Process: Structure and Anti-Structure* (Piscataway, NJ: Aldine de Gruyter, 1969).

18. Under this conception, the very institution of the temple is liminal, as it bridges the heavenly and the earthly realms.

19. The other primary element is as God's heavenly chariot, a concept which both the mercy seat and Ezekiel bring together. See T. N. D. Mettinger, "Cherubim," in *Dictionary of Deities and Demons in the Bible*, ed. Karel Van der Toorn, Bob Becking, and Pieter W. van der Horst, 2nd ed. (Leiden: Brill; and Grand Rapids, MI: Eerdmans, 1999), 189–92.

20. Mettinger, "Cherubim," 190, and especially Freedman and O'Connor, "cherub," *Theological Dictionary of the Old Testament*, ed. G. Johannes Botterweck, Helmer

Ringgren, and Heinz-Josef Fabry, trans. David E. Green (Grand Rapids, MI: Eerdmans, 1995), 7:307–19.

21. Donald W. Parry, "The Garden of Eden: Prototype Sanctuary," in *Temples of the Ancient World*, ed. Donald W. Parry (Salt Lake City: Deseret Book; and Provo, UT: FARMS, 1994), 126–51, and the bibliography cited therein.

22. The King James Version of the Bible has the incorrect double plural "cherubims." This is correctly either *cherubs* or *cherubim*. See Alma 12:21, which reads "cherubim," for an example of the correct way to render the plural of *cherub* in English.

23. See Paul Hoskisson, "Aaron's Golden Calves," in *FARMS Review* 18, no. 2 (2006): 375–87, http://maxwellinstitute.byu.edu/publications/review/?vol=18&num=1&id=612.

24. The cherubim in Ezekiel illustrate the other function of the cherubim as described in the scriptures: to serve as the chariot of God. This is particularly clear in Psalm 18:10, where God saves the Psalmist while riding upon a cherub. Thus, in the imagery of the Psalm, the cherubim guard the way to the temple, but just as importantly, they protect God when he rides out to battle or even when he rejects his house entirely, as happens in Ezekiel 10.

25. Although the temple described is presented as the First Temple of Solomon, it is generally considered by scholars to be primarily modeled around the Second Temple, current at the time of the composition of the books of 1 and 2 Chronicles. For a discussion of 1 and 2 Chronicles and where they fit in the history of the Old Testament, see Holzapfel, Pike, and Seely, *Jehovah and the World of the Old Testament*, 214.

26. The Aramaic equivalent to *shoʻarim*, *taraya*, appears in Ezra 7:24 alongside the priests, Levites, and other temple personnel who were exempt from taxes.

27. There is a general trend in English to trivialize the role of these kinds of officers, as the modern connotations of the conceptually similar "janitor" and "custodian" indicates.

28. John Jarick, *1 Chronicles* (New York: Sheffield Academic, 2002), 149.

29. There is a group called the sons of Korah who are mentioned in the book of Psalms, in Psalm 42, 44–49, 84–85, and 87–88.

30. As noted, the composition of the books of Chronicles is generally dated later than the books of Samuel and Kings.

31. John Wesley Wright, "Guarding the Gates: 1 Chronicles 26.1–19 and the Roles of the Gatekeepers in Chronicles, *Journal for the Study of the Old Testament* 48 (1990), 69–81, 76.

32. So it appears in the King James Version, and most of its daughter translations, including the NRSV. The English Standard Version and the New American Standard Bible have "I would rather stand at the threshold" for "I would rather be a gatekeeper."

33. A. Robinson, "Three Suggested Interpretations in Psalm LXXXIV," *Vetus Testamentum* 24 (1974): 378–81. See the further discussion in Th. Booij, "Royal Words in Psalm LXXXIV 11," *Vetus Testamentum* 36 (1986): 117–21.

34. Margaret Huxley, "The Gates and Guardians in Sennacherib's Addition to the Temple of Assur," *Iraq* 62 (2000): 109–37.

35. John Gee, "The Keeper of the Gate," in *The Temple in Time and Eternity*, ed. Donald W. Parry and Stephen D. Ricks (Provo, UT: FARMS, 1999), 233–74.

36. Gee, "Gatekeeper," 250–51. There is an excellent discussion and introduction to Hekhalot literature including a detailed discussion on this phenomenon in Peter Schäfer, *The Hidden and Manifest God: Some Major Trends in Early Jewish Mysticism*, trans. Aubrey Pomerance, (Albany: State University of New York, 1992).

37. Day, *Psalms* (Sheffield: Journal for the Study of the Old Testament, 1990), 14–15; Donald W. Parry, "Temple Worship and a Possible Reference to a Prayer Circle in Psalm 24," *BYU Studies* 32 (1994): 57–62, and the bibliography mentioned in note 1.

38. See also Genesis 22:14, Isaiah 2:2–3, Isaiah 27:13, Micah 4:1–2.

39. Day, *Psalms*, 60.

40. Parry, "Temple Worship," 57.

41. Richard J. Clifford, *Psalms 1–72* (Nashville: Abingdon, 2002), 92, 134.

42. See the discussion and bibliography in Alan Cooper, "Mythology and Exegesis," *Journal of Biblical Literature* 102 (1983): 37–60, especially notes 2, 3, and 4.

43. Brigham Young, *Discourses of Brigham Young*, ed. John A. Widtsoe (Salt Lake City: Deseret Book, 1978), 416.

6

Clothed in Holy Garments: The Apparel of the Temple Officiants of Ancient Israel

Alonzo L. Gaskill

There are a variety of approaches to holy writ.¹ Some feel the most valid methodological approach is <u>exegetical—seeking to discover what the authors meant when they originally penned the words many centuries ago</u>.² Some, on the other hand, feel that an <u>apologetic approach is most correct— reading scripture in an effort to find "evidences" for one's personal denominational persuasion.</u> Certain students of scripture approach God's word as literature—looking not for its doctrinal or theological teachings but for its beauty in structure or language. And there are, of course, a number of individuals who read scripture for its moral teachings—seeking to draw an application-oriented homily from what they read.

Perhaps it is no surprise that subscribers to these various schools of thought do not always agree with each other on which approaches are valid and which are not. Those in the exegetical camp, for example, sometimes feel that the homiletic approach "does violence to scripture," as they say, by offering applications which were never intended by the original author. Those in the homily camp, on the other hand, sometimes argue that to not apply scripture to one's personal

---

Alonzo L. Gaskill is an associate professor of Church history and doctrine at Brigham Young University.

situation is to miss the entire point of God's word. The dispute, which is more heated than many lay Christians realize, brings to mind the words of the Prophet Joseph: "Who of all these parties are right; or, are they all wrong together? If any one of them be right, which is it, and how shall I know it?" (Joseph Smith—History 1:10). Regardless of which camp the reader falls into, what *is* certain is that many Christians throughout the centuries have felt comfortable with a homiletic approach to scripture. Such an approach was very common in the early post–New Testament Church, and it has been a popular approach for many modern commentators—including a fair number of Latter-day Saint authors.[3]

Among those who read scripture for its homiletic value, it has long been noted that the garments of the Aaronic high priest[4] were, through their symbolic design, a teaching device given by divine revelation to the prophet Moses. Many Christian commentators suggest that the articles of apparel associated with this priestly office were designed as a type or foreshadowing of Jesus Christ.[5] The author of the book of Hebrews goes so far as to call Christ the "great high priest" (Hebrews 4:14). Thus one commentator noted that "Aaron, as a High Priest, was a breathing statue—a type—of Christ."[6] Another suggested, "The ways in which Aaron typified Christ are numerous and varied. In many respects he is to be considered the most illustrative type of the spiritual work of Christ to be found in the entire Old Testament."[7] If this is the case, the symbolism associated with the priestly officiant's dress should have significance for followers of Jesus Christ, who in baptism "put on Christ" (Galatians 3:27), thereby becoming "the body of Christ, and members individually" (1 Corinthians 12:27, New King James Version). "When we *put on* Jesus Christ we accept him and his atonement, and we become like him."[8] Consequently, the robes of the Aaronic high priest have the potential to teach us much about Christ and his attributes. They can also teach us about the corporate body of Christ and the ideal attributes of a faithful follower of the Savior. One expert on the garments of the ancient temple has noted: "As the High Priest was a type of the Great High Priest, Jesus, so the garments of the High Priest were typical of the character of Jesus Christ. Likewise, as the sons of the High Priest were priests and as we who are the sons of God are called to be priests, even so the dress of the priests typifies the character of the believers."[9] Elsewhere we read that the officiant "represented all Israel when he ministered in the tabernacle."[10] Accordingly, in the symbolic clothing of the temple high priest we may draw a message about the nature and attributes of the Messiah and also of the characteristics each sincere follower of Christ should seek to develop if he or she seeks for an eternal inheritance in God's kingdom.[11]

Naturally, this understanding of the priestly garments implies a reading of scripture done through the lens of a "believer"—one who acknowledges Jesus Christ as the promised Messiah, of whom *all things*, including the Old Testament, testify (see Moses 6:63). This being the case, it is expected that those who do not share this belief are prone to arrive at different conclusions. Reading the scriptures through a Latter-day Saint lens, or even through a general Christian lens, will lead one to interpret symbols differently than would be the case otherwise. For this reason, a strictly exegetical analysis is unlikely to produce the same Christocentric results. Instead, we may hope to find Christ in the garments of the ancient high priests through a more homiletic approach.[12] From a traditional Latter-day Saint perspective, however, we can assume that those ancient Israelites who were enlightened by the Holy Ghost understood the ultimate messianic types embedded in the garments.[13] After all, the didactic symbols of which God makes abundant use are meant to open our eyes to greater truths—often, in fact, to the *greatest* truths.

The Linen Coat (Leviticus 8:7; Exodus 28:4, 39; 39:27)

The first item that was placed upon the high priest, immediately after washing (see Leviticus 8:6–7), was the linen coat. In Exodus 28:39 we read: "And thou shalt embroider the coat of fine linen." The Hebrew of this verse may also be rendered: "And thou shalt weave a shirt-like undergarment of fine white cloth."[14] Josephus suggested that (according to the understanding of those in the first century) the coat or undershirt was "made of fine flax doubled" and that the "vestment reaches down to the feet, and sits close to the body."[15] Another source submits that this undershirt's sleeves reached "to the wrists."[16] Thus, this linen coat appears to have covered the entirety of the high priest's body.

Not only was this undergarment made of the finest of materials, but the making of it apparently required significant effort. Indeed, the Hebrew root word used for "embroidered" implies something akin to our modern damask[17] (i.e., a lustrous fabric made with flat patterns in a satin weave). Thus, the garment is believed to have been skillfully woven so as to have a pattern within the fabric.[18] The embroidery may have been a "checkered" pattern[19] or one which utilized a design that looked like the Greek letter gamma (e.g., Γ).[20]

The symbols contained in this single article of clothing are manifold. For example, the material of its construction, being pure white, is often seen as "an emblem of moral purity."²¹ The ultimate referent of this symbol is Jesus Christ, who is our exemplar in moral purity and perfection.²² Thus on Yom Kippur (the Day of Atonement) the priest wore the linen coat, which (in the minds of many Christians) indicated that he was officiating as a type of Christ (see Leviticus 16). It is important that the linen coat was placed upon the high priest as the very first article of clothing, since this demonstrates that moral purity is foundational. Likewise, this sacred undergarment "was a full-length garment covering the entire body," which suggests to Christian commentators that Christ's salvation is "for the whole man; body, soul and spirit."²³ True moral purity requires totality, nothing lacking.

The embroidery pattern also contains important symbolic implications for the wearer and the viewer. One commentator notes that from a distance the linen coat may have appeared plain. However, "upon a closer examination there was skill and beauty attached to the make up [sic] of the fabric."²⁴ If this is the case, the implications this has for Jesus Christ are significant.

> To the many who take a casual glance at the "Jesus of Nazareth" and the "Man of Galilee" they see an ordinary yet good man, but study that character, look into that life, note those works, and meditate upon His words. Here is no ordinary person, even though he is found in fashion as a man. There is a Divine pattern most intrinsically worked into the human frame which reveals Him to be the Son of God.²⁵

Thus, the garment can remind us that something more than a casual look at the sacred is required if we wish to see and recognize the divine imprint.²⁶ This is as applicable to the doctrines of Christ as it is to Christ the man.

Beyond its reference to the Messiah, this linen coat may also allegorically suggest that the Church,²⁷ as a community of Christ's followers, must be completely morally pure.²⁸ That moral purity can only be obtained *through* Christ, whom the garment is said to represent. The undershirt, therefore, can be seen as an invitation to the Church to "awake" and "put on thy strength, O Zion; put on thy beautiful garments, O Jerusalem" (Isaiah 52:1). Additionally, the symbolism suggests that the Church of Christ is, like the linen coat, a work of fine craftsmanship, designed by heavenly hands and often referred to as a "marvelous work."²⁹ The Church, like its namesake, often looks plain upon a cursory glance. However, when sincerely and closely examined, the divine miracles and handiwork of God manifested in bringing it forth are apparent.

The Breeches (Leviticus 6:8–10; Exodus 28:42–43)

While the Leviticus pericope doesn't specifically mention it, Baruch Levine points out that "it is to be assumed that at the beginning of the robing the priests were wearing their linen breeches,"[30] which reached to the knees. These breeches, or underpants, were made of linen, which is *not* a product of animals (which are subject to death and corruption). Thus, they become a fitting symbol of both incorruptibility and immortality.[31] From the perspective of a Christocentric reading of the passage, the implication is that Christ is both incorruptible and also immortal. By extension, the breeches can suggest to the observer that (in this increasingly immoral world) Christ's followers should not allow their lives to become corrupted. Significantly, the fact that these breeches cover the loins—in other words, the reproductive area—is itself a potential symbol that the wearer needs to control his appetites and passions, lest defilement and corruption ensue. As the faithful followers of Christ reject all that corrupts, they have reason to hope that through Christ they shall also obtain immortality and "eternal lives" (D&C 132:24, 55).

The Girdle (Leviticus 8:7)

The Aaronic high priest donned two separate girdles as part of his holy clothing: "one of which was fastened over the coat [or undershirt] and was assumed by the priests generally; the other was emphatically *the* curious, or embroidered, 'girdle of the ephod,' and belonged to the robes of the High Priest alone."[32] Our focus here will be on the former of these—that which was common to high priest and priest alike.

According to Josephus, this inner girdle (over which other vestments were worn) was rather long: it was wrapped twice around the high priest and yet still reached to the ankles.[33] It was apparently worn on top of the coat (undershirt) and breeches (underpants), but beneath the other garb of the priest. The symbols associated with the girdle buttress the symbols of the linen coat beautifully.

In certain periods, in the ancient Near East, a girdle represented chastity and fidelity, including fidelity to covenants.[34] The fact that this girdle was used to bind up the loins suggests a likely origin of its symbolism. It potentially reminded the wearer of those virtues which must be tightly bound to the righteous individual—virtues present in the character of Israel's God and future Messiah. The fact that the girdle bound the coat and breeches close to the wearer's body was important, for, as one commentator suggested, "This is nearly always a symbol of service, the girded loins denoting readiness for action. This must always be the attitude of the priest and it is certainly true of Christ."[35] By implication, this hidden girdle can remind the Church of its need to be closely tied to the virtues of Christ and to ever be willing and ready to serve. This manifests the reality of the Christian virtues that the girdle symbolizes. The Lord's words to the Saints in section 4 of the Doctrine and Covenants exemplify the implied meaning of the under-girdle. Saints must develop qualities such as "faith, virtue, knowledge, temperance, patience, brotherly kindness, godliness, charity, humility, diligence" (D&C 4:6). And in the spirit of those virtues, they must diligently attend to the needs of God's children: "O ye that embark in the service of God, see that ye serve him with all your heart, might, mind and strength, that ye may stand blameless before God at the last day" (D&C 4:2).

The Robe of the Ephod (Leviticus 8:7; Exodus 28:4)

The Lord informed Moses that this distinctive robe was to be made "all of blue" (Exodus 28:31)[36] and that it would reach past the ephod to the knee.[37] Remarkably, the robe of the ephod was constructed out of a single sheet of material; having no seams, only a hole for the head and arms. The neck hole was reinforced to insure "that it be not rent" (Exodus 28:32). Indeed, the garment was "made in such a way that it was not possible for man to rend it."[38] At the bottom of the robe, stitched onto the fringe of it, were a series of alternating gold bells and cloth pomegranates.[39] According to Josephus, the practical function associated with these bells was to inform the priests and those within the temple precinct as to when the high priest was approaching the veil. It was hoped that upon hearing this sound "the people might have notice of it, and might fall to their own prayers at the time of incense [at the veil]."[40] Concerning the pomegranates, it is quite probable that their pattern was chosen due to their association with the promised land (see Deuteronomy 8:7–8; Numbers 13:23), which is a symbol of the celestial city. However, as will be demonstrated, their symbolic depth goes beyond that.

As a teaching device, a number of components of the robe of the ephod seem significant. First of all, the blue color of the garments is often seen as representative of the heavens—the abode of God. This color can symbolize the spiritual or celestial nature of a thing.⁴¹ Thus Joseph Fielding McConkie associates the robe with Christ: "This [robe of the ephod] appears to have been a reference to the heavenly origin, character, and ministry of Christ, the great high priest."⁴² Another author suggests that if a person in the Bible was adorned in blue, it indicated that he or she was divinely sanctioned.⁴³ For members of the Lord's Church, then, the robe can symbolize the divine origin of the Church and the requirement that they maintain the Lord's sanction through striving to be a Zion people.

The fact that the garment was donned by the high priest *after* the linen coat has been seen is an indication that divine sanction comes only to those who have purified their lives and taken virtue to the entirety of their beings, confirming such virtue through their actions.

Additionally, the seamless design of the robe serves as a reminder that Christ's divinity has no beginning and no end. The inability to tear the robe, its having the strength of armor, can signify his divine call as God's Only Begotten.

> How many would strip Jesus our Great High Priest, of His Divinity? But they could not and cannot. Every time man inflicted a doubt, saying: "*If* Thou be the Son of God" God was there to prove that He was. The Devil said: "*If* Thou be the Son of God" in Judea's wilderness, but he was vanquished with the "It is written". While Christ was on the Cross the people said, "Let Him save Himself *if* He be Christ the chosen of God" (Luke xxiii. 35). The soldiers said: "*If* Thou be the king of the Jews save Thyself" (Luke xxiii. 37). One of the malefactors joined the cry of doubt, saying: "*If* Thou be Christ, save Thyself and us" (Luke xxiii. 39) But to all these "ifs" came the challenge of the resurrection on the third day. Man said "Is not this the carpenter's son?" (Matt. xiii. 55). God said: "This is My Beloved Son in Whom I am well pleased" (Matt. iii. 17).⁴⁴

The people were free to reject Jesus' chosen and divine status, but their rejection could not change the fact that he was heavenly in his origin, authorization, and nature. For the Church, the fact that the robe was seamless suggests that they too must be seamless (i.e., one), for "if ye are not one ye are not mine" (D&C 38:27). If they who make up his Church seek that unity, they will be covered (protected) by Christ, just as the high priest was covered by the garment. The indestructibility of the robe can symbolize the fact that the Church in its righteousness shall not be broken up by the cunning or strength of the natural man. The Lord brought to pass "the establishment of the kingdom of God in the latter days, never again to be destroyed nor given to other people" (D&C 138:44). The seamless garment reminds us of the necessity of seeking full obedience to God's commands, so that apostasy—individual or collective—may never breach the protective parameters which we call "the Church."

The pomegranates and golden bells along the bottom of the robe are equally rich in symbolism. Among other things, the pomegranate is known for its multiplicity of seeds. This seems to represent well both Christ's role as father of all who are reborn through him and also the laws and ordinances of his gospel—each of which typify the Master. The golden bells, on the other hand, have been seen as a symbol of divine protection.[45] Thus, one commentator states: "This robe is a type of that which preserves from death."[46] Owing to the fact that the sounding of these bells likely represented the "sounding forth" of the word of God, it is no wonder that they symbolize divine protection.[47] Christ, who sounded forth the word of God boldly and upon whose heart God's word was inscribed perfectly, was granted protection until his mission was complete. He offers that same protection to those who are faithful to their covenants and callings—to those who heed his warning and the warning of his prophets.

The Ephod (Leviticus 8:7; Exodus 28:4, 6–7)

To date, there continues to be some debate within the scholarly community as to what exactly the ephod was. Thus the term remains untranslated in the King James Version. Most scholars maintain that it was an apron of unsurpassable beauty, having gold woven into it (see Exodus 39:3)[48] and being very colorful in its appearance. Matthew B. Brown speculates that the ephod may have been decorated with "figures" or symbols.[49] Regardless, we know that it was the outermost garment upon which the onyx shoulder stones and the breast piece of judgment were fastened. It was the vestment upon which some of the most emblematic and important features of the high priest's dress were to be secured. And it was the location in which the Urim and Thummim was stored.

The symbolism in this particular garment is rich and extensive. First, upon the shoulder-straps of the ephod were found two stones—one on each shoulder. Inscribed on these were the names of the twelve tribes of Israel (six on either stone). By implication, the Messiah bares the burdens of covenant Israel, as do his authorized servants. For the Church, on the other hand, this symbol can be seen as an invitation to keep the baptismal covenant to "bear one another's burdens, that they may be light" (Mosiah 18:8). Christ, the high priest, and every member of the Church must each shoulder the burdens (spiritual and otherwise) of God's children. That is what followers of the Messiah are called to do.

Beyond the aforementioned symbolism, aprons also served anciently as symbols for "priesthood"[50] and "work."[51] For Christians, the ephod signified Jesus' diligence in moving forward the will and work of the Father; and it likely reminded the high priest of the ancient temple that he too was called to do the work of the Lord—a work that required priesthood power. For the Latter-day Saints, the ephod may suggest one of the major differences between them and other Christian denominations: restored priesthood keys and a divine call to build up the Latter-day kingdom before the return of the Son of God.

Lastly, the coloration on the ephod would have been deeply important. Exodus 28:6 commands, "Make the ephod of gold, of blue, and of purple, of scarlet." As previously pointed out, blue (being the color of the sky) typically represents the heavens. Scarlet (or red) would have commonly represented the earth. As one text on the clothing of the high priest states, red "is the colour of the earth. Blue and Red are therefore opposites. The name Adam comes from a root word 'Adham' which means 'red earth', and from this he was made." This same source notes that purple is "an intermediary colour to blend them [blue and red]."[52] Thus, the ephod can imply that Christ was made in the likeness of man (red) that he might bring us back to the likeness of God (blue). By taking upon himself flesh and blood, Jesus was equipped to meet our every need and also to set the perfect example for us to follow. He was a combination (purple) of the divine (blue) and the human (red)—as are each of us, being the literal "offspring of God" (Acts 17:29). Finally, that thread of gold, woven into the ephod, can remind us of his eternal and celestial nature: "[Gold] is not affected by exposure to the air and it will not deteriorate if buried for thousands of years. Acid will not destroy it, and fire will not burn it; from these it only comes out purified."[53] How perfectly this typifies Christ. And how significant is the invitation it offers to each of us to strive for life eternal though Christ's blood and through the faithful observance of his words.

The Curious Girdle of the Ephod (Leviticus 8:7; Exodus 28:5–8)

As with the ephod, information concerning the pattern and appearance of the "curious girdle" is limited. Since this vestment was directly associated with the ephod, it was only worn by the high priest. Unlike the inner girdle spoken of previously, the curious girdle would have resembled the pattern of the ephod in fabric and embroidery. One source notes, "The skillfully woven band [known as the curious girdle] seems to have been a girdle with which to fasten the ephod close about the waist (Leviticus 8:7). It was permanently attached to the ephod and made of the same material."[54] As discussed above, a girdle represents fidelity or faithfulness to covenants as well as preparation for action.

Regarding the symbolism, the fact that the curious girdle (and the ephod which it bound) was worn *only* by the high priest indicates that certain functions and responsibilities were his alone to perform.[55] In obvious ways this seems to typify both Christ and the presiding high priest of the Church today (i.e., the Latter-day Prophet). For members of Christ's Church, this symbol stands as a reminder that, while other Christians may serve in significant ways to spread the message of "Jesus Christ, and him crucified" (1 Corinthians 2:2), Latter-day Saints have a mission and ministry which is unique to them. Theirs is a call which cannot be performed by any other.

The Breastplate of Judgment and the Urim and Thummim (Leviticus 8:8; Exodus 28:4, 15–30)

The breastplate of judgment was made from the same materials and in the same manner as the ephod. It was made, like the ephod, out of one continuous piece of fabric. The fabric was folded in half "upward to form a sort of pouch."[56] It was a span in length and width (about 9x9 inches), thus forming a perfect square.[57] Upon the front of the breastplate were twelve stones, arranged in four rows of three, each stone being different from the others. Every stone was engraved with the name of one of the tribes of Israel. The breastplate was secured over the chest of the high priest by gold chains. The function of the breastplate of judgment was to serve as a pouch which held the Urim and Thummim—a device through which seers and prophets received revelation on behalf of covenant Israel. The book of Exodus records, "And thou shalt put in the breastplate of judgment the Urim and Thummim; and they shall be upon Aaron's heart, when he goeth before the Lord" (Exodus 28:30). According to the Jewish sage, Nachmanides, Moses didn't make the Urim and Thummim—nor did anyone in Israel. It was given to Moses by God as a divine instrument of knowing and receiving.[58]

The Christocentric symbolism associated with the breastplate of judgment and with the Urim and the Thummim is rich and diverse. To begin, the shape and the size of the breastplate are of significance. We are informed that the shape was a perfect square, 9x9 inches. In the description of the tabernacle the square is repeatedly present: we see it in the brazen altar (Exodus 38:1), the golden altar (Exodus 37:25), and the breastplate (Exodus 39:9). Each was required by God to be geometrically square—a symbol of balance, solidity, and equality. The number four typically symbolizes geographic completeness or totality.[59] In other words, if the number four is associated with an event or thing, the indication is that it will affect the entire earth and all its inhabitants. The breastplate over the heart of the high priest seems, therefore, to suggest Christ's love and awareness for *each* of God's children. The foursquare breastplate suggests that, through the Atonement of Christ, the entirety of the house of Israel shall be bound to Christ's heart just as the breastplate is bound to the heart of the priest. Significantly, unlike the twelve names written upon two stones on the shoulders of the High Priest, on the breastplate "each name is now on a separate stone so every individual believer in Him who has made the all-covering atonement has a special place in that all-prevailing intercession which is continually going on at the throne of grace."[60]

Since the Urim and Thummim within the pouch was a revelatory device, its placement in the squared pouch can suggest Christ's desire to reveal himself to all of God's children. It potentially implies that Christ's word will eventually fill the earth.

Interestingly, the various types of stones fastened into the breastplate itself may also be significant.[61] The stones in the breastplate are identical with the precious or semi-precious stones that, according to Ezekiel 28:13, were to be found in Eden, "the garden of God."[62] This reference to the original garden of God could have served as a reminder to the high priest that his work as mediator was to seek to return humanity to its spiritual station "in the Garden of Eden, when man was free from all sin."[63] Accordingly, when Christ performs his intercessory work, it is to bring us back into the state that we were in at Eden—a state of innocence wherein we were permitted to dwell in the presence of the Lord.

Finally, two facts about the Urim and Thummim, that it was likely not of earthly make and that it was also concealed, can teach us two significant truths about Christ. First, his origins are not of this earth. Matthew records the query of the Jews:

> And when he was come into his own country, he taught them in their synagogue, insomuch that they were astonished, and said, Whence hath this man this wisdom, and these mighty works?
>
> Is not this the carpenter's son? is not his mother called Mary? and his brethren, James, and Joses, and Simon, and Judas?
>
> And his sisters, are they not all with us? Whence then hath this man all these things? (Matthew 13:54–56)

Jesus was the Son of God—not the son of a lowly carpenter. Yet, as Isaiah reminds us: "He hath no form nor comeliness; and . . . there is no beauty that we should desire him" (Isaiah 53:2). His divinity truly is hidden from most.

In regard to the Church of Christ and how each of these symbols applies, note the following. Just as Christ's message and mission is to all the world, Latter-day Saints have a vocation to bless, serve, and convert the world to Christ and his ways. A requisite part of fulfilling that mission is having a love for our fellow human beings and a spirit of revelation that will guide us in teaching and ministering to individuals. Both of those necessary qualities are gifts of the Spirit.[64] Like the Urim and Thummim (with its individual names) over the heart of the high priest, we too must seek revelation and a spirit of love and compassion if we, as the Bride of Christ, will be of use to our Groom in this most sacred work. And like the stones with individual names, we are reminded through the symbolism that Christ knows us intimately; he knows our needs and our gifts. He can aid us in all that we seek to do in his name, and on his behalf. Finally, like the Urim and Thummim, this work is of God, not of mortals. Yet, it is as a bed of gold concealed. It is our responsibility to uncover it and bring it to the entire world.

The Miter and the Holy Crown (Leviticus 8:9; Exodus 28:4, 39–40; 39:30–31)

The miter of the high priest was made of linen. It was "of the distinctive design worn by royalty."[65] Upon the front of the miter was fastened the "Holy Crown" which consisted of a golden plate that bore the inscription "HOLINESS TO THE LORD" (Exodus 28:36). Additionally, the holy crown was secured to the miter with "a blue lace" ribbon (Exodus 28:37).

Christ-centered symbolism can be found in the miter. For example, one commentator notes: "The head is that which denotes authority. It is the head that controls the whole of the body. Christ as the Head of the Church controls that Church."[66] Since linen is a "symbol of holiness and righteousness,"[67] it seems clear that "the linen of the miter speaks of the righteousness of the Lord."[68] The fact that it was the attire of royalty suggests he is the King of Kings (Revelation 17:14). Additionally, the blue ribbon attaching the holy crown to the miter can point to the reality that Christ's mind is that of the Father. He knows the Father's will, and all that he says and does is an attempt to bring that will to pass.

For the priest and the parishioner, the miter is a potential reminder of what God has promised each of us: that we might become "kings and priests unto God" (Revelation 1:6).[69] It also informs us as to how this is to be done: we must develop the mind of God. As Elder Bruce R. McConkie noted, "[when we] walk in the light as he is in the light . . . [we] thereby have his mind. [We then] think what he thinks, know what he knows, say what he would say, and do what he would do . . . all by revelation from the Spirit."[70] Though only the high priest was commanded to wear such an inscription, certainly what it represented was expected of all of God's servants. Without personal worthiness, all we do in the temple or in the Church is but a mere form and a mockery of holiness! The high priest represented the people before God. Thus, God's call to him to be holy before the Lord was, by application, a call to all in Israel to be holy before the Lord and to consecrate their hearts and minds to Jehovah. That declaration of "holiness to the Lord" was to influence their labors, their utterances, their thoughts and desires, and the paths they pursued—not just in the temple, but in their daily walk.[71] Thus, symbolically speaking, all who donned the cap of the priest were really donning a commitment to live in holiness *before* the Lord because they had dedicated their lives *to* the Lord.[72] The placement of the plate on the forehead can remind us of the fact that "it is the head that controls the whole of the body."[73] "For as he thinketh . . . so is he" (Proverbs 23:7).

Conclusion

What we have offered above is but a homily—an application of ancient Jewish symbols seen through Christian lenses. But lest we assume we have looked "beyond the mark" (Jacob 4:14), let us remember the words of Nephi, who wrote: "Behold . . . *all things* which have been given of God from the beginning of the world, unto man, are the typifying of [Christ]" (2 Nephi 11:4, emphasis added). "The literary evidence of that," Elder Jeffrey R. Holland pointed out, "is seen throughout the holy scriptures."[74] Jacob recorded that the scriptures "truly testify of Christ" (Jacob 7:11). In the book of Moses the Lord stated, "And behold, all things have their likeness, and all things are created and made to bear record of me, both things which are temporal, and things which are spiritual; things which are in the heavens above, and things which are on the earth, and things which are in the earth, and things which are under the earth, both above and beneath: all things bear record of me" (Moses 6:63). Clearly, the scriptures are replete with testaments of Jesus' Messianic call and divine nature. As we have pointed out above, much of Christianity acknowledges that the sacred clothing of the high priest can serve as a symbol of the consecrated attributes of the Holy Messiah.

As the priest of the temple served to mediate Israel's relationship with God, he too functioned as a type for the Redeemer. In donning the sacred garments, he served well as a representation of Jesus' role on behalf of the covenant people.

Finally, the attire of the high priest has much it can teach those who trust in Christ for their salvation. Peter reminded us that, in all things, Jesus is our exemplar (1 Peter 2:21). As the clothing of the high priest has the ability to teach us what the Savior is like, it also has the potential to teach us what we must become if we wish to inherit eternal life in God's presence. One commentator suggested that the function of the priestly garments "was to remind the Israelites that a powerful, holy and just God was indeed present with them in so far as the wearer of the garments was held to be linked to Him."[75] As covenant Israel continues seeking to develop the attributes of the Great High Priest, they have reason to trust in his promises. The Apostle Paul reminded us, "Wherefore the law was our schoolmaster to bring us unto Christ, that we might be justified by faith. But after that faith is come, we are no longer under a schoolmaster . . . For as many of you as have been baptized into Christ have put on Christ" (Galatians 3:24–25, 27). For Christians, this is the invitation of the garments of the high priest: to "put on Christ"!

Notes

1. See William W. Klein, Craig L. Blomberg and Robert L. Hubbard Jr., *Introduction to Biblical Interpretation* (Dallas: Word Publishing, 1993).

2. An exegetical approach typically includes word-studies—trying to find the various shades of meaning behind the original Greek or Hebrew words.

   3. Though this paper is a homily, I am not arguing generally for or against a homiletic approach either to scripture or to the clothing of the high priest. What this paper seeks to do is to report the Christocentric reading of these things by various interpreters and to suggest the implications of those readings for practicing Christians today.

   4. The term *Aaronic high priest* in this paper will refer to the high priests of the Mosaic dispensation, primarily the direct firstborn male descendants of Aaron. See Richard Neitzel Holzapfel and David Rolph Seely, *My Father's House: Temple Worship and Symbolism in the New Testament* (Salt Lake City: Bookcraft, 1994), 59. However, the term should not imply that each held only the Aaronic Priesthood. We know, for example, that Moses' brother, Aaron, and his sons held the Melchizedek Priesthood. See John A. Widtsoe, *Priesthood and Church Government in the Church of Jesus Christ of Latter-day Saints* (Salt Lake City: Deseret Book, 1961), 14; Bruce R. McConkie, *The Promised Messiah: The First Coming of Christ* (Salt Lake City: Deseret Book, 1981), 411.

   5. Along with the examples quoted directly within this paper, see also B. Maureen Gaglardi, *The Path of the Just: The Garments of the High Priest* (Dubuque, IA: Kendall/Hunt, 1971), 5: "There are, I suppose, numerous and undoubtedly profound volumes obtainable on the ministry and vestments of the High Priest. The great High Priestly office of Christ is the supreme lesson taught us by this type." Likewise, see Paul F. Kiene, *The Tabernacle of God in the Wilderness of Sinai*, trans. John S. Crandall (Grand Rapids, MI: Zondervan, 1977), 164: "The details of the high priest's garments speak of the Lord Jesus in His glory. They help us the better to recognize His incomparable qualities and the worth of His person, in order that we will love and honor our Lord more." Also, Stephen F. Olford, *The Tabernacle: Camping with God*, 2nd ed. (Grand Rapids, MI: Kregel, 2004), 123: "Each part of [Aaron's] attire speaks eloquently of the glories, virtues, and excellencies of our Great High Priest, the Lord Jesus Christ."

   6. David Fenton Jarman, *The High Priest's Dress; Or, Christ Arrayed in Aaron's Robes* (London: W. F. Crofts, 1850), ix.

   7. Kenneth E. Trent, *Types of Christ in the Old Testament: A Conservative Approach to Old Testament Typology* (New York: Exposition Press, 1960), 52. See also Ada R. Habershon, *Study of the Types* (Grand Rapids, MI: Kregel, 1974), 183.

   8. Donald W. Parry and Jay A. Parry, *Symbols and Shadows: Unlocking a Deeper Understanding of the Atonement* (Salt Lake City: Deseret Book, 2009), 27; emphasis in original.

   9. C. W. Slemming, *These Are the Garments: A Study of the Garments of the High Priest of Israel* (London: Marshall, Morgan & Scott, 1945), 22.

   10. Walter C. Kaiser Jr., "Exodus," in *The Expositor's Bible Commentary*, ed. Frank E. Gaebelein (Grand Rapids, MI: Zondervan, 1976–92), 2:466.

   11. In this paper we will be examining the garments in the order in which they are described in Leviticus 8:7–9, while also drawing upon descriptions of these same articles in the book of Exodus. I freely acknowledge that the garments of the high priest likely underwent modification in Israel's later periods; see Margaret Barker, *The Great High*

Priest: The Temple Roots of Christian Liturgy (New York: T&T Clark, 2007), 210. This article will be concerned primarily with the information Moses preserved for us in the Pentateuch, though (due to lack of detail in certain areas) we may occasionally look at other descriptions of the garments to arrive at a more complete picture. The reader will be benefited by briefly reviewing Exodus 25–30 (the revelation), Exodus 36–39 (the making), and Leviticus 8–9 (the investiture and inauguration of temple service). The scope of this article will not allow for a discussion of those details here. Suffice it to say, these three units are intimately related but describe different stages of implementation of God's revelation to Moses.

12. Moreover, this homily will occasionally analyze symbols from a Latter-day Saint perspective, showing possible meanings hidden in the garments that provide one with a greater understanding of the specific work of this last dispensation.

13. Just like the New Testament writers who were quick to identify Christ in Old Testament symbolism, all men and women can benefit from understanding the symbolism which God has embedded in all things. This symbolism is designed to bear testimony of his Son. While we must "be watchful that we do not force the text and make it say things it does not say" (Sidney Greidanus, *Preaching Christ from the Old Testament* [Grand Rapids, MI: William B. Eerdmans, 1999], 37), our homiletic approach will imitate the allegorical methodology found in the New Testament and in the early church fathers; see, for example, Luke 24:27 or Augustine, "The Epistle of John," Homily 2.1, in *Nicene and Post-Nicene Fathers: First Series*, ed. Philip Schaff (Peabody, MA: Hendrickson, 2004), 7:469. Augustine states that *everything* in the Old Testament speaks of Christ, *but only to those who have the ears to hear it.*

14. This optional rendering is based on the following: "And thou shalt *embroider* [Hebrew: *shabats*, meaning to 'weave' or 'plait'] the *coat* [Hebrew: *kthoneth* or *kuttoneth*, meaning an 'under-garment' or 'shirt-like garment,' sometimes rendered 'tunic'] of fine *linen* [Hebrew: *shesh* or *shshiy*, meaning something 'bleached white' or of white 'linen']." Admittedly, scholars have translated the passage variously. I have offered only one rendering, but it does appear to be a valid rendering of the Hebrew. See Kenneth Barker, ed., *The NIV Study Bible* (Grand Rapids, MI: Zondervan, 1995), 128, s.v. Exodus 28:39 and footnote 28:39; *Good News Bible* (New York: American Bible Society, 1978), 96, s.v. Exodus 28:39.

15. Flavius Josephus, *Antiquities of the Jews* 3.7.2, in *The Complete Works of Josephus*, trans. William Whiston (Grand Rapids, MI: Kregel, 1981), 73. See also Kaiser, "Exodus," 2:467 and J. H. Hertz, *The Pentateuch and Haftorahs* 2nd ed. (London: Soncino Press, 1962), 343. Josephus may or may not be right about the design of the clothing of the Aaronic high priest. Nevertheless, his explanation represents the views of his day—both Jewish and Christian. It is quite possible that the Christocentric reading of these items by Christians of the post–New Testament era was colored by explanations of the design given by first century witnesses like Josephus. In that regard, his views are germane to our study—particularly since our examination is homiletic rather than exegetical.

16. Leslie F. Church, ed., *The NIV Matthew Commentary in One Volume: Based on the Broad Oak Edition* (Grand Rapids, MI: Zondervan, 1992), 107. See also Patrick Fairbairn, *Typology of Scripture* (Grand Rapids, MI: Kregel, 1989), 242, n.1.

17. See Slemming, *These Are the Garments*, 25.

18. See Parry and Parry, *Symbols and Shadows*, 130–31 and Slemming, *These Are the Garments*, 25.

19. See Jacob Milgrom, *The Anchor Bible: Leviticus 1–16* (New York: Doubleday, 1991), 502 and fig. 11, 506; James G. Murphy, *A Critical and Exegetical Commentary on the Book of Exodus, with a New Translation* (Boston: Estes and Lauriat, 1874), 320; Willem A. VanGemeren, ed., *The New International Dictionary of Old Testament Theology and Exegesis* (Grand Rapids, MI: Zondervan, 1997), 4:340–41.

20. See Matthew B. Brown, *The Gate of Heaven: Insights on the Doctrines and Symbols of the Temple* (American Fork, UT: Covenant Communications, 1999), 104, n. 139. See also Hugh Nibley, *Temple and Cosmos* (Provo, UT: FARMS, 1992), 91–138; John W. Welch and Claire Foley, "Gammadia on Early Jewish and Christian Garments," *BYU Studies* 36, no. 3 (1996–97): 253–58. Brown states: "In the paintings of the Dura Europos synagogue (ca. 245 A.D.), Moses is depicted standing before the tabernacle dressed in a white robe that is decorated at chest and knee level with two different checkered marks. . . . Examples of Jewish clothing with marks shaped like the Greek letter *gamma* (Γ) have been recovered in archeological sites at Masada, Bar-Kokhba, and Dura-Europos."

21. Murphy, *Critical and Exegetical Commentary on the Book of Exodus*, 320.

22. Parry and Parry have suggested: "Various parts of the ancient priestly sacred vestments symbolize aspects of the atonement" (*Symbols and Shadows*, 138). The whiteness of the linen coat has obvious connections to Christ's ability to cleanse.

23. Gaglardi, *Path of the Just*, 28.

24. Slemming, *These Are the Garments*, 25.

25. Slemming, *These Are the Garments*, 25.

26. See Augustine, "The Epistle of John," Homily 2.1, in *Nicene and Post-Nicene Fathers: First Series*, ed. Philip Schaff and Schaff, *Nicene and Post-Nicene Fathers—Series 1*, 7:469, who states that everything in the Old Testament "tells of Christ," but only if you and I have the ears to hear what is being symbolically taught.

27. The "Church" of the Old Testament was quite different from the "Church" of the New Testament, just as the Church of today is quite different from the "Church" of antiquity; see John A. Tvedtnes, *The Church of the Old Testament* (Salt Lake City: Deseret Book, 1967). The use of the term "Church" here is intended generically, referring only to followers of YHWY or Christ in any gospel dispensation.

28. Of course, commentators are extrapolating a meaning which was quite possibly foreign to Jews of the Mosaic dispensation, but which would have meaning to Christian readers of the Hebrew Bible. Holzapfel and Seely have written: "There is no scriptural evidence for the clothing of the Levites, but Josephus records that at the time of Jesus the Levites had gained the privilege of wearing priestly linen robes" (*My Father's House*, 60). Though we cannot be certain of how far back this practice goes, it is clear that it would have allowed all Levites to gain a greater appreciation for and understanding of the symbolism behind the linen robe—not just the high priest and Aaronic priests.

29. For examples, see Doctrine and Covenants 4:1; 6:1; 11:1; 12:1; and 14:1.

30. Baruch A. Levine, *The JPS Torah Commentary: Leviticus* (Philadelphia: The Jewish Publications Society, 1989), 50. Eight articles of sacred clothing are mentioned in

association with the high priest. The four undergarments—the linen coat, the breeches, the girdle or sash, and the headband—were worn by all Aaronic priests who worked in the tabernacle or the temple. The four outer garments—the breastplate with the Urim and Thummim, the ephod, the robe, and the miter—were worn only by the high priest. See Kaiser, "Exodus," 2:465.

31. See Brown, *The Gate of Heaven*, 81–82; Stephen D. Ricks, "The Garment of Adam," *Temples of the Ancient World*, ed. Donald W. Parry (Salt Lake: Deseret Book, 1994), 709, 727, n. 23. While plants were technically also subject to corruption and death, they were not seen as symbols of such because their level of life was not equivalent to the level of life of an animal. Thus, animal products carried negative symbolic connotations, whereas linen carried positive ones. See also Trent, *Types of Christ in the Old Testament*, 56, who associates the "linen breeches" with "the righteousness of Christ."

32. Jarman, *High Priest's Dress*, 19; emphasis in original.

33. See Josephus, *Antiquities of the Jews* 3.7.2. See also Brown, *The Gate of Heaven*, 84.

34. See Douglas R. Edwards, "Dress and Ornamentation," in *The Anchor Bible Dictionary*, ed. David Noel Freedman (New York: Doubleday, 1992), 2:237; James Hall, *Dictionary of Subjects and Symbols in Art* (New York: Harper and Row, 1974), 138; Jack Tresidder, *Symbols and Their Meanings* (London: Duncan Baird Publishers, 2000), 134. See also J. C. Cooper, *An Illustrated Encyclopaedia of Traditional Symbols* (London: Thames and Hudson, 1995), 73–74; Hugh T. Henry, *Catholic Customs and Symbols* (New York: Benziger Brothers, 1925), 69–70.

35. Slemming, *These Are the Garments*, 28. See also Gaglardi, *The Path of the Just*, 45: "Biblical girdles had various uses, the most common of which was to tighten the coat or clothes, bringing the folds together to enable the party wearing it to be prepared for work, or action such as running." See also 1 Peter 1:13; Walter L. Wilson, *A Dictionary of Bible Types* (Peabody, MA: Hendrickson, 1999), 196; Ralph Gower, *The New Manners and Customs of Bible Times* (Chicago: Moody Press, 1987), 14.

36. The Hebrew word translated as "blue" here is also sometimes translated as "violet." Though we are not explicitly told within the text whether the robe was made from linen, wool, or some other comparable fabric, commentators suggest it was most likely made of wool. See Levine, *The JPS Torah Commentary: Leviticus*, 50; Sol Scharfstein, *Torah and Commentary: The Five Books of Moses* (Jersey City, NJ: KTAV Publishing, 2008), 259.

37. See Brown, *The Gate of Heaven*, 82; Milgrom, *The Anchor Bible: Leviticus 1–16*, 506, figure 11; Hertz, *The Pentateuch and Haftorahs*, 342; *Eerdmans' Handbook to the Bible* (Grand Rapids, MI: Eerdmans, 1973), 169.

38. Slemming, *These Are the Garments*, 34.

39. See Levine, *JPS Torah Commentary: Leviticus*, 50.

40. See Whiston, *Complete Works of Josephus*, 74, note.

41. See Ada R. Habershon, *Study of the Types* (Grand Rapids, MI: Kregel Publications, 1974), 95; Cooper, *An Illustrated Encyclopaedia of Traditional Symbols*, 40.

42. Joseph Fielding McConkie, *Gospel Symbolism* (Salt Lake City: Bookcraft, 1985), 111.

43. See Kevin J. Conner, *Interpreting the Symbols and Types* (Portland, OR: City Bible Publishing, 1992), 61.

44. Slemming, *These Are the Garments*, 34; emphasis in original.

45. They represent "divine protection" because they are said to scare away demons. See Milgrom, *The Anchor Bible: Leviticus 1–16*, 504.

46. Murphy, *Critical and Exegetical Commentary on the Book of Exodus*, 319.

47. Charles F. Pfeiffer and Everett F. Harrison, eds., *The Wycliffe Bible Commentary* (Chicago: Moody Press, 1975), 79.

48. See, for example, Carol Meyers, "Ephod," in *The Anchor Bible Dictionary*, ed. David Noel Freedman, 2:550; John L. McKenzie, *Dictionary of the Bible* (Milwaukee: The Bruce Publishing Company, 1965), 241; Allen C. Myers, ed., *The Eerdmans Bible Dictionary* (Grand Rapids, MI: Eerdmans, 1987), 342; Kaiser, "Exodus," 2:468; George Arthur Buttrick, ed., *The Interpreter's Bible* (New York: Abingdon Press, 1951–57), 1:1039; Michael D. Coogan, ed., *The New Oxford Annotated Bible*, 3rd ed. (New York: Oxford University Press, 2001), 122 (Hebrew Bible section). Some English translations render the Hebrew word "ephod" as "apron." See, for example, James Moffatt, trans., *A New Translation of The Bible: Containing the Old and New Testaments* (New York: Harper & Brothers, 1950), 92 (Hebrew Bible section); J. M. Powis Smith and Edgar J. Goodspeed, trans., *The Complete Bible: An American Translation* (Chicago: University of Chicago Press, 1949), 76 (Hebrew Bible section).

49. Brown, *The Gate of Heaven*, 86.

50. Conner, *Interpreting the Symbols and Types*, 141; Merrill F. Unger, *Unger's Bible Dictionary* (Chicago: Moody Press, 1975), 317.

51. Nadia Julien, *The Mammoth Dictionary of Symbols* (New York: Carroll and Graf Publishers, 1996), 24. Cooper writes "fertility" (*Illustrated Encyclopaedia of Traditional Symbols*, 14).

52. Slemming, *These Are the Garments*, 41.

53. Slemming, *These Are the Garments*, 39–40.

54. Buttrick, *Interpreter's Bible*, 1:1039.

55. See Jarman, *High Priest's Dress*, 3.

56. Kaiser, "Exodus," 2:467.

57. Murphy, *Critical and Exegetical Commentary on the Book of Exodus*, 315.

58. See Ramban Nachmanides, *Commentary on the Torah*, trans. Charles B. Chavel (New York: Shilo Publishing House, 1973), 2:481. Whether Nachmanides is right on this point is anyone's guess. However, there seems to be scriptural support for his claim. For example, the Urim and Thummim mentioned time and again in the Hebrew Bible (Exodus 28:30; Leviticus 8:8; Numbers 27:21; Deuteronomy 33:8; 1 Samuel 28:6; Ezra 2:63; Nehemiah 7:65) never has an origin attached to it, and the one given to Joseph Smith by Moroni (see Joseph Smith—History 1:35) had belonged to Mahonri Moriancumer, and it was "given to the brother of Jared upon the Mount, when he talked with the Lord face to face" (D&C 17:1). Additionally, section 130 and Revelation 2 speak of a Urim and Thummim which will be given to "each individual" who proves worthy of an inheritance in the celestial kingdom—again implying divine origin. Abraham spoke of "the Urim and Thummim, which the Lord my God had given unto me" (Abraham 3:1). Thus, Nachmanides's claim that this was not a man-made device finds support.

59. See Richard D. Draper, *Opening the Seven Seals: The Vision of John the Revelator* (Salt Lake City: Deseret Book, 1991), 24, 77, 94; Mick Smith, *The Book of Revelation: Plain, Pure, and Simple* (Salt Lake City: Bookcraft, 1998), 288; Robert D. Johnston, *Numbers in the Bible: God's Design in Biblical Numerology* (Grand Rapids, MI: Kregel Publications, 1990), 61; Carol L. Meyers and Eric M. Meyers, *The Anchor Bible: Haggai, Zechariah 1–8* (New York: Doubleday, 1987), 317.

60. Murphy, *Critical and Exegetical Commentary on the Book of Exodus*, 316.

61. The stones of the breastplate were sardius, topaz, carbuncle, emerald, sapphire, diamond, ligure, agate, amethyst, beryl, onyx, and jasper (Exodus 28:17–20).

62. The stones mentioned in Ezekiel 28:13 are sardius, topaz, diamond, beryl, onyx, jasper, sapphire, emerald, and carbuncle.

63. Umberto Cassuto, *A Commentary on the Book of Exodus*, trans. Israel Abrahams (Jerusalem: Magnes Press of the Hebrew University, 1983), 375–76.

64. See Marvin J. Ashton, "There Are Many Gifts," *Ensign*, November 1987, 23; Bruce R. McConkie, *Mormon Doctrine*, 2nd ed. (Salt Lake City: Bookcraft, 1966), s.v. "Gifts of the Spirit."

65. Brown, *The Gate of Heaven*, 84.

66. Slemming, *These Are the Garments*, 118.

67. Slemming, *These Are the Garments*, 118.

68. Gaglardi, *Path of the Just*, 216.

69. "Dressing in special clothing in the temple denotes a change in role, from that of mortal to immortal, from ordinary human to priest or priestess, king or queen." John A. Tvedtnes, "Priestly Clothing in Bible Times," in *Temples of the Ancient World*, ed. Donald W. Parry (Salt Lake City: Deseret Book, 1994), 666.

70. Bruce R. McConkie, *Doctrinal New Testament Commentary* (Salt Lake City: Bookcraft, 1987–88), 2:322.

71. Slemming wrote: "The mitre that adorned [the temple priest's] head would speak of holiness of thought and control" (*These Are the Garments*, 127).

72. See Slemming, *These Are the Garments*, 124–25.

73. Slemming, *These Are the Garments*, 118. See also Gaglardi, *Path of the Just*, 216: "'HOLINESS TO THE LORD' is the ultimate complete holiness of the body, soul and spirit, essential in order for this old mortal to put on immortality when Jesus returns. All who have this hope certainly are purifying themselves today."

74. Jeffrey R. Holland, *Christ and the New Covenant: The Messianic Message of the Book of Mormon* (Salt Lake City: Deseret Book, 1997), 159.

75. R. K. Harrison, *Leviticus: An Introduction and Commentary* (Downers Grove, IL: Inter-Varsity Press, 1980), 92.

7

Gestures of Praise: Lifting and Spreading the Hands in Biblical Prayer

David M. Calabro

Prayer, including praise as well as supplication, tends to be understood as the offering up of words that are enunciated and heard.[1] However, prayer also has an important visual component, especially in the context of the temple, where ritual actions are a focus.[2] The quintessential type of gesture associated with prayer in the ancient world was the lifting of the hands, a visual sign that accompanied verbal expressions of praise and entreaty.[3]

The ancient Israelite gesture of raising both hands in praise or supplication is mentioned in twenty-four scriptural passages, of which twenty-two are from the Old Testament, one is from the New Testament, and one is from the Book of Mormon.[4] Similar references are also found in a small group of inscriptions from cultures closely related to ancient Israel (two Ugaritic and two Aramaic).[5] In addition, art from the ancient Levant bears witness to this gesture (see figs. 1–4 and discussion below). However, scholars who have studied the gesture based on the biblical text have tended either to rely on comparisons with the more distant cultures of Mesopotamia and Egypt or to ignore the evidence from art, leading to a distorted picture of what the gesture looked like. This is

---

David M. Calabro is a graduate student at the University of Chicago.

important because, in some cases, the precise meaning of the gesture depends on its appearance. For example, Mayer Gruber, based on analysis of biblical and Mesopotamian textual sources and perhaps influenced by Mesopotamian art, suggests that the gesture symbolizes a request for one's empty hands to be filled, which assumes that the hands are raised with the palms upward.[6] At the same time, those who have commented on this gesture as it appears in Levantine art have generally given only cursory attention to the meaning of the gesture, as if the meaning is obvious and not worthy of in-depth study. An example of this kind of cursory interpretation is found in James Pritchard's description of a relief on a sarcophagus from ancient Byblos: "The last four figures *merely salute* the king with upraised and out-turned hands."[7]

My purpose in this study is to present the evidence for this gesture in the literature and art of the biblical world, combining the textual and artistic sources to establish the form and then the meaning of this gesture. I will begin by reviewing the examples of this gesture: first those from the biblical passages, then those from the inscriptions, and finally those from the artistic sources. Along the way, I will explain what these examples tell us about the gesture's form. I will then discuss the gesture's meaning, including how raising the hands in prayer may relate to other ritual actions that were performed in the same context.

Biblical Instances of Raising Both Hands in Prayer

Six Hebrew idioms are used in the Old Testament to describe the gesture of raising both hands in prayer. One of these is *nāśā' yādayim*, "lift up the hands," which is used twice in the Psalms:

> Hear the voice of my supplications, when I cry unto thee, when I *lift up my hands* toward thy holy oracle. (Psalm 28:2; emphasis added in scriptures quoted)[8]

> *Lift up your hands* in the sanctuary, and bless the Lord. (Psalm 134:2)

An additional example of this idiom is found in the book of Habakkuk:

> The mountains saw thee, and they trembled: the overflowing of the water passed by: the deep uttered his voice, and *lifted up his hands* on high. (Habakkuk 3:10)

The Hebrew text of the passage including Habakkuk 3:10 contains many problems, and scholars differ as to whether it was the deep or the sun (mentioned in the following verse) that was originally described as lifting up its hands, or whether an entirely different idiom was originally used.[9] In any case, the text as it now stands seems to describe the personified deep raising its "hands" (perhaps referring to waves) in praising God.

The second idiom used for this gesture is *nāśāʾ kappayim*. This idiom is also translated as "lift up the hands" in most English translations.[10]

> Let my prayer be set forth before thee as incense; and *the lifting up of my hands* as the evening sacrifice. (Psalm 141:2)

> Arise, cry out in the night: in the beginning of the watches pour out thine heart like water before the face of the Lord: *lift up thy hands* toward him for the life of thy young children, that faint for hunger in the top of every street. (Lamentations 2:19)

> Let us *lift up* our heart with *our hands* unto God in the heavens. (Lamentations 3:41)[11]

A third idiom, *pāraś kappayim*, means "spread or stretch out the hands." This is the most common Hebrew idiom used for the raising of both hands in worship, and it is found in many biblical books, including the historical books:

> And Moses said unto him, As soon as I am gone out of the city, I will *spread abroad my hands* unto the Lord; and the thunder shall cease, neither shall there be any more hail; that thou mayest know how that the earth is the Lord's. . . . And Moses went out of the city from Pharaoh, and *spread abroad his hands* unto the Lord: and the thunders and hail ceased, and the rain was not poured upon the earth. (Exodus 9:29, 33)

> And Solomon stood before the altar of the Lord in the presence of all the congregation of Israel, and *spread forth his hands* toward heaven: . . . And it was so, that when Solomon had made an end of praying all this prayer and supplication unto the Lord, he arose from before the altar of the Lord, from kneeling on his knees with *his hands spread* up to heaven. (1 Kings 8:22, 54)

> What prayer and supplication soever be made by any man, or by all thy people Israel, which shall know every man the plague of his own heart, and *spread forth his hands* toward this house: then hear thou in heaven thy dwelling place, and forgive, and do, and give to every man according to his ways, whose heart thou knowest. (1 Kings 8:38–39)[12]

The fourth idiom is *pēraś (bə)yādayim* "spread or stretch forth the hands." This idiom occurs once in Psalms and once in Lamentations:

> I *stretch forth my hands* unto thee: my soul thirsteth after thee, as a thirsty land. (Psalm 143:6)

> Zion *spreadeth forth her hands*, and there is none to comfort her: the Lord hath commanded concerning Jacob, that his adversaries should be round about him: Jerusalem is as a menstruous woman among them. (Lamentations 1:17)

The idiom *pēraś (bə)yādayim* is also used in Isaiah 25 to describe quite a different action, namely the strokes of a swimmer. However, in using this figure of a swimmer, the prophet may also be making an allusion to raising the hands in worship:

> For in this mountain shall the hand of the Lord rest, and Moab shall be trodden down under him, even as straw is trodden down for the dunghill. And he shall *spread forth his hands* in the midst of them, as he that swimmeth spreadeth forth his hands to swim: and he shall bring down their pride together with the spoils of their hands. (Isaiah 25:10–11)

The setting in which personified Moab will "spread forth his hands" is "this mountain," referring to the mountain of the Lord (that is, the temple). It is likely that a double meaning of the gesture is intended: Moab, as he is being trodden down in the temple, will "spread forth his hands" in urgent prayer like that of the Psalmist in Psalm 143:6 and that of personified Zion in Lamentations 1:17, and the motions of his hands will be so desperate that they will be comparable to a swimmer's strokes.

The idiom *pēraś kappayim*, which also means "spread forth the hands," occurs twice in the prophetic books:

> And when ye *spread forth your hands*, I will hide mine eyes from you: yea, when ye make many prayers, I will not hear: your hands are full of blood. (Isaiah 1:15)

> For I have heard a voice as of a woman in travail, and the anguish as of her that bringeth forth her first child, the voice of the daughter of Zion, that bewaileth herself, that *spreadeth her hands*, saying, Woe is me now! for my soul is wearied because of murderers. (Jeremiah 4:31)

Finally, the phrase *mōʿal yādayim* "lifting up hands" is used once in the description of a prayer in the book of Nehemiah:

> And Ezra blessed the Lord, the great God. And all the people answered, Amen, Amen, with *lifting up their hands*: and they bowed their heads, and worshipped the Lord with their faces to the ground. (Nehemiah 8:6)

The gesture of stretching forth or lifting up the hands, while most frequently found in the Old Testament, is also mentioned once in the Book of Mormon and once in the New Testament. In the Book of Mormon, this ancient Israelite gesture is part of the apostate worship practices of the Zoramites, although it is not stated whether the gesture itself was regarded as inappropriate:

> Therefore, whosoever desired to worship must go forth and stand upon the top thereof, and *stretch forth his hands* towards heaven, and cry with a loud voice, saying: Holy, holy God. (Alma 31:14–15)

A statement in Paul's letter to Timothy shows that this gesture was known among members of the Church in New Testament times:

> I will therefore that men pray every where, *lifting up* holy *hands*, without wrath and doubting. (1 Timothy 2:8)

The Greek phrase used for the gesture in this verse is *cheiras epairō* "lift up the hands," which is a phrase used in the Septuagint (the Greek translation of the Old Testament) to translate the Hebrew *nāśāʾ yādayim*.[13] Many ancient Jewish and early Christian sources also mention raising the hands in the context of worship.[14] Thus, when Paul expresses the wish "that men pray every where, lifting up holy hands," he is speaking of a common Jewish and Christian practice, with very ancient roots; Paul is not wishing for a new practice but for its faithful observance and the sanctification of those who participate in it.

One scholar, Mayer Gruber, has suggested that two different prayer gestures are referred to in the Bible: a generic gesture of worship indicated by the verb *nāśāʾ* "lift up," and a gesture of supplication indicated by the verb *pāraś/pēraś* "spread forth."[15] However, I suggest instead that all of the passages quoted above refer to a single gesture of raising the hands in prayer. My reasons for this are fourfold. First, contrary to what Gruber suggests, the biblical examples do not divide neatly into function categories corresponding to the verb used. The gesture in Psalm 28:2, for example, is indicated by the verb *nāśāʾ*, yet it is explicitly a gesture of supplication; moreover, the gestures in Lamentations 2:19 and Jeremiah 4:31 use different expressions (*nāśāʾ yādayim* and *pēraś kappayim* respectively), yet they portray a practically identical kind of petitionary prayer. Second, the various expressions used to refer to raising the hands in prayer are not mutually exclusive. The hands can be both lifted and spread at the same time, and expressions using both *nāśāʾ* and *pāraś/pēraś* may have a prepositional phrase indicating that the gesture is performed "toward" or "unto God." Third, while Gruber relies on comparison with Mesopotamian material, geographically and chronologically closer parallels are found in the inscriptions and art of the Levant, and these do not seem to me to support the division into two prayer gestures proposed by Gruber. (These sources are discussed below.) Fourth, it seems inadvisable to make a sharp distinction between worship and supplication in the context of biblical prayer, since these functions are often intermingled in the same prayer (as in some of the examples cited above). I will thus proceed on the assumption that the expressions listed above refer to one prayer gesture; this assumption is not conclusive (given that ancient Hebrew culture can no longer be observed directly), but it represents my best guess from the available evidence.

From the passages quoted above, we can gather some clues as to the form of the raised-hand gesture. For example, the verb *nāśāʾ* "raise" indicates that the hands are held high, perhaps at the level of the face or higher. Some passages refer to lifting or spreading the hands "to heaven," "to God in heaven," or "on high" (see 1 Kings 8:22, 54; Lamentations 3:41; Habakkuk 3:10; Alma 31:14–15); these passages seem to describe instances in which the hands are held especially high. In other cases, the target of the gesture appears to be roughly on the same level as the person performing it, such as when the hands are raised to the temple or to the Holy of Holies (see 1 Kings 8:38–39; Psalm 28:2). The reference to the swimmer's strokes in Isaiah 25:10–11, if this does indeed allude to the prayer gesture, would imply that the gesture could involve some motion of the arms comparable to swimming (such as, perhaps, raising the hands and then lowering them). Also, the phrase *spread forth the hands* implies that the hands are held apart from each other, held open, or both.

The Raised-Hand Prayer Gesture in Ancient Inscriptions

A small handful of inscriptions from the area around ancient Israel mention a gesture that is identical or similar to that described in the biblical passages quoted above. Two of these inscriptions come from Ugarit, a city on the Mediterranean coast north of Israel that was destroyed in about 1185 BC. The first of these recounts instructions given by the god El to the hero Kirta, telling him how to approach and entreat the god Baal; the text then describes Kirta carrying out the instructions:

> Ascend to the top of the tower, mount the shoulder of the wall. *Lift up your hands* to heaven, sacrifice to the Bull, your father El. Bring down Baal with your sacrifice, the son of Dagon with your prey.... He ascended to the top of the tower, he mounted the shoulder of the wall. He *lifted up his hands* to heaven, he sacrificed to the Bull, his father El. He brought down Baal with his sacrifice, the son of Dagon with his prey. (Kirta, *KTU* 1.14 ii 21–26, iv 2–8)[16]

The second Ugaritic inscription describes a ritual to be carried out at the time of vintage. As part of the ritual, the king is to offer a prayer:

> When the sun rises, the king will be free of cultic obligations.... You shall take him back to [the palace].[17] When he is there, he shall *lift up his hands* to heaven. (Rites for the Vintage, *KTU* 1.41 50–55)

The Ugaritic idiom used in both of these inscriptions is *naša'a yadêmi* "lift up the hands," which is cognate with the Hebrew *nāśā' yādayim*.

Two Aramaic inscriptions also refer to a gesture of raising the hands in worship. The first is from a stela dating to ca. 780 BC; it records a battle in which the king of Hamath, named Zakkur, lifted up his hands in prayer to the god Baal:

> All these kings laid siege to Hadhrak. They raised a wall higher than the wall of Hadhrak, they dug a ditch deeper than its ditch. I *lifted up my hands* to Baal-shemayn. Baal-shemayn answered me, Baal-shemayn spoke to me through seers and through diviners. (Zakkur, KAI 202 A:9–12)

The other Aramaic example comes from a papyrus that contains several Aramaic texts written in Demotic Egyptian characters and was probably composed in Egypt around 300 BC. One of these texts makes reference to a widow to whom God has granted blessings:

> Lord, God who judges the orphan, the widow who *raised her hands* towards you will straightway receive good tidings and will laugh; behold, she *raised her hands*, will straightway receive good tidings, and will laugh. (pAmherst 63 ix 17–19)[18]

The idiom used in both of these instances is *nəśāʾ yədayn* "lift up the hands," which is cognate with the Hebrew *nāśāʾ yādayim* and the Ugaritic *našaʾa yadêmi*.

These inscriptions confirm that the gesture of lifting the hands in prayer was not unique to Israelite scripture but was part of a cultural heritage that was shared between Israel and surrounding peoples. As in the scriptural passages quoted above, the gesture as described in the inscriptions accompanies various kinds of prayer, including ritual prayer as well as spontaneous supplication. The inscriptions, like the scriptural passages, also sometimes indicate the height of the gesture with the terms "lift up" and "to heaven." Many similar examples from elsewhere in the Near East could be added, showing that this cultural heritage extends beyond the area occupied by Israel's closest neighbors. Some of these other examples will be touched on below.

The Raised-Hand Prayer Gesture in Ancient Levantine Art

When we survey the art of the ancient Levant (the area adjacent to the eastern Mediterranean, including the land of Israel) in search of a gesture of raising both hands in the context of prayer, we find one very prominent match: the raising of both hands to about the level of the mouth (sometimes higher or lower, depending on the locations of the one performing the gesture and of the gesture's target), the palms slightly concave and facing outward. The gesture is performed kneeling or standing. This gesture is found depicted on ivory carvings, stone reliefs, stamp seals, and other art pieces from the

Gestures of Praise: Lifting and Spreading the Hands in Biblical Prayer

Figures 1–4. Balu'ah stela; carved ivory panel from Ugarit; carved ivory panel from Nimrud; Hebrew or Phoenician stamp seal. Figure 1 redrawn from *ANEP*, 167 (no. 488). Figure 2 redrawn from Robert du Mesnil du Buisson, "Les ivoires du palais royal de Ras Shamra, du Musée de Damas," in *Nouvelles études sur les dieux et les mythes de Canaan* (Leiden: Brill, 1973), pl. 11. Figure 3 redrawn from Georgina Herrmann, *Ivories from Room SW37 Fort Shalmaneser* (London: The British School of Archaeology in Iraq, 1986), pl. 2 (no. 12), bottom right portion reconstructed based on similar ivories. Figure 4 redrawn from Nahman Avigad and Benjamin Sass, *Corpus of West Semitic Stamp Seals* (Jerusalem: Israel Exploration Society, 1997), 445 (no. 1175). All drawings herein are by David M. Calabro.

Levant; it is also shown in Egyptian scenes showing Levantine people in an attitude of praise and supplication.

The number of relevant art pieces from the Levant is great, and it is possible to provide only a few examples and minimal discussion here. Figures 1–4 show a stela from Balu'ah in Jordan (ca. 1200 BC), a carved ivory furniture panel from Ugarit (ca. 1350 BC), a carved ivory of Phoenician manufacture found at the Assyrian fortress of Nimrud (ca. 750 BC), and a Phoenician or Hebrew stamp seal (ca. 750 BC), respectively. Each of the examples is consistent with the idea that the gesture is one of prayer (defined in the introduction above as praise and supplication). Figure 3, for example, shows the person performing the gesture directly before a god, and figure 4 shows the two gesturing figures flanking a sacred scarab motif.

Further examples of this gesture can be found in Egyptian representations of Semitic people addressing the pharaoh. A painting from the tomb of Menkheperresonb in Thebes (ca. 1450 BC), for example, shows a group of non-Egyptians (mostly Levantine Semitic people) approaching the pharaoh with gifts, at the same time supplicating him for "the breath of life" (fig. 5). The first one prostrates himself, while the second kneels and raises both hands in

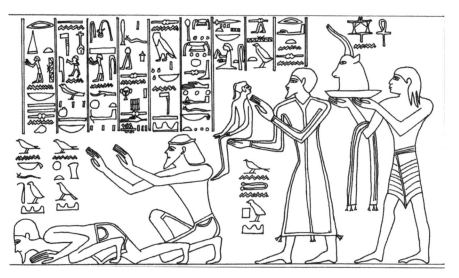

Figure 5. Painting from tomb of Menkheperresonb. Redrawn from *ANEP*, 15 (no. 45). The hieroglyphic inscription at the top reads: "Giving of praise to the Lord of the Two Lands, prostration to the beautiful god by the chiefs of every land, as they pay homage to the might of his majesty, bringing on their backs some of every product of the god's land—silver, gold, lapis lazuli, turquoise, and every costly gemstone, in hopes that the breath of life might be granted them."

the prayer gesture, and the next two approach with offerings of a child and a drinking vessel in the shape of an animal's head. This example shows the gesture as one stage of an elaborate ritual performed as a means of approaching the presence of the pharaoh. Since ancient Egyptians and tributary peoples regarded the pharaoh as a god, this example is relevant to understanding how Semitic people from the Levant used the gesture in the worship of their gods, including the Hebrew God, Jehovah.

An Egyptian relief from the tomb of Horemheb in Saqqara (ca. 1320 BC) shows a group of non-Egyptians (including some Semitic people) who are putting up a petition for help to the pharaoh (fig. 6). Some prostrate themselves with their arms fully extended, while others spread their arms wide. In all cases, however, the gesture is essentially the same, the hands raised with the palms facing outward. This example illustrates the different varieties of this gesture.

These illustrations show that the prayer gesture essentially consisted of raising both hands with the palms facing outward. There was also a dynamic element, however, in the degree to which the hands were extended upward: the hands were held sometimes at the level of the face (as in figs. 2 and 3) and sometimes high above the head (as in fig. 4). The latter form of the gesture provides a suitable comparison for those textual passages that use the phrases "to heaven," "to God in heaven," or "on high" to describe the hands being held up high. The one physical aspect of this gesture that is not represented in art, which can only depict moments of action frozen in time, is the movement of the hands alluded to by Isaiah 25:10–11.

Gestures other than the lifting of both hands with the palms facing outward occur in Mesopotamian and Egyptian art in contexts that could be equated with prayer. Among these other gestures are the raising of one or both hands with the palm inward, the raising of one finger to the mouth, and the extending of the hands to the sides with the palms upward.[19] However, while comparisons with the closely related

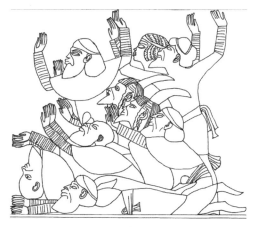

Figure 6. Relief from the tomb of Horemheb, Memphis. Redrawn from *ANEP*, 2 (no. 5).

cultures in Mesopotamia and Egypt are often very informative, it must be emphasized that Hebrew culture is Levantine, not Mesopotamian or Egyptian. Some of these other prayer gestures may be frequently attested in Mesopotamia or Egypt, but they are rare or nonexistent in native Levantine sources from the biblical period. The relatively high number of examples of the palm-out gesture in Levantine sources and the certainty of its analysis as a prayer gesture based on context make this the most logical match for the biblical prayer gesture.

Being able to match the biblical descriptions of this gesture with ancient Near Eastern depictions is useful because it allows readers of the Bible to picture what is going on in the biblical passages. Matching these two sources also helps readers to understand the symbolism of the gesture, which I will now discuss.

The Meaning of the Raised-Hand Prayer Gesture

What is the meaning of raising both hands in prayer? Many answers to this question have been suggested. According to Gruber, as we have seen, there are two different gestures with different meanings in the textual sources. One of these gestures (denoted by the verb *nāśā'* "lift up") is a way of pointing to God's abode in heaven, while the other (denoted by *pāraś/pēraś* "spread forth") symbolizes a request for the empty hands to be filled.[20] This interpretation, however, is difficult to sustain in light of the evidence from art. Like most gestures, this one does have a directional component: the direction in which the palms face may be said to indicate the target or addressee of the prayer. However, it would be somewhat of a stretch to call this directing of the palms "pointing." As for the empty hands being filled, this symbolism is impossible for the gesture as depicted in art, since the palms are held outward and roughly perpendicular to the ground.

Othmar Keel, a specialist in ancient Near Eastern art, suggests that the gesture was originally a response to coming into the holy presence of a deity: throwing up the hands to protect oneself and to ward off the potentially dangerous power of the divine being.[21] This suggestion would have interesting implications for a number of the textual passages discussed above. For example, in Isaiah 1:15, there could be irony in God's statement: "And when ye spread forth your hands, I will hide *mine* eyes from *you*" (emphasis added). However, this interpretation is not very well supported by the Ugaritic narrative of Kirta and the Aramaic inscription of Zakkur, in which the gesture is performed before and not after the god's response; it seems that in these passages and elsewhere, the gesture's purpose is to invite rather than react to a manifestation of the god.

Other possibilities for the interpretation of this gesture are perfectly plausible in light of the evidence from texts and art. These include the following: (1) The gesture has the purpose of exposing the hands and heart to divine view, showing that one is pure and therefore qualified to be in God's presence.[22] This suggestion is strongly supported by Isaiah 1:15, in which the gesture fails because the supplicants' "hands are full of blood." (2) A related possibility is that the gesture expresses surrender, displaying the hands empty of weapons and simultaneously exposing the vital organs. (3) The gesture has the purpose of attracting God's attention.[23] (4) The gesture expresses a desire for contact with God.[24] (5) The gesture symbolizes life, and performing it in the context of prayer is equivalent to petitioning God to grant life.[25] (6) The gesture marks the relationship between the one performing it and the target, asserting that the former is lowly with respect to the latter and is at the latter's service. These six interpretations are not mutually exclusive; in fact, it is not out of the question that all of these interpretations of the raised-hand gesture coexisted even in ancient times.

So far, I have focused on the meaning of the raised-hand gesture as an isolated action, independent of other actions or of the prayer ritual as a whole. An additional facet of this gesture's meaning is how it functioned in concert with other gestures as part of a larger ritual. Combining textual and artistic sources gives us the opportunity to explore this facet of the prayer gesture from a fresh perspective. For example, the fact that examples in art show the gesture being performed both while standing and while kneeling raises the possibility that a prayer ritual would include both standing and kneeling in sequence. This may have taken the form of a repeated cycle of actions similar to Muslim prayer, which includes standing, raising the hands, clasping the hands in front of the torso, and prostrating oneself, all performed while remaining in one spot. Nehemiah 8:5–6 would support the idea that such a cycle existed in ancient Israelite prayer after the Babylonian captivity. At the reading of the "book of the law," the people first stand up, then they lift up their hands while saying "Amen, amen," then they kneel and finally prostrate themselves to the earth. After these actions, they apparently stand again (see verse 7).

The prayer gesture of raising the hands may also have been part of a series of "gestures of approach" performed as one drew near to the presence of deity.[26]

In Psalm 63, in the explicit context of seeking God in the temple (verses 1–2), the Psalmist first mentions lifting up his hands (verse 4); then he mentions rejoicing "in the shadow of [God's] wings," perhaps alluding to an embrace (verse 7); and finally he mentions clasping God's right hand (verse 8). While these actions may have been understood metaphorically, it is also possible that they were part of a concrete ritual in which a human priest represented the Lord by proxy, as Matthew Brown has suggested.[27] The Ugaritic Kirta epic describes a series of ritual actions that includes washing the hands, putting on red pigment, climbing atop a wall, raising the hands, and offering sacrifice; the progression is upward, and the god responds by coming down to meet Kirta. The tomb painting of Menkheperresonb (fig. 2 above) also shows a progression of gestures as people approach the presence of the pharaoh. The sequence includes presenting a gift with one hand while raising the other, raising both hands while kneeling, and finally prostrating oneself.

This exploration of the gesture associated with prayer in the biblical world should help us to appreciate how ancient Israelites understood prayer. The gesture is different from those typically used for private prayer by Latter-day Saints and other Christians today, such as the folding of the arms across the chest or the clasping of the hands in front of the chest or face. Nevertheless, the ancient raising and spreading of the hands may express concepts of prayer with which we can identify, such as God's holiness, his knowledge of our moral state and of our private thoughts, submission to his will, and the desire to approach and achieve contact with him (see the possible interpretations of this gesture as discussed above). The characteristics of this gesture are in harmony with the Psalmist's confidence and intense desire to approach God as expressed in Psalm 26:

> Judge me, O Lord; for I have walked in mine integrity: I have trusted also in the Lord; therefore I shall not slide. Examine me, O Lord, and prove me; try my reins and my heart. For thy lovingkindness is before mine eyes: and I have walked in thy truth. (vv. 26:1–3)

My discussion about the context and form of the raised-hand prayer gesture thus helps to clarify some of its possible meanings. Matching textual descriptions with pictorial representations makes it possible to more effectively evaluate how accurately an interpretation fits the gesture as it was originally performed. It also reveals ways in which raising the hands may have been used

Gestures of Praise: Lifting and Spreading the Hands in Biblical Prayer 119

together with other gestures in ritual contexts. The saying that "a picture is worth a thousand words" holds true, but the value of both the picture and the words increases when the two are united.

Notes

1. The verb *pray*, for example, is defined as "to utter a prayer or prayers" in *The American Heritage College Dictionary*, 3rd ed. (Boston and New York: Houghton Mifflin, 1993), 1075, definition 1. In some modern Romance languages, the word for "pray" is derived from Latin *ōrāre* "speak."

2. It is noteworthy that the Latter-day Saint Bible Dictionary entry on "prayer" contains a paragraph on the "attitude of prayer," meaning the postures and gestures that accompany prayer.

3. See the many illustrations from ancient art in Heinz Demisch, *Erhobene Hände: Geschichte einer Gebärde in der bildenden Kunst* (Stuttgart: Urachhaus, 1984), 107–68. The Egyptian hieroglyph standing for the word *yau* "praise" shows a man standing and raising both hands; see Alan Gardiner, *Egyptian Grammar*, 3rd ed. (Oxford: Griffith Institute, 1957), 445 (no. A30). Other gestures are also found in the context of prayer in ancient times. For example, Mesopotamian statuettes placed in temples as substitutes for petitioning individuals have both hands clasped in front of the torso, with the left hand inside the right hand. In Biblical Hebrew, the very common verb *hištaḥăwâ* "bow oneself" is used to signify "worship" (see, for example, Genesis 24:52; Exodus 20:4–5), the concept of worship being related to that of prayer. For the purposes of this paper, I distinguish between "gestures" involving primarily the movement of the hands and "postures" involving primarily the whole body; with this distinction, raising the hands is classified as a gesture, while bowing oneself is classified as a posture.

4. Exodus 9:29, 33; 1 Kings 8:22, 38–39, 54; 2 Chronicles 6:12–13, 29–30; Ezra 9:5–6; Nehemiah 8:6; Job 11:13–15; Psalms 28:2; 44:20–21; 63:4; 119:48; 134:2; 141:2; 143:6; Isaiah 1:15; Jeremiah 4:31; Lamentations 1:17; 2:19; 3:41; Habakkuk 3:10; 1 Timothy 2:8; Alma 31:14–15.

5. Manfried Dietrich, Oswald Loretz, and Joaquín Sanmartín, eds., *Die keilalphabetischen Texte aus Ugarit* (Neukirchen: Verlag Butzon & Bercker Kevalaer, 1976) (hereafter *KTU*), nos. 1.14 ii 21–26, iv 2–8; 1.41 50–55; H. Donner and W. Röllig, *Kanaanäische und aramäische Inschriften* (Wiesbaden: Otto Harrassowitz, 1976) (hereafter *KAI*), no. 202 A:9–12; pAmherst 63 ix 17–19. Each of these inscriptions is quoted and discussed below.

6. Mayer Gruber, *Aspects of Nonverbal Communication in the Ancient Near East* (Rome: Biblical Institute Press, 1980), 35–37; cf. Stephen Langdon, "Gesture in Sumerian and Babylonian Prayer: A Study in Sumerian and Assyrian Archaeology," *Journal of the Royal Asiatic Society* (October 1919): 542–43.

7. James B. Pritchard, *The Ancient Near East in Pictures Relating to the Old Testament* (Princeton, NJ: Princeton University Press, 1954) (hereafter *ANEP*), 157, 302 (no. 456); emphasis added.

8. The biblical quotations in this paper are drawn from the King James Version. I consider this translation to be generally accurate as far as the interpretation of gesture idioms is concerned.

9. George Stonehouse, *The Book of Habakkuk: Introduction, Translation, and Notes on the Hebrew Text* (London: Rivingtons, 1911), 142, 239–42; Baruch Margulis, "The Psalm of Habakkuk: A Reconstruction and Interpretation," *Zeitschrift für die alttestamentliche Wissenschaft* 82 (1970): 422–25; Yitzhak Avishur, *Studies in Hebrew and Ugaritic Psalms* (Jerusalem: Magnes Press, 1994), 181–83; W. F. Albright, "The Psalm of Habakkuk," in *Studies in Old Testament Prophecy*, ed. H. H. Rowley (Edinburgh: T. & T. Clark, 1950), 11; Theodore Hiebert, *God of My Victory: The Ancient Hymn in Habakkuk 3* (Atlanta: Scholars Press, 1986), 6, 30–31; Francis I. Andersen, *Habakkuk*, Anchor Bible 25 (New York: Doubleday, 2001), 312, 326–33.

10. The word *yād* means "hand, forearm," while *kap* means "palm, hand"; in the case of expresssions referring to the raising or spreading of the extremities, the parallel between expressions using *yād* and those using *kap* suggests that these two words should be translated identically as "hand" in these expressions.

11. See also Psalms 63:4 (verse 5 in the Hebrew) and 119:48.

12. Additional occurrences of this idiom are found in 2 Chronicles 6:12–13, 29–30, which is parallel to the passages from 1 Kings 8 quoted above, and in Ezra 9:5–6; Job 11:13–15; and Psalm 44:20–21 (verses 21–22 in the Hebrew).

13. Psalm 134:2. The most common Greek phrase used to translate the Hebrew *nāśāʾ yādayim* and *nāśāʾ kappayim* is *cheiras airō* "lift the hands," which is related to *cheiras epairō*. Different Greek phrases, including *cheiras diapetannumi* "spread out or open the hands," are used to translate *pāraś kappayim*, *pēraś (bə)yādayim*, and *pēraś kappayim*. These various Greek phrases tell us little about the meaning of the Hebrew phrases or of the gesture itself, since they are basically direct, "wooden" translations of the Hebrew phrases.

14. For an excellent survey of Jewish and early Christian sources mentioning the raising of both hands in prayer, see John A. Tvedtnes, "Temple Prayer in Ancient Times," in *The Temple in Time and Eternity*, ed. Donald W. Parry and Stephen D. Ricks (Provo, UT: FARMS, 1999), 81–84.

15. Gruber, *Aspects of Nonverbal Communication*, 35–37.

16. The translations from Ugaritic, Aramaic, and Egyptian are my own unless otherwise indicated.

17. Or, perhaps, "to [the temple]." The latter restoration is adopted by Baruch A. Levine, Jean-Michel de Tarragon, and Anne Robertson, "Ugaritic Rites for the Vintage (KTU 1.41//1.87) (1.95)," in *The Context of Scripture*, vol. 1: *Canonical Compositions from the Biblical World*, ed. William W. Hallo and K. Lawson Younger Jr. (Leiden: Brill, 1997), 301.

18. The translation given here of this very difficult text relies on that of S. P. Vleeming and J. W. Wesselius, *Studies in Papyrus Amherst 63: Essays on the Aramaic Texts in Aramaic/Demotic Papyrus Amherst 63* (Amsterdam: Juda Palache Instituut, 1990), 2:46–51.

19. Langdon, "Gesture in Sumerian and Babylonian Prayer"; Richard Neitzel Holzapfel, Dana M. Pike, and David Rolph Seely, *Jehovah and the World of the Old Testament* (Salt Lake City: Deseret Book, 2009), 231.

20. Gruber, *Aspects of Nonverbal Communication*, 35–37.

21. Othmar Keel, *The Symbolism of the Biblical World: Ancient Near Eastern Iconography and the Book of Psalms* (New York: Crossroad, 1985), 312–13.

22. Tvedtnes, "Temple Prayer," 81–84.

23. In Isaiah 65:1–2, the phrase "spread out [the] hands," though referring not to prayer but to an action carried out by God, is parallel to saying, "Behold me, behold me."

24. Keel, *Symbolism of the Biblical World*, 322; David Calabro, "'When You Spread Your Palms, I Will Hide My Eyes': The Symbolism of Body Gestures in Isaiah," *Studia Antiqua* 9, no. 1 (Spring 2011): 30–31.

25. Demisch, *Erhobene Hände*, 107–68.

26. Mircea Eliade, *Patterns in Comparative Religion*, trans. Rosemary Sheed (New York: Sheed and Ward, 1958), 370–71; Hugh Nibley, "Temples Everywhere," *Insights* 25, no. 1 (2005): 14.

27. Matthew Brown, "The Handclasp, the Temple, and the King" (unpublished paper, August 2008). If this is to be taken as a metaphor, the imagery of praying with uplifted hands, embracing the god, and finally clasping his hand may still be rooted in earlier rituals in which physical contact occurred with a divine image or a human proxy.

8

Worship: Bowing Down and Serving the Lord

Jennifer C. Lane

The Old Testament provides foundational insights into worship that help us rethink our understanding of worship throughout the scriptures and also help us more fully understand what worship means for us as Latter-day Saints. In the vocabulary of the Old Testament, the Hebrew verbs "bow down" (*ḥwh*) and "serve" (*ābad*) are often translated "worship." These verbs describe the physical expression of a relationship of submission to authority—to "bow down" and to "serve" (e.g., Exodus 20:5). In the practice of Old Testament temple worship, we see this embodiment of relationship when those worshipping the Lord in his holy house literally "bow down" and "serve." In addition to these more narrow usages, the Old Testament also shows that "bowing down" and "serving" in worship is a way of life. It illustrates how obedience and covenant faithfulness is worship; lack of obedience and unfaithfulness to a covenant is betraying the relationship of submission and loyalty required of one who should be in the position of "bowing down" and "serving."

In this paper I will first explore worship in the Old Testament vocabulary and usage and then examine what this suggests about worship in our day. Both

---

Jennifer C. Lane is an associate professor of Religious Education at BYU–Hawaii.

the vocabulary and temple context of worship in the Old Testament give us a vision of worship as the embodiment of a true relationship of submission to God. These insights can transform how we experience ritual worship in our day and teach us how to live a life of worship by bowing down and serving the Lord in our daily lives.

As we look at these two verbs, keep in mind how they describe the concrete performance or embodiment of a relationship of submission to authority—to "bow down" and to "serve." In other words, these verbs illustrate that worship is something that we do and that we are in a relationship with the one whom we are worshipping. Rather than merely being about what we think or feel, these Old Testament terms point us to an "embodied" understanding of worship—<u>a way of life and a relationship with God expressed by the physical actions of bowing down or serving</u>.

Bowing Down and Serving in the Old Testament

In the Ten Commandments the Lord directly forbids worship of other gods. God is to be in the sole position of authority in our lives: "I am the Lord thy God, which have brought thee out of the land of Egypt, out of the house of bondage. Thou shalt have no other gods before me" (Exodus 20:2–3). In the next verse we find two Hebrew terms that are commonly translated as "worship" in English: "Thou shalt not bow thyself to them, nor serve them: for I the Lord thy God am a jealous God" (Exodus 20:5). These two terms, "bow down" and "serve," have important similarities, but each expresses distinct aspects of what worship is and what it means to worship God.

Scholars today believe that the Hebrew verb *ḥwh* is the root of the forms which express "bowing down" in the Old Testament.[1] A concise summary of the usage of the verb *ḥwh* captures the physical quality of this form of worship:

> [*ḥwh*] always refers to the action/attitude directed toward a human or divine figure who is recognized (appropriately or inappropriately) as being in a position of honor or authority. Depending on the figure and the situation, it may be a gesture of greeting, respect, submission, or worship. The action may entail falling to one's knees, in front of which one places the hands or between which one bows the face (nose, forehead) to the ground (or comparable gesture). . . . The gesture is an external sign of the inner spirit (though hypocrisy is possible); the

word can also simply express the inner attitude. The prayer posture (hands outstretched) normally does not entail prostration.[2]

So, simply put, in the Old Testament *ḥwh*—expressed in the noun form as *hishtachᵃvāh*—is a physical enactment of one's relationship with a superior. It was understood as an outward expression of an inward attitude. Translations include "to bow," "to prostrate oneself," "to make obeisance," or "to bend low."[3] This gesture of bowing down was widespread in ancient Near Eastern religious practice and was a daily part of the ritual worship of the gods in ancient Near Eastern temples. In Egyptian this prostration is expressed as "kissing the ground."[4]

In the world of the Old Testament, people bowed down to physically embody a relationship of submission to the Lord, to other gods, and to mortals. Preuss notes that "very often we find *hishtachᵃvāh* in the sense of 'homage to the king.' Many of the occurrences belonging here make it clear that we are dealing with a gesture of submission or surrender."[5]

We find examples of "bowing down" (*ḥwh*) to mortals as a sign of respect throughout the Old Testament. In Genesis 23:7, as Abraham was seeking for a place to bury Sarah, we read that "Abraham stood up, and bowed himself to the people of the land, even to the children of Heth" (see also Genesis 23:12). Likewise, when the three strangers appeared in the plains of Mamre, Abraham "ran to meet them from the tent door, and bowed himself toward the ground" (Genesis 18:2). Bowing down clearly indicates relative position in the story of Joseph and his brothers, both in his dreams and when they appear in Egypt. "And Joseph was the governor over the land, and he it was that sold to all the people of the land: and Joseph's brethren came, and bowed down themselves before him with their faces to the earth" (Genesis 42:6). Another important biblical scene where bowing expresses relationships is the story of Esther, where Mordecai refuses to recognize the status and position of Haman. "And all the king's servants, that were in the king's gate, bowed, and reverenced Haman: for the king had so commanded concerning him. But Mordecai bowed not, nor did him reverence" (Esther 3:2). In all of these examples we can see the physical expression of a relationship of submission through the performance of bowing and prostration.

The second verb in the couplet of the Ten Commandments "Thou shalt not bow thyself to them, nor serve them" is the Hebrew term *'ābad*, which, when used without an object, is usually translated as "to work."[6] Those who work for another are in that person's service and thus "with personal objects *ʿābad* means 'serve' and expresses the relationship between an *ʿebed* and his or her *ʾādôn*, 'lord, master.'"[7] The lord is the one who is served, and the servant or slave is the one who does the work.[8] This term brings with it an understanding of the submission and loyalty of a servant to his or her master that directly connects with "religious loyalty expressed through worship," particularly in Deuteronomy.[9] The Hebrew verb *ʿābad* naturally becomes paired with the verb *ḥwh*; serving and bowing down are the proper expression of a relationship of submission and subservience.

The Old Testament helps us understand why we should see ourselves as God's servants, those who are grateful to bow down and serve only him. This insight comes in a simple passage in Leviticus, but it has already been hinted at in the Ten Commandments. Remember that the Lord told Israel, "I am the Lord thy God, which have brought thee out of the land of Egypt, out of the house of bondage. Thou shalt have no other gods before me" (Exodus 20:2–3). The Lord's position as *our* Lord derives from his having brought us out from bondage to another lord. Because of the redemption, the Israelites became God's *ʿăbādîm*, his servants or slaves.

In Leviticus 25, in a discussion of slavery under the law of Moses, the Lord explains that Israelites who become slaves have a different status than foreign slaves. "For they are my servants, which I brought forth out of the land of Egypt: they shall not be sold as bondmen" (Leviticus 25:42). In this chapter we learn that fellow Israelites cannot be "actual property," as can a foreign slave, because "the Israelites themselves are actually Yahweh's *ʿăbādm* whom he liberated from Egypt. The ultimate point of this is that, strictly speaking, no Israelite can really ever become the slave of another Israelite."[10] This sense of belonging to the Lord as his servants or slaves because of the redemption from bondage in Egypt is a foreshadowing of the spiritual principle taught by Paul, "ye are not your own . . . for ye are bought with a price" (1 Corinthians 6:19–20).

Paul elaborates this concept, explaining that since we belong to the Lord through the purchase price of the blood of Christ, we should not bow down and serve anyone else: "Ye are bought with a price; be not ye the servants of men" (1 Corinthians 7:23). In Exodus and Leviticus, the Israelites were being taught this principle that we need to understand as well—we have been bought out of bondage, but we are not free from obligation. We belonged to another master, but now we have been delivered to be the servants of the Lord. Paul expresses the spiritual implications of Leviticus 25 by saying, "But God be thanked, that ye were the servants of sin, but ye have obeyed from the heart that form of doctrine which was delivered you. Being then made free from sin, ye became the servants of righteousness" (Romans 6:17–18).

Bowing Down and Serving in a Temple Context

The social and cultural use of "bow down" and "serve" in the world of the Old Testament illustrates the sense of respect and submission that is owed to the one who is worthy of worship. These insights are complemented by an examination of how these terms function in the context of temple worship in ancient Israel where both "to bow down" and "to serve" have very clear roles in cultic activity (i.e., formal worship practice in the temple). In the enactment of "bowing down" and "serving" in the temple we can see the relationship of obedience and submission made visible.

The verb "bow down" (ḥwh) can be used in the context of divine worship to express gratitude both outside of the context of the temple and also within it.[11] In the setting of the temple "this action joins other forms of cultic activity, such as sacrifices and various types of music."[12] An early usage of "bow down" (ḥwh) in the context of offering sacrifices can be seen in the story of Abraham preparing to offer up Isaac: "And Abraham said unto his young men, Abide ye here with the ass; and I and the lad will go yonder and *worship*, and come again to you" (Genesis 22:5; emphasis added).

Another early example of where the term ḥwh appears to describe bowing down as part of sacrificial worship is in the scene with the molten calf. While Moses was away, the children of Israel "turned aside quickly out of the way which I commanded them: they have made them a molten calf, and have *worshipped* it, and have sacrificed thereunto, and said, These be thy gods, O Israel, which have brought thee up out of the land of Egypt" (Exodus 32:8; emphasis added). Here the verb ḥwh is used to indicate they bowed down.[13]

Other examples of ḥwh or bowing in worship can be seen in the book of Exodus. The Lord "said unto Moses, Come up unto the Lord, thou, and Aaron, Nadab, and Abihu, and seventy of the elders of Israel; and *worship* ye afar off" (Exodus 24:1; emphasis added). And once the Israelites had moved from worshipping on high mountains to worshipping at the tabernacle, we find the same verb describing how the people worshipped as Moses was in the tabernacle speaking with the Lord: "And all the people saw the cloudy pillar stand at the tabernacle door: and all the people rose up and *worshipped*, every man in his tent door" (Exodus 33:10; emphasis added). Here the verb *ḥwh* expresses how the people showed their awe and reverence for the presence of the Lord in the tabernacle—they bowed down and prostrated themselves.

While the expression of prayer in the Old Testament was typically not prostration but rather the lifting up of the hands, other specific references show that there was a place for prostration, or bowing down, as part of the worship practices of the law of Moses. In Deuteronomy we learn that bringing the firstfruits was tied to prostration or bowing down: "And now, behold, I have brought the firstfruits of the land, which thou, O Lord, hast given me. And thou shalt set it before the Lord thy God, and *worship* before the Lord thy God" (26:10; emphasis added). Within the Psalms we can find several examples of *ḥwh* in the context of worship in the temple: Psalm 5:7, "But as for me, I will come into thy house in the multitude of thy mercy: and in thy fear will I worship toward thy holy temple"; Psalm 95:6, "O come, let us worship and bow down: let us kneel before the Lord our maker"; Psalm 99:5, "Exalt ye the Lord our God, and worship at his footstool; for he is holy."

Just as the use of the root *ḥwh* illustrates how bowing down was an expression of worship in the temple, so the Hebrew term *ʿābad*, "to serve," very often has a cultic—or formal worship—usage.[14] These connections can help us see how temple worship, temple service, and temple work are literally synonymous in the Old Testament—they share the same term. In certain verbal forms, *ʿābad* was regularly used to describe the routine responsibilities of formal worship "of Israel in its service and care for the tabernacle, temple, its appurtenances, and its personnel."[15] We see this charge to the Levites in Numbers 3:5–8: "And the Lord spake unto Moses, saying, Bring the tribe of Levi near, and present them before Aaron the priest, that they may minister unto him. And they shall keep his charge, and the charge of the whole congregation before the tabernacle of the congregation, to do the service of the tabernacle. And they shall keep all the instruments of the tabernacle of the congregation, and the charge of the children of Israel, to do the service of the tabernacle." Doing the service of the tabernacle was the sacred responsibility for which the priesthood was given (see also Numbers 4:21–24).

In addition to the sacred charge to care for the sacred space and possessions of the temple, this verb was also "used specifically regarding sacrifices to worship ('*bd*) Yahweh" as can be seen in Isaiah: "And the Lord shall be known to Egypt, and the Egyptians shall know the Lord in that day, and shall do sacrifice ['*ābad*] and oblation" (19:21).[16] So, '*ābad* "refers to the performance of the cult in the sense of worship, honor, serve in a purely religious sense, in addition to caring ('*bd*) for its physical upkeep and maintenance."[17] Another scripture that captures this use of "to serve" as performing offerings in the temple is found in Ezekiel 20:40: "For in mine holy mountain, in the mountain of the height of Israel, saith the Lord God, there shall all the house of Israel, all of them in the land, serve me: there will I accept them, and there will I require your offerings, and the firstfruits of your oblations, with all your holy things."

The identification between "serving" the Lord and formal worship with sacrifices in a sacred place is made explicit as seen in the Lord's explanation of *why* the children of Israel were to be redeemed from bondage in Egypt.[18] When the Lord spoke to Moses on Mount Sinai, he explained, "Certainly I will be with thee; and this shall be a token unto thee, that I have sent thee: When thou hast brought forth the people out of Egypt, ye shall serve God upon this mountain" (Exodus 3:12). Israel was serving another master in bondage but was going to be brought out of Egypt to serve a new master. That this service was temple service is emphasized by the location—redeemed Israel was to serve the Lord "upon this mountain."

This relationship between the redemption and Israel's responsibility to serve and worship their true Lord is repeated in what Moses is told what to say to Pharaoh: "And thou shalt say unto Pharaoh, Thus saith the Lord, Israel is my son, even my firstborn: and I say unto thee, Let my son go, *that he may serve me*: and if thou refuse to let him go, behold, I will slay thy son, even thy firstborn" (Exodus 4:22–23; emphasis added). Serious consequences fell upon the Egyptians for refusing to allow the Israelites to perform the service that belonged to the Lord. This interchange highlights the central themes of idolatry and worship in the Old Testament. Simply put, "worshipping other gods is the antithesis to serving Yahweh."[19]

Throughout the Old Testament, Israel was warned that when they strayed from the service and worship of the Lord so that they could serve and worship other gods, they would receive the pay of him whom they had served: "Because thou servedst not the Lord thy God with joyfulness, and with gladness of heart, for the abundance of all things; Therefore shalt thou serve thine enemies which the Lord shall send against thee, in hunger, and in thirst, and in nakedness, and in want of all things: and he shall put a yoke of iron upon thy neck, until he have destroyed thee" (Deuteronomy 28:47–48). Alma draws a similar message from Korihor's fate for serving another master: "And thus we see the end of him who perverteth the ways of the Lord; and thus we see that the devil will not support his children at the last day, but doth speedily drag them down to hell" (Alma 30:60). Paul puts it even more simply: "The wages of sin is death" (Romans 6:23).

On a happier note, the Lord's invitation to serve and worship him is universal: "Make a joyful noise unto the Lord, all ye lands. Serve the Lord with gladness: come before his presence with singing" (Psalm 100:1–2). All lands and all people were invited to be the Lord's servants and to come before his presence in his holy house to worship and praise. "Bowing down" and "serving" the Lord in the context of temple worship is a commandment, but it is also an expression of love and gratitude for our redemption. In ritual action we express and enact the relationship with God so that we can go forward to live out that relationship in the rest of our lives.

As we have seen, both *ḥwh* and *'āḇaḏ* are consistently used in formal worship at the temple and help us understand temple worship with the enactment of a relationship of humility and submission in "bowing down" and of faithful obedience in "serving." But worship is more than just the external, formal requirements of ordinances, although it does include them. The Savior reminded the religious leaders of his day that the diligent performance of externals alone would not suffice: "Ye pay tithe of mint and anise and cummin, and have omitted the weightier matters of the law, judgment, mercy, and faith: these ought ye to have done, and not to leave the other undone" (Matthew 23:23).

It is important, however, that Christ notes we are "not to leave the other undone." Formal religious behavior alone will not save us without a change of nature, but it is essential to the process of becoming changed. In the ritual action that reflects a relationship of obedience and submission, we learn about and learn to live out our true relationship with God. The world would have us believe that being in this relationship is demeaning and limiting, that we are free only when we are not bound by covenant obligations to serve and obey. The scriptures and the ordinances teach us instead that through taking on covenant obligations to serve and obey God, we are redeemed and brought back into his presence. The more often we have that reinforcing message and experience, the stronger we can stand against the siren call of autonomy, individualism, and finally rebellion against God as a way of asserting ourselves and finding ourselves.

Thus the repetition of embodiment of our real and saving relationship with God, in our worship services and temple worship, becomes as critical for us as it was for ancient Israel to ritually "bow down" and "serve" in the Old Testament temples. In the ritual process of submitting our will to God through temple service, we can let our spirits and minds be changed and more truly learn what it means to worship not only in ritual context but also in a life of obedience and covenant faithfulness.

Worship as a Way of Life: Covenant Faithfulness

The term "to serve Yahweh" ([ʿbd] yhwh) is found fifty-six times in the Old Testament, each instance "referring to worship, cultic service or faithfully keeping his covenant as his people."[20] In the Old Testament, "serve" (ʿābad) means formal ritual worship of Jehovah or other gods, but it can also have "an extended meaning . . . in the sense of 'venerate,' 'follow.'"[21] Thus <u>"serving" the Lord can mean both ritual worship practices and also a life of faithfulness and loyalty—living as a faithful servant</u>. It is to this broader sense of "bowing down" and "serving" that we now turn.

The Old Testament teaches us that serving the Lord is not just formal worship, although it does include that. Many passages including "bow down" and "serve" illustrate how worship is a life of faithfulness and obedience. In Deuteronomy in particular, the joint usage of the Hebrew verbs ḥwh and ʿābad together show that "what is forbidden is not only the cultic worship of other gods, but a way of life that departs in general from that of the people of Yahweh."[22] The Israelites are warned, "Thou shalt fear the Lord thy God, and serve him, and shalt swear by his name. Ye shall not go after other gods, of the gods of the people which are round about you" (Deuteronomy 6:13–14). They are taught, "Ye shall walk after the Lord your God, and fear him, and keep his commandments, and obey his voice, and ye shall serve him, and cleave unto him" (Deuteronomy 13:4). Ringgren insightfully observes that serving (ʿābad) the Lord throughout Deuteronomy "far transcends any specifically cultic context. Thus we read in [Deuteronomy] 6:13: 'Yahweh your God you shall fear; him you shall serve, and by his name alone you shall swear.' . . . Hence here the correct posture toward Yahweh is circumscribed . . . and the issue is thus faithfully to worship Yahweh alone. . . . This is thus a religious and ethical disposition encompassing a person's entire life, one coming to an expression especially in the obedient keeping of the commandments."[23] It is significant that Ringgren uses the language of embodiment, explaining that in the command to serve only God "the correct posture toward Yahweh is circumscribed."

When we live out a covenant relationship with God, it requires a whole-souled and embodied acceptance of our relationship as his servants, to live our lives for him—spirit and body. Embracing that covenant relationship of being the Lord's servant is a full reshaping of ourselves—our minds and bodies oriented to his worship and his service. "And now, Israel, what doth the Lord thy God require of thee, but to fear the Lord thy God, to walk in all his ways, and to love him, and to serve the Lord thy God with all thy heart and with all thy soul" (Deuteronomy 10:12).

One of the most sobering and consistent messages of the Old Testament is that there are other places we can choose to bestow our loyalty and service, but we are not to go down these paths. We are to serve the Lord. We are redeemed from the bondage of sin in order to serve the Lord, and we must be careful not to ignore or despise that obligation. We must watch ourselves to see if we are choosing to serve other gods, even if that god is in our own image. And when we begin to reap what we sow, we can remember the warning in Deuteronomy: "Even all nations shall say, Wherefore hath the Lord done thus unto this land? what meaneth the heat of this great anger? Then men shall say, Because they have forsaken the covenant of the Lord God of their fathers, which he made with them when he brought them forth out of the land of Egypt: For they went and served other gods, and worshipped them, gods whom they knew not, and whom he had not given unto them" (29:24–26).[24] Covenant faithfulness requires complete fidelity.

When we understand that the Lord has redeemed us from the bondage of sin so that we can serve him in lives of righteousness, then we realize the privilege it is to serve him and leave the other gods behind. But even after we are redeemed, we must continue to choose to put away other gods completely and to cease serving and bowing down to anything other than the Lord. Joshua invites us as well: "Now therefore fear the Lord, and serve him in sincerity and in truth: and put away the gods which your fathers served on the other side of the flood, and in Egypt; and serve ye the Lord. And if it seem evil unto you to serve the Lord, choose you this day whom ye will serve; whether the gods which your fathers served that were on the other side of the flood, or the gods of the Amorites, in whose land ye dwell: but as for me and my house, we will serve the Lord" (Joshua 24:14–15).

Worship as a Way of Life: The Example of the Servants

Because of contemporary cultural values, we may struggle to see ourselves as servants who should be bowing down to God by submitting our will to his. In our efforts to come to grips with the deep implications of being in a relationship of submission to God, the Old Testament offers us hopeful and inspiring models of servanthood and how we can live in a true relationship with God. In the Old Testament we can see a very positive status of a servant for redeemed Israel, the Lord's prophets, and the Suffering Servant.

While the noun form 'e<u>b</u>ed ("servant") generally "expresses the position of a human being before God,"[25] it can also have particular uses such as the servant who is an instrument in the Lord's hands to accomplish his work and bring about his righteousness. As we have seen earlier, this status of servant was particularly tied to the house of Israel who had been purchased or redeemed from the bondage of serving another master to become the Lord's servants exclusively. Likewise, the prophets were consistently referred to as the servants of the Lord and, the image of the Suffering Servant describes the redemptive role of Christ in the prophetic writings of Isaiah. Carpenter shares an inspiring vision of the servant that can help us appreciate all these usages of "servant" in the Old Testament and thereby help us gain a greater desire to more fully become God's servants in our own lives.

> The "servant of God" is further singled out as one who had a specific task to perform. Moses the servant of God wrote the law of God (Dan 9:11). The one who was chosen as the servant of God always had a good Master, always had a task to perform that involved doing the will of the covenant God, did not speak or act on his own behalf, but solely at the behest of his divine Sovereign Master. <u>To be a servant of Yahweh was an honor, raising the status of the person involved. It did not mean degradation but exaltation in Yahweh's service.</u> To be a servant of God had no negative connotations for the servant, after all things were considered, even though his task might have been one of delivering a word or parable of judgment.[26]

This principle—namely, the honor of being chosen, obedient, and working as representatives of God, the "good Master"—applies to the expectations for redeemed Israel, the example of the prophets, and the foreshadowing of the mission of the Suffering Servant.

In the Old Testament, *'ebed* describes the one who lives in the true relationship with God—always obedient, always on the Lord's errand. Another biblical scholar also captures the exemplary nature of the "servant of the Lord" in the Old Testament: "A true prophet and a true *'ebed YHWH* does everything at the bidding of his God."[27] In 1 Kings we see the example of Elijah as an obedient servant in the contest with the priests of Baal: "And it came to pass at the time of the offering of the evening sacrifice, that Elijah the prophet came near, and said, Lord God of Abraham, Isaac, and of Israel, let it be known this day that thou art God in Israel, and that I am thy servant, and that I have done all these things at thy word" (18:36). With servants, the criterion is obedience. A good and faithful servant is an obedient servant, doing "all these things at thy word."

President Benson invited all of us to seek to "do everything at the bidding of our God" by describing how "Paul asked a simple eight-word question" and stated "the persistent asking of the same question changed his life. 'Lord, what wilt thou have me to do?' (Acts 9:6)." This modern-day prophet promised that "the persistent asking of that same question can also change your life. There is no greater question that you can ask in this world. 'Lord, what wilt thou have me to do?' I challenge you to make that the uppermost question of your life."[28] When we are asking that question, then we are seeking to be the Lord's servant—to do his bidding and to be on his errand.

We do not need to have a messianic or prophetic mission in life in order to worship the Lord as his servants. In fact, recognizing that we are all called to be servants but given different missions is a humbling and also equalizing vision that can free us from envy, resentment, pride, or any desire to boast or compare. To the extent that we are all seeking to worship by doing the Father's will, we can feel the meaning of John the Baptist's address to Joseph Smith and Oliver Cowdery: "upon you my fellow servants" (D&C 13:1). Our lives of worship as submissive and obedient servants puts us in a position of unity not only with the prophets, but with Deity. As we serve our Master, we come to know him, becoming aligned with his thoughts and the intents of his heart (see Mosiah 5:13). The Lord has explained that "he that exalteth himself shall be abased, and he that abaseth himself shall be exalted" (D&C 101:42). The Son came as the obedient servant of the Father, doing "always those things that please him" (John 8:29). As we become servants in Christ's image, willing to bow down and serve, we find that our submission is the means of being raised up to an eternal unity of will and purpose: "that they all may be one; as thou, Father, art in me, and I in thee, that they also may be one in us" (John 17:21).

Notes

1. For some additional background on how scholars' understanding of the Hebrew term has changed, see Preuss, "ḥwh," in *Theological Dictionary of the Old Testament* (Grand Rapids, MI: Eerdmans, 1980), 4:249, and Terence E. Fretheim, "ḥwh," in *New International Dictionary of Old Testament Theology and Exegesis* (Grand Rapids, MI: Zondervan, 1997), 2:42.
2. Fretheim, "ḥwh," 2:43.
3. Preuss, "ḥwh," 4:249.
4. "The gesture designated by *hishtachᵃvāh*, which also expresses an inward attitude, is also familiar among Israel's neighbors. It is attested both pictorially and in texts, since 'prostration' formed part of the cult of all deities (2 K. 5:18). Egyptian speaks of 'kissing the ground' . . . and obeisance was a common part of the daily ritual before the statues of the gods" (Preuss, "ḥwh," 4:250).
5. Preuss, "ḥwh," 4:251–52. While some might argue that the use of *ḥwh* is to express the relationship of worship through bowing down moved from human political and social spheres to the religious, Preuss argues that the sacred meaning does not come from the secular but probably the reverse.
6. Helmer Ringgren, "'āḇaḏ," in *Theological Dictionary of the Old Testament* (Grand Rapids, MI: Eerdmans, 1980), 10:381.
7. Ringgren, "'āḇaḏ," 10:383.
8. The relationship between *'eḇeḏ* and *'āḏôn* can have various connotations. Those who have no freedom are slaves that serve masters. Those who wish to be close to those in power are vassals serving their lord. Ringgren notes that the various nuances of this relationship "can be one of subjugation and dependence, or total claim on a person, or of loyalty. Indeed, all these nuances resonate, with one or another feature being more or less emphasized in any given case" (10:383). The different kinds of subordination potentially expressed by the term *'eḇeḏ* can been seen in various positions: "slave, servant, subject, official, vassal, or 'servant' or follower of a particular god" (10:387).
9. "Especially in Deuteronomy and in the DtrH, 'to serve' is frequently used more generally to indicate religious loyalty expressed through worship. 'To bow down' to high-status humans is a sign of respect or submission. Used in the context of prayer or sacrifice, the verb describes the physical gesture of prostration. However, because the gesture reflects an inner attitude, 'to bow down' also signifies worship in a broader sense." Richard D. Nelson, "Worship, OT," in *The New Interpreter's Dictionary of the Bible* (Nashville: Abingdon, 2009), 5:924.

10. Ringgren, "'āḇaḏ," 10:388.
11. Fretheim, "ḥwh," 2:43.
12. Fretheim, "ḥwh," 2:43.
13. Pruess notes that although bowing is not specified in verse six, the use of ḥwh in verse eight implies that prostration in worship "must have been a regular part of the sacrifice ritual" (4:254).
14. Ringgren, "'āḇaḏ," 10:384.
15. Eugene Carpenter, "'bd," in *New International Dictionary of Old Testament Theology and Exegesis* (Grand Rapids, MI: Zondervan, 1997), 3:305.
16. Carpenter, "'bd," 3:305.
17. Carpenter, "'bd," 3:305.
18. See also Ringgren, "'āḇaḏ," 10:384–85 on Exodus 3:12, why Moses brought the children of Israel out of captivity.
19. Ringgren, "'āḇaḏ," 385.
20. Carpenter, "'bd," 3:306.
21. Ringgren, "'āḇaḏ," 10:386.
22. Preuss, "ḥwh," 4:254.
23. Ringgren, "'āḇaḏ," 10:386.
24. "A passage such as [Deuteronomy] 29:24f. (25f.) shows that 'serving other gods' simultaneously means 'forsaking Yahweh's bᵉrît' . . . . In a reverse fashion, serving Yahweh means keeping his covenant" (Ringgren, 10:386).
25. Carpenter, "'bd," 3:306.
26. Carpenter, "'bd," 3:307.
27. Ringgren, "'āḇaḏ," 10:395.
28. Ezra Taft Benson, "Think on Christ," *Ensign*, April 1984, 11.

9

"I Will Bless the LORD at All Times": Blessing God in the Old Testament

Dana M. Pike

Because of his love for them, God is disposed to bless all his children to some extent (see Matthew 5:45). However, in addition to God's graciously bestowed blessings on all people, many divine blessings are primarily relationship dependent; that is, existing in a particular relationship with God allows one to obtain certain blessings that are often greater than those bestowed upon someone outside such a relationship.[1] The Bible indicates that by his power God blessed Adam and Eve (Gen 1:22, 28) and their faithful descendants, including Noah, Abraham, Sarah, and many others. For example, after Noah's family left their ark, "God blessed Noah and his sons, and said unto them, Be fruitful, and multiply, and replenish the earth. . . . I establish my covenant with you, and with your seed after you" (Genesis 9:1, 9).[2] To Abraham, God promised: "I will make of you a great nation, and I will bless you, and make your name great. . . . I will bless those who bless you, and the one who curses you I will curse" (NRSV, Genesis 12:2–3). These specific covenant relationships required human obligation and participation for the covenant makers to receive the fullest measure of God's blessings.

Dana M. Pike is a professor of ancient scripture at Brigham Young University.

In a religious context, "to bless" is commonly defined as bestowing divine assistance, favor, or power on someone.[3] Thus, "blessing presupposes a benefactor [God, who grants the blessing] and a recipient, and not infrequently there is a mediator who pronounces or confers the prospect of blessing from God to a human recipient."[4] In ancient Israel, this "mediator" who verbalized "the prospect of blessing" was most often a prophet or priest.

However, the Old Testament also contains many passages in which individuals such as Abraham, Moses, David, Solomon, and Daniel, in a seeming reversal of roles, invoked a blessing *on* God or encouraged other people *to bless* God. For example, Moses taught the Israelites, "You shall . . . bless the Lord your God" (NRSV, Deuteronomy 8:10). Under Joshua's leadership, "the children of Israel blessed God" (Joshua 22:33). A few centuries later, when dedicating the Jerusalem Temple, Solomon proclaimed, "Blessed be the Lord God of Israel" (1 Kings 8:15). And in Psalms, Israelites are encouraged to "bless our God, ye people" (66:8). This practice of people blessing God is also attested in the Jewish Apocrypha;[5] in the New Testament, as found in the writings of Luke, Paul, James, Peter, and John;[6] and in later Jewish liturgical texts.[7] For example, James, in speaking of peoples' mouths and tongues, wrote, "Therewith bless [*eulogoumen*] we God, even the Father" (James 3:9). But what does it mean to "bless God"? Since the word "bless" is generally defined as bestowing divine favor or assistance on someone or something, the very notion that a human can "bless" God may seem inconceivable.

The purpose of this paper is to explicate what this practice of "blessing God" consisted of among ancient Israelites, as reflected in the Old Testament, and to determine if it has any relevance for our worship of God in modern times. I will accomplish this by first reviewing the lexical root *b-r-k*, "to bless," in the Hebrew Bible (or Old Testament), after which I will give an overview of blessing passages, with a specific focus on passages in which people "bless" God. I will then analyze and explain what is intended by these passages, discuss how this practice fits into the worldview of ancient Israelites, briefly review how modern English translations render such passages, and conclude with some pertinent comments on how this practice relates to us in this latter-day dispensation.

The Hebrew Word for "Bless"

The Hebrew lexical root *b-r-k* means "bless." It occurs in verbal forms, usually in the *Piel* verbal stem, *bērēk*, "to bless." The nominal form is *bĕrākâ*, "a blessing." The lexical root *b-r-k* is most often attested in Genesis, Deuteronomy, and Psalms, but it is found in most of the books in the Hebrew Bible and in all the major genres (e.g., narrative, prophetic, wisdom, and psalmic) except legal texts.[8] Together, verbal and nominal forms of *b-r-k* occur nearly four hundred times in the Bible. The Hebrew root *b-r-k* is cognate with similar forms in other Northwest Semitic languages and is semantically related to the Akkadian *karabu*.[9] All forms of the English words "bless" or "blessing" in the biblical quotations that follow are derived from the Hebrew lexical root *b-r-k*.

God Blessing People and Things in the Old Testament

Not surprisingly, numerous passages in the Old Testament relate incidents of God blessing people as well as things. The following passages briefly represent such activity:[10]

To the Israelites as a group, if they kept their covenant with God:

Deuteronomy 7:12–13: "Wherefore it shall come to pass, if ye hearken to these judgments, and keep, and do them, that the Lord thy God shall keep unto thee the covenant and the mercy which he sware unto thy fathers: and he will love thee, and bless thee, and multiply thee: he will also bless the fruit of thy womb."

Deuteronomy 26:15: "Look down from thy holy habitation, from heaven, and bless thy people Israel."

To individuals:

Genesis 17:16: God spoke to Abraham about Sarah: "And I will bless her, and give thee a son also of her: yea, I will bless her, and she shall be a mother of nations."

NET, Job 42:12: "So the Lord blessed the second part of Job's life more than the first."

To nonhumans:

Genesis 1:22: "And God blessed them [the water creatures and fowl, created on the "fifth day"], saying, Be fruitful, and multiply, and fill the waters in the seas, and let fowl multiply in the earth."

NRSV, Genesis 2:3: "So God blessed the seventh day and hallowed it, because on it God rested from all the work that he had done in creation."

NRSV, Exodus 23:25: "You shall worship the LORD your God, and I will bless your bread and your water; and I will take sickness away from among you" (similarly, see Deuteronomy 7:12–13; 26:15; 28:4).

Throughout time, people have regularly petitioned God for blessings. One of many examples of this in the Old Testament is Hannah, who earnestly sought the Lord's blessing to conceive and bear a son (see 1 Samuel 1:10–11, 27). Hezekiah's plea to be healed when he was "sick unto death" provides another illustration of people petitioning God for a blessing (2 Kings 20:1-5). Significantly, the Bible consistently depicts YHWH (or Jehovah, usually rendered "the LORD" in English)[11] as the sole source of the Israelites' blessings. As an aside, it is worth mentioning that the Bible also declares that Israel's God is the source of and power behind all curses (see, for example, 1 Samuel 17:43). Curses are experienced as challenges, problems, and disasters. And according to the Bible, curses generally came upon the Israelites as the result of covenant violations, or ruptures in their relationship with God. Classic illustrations of the juxtaposition of blessings and curses are found in the extended covenant formulations in Leviticus 26 and Deuteronomy 28–29, which outline collective blessings to result from the Israelites' covenant loyalty to Jehovah and curses that would just as surely follow disobedience or apostasy. This contrast between blessings and curses is also evident in the Moabite king Balak's expression of frustration towards Balaam: "What have you done to me? I brought you to curse my enemies [the Israelites], but now you have done nothing but bless them" (NRSV, Numbers 23:11).[12]

People Blessing People on Behalf of God[13]

Scripture often relates that an intermediary acted to announce, pronounce, or invoke God's blessings on people. Such blessings are related as primarily verbal acts, but sometimes they involve physical actions as well. For example, the account of Jacob blessing Ephraim and Manasseh relates that he laid a hand on each of their heads (see Genesis 48:14–20).

People often acted as divinely appointed intermediaries who were authorized to pronounce blessings. From a Latter-day Saint perspective, we assume these individuals had priesthood authority to act and bless on behalf of God. However, given the current state of the Old Testament, the text does not always indicate whether these individuals had the priesthood (as in the example just cited of Jacob blessing his grandsons). Additional illustrations of such activity include the following:

> Genesis 14:19: "And he [Melchizedek] blessed him, and said, Blessed be Abram of the most high God."

> Genesis 47:7: "And Joseph brought in Jacob his father, and set him before Pharaoh: and Jacob blessed Pharaoh."

> 1 Samuel 2:20: "And Eli [the Aaronic high priest] blessed Elkanah and his wife [Hannah], and said, The LORD give thee seed of this woman for the loan which is lent to the LORD. And they went unto their own home."

The Aaronic priestly blessing recounted in Numbers 6:24–26 provides an important view of the mediating role of the Aaronic priests in ancient Israel: "The LORD spoke to Moses, saying: Speak to Aaron and his sons, saying, Thus you shall bless the Israelites: You shall say to them, The LORD bless you and keep you; the LORD make his face to shine upon you, and be gracious to you; the LORD lift up his countenance upon you, and give you peace. So they shall put my name on the Israelites, and I will bless them" (NRSV, Numbers 6:22–27).[14] The Old Testament does not specifically indicate when and how often the priests or high priest pronounced this blessing upon Israelites, although this presumably occurred when Israelites gathered for major holidays at the tabernacle and later at the temple. Leviticus 9:22 recounts one possible illustration of such activity:

"Aaron lifted up his hand toward the people, and blessed them, and [then] came down from offering . . . offerings." Later Jewish texts indicate that priests in the late Second Temple period would emerge from the temple and raise their hands above their heads as they invoked the Aaronic priestly blessing upon the people, providing a dramatic reminder of their role in representing the Lord to his covenant people.[15]

In addition to authorized intermediaries, people with no special authority invoked God's blessings on other people. These blessings are best considered thoughtful requests that God's beneficence be extended to someone (presumably uttered with more faith than exhibited in the modern polite practice of saying "God bless you" when someone sneezes). Other passages indicate that a greeting, farewell, or expression of gratitude often included an invoked blessing:

> NRSV, Genesis 24:60: "And they [her family] blessed Rebekah and said to her, "May you, our sister, become thousands of myriads; may your offspring gain possession of the gates of their foes.'"

> NRSV, Ruth 2:4: "Boaz came from Bethlehem. He said to the reapers, 'The Lord be with you.' They answered, 'The Lord bless you.'"

> NRSV, Ruth 2:20: "Naomi said to her daughter-in-law [Ruth], 'Blessed be he [Boaz] by the Lord, whose kindness has not forsaken the living or the dead!'"

> NRSV, 2 Samuel 14:22: "Joab prostrated himself with his face to the ground and did obeisance, and blessed [$y\check{e}b\bar{a}rek$] the king" (KJV reads "thanked the king").

These examples sufficiently illustrate the biblical depiction of God blessing people and things, as well as people blessing others on behalf of God. Our focus now turns to the biblical depiction of people blessing God.

People Blessing God

In addition to passages in which the Old Testament depicts God blessing people, there are a number of passages in which people "bless God," or invoke a blessing upon him. In these scriptures, some of which were quoted at the beginning of this article, God is the object or recipient of a blessing, not the dispenser. Such passages divide easily into two broad categories: (1) what appear to be spontaneous expressions of blessing and (2) more formal expressions of worship, probably having functioned in some liturgical context. Two broad grammar-based categories of usage are also evident in these passages: (1) those expressions reported with an active verb form, "to bless," and (2) those employing a passive verbal form, "to be blessed."

Less formal expressions of "blessing God." The following three passages illustrate narrated declarations of individuals and groups blessing God. These seem to be nonformal, or nonliturgical, expressions of blessing.

Grateful that the Lord had answered his prayer to find a fitting mate for Isaac, Abraham's servant related to Laban and his household, "I bowed down my head, and worshipped the Lord, and blessed the Lord God of my master Abraham" (Genesis 24:48). The servant is certainly grateful, but the phrases "worshipped the Lord" and "blessed the Lord God" imply something greater than mere gratitude.

When the leaders of the Israelite tribes resolved an issue of concern (certain tribes had built a memorial altar near the Jordan River), scripture reports that "the thing pleased the children of Israel; and the children of Israel blessed God" (Joshua 22:33). Relief and thanksgiving were natural outcomes of this intertribal settlement. But again, the phrase "the children of Israel blessed God" seems to convey something more.

Following a joyous celebration of Passover and the Feast of Unleavened Bread (2 Chronicles 30), Chronicles records that King Hezekiah asked his people to contribute sacrifices to be offered at the Jerusalem temple during the coming year. "When Hezekiah and the princes came and saw the heaps" of contributions, they were impressed with the people's generosity; therefore "they blessed the Lord, and his people Israel" (2 Chronicles 31:8). Gratitude was clearly part of their response, but more is implied in this and other biblical reports of Israelites "blessing" God.

More formal expressions of blessing God. Passages in the book of Psalms and elsewhere provide a similar depiction of people blessing God, often arising from gratitude for *his* blessings to them. These formulations, however, have a more formal tone, and they were likely used liturgically by Israelites worshipping at the temple and elsewhere, sometimes collectively. For example, Psalm 16:7 reads, "I will bless the Lord, who hath given me counsel," and Psalm 26:12 (NRSV) declares, "My foot stands on level ground; in the great congregation I will bless the Lord." Other examples of more formal or liturgical use include:

> Nehemiah 9:5: "Then the Levites . . . said, "Stand up and bless the Lord your God for ever and ever."
>
> NRSV, Psalm 68:26: "Bless God in the great congregation, the Lord, O you who are of Israel's fountain!"[16]
>
> Psalm 134:1: "Behold, bless ye the Lord, all ye servants of the Lord, which by night stand in the house of the Lord."

What does it mean to bless God? These and other biblical passages confront us with the questions: What did it mean to the Israelites to "bless" Jehovah, their God? And more fundamentally, how can humans possibly "bless" God in the sense of bestowing a beneficial gift or power on him?

Some earlier biblical scholars thought such biblical passages as those quoted above represented a belief in the magical power of pronouncing words of blessing, that humans could thereby transfer power to God and thus increase his ability to bless others.[17] However, as the academic understanding of ancient religions has further developed, such perceptions are no longer viewed as tenable.

The realization that humans cannot bless God in the way that he blesses humans invites us to analyze what *is* intended in biblical passages in which people "bless" God. For some time now, many scholars have suggested that help in understanding the intent of these expressions is available in the Old Testament itself. Consider these four psalm passages:

> Psalm 34:1: "I will bless the Lord at all times: his praise shall continually be in my mouth."[18]
>
> Psalm 113:1–3: "Praise ye the Lord. Praise, O ye servants of the Lord, praise the name of the Lord. Blessed be the name of the Lord from this time forth and for evermore. From the rising of the sun unto the going down of the same the Lord's name is to be praised."

Psalm 115:17–18: "The dead praise not the Lord, neither any that go down into silence. But we will bless the Lord from this time forth and for evermore. Praise the Lord."

Psalm 145:2: "Every day will I bless thee; and I will praise thy name for ever and ever."

In these and other passages, a verbal form of *b-r-k*, "bless," is parallel with a verbal form (often a masculine plural imperative) of *h-l-l*, "praise." From the latter verb comes *halĕlû-yāh*, or "hallelujah": the plural imperative *halĕlû*, "praise," plus *yāh*, an abbreviated form of the divine name YHWH, or Jehovah. This and related biblical evidence that combines blessing and praising God suggest that when humans "bless" God, they are, at the very least, praising him.[19] This is evident even when the lexical root *h-l-l* does not occur in a passage. For example, Psalm 63:4—"Thus will I bless thee while I live: I will lift up my hands in thy name"—uses the act of lifting up one's hands to convey an attitude that is parallel to the expression "I will bless thee [the Lord]," even though a verb specifically meaning "praise" is not included.[20]

In these passages in which people "bless" Jehovah, it is the *context* of the verb *b-r-k* that provides the intended meaning rather than its etymology. While etymological information is important, it cannot always be the main guide to accurately interpreting the meaning that a word has acquired over time.[21] Because the lexical root *b-r-k* acquired the meaning "praise" when used by people praising God, it is an example of polysemy, a term indicating that a word can have more than one meaning, depending on how and where it is used.

Thus, when individuals, such as Abraham's servant, or groups of Israelites "blessed" God, they were not only expressing gratitude but praising him. All the passages quoted above, as well as others that follow below, are best understood as employing the word *bless* to mean "praise."

Some scholars see this development of *bless* conveying praise for God as an "entirely inner-biblical development," something not attested outside of the Bible, although we cannot tell exactly when, where, or how this development occurred.[22] Other scholars have questioned this assertion and have claimed that inscriptions contemporary with the Bible also express praise to

God using a form of *b-r-k*; however, the epigraphic evidence they muster to support their notion is not conclusive.[23]

Interestingly, verbal forms of *b-r-k* do occur in Israelite inscriptions, although many are in poorly preserved texts. Examples include the blessing invoked in the salutation of Arad ostracon 16, lines 2–3: "I bless you to [or by] YHWH." This formulation has essentially the same force as the grammatically passive biblical expression "may YHWH bless you" (see discussion below). Similarly, the dedicatory inscription on the edge of a stone bowl from Kuntillet Ajrud reads, "To Obadyaw (Obadiah), the son of Adnah. Blessed be he by YHW."[24] These invocations of blessings on other people parallel those found in the Bible. However, there is no thoroughly accepted instance of someone "blessing God" in an Israelite inscription. For now, the best we can say is that this phenomenon is only clearly attested in Hebrew scripture and its subsequent textual traditions.

The bārûk *formula.* The last aspect of our discussion of blessing God deals with what is sometimes referred to as the *bārûk* formula. This designation derives from the fact that the *Qal* passive participial form of the lexical root *b-r-k* is *bārûk*.[25] This form commonly occurs in biblical texts in which people invoke God's blessing on someone *and* in which people invoke a blessing, or praise, *on God*.[26] Examples of occasions on which people invoked a divine blessing on other people, sometimes in a greeting, include the following:

> Judges 17:2: "And his mother said, Blessed be thou of the Lord, my son."

> NRSV, Ruth 2:19: "Her mother-in-law said to her, 'Where did you glean today? And where have you worked? Blessed be the man who took notice of you.'"

> NRSV, 1 Samuel 15:13: "When Samuel came to Saul, Saul said to him, 'May you be blessed by the Lord.'"

There are many passages in which God is the object of invoked blessings. (Grammatically speaking, deity is the syntactic subject of these sentences, but because the blessing was invoked on God, he is semantically the object or recipient of the blessing, so I will refer to deity as the object of blessing even in this passive formulation in the Bible).[27] The use of the *bārûk* formula in this context parallels the expressions of "blessing" God mentioned above in that some expressions seem more spontaneous, while others are clearly part of formal worship. As is evident in all these passages, Jehovah is most often referred to in the third person, and the text often includes a justification for invoking a "blessing" on God. Examples of both the less and more formal uses of *bārûk* with God as object include the following:

> Exodus 18:10: "And Jethro said, Blessed be the Lord, who hath delivered you out of the hand of the Egyptians."

> NRSV, Ruth 4:14: "Then the women said to Naomi, 'Blessed be the Lord, who has not left you this day without next-of-kin.'"

> 1 Kings 8:56 (Here Solomon is dedicating the temple in Jerusalem): "Blessed be the Lord, that hath given rest unto his people Israel, according to all that he promised."

> 1 Chronicles 29:10: "Wherefore David blessed the Lord before all the congregation: and David said, Blessed be thou, Lord God of Israel our father, for ever and ever."

> Psalm 28:6: "Blessed be the Lord, because he hath heard the voice of my supplications."

> NRSV Psalm 72:18: "Blessed be the Lord, the God of Israel, who alone does wondrous things."

> Psalm 89:52: "Blessed be the Lord for evermore. Amen, and Amen."

In harmony with the assessment presented above, passages in which the *bārûk* formula is used to invoke a blessing on God are best understood as expressions of praise born of gratitude. Gratitude and praise seem to be the predominant Israelite responses to the greatness, the goodness, the mercy, and the holiness of the Lord.[28] A blessing was invoked upon—or in other words, praise and gratitude were expressed to—the true giver of life's blessings. As one scholar has observed, "Instead of calling for God to be blessed, i.e., to receive prosperity, fertility, etc., *bārûk* called for the praise of God. Praise was what man could give to God *in lieu* of material benefits as an expression of appreciation for God's benefaction."²⁹ It is thus not surprising that the *bārûk* formula occurs in parallel with verbs of praise. For example:

> 1 Chronicles 16:36: "Blessed be the LORD God of Israel for ever and ever. And all the people said, Amen, and praised [*hallēl*] the LORD."

> NRSV, Psalm 68:32, 34–35: "Sing to God, O kingdoms of the earth; sing praises to the Lord. . . . Ascribe power to God, whose majesty is over Israel; and whose power is in the skies. Awesome is God in his sanctuary, the God of Israel; he gives power and strength to his people. Blessed be God!"

> Psalm 106:48: "Blessed be the LORD God of Israel from everlasting to everlasting. . . . Praise ye the LORD [*halĕlû-yāh*]."

Modern English Translations

As is evident from the foregoing review, the King James Version regularly translates the Hebrew verb *b-r-k* as "bless" whenever God is the object or the recipient of expressions of blessing. However, a number of modern English translations of the Hebrew Bible, such as the NIV (New International Version) and the NET (New English Translation), follow the scholarly perspective just presented and render most occurrences of *b-r-k* as "praise" when God is the object or recipient of human blessing. For example, Psalm 28:6 is translated in the KJV as "Blessed be the LORD, because he hath heard the voice of my supplications," but the NIV reads "Praise be to the LORD, for he has heard my cry for mercy," and the NET has, "The LORD deserves praise, for he has heard my plea for mercy!" Similarly, Psalm 34:1 is translated in the KJV as "I will bless the LORD at all times," but the NIV has, "I will extol the LORD at all times," and the NET reads "I will praise the LORD at all times." Somewhat differently, the NRSV (New Revised Standard Version) retains the older rendition of *b-r-k* as "bless" in some passages in which God is the object but renders *b-r-k* as "praise" in others, while the New Jewish Publication Society translation most often uses "bless" in the passages under review but occasionally renders *b-r-k* as "praise" or "thanks."

Thus, when God is the object of verbal forms of *b-r-k*, the KJV accurately translates the basic etymological sense of the Hebrew word. But some modern English Bible translations (and many modern scholars) render verbal forms of *b-r-k* as "praise" in expressions in which God is the recipient of human "blessing."

Summary and Application: Expressing Praise

Based on the assessment just presented, when ancient Israelites "blessed" Jehovah, either in spontaneous expression or through more formal means, they were in effect praising and worshiping their God. Using active and passive verbal forms of *b-r-k*, they pronounced and invoked blessings or praise upon God. Praise is any worshipful expression in which the greatness and goodness of God are affirmed. As illustrated in the passages quoted above, as well as others found in the Bible, there were many reasons why people blessed or praised God. One example is found in 1 Kings 8:56 (quoted above): "Blessed be the Lord, that hath given rest unto his people Israel."

As depicted in the Old Testament, praising Jehovah was a central feature of Israelite religion. Biblically preserved expressions of praise are "found sporadically throughout the historical writings [of the Bible] and rarely in the prophets. In the cult [priestly and temple activity], however, praise became a dominant theme. . . . The psalms describe the proper attitude toward God of pious individuals as well as of the nation as praise. . . . Praise expressed Israel's faith in God's goodness and trust in his future benefaction."[30]

Israelite praise of the Lord was not restricted to mere verbal exclamations. Singing was also a part of Israelite worship, as indicated in Psalm 135:3: "Praise the Lord; for the Lord is good: sing praises unto his name; for it is pleasant" (see also Psalm 68:32–35). Furthermore, Psalm 150, the concluding psalm in the book of Psalms, illustrates well that instrumental music was incorporated into the praise and worship of Jehovah:

> Praise ye the Lord [*halĕlû-yāh*]. Praise God in his sanctuary: praise him in the firmament of his power. . . .
> Praise him with the sound of the trumpet: praise him with the psaltery and harp.
> Praise him with the timbrel and dance: praise him with stringed instruments and organs.

Praise him upon the loud cymbals: praise him upon the high sounding cymbals.
Let every thing that hath breath praise the Lord. Praise ye the Lord [*halĕlû-yāh*]. (Psalm 150:1, 3–6)

Physical movement often (or perhaps always) accompanied verbal or musical expressions of praising and blessing God, as exemplified in these three biblical passages:

1 Kings 8:22: "And Solomon stood before the altar of the Lord in the presence of all the congregation of Israel, and spread forth his hands toward heaven."

Psalm 95:6: "O come, let us worship and bow down: let us kneel before the Lord our maker."

Psalm 134:1–2: "Behold, bless ye the Lord, all ye servants of the Lord, which by night stand in the house of the Lord.
Lift up your hands in the sanctuary, and bless the Lord.

It is likely that less formal, more spontaneous expressions of "blessing" God regularly included physical gestures or movement as well, as indicated in Genesis 4:48: "I bowed down my head, and worshipped the Lord, and blessed the Lord God of my master Abraham."

Scriptural passages in which praise is expressed to God are not limited to the Old Testament. They are well attested in the New Testament and Book of Mormon, and to a lesser extent in the Doctrine and Covenants.[31]

Personally, although I largely agree with the generally accepted academic perspective that "blessing God" essentially overlaps with the concept of praising him, collectively these biblical passages suggest to me something greater than that; otherwise, why use the verb "bless" at all when God is the object or recipient of the blessing, when *h-l-l* or some other Hebrew verb would serve just fine?[32] In this regard, I agree with Jacob Milgrom's assessment that "to bless God is more than to praise . . . Him; it implies that one must demonstrate to Him reverence and loyalty in deeds as well as words."[33] Thus, biblical expressions of blessing God include but can be said to go beyond expressing praise. Blessing God seems to me to convey a whole-souled worship of and commitment to him from whom all true blessings flow. Just as many divine blessings are primarily covenant-relationship dependent, so, I believe, the act of "blessing God" demonstrates a vital dimension of such a relationship. This attitude is demonstrated by a person's faith, love, obedience, and consecration.[34]

Based on my own experience, the practice of using this language of "blessing God" is not evident in modern Latter-day Saint culture (although it still is in orthodox Jewish culture).[35] Furthermore, it seems to me that, other than verbalizing expressions of praise while singing hymns, many Latter-day Saints are less likely than ancient Israelite worshippers to verbally express praise to God, whatever the verb employed. Something is lost, in my opinion, when both spontaneous and more formal expressions of praising and blessing are absent from the vocabulary we employ in our relationship with God our Father and his Son. I hope this presentation encourages us all to think about reasons for and expressions of praise and worship in our own lives.

As a whole, Psalm 103 gives wonderful voice to the might and mercy of the Lord. In the spirit of offering praise and worship to the great God of Israel, YHWH or Jehovah, who Latter-day Saints understand is Jesus Christ, I conclude this presentation with a few verses from this psalm in which participants are exhorted to "bless" the Lord. Notice the prominent use of *b-r-k* in expressing praise to, but also a sense of adoration for, the Lord:

> Bless the Lord, O my soul: and all that is within me, bless his holy name.
> Bless the Lord, O my soul, and forget not all his benefits. . . .
> Bless the Lord, ye his angels, that excel in strength, that do his commandments, hearkening unto the voice of his word.
> Bless ye the Lord, all ye his hosts; ye ministers of his, that do his pleasure.
> Bless the Lord, all his works in all places of his dominion: bless the Lord, O my soul. (Psalm 103:1–2, 20–22)

Notes

The title quotes Psalm 34:1 (34:2 in the Hebrew version of the Bible). I express my thanks to my former student assistant, Courtney Dotson, for helping gather materials used in preparing this paper. I also thank my wife, Jane Allis-Pike, for providing feedback on an earlier draft of this paper.

1. For a discussion of this point, see Josef Scharbert, "brk," in *Theological Dictionary of the Old Testament*, ed. G. J. Botterweck and H. Ringgren, trans. J. T. Willis, G. W. Bromiley, and D. E. Green (Grand Rapids, MI: Eerdmans, 1975), 2:293–94, 305 (hereafter *TDOT*); and Christopher Wright Mitchell, *The Meaning of BRK "To Bless" in the Old Testament* (Atlanta: Scholars Press, 1987), 26.

2. Biblical quotations cited in this paper are from the King James Version (KJV) unless otherwise indicated. Other cited translations are the New Revised Standard Version (NRSV), the New International Version (NIV), and the New English Translation (NET).

3. See, for example, the definition in the *Guide to the Scriptures*: "to confer divine favor upon someone." *Guide to the Scriptures*, "bless, blessed, blessing," accessed April 8, 2013, http://www.lds.org/scriptures/gs/bless-blessed-blessing?lang=eng&letter=b.

4. *Dictionary of Biblical Imagery*, ed. Leland Ryken, James C. Wilhoit, and Tremper Longman III (Downers Grove, IL: InterVarsity, 1998), "blessing, blessedness." See also Mitchell, *Meaning of* BRK, 2.

5. See, for example, Tobit 8:15; 12:6, 17–20; 2 Maccabees 15:29, 34. It is also worth noting that the biblical passages in which deity is the object of human "blessing" are routinely translated with a form of the verb *eulogeō*, "to bless," in the Septuagint, the early Greek translation of the Hebrew scriptures (third to second centuries BC). This indicates that the Jewish translators of the Septuagint were comfortable in continuing to use a word meaning "bless" in expressions with God as the object or recipient.

6. See, for example, Luke 1:68; 2:28; 24:53; Ephesians 1:3; 1 Peter 1:3.

7. For example, the ʿămîdâ, "the main statutory prayer in Jewish public and private worship since the [Roman] destruction of the Second [Herod's] Temple"—the "prayer par excellence"—begins with the phrase, "Blessed are You, Lord our God," which is repeated multiple times (sometimes without "our") throughout the prayer. Peter Lenhardt, "'Amidah," in *The Oxford Dictionary of Jewish Religion*, ed. R. J. Zwi Werblowsky and Geoffrey Wigoder (New York: Oxford University Press, 1997), 42.

8. For convenience, see the charts of attestation accompanying the entry "brk," in Ernst Jenni and Claus Westermann, *Theological Lexicon of the Old Testament*, trans. Mark E. Biddle (Peabody, MA: Hendrickson, 1997), 1:267 (hereafter *TLOT*); and in Mitchell, *Meaning of* BRK, 185.

9. See, for example, L. Koehler, W. Baumgartner, and J. J. Stamm, *The Hebrew and Aramaic Lexicon of the Old Testament*, trans. and ed. under the supervision of M. E. J. Richardson (Leiden: Brill, 1994), 1:160–61 (hereafter *HALOT*). For discussions of the possible relationship between Hebrew b-r-k I, "to kneel," and b-r-k II, "to bless," and of the cognate evidence, see Scharbert, "brk," in *TDOT*, 2:279–84; Mitchell, *Meaning of* BRK, 8–16; and Timothy G. Crawford, *Blessing and Curse in Syro-Palestinian Inscriptions of the Iron Age* (New York: Peter Lang, 1992), 7–12.

10. There are more examples of most of these categories, but space is a limiting factor here. Furthermore, the examples provided here represent broad categories of usage. The

interested reader can pursue the finer points of this discussion by consulting Mitchell and other sources cited in my notes.

11. For a discussion of the form of the divine name YHWH, usually vocalized "Yahweh" by scholars and traditionally rendered "Jehovah" by English speakers, see Dana M. Pike, "The Name and Titles of God in the Old Testament," *Religious Educator* 11, no. 1 (2010): 17–31, especially 19–21; and Dana M. Pike, "Biblical Hebrew Words You Already Know, and Why They are Important," *Religious Educator* 7, no. 3 (2006): 97–114, especially 106–9.

12. See Jeremiah 17:5–8 for another pointed example of the contrast between blessing and cursing. I note, without further discussion in this paper, that traditionally it has been accepted that occasionally biblical scribes euphemistically used b-r-k, "bless," to avoid writing that someone "cursed God" (commonly suggested examples include 1 Kings 21:10, 13; Job 1:5, 11). See comments on this by J. K. Aitken, *The Semantics of Blessing and Cursing in Ancient Hebrew* (Louvain: Peeters, 2007), 112 (A.9), 114 (A.6). See also Jacob Milgrom, *The JPS Torah Commentary: Numbers* (Philadelphia: Jewish Publication Society, 1990), 360: "The Bible records another nuance to *berekh*: With God as the object it is [sometimes] a euphemism for *killel*, 'to treat God lightly, disparagingly' (e.g., 1 Kings 21:13; Job 1:5, 11; 2:9)."

13. Deuteronomy 29:18–20 and Psalm 49:16–19 (in the Hebrew Bible, verses 17–20) suggest the futility of trying to "bless" oneself. As emphasized above, the blessing comes from God when one is in a proper relationship with him.

14. For brief remarks on the contents of the Aaronic priestly blessing, its occurrence on two small silver foil amulets found at Ketef Hinnom (western Jerusalem), and related matters, see Dana M. Pike, "Israelite Inscriptions from the Time of Jeremiah and Lehi," in *Glimpses of Lehi's Jerusalem*, ed. John W. Welch, David Rolph Seely, and Jo Ann H. Seely (Provo, UT: FARMS/BYU, 2004), 213–15; and Richard Neitzel Holzapfel, Dana M. Pike, and David Rolph Seely, *Jehovah and the World of the Old Testament* (Salt Lake City: Deseret, 2009), 129, 329.

15. The late Second Temple period includes the last few centuries BC until AD 70, when the Romans destroyed the Jerusalem temple. The late Second Temple–period text most cited in connection with this priestly blessing is in the book of the Apocrypha known as the Wisdom of Ben Sira(ch); see 50:14–21, especially verses 20–21 (NRSV): "Then Simon [the Aaronic High Priest] came down and raised his hands over the whole congregation of Israelites, to pronounce the blessing of the Lord with his lips . . . and they bowed down in worship a second time, to receive the blessing from the Most High." For a discussion of whether the text in Ben Sira 50 is describing a daily practice or that of the holiday Yom Kippur, see Jeremy Penner, *Patterns of Daily Prayer in Second Temple Period Judaism* (Boston: Brill, 2012), 45–48. Post-temple sources on the priestly blessing include the Mishnah, *Sota* 7:6 and *Tamid* 7:2.

16. Psalm 68:26 is 68:27 in the Hebrew Bible.

17. For references to and a brief overview of older theories on God blessing people and people blessing God, see Mitchell, *Meaning of* BRK, 17–27, 143, 171–77.

18. Psalm 34:1 is 34:2 in the Hebrew Bible.

19. Publications providing an explanation of "blessing God" similar to what is presented herein include Aitken, *Semantics of Blessing and Cursing*, 112–16; Mitchell, *Meaning of* BRK, 133–64; Jenni and Westermann, *TLOT*, 269–70, 281–82; Scharbert, "brk," in *TDOT*, 2:292–93; *HALOT*, 1:160; and Herbert Chanan Brichto, "Blessing and Cursing," in *Encyclopedia Judaica* (Jerusalem: Macmillan, 1971), 4:1084: "When man is the subject of the verb *berekh* and the Deity is the object, the verb denotes praise, for nowhere in the Bible is there any indication that the power of God is itself increased by man's pronouncements."

20. Psalm 63:4 is 63:5 in the Hebrew Bible.

21. See, for example, Aitken, *Semantics of Blessing and Cursing*, 3–4, for comments on the role of context in determining the meaning of a given term. An analogous situation, in my opinion, is what occurred with the expression rendered "hosanna" in the New Testament (*hōsanna* in Greek). This term, exclaimed in Aramaic by some Jews during Jesus' triumphal entry into Jerusalem (Matthew 21:9; John 12:13)—"Hosanna to the Son of David"—conveyed praise and adoration. However, it is derived from a Hebrew imperative form of the verb *y-š-ʿ*, with an appended particle (*-nnāʾ*) that strengthens the request conveyed by the imperative. Thus, viewed etymologically, "hosanna" translates as "save, please" or "save now." Although this exact form does not occur in the Hebrew Bible, it is presumably based upon, or is at least related to, *hôšîʿâ-nnāʾ*, which occurs in Psalm 118:25. In its context in the New Testament, the imperative form "save now," a plea for deliverance, had become an expression of praise to the one divine being who was actually capable of saving them (and us). See Marin H. Pope, "Hosanna," in the *Anchor Bible Dictionary*, ed. David Noel Freedman (New York: Doubleday, 1992), 3:290–91, for a survey of theories on the history of the development of "hosanna." Subsequent Christian usage continued employing "hosanna" as a form of praise for Jesus. For example, the term "hosanna" as an expression of praise was "introduced into the Christian liturgy at a very early date. . . . The words 'Glory be to thee, O Lord, most High' in the Sanctus of the Anglican BCP [Book of Common Prayer] are a rendering of the *Hosanna in excelsis* ('Hosanna in the highest') in the medieval and modern Latin rite." "Hosanna," in *The Oxford Dictionary of the Christian Church*, 3rd ed., ed. F. L. Cross and E. A. Livingstone (New York: Oxford, 1997), 792. This trend is also evident in Latter-day Saint hymns, such as "The Spirit of God," with its line "Hosanna, hosanna, to God and the Lamb." William W. Phelps, "The Spirit of God," *Hymns* (Salt Lake City: The Church of Jesus Christ of Latter-day Saints, 1985), no. 2. Whatever one's view on the development and meaning of "hosanna" in the New Testament and the era in which it was produced, "hosanna" clearly became an expression of praise.

22. Mitchell, *Meaning of* BRK, 12 (see also 134). Mitchell is aware that "the root [*b-r-k*] is used [elsewhere] for the praise of divinities only in Palmyrene dedication formulas from the second to fourth centuries A.D., aside from post-biblical Jewish literature," but he attributes this later use to biblical influence (as do others).

23. Aitken, *Semantics of Blessing and Cursing*, 113, for example, cites a line from an inscription often designated En Gedi 2 as "an extra-biblical example of man 'praising' God" by use of the verb *b-r-k*. The line in question (4) is fragmentary, however, as is the rest of the inscription. Line 4 reads *brk yhw*[—]. Aitken cites Crawford, *Blessing and Curse*, 157–58,

as agreeing with his assertion. However, F. W. Dobbs-Allsopp observes, "It is possible that this [*yhw*] is the complete DN [divine name] . . . or that one should read *yhw*[*h*]. Yet it seems more likely that we have here the beginning of a theophoric PN [personal name]." F. W. Dobbs-Allsopp and others, *Hebrew Inscriptions: Texts from the Biblical Periods of the Monarchy with Concordance* (New Haven: Yale, 2005), 151. Likewise, I do not consider the claim by Crawford and Aitken (including their comments on line 7 of the same inscription) to be conclusive at the present time.

24. For these texts (Arad 16; KAjrud 9) and references to related ones, see Dobbs-Allsopp and others, *Hebrew Inscriptions*, 32–33, 283–84. See also the discussion in the previous note. Besides that disputed reading, the only other possible example in an Israelite inscription of a human invoking a blessing on Deity is line 5 of KAjrud 15, in the faded remains of ink writing on plaster. The text in question is presented in *Hebrew Inscriptions*, 287, as *lbrk bʻl bym mlḥ*[*mh*], which has been translated as "for the blessed one of the lord on the day of the bat[tle]" (brackets in original). However, Aḥituv translates this as "to [b]less Baal on the day of wa[r]." Shmuel Aḥituv, *Echoes from the Past* (Jerusalem: Carta, 2008), 325; brackets in original. Due to differing translation possibilities (and in some cases, differences in proposed readings), this text cannot be taken as conclusive inscriptional evidence for the practice of "blessing" Deity.

25. A relatively rare alternative to the *bārûk* formula is *mĕbōrak*, a *Pual* participle. This participle occurs in conjunction with the name of God, and has essentially the same meaning as *bārûk*, in Psalm 113:2; Job 1:21; and Daniel 2:20 (here in the Aramaic *Pael*). This form is not dealt with further in this study.

26. This is the same Hebrew form used in the name of Jeremiah's scribe, Baruch (see Jeremiah 36:4–5).

27. I thank Jonathon Owen for reviewing with me the grammatical particulars of passive subjunctives and the translations of these biblical passages in particular.

28. It is possible that other emotions were expressed by Israelites as they "blessed" God, but it is not possible to identify these from what is included in the biblical text. Furthermore, Israelites in antiquity and in the present may conclude that living a faithful, virtuous life is a form of praising God; however, that is not the focus of this study.

29. Mitchell, *Meaning of* BRK, 147.

30. Mitchell, *Meaning of* BRK, 133.

31. This claim can easily be verified by searching for the word "praise" at http://www.lds.org/search?lang=eng&collection=scriptures&query=praise&sortBy=book, or with any other search engine that includes all Latter-day Saint scripture.

32. Besides *h-l-l*, another verb meaning "to praise" that commonly occurs in the Hebrew Bible is *y-d-h* (*Hiphil* verbal stem). This latter verb, sometimes rendered "give thanks," occurs in parallel with *h-l-l* (e.g., Psalms 35:18; 106:1; 109:30) and a few times in parallel with *b-r-k* (Psalms 100:4; 145:10). Such attestations do not negatively impact the view of "blessing God" presented in this paper, in my opinion.

33. Milgrom, *Numbers*, 360.

34. This understanding of "blessing God" thus involves consecrating oneself to him. For a classic sermon on consecration, see Neal A. Maxwell, "Swallowed Up in the Will of the Father," *Ensign*, November 1995, 22–24.

35. Some Latter-day Saints have occasionally used the language of blessing God. For example, in a letter written to Vienna Jacques, dated September 4, 1833, Joseph Smith wrote, "I received your Letter some time since containing a history of your Journey and your safe arrival for which I bless the Lord." Quoted in Steven C. Harper, *Making Sense of the Doctrine and Covenants* (Salt Lake City: Deseret Book, 2008), 338. In my experience, such usage, presumably influenced by familiarity with the Bible, is rarely if ever employed by Latter-day Saints in the twenty-first century. For Jewish usage of the phrase "bless God," see note 7 above.

10

The Context of Old Testament Temple Worship: Early Ancient Egyptian Rites

John S. Thompson

Comparative studies in religion can be useful due to the discipline's ability to reveal ideas in one tradition because of similar concepts found in another. Bible scholars have long collected and studied the art and texts of ancient Israel's contemporary societies in hopes that comparisons might reveal or provide greater understanding of biblical culture and ideas. Pritchard's *Ancient Near Eastern Texts*, Hallo and Younger's *The Context of Scripture*, and the Society of Biblical Literature's *Writings from the Ancient World* series have been important publications over the last several decades for such a purpose.[1]

Of course, care should be taken not to overstate the influence of one tradition upon another or to assume that parallel art or texts also have parallel meaning in separate traditions.[2] One must also acknowledge the differences that exist between cultures.[3] Ultimately, and this idea cannot be stressed enough, a culture's texts and art must be studied and interpreted within the parameters of its own tradition to gain a proper understanding of the meaning they may have had to the people who produced them. But again, comparative studies can help us to view things from different perspectives and to ask questions of a text

---

John S. Thompson is completing a PhD in Egyptology at the University of Pennsylvania and is an instructor at the Orem Utah University Institute of Religion.

or work of art that we might never have asked had we ignored what neighboring traditions did with similar concepts.[4]

Temple worship in the Old Testament did not exist in a vacuum. Neighboring cultures also had temples that appear to share some similarities with those in the Old Testament.[5] A passage from the Book of Abraham invites particularly a comparison between the priesthood, temple, and government of the early Old Testament patriarchal fathers with early Egyptian culture, for it claims that the first pharaoh of Egypt sought earnestly to "imitate that order" established "in the days of the first patriarchal reign," namely from Adam to Noah (see Abraham 1:25–26).

Efforts to explore corollaries between Egyptian temple rituals and the Old Testament temple traditions often conflate all of Egyptian history and their many different rituals into a single whole, which is a problematic methodology. In order to have a more focused basis for comparison, this study concentrates on one of the earliest known rituals that appears in the art of the ancient Egyptian Old Kingdom nonroyal elite tomb chapels (c. 2600–2100 BC), a sequence of rites that, at its core, also appears in the Old Kingdom Pyramid Texts (c. 2350–2100 BC) and in the daily ritual program of ancient Egyptian temples until later periods. These rites, appearing in the Old Kingdom nonroyal tombs and Pyramid Texts, provide a glimpse into the temple theology and worship of this culture from its earliest times.

Ideally, in light of Abraham 1:25–26, <u>this early Egyptian ritual program should be compared to what is known</u> of temple worship from Adam <u>to Noah</u>. However, no original sources have survived from these first patriarchs. Consequently, this paper can only compare the Egyptian sources with later scriptural traditions about the first patriarchs and with the forms of temple worship and priesthood that, according to tradition, the later patriarchs received either from the earlier patriarchs directly or as a restoration of earlier patriarchal ideas by heavenly messengers (see Abraham 1:28, 31; Moses 5:58–59; Acts 7:52–53; D&C 112:31–32; 128:21). Uniquely Latter-day Saint scriptural traditions about Old Testament temple worship will be included in this analysis.

Due to the lack of details concerning early Old Testament temple worship, modern biblical scholars have concluded that the early rites of worship appear mainly to be simple sacrifices and then became more complex in later time periods. Such a conclusion serves, in part, to bolster modern scholarship's assumptions that the most complex temple-related texts in the Old Testament, such as Leviticus and Exodus 25–40, must have been written at much later dates and then falsely attributed to earlier biblical figures such as Moses. However, the similarities of the early Egyptian ritual program (which is complex and dates to periods centuries before the days of Abraham) with the Old Testament temple tradition suggests that the more complex Old Testament ritual programs have a cultural context into which they can fit dated much, much earlier than assumed.

Scriptural Perspectives on True Temple Worship in the Earliest Patriarchal Period

Scriptural tradition affirms that temple worship began in the days of Adam and Eve. Tradition mentions temple-related concepts such as Adam and Eve receiving Abrahamic covenant-like promises from God of "all the earth" as their kingdom, priesthood powers of "dominion," and being "fruitful" as they "multiply, and replenish the earth" with their seed (Genesis 1:26–28), "worship[ping] the Lord their God" via sacrificial offerings (Moses 5:5–6), Adam's receipt of "an holy ordinance" that "confirmed all things" (Moses 5:59),[6] as well as an "order" in which Adam became a "son of God" (Moses 6:67–68).[7] Arguably, tradition portrays the Garden of Eden as the first temple—with its eastern entrance (see Genesis 2:8, 3:24), sacred center (see Genesis 2:9), purity required to remain inside (see Genesis 3:23), seraphim guards (see Genesis 3:24), and, most importantly, the enduring presence of God (see Moses 5:4).[8] Presumably, Adam built an altar outside the Garden of Eden (see Moses 5:5–6),[9] and this altar may prefigure the sacrificial altars of later temples placed in courtyards outside their associated sacred buildings.

True Adamic temple worship seems to have continued through some of Adam's descendants. Scripture declares that both Abel and Seth offered acceptable sacrifices (see Moses 6:3). Seth's descendant Enoch bowed down "before the Lord," and the Lord told Enoch to "open thy mouth" and promised him an endowment of power to move mountains and turn rivers with his words (see Moses 6:31–34). The Lord also told Enoch to "wash" his eyes, whereby he beheld premortal spirits and other things (see Moses 6:34–35; cf. Abraham 3:22, Moses 1:8, 28). Possibly referring to this same moment, Enoch also spoke of being in a "high mountain" wherein he was "clothed" and saw the "world for the space of many generations" (see Moses 7:2–4).

Prior to the Flood, Enoch's great-grandson Noah entered the highest "order" of the temple, whereby he also became a "son of God" with some of his children (see Moses 8:13, 19). After the Flood, he built "an altar unto the Lord," and God "established [his] covenant" with Noah and his sons, giving them priesthood dominion over the earth and also seed (see Genesis 8:20–22; 9:1–17).

Among the later patriarchs, scriptural tradition indicates that Melchizedek was tested by the "violence of fire" and ultimately was "approved of God" and thus entered into the highest order of the temple and became a "Son of God" (see JST, Genesis 14:26–28). As a member of this highest temple order, Melchizedek received an endowment of power by means of an oath from God (see JST, Genesis 14:30–31, Bible appendix; cf. Helaman 10:6; D&C 84:35–39) and obtained supernal titles such as "prince of peace," "king of heaven," and "high priest" (see JST, Genesis 14:33, 36–37).[10]

Abraham also sought for these highest temple blessings. He desired to "receive instruction" that would allow him to move from a lesser to a "greater" order wherein he, like Melchizedek and the fathers before him, would be called a "prince of peace" and "High Priest" (Abraham 1:2). In connection with his marriage to Sarah, Abraham received the temple covenant promises of a kingdom, priesthood power, and seed (see Genesis 11:27–12:5; Abraham 2:1–16), just as Adam and Noah did. Like Enoch, he saw the premortal spirits of mankind and also the Creation (see Abraham 3–5). Finally, after a series of tests, Joseph Smith declared that Abraham obtained the highest order of the temple "by the offering of his son Isaac" at the figurative altar of consecration, whereupon his temple covenant blessings were repeated and confirmed or made sure with an oath by God (see Genesis 22:15–18; cf. Hebrews 6:13–17).[11]

Like his father, Abraham, Isaac married and received the temple covenant promises of a kingdom, powers, and seed (see Genesis 26:1–5). This was followed by periods of testing and actions that mirror those of Abraham and Sarah (see Genesis 26:6–22) and culminated in a repetition of the temple blessings with a more sure word or oath by God at the same well associated with Abraham's receipt of the oath by God (see Genesis 26:23–25, 32; cf. 22:19).

Likewise, Jacob's meeting and subsequently marrying Rachel was the immediate context for his receiving the temple covenant promises of a kingdom, power, and seed, in connection with a ladder that "reached to heaven" that Jacob stated "is none other but the house of God" and "gate of heaven" (Genesis 28:10–22; cf. Moses 7:53). After a period of testing and struggling symbolized by a culminating wrestle with "a man," Jacob was called a "prince," having "power with God and with men" because he "prevailed" (Genesis 32:28), and the temple covenant blessings were repeated with an oath by God, making sure his promises (see Genesis 35:9–15). In this context, Jacob poured out drink and oil libations.

During the Mosaic era, scriptural tradition suggests that God desired to give to the whole house of Israel the same temple promises given to the first patriarchs, for he would make them all a "kingdom of priests"—i.e., king-priests like Adam, Enoch, and Melchizedek—via a covenant at the temple-mountain of Sinai (see Exodus 19:3–6). In connection with this desire of God, a temple building and ritual program is revealed to Moses (see, for example, Exodus 25–40).

Scriptural Perspectives on False Temple Worship in the Earliest Patriarchal Period

The scriptures contrast the above traditions of true temple priesthood and rites among Seth's descendants with counterfeit priesthoods and temples found among other lineages. For example, Cain practiced temple rites of sacrifice and oath making (see Moses 5:19, 29); however, he "loved Satan more than God" (Moses 5:18) and distorted the use of the sacred rites for the purpose of getting gain (see Moses 5:31); consequently, Cain's rites were not done with repentance nor in the "name of the Son" as commanded by the angel of the Lord (Moses 5:8) and were thus rejected by God. Some of Cain's descendants also used these counterfeit temple rites or secret combinations for continuing works of darkness (see Moses 5:49–55).

The wicked "sons of men" during the days of Noah claimed that they, not Noah and his sons, were the true "sons of God" and had the correct temple worship and blessings, including marriage rites and having power in their posterity—"children" who are "mighty men, which are like unto men of old" (Moses 8:21).[12] Blinded by their own "imagination," they hearkened not unto Noah's words and became "evil continually" (Moses 8:22).

Following the Flood, the Tower of Babel appears to be a false temple that, like the true temples, promised its worshippers an ascension to God (see Genesis 11:4); however, the language of this false temple was confounded by God and stands in contrast to the preserved language of Jared and his brother and to the power of all those who would "call upon the

The Context of Old Testament Temple Worship 161

name of the Lord" in true priesthood and temple worship (see Ether 1:35, Moses 6:4–7; 7:13).

The scriptures identify the Egyptians as another example of people practicing unauthorized early temple worship. The first pharaoh of Egypt was "righteous" and "established his kingdom" and judged his people "justly" and "wisely;" however, because he could not inherit the priesthood and other blessings of the covenant due to the choices of his forefathers, he could only "imitate that order" had among the patriarchs of the "first generations" (Abraham 1:26–27). It is upon the temple worship of this declared imitation we now focus.

The Earliest Egyptian Temple Ritual Sequence

Fig. 1. Tomb of N̠t̠r-w s r.

Recent research has demonstrated that combining the images of priests appearing on the walls near the cult-center places of nonroyal tomb chapels in Egypt's Old Kingdom reveals a ritual program sequence that matches but effectively predates the main offering ritual in the royal Old Kingdom Pyramid Texts, the oldest known fully developed religious text in the world.[13] Due to similarities with the core daily rituals performed before deity into the later periods of Egyptian history,[14] this sequence arguably provides a glimpse into the earliest program of temple worship in Egypt. Indeed, nonroyal Egyptians claimed that their tombs were temples and that one should enter them in a state of purity as one enters the temple of a god.[15]

The ritual sequence outlined in both the nonroyal tombs and in the Pyramid Texts can be divided into four segments by means of three censings that occur throughout:

First segment. The first segment of the ritual sequence in both the elite tomb chapels and royal Pyramid Texts is a single *z̠ȝt* libation. The elite tombs depict this initial ritual with one or two priests pouring liquid. When two priests occur, the first typically kneels in front and receives water onto an offering table or slab poured from over his head by another priest standing behind (Fig. 1).[16] This combination creates an artistic parallel of the hieroglyphics sign for wʿb "to purify."[17] In the Pyramid Texts of Unas, Teti, and Pepi I, the z3t̲ is performed as a purification against those who "speak evil of [the king's] name."[18] Purifying by removing evil via water is a common initial ritual in ancient Egypt.[19]

First censing. Between the first and second segments of the ritual sequence is a censing. In the non-royal tomb chapels, this is typically depicted by a priest holding a censing cup in one hand while holding or lifting the lid of the censer in the other (Fig. 2).[20] In the PT offering rituals of Unas, Teti, and Pepi I, this rite consists of the command to "let the smell of Horus's eye [the incense as offering] adhere to you."[21] Later in the final censing of Unas's offering list, the text states, "let your scent be on Unas and purify Unas."[22] This suggests that censing includes the idea of removing impurities with a sweet smell.

Fig. 2. Tomb of *Mrj-ttj*.

Second segment. The second segment of the Old Kingdom ritual sequence includes the Opening of the Mouth ritual, featuring a washing and small meal, followed by an anointing and a clothing rite. According to the Pyramid Texts, the "Opening of the Mouth" begins with a washing with k̲bḥw "cool water" that is mixed with natron pellets, giving the water the appearance of milk. This "milk" will "part the mouth" of the recipient, whose mouth is like the mouth of a "calf on the day it is born."[23] The natron solution placed "on [the] mouth" appears to "clean all your bones and end that which is against you."[24] A flint tool is mentioned, which is used in later periods to symbolically part or open the mouth, after which the recipient receives instruction to drink the "milk."[25] Following the mouth cleansing and opening, the Pyramid Texts prescribe a small meal of onions, bread, wine, and beer, among other things.[26]

E. Otto's reconstruction of the Opening of the Mouth ritual portrays this meal with a priest kneeling with hands palm down on an offering table, and a priest pouring water from behind over the head of the first priest (Fig. 3).[27] Following is another priest making an offering gesture—i.e., a hand extended forward with the palm up—and three more priests who kneel crossing one

Fig. 3. Opening of the mouth meal offering.

Fig. 4. Tomb of K3r.

arm across their chests with the hand closed in a fist, while they raise the other arm to the square with hand closed in a fist as well. This latter gesture is called *hnw* based upon its later appearance as a determinative in the hieroglyphics for the word *hnw* "cheer, jubilation." However, the actual purpose of these three priests in this context is difficult to determine. All of this takes place before a standing image of the deceased with a table piled with the opening of the mouth meal offerings.

The priestly iconography associated with the Old Kingdom Memphite elite tomb offering lists reflect the same elements outlined above. On the west wall in the tomb of *K3r* (VI.4, Giza)[28] the initial *z3t* libation is followed by an individual who holds out a basin in front of him, a small offering before him contains a natron ball and a few food offerings. The caption above states "sending the voice with the offering necessities" (Fig. 4).[29]

The presence of the basin, natron ball, and other edible goods on the small table following a *z3t* libation appear to signify both the natron solution for the mouth washing as well as the small Opening of the Mouth meal that closely follows. After depictions of the natron washing or placing of goods for the "opening of the mouth" meal, several of the elite tomb chapels include the three

Fig. 5. Tomb of *Mtn*.

priests making the *hnw* gesture outlined above. The only two occurrences of the actual words *wpt-r* "opening of the mouth" in the Memphite elite tomb chapels appear in the tomb of *Mtn* (see Fig. 5).[30] In both cases the term appears next to a *wtj* priest who makes a variation of the *hnw* gesture,[31] suggesting that this pose does indeed relate to the opening of the mouth ritual.

A scene of anointing immediately follows those poses depicting the Opening of the Mouth in the tomb of *K3r* (VI.4, Giza).[32] The first person in the scene extends out his little finger on each hand in the standard gesture of anointing (Fig. 6).[33] The accompanying label, *wrh* "anointing," describes the action. Stephen Thompson demonstrated that the term *wrḥ* is the term for anointing the head throughout Egyptian history, whereas other terms appear for the anointing of other parts of the body.³⁴ Another person follows, carrying various jars on a table. Accompanying him is the label *mrḥwt* "oils" and an accompanying texts that states "It is for salving him."³⁵

Likewise, the Pyramid Texts indicate an anointing with seven oils occurs after the Opening of the Mouth. In Unas's pyramid the text reads, "Oil, Oil, where should you be? You on Horus's head, where should you be? You were on Horus's head, but I will put you on this Unis's head. . . . You will glorify him under you."³⁶ The text here focuses upon placing oil on Unas's head. Thompson indicates that the seven sacred oils correspond to the anointing of the seven openings of the head—namely the two eyes, two ears, two nostrils, and mouth.³⁷ *Wrḥ* does not actually appear at this point in the Pyramid Texts, but the mention of putting oil on the head of Unas implies it.

Fig. 6. Tomb of *K3r*.

The next rite in both the elite tomb chapels and the Pyramid Texts is the offering of two strips or rolls of linen. In the tomb scenes, priests extend both hands forward while grasping a strip or roll of linen in each (Fig. 7. Tomb of NTr-wsr.).[38] The label *wnḫw(j)* "two rolls/strips of cloth" identifies the product they are holding out.

The PT seem to indicate that these are not just strips or bolts of cloth but actually represent wearable apparel. In relationship to the two strips of linen, PT 81 summons Ta'it, the goddess of linen or weaving, to awake and describes her as the one "whom the made-up woman receives" and "who adorns the great one in the sedan chair."[39] That a "made-up" woman personified as a goddess receives the linen and that it "adorns" implies that it is something one wears. Indeed, Teti's pyramid states, "your mother Ta'it will clothe you," linking this goddess, and by extension the linen she represents, explicitly to the idea of clothing.[40] Likewise, Middle Kingdom copies

Fig. 7. Tomb of *Nṯr-wsr*.

of the Pyramid Texts actually label this part of the offering list sequence as "clothing" rather than $wnḫw(j)$ "two strips/rolls of linen" indicating that is how they understood this passage.[41]

Second censing. Between the second and third segments of the ritual sequence is another censing ritual. The Pyramid Texts repeat the text of the first incense offering immediately following the anointing and presentation of two strips/rolls of linen.[42] Likewise, a secondary censing follows the presentation of cloth in the elite tombs such as $Nṯr-wsr$'s (Fig. 7. Tomb of NTr-wsr.).[43]

Third segment. Following the second censing, the third segment in both the Pyramid Texts and elite tomb chapels include rites related to a meal offering of a grand scale as well as a ritual bestowal of insignia. The Pyramid Texts begins this segment by repeating the spell for the natron solution that washes the mouth in preparation for the small meal in the former segment, including the specific prescription of two natron balls.[44] The text then continues with the preparation of the offering table and a lengthy list of various food items, including several meat offerings that start with a bovine foreleg and conclude with geese, duck, and pigeon.[45]

Several of the elite tombs have scenes that portray a similar sequence. Following the second censing in the tomb of $K₃r$, two additional priests prepare a natron solution with $kbḥw$ "cool water" and two pellets of natron, exactly as the Pyramid Texts prescribe (Fig. 8).[46]

After the natron libation, several tombs portray either a kneeling priest who places offerings on an offering table or a standing priest who makes an offering gesture. On the north wall of $ᶜnḫ-mrj-Rᶜ$'s tomb, a priest kneels and makes an offering at an offering table (with lectors holding open scrolls standing by) representing the presentation of this great meal offering, while priests bearing forelegs and other goods follow immediately.[47] Many tomb chapels often display large groups of priests carrying goods towards the false door of the elite chapels carrying forelegs first and then fowl. In the tomb of $K₃-gm-nj$, priests bear forelegs followed by other priests bringing geese, ducks, and pigeons corresponding precisely to the order of meat offerings in the Pyramid Text for this meal. These connections suggest that the long line of offering bearers bringing goods belong to the great meal portion of the ritual sequence, even though these long lines often appear outside the actual ritual sequence due to their great numbers.

Fig. 8. Tomb of *K3r*.

The next ritual after the Great Meal offering in the Pyramid Text offering list of Unas consists of bestowing scepters, staves, and other insignia that indicate the deceased king's power to "govern."[48] In this context the recipient is commanded to "get dressed" four times, including, in Teti's pyramid texts, in a leopard skin, kilt, and sandals. This stands in contrast to the simple linen cloth offerings in the previous segment. The elite tomb of *Hsj* contains a brief sequence on the south wall that reflects this PT ritual (Fig. 9).[49] A lector priest, making the offering gesture with the label "offering things by the lector," stands before the deceased who sits behind his offering table, possibly indicating the great meal offering represented by the offering list above the table. Behind the lector stands a figure who carries a scepter or baton in his hand. The label above him states "reciting a great many glorifications."

After the bestowal of insignia, the Pyramid Texts and the elite tomb sequence indicate a *wdb* "reversion [of the offerings]" rite took place.[50] This is typically understood as a redistribution rite in which a priest or some other entity takes the offering goods that were given to a god, king, or private individual and then distributes them elsewhere, mainly to other subordinate entities.[51] In the elite tomb chapels, the reversion rite appears to be closely connected

The Context of Old Testament Temple Worship 169

Fig. 9. Tomb of *Ḥzj*.

with the *jnt rd* "bringing the foot" rite, which typically includes a depiction of a priest sweeping with a broom. Not mentioned in the PT, this sweeping ritual was a terminal rite in the daily temple ritual wherein the priests swept away their own footprints after closing the shrine of the god and vacating the premises.[52]

The last two sets of squares in the offering list grid in the tomb of Mehu contains two figures with text above each (Fig. 10).[53] On the left is an offering bearer who carries a table of offerings. The text above states: *wḏb ḥt* "reverting offerings." To the immediate right is an individual with a broom. The text above him states: *jnt rd* "bringing the foot." Even though the text is oriented in the same direction as the other offerings in the grid, suggesting they are a part of that scene, the bodies of both individuals are in reverse with their feet

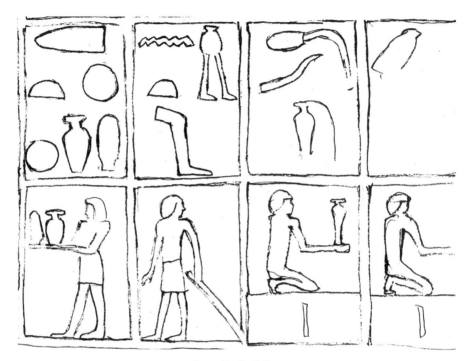

Fig. 10. Tomb of *Mḥw*.

Fig. 11. Tomb of *K3-gm-nj*.

apart, suggesting they are walking away from the image of the owner seated at the offering table. The head of the one with the broom turns to face back towards the seated owner, which is typical for this pose, but his body and trailing broom indicate clearly the direction he moves. The lector priest who is *jnt rd* appears, in this context, to follow the priest who has already picked up the offerings and is walking out.

In contrast, an individual kneels at an offering table with the label *wdb ḫt* in the same direction at the main offering list sequence in *K3-gm-nj*'s tomb (Fig. 11).[54] To his right is a lector in reverse pose, dragging a broom towards the reversion pose. The reason the individual in the reversion pose in not in reverse as in Mehu's tomb may simply be a difference in the representation of time. Here he is kneeling and the offering table is on the ground, whereas in Mehu he is standing with the table in his hand and walking out.

After the reversion of offerings, the elite tombs and Pyramid Texts indicate a double libation takes place. The first libation is a final natron-washing spell that we encountered twice before as it preceded meals, only this time there is no indication of a meal. The second libation is a *z3t* libation, the same libation as the one at the beginning of the sequence. The tomb of *K3-gm-nj* portrays this double libation in the proper sequence (Fig. 12).[55]

Final (third) censing. In the Pyramid Texts and elite tomb chapels, a third and final offering of incense occurs after the final libations. The Pyramid Texts repeat the script associated with the previous two censings; however, some material is added. Unlike the previous two censings, the text indicates that this

Fig. 12. *K3-gm-nj*.

third censing is of "great purity" and is to become "high and big," and the king is to become pure through it.[56] The use of "great," "high," and "big" magnify its purpose in comparison with the earlier censings. This may indicate a progression as the recipient attains a higher or greater degree of purity than before.

Fourth and final segment. The concluding rite in the Pyramid Text offering lists is the "smashing red pots." Sethe links the breaking of red pots to execration, which is a rite used to curse an enemy.[57] The Pyramid Text offering list indicates that the purpose of the smashing of red pots is "that you may become powerful and that he [an enemy] may become terrified of you," providing proof for Sethe's conclusion.[58]

In the elite tomb chapel offering-list grid of *Ḥsj* (VI.1–2, Saqqara), "smashing red pots" is also the concluding rite. However, this rite sometimes occurs in the same position as the reversion of offerings; i.e., immediately after the *jnt rd* and before the concluding rites. In fact, the tombs of *Mrrw-k3.j* and *Mry-ttj* depict the individual "breaking red pots" in the same pose as the reversion of offerings pose—i.e., kneeling with both hands extended palm down with finger tips on a small offering table or slab (see Fig. 13 and compare with Fig. 11 above). The only indicator that this is a "breaking red pots" pose and not the reversion of offerings is the text label.[59]

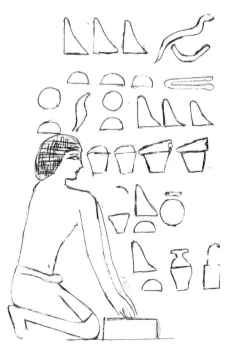

Fig. 13. *Mry-ttj*.

At the end of the offering sequence in a few elite tomb chapels is a man who carries a bag. In the tombs of *K3.j-m-ʿnḫ* and *Nj-ḥtp-Ptḥ*, this figure crosses one of his arms across his chest grabbing the opposite shoulder as a sign of veneration (see Figs. 14–15).[60] In *K3.j-m-ʿnḫ* he is shown in a reverse pose, and in *Nj-ḥtp-Ptḥ* two appear in a row with a title for each—*ḥtmw* "sealer."

Due to the lack of a Pyramid Text parallel, the purpose of the sealer in this ritual sequence is difficult to ascertain. The reverse pose of

The Context of Old Testament Temple Worship 173

Fig. 14. Tomb of *K3.j-m-ʿnẖ*.

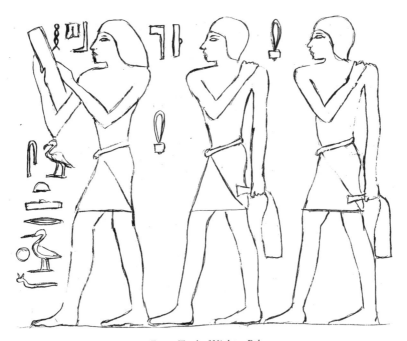

Fig. 15. Tomb of *Nj-ḥtp-Ptḥ*.

the sealer in *K3.j-m-ʿnḫ* may provide a clue. The only other characters in the elite tombs in a reverse pose are those "bringing the foot" and "reverting offerings," actions pertaining to leaving the offering place. A sealer departing a sanctuary at the end of a series of rites brings to mind the sealers who complete the daily temple services of the statue rites in royal and divine temples of later periods by sealing the shrine doors closed and walking out.[61]

Another idea is suggested by the hieroglyphics before the sealer's face in *Nj-ḥtp-Ptḥ* that relate him to a *mdȝt nṯr* "divine document." Some tomb biographies of the Old Kingdom contain statements of the deceased regarding knowledge of such documents. For example, the tomb of Tjy declares, "I am initiated in all secrets of the house of divine documents."[62] Since sealing, as a general practice, "was used to guarantee the identity of the sender and authenticate the contents of private, legal, and official documents,"[63] a sealer in this context may provide an official stamp of approval on the rituals by which the deceased was initiated into the secrets of the document, having the legal status of a sealed document.

Finally, Kuraszkiewicz concludes that the *ḥtmtj nṯr* "god's sealer", meaning the king's sealer, in the Old Kingdom is "responsible for supplying rare and valuable materials,"[64] perhaps this title's stewardship over goods in the royal sphere reflects some purpose of the *ḥtmw* in the elite tomb as well as goods are central to the offering rites.

Some Comparisons between the Egyptian and Old Testament Temple Traditions

The Egyptian sequence outlined above has some similarity with the Old Testament temple tradition that, outlined here, may be of use for a further in-depth study.

The three Egyptian censings and the three areas of the Old Testament sanctuary. Segmenting the rites in connection with burning incense three times in the Egyptian sequence may have some corollaries with the Old Testament temple tradition: (1) In the Old Testament sources, burning incense on the sacrificial altar (with the grain offering) and the use of portable censers for other purposes occurred outside the temple in the courtyard (e.g., Leviticus 2:1–3, 14–16; Numbers 16:17–18). The courtyard is also the place where priests were washed, anointed, clothed and ate the sacrifices (see Exodus 29:1–9, 31–33;

Deuteronomy 12:17–19). Likewise, in the Egyptian sequence the first censing appears in connection with the "Opening of the Mouth" washing and meal, followed by anointing and clothing rites. (2) In Old Testament temple worship, daily censing occurred on the altar of incense in the Holy Place in connection with the lamp lighting (see Exodus 30:7–8) and in the same room as the table of shewbread, which is meant to indicate a feast of some kind. Likewise, a second censing appears in connection with a great offering meal in the Egyptian sources. (3) In the Old Testament tradition, a third censing occurred with a portable censer, on the Day of Atonement in the Holy of Holies, as the high priest enters the presence of God (Leviticus 16:12–13). This censing, the holiest of all, may echo the third and final censing in the Egyptian sources which was "big," "great" and "high" in comparison with the previous censings and which preceded the final rites.[65]

Segment 1 of the Egyptian sequence and initial approaches to God in the Old Testament tradition. Additional more specific corollaries appear in the details of the individual rituals within each segment. As outlined above, the first ritual segment preceding the first censing in the Egyptian sequence is an initial libation that they viewed as a purification against those who "speak evil of [the king's] name." While no initial libation is explicitly mentioned in the daily offering program of the Israelite temple, ritual libations are mentioned elsewhere. In 1 Samuel 7:6 it states, "And they gathered together to Mizpeh, and drew water, and poured it out before the Lord, and fasted on that day, and said there, We have sinned against the Lord. And Samuel judged the children of Israel in Mizpeh." Pouring water out "before the Lord" because one has sinned "against the Lord" is similar to the Egyptian sources that state the water is poured out because one has spoken against the king.

In the Old Testament tradition, pouring out water signifies lowliness, repentance, and the hopeful dissipation of sin, like water seeping into the earth, as seen in passages such as 1 Samuel 1:15; 2 Samuel 14:14; Job 11:16; Psalms 22:14, 62:8. Likewise, Jeremiah, using temple imagery, pleads with Israel to "lift up their hands toward [God]" and pray, in the "beginning of the watches," they should "pour out thine heart like water before the face of the Lord" (Lamentations 2:19). This emphasizes their need to repent as the first thing one does, at the beginning of the watch, when approaching the Lord. The pouring of the blood of the sacrifices "upon the earth as water" in Deut. 12:24 may have some connection here.

Segment 2 of the Egyptian sequence and the Old Testament temple courtyard. The Egyptian rituals in the second segment outlined above include the "Opening of the Mouth" washing and eating followed by an anointing and clothing. These closely match similar rituals performed in the courtyard of the Israelite temple wherein the priests were prepared by means of a washing, clothing, and anointing ritual (see Exodus 29:4–9), followed by the eating of ram meat and bread (see Exodus 29:31–33). This Aaronic ordination includes the command to "consecrate (literally "to fill the hand of") Aaron and his sons" (Exodus 29:9). The image of the Aaronic priests with outstretched hands ready to be filled matches the offering gesture of the Egyptian priests, who stand with one arm outstretched and palm up, in connection with these rites.

The "Opening of the Mouth" also has parallels in the preparations of Old Testament patriarchs and prophets in temple settings as well. In the temple before God, Isaiah declared himself a man of "unclean lips," and thus a seraphim took "a live coal in his hand" and "laid it upon [his] mouth," "touched [his] lips," and declared Isaiah's sin "purged" (Isaiah 6:1, 5–7). God then tells Isaiah to "go, and tell" (Isaiah 6:9). When Jeremiah was being called to serve, he stated, "I cannot speak: for I am a child," but God "put forth his hand, and touched [his] mouth" and said, "I have put my words in thy mouth" (Jeremiah 1:6–9). Likewise, the Lord commanded Ezekiel while in the temple to "open thy mouth, and eat that I give thee." He was given a book. Ezekiel then said, "So I opened my mouth, and he caused me to eat that roll. . . . And he said unto me, Son of man, go, . . . and speak" (Ezekiel 2:8; 3:2–4). Moses and Enoch's declaration of being "slow of speech" fits this scenario as well (see Exodus 4:10; Moses 6:31).[66] Not only may a prophet's mouth be ritually opened, but their eyes may be ritually opened also, as was the case with Enoch mentioned at the beginning of this study (see Moses 6:35–36). As outlined above, the "opening" and anointing in the Egyptian material include the mouth, eyes, ears, and nose.

Segment 3 of the Egyptian sequence and the Holy Place. The main focus of the third segment in the Egyptian sources is the great meal offering with its long lists of food offerings in the PT or long lines of offering bearers in the nonroyal tombs. In the Holy Place, the table of shewbread appears to represent some sort of feast as well. While bread and frankincense are the only consumables mentioned in scripture with regard to this table, the placement of all manner of vessels and utensils suggest a grander fare (see Exodus 35:13; Numbers 4:7; 1 Chronicles 28:16–17).

The bestowal of scepters and staves along with a leopard skin covering, kilt, and sandals in this segment of the Egyptian tradition stands in contrast to the simple linen offering in the clothing ritual of the previous segment. This can reflect similar concepts in the clothing differences between the more simply clothed priest and the more elaborately clothed high priest in the Old Testament temple tradition (see Exodus 28). In the earlier sources of Israelite temple tradition, the priests appear confined to the courtyard as far as temple service is concerned. Only the high priest performed the services in the holy place such as lighting the lamps, burning incense, and changing the shewbread (e.g., see Exodus 30:7–9; Leviticus 24:2–3, 8). The investiture of Joshua in the high priestly clothing of the Second Temple period is also placed in a temple context, including an associated ritual drama starring various heavenly hosts, including Satan who is cast out (see Zechariah 3). Enoch's declaration that he was "clothed with glory" during his "high mountain" experience may relate (see Moses 7:3).

The Egyptian offering list sequence of the Old Kingdom outlined herein does not appear to have a ritual of lamp lighting that would correlate to the lamp of the Old Testament temple's holy place; however, in the Pyramid Texts as a whole, there is one mention of lighting a lamp and it is in connection with opening the "gate of heaven" (temple doors?) and entering into the "darkness" beyond.[67] However, this appears outside the standard offering list sequence and thus would be a difference between these two traditions that could be explored further.

The last libations, preceding the final censing and final rites, in the Egyptian sequence may echo the final libation Jacob performs near the end of his life in connection with God making sure his covenant promises in Genesis 35:9–15.

The fourth segment of the Egyptian sequence and the Holy of Holies. The last rites of the Egyptian sequence have two purposes: (1) to affirm power over one's enemies via the execration ritual of smashing the red pots, and (2) to seal, or make legally binding in relation to a "divine document," the rituals. Likewise, as outlined in the first section of this study concerning true temple worship in the early patriarchal period, those who enter the highest order of the temple, represented by the Holy of Holies, are given great power in the priesthood with which they can confound their enemies (see JST, Genesis 14:30–31, wherein they receive power to "put at defiance the armies of nations" and "break every band." Even "break[ing] mountains" and "divid[ing] the seas" were powers used against enemies (see Moses 7:13–14; Exodus 14:27)).[68]

While "sealers," "sealing," and "divine documents" as a conclusion of temple rituals is not explicit in the Old Testament temple worship, Nehemiah 9:38 may be a distant Second Temple period corollary: "And because of all this we make a sure covenant, and write it; and our princes, Levites, and priests, seal unto it." The mention of Levites and priests sealing a writing relative to the covenant points to the temple, since the covenant itself is explicitly associated with the temple in Malachi 3:1.[69]

Conclusion

The above are just a few points of comparison between temple rituals of an early period in Egyptian history with the scriptural tradition concerning temple worship among the early patriarchs and those descendants who preserved it. It is hoped that these comparisons increase awareness of the similarities between these two cultures from a very early period and provide an additional cultural comparison and contrast in order to deepen understanding of Old Testament temple worship. Further, it is hoped that the complexity of the early Egyptian ritual program dating from 2600–2100 BC and its similarity to scriptural traditions concerning Old Testament worship reveals just how complex the Old Testament temple rites could actually be at a very early date, calling into question some assumptions of modern scholars concerning the dating and nature of early Old Testament temple worship in general.

Notes

1. James B. Pritchard, *Ancient Near Eastern Texts Relating to the Old Testament*, 3rd ed. (Princeton: Princeton University Press, 1969); William W. Hallo and K. Lawson Younger, *The Context of Scripture* (Leiden, New York: Brill, 1997). For a current list of the Writings of the Ancient World series, see http://www.sbl-site.org/publications/Books_WAW.aspx.

2. A standard and important article on the dangers of overreaching conclusions based on similarities between two traditions is Samuel Sandmel, "Parallelomania," *Journal of Biblical Literature* 81 (1962): 1–13.

3. William W. Hallo, "The Bible in Its Near Eastern Setting: The Contextual Approach," in *Scripture in Context: Essays on Comparative Method*, ed. C. Evans and others

(Pittsburgh: Pickwick Press, 1980), 1–26, argues that comparative methods (highlighting similarities) must be supplemented with contrastive methods (highlighting differences). Blending the two makes a "contextual" method.

4. In addition to the important essays on the comparative method mentioned in notes 2 and 3, see also Shemaryahu Talmon, "The 'Comparative Method' in Biblical Interpretation—Principles and Problems," in *Congress Volume: Göttingen, 1977*, ed. J. A. Emerton, *Supplements to Vetus Testamentum* 29 (Leiden: E. J. Brill, 1978), 320–56.

5. For some broad examples of shared temple ideologies, see John M. Lunquist, *The Temple* (London: Thames & Hudson, 2012) and his "What Is a Temple? A Preliminary Typology," in *Temples of the Ancient World*, ed. Donald W. Parry (Salt Lake City: Deseret Book, 1994), 83–117.

6. A culminating temple ordinance that confirms all things is also mentioned in D&C 124:39, wherein the Lord states that all the washing, anointings, work for the dead, solemn assemblies, revelations, statutes, and judgments are confirmed or "ordained" by "*the* ordinance of my holy house"(emphasis added). D&C 132:7 refers to this culminating ordinance as a "seal."

7. The teachings of Joseph Smith and others demonstrate that entering an "order" wherein one is called a "son of God" is more than just the initial bestowal of Melchizedek Priesthood by the laying on of hands, though it begins there. Rather, after the laying on of hands, one must progress through various orders by making and keeping temple covenants until they attain to the highest order. For example, the Doctrine and Covenants declares that temple marriage is one particular "order" of the priesthood that a person can enter (see D&C 131:2). Joseph Smith explained that the highest order, which he called the "Melchizedek order," is entered when one has been "called, elected, and made sure." (*The Words of Joseph Smith*, ed. Andrew F. Ehat and Lyndon W. Cook (Orem, UT: Grandin, 1991), 244; spelling and punctuation standardized). Those who enter this highest order, having first been "tried so as by fire," are given the title "sons of God" (Joseph Smith Translation [hereafter JST], Genesis 14:35) and are given great powers in the priesthood such as the power to move mountains and divide the seas (JST, Genesis 14:30–31; cf. Helaman 10:1–11). President Ezra Taft Benson indicated that when scripture declares that Adam entered this "order" wherein he was called a "son of God," it means that Adam received "the fullness of the Melchizedek Priesthood, which is only received in the house of the Lord." "What I Hope You Will Teach Your Children about the Temple," *Ensign*, August 1985, 8; cf. D&C 124:25–28.

8. For more discussion of Garden of Eden as temple, see G. K. Beale, *Temple and the Church's Mission* (Downers Grove, IL: InterVarsity Press, 2004); Donald W. Parry, "Garden of Eden: Prototype Sanctuary," in *Temples of the Ancient World*, ed. Donald W. Parry (Salt Lake City: Deseret Book, 1994), 126–51.

9. While the scriptures do not explicitly mention an altar built by Adam, one can be implied from the fact that he made sacrificial offerings (see Moses 5:4–5). Additionally, Joseph Smith appears to have taught Brigham Young that Adam did indeed build an altar: "Joseph the Prophet told me that . . . when Adam was driven out of the Garden of Eden he . . . built an altar of stone and offered sacrifice." (Brigham

Young as quoted by Wilford Woodruff, *Waiting for World's End: The Diaries of Wilford Woodruff*, ed. Susan Staker (Salt Lake City: Signature Books, 1993), 305; spelling and punctuation standardized.)

10. The title "high priest" in such contexts is indicative of one who has entered the highest order of the priesthood (as Jesus himself is called a high priest after the order of Melchizedek in Hebrews 6:20) and is a different use of the title than the office of high priest in the LDS Church today. Consequently, being "ordained an high priest" (JST, Genesis 14:27) is also different than the modern idea of receiving the laying on of hands for the conferral of an office. Rather, "ordained" can have reference to temple ordinances as Alma 13:2 (cf. 13:16) makes clear.

11. *Words of Joseph Smith*, 245. Joseph Smith and the Epistle to the Hebrews give clarity to Genesis 22:15–18, wherein the Lord repeats the Abrahamic covenant after the binding of Isaac, only this time he swears an oath in order to confirm or make sure the blessings of the covenant upon Abraham.

12. The phrase "do we not eat and drink" as a justification for the wicked's claim to be "sons of God" in this verse may have reference to counterfeit ritual meals that they practice, especially since they mention their marriage rituals next, or, at least, it may be they are claiming prosperity as a supposed means of proving their righteousness to Noah.

13. For the most complete treatment of this idea, see John S. Thompson, "The Iconography of the Memphite Priesthood in Egypt's Elite Tombs of the Old Kingdom" (PhD diss., University of Pennsylvania, forthcoming). See also Harold M. Hays, "The Death of the Democratization of the Afterlife," in *Old Kingdom: New Perspectives: Egyptian Art and Archaeology, 2750–2150 BC*, ed. Nigel Strudwick and Helen Strudwick (Cambridge, England: Oxbow Books, 2011), 115–30.

14. See, for example, A. Rosalie David, *A Guide to Religious Ritual at Abydos*, Rev. ed., Modern Egyptology Series (Warminster, England: Aris & Phillips, 1981); Alexandre Moret, *Le Rituel Du Culte Divin Journalier En Égypte, D'après Les Papyrus De Berlin Et Les Textes Du Temple De Séti 1er, À Abydos*, Annales Du Musée Guimet Bibliothèque D'études (Paris: E. Leroux, 1902).

15. Nigel Strudwick, *Texts from the Pyramid Age* (Atlanta: Society of Biblical Literature, 2005), 236, 358. Noted also in John Laurence Gee, "The Requirements of Ritual Purity in Ancient Egypt" (PhD diss., Yale University, 1998), 36, 38.

16. Figure based on Margaret Alice Murray, *Saqqara Mastabas*, 2 vols. (London: British School of Archaeology in Egypt and B. Quaritch, 1905–37), I: XXIII. I would like to acknowledge Hannah Thompson and Hyrum Thompson for their work on and drawings of all the figures herein.

17. Alan Henderson Gardiner, *Egyptian Grammar*, 3rd ed. (Oxford: Griffith Institute Ashmolean Museum, 1957), Sign List, A6.

18. PT 23.

19. Dmitri Meeks, *Pureté Et Purification En Égypte* (Paris: Letouzey & Ané, 1976), 434–35; Robert Krioch Ritner, *The Mechanics of Ancient Egyptian Magical Practice*, Studies in Ancient Oriental Civilization (Chicago: Oriental Institute of University of Chicago, 1993), 101–2, and n. 496.

20. Figure based on Naguib Kanawati and Mahmoud Abder-Raziq, *Mereruka and His Family, Part 1, the Tomb of Meryteti* (Oxford: Aris and Phillips, 2004), pl. 49; James Edward Quibell and others, *The Ramesseum* (London: Histories & Mysteries of Man, 1896), pl. XXXVIII.

21. PT 25.

22. PT 200.

23. PT 32, 34–35.

24. PT 36.

25. PT 37–42.

26. PT 44–57.

27. Figure based on Eberhard Otto, *Das Ägyptische Mundöffnungsritual* (Wiesbaden: Otto Harrassowitz, 1960), 153–55, scene 69A-C.

28. Roman and Arabic numerals as here indicate the relative dates of tombs. Roman numerals indicate the Egyptian Dynasty and Arabic numerals indicate the ruler within the Dynasty, following the convention outlined in Yvonne Harpur, *Decoration in Egyptian Tombs of the Old Kingdom* (London; New York: Kegan Paul, 1987).

29. Figure based on William Kelly Simpson, *The Mastabas of Qar and Idu (G7101 and 7102)*, Giza Mastabas (Boston: Museum of Fine Arts, 1976), fig. 25.

30. Figure based on Richard Lepsius, *Denkmäler aux Aegypten und Aethiopien*, 12 Vols. (Berlin: Nicolaische Buchhandlung, 1849–1859), Vol. II: B1.4.

31. Brigitte Dominicus, *Gesten Und Gebärden in Darstellungen Des Alten Und Mittleren Reiches*, Studien Zur Archäologie Und Geschichte Altägyptens (Heidelberg: Heidelberger Orientverlag, 1994), 61–65.

32. Figure based on Simpson, fig. 25.

33. See Stephen E. Thompson, "A Lexicographic and Iconographic Analysis of Anointing in Ancient Egypt" (PhD diss., Brown University, 1991), 255.

34. Thompson, 253–54.

35. Simpson, 7.

36. PT 77.

37. Thompson, 220–21.

38. Figure based on Murray, I: XXIII.

39. PT 81. See James P. Allen, *The Ancient Egyptian Pyramid Texts*, Writings from the Ancient World, No. 23 (Atlanta: Society of Biblical Literature, 2005), 22.

40. PT 417.

41. Allen, 62, n.18.

42. Allen's category labels are sometimes confusing with regard to the rituals being performed. For example, he indicates the second censing spell is part of a "Libation and Cleansing" (p. 23) when in fact it is a censing followed by a natron solution cleansing so "Censing and Cleansing" would be a more appropriate header.

43. Figure based on Murray, I: XXIII; Simpson, fig. 25.

44. PT 32.

45. PT 126–140.

46. Figure based on Simpson, fig. 25.

47. Hartwig Altenmüller, *Die Wanddarstellungen Im Grab Des Mehu in Saqqara* (Mainz: Philipp von Zabern, 1998), Tafel 90.

48. PT 224.

49. Figure based on Naguib Kanawati and Mahmoud Abder-Raziq, *The Teti Cemetery at Saqqara. Vol. 5, the Tomb of Hesi* (Warminster: Aris and Philips, 1999), pl. 64.

50. PT 199.

51. Paule Posener-Kriéger, *Les Archives Du Temple Funéraire De Néferirkarê-Kakaï (Les Papyrus D'abousir): Traduction Et Commentaire*, Bibliothèque D'étude, T. 65/1–2 ([Le Caire]: Institut français d'archéologie orientale du Caire, 1976), 405–12.

52. Harold H. Nelson, "The Rite of 'Bringing the Foot' as Portrayed in Temple Reliefs," *The Journal of Egyptian Archaeology* 35 (1949): 82–86.

53. Figure based on Altenmüller, Tafel 58.

54. Yvonne Harpur and Paolo J. Scremin, *The Chapel of Kagemni: Scene Details, Egypt in Miniature* (Reading, England: Oxford Expedition to Egypt, 2006), context drawing 31.

55. Harpur and Scremin, Context Drawings 31.

56. PT 200.

57. Kurt Heinrich Sethe, *Die Achtung Feindlicher Fürsten, Völker Und Dinge Auf Altägyptischen Tongefässcherben Des Mittleren Reiches. Nach Den Originalen Im Berliner Museum Herausgegeben Und Erklärt Von K. Sethe, Etc.* [Abhandlungen Der Preussischen Akademie Der Wissenschaften; Jahrg. 1926; Phil.-Hist. Klasse no. 5], p. 74., pl. 33.

58. As indicated by Ritner, 146. For a more complete discussion of this rite, see 144–53.

59. Figure based on Kanawati and Abder-Raziq, *Mereruka and His Family. Part 1, The Tomb of Meryteti*, I, pl. 49.

60. Figure based on Hermann Junker, *Gîza*, 12 vols., Denkschriften / Akademie Der Wissenschaften in Wien. Philosophisch-Historische Klasse (Wien; Leipzig: Hölder-Pichler-Tempsky A.-G., 1929–55), vol. 4, abb. 7; Naguib Kanawati, *Tombs at Giza. Vol. 1, Kaiemankh (G4561) and Seshemnefer (G4940)*, The Australian Centre for Egyptology. Studies (Warminster: Aris and Phillips, 2001), pl. 29, and Alexander Badawy, *The Tomb of Nyhetep-Ptah at Giza and the Tomb of 'ankhm'ahor at Saqqara* (Berkeley: University of California Press, 1978), pl. 7; Richard Lepsius, *Denkmäler Aus Aegypten Und Aethiopien*, 12 vols. (Berlin: Nicolaische Buchhandlung, 1849–59), abb. II, bl. 71, respectively.

61. P. Berlin 3055 3/5–8 in *Hieratische Papyrus Aus Den Königlichen Museen Zu Berlin*, 5 vols. (Leipzig: J.C. Hinrichs, 1901), vol. 1, pl. 3.

62. Henri Wild, "L'adresse Aux Visiteurs Du Tombeau De Ti," *BIFAO* 58 (1953): 101–13.

63. Stuart Tyson Smith, *Administration at the Egyptian Middle Kingdom Frontier: Sealings from Uronarti and Askut* (Liege: Université Liege, 1990), 201.

64. Kamil O. Kuraszkiewicz, "The Title *Xtmtj Ntr*—God's Sealer—in the Old Kingdom," in *The Old Kingdom Art and Archaeology: Proceedings of the Conference in Prague 2004*, ed. Miroslav Bárta (Prague: Czech Institute of Egyptology, 2006), 200.

65. For further discussions of incense usage in Israel including its possible connection with Egypt in general, see Menahem Haran, *Temples and Temple-Service in Ancient Israel: An Inquiry into the Character of Cult Phenomena and the Historical Setting of the*

Priestly School (Oxford: Clarendon Press, 1978), 239–41; Paul Heger, *The Development of Incense Cult in Israel* (Berlin: Walter de Gruyter, 1997).

66. For further discussion of this motif, including Egyptian and biblical parallels, see Gregory Galsov, *The Bridling of the Tongue and the Opening of the Mouth in Biblical Prophecy* (Sheffield: Sheffield Academic Press, 2001).

67. PT 361–62 from the pyramid of Teti.

68. The explicit relationship between these final blessings of having power over the wicked and sealing appears when God swears the oath to Nephi in Helaman 10:6-10.

69. For sealed documents in ancient tradition in general, see John W. Welch, "Doubled, Sealed, Witnessed Documents: From the Ancient World to the Book of Mormon," in *Mormons, Scripture, and the Ancient World*, ed. Davis Bitton (Provo, UT: FARMS, 1998), 391–444.

11

The Rejection and Rehabilitation of Worship in the Old Testament

Jared M. Halverson

Throughout history, much of worship's role in revealed religion has been to give voice to the ineffable, form to the invisible, and outlet to the inexpressible. Worship is a conduit—not only to give God a way of revealing himself to his children, but to give those children a means whereby they can express themselves to God. Whether sacrificial offerings in ancient Israel or temple work in the Church today, liturgical forms and ritualistic practices have allowed the faithful to communicate their devotion to and reverence for God in ways that convert the internal and invisible into the external and discernible—providing embodiment for those heartfelt "groanings which cannot be uttered" (Romans 8:26). True worship has always been a delicate balance between belief and behavior, in which sacraments and sentiments merge into one.

Of course, worship's outward actions and inward attitudes are not inherently coexistent. The presence of the first does not necessarily verify the reality of the second, as evidenced by the Lord's lament to both Isaiah and Joseph Smith that some who "draw near [him] . . . with their lips" have "hearts [that

---

Jared M. Halverson is director of the Nashville Tennessee Institute of Religion.

are] far from [him]" (Isaiah 29:13; Joseph Smith—History 1:19). Unfortunately, the very process of externalization sometimes substitutes for the true purposes of worship, until ritual becomes routinized and form supplants function. Thus debased, mere participation in worship often passes for true engagement with God, fooling some adherents into settling for outward compliance when inward conversion is required. More hollowed than hallowed, such empty exteriority leaves so-called worshippers following the "form of godliness," even while denying themselves "the power thereof" (2 Timothy 3:5; see also Joseph Smith—History 1:19). No wonder it is "true worshippers," as Jesus told the woman at the well, that the Father "seeketh," for harder to find than mere church-goers are those who truly "worship [God] in spirit and in truth" (John 4:23–24).

If finding true worship was something of a selective search when this New Testament conversation took place, the same could be said of the Old Testament history which precedes it. The same Samaritan woman, for example, defined her ancestors' worship in terms of place rather than piety and described Jewish worship in the same light (see John 4:20), as if location had become more important than intent. Indeed, throughout much of the Old Testament text, in which Israelite worship entailed a complex assemblage of sacrificial rites and elaborate rituals, whenever prophets cautioned Israel against mistaking worship's external means for its internal ends, they were sounding a familiar theme, one that constitutes the subject of this study. In examining this issue, I will show, first, that much of the worship decried as degenerate in the pages of the Old Testament entailed Israel losing sight of worship's inner purposes while remaining active in its outer forms. Second, I will argue that in order to rehabilitate Israelite worship internally, God often rejected it externally. At times literally, though more often rhetorically, God frequently stripped away the external forms to reveal the lack of internal function, reenthroning the inner purposes of worship by calling into question the outer practices such ritual entailed. In doing so, God also pointed worshippers forward to a time of even greater internalization to come, one embodied in the new covenant of Jesus Christ.

True Worship: "An Outward Expression of an Inner Commitment"

With the law of Moses determining the worship patterns throughout most of the Old Testament text, it is an easy mistake to assign outer form to the Old Testament and inner faith to the New Testament. The law was, after all, a system of external "performances and ordinances," as the Book of Mormon repeatedly attests (see 2 Nephi 25:30; Mosiah 13:30; Alma 30:23; 4 Nephi 1:12), and it was administered under Aaronic authority with its keys concerning "outward ordinances [and] the letter of the gospel" (D&C 107:20). However, like the unfair oversimplification that assigns justice to the Old Testament and mercy to the New Testament, this approach ignores the interiority of worship emphasized long before the Savior came to fulfill the Mosaic law. Adam and Eve were not engaged in the "outward ordinance" of sacrifice for long before they received an inner understanding of its significance and symbolism (see Moses 5:5–8). Cain's offering—though outwardly compliant in some sense—was rejected because it was devoid of an inward faith.[1] The people of Enoch's Zion, while well versed in visible rituals of "water, and blood, and the spirit," were defined more by their internal oneness of heart and mind (Moses 6:59; see also 7:18). Even Moses, whose law has become synonymous with external forms and ritual practices, was far more intent on "sanctify[ing] his people" internally, "that they might behold the face of God" (D&C 84:23). Elder Neal A. Maxwell observed, "Real, personal sacrifice"—one of the most visible forms of worship at the time—"never was placing an animal on the altar. Instead, it is a willingness to put the animal in us upon the altar and letting it be consumed!"[2] In short, throughout Old Testament history, worship was meant to be what signs and sacraments have always been: "an outer expression of an inner commitment."[3]

Old Testament prophets, therefore, taught the external with an eye to the internal, pointing their people to the spirit by upholding the letter. They knew, as did the Apostle Paul, that "he is not a Jew, which is one outwardly, . . . but he is a Jew, which is one inwardly," whose worship "is that of the heart, in the spirit, and not in the letter" (Romans 2:28–29). Thus Jeremiah prophesied of a "law in their inward parts" (Jeremiah 31:33), and Ezekiel wrote of "a new spirit . . . within" (Ezekiel 36:26). Old Testament–era prophets in the Americas were even more explicit, "teaching the law of Moses, *and the intent for which it was given*" (Jarom 1:11; emphasis added), such that the Nephites could simultaneously "keep the law of Moses" (the external) and "look forward to the coming of Christ" (the internal) (Alma 25:15). With such a forward-looking faith in Christ, worshippers could be given outward "performances and ordinances" with the counsel to look through them rather than looking to them, as was the case with the serpent Moses fashioned of brass. It was not the brazen serpent as object but as symbol that allowed the stricken Israelites to look and live, and that symbol pointed both forward to Jesus Christ and inward to the requisite acceptance of his sacrifice. As Nephi, son of Helaman, explained, the outward action of looking had to be accompanied by a pair of inward qualifiers: they had to look "with faith" while "having a contrite spirit" (Helaman 8:15).

Perhaps true worship—in the Old Testament era as well as in any other age—can therefore be summarized as follows: Worship is not merely something we do, but something we do because of something we feel about something we believe. And of those elements—doing, feeling, and believing—doing, while important, is the least imperative of the three. Thus Abraham's interrupted offering of Isaac "was accounted to him for righteousness" (Galatians 3:6) even without the actual act of sacrifice. Abraham proved what he felt about what he believed, and that was sufficient. That was worship. In fact, the first time the word worship appears in the King James Version of the Bible is in Abraham's statement concerning what he and his son were going up to Mount Moriah to do (see Genesis 22:5).[4] Obviously, the outward expression Abraham was initially commanded to perform was never completed, but only because his true acts of worship had already occurred. As the angel reassured him, "Now I know that thou fearest God" (Genesis 22:12). In short, Abraham had "bowed down" internally, and offered the sacrifice of a broken heart and a contrite spirit. His external hand was stayed because his internal heart was right. Compare this to the external obedience of Laman and Lemuel, who did in fact follow their father into the wilderness, making, at least in the technical sense, the same sacrifice as their brothers—indeed, in Laman's case, making a greater sacrifice, since his inheritance would have been a birthright double-portion. Unfortunately for Laman and Lemuel, however, and in contradistinction to the example of Abraham, absent from the story of their sacrifice is the inward-pointing adverb that typically accompanies acceptable offerings: they did not do it "willingly."[5] Though not an instance of worship in the ritual sense, the same principle applies to their outward offering. What they did was not an outgrowth of how they felt about what they believed. It was in no way an act of true worship.

False Worship: "An Outward Expression Devoid of Inner Commitment"

As a record of God's dealings with his chosen people and their covenant relationship with him, the Old Testament is replete with powerful examples of the kind of willing obedience, deep devotion, and heartfelt faith that constitute true worship.[6] Even during a time of gross idolatry, when Elijah worried that he alone was left a righteous worshipper, God reminded him that there were still seven thousand others who had not "bowed unto Baal" (1 Kings 19:14–18). This prevalence of true worship, as well as those righteous exceptions whenever wickedness became the rule, should be kept in mind as we turn our attention to the accounts of false worship that also abound in the Old Testament, accounts that can generally be categorized into three overlapping types. First are the Old Testament's frequent references to Asherah and Baal, the false gods of Egypt or Babylon, or the groves and high places honored by the apostate kings of Israel and Judah. A second type of false worship entails the willful neglect of true worship, times when some in Israel "despised mine holy things, and . . . profaned my sabbaths" (Ezekiel 22:8) or allowed themselves to "forget my holy mountain" (Isaiah 65:11). The third form of false worship (the focus of this study) is more subtle and therefore more insidious than these examples of blatant idolatry and willful disregard—those involving external compliance devoid of internal commitment. To borrow more modern terms, the problem did not have to be one of apostasy or inactivity, but lack of interiority.

This inward defiance hidden behind outward compliance accounts not only for Laman and Lemuel's halfhearted obedience mentioned earlier, but more significantly, for their wholehearted defense of the unrepentant people of Jerusalem—friends and neighbors whom they accused their prophet father of judging incorrectly. "We know that the people who were in the land of Jerusalem were a righteous people," Laman and Lemuel affirmed defensively, "for they kept the statutes and judgments of the Lord, and all his commandments, *according to the law of Moses*" (1 Nephi 17:22; emphasis added). In this revealing comment, we see Laman and Lemuel's perspective on what constituted obedience to the law of Moses (a view most likely shared by those who remained in Jerusalem), and by implication, their view of worship: it was tied, in their minds, to ritual sacrifice rather than love of God and neighbor. It seems that they had separated the law's internal intangibles from its external expressibles and assumed that compliance with the latter would compensate for an absence of the former. In other words, Laman and Lemuel had observed the "performances and ordinances" taking place without fail in Jerusalem and assumed that obeying the law of Moses entailed little else. As long as they complied with the legalistic outer requirements of the law, its moralistic inner elements might be safely underemphasized.

Malachi identified this type of inner apostasy when he accused Israel's priests of despising the Lord's name. "Wherein have we despised thy name?" the priests protested. By offering "polluted bread upon mine altar," the Lord replied. Again in mock protest they asked, "Wherein have we polluted thee?" In their minds they were performing the required rituals, worshipping at the altar as expected. But as Malachi revealed, their outer observance betrayed an inner contempt, for they were offering the blind, the lame, and the sick for sacrifice when only the unblemished were acceptable to God. "Ye said also, Behold, what a weariness is it!" the Lord continued, "and ye snuffed at it." It is true, the Lord admitted, that "ye brought an offering," but "should I accept this of your hand?" Why "kindle fire on mine altar for nought[?] I have no pleasure in you, saith the Lord of hosts, neither will I accept an offering at your hand" (Malachi 1:6–8, 10, 13), for it was never an offering of their hearts.[7]

This artificial obedience was not a priestly problem in Malachi's day alone. Centuries earlier the same had been true of Eli's sons Hophni and Phinehas, who "abhorred the offering of the Lord" even while administering it (1 Samuel 2:17; see also 1 Samuel 2:13–16, 22, 29). It was not that they offered sacrifices to false gods or abandoned sacrifice altogether, but the offerings, taken "by force" (1 Samuel 2:16), were not offered in faith. They maintained their post "at the door of the tabernacle," but their actions there were adulterated, in more ways than one (1 Samuel 2:22). Morally bankrupt within, Hophni and Phinehas mistakenly maintained some level of confidence in God's companionship because of their continued participation in the visible trappings of Israelite religion.

A focus on the tangible in the days of Hophni and Phinehas led some to the false assumption that the power of God remained with Israel merely because the vessels of God were in their possession, as best evidenced by their misplaced trust in the ark at the expense of the covenant. Having been defeated by the Philistines at Aphek—a loss their false sense of security made difficult to explain—the elders of Israel decided, "Let us fetch the ark of the covenant of the Lord out of Shiloh unto us, that, when it cometh among us, it may save us out of the hand of our enemies" (1 Samuel 4:3). Notice their assumption that "it," the ark, would save them, as opposed to faith that he, God, would deliver them. In other words, they mistook the symbol for the source and the object for the agent. The men of Israel were no better, for when they saw the ark among them, along with the presence of their priests, Hophni and Phinehas, the men of Israel shook the earth with their shouts of self-assurance. On the other side of the battlefield, meanwhile, the Philistines showed the same mistaken trust in the tangible: hearing the shouts of their opponents, "they understood that the ark of the Lord was come into the camp" and cried fearfully, "*God* is come into the camp . . . the *Gods* that smote the Egyptians" (1 Samuel 4:3–8; emphasis added).

While there may have been some in either camp still able to distinguish between *signified* and *signifier*, these verses suggest that in the eyes of many Israelites and Philistines, the ark was Israel's graven God, and its presence alone ensured victory. Thus, when the battle ended, the Philistines celebrated the ark's capture and the Israelites mourned its loss. In fact, textually, the entire narrative centers on the ark's physical presence. During the battle, Eli's "heart trembled for the ark of God," with no mention made of his two sons who accompanied it. When a messenger returned to Eli with news, he ordered his report in increasing degrees of disaster: the retreat of the army, the slaughter of the people, the death of Hophni and Phinehas, and, last and apparently worst, the news that "the ark of God is taken." As devastating as each of those four news flashes was (especially the third, one would think), it was only "when he made mention of the ark of God" that Eli "fell from off the seat backward" and died. Moments later, the news reached Eli's daughter-in-law, and again the ark is given pride of place. The "tidings that the ark of God was taken" was the first report that registered, and naming her newborn Ichabod—meaning "Where is the glory?"—as she lay dying, she bemoaned Israel's loss of glory in terms that made the deaths of her father-in-law and husband seem like secondary sorrows. "The glory is departed from Israel: because the ark of God was taken, and because of her father in law and her husband. And [again] she said, The glory is departed from Israel: for the ark of God is taken" (1 Samuel 4:10–22). Subsequently, when the Philistines installed the ark in the temple of their own god, Dagon, a contest between the two images ensued, followed by a seven-month tour of devastation in the wake of the Israelite ark. Passed around Philistia like a hot potato, it was eventually returned to the people from whom it was taken (1 Samuel 5–6), having dramatized the danger of treating as an outward trophy what was meant to be a token of inward covenants. From start to finish, this was not a story of reverence for Israel's God, but reliance on an object meant to symbolize him. Not unlike the golden calf of their ancestors, the ark became for some merely an object of affection, one that was literally lost in battle in order to illustrate a more significant loss that had already occurred—the loss of the interior attitudes that truly herald the presence of God.

No wonder young Samuel grew to distinguish between such inner attributes as obedience and such outer actions as sacrifice (see 1 Samuel 15:22). No wonder he bemoaned Israel's confidence in a visible king and their lack of faith in an invisible God (see 1 Samuel 8:6–22). No wonder he was able to discern the heart by looking past "the outward appearance" (1 Samuel 16:7). Others in Israel were often not so discerning. As Isaiah lamented, many in his day were "called by the name of Israel, and [were] come forth out of the waters of Judah," but did not act "in truth, nor in righteousness." As was often the case, they mistook identity for integrity. Word and ritual had told them who they were, but they had not internalized those acts of worship. They "call[ed] themselves of the holy city," but could not be called holy themselves (Isaiah 48:1–2). As God had told Isaiah earlier, many in Israel had all of the objects—eyes, ears, and hearts—but none of the abilities required to see, hear, and feel (see Isaiah 6:9–10).

The prophet Jeremiah directed similar words to the people of his day (see Jeremiah 5:21), for they had similar problems internalizing the attitudes and attributes that worship's external forms were meant to engender. In fact, beyond echoing Isaiah, Jeremiah also alluded to the formalism of Eli's day discussed earlier, drawing a parallel between his people's trust in the temple at Jerusalem and Israel's earlier trust in the ark at Shiloh. "Trust ye not," he warned, "in lying words, saying, The temple of the Lord, The temple of the Lord, The temple of the Lord, are these." The mere presence of the ark had not delivered Israel in Eli's day, and the mere presence of the temple would not deliver Judah in Jeremiah's.[8] Those who doubted the prophet's words were invited, "Go ye now unto my place which was in Shiloh, where I set my name at the first, and see what I did to it for the wickedness of my people Israel." The people in both periods felt "delivered to do all these abominations" because they could always, at least outwardly, "come and stand before

[God] in [his] house." Therefore, to eliminate the empty assurance derived from outward expressions devoid of inner commitments, both Shiloh and Jerusalem were destroyed. As God warned the people through Jeremiah, "Therefore will I do unto this house, which is called by my name, wherein ye trust, . . . as I have done to Shiloh. And I will cast you out of my sight" (Jeremiah 7:4–15). Perhaps to make it even more obvious that no amount of external worship would compensate for their lack of internal worthiness, the Lord then commanded Jeremiah, "Therefore pray not thou for this people, neither lift up cry nor prayer for them, neither make intercession to me: for I will not hear thee" (Jeremiah 7:16).

Rejection of the External

Whether embodied in torn-down temples, captured vessels, broken relics, or even ages of apostasy, the literal destruction of Israelite worship would have been dramatic indeed. However, the Old Testament's rhetorical rejection of hollow formalism is in some ways equally striking. Consider the Lord's forceful words as recorded by Amos: "I hate, I despise your feast days, and I will not smell in your solemn assemblies. Though ye offer me burnt offerings and your meat offerings, I will not accept them: neither will I regard the peace offerings of your fat beasts" (Amos 5:21–22). An even more eloquent example comes from the prophet Isaiah, who both began and ended his prophesying with rhetorical rejections of worship that had grown disingenuous. The first chapter includes a protracted denunciation worth quoting at length, in which the Lord asks the following:

> To what purpose is the multitude of your sacrifices unto me? saith the Lord: I am full of the burnt offerings of rams, and the fat of fed beasts; and I delight not in the blood of bullocks, or of lambs, or of he goats.
>
> When ye come to appear before me, who hath required this at your hand, to tread my courts?
>
> Bring no more vain oblations; incense is an abomination unto me; the new moons and sabbaths, the calling of assemblies, I cannot away with; it is iniquity, even the solemn meeting.
>
> Your new moons and your appointed feasts my soul hateth: they are a trouble unto me; I am weary to bear them.

And when ye spread forth your hands, I will hide mine eyes from you: yea, when ye make many prayers, I will not hear: your hands are full of blood. (Isaiah 1:11–15)

In this scathing rebuke, the Lord rejects what he had once required—more accurately, he rejects the people's artificial observance of what should have been worship's true forms. Israel's oblations were vain, their offerings an abomination. Evidently they were still engaging in these ritual behaviors, but God refused to accept them. By the end of the book of Isaiah, God's words of rejection are some of his most forceful: "He that killeth an ox is as if he slew a man; he that sacrificeth a lamb, as if he cut off a dog's neck; he that offereth an oblation, as if he offered swine's blood; he that burneth incense, as if he blessed an idol." In summary, he concludes, "They have chosen their own ways, and their soul delighteth in their abominations" (Isaiah 66:3).[9]

Rhetorically, there may be no more graphic rejection of the ritualistic worship practices of ancient Israel.[10] On the one hand, throughout this string of comparisons are prescribed acts of worship: the sacrificing of an ox or a lamb, the offering of an oblation, or the burning of incense. But paired with each practice is its equivalent as perceived by an offended God, each one suggesting the height of idolatry and degradation.[11] Dogs were seen as an abomination in Israel; few things would have been considered as unclean as the blood of swine (see Deuteronomy 23:18; Leviticus 11:7); and idols had been forbidden at least since the days of Sinai. But devoid of the faith that made true ritual worshipful, Israel's animal sacrifices were no better than human sacrifice or even murder. As an early scholar said of such language, "Nothing could more emphatically express the detestation of God for the spirit with which they would make their offerings."[12]

Within these two passages of Isaiah—the bookends of his volume—we see the rhetorical rejection of worship as known and practiced by many in ancient Israel and Judah.[13] We also see where these people had gone wrong in their worship and how true worship was intended to make things right. In the earlier passage, Isaiah asks two questions that lie at the heart of the issue. The first ("To what purpose?") asks the *why* and the second ("Who hath required this?") asks the *who* (Isaiah 1:11, 12). With regard to the first, even while remaining compliant with the *what* of worship—its outward forms and visible gestures—Isaiah's audience had lost sight of the reason those actions were required. Jeremiah asked similarly, "To what purpose cometh there to me incense . . . ? your burnt offerings are not acceptable, nor your sacrifices sweet unto me" (Jeremiah 6:20). By its very nature, ritual is susceptible to the charge of "vain repetition" that Jesus condemned in the praying habits of the heathen (see Matthew 6:7). The purpose behind such repetitive acts must therefore be constantly kept in mind. Otherwise, such outward repetitiveness will indeed become vain, which, depending on the meaning one chooses for that word, leaves it either ineffective or self-centered. Either way, whether purposeless or proud, such so-called worship loses its power by losing its aim, a frequent problem among those for whom worship has become ritual monotony. Each instance becomes a sad illustration of the aphorism of H. W. Schneider: "Beliefs seldom become doubts; they become ritual."[14]

As for the question of *who*, at times the people of Israel were quick to rejoice in the blessings of God but slow to acknowledging the source. As Isaiah lamented, even farm animals know who provides for them, "but Israel doth not know, my people doth not consider" (Isaiah 1:3). Like the Nephites condemned by Samuel the Lamanite, they did "not remember the Lord [their] God in the things with which he ha[d] blessed [them]." They "always remember[ed]" their blessings, but "not to thank the Lord [their] God for them" (Helaman 13:22). Under such circumstances, acts of worship can be dutifully performed without becoming personally directed, leaving ritual devoid of any feeling toward God. Habakkuk likened such disengaged worshippers to fishermen who "catch [fish] in their net, and gather them in their drag" only to "sacrifice unto their net, and burn incense unto their drag" instead of rendering thanks and praise unto God (Habakkuk 1:15–16). Even when counting their blessings Israel sometimes honored the visible and tangible *instruments* rather than the invisible and intangible *instrumentality* of God.

But to what degree is the *what* of worship affected by the absence of its requisite *why* and *who*? As the passage in Isaiah 66:3 makes clear, purposeless worship is not merely a neutral endeavor, but a negative one. Isaiah equates it with serious sin, not mere ignorance or indecision. Describing similar halfheartedness, Mormon at first dismisses it as simply ineffectual—"except he shall do it with real intent it profiteth him nothing"—but immediately intensifies his judgment to condemn it as an actual wrong. "It [is] counted *evil*," he warns, to engage in such acts "and not with real intent" (Moroni 7:6–9; emphasis added). Similarly, after the brother of Jared endured his three-hour chastening for an offense as simple as neglected prayer, he "repented of the *evil* which he had done" in forgetting God (Ether 2:15; emphasis added).

If forgetting God by neglecting worship is considered evil, then forgetting God while engaging in worship adds an element of hypocrisy to that sin. A measure of mercy therefore exists in the rejection of such ritual, for it helps remove that hypocritical aspect. Gone is the external veneer behind which to hide. Also eliminated is the false sense of security that comes from outward-only obedience. In the absence of worship's exterior forms, what would have come of Laman and Lemuel's overconfidence in their countrymen's outward compliance with the law of Moses? Who would have followed Hophni and Phinehas if they had had no observable ordinances with which to "cover [their] sins" (D&C 121:37)? Allowing formalism to continue uncorrected would only lull Israel into thinking that their outward obedience could substitute for inner adoration, and therefore the external had to be removed—either literally or rhetorically—in order to lay bare the internal (or its absence). The reality had to match the perception. An empty Holy of Holies in Eli's day bore witness to the emptiness of worship that took place there. A temple destroyed by Babylon mirrored a devotional life that had been overrun by the cares of the world. Returning to the Lord's words in Isaiah's first chapter, God simply gave voice to Israel's true feelings: he saw no purpose in their sacrifices because Israel had lost its purpose in performing them; he took no delight in their offerings because they found no delight in their gifts; he was weary with their holy days because the feasts were a weariness to them. In rejecting the outward appearance of piety, God placed his people before a mirror that reached within. Similar rhetorical work is accomplished in Isaiah 3, where the apostate daughters of Zion are likewise shown their true reflection: not the well-dressed, perfumed beauty they saw on the surface, but the ill-clad, putrid ugliness that an all-seeing God perceived within (see Isaiah 3:24). In essence, like the "whited sepulchers" in Jesus' rebuke (see Matthew 23:27), Isaiah was turning these daughters of Zion inside-out, making bare the inner reality in an externally visible way.

In times of empty, insincere worship, because Israel had in effect come to assume an equivalence between the external and the internal, with the visible standing in for the invisible, God concretized their assumption to prove it false. Whereas Israelite worship evinced a high degree of exteriority, with the assumption that its interiority would be judged as being on the same level, God knew the true level of its interiority and brought down its exteriority to be in line. In short, Israel hoped that both sides would be deemed equally visible; God proved that both were equally invisible. Israel hoped the internal would be judged by the external; God made sure that it would. By rejecting worship's outer forms, God left Israel to face its inner inclinations, and without the crutch of superficial sacrifice or the veneer of hypocritical praise, Israel stood in a position to honestly look inward and truly repent.

Rehabilitation of the Internal

In a way, the process of rehabilitation through rejection mirrors the fall and rise of buildings, communities, or civilizations. When the old structure has been abandoned and allowed to decay, its hollow exterior eventually crumbles or is torn down, clearing the ground for a new foundation to be laid and a new structure to be built and inhabited. Isaiah seems to suggest this process when he follows his diatribe against hollow temple worship in chapter 1 with the promise of a new "mountain of the Lord's house" in chapter 2.[15] In worship, the order of this rehabilitation typically follows the order in which worship was meant to arise in the first place—an emphasis on the internal, the spiritual, and the relational, which then gives meaning to the forms of devotion that give it visible shape and experiential regularity. Continued engagement in the external then allows for greater understanding and internalization, provided that the original emphases are not lost in the process. In other words, what we feel gives rise to what we do, and in turn, what we do gives structure to what we feel.

An inner-oriented type of worship seems to have been God's original intention, before its spirit became entangled in the letter of ritual complexity. As Moses reminded his people, the reason they "saw no manner of similitude" at Sinai was because the Lord feared they would "corrupt [them]selves, and make [themselves] a graven image." Moses then listed three verses of potential externalities that the Israelites may have been prone to employ as an outward symbol of—or worse, a substitute for—the true God (Deuteronomy 4:15–19). Thus it was not only the law (with its prohibition of graven images) but also the manner in which it was given that was meant to counter that inclination. God chose to remain invisible to them in that instance, and thereby pointed Israel inward, both to inner worship and to an emphasis on the inner attributes of God and the inner principles of his redemptive plan. Jeremiah recalled this order—the spiritual before the physical—in his lament, discussed earlier, that Judah's unmerited trust in the temple would prove no more effective than Israel's trust in the ark of the covenant. "I spake not unto your fathers, nor commanded them in the day that I brought them out of the land of Egypt, concerning burnt offerings or sacrifices: But this thing commanded I them, saying, Obey my voice, and I will be your God, and ye shall be my people" (Jeremiah 7:22–23). In other words, inner obedience was the original end, with outer ordinances the superadded means. The shell meant nothing without the core. Without inner righteousness and real intent, Jeremiah suggests, they might as well eat their sacrificial offerings themselves.[16]

Jesus similarly turned to the Old Testament to privilege internal ends over external means. Twice when dealing with certain Pharisees—often presented as the personification of the external devoid of the internal in Jesus' day—the Lord quoted Hosea's words to ancient Israel, "For I desired mercy, and not sacrifice; and the knowledge of God more than burnt offerings" (Hosea 6:6; see Matthew 9:13 and 12:7). Micah acknowledged this dichotomy as well when questioning the sufficiency of outward offerings: "Wherewith shall I come before the Lord, and bow myself before the high God? shall I come before him with burnt offerings, with calves of a year old? Will the Lord be pleased with thousands of rams, or with ten thousands of rivers of oil? shall I give my firstborn for my transgression, the fruit of my body for the sin of my soul?" Recognizing the insufficiency of these physical manifestations, Micah eventually settled on the offering God really requires: "to do justly, and to love mercy, and to walk humbly with thy God" (Micah 6:6–8).[17]

Like Hosea and Micah, Isaiah likewise elevated attributes over actions. He addressed the issue at length in his description of "the fast that I have chosen" (see Isaiah 58), but perhaps his most powerful treatment of this concept appears in his final chapter, in the verses leading up to the scathing rejection, discussed earlier, of Israelite offerings as swine's blood. "Thus saith the Lord," Isaiah begins, "The heaven is my throne, and the earth is my footstool." Compared to this universal creation, "where is the house that ye build unto me? and where is the place of my rest?" (Isaiah 66:1). Echoing Solomon's lament of centuries earlier, Isaiah wonders what the temple—if devoid of empowering authenticity—could possible mean to a Being that even the "heaven of heavens cannot contain" (1 Kings 8:27). "For all those things hath mine hand made, and all those things have been, saith the Lord: but to this man will I look, even to him that is poor and of a contrite spirit, and trembleth at my word" (Isaiah 66:2). In essence, Isaiah is asking his people to consider what good their physical offerings are to God when they all came from God to begin with. By asking for a portion of those offerings in worshipful return, what God was really seeking was the interest on that investment—an increase in the gratitude, love, and reverence those gifts were meant to convey. Like the bulging fishnets abandoned by the Savior's apostles, it was the Lord who had filled them in the first place, a gift given that they might have something to offer in return. Their real gift was the faith and submissiveness their sacrifice embodied, the external providing proof of the internal. Returning to Isaiah's words, what God really requires in worship is what he cannot create himself ("all those things hath mine hand made"), something that does not already exist ("all those things have been"), namely, a person who is "poor and of a contrite spirit"—an independent offering, born of agency, of uniquely human creation. Such willing submission is, in Elder Neal A. Maxwell's oft-quoted words, "really the only uniquely personal thing we have to place on God's altar," everything else being only what "He has already given or loaned to us."[18] Borrowing again from Isaiah, if "Lebanon is not sufficient to burn, nor the beasts thereof sufficient for a burnt offering" (Isaiah 40:16), then what good is feigned faith or forced ritual observance? What God truly desires from us are expressions of realities within.

Conclusion

As history can attest, emphasizing outward expressions at the expense of inner commitments is a continual danger in any age, even after certain "performances and ordinances" were eclipsed by the Atonement of Christ. The Saints in Joseph Smith's day were warned against relying on "dead works" (D&C 22), and later, they still needed clarifying revelation to teach them "how to worship" and "what [to] worship" (D&C 93:19). Their struggles in Missouri suggest that some relied too much on Zion-as-place—like Jerusalem or Shiloh anciently—and neglected becoming Zion-as-people. Much more recently, during the first general conference held in the much-anticipated Conference Center in Salt Lake City in April 2000, President Boyd K. Packer asked, "Do you think it possible for those of us who are called upon to speak to draw attention away from this wonderful building long enough to focus on the purpose for which it was built?"[19]

Indeed, the Saints are still seeking the proper balance between outer forms and inner feelings, and God is still seeking those who will "worship him in spirit and in truth" (John 4:24). As Elder Donald L. Hallstrom of the Seventy recently observed, we still sometimes allow external activity in the Church to substitute for internal conversion to the gospel. As a result, he warned, "Many of us are not being regularly changed by [the] cleansing power [of outer ordinances] because of our lack of [inner] reverence."[20] We must therefore continue striving to bend our wills as we bend our knees, to lift our hearts as we raise our hands, to "praise the Lord with heart [as well as] voice."[21] In short, we must worship God, not only in our external gestures, but, as the Psalmist said, "in the beauty of holiness" (Psalms 29:2; 96:9).

Eventually, that beautiful, holy worship will be such that no outward manifestation could possibly do it justice. As Jeremiah prophesied, "in those days, saith the Lord, they shall say no more, The ark of the covenant of the Lord: neither shall it come to mind: neither shall they remember it; neither shall they visit it; neither shall that be done any more" (Jeremiah 3:16). Or as Isaiah foretold, "At that day shall a man look to his Maker, and his eyes shall have respect to the Holy One of Israel. And he shall not look to the altars" (Isaiah 17:7–8), even those dedicated in service to God. By then, as John the Revelator was shown, the righteous who worshipped the Lamb premortally will do so again (see Revelation 5:8–14; 19:1–6), but with no need for tangible temples, "for the Lord God Almighty and the Lamb [will be] the temple" where they dwell (Revelation 21:22). In the meantime, we would be wise to learn from the Old Testament to engage in the outward but with our focus on the inward, until worship becomes an unaffected externalization of our love, faith, and reverence for God—a means by which our soul can speak when we "cannot say the smallest part which [we] feel" (Alma 26:16). If we come to know God and reverence him at that depth, our worship will naturally break through to the surface—an eruption occasionally, as when "David danced before the Lord with all his might" (2 Samuel 6:14), but more often a spring, like the one of which Jesus spoke to a would-be worshipper in his day, "a well of water springing up into everlasting life" (John 4:14).

Notes

1. Genesis 4:3–5. See *History of the Church of Jesus Christ of Latter-day Saints*, ed. B. H. Roberts, 2nd ed. rev. (Salt Lake City: Deseret Book, 1976), 2:15–16.

2. Neal A. Maxwell, in Conference Report, April 1995, 91.

3. This phrase has been used by numerous writers from various faiths to describe the visible forms of religious experience. Perhaps the most famous Latter-day Saint instance is Elder Carlos E. Asay's use of the phrase to describe the temple garment. See Carlos E. Asay, "The Temple Garment: 'An Outward Expression of an Inward Commitment,'" *Ensign*, August 1997, 18–23.

4. The Hebrew word translated in this verse as "worship" appears earlier in the book of Genesis twice (see Genesis 18:2; 19:1), but is translated as "bow down" in both instances, and is not a "bowing down" before God, but before other messengers.

5. The expectation that sacrifice be "willing" appears frequently in the Old Testament text. See Exodus 25:2; Judges 5:2, 9; 1 Chronicles 28:9, 21; 2 Chronicles 17:16; 35:8; Ezra 3:5; 7:16. Significantly, the most notable examples of willingness in sacrifice concerned the building of the tabernacle and the Temple of Solomon, as shown in Exodus 25 and 1 Chronicles 29, respectively. In the first instance, the word "willing" appears five times; in the second, it appears seven times.

6. For an excellent discussion of these more positive examples of ritual worship in the Old Testament, see Carol Frogley Ellertson, "The Sanctifying Power of True Ritual Worship," in *The Gospel of Jesus Christ in the Old Testament, the 38th Annual Brigham Young University Sidney B. Sperry Symposium*, ed. D. Kelly Ogden, Jared W. Ludlow, and Kerry Muhlestein (Provo, UT: Religious Studies Center, Brigham Young University; Salt Lake City: Deseret Book, 2009), 86–108.

7. Rex C. Reeve Jr. briefly treats these verses in his discussion of Malachi during the 1986 Sidney B. Sperry Symposium on the Old Testament, observing, as I have, that "Israel's lack of reverence and their polluted sacrifices caused God to reject them." Rex C. Reeve Jr., "Malachi and the Latter Days," in *The Old Testament and the Latter-day Saints* (Orem, UT: Randall Book, 1986), 310.

8. Ellis Rasmussen said of these verses, "They [the temple worshippers] could not assume that by going to the temple and making perfunctory sacrifices in it, they could be excused from repenting. They must learn to do good and cease to do evil. They must not make the temple 'a den of robbers' and hope to hide in it, thinking it would not be destroyed." *A Latter-day Saint Commentary on the Old Testament* (Salt Lake City: Deseret Book, 1993), 547.

9. For an alternate translation of this verse and a discussion of the possibility that it ties Israel's legitimate offerings to pagan sacrifice, see Jack M. Sasson, "Isaiah LXVI 3–4a," *Vetus Testamentum* 26, no. 2 (April 1976): 199–207.

10. The strong rhetoric in these verses has even led some scholars to wonder if the author is rejecting the temple outright. See Wim Beuken, "Does Trito-Isaiah Reject the Temple? An Intertextual Inquiry into Isa. 66. 1–6," in Sipke Draisma, ed., *Intertextuality in Biblical Writings: Essays in Honour of Bas van Iersel* (Kampen, Netherlands: Uitgeversmaatschappij J. H. Kok, 1989), 53–66. Latter-day Saint scholars would see in this text a less sweeping rejection: "The old rituals, so often

hypocritically performed, will be done away, and they who have only such worship to their credit shall suffer the consequences." Rasmussen, *Latter-day Saint Commentary*, 539.

11. A group of Latter-day Saint scholars said of these verses, "The parallels in this verse illustrate how men may outwardly appear to worship Jehovah while in reality continuing their sinful ways, whether outwardly or in their hearts (James 3:9–10). Certainly the Lord wants our sacrifices, the outward signs of our devotion. But he also wants us to understand that outward symbols are empty without the inward devotions: obedience, repentance, humility, gratitude (1:11 – 13)." Donald W. Parry, Jay A. Parry, and Tina M. Peterson, *Understanding Isaiah* (Salt Lake City: Deseret Book, 1998), 584.

12. Albert Barnes, *Notes, Critical, Explanatory, and Practical, on the Book of the Prophet Isaiah*, vol. 2 (New York: Leavitt & Allen, 1853), 439.

13. Many scholars agree that Isaiah 1 "recapitulates themes found throughout Isaiah, and that it runs parallel thematically and linguistically with the final chapters of the book," specifically, "the diatribe against the sacrificial cult." See Joseph Blenkinsopp, *Isaiah 1–39: A New Translation with Introduction and Commentary*, The Anchor Bible 19, ed. William Foxwell Albright and David Noel Freedman (New York: Doubleday, 2000), 181.

14. Herbert Wallace Schneider, *The Puritan Mind* (New York: Henry Holt, 1930), 98.

15. For an extended discussion of this comparison, see Francis Landy, "Torah and Anti-Torah: Isaiah 2:2–4 and 1:10–26," *Biblical Interpretation* 11, nos. 3–4 (January 2003): 317–34.

16. This sense is clearer in translations other than the King James Version. The New International Version, for example, translates Jeremiah 7:21 as follows: "Go ahead, add your burnt offerings to your other sacrifices and eat the meat yourselves!"

17. In the 1986 Sidney B. Sperry Symposium on the Old Testament, Monte S. Nyman similarly noted Micah's elevation of inner attributes over "the ritual of the law," and linked this text to Isaiah's words in Isaiah 1 and Abinadi's words in Mosiah 13. See Monte S. Nyman, "Micah, the Second Witness with Isaiah," in *The Old Testament and the Latter-day Saints* (Orem, UT: Randall Book, 1986), 219, 222.

18. Neal A. Maxwell, in Conference Report, October 1995, 30.

19. Boyd K. Packer, in Conference Report, April 2000, 6.

20. Donald L. Hallstrom, "Converted to His Gospel through His Church," *Ensign*, May 2012, 13–15.

21. Tracy Y. Cannon, "Praise the Lord with Heart and Voice," *Hymns* (Salt Lake City: The Church of Jesus Christ of Latter-day Saints, 1985), no. 73.

12

Approaching Holiness: Sacred Space in Ezekiel's Temple Vision

Jacob Rennaker

A living, breathing temple tradition dramatically sets Latter-day Saints apart from contemporary Christianities and Judaisms. However, because Latter-day Saints are so familiar with the rituals performed and the concepts taught in these temples, it is easy for them to become complacent in their temple worship and to overlook the beauties of this tradition. Thankfully, Latter-day Saint scholars have produced a number of edifying and thought-provoking books and articles dedicated to the subject of the temple.[1] In general, these scholars have looked at the "big picture," synthesizing statements and themes from Restoration scripture, the Bible, nonbiblical religious texts, and religious scholars in order to understand their own temple tradition. However, detailed studies focusing on specific ancient temple texts have been significantly less frequent.[2] Since religious scholarship outside of the Latter-day Saint community has tended to focus more on individual temple texts, Latter-day Saint scholars would do well to benefit from this scholarship and to take this approach themselves. This study hopes to demonstrate the insights that a close study of individual temple texts can

---

Jacob Rennaker is a PhD candidate in Hebrew Bible at Claremont Graduate University.

provide regarding the nature of temples by examining non-Latter-day Saint scholarship on Ezekiel's temple vision (Ezekiel 40–48). I will provide examples of two ways that scholars have tried to make sense of the sacred space that Ezekiel describes. While these two approaches may seem contradictory, I will suggest a way to reconcile these views. Ultimately, I hope to show how open-mindedness in engaging with a variety of scholarly and religious literature (both biblical and nonbiblical) can help Latter-day Saints better appreciate their own temple tradition.

Ezekiel's Vision

Born into a priestly family (Ezekiel 1:3), Ezekiel had every right to expect that his life would be both predictable and stable. However, with the Babylonian conquest of Jerusalem (2 Kings 24:11–14), he was torn from his homeland and its sacred temple, his priestly home away from home. Having been thrust into a Babylonian world dominated by ziggurats (pyramid-like temple structures), each one dedicated to a different deity, Ezekiel would have been reminded of his precious temple's loss at every turn. It was in this setting that Ezekiel received one of the most spectacular and detailed visions in all scripture, which, unsurprisingly, centered on the temple.

After twenty-five years in captivity, Ezekiel had a homecoming of sorts: the Lord gave him a vision of his native Israel and a glorious, complete temple in the midst of the land (Ezekiel 40–48).[3] In this vision, Ezekiel is not alone—he is guided on a tour of the temple by an angelic figure (Ezekiel 40:3) who measures the temple's dimensions. Ezekiel then describes in detail the appearance of this temple, as well as its inner workings and its rejuvenating effects on the surrounding land. Finally, his temple vision concludes with the city of Jerusalem receiving the comforting new name of "The Lord is there" (Ezekiel 48:35).

While almost all biblical scholars recognize that some areas of Ezekiel's temple are holier than others, there is no consensus on how these degrees of holiness relate to how humanity should approach God. Two options proposed by scholars are 1) a vertical approach to sacred space, with the altar as its focus of worship, requiring the worshipper to ascend to reach God, or 2) a horizontal approach, with the Holy of Holies as its focus of worship, requiring the worshipper to move westward to reach God. Those who champion a vertical approach argue that Ezekiel was influenced by Mesopotamian ideas about temples because he was in Babylon at the time of his vision (Ezekiel 1:3; 40:1). According to this view, the highest point of the temple is the holiest, and humanity approaches God by ascending symbolically through a vertically aligned world. On the other hand, those who champion a horizontal approach point to the story of Eden and other Old Testament texts relating to priests (e.g., Leviticus), claiming that Ezekiel's description was largely influenced by these biblical texts. This perspective emphasizes an approach toward sacred space along a horizontal axis, where one progresses toward increasingly sacred space the closer one gets to the Holy of Holies (which is situated toward the western end of the temple). This paper will explore both of these views and suggest that each can be valuable in illuminating the meaning of Ezekiel's temple vision, and, as a result, illuminate Latter-day Saints' understanding of their own temple tradition.

Vertical Conceptualization of Sacred Space

As mentioned above, Ezekiel's vision begins with an angelic figure who carefully measures the temple. Some scholars look to these measurements for clues to determine Ezekiel's emphasis. Walter Zimmerli's foundational study of Ezekiel made this claim: "What dominates the picture [described by Ezekiel] as a whole is not the sight of a building rising before one's eyes, as one would expect in a spontaneous vision, but a ground plan."[4] While Zimmerli correctly notes the scarcity of height measurements in the otherwise meticulous description of temple architecture,[5] there *are* vertical architectural elements that suggest the symbolism of ascending vertically towards increasingly sacred space.

While no specific measurements are given, the vertical ascent is implicit in the description of stairs in the temple vision. After orienting Ezekiel on the east side of the outermost temple walls, the visionary guide ascends (ויעל) a flight of stairs (מעלות) in order to measure the first temple gate (Ezekiel 40:6). There is another description of stairs as Ezekiel moves from the outer courtyard to the inner courtyard (Ezekiel 40:34), followed by a final set of stairs leading up to the sanctuary (Ezekiel 40:49). In the systematic description of the temple's stairs, the audience moves progressively higher up the temple compound. Daniel Block notes that "the difference in elevation increases with each unit in this sacred complex, as one moves from the outside toward the center. . . . The scene is impressive. The observer's eyes are drawn ever upward to the top of this temple mount."[6] This description of vertical progression, however, does not seem to be concerned with precise measurements of physical elevation. In the verse first mentioning ascent (Ezekiel 40:6), the stairs are not numbered (and they remain unnumbered until verse 22). Similarly, in the account of Ezekiel's final ascent, the stairs are never numbered (Ezekiel 40:49). Taken together, these passages suggest that the emphasis of the author was on the general concept of height, not on a precise physical measurement.

The subsequent description of Ezekiel's temple altar also sheds light on the use of vertical sacred space within the vision. One of the most noticeable features of this altar's description in Ezekiel 43:13–15 is the explicit mention of its height. The height itself is not remarkable (four cubits), but rather the peculiar language used to describe these measurements. Block notes that "the observations on the altar's height represent a significant departure from the preceding description, which has been satisfied to provide horizontal dimensions of the temple complex."[7] In addition, the author depicts this altar in terms that suggest a cosmic conceptualization of the space within the temple compound. Steven Tuell notes that "the contrast between the description of the altar and Ezekiel's description of the Temple comes . . . in the [cosmic] designations given to the parts of the altar in 43:13–17."[8] Of particular interest is the terminology used for the altar's base (חיק הארץ "the bottom upon the ground") and its hearth (הראל "altar") (Ezekiel 43:14–15).

Michael Fishbane notes that these terms did not merely describe architectural elements of the altar, but carried with them a much more significant connotation: "It is striking that Ezekiel describes the base platform of the altar of the envisaged Temple as *ḥēq hāʾāreṣ* 'bosom of the earth' (43:14 [translated in the KJV as "the bottom upon the ground"]) and its summit, with four horns, as *harʾēl* 'mountain of God' (43:15 [translated in the KJV as "the altar"])."[9] These terms immediately bring to mind both depth and elevation. Regarding the significance of this conceptualization of the temple altar, Fishbane writes, "From this axial point . . . the new Temple, like the old, will be a font of blessing for Israel, a 'mountain of god,' linking the highest heaven to the nethermost earth."[10] Fishbane, then, sees the altar in this passage functioning as a metonymy for the entire temple compound, a sacred part representing the sacred whole.[11] Just as the altar is described in cosmic terms, the temple, too, can be seen as taking on cosmic dimensions.

The Mesopotamian temples that would have surrounded Ezekiel are described in some texts as filling the expanse of creation.¹² Esarhaddon, king of Assyria, portrayed his temple-building efforts in this inscription: "I raised the top of Esharra [the temple] to heaven, / Above, to heaven I elevated its top. / Below in the netherworld / I made firm its foundations."¹³ This temple (and, by extension, the king who built it) was so grand that its power extended vertically from heaven to the "netherworld."¹⁴

Ezekiel describes the temple altar using similar terminology. As Fishbane states above, the author is using a play on words to make a point. The uppermost tier of this altar is described using a word that can either be translated as "altar" or "mountain of God" (Ezekiel 43:15), and the word used to describe the base of the altar can either be translated as "the bottom upon the ground" or the "bosom of the earth" (Ezekiel 43:14). Many note the unique spelling of this first term (הראל in verse 15) and suggest that it serves to explain the subsequent terms used for "altar" (הראיל in verses 15 and 16, a difference of only one letter). Tuell explains that by using this unique spelling of "altar" to evoke images of the "mountain of God," the author

> accomplishes two purposes. First, it explains the ancient name for the altar hearth in a way that complements and contrasts with the designation of the foundation as הארץ חק ["bosom of the earth"], thereby making a profound statement in [cosmic] terms about the altar's significance. Second, however, it ties the altar description firmly into its literary context. The designation of the altar hearth as הראל ("mountain of God") recalls the הר גבה מאד ("very high mountain") of 40:2, as well as the ההר ראש ("mountaintop") of 43:12.¹⁵

Both of the purposes that Tuell mentions deal with height, suggesting that the description of Ezekiel's altar emphasized a vertical element of sacred space in this text.

In his discussion of the altar's significance, Block writes, "All that matters are its size and shape, the latter of which is seen to match the symmetry of the temple complex as a whole."¹⁶ Indeed, this three-tiered altar corresponds nicely to the three-tiered temple compound described in Ezekiel 40–43,¹⁷ the top tier of which contains the sanctuary, the "place of my throne, and the place of the soles of my feet" (Ezekiel 43:7).¹⁸ It is here that humanity touches divinity.

According to these scholars, the temple appears as a vertical representation of the cosmos with the altar at its sacred summit, where one must ascend to approach God. Commenting upon the aforementioned altar language in Ezekiel 43, Jon Levenson writes the following: "What all this suggests is that the Temple is not a place in the world, but the world in essence. . . . In the Temple, God relates simultaneously to the entire cosmos, for the Temple . . . is a microcosm of which the world itself is the macrocosm."[19] He also explains that "the Temple is the epitome of the world, a concentrated form of its essence, a miniature of the cosmos."[20] This was true of both Mesopotamian temples and Ezekiel's temple. Therefore, both the altar and the temple compound in which it was enshrined should be viewed with a vertically aligned cosmos in mind.[21] As demonstrated above, Ezekiel goes to great lengths to emphasize the element of a sacred, vertical ascent toward God in the account of Ezekiel's temple vision. However, is this the only possible way to understand sacred space within that temple?

Horizontal Conceptualization of Sacred Space

Despite the plentiful evidence for Ezekiel's emphasis on a vertical ascent toward the holy, some scholars argue for a completely different emphasis in the text. While recognizing the importance of the altar and its vertical position within the temple compound, Margaret Odell finds an alternative framework for understanding the directional emphasis in Ezekiel: "If [Jehovah] dwells in the temple, then it is no longer appropriate to think of [Jehovah] as 'coming down' to the altar to accept the offerings, which 'go up' to God (Hebrew *ʿôlah*, 'go up'). The altar remains the meeting place between deity and people; in Ezekiel's temple, however, the intersection is worked out on a horizontal, *not vertical* plane, as offerings are brought in to the altar and [Jehovah] moves out from the temple to accept them there."[22] This emphasis on a horizontal framework within Ezekiel's temple description is far from theoretical; it finds a great deal of support within the text of Ezekiel 40–43.

Significantly, the sanctuary (the holiest building within the temple compound, comprising the "holy place" and the Holy of Holies) receives special attention in these chapters. This significance is signaled by the order in which the angelic figure directs Ezekiel around the different locations of the temple compound. Ezekiel is guided through six gates, which he describes in detail (Ezekiel 40:6–46). After passing the initially nondescript altar (Ezekiel 40:47), he reaches the sanctuary. It is at *this* location that the heavenly guide finally breaks his silence and gives a name to one of the rooms within the sanctuary. Zimmerli notes, "The prophet's way leads through six gates to the building in which he reaches his goal, to the threshold of the holy of holies which alone is given a name by the figure of the guide."[23] The sanctuary, with its most sacred room lying at the westernmost end of the building, is the climax of this tour.

A consideration of creation imagery suggests the prominence of this building within the temple compound. Each of the aforementioned gates had three chambers on each side (Ezekiel 40:10), creating a tripartite passageway.[24] It is only after recording all six of these unique tripartite gates that Ezekiel approaches the sanctuary, which also exhibits a three-part structure—the porch (אלם), the great hall (היכל), and the Holy of Holies (הקדשים קדש) (see Ezekiel 40:48–49; 41:1–4). Zimmerli suggests that "in two times three gates there is opened the access to the similarly tripartite seventh structure at the goal of this whole guidance. In this there seemed to be discernible something of the rhythm of the Priestly creation narrative with its culmination in the seventh, sanctified day."[25] The focus on a most sacred seventh space by the priestly Ezekiel, who would have been concerned with both preaching and keeping the Sabbath day holy (see Exodus 20:8–11), can hardly be accidental.[26]

In light of this discussion, the Holy of Holies (הקדשים קדש) appears to be the climax of Ezekiel's initial view of the temple compound. Zimmerli explains, "In the continuation of the leading of the prophet, which has its goal *not* at the altar, but in the temple building to the west of the altar and there in the most westerly room of that building, the holy of holies,"[27] sacred space within the temple compound appears to be oriented along a horizontal plane, rather than a vertical plane. The west, then, takes on a clear significance in the sacred orientation (or "occidentation") of the temple compound, becoming the most appropriate way to approach God.

Imagery of the Garden of Eden is also prevalent in the architecture of the sanctuary, and it, too, suggests a horizontal emphasis.. While the six gates of the temple courtyards were all decorated with palm trees, the walls of the sanctuary were decorated with both palm trees *and* cherubim (Ezekiel 41:20). In addition to these wall decorations, the two doors located on the east side of the innermost rooms of the sanctuary (Ezekiel 41:2–3) are described in the following manner:[28] "And there were two doors to both the great hall and the Holy [of Holies]. . . . And there were made upon them—upon the doors of the great hall—cherubim and palm trees, like [those] made for the walls [of the sanctuary]" (Ezekiel 41:23, 25, translation my own). The author of Genesis uses this same imagery when God expels Adam from the Garden of Eden: "When he drove out the man, he placed on the east of the Garden of Eden the cherubim and a flaming sword continually turning to guard the way of the tree of life" (Genesis 3:24, translation my own). Here, God drives Adam eastward from Eden. Cherubim are placed "at the east of the Garden of Eden" (לְגַן־עֵדֶן מִקֶּדֶם) to prevent a westward return to the sacred garden and the presence of God. Similarly, the cherubim on the doors that Ezekiel describes are stationed at the east entrances to the sacred inner chambers of the sanctuary. This positioning of protective figures indicates the supreme sacredness of a western direction within Ezekiel's temple compound.

In the period immediately following the Babylonian exile of the Jewish people, imagery of Adam, Eden, and the temple became much more prevalent. Marvin Sweeney explains: "Later texts of the Second Temple period . . . note that the priest in the Temple represents Adam in the Garden of Eden, which may explain the appellation *ben-'ādām*, 'son of Adam' or 'mortal,' that is consistently applied by [Jehovah] to Ezekiel throughout the book. The fact that only the high priest may enter the Holy of Holies, where the ark of the covenant is guarded by cherubim much like the Garden of Eden, reinforces this image."[29] The text of Ezekiel 40–43 demonstrates that this conceptualization was prevalent in the mind of the author. However, Ezekiel's use of Eden-related imagery does not begin with this spectacular temple vision in chapters 40–43.

There is precedent for the use of Eden-related imagery elsewhere in the book of Ezekiel. In chapter 28, Tyre is compared to "Eden, the garden of God" (גַּן־אֱלֹהִים עֵדֶן) (v. 13). In Ezekiel 31, Assyria, Egypt, and other unidentified nations are compared to the "trees of Eden" (עֲצֵי־עֵדֶן) that were found within the "garden of God" (גַּן הָאֱלֹהִים) (see Ezekiel 31:9, 16, 18).[30] Fishbane suggests that the imagery of Eden was also used in Ezekiel 36–37. He describes the use of this imagery in the following way:

> Longing for order and spatial restoration, the prophets imagined the ancient national centre [of Jerusalem] as an old-new Eden from which the people were evicted. But, quite unlike the old Adam, this new national counterpart will return to Edenic bliss—this being the return to Zion and to national dignity in the land. Perhaps for this reason,

Ezekiel . . . juxtaposed the oracle of hope that the old Eden would be restored (36:35) with the parable of dry bones, whereby he envisages the re-creation of the corporate body of Israel—much like a new Adam—with a new flesh and a new spirit (37:4–9). By this coupling of Edenic and Adamic imagery, national nostalgia and primordial fantasies are blended.[31]

The yearning for a symbolic return to Eden was, in part, a result of the trauma experienced by those who had been exiled to Babylon.[32] From the perspective of these exiles, they, like Adam, had been driven eastward. A return to Eden meant a return to the sacred land of *their* inheritance, the land of Israel. Regarding this view in Ezekiel 40–48, Levenson explains, "[Ezekiel's] stress on Eden traditions in his description of Zion is a way of reorienting the hopes of his audience from the east, where Eden had been thought to lie, to the west, the direction of Israel's future."[33] Thus, the literary allusions in Ezekiel 40–43 to the account of the Garden of Eden, combined with the exilic situation of the author, strongly suggest the west as the sacred direction of returning to the presence of God.[34]

The *Lamassu* Statue: A Reconciling Paradigm

In light of the previous discussion, both the vertical and horizontal conceptualizations of sacred space seem valid, as they are both backed by ample evidence. However, many scholars have implicitly assumed from the description of his temple vision that Ezekiel could have held only one of these views. As seen above, one group of scholars assumes that Ezekiel had in mind a vertical conceptualization of sacred space, with the altar as its focus atop the sacred summit of the temple, requiring an ascent to reach God. Other scholars argue instead for a horizontal conceptualization of the temple with its sacred endpoint in the Holy of Holies situated at the western end of the sanctuary, requiring a horizontal, westward movement to reach God. These two groups of scholars appear to be in conflict regarding the "correct" conceptualization of sacred space within Ezekiel's temple compound, including the proper way to approach Deity. However, did such a conflict exist for Ezekiel?

Iconographic evidence from the Mesopotamian temples and palaces that surrounded Ezekiel would argue that these two conceptualizations are not mutually exclusive. Figure 1 depicts a statue commonly identified

Fig. 1. *Lamassu* statue, British Museum.
Photo by Jacob Rennaker.

as a *lamassu* (or *šēdu*), which was recognized as a protective deity.³⁵ Such statues or deities were often guardians of temples³⁶ and were sometimes referred to as the *lamassi É puzra*, "the protective spirit of the temple."³⁷ While there is a strong similarity between the function of the *lamassu* and the cherubim (כרבים) in Ezekiel's earlier vision (see Ezekiel 9–10), the artistic technique used to depict these beings deserves special attention, as it provides a possible paradigm for understanding Ezekiel.

This *lamassu* statue is an example of a unique artistic device employed by Mesopotamian artists. In examining these particular statues, Julian Reade explains: "If one looks at one of these monsters from the side, one sees that it has four legs, striding purposefully forward. If one moves to look at it head-on, from the front, it has two front legs at rest. Both views in isolation are satisfactory and logical, as the figure might have been drawn by an artist looking at it either from one direction or from the other. The three-quarter viewpoint, in contrast, with both front and side visible at once, shows an animal that has not four legs but five."³⁸ Using this artistic device as a paradigm for understanding Ezekiel's temple description, any perceived tension between vertical and horizontal conceptualizations of sacred space and the direction of sacred approach to reach God is relieved. The position that only one of these approaches is valid is akin to an observer's confusion at noticing five legs on a *lamassu* statue. Just as the artist did not intend for the viewer to examine the statue from multiple viewpoints at once, perhaps the author of Ezekiel 40–43 did not intend for the audience to view the temple from both vertical and horizontal perspectives at the same time.

With this in mind, it becomes clear that both the vertical and the horizontal representations are appropriate ways of conceptualizing sacred space in Ezekiel's temple compound, and both appropriately conceptualize how one may approach God. The tension comes when one stands at a conceptual "three-quarter viewpoint," seeing both possibilities present at the same time yet assuming that only one conceptualization can have precedence. For the artist of the five-legged *lamassu*, "this device was used to make them appear complete from both points of view,"[39] without respect for which view was "superior." Likewise, *both* the vertical *and* the horizontal representations of sacred space in Ezekiel's temple vision appear complete when viewed in isolation, and both are clearly significant.[40] These multiple emphases uniquely describe how humans must progress through increasingly sacred space in order to approach God. Ezekiel skillfully weaves together two different spatial paradigms: a vertical approach to a sacred summit and a westward approach to a Holy of Holies. In doing so, the exilic Ezekiel displays a level of literary sophistication that might confuse those rooted in an "either-or" interpretive paradigm but which, when understood, leads to an increased appreciation of Ezekiel's unique perspective on the temple and what is symbolizes.

As demonstrated above, biblical scholarship provides valuable perspectives on understanding Ezekiel's temple vision; it shows ways to understand progression through increasingly sacred space and the relationship between the temple and Eden. These lessons can be applied easily to architecture and worship within Latter-day Saint temples, as well as the doctrines taught within their sacred walls. Such scholarship can also provide alternative paradigms and categories for thinking about Latter-day Saint temples that can help breathe new life into temple worship. For example, the categories of sacred height and sacred direction discussed here are noticeably present in Latter-day Saint temples—worshippers experience a rise in elevation by steps or ramps as they physically approach the temple's holiest space (the direction one approaches this space, however, differs from temple to temple). What do these changes in height and direction mean? How would a Latter-day Saint describe his or her approach to God in the temple? In addition to these directional questions, what sort of role does Eden play (architecturally, symbolically, theologically, and so forth) in temple worship for Latter-day Saints? In light of the significance these questions held for biblical authors, Latter-day Saint worshippers would do well to consider such questions themselves.

Latter-day Saints need not fear using scholarship from those of other faiths to better understand our own. This, however, requires Latter-day Saints to be humble about what they think they know and how they know it, as well as where they are willing to look for truth.[41] While the results of such studies may sometimes appear contradictory to our own current understanding and assumptions, there may be ways of reconciling these views.[42] As seen above, biblical scholars provided valuable information on Ezekiel's use of vertical and horizontal sacred space, but they appeared to be at odds regarding which was more significant. However, by thinking outside the box and using the example of the Mesopotamian *lamassu* statue, we see that both views can actually work together. Similarly, for Latter-day Saints, insights and answers to questions about the temple can come not only from the study of biblical scholarship, but also from the study of religious traditions outside of Christianity and Judaism. Due to such an incredible wealth of available information, Latter-day Saints should never feel complacent in the understanding of their temples or temple worship. It is only through the arduous process of both study and faith (see D&C 88:118) that such illuminating insight is available. And, though challenging, it is this very process of reaching for divine truth—wherever it may come from—that allows us to approach holiness ourselves.

Notes

1. One of the pioneers of Latter-day Saint temple scholarship was Hugh Nibley, whose *Temple and Cosmos: Beyond This Ignorant Present* (Salt Lake City: Deseret Book; Provo, UT: FARMS, 1992) is still invaluable. A good sampling of the sorts of studies that Latter-day Saint scholars have engaged in more recently is *Temples of the Ancient World: Ritual and Symbolism*, ed. Donald W. Parry (Salt Lake City: Deseret Book; Provo, UT: FARMS, 1994).

2. Notable exceptions are Jeffrey Bradshaw's *Temple Themes in the Book of Moses* (Salt Lake City: Eborn Publishing, 2010) and *Temple Themes in the Oath and Covenant of the Priesthood* (Salt Lake City: Eborn Publishing, 2012).

3. Scholars still debate the nature of this temple: Was it a heavenly pattern, similar to the one shown to Moses before he constructed the tabernacle (see Exodus 24) or to the one shown to David before he attempted to build the temple at Jerusalem (see 1 Chronicles 28:2–5, 11–12)? Was it a vision of the actual temple in Jerusalem that Ezekiel had grown up with? Or was it a vision of a temple that would be built at a future time of paradisiacal splendor? Because Ezekiel never clearly answers these questions, this paper will focus on the imagery that Ezekiel used in describing the temple itself, and it will explain the imagery in order to help better understand what this temple meant to him.

4. Walter Zimmerli, *Ezekiel 2: A Commentary on the Book of Prophet Ezekiel Chapters 25–48* (Philadelphia: Fortress Press, 1983), 343. Daniel Block similarly notes: "The dimensions recorded are exclusively horizontal measurements, apparently without regard for

the vertical distances required by architectural plans." Daniel Block, *The Book of Ezekiel: Chapters 25–48* (Grand Rapids, MI: Eerdmans, 1998), 510–11.

5. The only two measurements of height (גבה) appear in the description of the sacrificial tables (Ezekiel 40:42) and in the description of the sanctuary's golden altar/table outside the Holy of Holies (קדש הקדשים) (Ezekiel 41:22).

6. Block, *Book of Ezekiel: Chapters 25–48*, 542–43.

7. Block, *Book of Ezekiel: Chapters 25–48*, 595.

8. Steven Tuell, *The Law of the Temple in Ezekiel 40–48* (Atlanta, GA: Scholars' Press, 1992), 46. Throughout this paper, I have replaced the word *mythic* with *cosmic* to avoid any negative connotations associated with *myth*. Technically, a myth is a story that cultures use to explain and give meaning to their history, the supernatural, and the world around them. In popular use, however, because greater preference is given to straightforward and technical descriptions of the world, *myth* has come to mean "something false." In using the term *cosmic* in this paper, I am referring to a way of viewing the world that describes it using the largest scale possible.

9. Michael A. Fishbane, *Biblical Interpretation in Ancient Israel* (Oxford: Clarendon Press, 1985), 370, n. 132.

10. Fishbane, *Biblical Interpretation in Ancient Israel*, 370.

11. Other scholars agree with this interpretation of "bosom of the earth" (חיק הארץ) and "mountain of God" (הראל), likewise suggesting that the cosmic properties here ascribed to the altar also apply conceptually to the entire temple compound. See Jon Levenson, *Sinai and Zion: An Entry into the Jewish Bible* (Minneapolis, MN: Winston Press, 1985), 139; and Marvin Sweeney, "Ezekiel: Zadokite Priest and Visionary Prophet of the Exile," in *Form and Intertextuality in Prophetic and Apocalyptic Literature* (Tübingen, Germany: Mohr Siebeck, 2005), 142. Block, on the other hand, finds this etymology of הראל as "mountain of God" suspect. He points out that this same hearth is spelled differently (הראיל) twice: once in the same verse (Ezekiel 43:15) and once in the verse immediately following (Ezekiel 43:16), and therefore the extra letter in these subsequent descriptions needs explaining. At the very least, however, he admits that "it seems best . . . to treat har'ēl [הראל, "mountain of God"] as an intentional theological play on an architectural designation for the flat surface of the altar on which the offerings were presented." Block, *Book of Ezekiel: Chapters 25–48*, 600.

12. Margaret Odell's commentary does an excellent job of showing how Ezekiel's writings reflect his Babylonian environment. See Margaret Odell, *Ezekiel* (Macon, GA: Smyth & Helwys, 2005).

13. Victor Hurowitz, *I Have Built You an Exalted House: Temple Building in the Bible in Light of Mesopotamian and Northwest Semitic Writings* (Sheffield, England: JSOT Press, 1992), 336.

14. Similarly, the Papulegara hymn describes the temple of Kesh in the following words: "The head of the temple is lofty / Below its roots touch the netherworld / The head of the Kesh temple is lofty / Below its roots touch the netherworld / Above may its . . . rival heaven / Below its roots touch the netherworld." Hurowitz, *I Have Built You an Exalted House*, 335–36; ellipsis in original.

15. Tuell, *Law of the Temple*, 50–51.

16. Block, *Book of Ezekiel: Chapters 25–48*, 597.

17. Identified as such in Richard J. Clifford, *The Cosmic Mountain in Canaan and the Old Testament* (Cambridge, MA: Harvard University, 1972), 179. See also the depiction of this altar in Odell, *Ezekiel*, 500.

18. Another Mesopotamian temple description also equates the heights of the temple with heaven. The temple hymn to Ezida in Barsippa reads: "Barsippa resembles heaven, / Rivaling Esarra, is lofty Ezida, / Its foliage reaches the clouds, / Its roots are founded piercing the netherworld" (Hurowitz, *I Have Built You an Exalted House*, 336). Likewise, Odell notes the similarity between the stepped nature of this altar and ziggurats, the stepped Mesopotamian temple structures that Ezekiel would have certainly seen in Babylon. See Odell, *Ezekiel*, 501.

These three tiers or levels of the altar and the temple correspond with and may be representative of the three levels of the cosmos as envisioned by both Mesopotamians and Israelites: the heavens, the earth, and the netherworld. The thoroughly Jewish Apostle Paul mentions these three levels in his letter to the Philippians, explaining the scope of Jesus' lordship: "At the name of Jesus every knee should bow, of things in heaven [επουρανίων], and things in earth [επιγείων], and things under the earth [καταχθονίων]; and that every tongue should confess that Jesus Christ is Lord, to the glory of God the Father" (Philippians 2:10–11). Paul uses the first two of these three words elsewhere in his discussion of the Resurrection, where they are translated as follows: "There are also celestial bodies, and bodies terrestrial: but the glory of the celestial [επουρανίων] is one, and the glory of the terrestrial [επιγείων] is another. There is one glory of the sun, and another glory of the moon, and another glory of the stars" (1 Corinthians 15:40–41). In light of this information, one may translate Paul's earlier statement to the Philippians as follows: "At the name of Jesus every knee should bow, those who are celestial, terrestrial, and telestial." Thus, these three levels of the universe mentioned by Paul may correspond to the three degrees of glory: celestial, terrestrial, and telestial (see D&C 76). Likewise, the three levels of the temple and its altar may also correspond to these three degrees of glory.. My thanks to John Gee for suggesting this interpretive possibility in Philippians 2:10.

19. Levenson, *Sinai and Zion*, 139. This view is strengthened by the fact that the author describes the temple as being positioned "upon the top of the mountain" (על-הר ראש) (Ezekiel 43:12), which is itself a location with cosmological overtones. See Clifford, *Cosmic Mountain in Canaan and the Old Testament*, 5–8.

20. Levenson, *Sinai and Zion*, 138.

21. Latter-day Saint scholar John Lundquist makes a similar argument regarding all temples. See John M. Lundquist, "What Is a Temple? A Preliminary Typology," in *Temples of the Ancient World*, 83–117.

22. Odell, *Ezekiel*, 502; emphasis added.

23. Zimmerli, *Ezekiel 2*, 361.

24. "Tripartite" simply means "three-part." The tripartite gate structure described by Ezekiel here is similar to the city-gate structures archaeologists have uncovered at some of Solomon's cities. See Zimmerli, *Ezekiel 2*, 352 and footnotes.

25. Zimmerli, *Ezekiel 2*, 362. Many scholars argue that there are actually two creation stories present in Genesis 1–3. Because the emphasis in this first section (Genesis 1:1–2:3)

is on sacred boundaries and sacred time, scholars argue that this portion of the creation story was written by a priest (someone who would have been especially concerned with such sacred divisions).

26. Israelite priests were responsible for teaching their people the difference between the sacred and the profane (see Leviticus 10:8–11). For an excellent discussion of Ezekiel's priestly concerns throughout the book of Ezekiel, see Sweeney, "Ezekiel: Zadokite Priest and Visionary Prophet of the Exile," 125–43.

27. Zimmerli, *Ezekiel 2*, 355; emphasis added.

28. Both of the following translations of Ezekiel 41:23, 25 and Genesis 3:24 are my own.

29. Sweeney, "Ezekiel: Zadokite Priest and Visionary Prophet of the Exile," 141–42.

30. For a more complete examination of the imagery of these two chapters, see Jon Levenson, "The Mountain of Ezekiel's Vision as the Garden of Eden," in *Theology of the Program of Restoration of Ezekiel 40–48* (Missoula, MT: Scholars' Press, 1976), 25–36.

31. Fishbane, *Biblical Interpretation in Ancient Israel*, 370.

32. Fishbane writes, "It was not until the woe and dislocation of the exile, and with it the destruction of the land and Temple, that the symbolism of Eden emerges with singular emphasis. In the mouths of the post-exilic prophets, this imagery serves as the organizing prism for striking visions of spatial renewal." Fishbane, *Biblical Interpretation in Ancient Israel*, 369–70.

33. Levenson, *Theology of the Program of Restoration of Ezekiel 40–48*, 32.

34. Latter-day Saint scholar Donald Parry makes a similar argument regarding the Israelite tabernacle and temple. See Donald Parry, "Garden of Eden: Prototype Sanctuary," in *Temples of the Ancient World*, 126–51.

35. Jeremy Black and Anthony Green, *Gods, Demons and Symbols of Ancient Mesopotamia: An Illustrated Dictionary* (Austin: University of Texas, 1992), 51, 115.

36. Karel van der Toorn, Bob Becking, and Pieter W. van der Horst, eds., *Dictionary of Deities and Demons in the Bible* (Leiden, Netherlands: Brill; Grand Rapids, MI: Eerdmans, 1999), 181.

37. Miguel Civil and others, eds., *The Assyrian Dictionary*, vol. 9 (Chicago: The Oriental Institute, 1973), 63. In the Neo-Babylonian period, these protective deities "usually introduc[ed] worshippers into the presence of important deities" (Black and Green, *Gods, Demons and Symbols of Ancient Mesopotamia*, 115).

38. Julian Reade, *Assyrian Sculpture* (Cambridge, MA: Harvard University, 1999), 28.

39. Cyril John Gadd, *The Assyrian Sculptures* (London: The British Museum, 1934), 14.

40. In fact, the measurements of both the altar and the Holy of Holies (הקדשים קדש) suggest that these two seemingly opposed locations are equally significant. Odell notes, "The altar's size in comparison with other elements in the temple also indicates its importance. . . . In area, it equals that of the holy of holies." Odell, *Ezekiel*, 502–3. See also the reconstructions of these two locations in Block, *Book of Ezekiel: Chapters 25–48*, 541, 598.

41. Ever a student, Joseph Smith stated, "One [of] the grand fundamental principles of Mormonism is to receive truth, let it come from where it may." *The Words of*

Joseph Smith: The Contemporary Accounts of the Nauvoo Discourses of the Prophet Joseph, ed. Andrew F. Ehat and Lyndon W. Cook (Orem, UT: Grandin Book, 1991), 229; spelling and punctuation standardized.

Following Joseph's lead, Brigham Young expanded upon this principle:

> It is our duty and calling, as ministers of the . . . Gospel, to gather every item of truth and reject every error. Whether a truth be found with professed infidels, or with the Universalists, or the Church of Rome, or the Methodists, the Church of England, the Presbyterians, the Baptists, the Quakers, the Shakers, or any other of the various and numerous different sects and parties, all of whom have more or less truth, it is the business of the Elders of this Church . . . to gather up all the truths in the world pertaining to life and salvation, to the Gospel we preach, . . . wherever it may be found in every nation, kindred, tongue, and people, and bring it to Zion.
>
> The people upon this earth have a great many errors, and they have also a great many truths. This statement is not only true of the nations termed civilized—those who profess to worship the true God, but is equally applicable to pagans of all countries, for in their religious [rites] and ceremonies may be found a great many truths which we will also gather home to Zion.

Brigham Young, in *Journal of Discourses* (London: Latter-day Saints' Book Depot, 1854–86), 7:283–84.

42. Encouragement for such an endeavor can be found in the words of Joseph Smith, who once said, "By proving contraries, . . . truth is made manifest." *History of the Church of Jesus Christ of Latter-day Saints*, ed. B. H. Roberts, 2nd ed. rev. (Salt Lake City: Deseret Book, 1980), 6:428.

13

Theophany on Sinai

Amy B. Hardison

Mount Sinai looms large in the theological landscape of the Old Testament. It is "the mountain of God" (Exodus 3:1) and the first Israelite sanctuary.[1] It is where the law is revealed and where an incipient nation is set apart to God. It is where Moses enters into the presence of God, not once, but on at least three different occasions.[2] In Old Testament thought, bringing corruptible, consumable flesh into the presence of a being whose very essence is infinite glory, perfection, and holiness is imbued with danger. A mere mortal who attempts this must first engage in gestures of approach, religious acts that purify and prepare. However, ritual and spiritual preparation alone do not qualify one to enter into the presence of God. Theophanies are not gratuitous. They have purpose—a prophet is called, truth is revealed, a person is endowed with the power of God. Thus, theophanies transform. Having encountered the Divine, the person is never—or should never be—the same.

This paper will explore the three different theophanies that occur on Sinai: the commissioning call of Moses (Exodus 3–4), the establishment of the Mosaic covenant (Exodus 19–20, 24), and the renewal of the covenant after the rebellion

---

Amy B. Hardison is an independent scholar in Mesa, Arizona.

of the golden calf (Exodus 32–34). In particular, we will examine the rituals of approach and the ritual responses that accompany these theophanies, the ensuing transformation, and the revelation of the nature of God.

Moses' Commission (Exodus 3–4)

Moses' first encounter with God begins nondescriptly. He is simply doing what he has probably done many times in his forty years of shepherding, leading Jethro's flock into the remote pasturelands on the far side of Sinai. This time, however, "the angel of the Lord appeared unto him in a flame of fire out of the midst of a bush" (Exodus 3:2). In the Old Testament, the phrase "angel of the Lord" often refers to a "manifestation of God that is visible to the human eye."[3] The phrase "in a flame of fire" suggests that the Lord appears with the ineffable brilliance of celestial glory that is often described as fire.

God calls Moses by name, and Moses responds with the Hebrew idiom of readiness, "Here am I" (Exodus 3:4). In spite of this answer, Moses is not ready to enter into the presence of God. "Draw not nigh hither," God commands. "Put off thy shoes from off thy feet, for the place whereon thou standest is holy ground" (Exodus 3:5). Moses has been tramping through the dusty, dirty wilderness. Undoubtedly, the impurities of the world adhere to his sandals. It goes without saying that "one should not track dirt into God's house."[4] However, purity of the sole is not nearly as important as purity of the soul. The act is primarily symbolic. It is a gesture of approach that represents the ritual cleansing that must occur before one enters into the presence of God. At the same time, because only people of means wore sandals in Egypt and Israel, when Moses removes his sandals he demonstrates deference and humility.

Moses reacts to the appearance of God with the typical Old Testament response: fear. Too frightened to look upon God, he hides his face. While Moses cowers, God speaks; in doing so, God reveals himself. "I have surely seen the affliction of my people which are in Egypt and have heard their cry by reason of their taskmasters; for I know their sorrows; and I am come down to deliver them out of the hand of the Egyptians and to bring them up out of that land unto a good land and a large, unto a land flowing with milk and honey" (Exodus 3:7–8). By this statement, God reveals that he is not a remote God dispassionately observing earthlings. God sees. He listens. He knows. He comes down (an idiom for describing divine intervention in human affairs).[5] He delivers. And he brings them into a spacious and bountiful land.

This is a God who cares deeply, who responds to calls of distress and anguish, but not prematurely. This is a God who desires to bless and bestow abundance and above all to take his people out of the world and bring them unto himself, where they may rest in him.

Listening to this being of unimaginable power and glory declare that he will deliver the Hebrews from bitter and oppressive bondage would presumably amaze and delight Moses—until Moses learns that he is not to be a mere spectator. He has a key role in this deliverance. Understandably, Moses gasps, "Who am I, that I should go unto Pharaoh, and that I should bring forth the children of Israel out of Egypt?" (Exodus 3:11).

Interestingly, God does not dispute Moses' conclusion of inadequacy. He does not remind Moses that he had been raised in the royal courts of Egypt and thus is uniquely prepared for this mission. He does not tell him that he had been foreordained to this role. In fact, the absence of a direct reply to Moses' question "Who am I?" (an idiom for expressing insufficiency) tacitly affirms Moses' fear. Moses is *not* equal to the task at hand. But God is, and he promises, "Certainly, I will be with thee" (Exodus 3:12). This statement is "a ubiquitous formula of divine reassurance"[6] and occurs over a hundred times in the Old Testament. It is most frequently used "when the addressee faces danger or a task where the risk of failure is very great."[7] God does not minimize the difficulty of what he asks Moses to do. Rather, he swears that he will empower Moses and will give him what he needs to succeed.

So important is God's promise that he offers a token to seal and affirm the oath. "And this shall be a token unto thee, that I have sent thee: When thou hast brought forth the people out of Egypt, ye shall serve God upon this mountain" (Exodus 3:12). It is not clear exactly what this token is. Carol Meyers writes, "God proclaims the sign [token], meant to corroborate a message from God, in language fraught with ambiguity."[8] She offers several possibilities for the token, including the burning bush, the presence of God, and the eventual success of Moses' mission. One possibility that Meyers does not mention is that the token might be a physical gesture intentionally left unrecorded because of its sacredness.

Moses has received a divine promise and a token confirming the promise. He next asks for God's name. Scholars do not agree on exactly why Moses needs to know God's name. Some propose that the name is a kind of test, either a test of God (if Moses already knows God's name, he may be testing this luminescent being to see if he is really Yahweh; cf. D&C 129) or a test of Moses (administered by the leaders of Israel to Moses to see if he has truly been in the presence of God). William Propp suggests another possibility: "Most likely, the divine name functions somehow as a password."⁹ Alternatively, he says, "Moses' desire to learn the Deity's name seems to be born, not of idle curiosity, but of a persistent aspiration to know God."¹⁰ How is God's name related to knowing God? In the ancient world, one's name was far more than an appellation. It revealed the very essence and nature of a person.

In Moses' first theophany on Sinai, God refers to himself with two different names. The first is "the God of Abraham, the God of Isaac, and the God of Jacob" (Exodus 3:6) and its variation "the God of your fathers" (Exodus 3:13). William L. Lane states that "the phrase 'the God of . . .' is synonymous with helper, savior."¹¹ Thus, when God says, "I am the God of thy father, the God of Abraham, the God of Isaac, and the God of Jacob" (Exodus 3:6), he is saying he has been the patriarchs' guide, helper, and sustainer and will be Israel's savior in their current affliction. This name-title recurs in Exodus 3:15, 16 and 4:5, "precisely in passages in which God promises salvation and deliverance to his people, and serves as a guarantee of that deliverance."¹² It also reveals one of God's defining attributes, that of Savior.

God reveals a second name when Moses asks what he should say to the children of Israel when they ask him for the name of the God who has sent him. God responds, "*'ehyeh 'ăšer 'ehyeh*," translated in the King James Version as "I AM THAT I AM" (Exodus 3:14). Propp writes, "Scholars call sentences with two identical (or nearly identical) verbs, usually connected by the relative pronoun *'ăšer* [who, which, that], *idem per idem* formulae. . . . The main function of this rhetorical device is to be vague, whether to convey infinite potentiality or to conceal information, by defining a thing as itself."¹³ The inherent ambiguity of *'ehyeh 'ăšer 'ehyeh* is reflected by the numerous translations proffered by scholars.¹⁴ David Noel Freedman renders "the enigmatic expression in Exod 3:14: 'I create what I create,' or more simply, 'I am the creator.'"¹⁵ It is not incidental that Jehovah would introduce himself to Moses as the Creator. In ancient Near Eastern thought, the god of creation subdued the violent, primordial powers of chaos and death and imposed peace, stability, and order on the earth. Such a powerful god definitely has power to overthrow one small pharaoh.

It is possible that *'ehyeh 'ăšer 'ehyeh* is not a name at all. John Durham writes, "The answer Moses receives is not, by any stretch of the imagination, a name. It is an assertion of authority, a confession of an essential reality."[16] In Exodus 3:12–14, "I AM" is repeated four times in quick succession (translated as "I will be" in verse 12). Durham continues: "The repetition of these 'I AM' verbs, as awkward as it may appear, is entirely intentional. The redactor's point is just too important to be missed, and so he has labored to make it obvious: Yahweh Is. However absent he may have seemed to the oppressed Israelites in Egypt, . . . his Is-ness means Presence."[17] Whether we understand *ehyeh 'aser 'ehyeh* to be a reference to Jehovah's role as creator, with all the power that entails, or a theological statement of his constant, unfailing presence, the name reveals something of the nature of God.

At one point in his encounter with God, Moses expresses his concern that the children of Israel will not believe that God has appeared to him. God responds by turning a rod into a serpent and back into a rod, by turning Moses' healthy hand into a leprous one and back again, and by promising him "a third sign, which will assuredly prove decisive. This sign, which cannot be performed here, but only in Egypt,"[18] is the turning of the water of the Nile into blood. These signs fill multiple purposes. They assure the children of Israel that Moses comes with the power of God. They bolster Moses' flagging confidence. They may also accompany and confirm the bestowal of priesthood power.

Since both the serpent and the Nile are deified in Egypt, these signs also testify that Israel's God is more powerful than the gods of the Egyptians. The cobra was the patron goddess of Lower Egypt, and the uraeus (a stylized rearing cobra with a flared hood) was worn on the forehead by all the pharaohs as a symbol of their imperial sovereignty. When Aaron's rod turns into a serpent, it devours the Egyptian magicians' rods, which also turned into serpents, demonstrating the supremacy of the God of Israel. In a similar vein, the Nile was the source of fertility for Egypt. Its annual flooding ensured bounteous crops and established Egypt as the breadbasket of the region, which in turn generated Egypt's enormous wealth and power. Not surprisingly, the Nile was regarded as a deity, the god Hapi, who unceasingly blessed the land. To threaten or destroy the Nile was to destroy Egypt itself. When Moses turns the Nile into blood, the God of Israel destroys the river's life-giving power and sends a strong message as to who reigns supreme.

Having stood in the presence of God and having received sacred promises confirmed by tokens, names, and signs, Moses is now ready to embark on his mission. He goes forth not as a shepherd but as a prophet, a servant appointed to represent God and endowed with power to perform miracles. He has not instantaneously transformed into a spiritual superhero; he is still reluctant and tentative. But his transformation has begun. The next time he stands on Sinai, he will have unflinchingly challenged one of the most powerful rulers in the ancient Near East, taken leadership of the Hebrew multitude, and parted the waters of the Red Sea through the power of the priesthood.

The Establishment of the Mosaic Covenant (Exodus 19–24)

Seven weeks after their deliverance from Egypt, the children of Israel arrive at Sinai, where they will remain for the better part of a year. On the very day they arrive, Moses ascends the mountain of God (see Exodus 19:1, 3).[19] In this second theophany, God invites Israel to enter into a covenant relationship with him. This invitation sheds additional light on the nature of God, particularly revealing his desire for an intimate relationship with his people.

God instructs Moses, "Thus shalt thou say to the house of Jacob, and tell the children of Israel; ye have seen what I did unto the Egyptians, and how I bare you on eagle's wings, and brought you unto myself" (Exodus 19:3–4). Here, God employs the image of a mother eagle that is teaching her eaglets to fly, who gently but firmly pushes them out of the nest so they can try their wings. If they falter, she will swoop down and bear them up on her own powerful wings.[20] The imagery is of tender, protective care that is ever present. According to Victor P. Hamilton, the phrase "and brought you unto myself" suggests that "God's primary purpose of bonding with Israel is for that rapturous enjoyment of each other's presence."[21] This corresponds with Terence Fretheim's view that "God desires to be as intimately present [with his people] as possible."[22] Hamilton's and Fretheim's views are echoed in scripture. Doctrine and Covenants 88:63 states, "Draw near unto me and I will draw near unto you." In 2 Nephi we read that God desires to encircle us in the arms of his love (see 2 Nephi 1:15; see also D&C 6:20). Truly, Jehovah's great invitation is "come unto me" (Matthew 11:28), and his great desire is unity and at-one-ment.

God's desire for intimacy with the children of Israel is also present in the phrase "ye shall be a peculiar treasure unto me" (Exodus 19:5). The word "peculiar treasure" is the Hebrew word *segulla*. It denotes a treasured possession or a personal treasure. The *segulla* must be understood "against the background of the absolutist monarchies of the ancient world, where the king was the theoretical owner of everything. Within this total ownership, he might gather and put to one side things that he specially prized and considered to be his own in a unique way. It was this that was his *sĕgullâ*, his choice, personal treasure."[23]

God also declares that Israel shall be "a kingdom of priests, and an holy nation" (Exodus 19:6). The great prerogative of priests is that they enjoy a privileged relationship with God. They can enter into sacred space and approach God in a way others cannot. They alone are exclusively dedicated to God and to his service. God is inviting all of Israel to be priests, to have an intimate, personal relationship with him. This is unique in the ancient world. Typically, the gods were above all, "'something grandiose, inaccessible, dominating, and to be feared.' . . . [They] were not the object of enthusiastic pursuit. The people sought the gods for protection and assistance, not for relationship."[24]

Moses returns to the children of Israel and extends to them God's invitation to be his people. They answer in unison, "All that the Lord hath spoken we will do" (Exodus 19:8). Once they give their preliminary commitment, God agrees to do something spectacular and amazing: he will "come down in the sight of all the people upon mount Sinai" (Exodus 19:11), and they will hear when he speaks with Moses (see Exodus 19:9). "This is the only instance in the Old Testament where the gathered community is confronted with such a direct experience of God, hearing God speak without an intermediary. It is *a unique divine appearance*."[25]

However, if the people are to experience the power and glory of God, they—like Moses, who was required to remove his shoes in the first theophany—must participate in gestures of approach. This time, the Lord requires the people to wash their clothes and to abstain from sexual relations for three days. The washing of clothes clearly represents the removal of impurities and contaminations. Various reasons are suggested for the requirement of sexual abstinence. One reason is that many ancient religions used sexual rites as a way of entreating the gods to bless their lands with fertility.[26] The God of Israel unequivocally separated sex and worship.[27] Another reason is that the emission of bodily fluids was believed to make one temporarily less than whole and thus ceremonially unclean.[28] It must also be remembered that temporary celibacy for worshippers was common in the ancient world. William Propp explains, "This temporary continence does not imply that sex was sinful for Israelites and other ancient Near Easterners—any more than eating is sinful because people sometimes fast for religious reasons. Rather, one subjects oneself to a trial by forgoing a licit pleasurable activity."[29]

After the people prepare themselves for three days, God descends onto Mount Sinai. He does so heralded by thunder, lightning, smoke, trumpets, fire, and the quaking of the mount. It would appear that a volcano is erupting—except there are no active volcanoes in the area. In the midst of intense meteorological phenomena, a ram's horn begins to sound and grows steadily louder. Propp writes, "While the ram's horn is rather faint by modern, symphonic standards, it probably made a greater impression on the ancients, who inhabited a quieter world."[30] Moreover, there is no mention as to who is blowing the horn.[31] It is not Moses or any Israelite, adding to the *mysterium tremendum*[32] of the occasion.

At this moment of spellbinding wonder and awe, God speaks. He delivers the Ten Commandments.[33] When God finishes, the people withdraw, terrified. They plead with Moses, "Speak thou with us, and we will hear; but let not God speak [or "keep speaking"[34]] with us, lest we die" (Exodus 20:19). Moses tries to convince the people to not fear God, "for God is come to prove you" (Exodus 20:20). The word translated as "prove," *nissa*, could also be translated as "train," "initiate by ordeal," "instruct,"[35] or "see, experience."[36] Whether testing or training, Israel fails. Doctrine and Covenants 84:24 tells us, "They hardened their hearts and could not endure his [God's] presence." This does not, however, amount to a wholesale rejection of the covenant. Rather, the children of Israel place the burden and privilege of personally experiencing God on Moses. They prefer a less direct and less demanding experience.

In Exodus 24, the people participate in a ceremony to ratify and seal the covenant. They once again verbally assent in unison to the covenant. The next morning, Moses arises early, builds an altar, and sets up twelve pillars. The altar represents Yahweh, and the pillars represent the twelve tribes of Israel. The pillars, or standing stones, also serve as a witness to or a memorial of the covenant. Moses appoints some young men to sacrifice burnt offerings and peace offerings upon the altar. It should be noted that these offerings are not the same as sin or guilt offerings. They are nonexpiatory. The burnt offering, which is burnt on the altar in its entirety, represents holding nothing back from God, a total consecration of one's being. The <u>peace offering</u> is apportioned between God, the priest, and the offerer. <u>The offerer takes the majority of the sacrifice back to his family and celebrates with a feast that represents fellowship and unity with God and fellow man.</u>

Moses next takes the blood of the sacrifices and sprinkles it upon the altar, which represents Yahweh, and upon the people, or more probably upon the pillars that represent the people. This mysterious rite is "heavily freighted with symbolism."[37] The sprinkling of blood on both the altar (Yahweh) and the pillars (the people) attests to the reciprocity of this covenant. Both God and Israel are bound—God to support and defend his people; the people to love and obey their God. The sprinkling of the blood was also a "symbolic action in which the people were identified with the sacrificed animal, so that the fate of the latter is presented as the fate to be expected by the people if they violated their sacred promise."[38] This kind of symbolic action was often accompanied by a self-execrative oath like, "If I transgress the terms of the covenant, may my blood be spilled as the blood of this animal was spilled."[39]

To further seal the covenant, seventy elders of Israel ascend the mount, where they see the God of Israel and participate in a covenantal meal. Durham writes, "The apparent purpose of the climb up onto Sinai of this special group is that they shall have the experience, as Moses has had already, of a still more intimate contact with the Presence of Yahweh. In such a manner are they uniquely equipped for their service of guidance and teaching, of leadership."[40] It is notable that God "laid not his hand" (Exodus 24:11) upon any of the elders. The apparent meaning here is that God did not harm these elders in spite of their proximity to the consuming glory and holiness of God. However, there is another possibility. The Hebrew word for "laid," *shalach*, also means "to stretch out," perhaps indicating that God did not extend his hand to these elders, a privilege he might have granted Moses, who enjoyed greater intimacy than did these seventy.

The effect of this second theophany is that all of Israel has transformed from the descendants of Jacob into a covenant community and a nation dedicated to God, his special treasure. While it is true that as the descendants of Abraham, Isaac, and Jacob, they are children of the covenant, it is also true that this is a new dispensation. The covenant has been renewed with them. The operative point is that in every dispensation "a covenant elevates a relationship to a more intimate, dynamic level."[41] As President Henry B. Eyring has said, "Every covenant with God is an opportunity to draw closer to him. . . . To have that bond made stronger and that relationship closer is an irresistible offer."[42]

The Renewal of the Covenant (Exodus 32–34)

Within forty days of experiencing God and entering into a holy covenant through sacred rituals, the children of Israel break their covenant. This happens so fast that it could be likened unto "committing adultery on one's wedding night."[43] Moses, who at the time of this egregious breach is still with God on the upper reaches of Sinai, pleads for his people. He implores God to restrain his anger, not because the people deserve leniency, but because God has so recently gone to such lengths to deliver them, because the Egyptians will gloat over this surprising turn of events and draw erroneous conclusions about God's intention and ability, and because of the promises made to the patriarchs (see Exodus 32:11–13).

Moses placates God, only to have his own anger "wax hot" (Exodus 32:19) when he sees Israel's raucous rebellion for himself. Moses breaks the tables of stone, signifying the nullification of the covenant, and punishes the people. He then returns to the heights of Sinai and into the presence of God. In this third theophany, God reveals to Moses another of God's names. Unlike the laconic name "I am that I am," this name contains thirty-two words, all describing various attributes of God. While "thirty-two words may seem an impossibly long appellation, even for a god,"[44] the "multiplication of names was one way to express the power and station of the deity"[45] in the ancient Near East.

God's first pronouncement is "The Lord, The Lord God, merciful and gracious" (Exodus 34:6). This could also be translated as "The Lord. The Lord. God is merciful and gracious." It is uncertain why God would begin his name with a twofold "The Lord." William Propp suggests that the "repetition itself constitutes invocation, whether God calls Man (Gen 22:11; 46:2; Exod 3:4; 1 Sam 3:10) or Man calls God (Josh 22:22; Ps 22:2 [Rashi]; cf. 1 Kgs 18:39). God can also, as here, cultically invoke himself; compare [Exodus] 20:24 (21): 'in any place where I announce my name, I will come to you and bless you.'"[46]

The next part of God's name is "merciful and gracious, longsuffering" (Exodus 34:6). This mercy, grace, and longsuffering is atypical in the ancient religious milieu. There is no doctrine in Canaanite religions supporting the idea that when people have offended their god, "divine favor can be restored when the people turn to righteousness as there is in Israel."[47]

God declares that he is "abundant in goodness and truth" (Exodus 34:6). "Goodness" is the Hebrew word *hesed*, a word for which no simple translation exists in English. It is used in covenantal contexts, as well as elsewhere, and it conveys the sense of steadfast loyalty to the covenant. This stands in stark contrast to the behavior of the children of Israel, who are far from steadfast and immovable.

The final phrase of God's name is "keeping mercy for thousands [that is, thousands of generations], forgiving iniquity and transgression and sin, and that will by no means clear the guilty; visiting the iniquity of the fathers upon the children, and upon the children's children, unto the third and to the fourth generation" (Exodus 34:7). While God's mercy and forgiveness are again emphasized, it is now revealed that justice is an essential part of God's nature. God will not clear the guilty or overlook sin. Mercy will not rob justice. God will visit the iniquity of the fathers unto the fourth generation. But his mercy will extend until the thousandth generation—250 times longer than his anger. No wonder when Moses hears the name of God and understands his nature he bows his head and worships the benevolent and merciful Redeemer.

Moses again implores God to forgive the stiffnecked people, to pardon their sin, and to take them as his inheritance (see Exodus 34:9). The word translated as "inheritance," *nahala*, refers to an eternal, inalienable possession. In other words, Moses is asking God to take Israel once again as his own special possession, his *segulla*. Could God possibly be *that* benevolent? *That* merciful? God responds, "Behold, I make a covenant: before all thy people I will do marvels, such as have not been done in all the earth, nor in any nation" (Exodus 34:10). God will not permanently revoke the privilege of a covenant relationship. Israel will once again be his people. He will be their God. He will do marvels. The root of the Hebrew word translated as "marvels" is *p-l-'* and means "wonderful, surpassing, extraordinary, or marvelous." When God says he will do things that "have not been done in all the earth" (Exodus 34:10), the word "done" is from the Hebrew word *bara'*, "to create." It is the word used in Genesis 1. In other words, as Fretheim writes, what God is about to do "is of such an unprecedented nature that only creation language, combined with language of marvel and awe, can adequately describe it."[48] What is this act? It is the miracle of forgiveness.

The effect of this third theopany is that God and Israel are reconciled. The people are restored to a nation of priests, though not collectively, for God with all his compassion will not abandon justice or judgment. A representative group, the Levites, will appear before God. They will bear the priesthood—a preparatory priesthood—of God.

Conclusion

Sinai was the setting for three theophanies that shaped the history of Israel. Theophanies often included preparatory gestures of approach and covenants that were sealed and ratified by holy actions. Those who experienced a theophany inevitably learned more about the nature of God and underwent individual or corporate transformation. Significantly, many of these aspects of theophanies became a ritualized part of temple worship. John Lundquist writes, "The temple of Solomon would seem ultimately to be little more than the architectural realization and the ritual enlargement of the Sinai experience."[49] This is true not only of Solomon's and Herod's temples, but also of the temples of the restored gospel. Our temple experience includes gestures of approach, covenants, ratifying signs and tokens, verbal assents, sacrifices of heart and will at an altar, coming to understand the nature of God, and personal transformation. Each time we figuratively climb the mountain of the Lord, we, like Moses, can enter into God's presence. We, like Moses, can experience the glory, grandeur, love, support, and mercy of our God. We, like Moses, can bow our head and worship in loving reverence and awe. This is the privilege and potential of temple worship for every endowed Latter-day Saint. As Karl G. Maeser has said, "There is a Mount Sinai for every child of God if he only knows how to climb it."[50]

Notes

1. Donald W. Parry, "Sinai as Sanctuary and Mountain of God," in *By Study and Also By Faith*, ed. John M. Lundquist and Stephen D. Ricks (Salt Lake City: Deseret Book, 1990), 1:482.

2. It is difficult to determine exactly how many trips Moses makes to the summit of Sinai and into the presence of God because of the "chronological morass" of Exodus 19 due to "profound redactional and source complexity." Carol Meyers, *Exodus* (New York: Cambridge University Press, 2005), 144. However, this paper rests not on how many trips Moses makes up Sinai but rather on the three different periods in which Moses ascends the mountain and enters the presence of God.

3. Victor P. Hamilton, *Exodus: An Exegetical Commentary* (Grand Rapids, MI: Baker Academic, 2011), 46.

4. William H. C. Propp, *Exodus 1–18*, Anchor Bible 2 (New York: Doubleday, 1999), 200.

5. Umberto Moshe David Cassuto, *A Commentary on the Book of Exodus* (Skokie, IL: Varda Books, 2005), 34.

6. Propp, *Exodus 1–18*, 203.

7. D. E. Gowan, *Theology in Exodus: Biblical Theology in the Form of a Commentary* (Louisville, KY: John Knox Press, 1994), quoted in Hamilton, *Exodus*, 59.

8. Meyers, *Exodus*, 56.

9. Propp, *Exodus 1–18*, 223; cf. D&C 130:11; see also Gaye Strathearn, "Revelation: John's Message of Comfort and Hope," in *The Testimony of John the Beloved* (Salt Lake City: Deseret Book, 1998), 292.

10. Propp, *Exodus 1–18*, 223.

11. William L. Lane, *The Gospel According to Mark*, New International Commentary on the New Testament 2 (Grand Rapids, MI: Eerdmans, 1974), 429.

12. Lane, *Gospel According to Mark*, 430.

13. Propp, *Exodus*, 225.

14. For instance, Alter suggests "I Am He Who Endures" and "He Who Brings Things into Being." Robert Alter, *The Five Books of Moses* (New York: Norton, 2004) 321. Fretheim prefers "I will be who I am/I am who I will be." Terence E. Fretheim, *Exodus*, Interpretation: A Bible Commentary for Teaching and Preaching (Louisville, KY: John Knox Press, 1991), 63); Propp supports "I will be who I will be." *Exodus 1–18*, 205.

15. David Noel Freedman, "The Name of the God of Moses," *Journal of Biblical Literature* 79, no. 2 (June 1960): 154. According to Freedman, although the Masoretic Text (MT) has the active verb form (Qal), it was originally causative (Hiphil). Thus, in his translation, Freedman uses the causative "I bring into being" or "I create" (152, 153). Paul Haupt, William F. Albright, and Frank Moore Cross all favor a similar interpretation. See Propp, *Exodus*, 225.

16. John I. Durham, *Exodus*, Word Biblical Commentary 3 (Waco, TX: Word Books, 1987), 38.

17. Durham, *Exodus*, 39.

18. Cassuto, *Exodus*, 48.

19. Verse two is a parenthetical note and obscures the urgency.

20. Fretheim, *Exodus*, 210.

21. Hamilton, *Exodus*, 302.

22. Terence E. Fretheim, *The Suffering of God*, Overtures of Biblical Theology (Philadelphia: Fortress, 1984), 65.

23. Alec Motyer, *The Message of Exodus*, The Bible Speaks Today (Downers Grove, IL: InterVarsity Press, 2005), 198, 199.

24. John H. Walton, *Ancient Near Eastern Thought and the Old Testament* (Grand Rapids, MI: Baker Academic, 2006), 161.

25. Fretheim, *Exodus*, 214; emphasis in original.

26. Scholars refer to this as "sympathetic magic." The idea is that the people would engage in actions that the gods would imitate. The copulation of gods was considered to bring fertility to the earth in Canaanite religious belief.

27. Rousas John Rushdoony, *The Institutes of Biblical Law* (Phillipsburg, NJ: Presbyterian and Reformed Publishing, 1973), 293.

28. Meyers, *Exodus*, 154.

29. William H. C. Propp, *Exodus 19–40*, Anchor Bible 2A (New York: Doubleday, 2006), 163.

30. Propp, *Exodus 19–40*, 164.

31. "One may assume this blast is of celestial origin probably blown by a member of God's angelic entourage, to announce the awe-inspiring descent of the King of all the earth." Alter, *Five Books of Moses*, 426.

32. This phrase was coined by Rudolf Otto to describe the numinous awe that comes from experiencing God. See Rudolf Otto, *The Idea of the Holy* (New York: Oxford University Press, 1950), 12, 13ff.

33. Some scholars believe that Exodus 19:19–25 are displaced and Exodus 19:19a should be followed not by vv. 19b–25, but by 20:1. See Durham, *Exodus*, 269, 270.

34. Durham, *Exodus*, 301.

35. Propp, *Exodus 19–40*, 182.

36. Durham, *Exodus*, 303.

37. Propp, *Exodus 19–40*, 308.

38. George E. Mendenhall and Gary A. Herion, "Covenant," in *The Anchor Bible Dictionary*, ed. David Noel Freedman (New York: Doubleday, 1992), 1:1185.

39. See Ruth 1:17; 1 Kings 19:2; Alma 44:13, 14; 46:21–24.

40. Durham, *Exodus*, 344; cf. D&C 95:3, 4; 105:9–11.

41. Hamilton, *Exodus*, 301.

42. Henry B. Eyring, "Making Covenants with God," in *Speeches, Brigham Young University 1996–1997* (Provo, UT: Brigham Young University Publications and Graphics, 1997), 15.

43. R. W. L. Moberly, "Exodus," in *Theological Interpretation of the Old Testament: A Book-by-Book Survey*, ed. K. J. Vanhoozer and others (Grand Rapids: Baker Academic, 2008), 48, quoted in Hamilton, *Exodus*, 531.

44. Propp, *Exodus 19–40*, 609.

45. Walton, *Ancient Near Eastern Thought*, 92.

46. Propp, *Exodus 19–40*, 610.

47. Francis I. Anderson and David Noel Freedman, *Hosea*, Anchor Bible 24 (New York: Doubleday, 1980), 476.

48. Fretheim, *Exodus*, 308.

49. John M. Lundquist, "What Is a Temple? A Preliminary Typology," in *Temples of the Ancient World*, ed. Donald W. Parry (Salt Lake City: Deseret Book, 1994), 85.

50. Harold B. Lee, *Teachings of Harold B. Lee* (Salt Lake City: Deseret Book 1996), 452.

14

Darkness, Light, and the Lord: Elements of Israelite Theophanies

Kerry Muhlestein

When readers of the Bible think of the divine presence in the Old Testament, the words *glory* and *power* are apt to come to mind. But in what way is this glory depicted? What were the authors of the Hebrew Bible trying to portray in their accounts? A careful study of the language of the theophanic scenes of the Old Testament reveals that after the Genesis accounts, light and "glory" are an important part of divine manifestations. In addition, we also encounter an interesting interplay between luminosity and darkness, or revealing and hiding. These ideas seem to be somehow tied together in the ancient Israelite concept of the presence of God.

While the theophanies[1] of the Hebrew Bible came from several different authors and passed through various redactional stages, there is remarkable uniformity in the elements accompanying the divine presence. Regardless of the source, the imagery of theophany remains the same. When this is not the case, the exception will be noted and discussed. However, even in these exceptions, the basic interplay of light and darkness remains constant. As we explore the textual evidence for theophanies in the Old Testament, we will

---

Kerry Muhlestein is an associate professor of ancient scripture at Brigham Young University.

proceed chronologically, and with each divine manifestation we will look at the references to light, called herein luminous references, and the interplay between revealing and hiding. Because we are investigating the physical presence of light and darkness, we will only examine theophanies where the physical presence of God is described or implied. Encounters with God that do not include a corporeal element, such as when Cain hears God's voice but no mention is made of seeing God (see Genesis 4:9), are not discussed in this paper.

Genesis

The first encounter with the divine presence is recorded in the Garden of Eden pericope. However, the scene at the Garden of Eden is not germane to this study, because mankind's relationship with God was different before the Fall. When Adam and Eve were cast out of the garden, they first heard "the voice of the Lord God walking in the garden" (Genesis 3:8).[2] While it is hard to determine what is meant by a "voice . . . walking," it is clear that the Lord is not before them.[3] The Book of Moses account portrays Adam and Eve as the beings that are walking (Moses 4:14). This change resolves the ambiguity of the Genesis phrasing and maintains the idea that in this text, God himself did not appear at this time. A conversation ensues, but never does the text portray Adam and Eve actually seeing the Lord. Thus, there is no description of his appearance in this account.

Similarly, Genesis 5:24 says that Enoch walked with God. It contains no description of God or his presence at all. For the purposes of this paper, there is no information to be evaluated in this encounter, whatever the form of that encounter may have been.

We first read of someone being truly in the presence of God in Genesis 17. Here we have this brief description: "The Lord appeared to Abram, and said unto him, I am the Almighty God; walk before me, and be thou perfect" (Genesis 17:1). This is one of the most salutary events of the Hebrew Bible, for it was on this occasion that God established his covenant with Abram (whose name was later changed to Abraham). However, the description of God's appearance is nothing more than that quoted above. We simply know that he "appeared." We gain no insight as to what that appearance was like. The Book of Abraham account merely mentions that Abraham spoke with God "face to face" but, consistent with the other Genesis accounts, includes no other information about the Lord's presence (Abraham 3:11).

Abraham's grandson Jacob also saw the Lord. Again we find no significant description of God's presence or physical appearance. In his famous dream, Jacob sees "a ladder set up on the earth, and the top of it reached to heaven: and behold the angels of God ascending and descending on it. And, behold, the Lord stood above it, and said, I am the Lord God of Abraham thy father, and the God of Isaac" (Genesis 28:12–13). This is the full extent of the description of the Lord in this vision.

In Genesis 32:30, it is intimated that Jacob saw God again, but since the appearance is only alluded to, we cannot expect to find a forthright description of that appearance.[4] Jacob sees God one final time, in the same place he had his first vision, towards the end of his life. Here it is recorded that "God appeared unto Jacob again, when he came out of Padan-aram, and blessed him" (Genesis 35:9). We find yet again that there is no description provided of God. All that is mentioned is that he appeared and renewed the covenant.

This lack of description in the Genesis accounts stands in stark contrast to the rest of the Bible. Interestingly, Abraham purportedly comes from Mesopotamian and then Canaanite origins, and descriptions of deities (other than sun or moon gods) in Mesopotamia and Canaan are likewise lacking in luminous references.[5] It is only after the Exodus from Egypt that the Israelites record a high degree of luminous terms in connection with the appearance of God. In these later descriptions, the Hebrew Bible contains luminous references that resemble those used by ancient Egyptians to describe divine appearances. While it is possible that Israel's cultural milieu was changed significantly while the Israelites were in Egypt, thus producing Egypt-like theophanic descriptions, such a causal relationship would be difficult to explore and lies well beyond the means of this study.[6] Still, it is fertile ground for some future exploration.

Exodus and Deuteronomy

Beginning in the book of Exodus, divine manifestations fit a pattern that will be followed throughout the rest of the Old Testament. In fact, it is the presence of light that caused Moses to turn aside and come into God's presence:

And the angel[7] of the Lord appeared to him in a flame of fire from the midst of a bush. And he looked, and, behold, the bush burned with fire, but the bush was not consumed.

And Moses said, I will turn aside, and see this great sight, why the bush does not burn.

And when the Lord saw that he turned aside to see, God called unto him from the midst of the bush, and said, Moses, Moses. And he said, behold me. (Exodus 3:2–4)[8]

The description of a bush that burned with fire but was not consumed seems to be a description of a bush that exuded light. The bush caught Moses' attention,[9] and from there, Moses heard the voice of the Lord and actually saw him "in a flame of fire," or, in other words, filled with light. From this brief account, it is clear that Moses' theophany was essentially luminous and that light was the element that indicated God's presence.

Sometime thereafter, Moses again sees God, as recorded in Moses 1. In this account, Moses makes repeated references to God's glory (see Moses 1:2, 5, 9, 11, 13, 14, 18, 20, 25, 31, 39), but the only reference made specifically to light is when Moses speaks of the "burning bush" (Moses 1:17). Some of the uses of the word *glory* clearly are not referring to light but to God's power and ability to transfigure Moses (see Moses 1:2, for example).[10] However, it is interesting to note that, while Moses uses the same phrase as Abraham when he describes seeing God "face to face" (Moses 1:31), he couples this experience with the glory of God, an idea missing from Abraham's account. We will more fully examine the Hebrew word for glory below.

Later, all of Israel also encountered the presence of God. Their first encounter may not be considered a theophany proper, but they definitely experienced Jehovah's presence. As they left Egypt, the Israelites were led by the Lord: "And the Lord went before them daily in a pillar of a cloud, to lead them in the way; and nightly in a pillar of fire, to give them light; to go by daily and nightly. He did not take away from before the people the pillar of cloud by day, nor the pillar of fire by night" (Exodus 13:21–22).[11] It is here that we first encounter the seemingly paradoxical appearance of the Lord as a fire and a cloud. This almost antithetical parallel use of the two ideas becomes a common motif of divine encounters throughout the Bible. The two elements signifying God's presence present a small conundrum. Is the Lord's presence indicative of fire, which connotes light, or of a cloud, which connotes darkness? Can his presence be symbolized by both?

The parallel yet antithetical pairing of these two elements is heightened when the Egyptian army approaches Israel. At this time, "the pillar of the cloud went from before them, and stood behind them. And it came between the camp of the Egyptians and the camp of Israel; and it was a cloud and darkness, but it gave light by night: so that the one came not near the other all the night" (Exodus 14:19–20). At this point, the pillar acted as a means of salvation for Israel, the primary role Jehovah takes in the Exodus story.[12] It is striking that the same pillar acted as both fire and cloud, light and darkness.[13] The text explicitly speaks of the cloud but says that the cloud gave light, implying that the fire element of the pillar was present as well. This idea is again strengthened when in the morning "the Lord looked at the camp of the Egyptians from inside a pillar of fire and cloud" (Exodus 14:24).[14] As it contained the Lord's presence, the pillar was simultaneously fire and cloud.

This cloud-fire motif is clearly seen in the next divine manifestation that Israel encountered. After the Lord leads them by his pillar to Mount Sinai, he tells them to prepare themselves so that he may "come down in the sight of all the people upon mount Sinai" (Exodus 19:11). For three days, the people prepared themselves, and then,

> on the third day in the morning, there were thunders and lightnings, and a heavy cloud upon the mount, and the voice of the trumpet was very strong; so that all the people who were in the camp trembled.
>
> And Moses brought forth the people out of the camp to meet God; and they stood at the nether part of the mount.
>
> And all of mount Sinai was smoky, because the Lord descended upon it in fire. And its smoke ascended as the smoke of a furnace, and the whole mount quaked greatly. (Exodus 19:16–18)

In this account, there seem to be four elements associated with the divine presence: smoke, light, thunder, and quaking.[15] The smoke, which would hide the personage of God, seems to be the most salient point of the above passage. This emphasis on smoke is heightened in the Deuteronomy account, which says that the "mountain burned with fire unto the midst of heaven, with darkness, clouds, and thick darkness" (Deuteronomy 4:11). In both texts, fire is associated with smoke. In fact, it seems to be the fire of the Lord's presence that causes the smoke—as actual fire does—and in this way, the very light which reveals God also causes the element which hides him.

Another Deuteronomy account is equally explicit, saying that the Lord spoke "out of the midst of the fire, of the cloud, and of the heavy darkness" (Deuteronomy 5:22).[16] As the account continues, an interesting comment adds another layer to the topic: "Ye heard the voice out of the midst of the darkness (for the mountain did burn with fire)" (Deuteronomy 5:23). The parenthetical aside indicates that the darkness is a direct result of the fire, much as we have postulated above: just as fire causes smoke, the light of the Lord also causes darkness. It almost seems that the nature of God is so glorious that as it is revealed, it must also be hidden.

I do not confess to understand the nature of God enough to fully explain why he might reveal his presence and simultaneously hide at least part of it. Latter-day scripture more plainly states this exact conundrum. In Moses 1:5, the Lord tells Moses that while he will partially reveal himself to Moses, he will not do so fully, because "no man can behold all my glory, and afterwards remain in the flesh on the earth." In other words, even when God reveals himself and his glory to mankind, he must withhold, or hide, at least some of his glory. For reasons that seem to be beyond our capacity to understand, God must hide part of his nature even as he reveals himself to us.

It would seem that the Israelites understood that God's presence is something beyond man's capacity to withstand because, after "all the people saw the thunderings,[17] and the lightnings, and the noise of the trumpet, and the mountain smoking: and when the people saw it, they removed, and stood afar off" (Exodus 20:18). They informed Moses that they felt God's presence was too glorious for them to encounter and survive.[18] Instead, they asked him to communicate with God for them (see Exodus 20:19–20). When Moses approached God, he "drew near to the thick darkness where God was" (Exodus 20:21). In both accounts, the whole theophany seems to be an intentional portrayal of God simultaneously surrounded by fire and smoke. It appears to be similar to the combined Amun-Ra, an Egyptian name that denotes a hidden and light-filled god; Jehovah too was both filled with light and hidden. This is not to posit that the Israelites thought of God as Amun-Ra, but it is possible that the lexicon they used to record encounters with God was influenced by the Egyptian tradition of writing about their deities.

This paradoxical light-darkness relationship is not expressed elsewhere in Deuteronomy. Twice Moses refers to the incident of the Lord providing the law without actually describing it. In both of these accounts, light is mentioned without any accompanying darkness: "And he said, The Lord came from Sinai, and rose up from Seir to them; he shined forth from mount Paran, and he came with ten thousand saints. From his right hand went a fiery law for them" (Deuteronomy 33:2). Also, "he wrote on the tables, according to the first writing, the ten words, which the Lord spoke to you in the mount out of the midst of the fire in the day of the assembly" (Deuteronomy 10:4). Here only the luminous nature of the experience is stressed. This lack of the element of darkness may be because this is not a description of the Lord's appearance, only a reference to the reception of the law, which emanated from the Lord and did not itself have to be hidden.

Likewise, in a more private encounter on Mount Sinai, the Lord seems to be accompanied by light and not at all hidden. The description reads: "Then went up Moses, and Aaron, Nadab, and Abihu, and seventy of the elders of Israel. And they saw the God of Israel. And under his feet it was like a paved work of a sapphire stone; and it was like the body of heaven in its clearness" (Exodus 24:9–10). While light is not specifically mentioned here, it is clear that these men see something beyond the capacity of description. The closest the writer can come to the reality of the scene is to compare aspects of what they saw to a work of sapphire and the body of heaven.[19] The bright blue of sapphire combined with the reference to heaven seems to indicate that the Lord is standing in a luminous sky or heaven.[20] There is no mention of clouds, and the Lord is not hidden here.[21] Perhaps this is because the select group was worthy to more fully come into God's presence. However, even this account is followed by combined hiding and revealing imagery.

After seeing God and eating and drinking, Moses left the rest of the group and went into the mount to visit with God. As Moses went further, "the cloud covered the mount" (Exodus 24:15). After this brief mention of God's presence being covered by a cloud, the interplay of light and darkness is further developed: "And the glory of the Lord tabernacled on mount Sinai, and the cloud covered it six days; and he called to Moses on the seventh day from the midst of the cloud. And the glory of the Lord appeared as a consuming fire on the top of the mount in the sight of the children of Israel" (Exodus vv. 16–17). Again we are presented with the image of God being surrounded by light, which is surrounded by darkness.[22] While the image seems paradoxical, it is, in fact, the scriptural language, and thus our task is to try to understand it.

The next divine encounter contains very little reference to light, fire, clouds, or darkness, but it does continue the interplay between the Lord being revealed and hidden. It starts by saying that as Moses entered the newly constructed tabernacle, "the cloud pillar descended, and stood at the door of the tabernacle, and he [the Lord] talked with Moses" (Exodus 33:9, translation mine). It is then that "the Lord spoke to Moses face to face, as a man speaks to his friend" (v.11). Strangely, shortly after this specific description of face-to-face conversation, the Lord informs Moses:

> You are not able to see my face: for no man will see me and live. And the Lord said, Behold, there is a place by me, and you will stand upon the rock. And it shall come to pass, when my glory passes by, that I will put you in the cleft of the rock, and will cover you with my hand until I have passed by. And I will take away my hand, and you will see after me. But my face shall not be seen. (Exodus 33:20–23)

The Joseph Smith Translation changes this passage to say that Moses cannot see God's face "at this time" because of God's anger (Joseph Smith Translation, Exodus 33:20). Even with this change, these are difficult texts to reconcile.[23] How can Moses both see the Lord face-to-face and yet not see his face, or why could he see it one moment and then soon thereafter be told he could not? Many have explained this seeming contradiction by positing one of the accounts as a later addition or as coming from a different source. Whether this is true or not, it cannot be ignored that the seeming paradox fits well into the larger interplay between light and darkness, seeing and hiding, which accompanies the Lord's presence throughout the book of Exodus and even later in the Hebrew Bible. It seems that with each divine encounter, the writers struggle with describing this dual essence of the divine presence. The Lord reveals himself, yet at the same time, his glory is too great to be fully revealed. Frequently, this conundrum is expressed by light revealing the Lord while darkness hides him. Here it is expressed by Moses seeing the Lord's face yet shortly thereafter only being allowed to see the back of him because of man's fallen and sinful actions. Clearly, this duality was difficult for the ancient writers to deal with. In some ways, this particular set of encounters with God highlights how God can reveal himself to us but also how our fallen natures and actions can prevent it.

Shortly after this incident, Moses again ascended the mount, where "the Lord descended in the cloud" (Exodus 34:5). After this encounter, it is Moses who is filled with light, which causes him to veil his face (Exodus 34:33–35). It seems that some of the Lord's qualities have now been transferred to Moses and that Moses is now so full of light that others could not fully behold him; he had to hide that light in much the same manner that the Lord does.

In the final chapter of the book of Exodus, we see the imagery of light and darkness again. The glory of the Lord filled the tabernacle, which was simultaneously covered by such a cloud that even Moses could not enter (Exodus 40:34–35). The tabernacle was covered by a cloud by day and fire by night, in a manner to which Israel was now accustomed (Exodus 40:38). The cloud preventing Moses from entering the tabernacle serves as a powerful image of the darkness motif protecting or hiding the image of the Lord.

There is one final account of the divine presence during the Exodus story. While in the wilderness, Aaron and Miriam complain that Moses has taken too much power upon himself. On this occasion, the Lord instructs the three to approach the door of the tabernacle. There "the Lord came down in the pillar of the cloud, and stood in the door of the tabernacle" (Numbers 12:5). Here only the hidden essence of the theophany is mentioned. This account continues the paradox well: even though Moses and Aaron seem to have beheld the unveiled presence of the Lord before,[24] here the Lord's personage is seen by no one. He is completely hidden. Interestingly, this concealing occurs as some are again exercising their fallen natures. This account serves to highlight that there are times when the Lord may reveal himself to us, but times where our fallen natures and actions cause him to be hidden from us.

Samuel, Psalms, and Kings

As we move on in the biblical story, one of David's psalms of praise describes the presence of God, though it is unclear whether David is speaking of an actual appearance to him or is just creating a poetic account based on the language of texts he was familiar with that described the presence of God. In his poetic praise, David says that when he called on God, "There went up a smoke out of his [God's] nostrils, and fire out of his mouth devoured: coals were kindled by it. He bowed the heavens also, and came down; and darkness was under his feet" (2 Samuel 22:9–10).[25] Whether David is describing a real appearance of God or not, it is clear that he conceives of God's presence as being attended by fire, smoke, and darkness.

Another psalm speaks of God's presence in terms of both light and darkness. "Clouds and darkness are round about him [God]: righteousness and judgment are the habitation of his throne. A fire goeth before him, and burneth up his enemies round about. His lightnings enlightened the world: the earth saw, and trembled. The hills melted like wax at the presence of the Lord, at the presence of the Lord of the whole earth" (Psalm 97:2–5). While no singular appearance of God is described here, this psalmist clearly felt that God sent forth light but was surrounded by darkness.

Similarly, while no one saw God in person at the dedication of Solomon's temple, there is no doubt that he was present. After the priests deposited the ark of the covenant in the Holy of Holies, "the cloud filled the house of the Lord, so that the priests could not stand to minister because of the cloud: for the glory of the Lord had filled the house of the Lord. Then spake Solomon, The Lord said that he would dwell in the thick darkness" (1 Kings 8:10–12). Because the glory of the Lord appeared on Sinai and at the tabernacle as a "fire," most likely this description from the temple dedication refers to the same aspect of the Lord's glory. If this is the case, then we again see God's presence denoted by light, which was associated with a cloud and thick darkness.

Isaiah

Isaiah contains one of the most famous accounts of biblical theophanies. In a description of his call to serve as Jehovah's prophet, Isaiah recorded his experience.

> In the year that king Uzziah died I saw also the Lord sitting upon a throne, high and lifted up, and his train filled the temple.
>
> Above it stood the seraphims: each one had six wings; with twain he covered his face, and with twain he covered his feet, and with twain he did fly.
>
> And one cried unto another, and said, Holy, holy, holy, is the Lord of hosts: the whole earth is full of his glory.
>
> And the posts of the door moved at the voice of him that cried, and the house was filled with smoke.

Then said I, Woe is me! for I am undone; because I am a man of unclean lips, and I dwell in the midst of a people of unclean lips: for mine eyes have seen the King, the Lord of hosts.[26]

Then flew one of the seraphims unto me, having a live coal in his hand, which he had taken with the tongs from off the altar:

And he laid it upon my mouth, and said, Lo, this hath touched thy lips; and thine iniquity is taken away, and thy sin purged. (Isaiah 6:1–7)

So many elements of this pericope are pertinent to our study that we must examine them one at a time. We start with the opening line. It is clear that Isaiah sees the Lord himself sitting on his heavenly throne in the heavenly temple. Accompanying these facts is the description that he is elevated[27] and that his "train" fills the temple. The train is a royal garment, not unlike what we currently call the train of a bridal gown.[28] It is unlikely that the garment is so big that it fills the entire temple, therefore not leaving room for any of the other elements which are, in fact, present in the temple. This phrasing seems, instead, to be an attempt at describing the idea that the Lord's majesty filled the temple by saying that an insignia of royalty, such as the royal train, filled the temple.

Above the throne stood the seraphim. While we do not know precisely what these creatures are, we can discern some idea about their nature by examining their appellation. It comes from the root word *seraph*, which means "to burn."[29] Derived from the plural participle of *seraph*, *seraphim* is a plural noun meaning "burning ones," or perhaps "fiery ones."[30] This makes it clear that light or fire was a part of the seraphim's very nature[31] and thus was a part of this theophany.[32]

As a part of the praise they give to God, the seraphim say that "the whole earth is full of his glory" (v. 3). The Hebrew word for glory, *kâbôd*, is very complex. We cannot fully explore the connotations of this word here, but some comment is necessary for us to understand how the word impacts our topic. The primary meaning of the word is connected with weight and heaviness.[33] Symbolically, this weight was also connected with social status and power. However, in many of its uses, *kâbôd* is also somehow tied up with fire or light. For example, in Isaiah 60, Zion is told, "Arise, shine; for thy light is come, and the glory of the Lord is risen upon thee. For, behold, the darkness shall cover the earth, and gross darkness the people: but the Lord shall arise upon thee, and his glory shall be seen upon thee. And the Gentiles shall come to thy light, and kings to the brightness of thy rising" (Isaiah 60:1–3). In this passage, light and glory are used in parallel twice:

a: thy light is come
a': the glory of the Lord is risen upon thee

and

a: the Lord shall arise upon thee
b: his glory shall be seen upon thee

a': the Gentiles shall come to thy light
b': kings to the brightness of thy rising

In both of these parallel patterns, we see glory compared to light or brightness. A few verses later, a similar meaning is conveyed: "The sun shall be no more thy light by day; neither for brightness shall the moon give light unto thee: but the Lord shall be unto thee an everlasting light, and thy God thy glory" (Isaiah 60:19). Again we see the parallelisms:

a: the sun shall be no more thy light by day
b: neither for brightness shall the moon give light unto thee

a': but the Lord shall be unto thee an everlasting light
b': and thy God thy glory

As before, we see that glory is clearly equated with fire, light or brightness. A host of other references provides the same connotation for this Hebrew word that normally denotes heaviness.[34]

This ambiguity leaves us wondering whether the Isaiah 6 reference to the earth being full of the Lord's glory has connotations of light or not. In the absence of parallelism to tie glory to light, and since most of the references to the Lord's presence within this passage have to do with power, weight, or heaviness, we must assume that light is not implied here, though we cannot do so conclusively.

Continuing with the Isaiah 6 pericope, we next are informed that the posts of the door moved, reminiscent of Mount Sinai quaking. We also read that "the house was filled with smoke" (v. 4). We know that an incense altar is present, which may account for the smoke.[35] However, even if this is so, it does not take away from smoke being listed as an essential quality of the experience. Coupled with the multiple smoke references of the Exodus story, we cannot dismiss the possibility that Isaiah's reference to smoke is integral to the Lord's presence.

Isaiah then bemoans that he is in an unclean state, as symbolized by his unclean lips. This problem is alleviated by the application of a live coal from the altar (presumably the incense altar present within the temple) is applied to his lips, which purges his sins. Here the fire in the theophany is a sanctifying element. It is likely that the fire of the altar makes Isaiah able to withstand the fire of the Lord's presence, though the fire of the Lord is not specifically mentioned here.

Throughout this description, Isaiah paints the picture of the Lord in a setting full of smoke, fire, and glory. In this pericope, these elements seem to be the integral aspects of coming into the Lord's presence.

Ezekiel

Ezekiel contains two descriptions of seeing the Lord in his heavenly temple, both of which are similar in many aspects to the Isaiah account. Ezekiel's book opens with his vision of the Lord. He first sees four fantastical beings with various human and animal features. In describing them, Ezekiel says, "The likeness of the firmament upon the heads of the living creature was as the colour of the terrible crystal, stretched forth over their heads above" (Ezekiel 1:22). While it is impossible to understand completely what Ezekiel is describing, the idea of a terrible crystal of firmament seems to be an attempt to describe a bright, refracting light above their heads, such as would emanate from a crystal held up to a bright sky. With this as background, Ezekiel goes on to describe the setting in which the creatures are found:

> And above the firmament that was over their heads was the likeness of a throne, as the appearance of a sapphire stone: and upon the likeness of the throne was the likeness as the appearance of a man above upon it.
>
> And I saw as the colour of amber, as the appearance of fire round about within it, from the appearance of his loins even upward, and from the appearance of his loins even downward, I saw as it were the appearance of fire, and it had brightness round about.

> As the appearance of the bow that is in the cloud in the day of rain, so was the appearance of the brightness round about. This was the appearance of the likeness of the glory of the Lord. (Ezekiel 1:26–28)

Here we read of the Lord—for so the man is identified at the end of the passage—sitting on a throne like sapphire, a description discussed above.[36] The upper half of the Lord has the appearance of amber—a fiery red—and fire. The lower half of the Lord[37] is also compared to fire, this time a bright fire—probably white as opposed to red. Then Ezekiel brings in the cloud element of Old Testament theophany in a surprising way. He is still attempting to describe the brightness of the Lord and compares it to a rainbow, which comes from rain, which is typically associated with a cloud. Even this simile cannot avoid the combination of cloud and light. While Ezekiel does not describe darkness as a part of his vision, he still carries the dichotomy into his account by use of this simile, possibly because the combination of cloud and fire as part of the divine presence was well ensconced in his mind.

All of this description of brightness is then said to be "the appearance of the likeness of the glory of the Lord" (v. 28). Thus Ezekiel combines the *kâbôd* of the Lord with light, fire, and brightness again. It would seem that in his mind, the power, weight, and status of the Lord are inextricably connected with light.

Ezekiel later sees another vision of the Lord. Apparently the same creatures are present, though now they are referred to as "cherubims."[38] Since it has been suggested that cherubim are symbolic of thunderclouds[39] and seraphim of lightning,[40] the attendance of either cherubim or seraphim in the Lord's presence adds to the fire-cloud motif. Of this vision, Ezekiel records that he saw the Lord and a man in white linen. After some conversation, he saw:

> In the firmament that was above the head of the cherubims there appeared over them as it were a sapphire stone, as the appearance of the likeness of a throne.
>
> And he [the Lord] spake unto the man clothed with linen, and said, Go in between the wheels, even under the cherub, and fill thine hand with the coals of fire from between the cherubims, and scatter them over the city. And he went in my sight.

> Now the cherubims stood on the right side of the house, when the man went in; and the cloud filled the inner court.
>
> Then the glory of the Lord went up from the cherub, and stood over the threshold of the house; and the house was filled with the cloud, and the court was full of the brightness of the Lord's glory. (Ezekiel 10:1–4)

Again, several elements of this description should be discussed. Elements from other theophanies that reappear here include the sapphire throne, a cloud that fills the inner temple, and the coals from the altar, which seem to be elements of light or fire.[41] After this, the description tells us that the glory of the Lord "stood over the threshold of the house [temple]" (v. 4), and then we find the cloud, brightness, and glory all used together in a parallel pattern.

a: and the house was filled with the cloud
b: and the court was full of the brightness of the Lord's glory

Here we see glory and brightness[42] combined and used in conjunction with the cloud, one filling the court and the other the house. Apparently, the presence of the Lord is accompanied by both elements. While at Sinai it seems that the light was around the Lord but that both were hidden by smoke. Here we see that the temple, where the Lord is, was filled with the cloud and surrounding that was brightness. The arrangement of clouds and light may change, but the one comes with the other consistently.

Finally, Ezekiel sees a vision of a future temple, wherein he again sees the Lord's presence:

> He brought me to the gate, even the gate that looketh toward the east:
>
> And, behold, the glory of the God of Israel came from the way of the east: and his voice was like a noise of many waters: and the earth shined with his glory.
>
> And it was according to the appearance of the vision which I saw, even according to the vision that I saw when I came to destroy the city: and the visions were like the vision that I saw by the river Chebar; and I fell upon my face.

And the glory of the Lord came into the house by the way of the gate whose prospect is toward the east.

So the spirit took me up, and brought me into the inner court; and, behold, the glory of the Lord filled the house. (Ezekiel 43:1–5)

Ezekiel explicitly compares this vision to those he had seen before.[43] Indeed, it has many similar elements. Glory is associated with light as it comes from the east, and instead of quaking, we have a voice "like a noise of many waters," a sound similar to that of thunder.[44] The Lord's glory "shined" on the earth, a connection that again equates glory with light.[45] This happens again when we see the glory entering the house from the eastern gate and filling the house.[46] There is little additional information in this vision. Instead, it provides an emphasis and reification of the essential theophanic elements discussed above.

Amos

The last account of seeing the Lord we'll consider, in the book of Amos, is similar to the Genesis accounts. Amos recounts, "I saw the Lord standing upon the altar" (Amos 9:1). There is nothing more concerning the actual appearance of the Lord. However, even this brief description is not devoid of references to either light or smoke. By simply saying that the Lord is standing "upon the altar," Amos brings in imagery of the fire and coals present there, as well as the smoke which was naturally a part of the incense altar. This interpretation assumes that it is the incense altar Amos sees; the altar he mentions is inside the temple, and the presence of an incense altar would parallel other accounts. Thus, this far into the theophanic tradition, even the briefest descriptions contain references to light and clouds as a part of theophany.

Indirect Presence

There are several biblical accounts which some have construed as indicating the physical presence of the Lord, and all of these accounts involve the consumption of offerings by fire. However, in none of these accounts is the Lord explicitly or necessarily present, and none even allude to his presence. We will examine them briefly.

In Genesis 15, Abraham is instructed to lay out a sacrifice and keep it from being consumed by animals. "It came to pass, that, when the sun went down, and it was dark, behold a smoking furnace, and a burning lamp that passed between those pieces" (Genesis 15:17). This account does include both smoke and light, but it does not necessitate that the Lord himself is present. Instead, it is likely that his power is present, not his actual personage.

Similarly, Gideon is instructed by an angel to present an offering which is then consumed by fire (Judges 6:21), and Samson's parents offer a kid which is consumed by fire in the presence of an angel (Judges 13:19–20). In neither of these cases is the angel equated with the Lord, and indeed, in Judges 13, the angel specifically states that the offering should not be made to him but to the Lord (Judges 13:16).

Elijah also calls down fire to consume offerings (1 Kings 18:38). Again, Elijah calls to the Lord, and it is the Lord's power that is manifest in the fire that licks up even the dust and water of the offering, but nowhere is it intimated that the Lord himself is present.

Conclusion

Little can be said of the theophanic accounts in Genesis, since little is said in these accounts about the countenance of God. However, the descriptions of the divine presence in the rest of the Old Testament contain many elements in common. Theophanies frequently contain references to loud noises or shaking. Both of these elements are indicative of power. Theophanic accounts also generally have a luminous element to them. Whether this is a description of the shining sky, of fire, of light, of coals, or of burning creatures, light or fire seems to be intrinsically connected to God's personage.

Surprisingly, this luminous presence is also connected with a dark element. In the preceding accounts, we also see either smoke or a cloud, which often hides the presence of the Lord. Thus Jehovah seems to simultaneously break forth in light, or reveal himself, and cover himself in a cloud or smoke, or hide himself. This tension between revealing and hiding is furthered by Moses' both being allowed to see the Lord's face and later not being allowed to see it. The various accounts paint for us a picture of the duality of the Lord's nature, something echoed in such natural elements as fire and its accompanying smoke or clouds and their accompanying lightning and rainbows.

The accounts which speak of both light and darkness seem to be attempts to grapple with an important problem in man's experience with God. Our loving Father wants to reveal himself to us and bring us back to his presence, but in our current fallen state, this cannot happen (see Moses 1:2). Even if we were transfigured, God's nature would still be so much more glorious than ours that he could not fully reveal himself to us (see Moses 1:5). Apparently, full communion with God must wait for our natures to more substantially and permanently change. In the meantime, God reveals himself to us as much as we are prepared for it (see Alma 12:9–10). The simultaneously competing and complementary images of light and darkness, fire and smoke, glory and cloud, symbolically convey this idea.

The power of the Lord seems to have been particularly hard for the biblical writers to convey. This difficulty may account for the ambiguous use of the term k~bôd. As has been noted, this term usually conveys the meaning of weight, or heaviness. However, it sometimes is associated with light, and this is frequently the case in theophanic accounts. Glory is often equated with light in divine manifestations, both of which are likely symbols of God's power and might. In any case, the term k~bôd may very well carry within itself the dualistic nature of God. God's glory is simultaneously heavy and full of light. The heaviness of his glory is sometimes symbolized by a train or cloud—two elements of hiding—but sometimes by light and shining—elements of revealing. It is this word, with its multiplicity of connotations, which may best describe the presence of the Lord, something so out of the experience of this world that it can only be described by similes, metaphors, and paradox.

Notes

1. For the purposes of this paper, a theophany is defined as God's physical presence being revealed or detectable.

2. Unless otherwise specified, all translations are from the King James Version.

3. For a possible context of the Lord's voice walking in the Garden of Eden, see Donald W. Parry, "Garden of Eden: Prototype Sanctuary," in *Temples of the Ancient World: Ritual and Symbolism*, ed. Donald W. Parry (Salt Lake City: Deseret Book, 1994), 144.

4. Andrew C. Skinner, "Jacob in the Presence of God," in *Sperry Symposium Classics: The Old Testament*, ed. Paul Y. Hoskisson (Provo, UT: Religious Studies Center, Brigham Young University; Salt Lake City: Deseret Book, 2005), 128–29, argues that Jacob saw God there.

5. After searching dozens of texts myself, I also consulted with Giorgio Buccellati, who studied this topic as well and who found the same results I did.

6. For a brief introduction to the topic of Egyptian influence on Israelite culture, see "Egypt and the Bible: An Interview with Kerry Muhlestein," *Religious Educator* 11, no. 3 (2010): 78–93.

7. It is clear later that it is the Lord speaking to Moses, but here the text states that an angel is in the bush. Walter Brueggemann, "Exodus," in *The New Interpreter's Bible*, ed. Leander E. Keck (Nashville: Abingdon Press, 1994), 711, is certain that this is a theophany but believes that an angel is present as well. William H. C. Propp, *Exodus 1–18, A New Translation with Introduction and Commentary*, ed. William Foxwell Albright and David Noel Freedman, The Anchor Bible 2 (New York: Doubleday, 1998), 198, notes that the mention of the angel may be a result of "Judaism's tendency to avoid direct reference to God, especially to his physical manifestations." However, he seems to be more convinced that the angel is acting on behalf of God and therefore speaks as if he were God. This is somewhat confusing since just paragraphs above, Propp asserts that while an angel was present, "God himself is within the bush." In either case, a theophany is occurring, since if it is an angel acting on behalf of God, he is playing the full part, with accompanying effects. Brevard S. Childs, *The Book of Exodus: A Critical, Theological Commentary*, ed. Peter Ackroyd and others, The Old Testament Library (Philadelphia: Westminster Press, 1974), 79n2, believes it is an angel of Yahweh "who assumes the form and speech of Yahweh himself." Childs also believes this to be a theophany.

8. In the Exodus and Deuteronomy section of this paper, all translations are my own, based closely on the King James Version.

9. Brueggemann, "Exodus," 711, and Propp, *Exodus 1–18*, 199, both believe that the initial light and the angel caught Moses' attention. After this, Moses communicated with the light-filled Lord.

10. For a Latter-day Saint discussion on glory and God in this context, see Daniel Belnap, "'Where Is Thy Glory?' Moses 1, the Nature of Truth, and the Plan of Salvation," *Religious Educator* 10, no. 2 (2009): 163–79. See also Rodney Turner, "The Visions of Moses (Moses 1)," in *Studies in Scripture: The Pearl of Great Price*, ed. Robert L. Millet and Kent P. Jackson (Salt Lake City: Randall Press, 1985), 46–49.

11. Propp, *Exodus 1–18*, 489, believes that this is the same pillar, which transforms itself from fire to cloud at the appropriate time. Childs, *Book of Exodus*, 224, also feels this way.

12. This is the first of many times that light is connected with the salvation of Jehovah. See Sverre Aalen, " 'ôr," in *Theological Dictionary of the Old Testament*, vol. 1, ed. G. Johannes Botterweck and Helmer Ringgren, trans. John T. Willis (Grand Rapids, MI: Eerdmans, 1974), 160, who connects light in general, and specifically the term for light, 'ôr, with salvation because of how such incidents connect light with God. Aalen maintains, however, that studies which connect Israelite worship with the sun have fallen out of acceptance in current scholarship (165).

13. Childs, *Book of Exodus*, 227, notes that as the Israelites flee into the sea, the Lord terrifies the Egyptians with the pillar of fire, and the Egyptians cry out that Jehovah is fighting for Israel. The Egyptians would have been particularly sensitive to gods that fought with fire, since this idea was such a part of Egyptian culture. Propp, *Exodus 1–18*, 498, writes that perhaps this happened at nightfall, as the cloud was turning into fire, or that it may mean that the pillar was dark by day and light at night.

14. Propp, *Exodus 1–18*, 499, again speculates that since it is morning, the pillar is in the process of turning from fire to cloud.

15. Brueggemann, "Exodus," 836, believes that the description of fire, smoke, and quaking is an attempt to convey the unconveyable. While this may be true, this description must still indicate that some sort of light, darkness, movement, and sound were present.

16. The word used for "heavy darkness" here, or "thick darkness" in Exodus 20:21 and Deuteronomy 4:11, is *arafel* or *ᶜrāpel*. While the etymology of this word is not completely understood, its closest cognates in other languages mean "to cover or wrap up." See Ludwig Koehler and Walter Baumgartner, *The Hebrew and Aramaic Lexicon of the Old Testament*, vol. II, ed. and trans. M. E. J. Richardson (New York: E. J. Brill, 1995), 888, who list these cognates and define the word as either "thick darkness" or "God's covering." While we may not fully understand this word's meaning, because it is often used in parallel with darkness, we can be sure that it has something to do with a darkness that covers or conceals. See also M. J. Mulder, "*ᶜrāpel*," in *Theological Dictionary of the Old Testament*, vol. 11, ed. G. Johannes Botterweck, Helmer Ringgren, and Heinz-Josef Fabry (Grand Rapids, MI: Eerdmans, 2001), 371–75. Mulder says that in each of the cognates, the word "suggests something like 'thick clouds, darkness'" (371). Mulder discusses the use of the phrase in the Exodus and Deuteronomy Sinai pericopes on pages 372–73.

17. John Day, "Echoes of Baal's Seven Thunders and Lightnings in Psalm XXIX and Habakkuk III 9 and the Identity of the Seraphim in Isaiah VI," *Vetus Testamentum* 29, no. 2 (1979): 143–51, notes the kinship between Jehovah's possessing both thunder and lighting and Baal's possession of the same. J. C. L. Gibson, *Language and Imagery in the Old Testament* (Peabody, Massachusetts: Hendrickson Publishers, 1998), 104, makes this same point, drawing on his vast experience as translator for most of the available Ugaritic literature. J. Glen Taylor, *Yahweh and the Sun: Biblical and Archaeological Evidence for Sun Worship in Ancient Israel*, ed. David J. A. Clines and Philip R. Davies, Journal for the Study of the Old Testament Supplement Series (Sheffield: JSOT Press, 1993), 237, believes that "the admixture of sun and storm language" may have conveyed an understanding that the Lord was identifiable as both a sun god and a storm god.

18. On the theological implications of this, see Kerry Muhlestein, "Israel, Exodus, Atonement, and Us," in *Covenants, Prophecies, and Hymns of the Old Testament*, ed. Victor L. Ludlow (Provo, UT: Brigham Young University Press, 2001), 89–100.

19. Brueggemann, "Exodus," 881, notes that the pavement was not sapphire, but was like it; the paved work was actually impossible to describe. Childs, *Book of Exodus*, 506–7, believes that lapis lazuli is being referred to here but makes the same point, that it is only "an approximate analogy to the reality itself."

20. U. Cassuto, *A Commentary on the Book of Exodus* (London: Magnes Press, 1967), 314, believes that the word here translated as "clear" is related to an Ugaritic cognate which describes the brightness of sapphire. This adds another luminous element to the account.

21. Childs, *Book of Exodus*, 506–7, comments that this account softens the actual beholding of God in this scene by using terminology usually associated with a vision. Thus God's presence was not necessarily hidden here, since he wasn't truly seen. In this way he "softens" the perceived textual difficulty of these men seeing God while later God says that he cannot be seen (see Exodus 33, treated later in this article). I do not think there is a tremendous difference between seeing God in a vision or in some other way.

22. Childs, *Book of Exodus*, 508, notes the relationship between Exodus 19 and 24: "The terrifying God of Ex. 19 who appeared in his theophany has not changed. He returns at the end of ch. 24 once again in majesty and awe-inspiring terror. What has changed is his relation to Israel."

23. Menahem Haran, *Temples and Temple Service in Ancient Israel* (Winona Lake, Indiana: Eisenbrauns, 1985), 267–68, speculates that in the first vision, Moses beheld the Lord only through the fabric of the tabernacle and that in the second, the cleft of the rock acts like the veil in the tabernacle which protects the sanctity of the Holy of Holies. While this interpretation solves many problems, it seems to ignore the explicitness of the phrase "face to face."

24. See discussions above on Exodus 24.

25. Psalm 18:9 contains a parallel account.

26. Tryggve N. D. Mettinger, "Jehovah Sabaoth—The Heavenly King on the Cherubim Throne," in *Studies in the Period of David and Solomon and Other Essays: Papers Read at the International Symposium for Biblical Studies*, ed. Tomoo Ishida (Winona Lake, IN: Eisenbrauns, 1982), 125, suggests that the "hosts" spoken of here are the seraphim, who form a part of Jehovah's heavenly council. They would then constitute the "us" in verse 8, not quoted above. His argument is particularly convincing. Gibson, *Language and Imagery*, 106, also makes this point.

27. Herbert G. May, "Some Aspects of Solar Worship at Jerusalem," *Zeitschrift fur die Alttestamentliche Wissenschaft* 55, no. 4 (1937b), 275, sees in the language of the lifted-up throne, and other aspects of the vision, evidence that Isaiah is referring to rites associated with enthronement and the equinox. See also F. J. Hollis, "The Sun Cult and the Temple at Jerusalem," in *Myth and Ritual: Essays on the Myth and Ritual of the Hebrews in Relation to the Culture Pattern of the Ancient Near East*, ed. S. H. Hooke (Oxford: Oxford University Press, 1934). While others, such as Gibson, *Language and Imagery*, 123, would agree that this is a Jehovah enthronement ceremony, there is no consensus that such a ceremony took place on the equinox.

28. Francis Brown, S. R. Driver, and Charles A. Briggs, *A Hebrew and English Lexicon of the Old Testament* (Oxford: Clarendon Press, 1951), 1002, list the meaning of the Hebrew word translated as "train" as the skirt of a robe, such as a high priest's robe. Because the Hebrew word is plural, more than one garment, hem, or robe is implied.

29. Donald W. Parry, Jay A. Parry, and Tina M Peterson, *Understanding Isaiah* (Salt Lake City: Deseret Book, 1998), 65, assert that a good translation would be "burning ones," or "bright shiny ones." See also Brown, Driver, and Briggs, *Hebrew and English Lexicon*, 976–77, who list the meaning of the root as "burn," with connotations of the ability to destroy by burning. See also B. Langer, *Gott als "Licht in Israel und Mesopotamien." Eine Studie zu Jes 60:1–3.19f* (Klosterneuburg: Österreichishces Katholisches Bibelwerk, 1989); and T. N. D. Mettinger, "Seraphim," in *Dictionary of Deities and Demons in the Bible*, ed. Karel van der Toorn, Bob Becking, and Pieter W. van der Horst, 2nd ed. (Leiden: Brill, 1999), 742–44.

30. Day, "Echoes of Baal's Seven Thunders and Lightnings,"149, among others, believes that the seraphim are the personification of lightning, which would explain why the foundations shook when they spoke. R. B. Y. Scott, "The Book of Isaiah," in *The*

Interpreter's Bible, vol. 5, ed. Nolan B. Harman (New York and Nashville: Abingdon Press, 1956), 208, believed that seraphim personified lightning in contrast to cherubim, which personified thunderclouds.

31. In this and other elements the *seraphim* have been thought of as Egyptian in origin. See Karen R. Joines, "Winged Serpents in Isaiah's Inaugural Vision," *Journal of Biblical Literature* 86, no. 4 (1967), 410–15; and Karen R. Joines, *Serpent Symbolism in the Old Testament* (Haddonfield, New Jersey: Haddonfield House, 1974), 42–60; and Day, "Echoes of Baal's Seven Thunders and Lightnings,"150.

32. Day, "Echoes of Baal's Seven Thunders and Lightnings,"149, believes that some of Jehovah's theophanic characteristics have here been "split off on" the *seraphim*.

33. The word comes from the root *k~bôd*. See C. Dohmen and P. Stenmans, "Kâbêd," in *Theological Dictionary of the Old Testament*, vol. 7, ed. G. Johannes Botterweck, Helmer Ringgren, and Heinz-Josef Fabry, trans. David E. Green (Grand Rapids, MI: Eerdmans, 1995), 13, wherein they show the meaning of this word in all Semitic languages as "be heavy." They demonstrate that the meaning of being heavy can refer to weight, burden, disability, social status, and honor. See also 17–19. The word *k~bôd* is in the nominal case. See Moshe Weinfeld, "Kâbôd," in *Theological Dictionary of the Old Testament*, vol. 7, 22–38, who examines the most common use of the word, namely as "weight." He also demonstrates its use as depicting power and might. Weinfeld ties its use as the glory of God to crowns and fire (27–31). See also Brown, Driver, Briggs, *Hebrew and English Lexicon*, 458–59, who link the meaning of heaviness to "abundance, honour, glory." The typical interpretation is similar to that of John Eaton, *Mysterious Messengers: A Course on Hebrew Prophecy from Amos Onwards* (Grand Rapids, MI: William B. Eerdmans, 1997), 22, who speaks of *k~bôd* for glory as meaning "an incomparable weight of excellence, a unique majesty," and yet admits that "although the Hebrew term has a basic sense of 'heaviness' rather than 'brightness,' the weight and worth of God's person are felt, as it were, to create a tremendous aura, more than enough to fill the whole earth."

34. See Exodus 24:15–17; Leviticus 9:23–24; Numbers 11:1; Deuteronomy 5:24–25; 2 Chronicles 7:1–3; Psalm 97:3–5; Isaiah 58:8; 60:1, 19; Ezekiel 1:28; 3:23. This list is an amalgam of passages found by Weinfeld, "Kâbôd," 31, and me.

35. Scott, "Book of Isaiah," 207, shares this point of view.

36. Herbert G. May, "The Book of Ezekiel," in *The Interpreter's Bible*, 74, believes that the sapphire here is lapis lazuli, which agrees with the scholars quoted above in the Exodus discussion.

37. Susan Niditch, *Ancient Israelite Religion* (New York: Oxford University Press, 1997), 44–45, notes that Ezekiel seems to be so nervous about seeing and describing God that he speaks of the "likeness" of God and describes the different parts of his body in separate ways, as if he could not look upon the entire presence of God at once.

38. David Noel Freedman and M. P. O'Connor, "Kerûb," in *Theological Dictionary of the Old Testament*, vol. 7, 307–19, believe that the word *cherubim* is semantically related to praying and blessing or to praising. See also T. N. D. Mettinger, "Cherubim," in *Dictionary of Deities and Demons in the Bible*, 189–92.

39. See Scott, "Book of Isaiah," 208. Freedman and O'Connor, "Kerûb," 318, note that cherubim have wings and are a counterpart to seraphim. They speculate that the

latter may be flying birds while cherubim are flying animals. They make no mention of the idea of thunderclouds, though since seraphim are typically strongly associated with lightning, it would seem logical that their counterpart version should have some sort of counterpart symbolism. Brown, Driver, Briggs, *Hebrew and English Lexicon*, 500–501, who find the word *cherubim* so enigmatic that they define it as "cherub"; they discuss the things it seems to be and the things it probably is not but provide no real definition. They do say that it is possible that the thundercloud underlies their conception. Since in Exodus 25:22, Jehovah says he will converse with Moses from between the two cherubim who cover the ark of the covenant with their wings, it seems that they must perform some sort of veiling or hiding function. Haran, *Temples and Temple Service*, 252, presents much convincing evidence that part of the nature of the cherubim was to cover things.

    40. See discussion above.

    41. Herbert G. May, "The Departure of the Glory of Yahweh," *Journal of Biblical Literture* 56, no. 4 (1937): 319, sees in this imagery evidence for solar and solstice rituals. See also May, "Book of Ezekiel," 109, 117; and May, "Aspects of Solar Worship," 270–73.

    42. Taylor, 158, *Yahweh and the Sun*, sees this as evidence for the glory of the Lord being connected to the sun. He does not seem to allow that there could be a source of light other than the sun.

    43. May, "Aspects of Solar Worship," 279, sees in this vision, and hence in Ezekiel's other visions, evidence which he believes points to rites associated with the equinox. See also J. Morgenstern, "The Gates of Righteousness," *Hebrew Union College Annual* 6 (1929).

    44. Mark S. Smith, "'Seeing God' in the Psalms: The Background of the Beatific Vision in the Hebrew Bible," *Catholic Biblical Quarterly* 50 (1988): 180, believes that like the Babylonian god Marduk, Jehovah here is exalted by attributing to him different natural powers. He does not discuss the possibility that the attributions are attempts to use familiar items to describe the unfamiliar.

    45. Taylor, *Yahweh and the Sun*, 158, again believes that this shining of the glory of the Lord is associated with the sun.

    46. See May, "Book of Ezekiel," 300.

15

"The Lord ... Bringeth Low, and Lifteth Up": Hannah, Eli, and the Temple

Julie M. Smith

The First Book of Samuel is a carefully crafted story that, when read closely, impresses upon the reader the importance of temple covenants. In the first chapter, we meet Hannah: a regular Israelite woman who lives some distance from the holy sanctuary.[1] She is devastated by her infertility, and it certainly doesn't help that her husband's other wife torments her about her barrenness. We also meet Eli: as high priest and judge, he lives in and has responsibility for the sanctuary. The natural expectation is that the house of the Lord will be central to Eli's life and that he will be a righteous man with an important role in the history of his nation; for Hannah, on the other hand, it seems that the temple will be peripheral at best, and she appears unlikely to leave any mark at all even on the history of her own family, let alone the nation. However, it will not take long for the story to completely reverse those expectations and teach the reader important lessons about the temple in the process. This paper explores this surprising turn of events and its implications for understanding temple worship, covenants, and songs of praise.

Julie M. Smith has an MA in biblical studies and homeschools her children near Austin, Texas.

Hannah's Sorrow

The first chapter paints a portrait of Hannah as a woman who focuses her life on the temple, despite overwhelming difficulties. She lived in a chaotic time of moral relativism: in Hannah's day, "there was no king in Israel: every man did that which was right in his own eyes" (Judges 21:25). The situation within her own family is also deeply troubling to her; she weeps often in the face of her own infertility, especially as Peninnah, her husband's other wife, makes a regular habit of using their yearly trips to the sanctuary to "provoke" Hannah and "make her fret" over her childlessness (1 Samuel 1:6). Hannah's husband, Elkanah, asks her, "Am I not better to thee than ten sons?" (1 Samuel 1:8). Scholars have understood that question in different ways: it is perhaps a kindhearted effort to soothe Hannah's mind, but it may also be interpreted as a self-centered dismissal of her concerns.[2] Either way, he is trying to encourage Hannah to become content with her situation. Hannah, however, has something else in mind: she takes her sorrow to the temple in an effort to change her circumstances.[3] She vows that if she is blessed with a son, that child will serve the Lord. At this point, the reader expects Hannah to find relief, but she has one more challenge to face: because Hannah prays silently, Eli accuses her of drunkenness (see 1 Samuel 1:13–14). We might expect this to be the straw that breaks Hannah's back, but instead she responds to Eli politely but firmly. Her response—cleverly explaining that instead of being drunken from having *taken in* wine, she was rather *pouring out* her spirit to the Lord (see 1 Samuel 1:15)—introduces the theme of reversals that will be so prominent in Hannah's story in the next chapter.

Note that Hannah—instead of lashing out at Peninnah, being disappointed in Elkanah's passive acceptance of her barrenness, or becoming offended at Eli's false accusations—focuses her attention instead on the temple and, more specifically, on her ability to enter into covenants. The story includes no response to Peninnah or Elkanah at all and only a modest, straightforward statement to Eli; despite the slights that Hannah would have felt from them, she chooses to focus on the Lord and on temple covenants.[4] We might suspect that Hannah prayed silently, which was contrary to usual practice,[5] because of the personal nature and depth of her anguish, but her silent prayer also reminds the reader that Hannah sees this issue as being solely between her and the Lord. She chooses not to get into a dispute with Peninnah, Elkanah, or the priest. Instead, she silently pours out her soul to the Lord. She sees a covenant with the Lord as the antidote to her emotional distress.

Hannah's Joy

Hannah is soon blessed with a baby boy, whom she names Samuel. While this would have brought her joy, it may also have brought a measure of anguish as well: she had vowed to give this child to the service of the Lord. It must have been enormously difficult for Hannah to keep this covenant. Under the best of conditions, it would mean having her young child live far away from her and under the care of others. But she would not have the best of conditions: for Hannah, keeping her covenant meant turning this young child over to the care of Eli. Hannah may not have known the full extent of the wickedness of Eli's family at this point, but she probably would have had at least some inkling of the situation, given the public nature of the sins of Eli's sons (see 1 Samuel 1:22). Perhaps Hannah entertained the idea that surely the Lord would understand if she decided to keep Samuel at home; this would violate her covenant, to be sure, but at home she could guard against unwholesome influences. However, Hannah was true to her word and brought young Samuel to live and serve in the sanctuary. With this decision, she becomes a model of keeping covenants even under the most difficult of circumstances.

There is another aspect to Hannah's understanding of the temple that literally gets lost in translation. When Hannah is telling her husband about her plans to go to the temple in 1 Samuel 1:22, the King James Version says that she will bring Samuel to the temple so that he may "appear before the Lord." But the Hebrew text can be translated as having Samuel going to "see the face of the Lord."[6] It is likely that the text was softened by later hands uncomfortable with the idea of seeing the Lord's face in the temple, but that idea appears to better reflect Hannah's understanding of temple worship.

In the very same narrative, there is another issue with the text: when Hannah tells her husband about her plan to take Samuel to the temple when he is weaned, Elkanah agrees and says (in the KJV and the Masoretic Text, the traditional Hebrew text), "Only the Lord establish his word" (1 Samuel 1:23). This sentence has puzzled interpreters because it is unclear what word of the Lord would be referenced here.[7] The Dead Sea Scrolls' version of that phrase concerns not the word of the Lord but rather the words of Hannah: Elkanah tells Hannah, "Only may the Lord fulfill what your mouth has uttered."[8] That reading makes more sense in context, since there is no specific word of the Lord in this story to which this phrase could refer. If the latter reading is more accurate, it sheds an interesting light on the text: Hannah has made a vow and will sing a song of praise in the next chapter. The fact that her words will be verified by the Lord strengthens our picture of Hannah as a woman possessed of a prophetic gift and a close connection to the Lord.

Chapter 2 begins with a hymn by Hannah. Note first the timing of this song: it is not at Samuel's birth but rather several years later at his dedication to the temple. Once again, Hannah has focused her attention on the keeping of covenants: this is the time for praising the Lord, even more so than the time of the birth of her long-awaited child. Also note the setting: she sings this song at the sanctuary itself (compare 1 Samuel 1:24 with 1 Samuel 2:11). Just as Hannah brought her sorrows to the temple in chapter 1, she now brings her joy to the temple. In fact, we can read the entirety of Hannah's story as a chiastically structured commentary on temple vows:

> A Hannah takes her sorrow to the temple (1:10)
>   B Hannah makes a covenant (1:11)
>   C Hannah defuses a potentially contentious interaction with a high-status man (1:12–16)
>   D Her desire is granted (1:17–20)
>   C' Hannah defuses a potentially contentious interaction with a high-status man (1:27–28)
>   B' Hannah keeps her covenant (1:27–28)
> A' Hannah takes her joy to the temple (2:1–10)

Note that the centerpiece of this structure is the Lord granting Hannah's desire for a child. The fulfillment of this desire is literally and metaphorically surrounded by the making (1:11) and keeping (1:27–28) of covenants. But those covenants are literally and structurally separated from the fulfillment of her desire by trials—in this case, the trials are the potentially contentious situations with her husband and Eli the priest. The careful reader concludes that making and keeping covenants leads to the fulfilling of righteous desires, but it does not insulate one from the challenges of life. Rather, those trying situations appear to be an essential part of the process. Also note that the story that began in sorrow ends in joy, continuing the parallel structure in the sense that they are both Hannah's emotions, but Hannah's faithfulness and endurance leads her from sorrow to joy.

No less important than the song's setting and structure is its content. The main theme is reversals: "The bows of the mighty men are broken, and they that stumbled are girded with strength" (1 Samuel 2:4). "They that were full have hired out themselves for bread; and they that were hungry ceased: so that the barren hath born seven; and she that hath many children is waxed feeble" (1 Samuel 2:5). Lastly, "The Lord maketh poor, and maketh rich: he bringeth low, and lifteth up" (1 Samuel 2:7). Throughout her song of praise, Hannah mentions multiple examples of reversals in order to develop the theme that the Lord is capable of causing these stunning changes to happen.[9] The immediate context for her praise song is her transition from a sorrowing, barren woman to a joyful mother, but the song also has greater implications. Hannah shares her testimony that though the Lord's changes might begin with the small and simple matter of a woman having a baby, they can affect the entire world. As Stanley D. Walters describes it, "The prayer opens with Hannah and closes with the King. It opens with her own personal praise and closes with a confident assertion of God's victory over every adversary and of his sovereign rule. It opens in Shiloh; it closes at the ends of the earth. It opens with a local reversal; it closes with a cosmic reversal. It opens in the present age; it closes with the age to come."[10] And the focus is, as always, on the temple as the hinge upon which these changes pivot; it is her experience with praying and making a vow in the temple that changes the course of Hannah's life and, as we will see, the course of her nation, as Samuel assumes an important role in the political and religious realms.

Another important theme in Hannah's song is found in its concluding lines: "The adversaries of the Lord shall be broken to pieces; out of heaven shall he thunder upon them: the Lord shall judge the ends of the earth; and he shall give strength unto his king, and exalt the horn of his anointed" (1 Samuel 2:10). This is a very significant use of the word *anointed*: it is the first time in the Old Testament that the word is used to refer to someone that will be sent by the Lord in a saving capacity (as opposed to previous uses of the word, limited to the book of Leviticus, where it refers to the anointed priest; see Leviticus 4:3, 5, 16; 6:22). It is also the only time that a prophecy of the coming Anointed One is spoken of by a regular Israelite, let alone a woman. It is therefore possible to read this part of the praise song as the exercise of a prophetic gift on Hannah's part; this view fits nicely with the temple setting and her position as a covenant-keeping and temple-focused woman, one who sees her own challenges and struggles as part of a larger context. Note also that her song begins with a reference to her horn (a symbol for strength) and ends with a reference to the horn of the Anointed. Hannah has linked her strength to the strength of the Lord's Anointed.

The hymn clarifies an important aspect of Hannah's story: she does not want a child for her own selfish ends. After all, she has already been assured by her husband that he is worth more to her than ten sons. And she will not enjoy the personal companionship or financial security that a son might bring if Samuel is living in another town—even as a child—and if he is serving in the temple for his entire life. Hannah's reasons for wanting a child seem then to have more to do with that child's ability to serve the Lord and change the world. Peninnah sees children as a bargaining chip used for status in a family, and Elkanah sees them as providing worth and companionship, but Hannah sees them as improving the world through service to the Lord. These contrasts heighten our appreciation for Hannah's view of the role of children compared to the views of the people around her. But the contrast with Eli is even starker.

Eli's Fall

Throughout this text, the writer has carefully interwoven Hannah's story with Eli's story in order to encourage the reader to ponder the contrasts. It has already been noted that the backgrounds of Eli and Hannah lead the reader to expect that Eli will be focused on the temple and Hannah will not, but the story presents precisely the opposite scenario. Even in the smallest details, we find a sharp contrast between Hannah and Eli. Note that Eli is always pictured sitting or lying down passively, unlike Hannah, who travels, prays, gives birth, vows, sings, and sews. First Samuel 1:9 contains a particularly compelling juxtaposition of Hannah's activity with Eli's passivity: "Hannah rose up after they had eaten in Shiloh, and after they had drunk. Now Eli the priest sat upon a seat by a post of the temple of the Lord."

Eli's first act in the story is to make a mistake: he sees Hannah's innovation of silent prayer and assumes that she is intoxicated. As Eli speaks to Hannah, he is cast in the role of a messenger of the Lord who announces the birth of an important person; this is evidenced by the fact that his words to

Hannah are in a poetic form as well as by the expectations for the scene in which Eli and Hannah interact. But rather than being a divine messenger with special knowledge to give to Hannah, he instead knows less than she does, as evidenced by the false accusation. The structure of the story leads the reader to expect an angel, but instead there is a very mistaken man. The portrayal of Eli is unsympathetic from the very beginning, but it deteriorates even further in chapter 2, where Hannah begins her song of praise to the Lord. The text immediately pivots to tell us that Eli's sons did not know the Lord (1 Samuel 2:12). The contrast with Hannah's family is heightened by the fact that Eli's sons are described as "sons of Belial" (1 Samuel 2:12), which means that they are wicked or worthless men. Hannah, when falsely accused by Eli, said that she should not be counted as a "daughter of Belial" (1 Samuel 1:16). The two references to Belial encourage the comparison, and the idea of being a son or daughter of Belial draws our attention to the theme of parenting in these stories.

Eli has sons who have been called to serve in the temple, but they abuse that role. Their behavior is truly shocking: as priests, they are to carefully follow the law of Moses to ensure that the sacrifices are properly performed in the sanctuary. They instead violate this sacred trust, take the best portions of the sacrificed meat for themselves, and, when questioned, threaten violence (see 1 Samuel 2:13–16). They seem to want to pick and choose the very best parts for themselves—a far cry from Hannah, who faithfully accepts whatever obstacles the Lord sends her way. Not only are their actions prohibited and a form of theft, but they also make a mockery of the sacred rituals that were instituted in order to prepare the Israelites to understand the Atonement of Jesus Christ.[11] The writer of this chapter heightens the contrast between Eli's sons and Samuel by breaking into the middle of the account of Eli's sons' wickedness to tell us that Samuel served the Lord faithfully (1 Samuel 2:18). There is a clear contrast between sacrifice, as performed by Hannah, and personal gain masquerading as sacrifice, as performed by Eli's sons.

In the middle of the story of Eli's sons, we get a final reference to Hannah: each year, she brings a new "little coat" to Samuel (1 Samuel 2:19). This is probably ritual clothing that he would have worn as he served in the temple.[12] We see here a strong contrast with Eli's sons, who used their authority in the temple to take that which did not belong to them. Hannah, who has no formal role, chooses instead to give more to the temple each year than was required of her by choosing to outfit her son for his duties—as if the sacrifice of her son to the temple was not already enough. This detail also serves to keep Hannah in the story—and in her son's life—past the point where we might have expected the spotlight to shift entirely to Samuel. It is probably no coincidence that her continual involvement in her son's life is centered on preparing him for his role in temple worship. These yearly donations of new clothing echo the scene in which Hannah brought Samuel to the temple for the first time: instead of withholding or even just bemoaning the sacrifice of her son, she instead also brought meat, flour, and wine to give to the temple (see 1 Samuel 1:24). Hannah is someone who always gives more to the Lord than is strictly necessary. The contrast with Eli's sons puts Hannah's own continual sacrifice into sharp relief.

The contrast between the path of Hannah's son and that of Eli's sons is made even starker as the text once again swings from Samuel and Hannah's service in the temple to Eli's sons' sins in their capacity as priests. We learn that Eli's sons have been engaged in inappropriate relationships with female temple workers (see 1 Samuel 2:22).[13] Eli lectures his sons, but his words have no effect. The story again pivots to Samuel's growth in righteousness. What is perhaps most stunning at this point is that Samuel is able to live morally when surrounded by such unrighteous leaders within the temple itself. The reader is left to conclude that Samuel's faith comes from the collaboration of Hannah and the Lord in raising and guiding him. The chapter ends with a man of God coming to Eli to tell him that, because he has honored his sons above the Lord, both sons will die on the same day and the Lord will raise up a faithful priest from another line (see 1 Samuel 2:29, 35).[14] Note the contrast with Hannah, who honored the Lord above her son by choosing to remain true to the covenant that she had made, even when it meant not enjoying her son's presence. Eli, on the other hand, has clearly not been faithful to his own obligation to ensure that the temple sacrifices are properly executed and that his sons behave righteously. We will later find out that Eli has poor eyesight, and this seems to be a metaphor for his lack of insight and his inability to see things as they really are. (There is a hint of this in 1 Samuel 1:16, where he doesn't seem to recognize Hannah.) Hannah, on the other hand, shows prophetic insight and a deep understanding of the Lord's will in her song. The contrast between Hannah and Eli could not be greater in their personal righteousness and in the effects of their choices on their children. The very themes of reversal found in Hannah's song of praise are evident in her own life as her devotion to the temple allows her to give birth to the prophet who will supplant Eli's failed line of authority.

Samuel's Rise

Once again, the author continues to switch between Eli's story and Samuel's story in order to emphasize the contrast. As soon as the Lord's messenger departs, we return to Samuel's story and find that the fall of Eli's family is mirrored by the rise of Hannah's family. Chapter 3 begins with the idea that there was very little revelation at this time: "And the word of the Lord was precious in those days; there was no open vision" (v. 1). (The NRSV reads: "The word of the Lord was rare in those days; visions were not widespread.") The end of the chapter (and the beginning of chapter 4, where the thought is continued) reflects a complete change: "And Samuel grew, and the Lord was with him, and did let none of his words fall to the ground. And all Israel from Dan even to Beer-sheba knew that Samuel was established to be a prophet of the Lord. And the Lord appeared again in Shiloh: for the Lord revealed himself to Samuel in Shiloh by the word of the Lord. And the word of Samuel came to all Israel" (1 Samuel 3:19–21; 4:1). How does this remarkable transition occur? Chapter 3 tells the story of Samuel learning to discern the voice of the Lord as he serves and lives in the holy sanctuary.

Samuel is not at first able to recognize the voice of the Lord, but the Lord is patient with him and Samuel is eventually able to respond and learn. While Eli gives him a little bit of guidance through this process, we also see Eli continue his physical decline—we are told that he has vision problems—and the reader sees that the difference between Eli's sons and Samuel is great and growing. The credit seems to belong to Hannah, particularly as her insightfully prophetic concept of reversals is seen when the Lord tells Samuel about the impending fall of Eli's house. So when Samuel takes up the prophetic mantle and shares this word with all of Israel, he is preaching about the same kind of reversals that his mother sang about in the temple.

In chapter 4, all that was prophesied comes to pass: Eli's sons die, Eli dies, and the ark of the covenant is lost in battle to the Philistines. This final blow would have been particularly troubling to the Israelites because they understood that one of the functions of the ark was to provide a place—a mercy seat— where the Lord could visit with the high priest in the temple's Holy of Holies (see Leviticus 16). They probably wondered how the Lord could visit them without it. Of course, the Lord had already raised up a prophet—Samuel—who could deliver the Lord's words to them. And it was not Samuel but his mother, Hannah, who originally anticipated the need of a child to serve the Lord for his entire life and who dedicated her own child to fill this need. When we meet Samuel again in chapter 7, he exhorts the Israelites to turn away from idolatry. And he anoints Israel's first and second kings—a complicated issue to be sure,[15] but he nonetheless fulfills the role of a prophet in Israel.

Hannah's Long Shadow

But Hannah's story is not quite over. She, unlike Eli, casts a long shadow not just on her son's life or on her immediate circumstances but also over the rest of the Bible. Note that 2 Samuel (which was not originally divided from 1 Samuel) ends with a song of praise—this time from the lips of David, but with remarkable similarities in language and theme to Hannah's song.[16] David's song also has reference to a rock, to sons of Belial (specifically mentioned twice in Hannah's story but not in her song), and to the ideas of exalting and debasing and killing and making alive. But where Hannah's song speaks of reversals and a future hope, David's song is full of praise for victories already achieved. In other words, Hannah's hopes are fulfilled in David's words. By bookending the books of Samuel with these two songs, the author has encouraged us to view Hannah as the initiator of the Davidic dynasty; in this sense she is parallel in importance with David, as Hannah's influence on Samuel becomes manifest in Samuel's anointing of David. Additionally, framing a history book with hymns makes clear that this is not a random chronicle of events but rather a sacred history in which the role of the Lord is clear and profound.

It is most significant, then, that these books of Israel's history begin not with kings, courts, and battles but rather with the personal, emotional struggles of an average woman. The genesis of the Davidic dynasty is to be found not on the battlefield but in a barren woman's prayer in the temple. This brokenhearted woman makes covenants that benefit not only herself and her family but also her nation.

We also find allusions to Hannah in the examples of several women in Luke's Gospel. Elisabeth, who is also tried by her barrenness, is, as Hannah was, blessed with a child who will have an important role to play in ushering in a king. Both Hannah and Mary have the rare experience of recognizing the coming Messiah (see Luke 1): Mary's song of praise after finding out that she will be the mother of the Son of God is very similar to Hannah's song, especially given that both have reversals as a theme and both women take their babies to the temple.[17] When Mary and Joseph bring Jesus to Jerusalem to present him to the Lord, they meet Anna (*Anna* being the Greek form of the name *Hannah*), a woman who is identified as a "prophetess" (Luke 2:36) who never leaves the temple but instead prays for the anticipated Messiah to come. When she is introduced to this infant Messiah, she rejoices and prophesies. The parallels to Hannah are many: they have the same name, the same gender, the same location (the temple), similar prophetic gifts, and a similar desire for God to raise up a righteous person who will set their world right. It seems that this constellation of similarities between Hannah and Elisabeth, Mary, and Anna is part of the well-recognized effort in Luke's Gospel to emphasize the role of regular, even dispossessed, people in welcoming the reign of the Messiah. It encourages us to read Hannah as one of the Old Testament templates of this desire for the Messiah and adds meaning to Hannah's own story.

One more New Testament event resonates with Hannah's story: on the day of Pentecost (see Acts 2), Peter prays in a way that his audience did not anticipate (Peter is speaking in tongues; Hannah prayed silently) and is he is accused of public drunkenness when he is actually engaged in spiritual communication (just as Hannah was). Peter clarifies and then prophesies of the reversals in the time to come, just as Hannah did. We might conclude that Hannah's story is once again a template—this time for Peter on the day of Pentecost. Just as Peter opened up a new time of increased spiritual witness, Hannah had done the same thing by preparing her child to become a prophet.

Hannah can also be seen as part of a group of women—including Miriam, Deborah, Mary, and Emma Smith—who were given special assignments related to the creation and compilation of praise songs. There appears to be a multi-dispensational tradition of women having a unique role in worshipful music, song, and prayer.[18]

Conclusion

The traditional reading of 1 Samuel 1–3 is of a barren woman who rejoices when she is blessed with the baby for whom she has earnestly prayed. While this is certainly an accurate and legitimate approach to the key events of the text, there is more to the story. By focusing on the contrast that the writer draws between Hannah's and Eli's families, we are able to find a potent commentary on the role of temple-based covenants. Hannah's story shows a rise in fortune that accompanies righteous choices, while Eli's fate reveals the devastating consequences that accompany sinful choices. This theme of reversals is highlighted in Hannah's own song of praise. And all of these choices—along with the song that commemorates them—are centered on the sanctuary and the idea of temple service. In Hannah we find a woman of low social status who struggles mightily with a challenging family dynamic: infertility compounded by a fecund sister-wife. Eli also grapples with a difficult family situation—unrighteous sons—but he does so from the high social standing of the high priest. The reader expects that Eli's physical and social proximity to the temple would make it central in his life (and peripheral for Hannah), but instead it is just the opposite: Hannah uses the temple as a refuge, with a focus on making and keeping covenants. There is a failure of priesthood leadership in Israel, and Hannah remedies it through committing her son to the service of the temple. Note that Eli's lack of oversight of his children is tied to military defeat (see 1 Samuel 4), while Hannah's desire for a son to serve in the temple leads to a new chapter of Israel's history, one with prophetic leadership and strong kings. There are interesting ramifications here about the ability of true temple worship to pierce the veil between the sacred and the secular. Note also that both Hannah's and Eli's lines innovate: Hannah through silent prayer, the use of the word *anointed*, and Samuel's anointing of a king; and Eli through modifying the sacrificial rituals to his family's own personal benefit. There is a commentary here on innovation: it is not condemned, but it must be done according to the will of the Lord and not for personal gain.

Hannah is able to change people: we see her changing her husband's and Eli's minds. But Eli is unable to change his sons' minds regarding their wicked behavior. Hannah's faithful worship gives her power. Note that Eli seems willing to police the temple to protect it from inappropriate behavior from people like Hannah (where he is wrong in his accusations), but he is unwilling to police inappropriate behavior when the source is his own sons. In other words, he seems to privilege family relationships over the sanctity of the temple. Hannah does just the opposite in her willingness to dedicate her son to the temple.

Hannah is living in difficult political and personal circumstances. But she chooses to focus on the Lord and the sanctuary and, by doing so, is able to change not only her own life but also the course of her entire nation.

Notes

1. 1 Samuel 1:7 refers to this shrine in Shiloh as "the house of the Lord." It is where Hannah's family worships and offers sacrifices (see 1 Samuel 1:3), and it is also called a temple (see 1 Samuel 1:9). It is a tabernacle, or "tent-shrine," and a precursor to the temple that will later be built in Jerusalem. While the historical distinction between the shrine at Shiloh and the temple should be maintained, I will refer to this structure as a temple throughout this paper, because it appears to fulfill the same function in Hannah's life.

2. For example, Jo Ann Hackett writes that Elkanah's statement shows a "lack of understanding for Hannah's unhappiness" and appears to be "naïve or even insensitive," but she acknowledges that it also "implies the possibility of a relationship in which love was more important than childbearing." Jo Ann Hackett, "1 and 2 Samuel," in *The Women's Bible Commentary*, ed. Carol A. Newsom and Sharon H. Ringe (Louisville, KY: Westminster/John Knox Press, 1992), 89. Robert Alter finds a "double-edged poignancy," as the statement "at once express[es] Elkanah's deep and solicitous love for Hannah and his inability to understand how inconsolable she feels." Robert Alter, *The David Story: A Translation with Commentary of 1 and 2 Samuel* (New York: W. W. Norton, 1999), 4.

3. While this concept is more than familiar to Latter-day Saints, it is not an idea that we find specifically in the Old Testament, where the temple is primarily a location for offering sacrifices, not explicitly for aid with personal issues or emotional comfort. In this instance, the story does imply that Hannah sought and received emotional comfort from the temple, and so we begin to get a glimmer of a theme that will develop throughout the narrative: Hannah is an innovator. Perhaps Hannah was thinking of the role that the temple plays in changing an individual's status (for example, from a layman to a priest or from a sinner to a "covered" sinner through offering a sacrifice), and she could have been hoping to change her status from barren to mother.

4. Note that these temple covenants are not identical to modern Latter-day Saint practice. Hannah is not entering into a covenant as part of the formal, prescribed temple worship but rather is initiating a covenant of her own (see 1 Samuel 1:11).

5. Prayers were normally offered out loud. The story itself implies that Hannah's prayer was regarded as unusual: Eli "marked" (or watched) her mouth as she prayed because it caught his attention. The narrator explains to the reader that Hannah "spake in her heart; only her lips moved, but her voice was not heard," and Eli is so unfamiliar with the idea of silent prayer that he assumes that Hannah is drunk (1 Samuel 1:12–13).

6. As Robert Alter explains, "The anthropomorphism of this ancient idiom [that is, the concept of seeing the Lord's face] troubled the later transmitters of tradition sufficiently so that when vowel points were added to the consonantal text, roughly a millennium after the biblical period, the verb 'we will see' (*nireh*) was revocalized as *nirah* ('he will be seen')." Alter, *The David Story*, 7.

7. See Stanley D. Walters, "Hannah and Anna: the Greek and Hebrew Texts of 1 Samuel 1," *Journal of Biblical Literature* 107, no. 3 (September 1988): 385–412.

8. Alter, *The David Story*, 7.

9. For more on the themes of Hannah's song, see Hackett, "1 and 2 Samuel," 89. See also Alter, *The David Story*, 9.

10. Stanley D. Walters, "The Voice of God's People in Exile," *Ex Auditu* 10 (1994): 76.

11. See 2 Nephi 25:24; Jacob 4:5; and Mosiah 16:14 as instances where Book of Mormon prophets explain that the purpose of the law of Moses was to prepare the people to understand the Atonement of Jesus Christ. See also Julie M. Smith, "Point Our Souls to Christ: Lessons from Leviticus," *Studies in the Bible and Antiquity* 1 (2009): 67–82.

12. See N. L. Tidwell, "The Linen Ephod: 1 Sam. 2:18 and 2 Sam. 6:14," *Vetus Testamentum* 24, no. 4 (October 1974): 505–7.

13. According to Douglas K. Stuart, the women here play a formal role in temple worship. The only other reference to female temple workers in the Old Testament is found in Exodus 38:3, where, as Stuart explains, a "quite fascinating detail is also included here: one that presumes some common knowledge that Moses and his audience shared, but that we do not. At some point after the tabernacle was built, certain women were employed to serve at its entrance—a practice that probably continued as long as the tabernacle was in use, judging from the mention of it in 1 Sam 2:22, hundreds of years after the time of the present description. How were these women chosen, and what exactly did they do? We have no firm information." Douglas K. Stuart, *Exodus*, vol. 2 of *The New American Commentary*, ed. E. Ray Clendenen, Kenneth A. Mathews, and David S. Dockery (Nashville: B&H Publishing, 2006), Kindle edition, chapter 7.

14. As Ralph W. Klein explains, verse 35 "announces the establishment of a faithful priest, who is not to be Samuel, as one might expect, but is clearly Zadok, David's other priest, who came to preeminence under Solomon. The Zadokites or sons of Aaron are the sure house (dynasty) referred to in the text." Ralph W. Klein, *1 Samuel* vol. 10 of *Word Biblical Commentary*, ed. David A. Hubbard and Glenn W. Barker (Nashville: Thomas Nelson, 2008), 27.

15. See 1 Samuel 8 for Samuel's initial reluctance for Israel to have a king.

16. See Randall C. Bailey, "The Redemption of YHWH: A Literary Critical Function of the Songs of Hannah and David," *Biblical Interpretation* 3, no. 2 (1995): 213–31.

17. See Raymond E. Brown, *The Birth of the Messiah: A Commentary on the Infancy Narratives in the Gospels of Matthew and Luke* (New Haven: Yale University Press, 1993), 357–61.

18. See Julie M. Smith, "'I Will Sing to the Lord': Women's Songs in the Scriptures," *Dialogue: A Journal of Mormon Thought* 45, no. 3 (Fall 2012): 56–69.

16

Seeing God in His Temple: A Significant Theme in Israel's Psalms

Andrew C. Skinner

The Hebrew Bible, or the Old Testament, contains several episodes in which God appears to mortals. Such an appearance is called a theophany (from the Greek *theophaneia*, "God appearance"). Theophanies were not everyday occurrences, and passages such as Exodus 19:5–11 imply that they resulted from obedience, covenant keeping, and faithful devotion to God: "Now therefore, if ye will obey my voice indeed, and keep my covenant, then ye shall be a peculiar treasure unto me above all people: for all the earth is mine: . . . And the Lord said unto Moses, Go unto the people, and sanctify them to day and to morrow, . . . for the third day the Lord will come down in the sight of all the people upon mount Sinai" (Exodus 19:5, 10–11).

While several other passages establish that theophanies occurred throughout the Old Testament, Exodus 29:42–46 tells us that after the Exodus from Egypt, the Lord said that he would appear to the Israelites mainly in the *'ohel moʿed* (the tent of meeting, or tabernacle) once it was established:

> For the generations to come this burnt offering is to be made regularly at the entrance to the Tent of Meeting before the Lord. There I will

---

Andrew C. Skinner is a professor of ancient scripture at Brigham Young University.

meet you and speak to you; there also I will meet with the Israelites, and the place will be consecrated by my glory. So I will consecrate the Tent of Meeting and the altar and will consecrate Aaron and his sons to serve me as priests. Then I will dwell among the Israelites and be their God. They will know that I am the Lord their God, who brought them out of Egypt so that I might dwell among them. I am the Lord their God. (NIV, Exodus 29:42–46)

Later, the First Temple in Jerusalem, Solomon's Temple, served this purpose—bringing worshippers into direct contact with Deity.

Thus a significant theme for the Psalmist,[1] as expressed in several of Israel's canonical psalms, was the idea that worshippers could come into the presence of God in his holy house in Jerusalem and see him face-to-face. As Professor Mark Smith of New York University put it, "'Seeing God' is the preeminent image [in the Psalms] for the experience of God in the temple (Psalms 17:15; 42:2; 63:2; 84:7; cf. 11:7; Job 33:26), and this is described as an experience of brilliant light or is expressed metaphorically by comparing God with the sun (Psalm 84:7, 11)."[2] If Margaret Barker is correct that "seeking the face/presence of the LORD had been at the heart of the temple cult [temple beliefs and rituals],"[3] the Psalter simply reflects this core message.

This should not surprise us, after all, since we know that there is a profound connection between the temple and many of the psalms—Israel's ancient hymns—as scholars both in and out of the Latter-day Saint community have noted. One scholar explains, "Many of the Psalms . . . though also sung at home or in the synagogue . . . were originally designed or later adapted for use in (or in connection with) the Temple."[4] Barker has stated flatly that "the Psalms were the hymns of the Temple."[5] Sigmund Mowinckel has emphasized that the psalms were centered in, and an important part of, Israelite and later Jewish temple worship.[6] Thus we should expect to find some discussion of one of the temple's central purposes—bringing worshippers into God's presence—in ancient hymns of Israel that were composed in or for the temple. In fact, several of the psalms express the spiritual journey of Israel's ancient pilgrims to find God, culminating in "the speaker in some psalms [asking] the face of God be allowed to shine upon him (Psalm 31:16)."[7] Therefore, in addition to looking at some examples of theophany in the Old Testament and some specific psalms about the great quest to see the face of God in the temple, we will consider *who* worshipped in the First Temple in order to see God.

Examples of Theophany

Ancient Israel's belief that mortals could enter God's presence and see him face-to-face is as old as the existence of Israel itself. We know this from the culminating experience of Jacob, the immediate father of the Israelites, when he wrestled with a divine messenger for a blessing:

> And he said unto him, What is thy name? And he said, Jacob.
>
> And he said, Thy name shall be called no more Jacob, but Israel: for as a prince hast thou power with God and with men, and hast prevailed.
>
> And Jacob asked him, and said, Tell me, I pray thee, thy name. And he said, Wherefore is it that thou dost ask after my name? And he blessed him there.
>
> And Jacob called the name of the place Peniel: for I have seen God face to face, and my life is preserved. (Genesis 32:27–30)

Even before Jacob had his life-altering experience, "the Lord appeared to Abram"—Jacob's grandfather and the father of multitudes—and commanded him to walk before the Lord in perfection (Genesis 17:1; see also 12:7; 18:1). The Lord spoke to Moses face-to-face as a man speaks to a friend (see Exodus 33:11). And Moses along with Aaron, Nadab, Abihu, and seventy of the elders of Israel "saw the God of Israel" (Exodus 24:10); this experience recalls that of Joseph Smith and Oliver Cowdery in the Kirtland Temple (compare Exodus 24:9–11 with D&C 110:1). During Israel's sojourn in the wilderness, the Lord said of Moses: "With him will I speak mouth to mouth, even apparently, and not in dark speeches; and the similitude of the Lord shall he behold" (Numbers 12:8). Deuteronomy refers to Moses as a prophet "whom the Lord knew face to face" (Deuteronomy 34:10).

The experiences of other witnesses attest to the real possibility of seeing God in mortality, especially in the temple. Amos, a prophet from the eighth century BC, straightforwardly stated that he "saw the Lord standing upon the altar" (Amos 9:1). Likewise, the great seer Isaiah declared emphatically that he saw the Lord, which humbled him immeasurably (see Isaiah 6:1). Additionally, see 1 Samuel 3:21 and 1 Kings 3:5–15, where the Lord's appearances to young Samuel and King Solomon are both associated with the tabernacle or temple. Enough preexilic examples can be marshaled to show that, though perhaps it was not common, there were several occasions when mortals enjoyed God's presence and saw him.

Indeed, in certain passages we even see the Israelites being encouraged, if not commanded, to seek the Lord's face. One of these is all the more interesting because it comes from a psalm of David not recorded in the Psalter but in the book of Chronicles, where the historical context for the psalm is presented. This psalm was uttered by King David after the ark of the covenant was brought safely to Jerusalem before the actual temple structure was built. David had prepared a special place to represent the temple, and it was ready for the ark.

> So they brought the ark of God, and set it in the midst of the tent that David had pitched for it: and they offered burnt sacrifices and peace offerings before God. . . .
>
> Then on that day David delivered first this psalm to thank the Lord into the hand of Asaph and his brethren.
>
> Give thanks unto the Lord, call upon his name, make known his deeds among the people.
>
> Sing unto him, sing psalms unto him, talk ye of all his wondrous works.
>
> Glory ye in his holy name: let the heart of them rejoice that seek the Lord.
>
> Seek the Lord and his strength, *seek his face continually*. (1 Chronicles 16:1, 7–11; emphasis added)

The whole of the psalm recounted in 1 Chronicles 16:8–36 seems to be an amalgamation of three other canonical psalms (1 Chronicles 16:8–22 corresponds with Psalm 105:1–15; 1 Chronicles 16:23–33 with Psalm 96:1–13; and 1 Chronicles 16:34–36 with Psalm 106:1, 47–48). While this may well mean that 1 Chronicles 16 was composed later than the psalms it resembles, I believe that 1 Chronicles 16 preserves the authentic historical setting for Psalm 105. First Chronicles 16 also contains the injunction to "seek his [the Lord's] face continually" (compare v. 11 and Psalm 105:4)—an injunction that perfectly fits the temple setting and the language of theophany in the canonical psalms.[8]

The Place of God's Dwelling

Of all the texts in the Old Testament, psalms of theophany, or of promised theophany, lay out most clearly the requirements for the unparalleled privilege of seeing God—perhaps because certain psalms connect that privilege with a specific locale, the Jerusalem temple, and define the temple as the Lord's dwelling place. Psalm 68:16, for example, speaks of the temple as "the hill which God desireth to dwell in; yea, the Lord will dwell in it for ever." The "hill" on which the temple was constructed was, of course, Mount Moriah (2 Chronicles 3:1).

Many biblical passages refer to the temple not as *built* on a hill or mountain, but *as* the hill or mountain of the Lord. Ezekiel 20:40 equates the expression "mine holy mountain" with the Lord's temple. Isaiah 2:2, a passage well known to Latter-day Saints, calls the Jerusalem temple, in Hebrew, the *har bet Yahweh*, literally "the mountain of the house of Jehovah." And Psalm 99:9 encourages all of righteous Israel to "exalt the Lord our God, and worship at his holy hill."

The belief that the temple was God's holy house dates back to the origins of the First Temple. Following King Solomon's dedicatory prayer over the temple, the Lord himself accepted the structure in these words: "I have heard thy prayer and thy supplication, that thou hast made before me: I have hallowed this house . . . to put my name there for ever; and mine eyes and mine heart shall be there perpetually" (1 Kings 9:3).

According to the Chronicler, as part of his acceptance of the temple, the Lord himself encouraged his people to seek his face, and he promised them an associated blessing. He declared:

> If my people, which are called by my name, shall humble themselves, and pray, and seek my face, and turn from their wicked ways; then will I hear from heaven, and will forgive their sin, and will heal their land.
>
> Now mine eyes shall be open, and mine ears attent unto the prayer that is made in this place. (2 Chronicles 7:14–15)

Clearly the Lord expected his people to seek his face in the temple. It was his dwelling place, a place of effectual, fervent prayer, and the place from which God himself would answer his people and in which he would dwell among them (note the parallel function of the tabernacle as described earlier in Exodus 29:42–45).[9]

In the Psalmist's worldview, God's earthly temple paralleled a heavenly temple. For he said, "The Lord is in his holy temple (bᵉheikhal qadᵉsho); the Lord is on his heavenly throne" (Psalm 11:4; translation mine). Here I believe the Psalmist is using antithetical parallelism to compare God's two dwelling places. The holy structure on earth called the temple (heikhal) has its counterpart: God's heavenly residence, his divine throne.

The Hebrew word heikhal is a well-known noun which is most often used to refer to the Jerusalem temple. Occasionally, it is translated as "palace" (1 Kings 21:1; 2 Kings 20:18). The term heikhal is a loan-word from the earlier Sumerian word e-gal, "large house, palace"[10]—the residence of the "big man," or king. Thus, even when the word heikhal clearly referred to God's holy temple in Jerusalem, it carried the connotation of a palace. Hence, we come to understand and appreciate that the Lord's earthly temple was also his earthly palace, home to his earthly throne. Just as God had a heavenly throne, so too he had an earthly throne in Zion, as the Psalmist declared (Psalm 9:11). Therefore, the Psalmist, one of the Heavenly King's earthly subjects, declared in a psalm which speaks of God's enthronement in his temple-palace,

> Lift up your heads, O ye gates; and be ye lift up, ye everlasting doors; and the King of glory shall come in.
>
> Who is this King of glory? The Lord strong and mighty, the Lord mighty in battle.
>
> Lift up your heads, O ye gates; even lift them up, ye everlasting doors; and the King of glory shall come in.
>
> Who is this King of glory? The Lord of hosts, he is the King of glory. Selah. (Psalm 24:7–10)

In another psalm, the Psalmist declared that he *had* seen God in his sanctuary and there beheld his power and glory (Psalm 63:2). Indeed, God was so great that even the mortal "king shall rejoice in God" (Psalm 63:11).

Temple Pilgrimages

Psalm 63 is also noteworthy as it relates to worshippers making pilgrimages to the Jerusalem temple. Three times a year, all males of the covenant were commanded to make a pilgrimage to the temple to "appear before the Lord God"—at the spring Feast of Unleavened Bread (Passover), seven weeks later at the Feast of Harvest (Weeks), and at the fall Feast of Ingathering (Tabernacles), according to Exodus 23:14–17.

I believe that over time, this passage came to be read differently from its original meaning, thus obscuring the powerful truth that God intended for mortals to strive to see his face. In this fundamental revelation about the liturgical calendar, Moses was told that there were three sanctuary festivals every year that *every* male of the covenant must observe. The King James Version of Exodus 23:17 reads, "Three times in the year all thy males shall appear (*yērā'eh*) before the Lord God." This is the standard translation. But it may be legitimately argued that the Hebrew word *yērā'eh* should be vocalized slightly differently (*yirᵉ'eh*) and that this passage should actually read, "Three times in the year every male of yours *will see the face of Lord*." The Samaritan Bible supports this reading (using a *Qal* form of the verb instead of the traditional *Nifal*),[11] and it harmonizes well with the collection of texts we have been exploring. I believe Deuteronomy 16:16 should be read this way as well: "Three times in the year every male of yours *will see the Lord your God* in the place that he will choose."[12] The place God first chose was, of course, the portable temple called the tabernacle, and he later chose the Jerusalem temple. Thus, seeing the face of the Lord was no inconsequential concept in ancient Israel. Its importance seems to have been lost in certain passages or, at the very least, downplayed over time. Thus, if the emended reading is correct, the original commandment to go to the temple to see the face of God was given to all, suggesting that all were at least to *strive* in righteousness to come into God's presence—if not to be wholly successful in that quest.

We have very little contemporary data about the details of these sanctuary festivals in First Temple times, how they were actually observed, the role of individual pilgrims, or how priests and Levites were expected to mediate between man and God. Most all of the information about these pilgrimage feasts comes from later rabbinic sources. Scholars have extrapolated the activities of pilgrims at the temple in preexilic times from sources from the

Second Temple period or later. Especially interesting is the glimpse we get of active participation on the part of the pilgrims themselves in the festivals, as well as the place of the psalms in all three pilgrimage festivals. During the Feast of Unleavened Bread (Passover), "each Israelite slaughtered his own offering, and priests caught the blood in gold and silver vessels. Meanwhile, Psalms 113–18, the Hallel psalms, traditionally the psalms for pilgrimage, were sung."[13] Upon arriving at the temple court during the Feast of Harvest (Weeks), the pilgrims were "met by the song of the Levites who are said to have sung Psalm 30."[14] Daily during the Feast of Ingathering (Tabernacles), "there was a procession around the altar; worshippers carried a branch in one hand and a piece of fruit in the other, and Psalm 118 was sung."[15]

Always the activities of the three pilgrimage festivals were accompanied by the singing of psalms and a feeling of joy centered on the temple. Each of the pilgrimages culminated in the experience of the temple, a feeling captured by one of the pilgrimage psalms:

> I was glad when they said unto me, Let us go into the house of the Lord.
> Our feet shall stand within thy gates, O Jerusalem.
> Jerusalem is builded as a city that is compact together:
> Whither the tribes go up, the tribes of the Lord, unto the testimony of Israel, to give thanks unto the name of the Lord.
> For there are set thrones of judgment, the thrones of the house of David.
> Pray for the peace of Jerusalem: they shall prosper that love thee.
> Peace be within thy walls, and prosperity within thy palaces.
> For my brethren and companions' sakes, I will now say, Peace be within thee.
> Because of the house of the Lord our God I will seek thy good.
> (Psalm 122:1–9)

Before entering the temple, the pilgrim was further elevated in purity through priestly rituals, "which provid[ed] a transition to the holy realm of the temple."[16] Inside the temple precinct, pilgrims would see architecture designed to enhance the feeling of holiness and closeness to God by symbolically replicating the Garden of Eden. All the temple walls were carved with "figures of cherubims and palm trees and open flowers," with "doors of olive tree" (1 Kings 6:29, 31). It seems that the pilgrim in the temple attempted to recapitulate symbolically the activities of the first inhabitants of the Edenic paradise, walking in the presence of God and feasting on the fruit of every tree of the garden (except one).[17] One Psalmist may have even drawn upon the recaptured setting of Eden in the Jerusalem temple when he described his successful quest to enter the divine presence: "I have seen you in the sanctuary and beheld your power and your glory. Because your love is better than life, my lips will glorify you. I will praise you as long as I live, and in your name I will lift up my hands. My soul will be satisfied as with the riches of foods; with singing lips my mouth will praise you" (NIV, Psalm 63:2–5).

From one perspective, "the experience of the temple was paradise regained."[18] The culmination of that experience—encountering God—was enhanced by the architectural designs in the temple.

Requirements for Worshippers

Certain psalms indicate that not everyone was permitted to enter the temple. There were requirements governing who could worship in the temple and thus seek to enjoy God's presence: "For the Lord is righteous, he loves justice; upright men will see his face" (NIV, Psalm 11:7). We might even say that *only* upright persons will see the Lord's face, for that is the message of the passage. The Hebrew word translated in this psalm as "upright" is *yashar*, which derives from a root that originally meant "to be straight," "honest," or "right."[19] The Lord's intent in this verse is not hard to discern.

Perhaps the best known of the psalms that describe the prerequisites for a personal encounter with God is Psalm 24, quoted in part above. Among the many scholarly treatments of Psalm 24, I still think that some of the older discussions are the best. Sigmund Mowinckel avers that Psalm 24 contains the "laws of the sanctuary," which are the "special rules and special demands as to the qualifications of those to be admitted" into the temple.[20] Psalm 24 is one of the so-called psalms of ascent or procession, sung by the Levites and priests as devotees went up to the temple to worship and participate in sacrifices offered there.

Biblical commentator Franz Delitzsch referred to this psalm as "preparation for the reception of the Lord who is about to come [into his temple]."[21] According to his scheme, the psalm was to be sung antiphonally, by a "chorus of the festive procession," starting out with verses 1 and 2 when the pilgrims were below the hill of the temple. Separate voices responded to the chorus with the critical questions and answers found in verses 3–4. The chorus in turn replied with verses 5 and 6 as the procession moved up the hill. Then, upon arriving at the gate of the temple, the chorus sang verses 7–10.[22] Psalm 24 reads:

> The earth is the Lord's, and the fulness thereof; the world, and they that dwell therein.
>
> For he hath founded it upon the seas, and established it upon the floods.
>
> <u>Who shall ascend into the hill of the Lord? or who shall stand in his holy place</u>?
>
> <u>He that hath clean hands, and a pure hea</u>rt; <u>who hath not lifted up his soul unto vanity, nor sworn deceitfully</u>. *Kept Covenants*
>
> He shall receive the blessing from the Lord, and righteousness from the God of his salvation.
>
> This is the generation of them that seek him, that seek thy face, O Jacob. Selah.
>
> Lift up your heads, O ye gates; and be ye lift up, ye everlasting doors; and the King of glory shall come in.
>
> Who is this King of glory? The Lord strong and mighty, the Lord mighty in battle.
>
> Lift up your heads, O ye gates; even lift them up, ye everlasting doors; and the King of glory shall come in.
>
> Who is this King of glory? The Lord of hosts, he is the King of glory. Selah. (Psalm 24:1–10)

Though the King James Version of Psalm 24:3 uses the words "hill of the Lord," the Hebrew literally translates to "who shall go up to the *mountain* of Yahweh," a reference to the Lord's mountain house, as we saw in Isaiah 2:2. And the phrase "who shall stand in his holy place" refers directly to the temple; a section of the Jerusalem temple was explicitly called "the Holy Place."[23]

The implication of the King James Version of Psalm 24 is that one could encounter God in the temple if worthy. Though the flow is a bit garbled, the text seems to be saying that "the generation of them that seek him [the Lord] . . . shall receive the blessing from the Lord [whose face they seek]." This was likely understood against the backdrop of several other psalms showing that when the Lord's face shines on a person, blessings—especially salvation—come (see

Psalms 4:6; 31:16; 67:1–2; 80:3, 7, 19; 119:135). The Psalmist's many petitions for God's face to shine upon him and his people seem to be part of a long-standing belief in God's anthropomorphic reality.

The problem is that the version of Psalm 24 preserved in the King James Bible appears to have something missing in verse 6, near the name Jacob. From the context provided in the rest of the verses, it is not Jacob's face that is sought but the Lord's. The Septuagint (LXX) points out much more explicitly (especially verse 6) that the ultimate purpose of going up to the temple was to "seek the face of the God of Jacob." And that opportunity rested on specific requirements of worthiness:

> Who shall go up to the mountain of the Lord, and who shall stand in his holy place?
>
> He that is innocent in his hands and pure in his heart; who has not lifted up his soul to vanity, nor sworn deceitfully to his neighbor.
>
> He shall receive a blessing from the Lord, and mercy from God his Saviour.
>
> This is the generation of them that seek him, that seek the face of the God of Jacob. . . .
>
> Who is this king of glory? The Lord of hosts, he is this king of glory. (LXX, Psalm 23:3–6, 10)[24]

Here the unobscured objective of the pure in heart is to see God in his temple. Why the Septuagint is clearer on this point is open to debate. Perhaps this clarity reflects the translator's interpretation of how the Hebrew text was supposed to be understood. Or perhaps the Hebrew manuscripts from which the LXX was translated truly did preserve the superior reading compared to other manuscript versions. Given available evidence, it seems not only possible but likely that different Jewish communities had slightly different versions of the same Old Testament books: the Babylonian community had one version, the Palestinian community had another version, and the Egyptian community had still another.[25] Whatever the reason, given all the scriptures we are able to examine, it is apparent to me that the LXX gives us the language and meaning that was originally intended.

In parallel fashion, Jesus Christ used the doctrinal foundation of Psalm 24 to make the same promise, in his Sermon on the Mount, to the pure in heart: they would see God (Matthew 5:8). In both cases, the condition upon which the promises rested was clean hands and a pure heart. It becomes even more apparent that Jesus based his promise on Psalm 24 when we compare the wording of the psalm in the Septuagint with the Greek New Testament wording of Matthew 5:8. The Septuagint phrase "pure in his heart" (*katharos te kardia*), used in the singular in verse 4, is equivalent to the phrase "pure in heart" (*katharoi te kardia*), used in the plural by Jesus in Matthew 5:8.

In First Temple times, it seems that both the outward actions and the inward thoughts of the worshipper had to conform to a holy standard for the person to gain entrance into the temple precinct. Hands were stained by such things as idolatry, murder, theft, adultery, Sabbath breaking, and mistreating others. The heart was corrupted by evil or impure thoughts. Ritual purity must also have been a concern, and thus participation in cleansing rituals to remove ritual impurity could also probably be expected of prospective temple attendees. Note the dozens of *mikvaoth*, or ritual baths, that archaeologists have uncovered around the precinct of the Second Temple.

The worthy temple worshipper in ancient Israel was also a member of the covenant community. Undoubtedly reflecting requirements from the First Temple period, Ezekiel included in his description of a glorious future temple the requirement of covenant membership for entering the temple: "Thus saith the Lord God: No stranger, uncircumcised in heart, nor uncircumcised in flesh, shall enter into my sanctuary, of any stranger that is among the children of Israel" (Ezekiel 44:9).

None of the other Old Testament theophanic passages we have examined place restrictions on who may worship in the temple. Neither do they provide many particulars concerning the ultimate quest of coming into the presence of God in the temple. Priests oversaw the sacrificial system and acted as mediators between man and God, but no detailed explanation of their role in guiding worshippers to see God is given in these passages. The language of all theophany texts in the Psalter is democratic. We know gradations of holiness existed—among classes of people as well as in the temple itself. Yet the language of the Psalter does not discriminate; all are invited to seek the face of God.

Some prominent biblical scholars, including Hermann Gunkel, Sigmund Mowinckel, K. Galling, and J. Begrich, have argued that during the existence of the First Temple, priests stood at the temple gates and ensured the worthiness of worshippers, and hence the sanctity of the temple, by posing questions to those seeking entrance.²⁶ Hans-Joachim Kraus suggested a similar, though reverse, scenario. The worshippers stood outside the gates of the temple and asked, "Who is worthy to enter the temple?" Then, "from the inside a priestly speaker answers them with the declaration of the conditions of entrance."²⁷ These conditions are found in other psalms beside Psalm 24.

Psalm 15 is another temple entrance hymn that presents qualifications required of those who seek the Lord in his sanctuary. It begins with a question directed to the Lord himself: "Lord, who shall abide in thy tabernacle? who shall dwell in thy holy hill?" (v. 1). The Lord's answer encompasses a series of requirements which seem very much the equivalent of an ancient certification of temple worthiness—a temple recommend, if you will, in Latter-day Saint parlance. The NIV Bible provides a helpful translation:

> He whose walk is blameless and who does what is righteous, who speaks the truth from his heart
> and has no slander on his tongue, who does his neighbor no wrong and casts no slur on his fellowman,
> who despises a vile man but honors those who fear the Lord, who keeps his oath even when it hurts,
> who lends his money without usury and does not accept a bribe against the innocent. He who does these things will never be shaken. (NIV, Psalm 15:2–5)

It has been asserted that these attributes were individual qualifications that formed a ten-part requirement. In sum, according to Psalm 15, a worshipper in ancient Israel who desired to enter the temple was one who

1. walked with integrity,
2. worked righteousness,
3. spoke truth,
4. despised reprobates,
5. had sworn to do no evil,
6. had not slandered ("trip on his tongue"),
7. had done no evil to his neighbor,
8. had not lifted up a reproach against his relative,
9. had not charged interest for his money,
10. and had not taken a bribe against the innocent.²⁸

Seeing God in His Temple 283

The number ten appears to have been used purposely by the Psalmist because of its symbolic value. It connoted wholeness, completeness, and correctness. The number ten was used symbolically in a number of other biblical passages, including, for example, the Ten Commandments, the ten plagues, tithing, and the parable of the ten virgins.[29] In Psalm 15, the number ten may have served another significant purpose in this confession of temple worthiness, according to Peter C. Craigie. He proposed that temple worshippers were required to recite from memory, using their ten fingers as memory devices, the "moral conditions prerequisite to participation in [temple] worship."[30] Psalm 15 seems to have recorded an ancient confession of faith and a pledge of worthiness that certified the uprightness of the temple participant or worshipper—priest, Levite, or Israelite.

Here one is reminded of the purity requirements demanded of ancient Egyptians who desired to enter the sacred space of their temples. Egypt was another intensely temple-oriented culture, closely associated with Israel. The Egyptians believed that their gods dwelt in temples just as the Israelites believed that the true and living God dwelt in his temple. Egyptian temples served as "mansions of the gods" and "portals to the divine."[31] Also, in Egypt, as in Israel, the identity between palace and temple is generally assumed. That is, the temple was likewise regarded as the throne room of deity. The declarations of purity required for entry into the temple comprised the Negative Confession in the Book of the Dead 125. A portion of the Negative Confession, an affirmation of uprightness stated as denial of any wrongdoing, reads as follows:

> Hail to thee, O great god, lord of the Two Justices! I have come to thee, my lord, I have been brought that I might see thy beauty. . . . I have come to thee, I have brought thee justice, I have banished deceit for thee.
>
> I have not done evil to men.
> I have not illtreated animals.
> I have not sinned in the temple. . . .
> I have not blasphemed the gods.
> I have not done violence to the poor.
> I have not done what the gods abhor.
> I have not defamed a slave to his master.

> I have not made anyone sick.
> I have not made anyone weep.
> I have not slain.
> I have not given orders to slay.
> I have not made anyone to suffer. . . .
> I am blameless.[32]

In Egypt, as in Israel, the temple was the place to see the face of the gods. According to Egyptologist John Gee, the Negative Confession constituted a list that certified the purity, capacity, and authorization of someone to enter the temple. It amounted to, in Professor Gee's words, "the ancient Egyptian equivalent of the modern temple recommend."[33]

Of course, the ancient Egyptians did not possess the priesthood, and their temples were not sacred precincts of the true and living God. But they understood very well the connection between the requirements of purity in thought and action and the ability to enjoy the presence of the gods. Their understanding of this principle, along with their attempt to imitate the powers of the ancient order of the priesthood, dates from the distant past, as the Patriarch Abraham's memoir in the Pearl of Great Price indicates (see Abraham 1:26).

Our Latter-day Dispensation

All of this sounds more than familiar to Latter-day Saints acquainted with their own temple theology and the requirements for temple entrance and worship. The concept of the temple as the place where the Lord may be seen face-to-face is one of the superlative doctrines restored by Joseph Smith. In his biography of the Prophet, eminent historian Richard Bushman commented on this aspect of the Restoration: "In the temple . . . Joseph hoped his Saints would face God as Moses' people never could. At the completion of Solomon's temple, God came in a cloud of glory. A fall 1832 revelation said that when the Kirtland temple was finished, 'a cloud shall rest upon it, which cloud shall be even the glory of the Lord.'"[34]

Indeed, a major part of Joseph Smith's ministry seems to have been devoted to helping latter-day Israel understand that the promise of seeing the Lord face-to-face in the temple was literal and real, just as ancient Israel's leaders and writers believed. But in presenting the authenticity and literal nature of this promise, both Joseph and the ancients were merely echoing the Lord himself, as we shall see.

In preparation for the building of the Kirtland Temple, the Lord emphasized to the Prophet the need for complete purity, using language about seeing the Lord face-to-face that sounds as if it were culled from something written by Israel's ancient Psalmist. The Lord said:

> And inasmuch as my people build a house unto me in the name of the Lord, and do not suffer any unclean thing to come into it, that it be not defiled, my glory shall rest upon it;
>
> Yea, and my presence shall be there, for I will come into it, and all the pure in heart that shall come into it <u>shall see God</u>.
>
> But if it be defiled I will not come into it, and my glory shall not be there; for I will not come into unholy temples. (D&C 97:15–17)

Several other passages in modern revelation hold up the promise of a face-to-face encounter with the Lord. But the requirement upon which the promise is predicated is uniform: purity. "Verily, thus saith the Lord: It shall come to pass that every soul who forsaketh his sins and cometh unto me, and calleth on my name, and obeyeth my voice, and keepeth my commandments, shall see my face and know that I am" (D&C 93:1).

Joseph Smith's emphasis on seeing God in the temple was not just a radical departure from the Christianity of his day—it was revolutionary. As Professor Bushman indicates, in an era when "many Christians were sloughing off the Hebrew Bible and taking their Gospel solely from the New Testament," Joseph was, by divine instruction, elevating and theologically enthroning temple themes from the Old Testament.[35] Joseph and the Psalmist, particularly, were at one.

The emphasis on purity as a requirement for temple participation in early Mormonism, as it was in certain psalms, is well exemplified in a comment by W. W. Phelps regarding the coming dedication of the temple: "We are preparing to make ourselves clean, by first cleansing our hearts, forsaking our sins, forgiving every body, all we ever had against them; anointing washing the body; putting on clean decent clothes, by anointing our heads and by keeping all the commandments. As we come nearer to God we see our imperfections and nothingness plainer and plainer."[36]

Praise and Petition

Above all, the biblical psalms are full of praise for God's goodness, greatness, righteousness, mercy, and loving-kindness (see, for example, Psalm 36:5–7). As a result, the Psalmist especially exulted in the opportunity to come into the Lord's presence, for "in [the Lord's] presence is fulness of joy" (Psalm 16:11).

The Psalmist was convinced that beholding the face of the Lord in righteousness would completely satisfy his soul. In contrast to the "men of the world," who "have their portion in this life," meaning wealth and worldly power, the Psalmist proclaimed, "I will behold thy face in righteousness: I shall be satisfied" (Psalm 17:14–15). Mitchell Dahood has noted that a "beatific vision, the face to face meeting with God, is clearly intended."[37] It was not metaphor.

The Psalmist declared, furthermore, that the countenance of the Lord made one "exceeding glad" (Psalm 21:6). "In [his] light shall *we* see light" (Psalm 36:9; emphasis added).

For these reasons, the Psalmist sought one thing above all others, had one overarching request of the Lord—that he "may dwell in the house of the Lord all the days of [his] life, to behold the beauty of the Lord, and to enquire in his temple" (Psalm 27:4).

Is this not the request of all true disciples in every age when the Lord's temples have been available? And can we not appreciate and relate to what ultimately kept the Psalmist faithful and motivated? For, he confessed, "I had fainted, unless I had believed *to see* the goodness of the Lord in the land of the living. Wait on the Lord: be of good courage, and he shall strengthen thine heart: wait, I say, on the Lord" (Psalm 27:13–14; emphasis added).

In these two verses do we not find something of an ultimate message for all those who worship in the Lord's temples in modern times? And is not the continued plea of the Psalmist our plea as temple-going Latter-day Saints?

> When thou saidst, Seek ye my face; my heart said unto thee, Thy face, Lord, will I seek.
>
> Hide not thy face far from me; put not thy servant away in anger: thou hast been my help; leave me not, neither forsake me, O God of my salvation. (Psalm 27:8–9)

This request becomes all the more significant in our discussion when we realize that the Psalmist uttered these words only three verses after he petitioned the Lord to be allowed to spend the rest of his days in the temple (see v. 4). Seeking the face of the Lord and seeking to be in the temple were twin thrusts of the same quest. In Psalm 42:2, the Psalmist longs to come to God in the temple: "When will I go and see the face of God?" (*māthai 'ābō' vᵉ'ērā'eh pᵉnê 'elōhîm*).[38]

Conclusion

Given all that we have examined, it is impossible for me to believe that seeking the face of God was a minor theme in the Old Testament or a passing fancy in the mind of the Psalmist. Rather, the Psalmist and other biblical writers seem, at times, to be consumed by this idea. Isaiah, for instance, regards his vision of the Lord in the temple as the apex of his call to be a prophet. "I saw also the Lord," he said, "and his train filled the temple" (Isaiah 6:1). In this vein, after discussing at great length "what the language of 'seeing God' or 'seeing God's face' refers [to]" in the psalms, Mark Smith concludes: "What the psalmists experienced of the divine in the temple was too great to reduce to natural phenomenon. . . . Perhaps the psalmists experienced God just as Moses, Isaiah, and Ezekiel did . . . human in form and dazzling in light."[39]

I think we should take very seriously the idea that in the minds of many biblical writers, especially the Psalmist, seeking the face of the Lord was *the* quest of mortality and that it was against the backdrop of this belief that the Psalmist encouraged every true follower of God to "seek the Lord, and his strength: *seek his face* evermore" (Psalm 105:4; emphasis added).

Jesus Christ renewed and revitalized this quest when he, quoting the Psalmist, promised the pure in heart that they would see God (Matthew 5:8). The Prophet Joseph Smith restored this quest and reported it to be the ultimate blessing of temple attendance within a religious system that began as a face-to-face encounter with Deity in an open-air, wooded temple called the Sacred Grove (D&C 97:15–17; Joseph Smith—History 1:14–17; see also D&C 93:1; 88:67–68). Thus, the belief of the ancient Psalmist—that God may be seen in his temple—is our conviction as well.

Notes

1. Hereafter I use *Psalmist* to refer to the author or authors of the particular psalm or psalms under discussion, not to suggest that all psalms were composed by a single author or that psalms, once written, were never edited by others.
2. Mark S. Smith, "The Psalms as a Book for Pilgrims," *Interpretation: A Journal of Bible & Theology* 46, no. 2 (April 1992): 162. Smith is Skirball Professor of Bible and Hebrew and Judaic Studies at New York University.
3. Margaret Barker, *The Great High Priest: The Temple Roots of Christian Liturgy* (London: T&T Clark, 2003), 6. Though some of Barker's positions regarding ancient Israel's history have been called into question, several scriptures support her view on this point.
4. John W. Welch, *The Sermon on the Mount in the Light of the Temple* (Surrey, England: Ashgate, 2009), 43.
5. Margaret Barker, *The Gate of Heaven* (London: SPCK, 1991), 45.
6. Sigmund Mowinkel, *The Psalms in Israel's Worship* (Nashville: Abingdon, 1962), 2:89–90.
7. Smith, "The Psalms as a Book for Pilgrims," 162.
8. First Chronicles 16 has also been used to support the argument that the Levites acted as the final compilers of the Psalter in the postexilic period since this chapter places the three sections of the canonical psalms "into the hand of Asaph and his brethren" (1 Chronicles 16:7)—a Levitical group. See Mark S. Smith, "The Levitical Compilation of the Psalter," *Zeitschrift für die Alttestamentliche Wissenschaft* 103 (1991): 258–59. This hypothesis also points to the temple, given the inextricable link between the temple and the Levites.
9. It is argued by interpreters that the author of Kings shaped and presented his material to speak to the needs of the exiled community of Israel while the Chronicler wrote for the restored community of Israel who had returned from exile. Perhaps some would dismiss the credibility of 2 Chronicles 7:14–15 on this basis. However, I believe that this passage does reflect a historical core—that at the dedication of the First Temple, God encouraged the Israelites to seek his face. I believe that Chronicles here is in harmony with several other scriptural writings that extend an invitation of theophany and that the language of the Psalmist about seeking the face of God develops from God's invitation at the First Temple dedication.
10. Ludwig Koehler, Walter Baumgartner, and others, *The Hebrew and Aramaic Lexicon of the Old Testament: Study Edition* (Leiden: Brill, 2001), 1:244–45.
11. The *Qal* form or stem of the Hebrew verb denotes action in the active voice; the *Nifal* form denotes action in the passive voice ("to see" versus "to appear"). Nearly 70 percent of verbs in Hebrew are *Qal* forms.
12. This is also the reading proposed by Margaret Barker in *Temple Themes in Christian Worship* (London: T&T Clark, 2010), 146.
13. Smith, "The Psalms as a Book for Pilgrims," 157.
14. Smith, "The Psalms as a Book for Pilgrims," 158.
15. Smith, "The Psalms as a Book for Pilgrims," 158.
16. Smith, "The Psalms as a Book for Pilgrims," 160.

17. The typology of feasting in God's presence in the temple is laid out in more detail in Smith, "The Psalms as a Book for Pilgrims," 161–62.

18. Smith, "The Psalms as a Book for Pilgrims," 161.

19. Koehler and Baumgartner, *Hebrew and Aramaic Lexicon*, 1:449.

20. Mowinckel, *The Psalms in Israel's Worship*, 1:177.

21. Franz Delitzsch, *Biblical Commentary on the Psalms* (Grand Rapids, MI: Eerdmans, n.d.), 1:332.

22. Delitzsch, *Biblical Commentary on the Psalms*, 1:332–33.

23. Alec Garrard, *The Splendor of the Temple: A Pictorial Guide to Herod's Temple and Its Ceremonies* (Grand Rapids, MI: Kregal, 2000), 21, 73.

24. Translation from Lancelot C. L. Brenton, *The Septuagint with Apocrypha: Greek and English* (Peabody, MA: Hendrickson Publishers, 1995), 711.

25. This notion is gathered from a variety of sources. See Karen H. Jobes and Moisés Silva, *Invitation to the Septuagint* (Grand Rapids, MI: Baker Academic, 2005), 177; Frank M. Cross Jr., "The History of the Biblical Text in Light of Discoveries in the Judaean Desert," in *Qumran and the History of the Biblical Text*, ed. Frank Moore Cross and Shemaryahu Talmon (Cambridge, MA: Harvard University Press, 1975), 177–95; and Frank Moore Cross, "The Evolution of a Theory of Local Texts," in *Qumran and the History of the Biblical Text*, 306–20.

26. Moshe Weinfeld, "Instructions for Temple Visitors in the Bible and in Ancient Egypt," in *Egyptological Studies*, ed. Sarah Israelit-Groll, Scripta Hierosolymitana 28 (Jerusalem: Magnes, 1982), 230–31, cited in Donald W. Parry, "'Who Shall Ascend into the Mountain of the Lord?' Three Biblical Temple Entrance Hymns," in *Revelation, Reason, and Faith: Essays in Honor of Truman G. Madsen*, ed. Donald W. Parry, Daniel C. Peterson, and Stephen D. Ricks, (Provo, UT: FARMS, 2002), 735.

27. Hans-Joachim Kraus, *Psalms 1–59: A Commentary*, trans. Hilton C. Oswald (Minneapolis: Augsburg, 1988), 227.

28. Parry, "'Who Shall Ascend into the Mountain of the Lord?,'" 732–33. Professor Parry follows the thinking of Peter C. Craigie, *Psalms 1–50* (Waco, TX: Word Books, 1983), 150.

29. Ethelbert W. Bullinger, *Number in Scripture: Its Supernatural Design and Spiritual Significance* (Grand Rapids, MI: Kregal, 1969), 243–50.

30. Craigie, *Psalms 1–50*, 151.

31. Richard H. Wilkinson, *The Complete Temples of Ancient Egypt* (New York: Thames & Hudson, 2000), 7.

32. Sabatino Moscati, *The Face of the Ancient Orient: A Panorama of Near Eastern Civilizations in Pre-Classical Times* (New York: Anchor Books, 1962), 126.

33. Personal conversation with John Gee, research professor, Neal A. Maxwell Institute for Religious Scholarship, Brigham Young University.

34. Richard Lyman Bushman, *Joseph Smith: Rough Stone Rolling* (New York: Knopf, 2005), 217.

35. Bushman, *Rough Stone Rolling*, 312.

36. Quoted in Bushman, *Rough Stone Rolling*, 314.

37. Mitchell Dahood, *Psalms I: 1–50*, Anchor Bible 16 (New York: Doubleday, 1981), 99.

38. My translation.

39. Mark S. Smith, "'Seeing God' in the Psalms: The Background to the Beatific Vision in the Hebrew Bible," *Catholic Biblical Quarterly* 50, no. 2 (April 1988): 173, 182–83. Professor Smith's comment appears in a detailed article responding to the late Professor Mitchell Dahood's thesis, in his three-volume Anchor Bible commentary on Psalms, that "numerous passages in the Psalter point to an ancient Israelite belief in the 'beatific vision' . . . that some psalms indicate a hope in 'beholding God throughout eternity, in afterlife.'"

17

Old Testament Psalms in the Book of Mormon

John Hilton III

The Psalms provide powerful messages of praise and worship. Their words reverberate not only throughout the Old Testament but also in the New. Elder Jeffrey R. Holland has written that "the book of Psalms may be the one biblical text admired nearly equally by both Christians and Jews, to say nothing of those of other faiths—or no faith at all—who find comfort in its verses and encouragement in the hope they convey."[1]

Over one hundred years ago Franz Delitzsch noted, "Next to the book of Isaiah, no book is so frequently quoted in the New Testament as the Psalter."[2] Henry Shires similarly states that "the N[ew] T[estament] has been influenced by Psalms more than by any other book of the O[ld] T[estament]. In 70 cases N.T. quotations of Psalms are introduced by formulas. There are 60 more quotations that have no introductory formula, and in an additional 220 instances we can discover identifiable citations and references."[3] These frequent New Testament allusions to the Psalms should not be surprising, for as Robert Alter writes, "Through the ages, Psalms has been the most urgently, personally present of all the books of the Bible in the lives of many readers."[4]

John Hilton III is an assistant professor of ancient scripture at Brigham Young University.

Given that the Psalms are frequently quoted in the New Testament, one wonders if a similar phenomenon occurs in the Book of Mormon. Although Psalms are not specifically mentioned as being on the brass plates (see 1 Nephi 5:10–16),[5] certainly some of what we today have as the book of Psalms could have been included on the plates.[6] Even if the Psalmic material did not appear in written form on the brass plates, early Book of Mormon authors such as Nephi could have been familiar with some Psalms based on their experience with temple worship in Jerusalem. Moreover, while there are no explicit references to Psalms in the Book of Mormon, David Larsen has found several textual connections between the biblical Psalter and the Dead Sea Scrolls, none of which were explicitly identified, leaving open the possibility of similar connections in the Book of Mormon as well.[7]

When making the case that Book of Mormon authors utilized the Psalms, some caveats are in order. First, the writings in the Book of Mormon have been both abridged and translated. Thus potential textual connections could have been created or obscured through these processes. The connections presented in this paper assume a literal English translation of the Book of Mormon from original text.[8] Second, because we do not have a complete record of the brass plates, several of the connections that appear to occur between Psalms and the Book of Mormon could in fact stem from other unknown sources.[9]

In this paper I provide forty-three phrases that have strong connections between the Book of Mormon and Old Testament Psalms. These demonstrate the extent to which the Psalms' language of praise and worship influenced Book of Mormon authors. I will then provide two extended examples of how these connections can deepen our understanding and appreciation of both texts.

Textual Allusions to Psalms in the Book of Mormon

Admittedly, uncovering allusions is a difficult and subjective endeavor. Given that "little or no consensus has emerged regarding what distinguishes a quotation from a mere verbal coincidence or vague reminiscence,"[10] it can be difficult to discern whether textual similarities are intentional or coincidental.[11] Robert Girdlestone cautioned, "We have to be on our guard against mistaking resemblances for references. Some expressions may have been common property to several Hebrew writers; they may have almost become idioms in the language; and we cannot say that the writers borrowed them from one another."[12] Moreover, finding allusions between the book of

Psalms and the Book of Mormon is particularly difficult, given the size of the two texts (43,760 and 268,323 words, respectively).

In this paper I focus on potential textual allusions, in this case, instances in which the phrasing of Psalms and Book of Mormon passages is identical.[13] In order to make these textual connections, I used WordCruncher[14] to identify every four-word phrase commonly held in the two texts. In total, WordCruncher found 1,567 four-word phrases that were in each of the two texts. Some of these were clearly commonly used phrases (for example, "the house of Israel") or relatively insignificant phrases (for example, "to the words of"), while others seemed potentially significant (for example, "enter into my rest"). Two research assistants, Alyssa Aramaki and Sam Woodall,[15] reviewed each of the 1,567 four-word phrases for potentially important allusions. I then synthesized their work and reviewed the phrases, looking for additional textual connections between the Psalms and Book of Mormon. In distinguishing between potential allusions and mere textual coincidences, we followed the criteria set forth by Richard Hays, such as significance of words in the two texts and thematic coherence.[16]

As a result of this analysis, I believe there are at least forty-three textual allusions to the book of Psalms in the Book of Mormon, as outlined in table 1.[17] It should be noted that the data in table 1 include not only the specific words listed but also variant phrases.[18] The purpose of the "appearances elsewhere" column is to indicate the relative scarcity of the phrase outside the Psalms and Book of Mormon. While some of these phrases may appear to be common (for example, "the goodness of the Lord"), this table clarifies the extent to which these phrases actually appear in scripture. While some phrases (for example, "that I may walk") appear in other Old Testament passages, the context indicates a particularly close relationship between the Book of Mormon and the Psalms.[19]

Table 1. Textual Connections between Old Testament Psalms and the Book of Mormon

Case	Book of Mormon	Psalms	Textual Connection	Appearances Elsewhere
Case 1	1 Nephi 1:20	Psalm 145:9	Tender mercies . . . are over all	0
Case 2	1 Nephi 8:8	Psalm 69:16	According to the multitude of tender mercies	0
Case 3	1 Nephi 8:19	Psalm 2:9	A rod of iron	Revelation 2:27; 12:5; 19:15
Case 4	1 Nephi 13:36; 15:15	Psalm 62:2, 6	My rock and my salvation	D&C 18:17, Abraham 2:16
Case 5	1 Nephi 16:5; Alma 7:19	Psalm 23:3	In the paths of righteousness	0
Case 6	2 Nephi 2:7, 3 Nephi 9:20, 12:19, Mormon 2:14, Ether 4:15, Moroni 6:2	Psalm 34:18	Broken heart . . . contrite spirit	D&C 20:37; 59:8
Case 7	2 Nephi 4:17	Psalms 27:13; 33:5	Goodness of the Lord	Jeremiah 31:13
Case 8	2 Nephi 4:25	Psalms 18:10; 104:3	Upon the wings of	2 Samuel 22:11
Case 9	2 Nephi 4:27, 29; 3 Nephi 3:26	Psalms 5:8; 27:11; 69:18	Because of mine enemies	0
Case 10	2 Nephi 4:30; Alma 36:28	Psalm 52:9	I will praise thee forever	0
Case 11	2 Nephi 4:30	Psalm 89:26	My god and the rock of my salvation	0
Case 12	2 Nephi 4:32; Mosiah 4:26; Alma 7:22	Psalm 56:13	That I may walk	Proverbs 2:20; Ezekiel 11:20; 1 Thessalonians 4:12
Case 13	2 Nephi 4:33	Psalm 5:8	Make . . . straight before	Joshua 6:5
Case 14	2 Nephi 4:34	Psalms 55:23; 56:3	I will trust in thee	0
Case 15	1 Nephi 21:22; 2 Nephi 4:35; 6:6	Psalms 63:4; 121:1	I will lift up my	Isaiah 49:22
Case 16	2 Nephi 4:35; Alma 33:11	Psalm 57:2	I will cry unto	0
Case 17	2 Nephi 9:40; Alma 36:1; Alma 38:1	Psalm 5:1	Give ear to my words	D&C 58:1

Case	Book of Mormon	Psalms	Textual Connection	Appearances Elsewhere
Case 18	2 Nephi 9:45	Psalms 62:7; 89:26; 95:1	The rock of ... salvation	2 Samuel 22:47; Isaiah 17:10; Deuteronomy 32:15
Case 19	2 Nephi 25:16; Alma 5:19	Psalm 24:4	Clean hands ... pure heart	0
Case 20	2 Nephi 26:5	Psalm 21:9	Shall swallow them up	Hosea 8:7
Case 21	2 Nephi 26:5; 3 Nephi 9:6, 8; 28:20	Psalm 71:20	The depths of the earth	0
Case 22	2 Nephi 30:10	Psalm 145:20	The wicked will he destroy	0
Case 23	2 Nephi 33:3	Psalm 6:6	Water my ... night	0
Case 24	Jacob 1:7	Psalm 95:8	As in the provocation	Hebrews 3:8
Case 25	Jacob 3:11; Alma 14:6, 26:13, 36:13	Psalm 116:3	The pains of hell	0
Case 26	Alma 12:35; Jacob 1:7	Psalm 95:11	Swear in my wrath	Hebrews 3:11; 4:3
Case 27	Jacob 4:10; Alma 37:12	Psalm 145:9	Over all his works	0
Case 28	Jacob 6:6	Psalm 95:7	Today if ye will hear his voice harden not your hearts	Hebrews 3:7
Case 29	Mosiah 7:33, 29:20; Alma 36:27; 38:5; 61:13	Psalms 7:1; 25:20, 31:1	Put my trust ... deliver	1 Chronicles 5:20; Isaiah 57:13; Jeremiah 31:18
Case 30	Alma 5:50	Psalm 47:7	The king of all the earth	0
Case 31	Alma 7:27	Psalms 113:2; 115:8; 121:8	From this time forth and forever	0
Case 32	Alma 26:8	Psalm 145:21	Praise ... his holy name ... forever	0
Case 33	Alma 26:12	Psalm 145:2	Will praise ... name forever	0
Case 34	Alma 26:36; Moroni 8:2	Psalm 115:12	Hath been mindful of us	0
Case 35	Alma 26:37	Psalm 30:12	I will give thanks unto [God] forever	2 Samuel 22:50
Case 36	Alma 37:15; Mormon 5:16	Psalm 35:5	As chaff before the wind	0
Case 37	Alma 60:34	Psalm 119:115	Keep the commandments of my God	0
Case 38	Helaman 6:34	Psalm 111:8	In truth and uprightness	(1 Kings 3:6 similar)

Case	Book of Mormon	Psalms	Textual Connection	Appearances Elsewhere
Case 39	Helaman 12:1	Psalm 34:8	See that the Lord . . . good . . . bless . . . trust in him	0
Case 40	3 Nephi 19:25	Psalms 4:6; 44:3; 89:15; 90:8	Light of . . . countenance	Job 29:24; Proverbs 16:15; D&C 88:56, 58
Case 41	Moroni 7:7	Psalm 106:31	Counted unto him for righteousness	Romans 4:3
Case 42	Moroni 7:22	Psalm 90:2; 103:17; 106:48	From everlasting to everlasting	D&C 20:17; 61:1; 109:77; 132:20
Case 43	Moroni 10:25	Psalms 14:3; 53:3	None that doeth good . . . no not one	Romans 3:12

Table 1 illustrates that some sections of the Book of Mormon have particularly high Psalmic concentrations. For example, ten (approximately 25 percent of the total) come from 2 Nephi 4, a subject which I will explore in a subsequent section of this paper. Sixty-three percent of the potential allusions to Psalms come from either Nephi or Jacob, a fact that makes sense given their cultural closeness to the brass plates and the culture of temple worship in Jerusalem.[20] In contrast, all other Book of Mormon speakers and authors combined (including important figures such as King Benjamin, Abinadi, Alma, Mormon, and Moroni) only account for one-third of the connections. This also is intuitive given that their relative distance from the brass plates. Another interesting finding is that Ammon's exultant praises in Alma 26 comprise approximately 10 percent of the cases in table 1. Perhaps also significant is that, with one exception that is clearly attributable to Moroni, there are no apparent allusions to Psalms in the book of Ether, sections of which are drawn from material that predates the brass plates.[21]

The data presented in table 1 can be reorganized by the order of Psalms in order to more clearly illustrate which Psalms have textual connections to the Book of Mormon. This information is presented in table 2.

Table 2. Allusions to Old Testament Psalms in the Book of Mormon, Organized by Reference to Psalms

Case	Psalms	Book of Mormon	Allusion	Appearances Elsewhere
Case 1	Psalm 2:9	1 Nephi 8:19	A rod of iron	Revelation 2:27; 12:5; 19:15
Case 2	Psalms 4:6; 44:3; 89:15; 90:8	3 Nephi 19:25	Light of . . . countenance	Job 29:24; Proverbs 16:15; D&C 88:56, 58
Case 3	Psalm 5:1	2 Nephi 9:40; Alma 36:1; Alma 38:1	Give ear to my words	D&C 58:1
Case 4	Psalms 5:8; 27:11; 69:18	2 Nephi 4:27; 2 Nephi 4:29; 3 Nephi 3:26	Because of mine enemies	0
Case 5	Psalm 5:8	2 Nephi 4:33	Make . . . straight before	Joshua 6:5
Case 6	Psalm 6:6	2 Nephi 33:3	Water my . . . night	0
Case 7	Psalms 7:1; 25:20; 31:1	Mosiah 7:33; 29:20; Alma 36:27; 38:5; 61:13	Put my trust . . . deliver	1 Chronicles 5:20; Isaiah 57:13; Jeremiah 31:18
Case 8	Psalms 14:3; 53:3	Moroni 10:25	None that doeth good . . . no not one	Romans 3:12
Case 9	Psalms 18:10; 104:3	2 Nephi 4:25	Upon the wings of	2 Samuel 22:11
Case 10	Psalm 21:9	2 Nephi 26:5	Shall swallow them up	Hosea 8:7
Case 11	Psalm 23:3	1 Nephi 16:5; Alma 7:19	In the paths of righteousness	0
Case 12	Psalm 24:4	2 Nephi 25:16; Alma 5:19	Clean hands . . . pure heart	0
Case 13	Psalm 27:13, 33:5	2 Nephi 4:17	Goodness of the Lord	Jeremiah 31:13
Case 14	Psalm 30:12	Alma 26:37	I will give thanks unto [God] forever	2 Samuel 22:50
Case 15	Psalm 34:8	Helaman 12:1	See that the Lord . . . good . . . bless . . . trust in him	0
Case 16	Psalm 34:18	2 Nephi 2:7; 3 Nephi 9:20, 12:19; Mormon 2:14; Ether 4:15; Moroni 6:2	Broken heart . . . contrite spirit	D&C 20:37; 59:8
Case 17	Psalm 35:5	Alma 37:15; Mormon 5:16	As chaff before the wind	0
Case 18	Psalm 47:7	Alma 5:50	The King of all the earth	0

Case	Psalms	Book of Mormon	Allusion	Appearances Elsewhere
Case 19	Psalm 52:9	2 Nephi 4:30; Alma 36:28	I will praise thee forever	0
Case 20	Psalms 55:23; 56:3	2 Nephi 4:34	I will trust in thee	0
Case 21	Psalm 56:13	2 Nephi 4:32; Mosiah 4:26; Alma 7:22	That I may walk	Proverbs 2:20; Ezekiel 11:20; 1 Thessalonians 4:12
Case 22	Psalm 57:2	2 Nephi 4:35; Alma 33:11	I will cry unto	0
Case 23	Psalm 62:2, 6	1 Nephi 13:36; 15:15	My rock and my salvation	D&C 18:17; Abraham 2:16
Case 24	Psalms 62:7; 89:26; 95:1	2 Nephi 9:45	The rock of … salvation	2 Samuel 22:47; Isaiah 17:10; Deuteronomy 32:15
Case 25	Psalms 63:4; 121:1	1 Nephi 21:22; 2 Nephi 4:35; 6:6	I will lift up my	Isaiah 49:22
Case 26	Psalm 69:16	1 Nephi 8:8	According to the multitude of tender mercies	0
Case 27	Psalm 71:20	2 Nephi 26:5; 3 Nephi 9:6, 8; 28:20	The depths of the earth	0
Case 28	Psalm 89:26	2 Nephi 4:30	My God and the rock of my salvation	0
Case 29	Psalms 90:2; 103:17; 106:48	Moroni 7:22	From everlasting to everlasting	D&C 20:17; 61:1; 109:77; 132:20
Case 30	Psalm 95:7	Jacob 6:6	Today if ye will hear his voice harden not your hearts	Hebrews 3:7
Case 31	Psalm 95:8	Jacob 1:7	As in the provocation… In the day of temptation	Hebrews 3:8
Case 32	Psalm 95:11	Alma 12:35; Jacob 1:7	Swear in my wrath	Hebrews 3:11; 4:3
Case 33	Psalm 106:31	Moroni 7:7	Counted unto him for righteousness	Romans 4:3
Case 34	Psalm 111:8	Helaman 6:34	In truth and uprightness	(1 Kings 3:6 similar)
Case 35	Psalms 113:2; 115:18; 121:8	Alma 7:27	From this time forth and forever	0
Case 36	Psalm 115:12	Alma 26:36; Moroni 8:2	Hath been mindful of us	0
Case 37	Psalm 116:3	Jacob 3:11; Alma 14:6; 26:13; 36:13	The pains of hell	0

Case	Psalms	Book of Mormon	Allusion	Appearances Elsewhere
Case 38	Psalm 119:115	Alma 60:34	Keep the commandments of my God	0
Case 39	Psalm 145:2	Alma 26:12	Will praise...name forever	0
Case 40	Psalm 145:9	Jacob 4:10; Alma 37:12	Over all his works	0
Case 41	Psalm 145:9	1 Nephi 1:20	Tender mercies...are over all	0
Case 42	Psalm 145:20	2 Nephi 30:10	The wicked will he destroy	0
Case 43	Psalm 145:21	Alma 26:8	Praise...his holy name...forever	0

When the multiple references to various Psalms are combined, we see that allusions are made to potentially forty-one different psalms.[22] Thirteen of these psalms appear to have multiple connections to the Book of Mormon.[23] Psalm 145 contains text that is utilized by Nephi, Jacob, Alma, and Ammon, including echoes of phrases as "his tender mercies are over all his works" (Psalm 145:9; compare 1 Nephi 1:20) and "my mouth shall speak the praise of the Lord: and let all flesh bless his holy name forever" (Psalm 145:21; compare Alma 26:8).

One interesting facet of allusions to Psalms is the fact that many psalms are *not* alluded to in the Book of Mormon. There may be a variety of reasons for this fact, including the idea that some psalms may have been considered to be less important by Nephite prophets. A similar phenomenon occurs in the New Testament. Shires points out that "as many as 29 of the psalms may have no direct relationship with the N[ew] T[estament] at any point, and these are well scattered throughout the Psalter. Some of the psalms seem to have been judged unsuitable by early Christian authors and so rejected or ignored."[24] It may be significant that the Book of Mormon likewise appears to not utilize these same twenty psalms that do not appear in the New Testament.[25]

While an analysis of each of the cases presented in table 1 is beyond the scope of the present article, I will provide two examples of how connections between Psalms and the Book of Mormon can deepen our understanding and appreciation of both texts. I begin with an analysis of Jacob's use of Psalm 95.

Jacob's Use of Psalm 95

As one of the earliest writers in the Book of Mormon, Jacob was surely familiar with the material on the brass plates, part of which may have been Psalm 95.[26] Even if Psalm 95 was not recorded on the brass plates, it could have been part of contextual worship services in Jerusalem, something Nephi could have discussed with Jacob. As we will see, sections of this psalm play a key role in Jacob's book. In Jacob 1:7, he records, "Wherefore we labored diligently among our people, that we might persuade them to come unto Christ, and partake of the goodness of God, *that they might enter into his rest*, lest by any means *he should swear in his wrath they should not enter in, as in the provocation in the days of temptation while the children of Israel were in the wilderness.*" The italicized portions of this verse bear a clear connection to Psalm 95:8 and 11, which state, "As in the provocation, and as in the day of temptation in the wilderness . . . Unto whom I sware in my wrath that they should not enter into my rest."

This shared text cannot be coincidental. This is doubly the case when we see another allusion to Psalm 95 at the end of Jacob's record. In Jacob 6:6, he exhorts, "Yea, today, *if ye will hear his voice, harden not your hearts*; for why will ye die?" These words directly echo Psalm 95:7–8: "To day if ye will hear his voice, harden not your heart."[27] Thus Jacob alludes to Psalm 95 at the beginning of his book (Jacob 1:7) and as he nears the end of it (Jacob 6:6).[28] Moreover, these introductory and concluding allusions use adjoining phrases from Psalm 95.[29] Psalms 95:7–8 reads, "To day if ye will hear his voice harden not your heart, as in the provocation, and as in the day of temptation in the wilderness." In Jacob 1:7, Jacob quotes the latter portion of these verses "as in the provocation in the days of temptation while the children of Israel were in the wilderness." In Jacob 6:6, he uses the first phrase, "Today if ye will hear his voice harden not your hearts," thus alluding to both halves, but reversing their order.[30]

Both Jacob 1:7 and Jacob 6:6 are portions of texts in which Jacob directly addresses readers. They are not part of a continuous discourse; rather, they are broken up by Jacob's sermon at the temple (Jacob 2:1–3:11) and his recording of the allegory of the olive tree (Jacob 5). Because Jacob is addressing the reader at each of the bookend allusions of Psalms 95:7–8, I believe he uses these two statements to cohesively communicate to readers of his book two of his core themes, those of not hardening our hearts and of coming unto Christ.

As I will demonstrate, Jacob uses textual connections to Psalm 95 to develop these themes.

Psalm 95 is an important psalm of worship. It is a hymn of praise focused on one of the three major Mosaic festivals, preparing worshippers to enter into God's presence.[31] As such, it certainly could predate the Babylonian exile and could have been in common use prior to Lehi's day. In context, Psalm 95:7–8 refers to an event in which the Israelites, while camped at Meribah, complained against Moses, leading Moses to miraculously provide water from a rock (see Exodus 17:1–7 and Numbers 20:1–13). Commenting on the connection between Psalm 95 and Exodus 17, Catherine Thomas states, "The Provocation refers not only to the specific incident at Meribah but to a persistent behavior of the children of Israel that greatly reduced their spiritual knowledge. . . . After a succession of provocations, the Israelites in time rejected and lost the knowledge of . . . the great plan of grace inherent in the doctrine of the Father and the Son."[32]

With this understanding of Psalm 95, a potential relationship between it and the book of Jacob becomes clearer and helps us see why Jacob would bracket his book with these verses. Psalm 95 refers to a people who were greatly blessed (not only in escaping Egypt but also in the riches of manna) but who out of pride sought for more. This mirrors the situation Jacob faced as he taught people who had received temporal blessings only to be "lifted up" in pride (Jacob 2:13). Psalm 95 refers to a people who counseled the Lord's prophet (see Psalm 95:8; compare Exodus 17:3), and Jacob states, "Seek not to counsel the Lord, but to take counsel from his hand" (Jacob 4:10). The continual provocations to which Psalm 95 alludes resulted in the Israelites losing important gospel principles. Jacob likewise spoke of a people who "despised the words of plainness . . . and sought for things they could not understand" (Jacob 4:14).

These connections carry into Jacob's quoting of the allegory of the olive tree. In Psalm 95:10 the Lord states, "Forty long years was *I grieved* with this generation." This could be related to the Lord of the vineyard saying on several occasions, "*It grieveth me* that I should lose this tree" (Jacob 5:7, 11, 13, 32, 46, 47, 51, 66).

Just before his second bookend reference to Psalm 95, Jacob makes a statement that could have been said by Moses to the Israelites: "God . . . remembereth the house of Israel, both roots and branches; and he stretches forth his hands unto them all the day long; and they are a stiffnecked and a gainsaying people; but as many as will *not harden their hearts* shall be saved in the kingdom of God. Wherefore . . . repent, and come with full purpose of heart, and cleave unto God as he cleaveth unto you. And while his arm of mercy is extended towards you in the light of the day, *harden not your hearts*" (Jacob 6:4–5). And then, after these two warnings against hardened hearts, Jacob turns to Psalm 95: "Yea, today, if ye will hear his voice, *harden not your hearts*; for why will ye die?" (Jacob 6:6; compare Psalm 95:7–8).

What should we do in place of hardening our hearts? Just before his first bookend reference to Psalm 95, Jacob records, "We labored diligently among our people, that we might persuade them to *come unto Christ*, and partake of the goodness of God" (Jacob 1:7). Likewise, prior to the second bracketed statement, he states, "*Come* with full purpose of heart, and *cleave unto God*" (Jacob 6:5). These two statements are similar to Psalm 95:6, which states, "*Come . . . : let us kneel before the Lord.*" The context of Psalm 95 as a hymn of praise connected with entering the presence of God, allows us to envision a powerful theme of coming unto Christ woven through Jacob's use of Psalm 95. Figure 1 illustrates how Jacob incorporates Psalm 95 in both the beginning and end of his book to develop a cohesive leitmotif of hardening not our hearts and coming unto Christ.

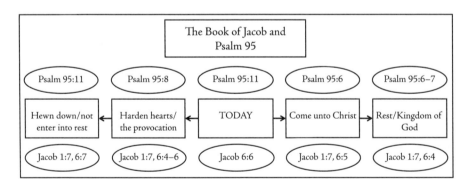

Fig. 1. Jacob and Psalm 95.

By invoking Psalm 95, Jacob reminds readers of a story of hardened hearts during the Exodus; he invites us to learn from them, to harden not our hearts, and to come unto Christ. Jacob wants us to choose *today* which path we will take. It may be that Jacob saw in the people of his day (and ours) many similarities to the rebellious Israelites in the wilderness. By echoing Psalm 95, Jacob ultimately encourages us to "enter into [God's] rest" and "obtain eternal life" (Jacob 1:7, 6:11).

The Old Testament Psalms and the "Psalm of Nephi"

The previous section focused on Jacob's use of one psalm throughout his entire book. I now discuss Nephi's use of a variety of psalms in one small part of his record, which is popularly called "the Psalm of Nephi."[33] S. Kent Brown has called this passage (2 Nephi 4:17–35) "a most poignant depiction of Nephi's own struggles with sin and with feelings about rebellious members of his family."[34]

It has been noted previously that the Psalm of Nephi shares several features with ancient Hebrew psalms. For example, Matthew Nickerson states that "Nephi's psalm plainly follows the format and substance of the individual lament as described by Gunkel and elaborated upon by numerous subsequent scholars."[35] Brown points out that Nephi's psalm "exhibits poetic characteristics found in the Old Testament."[36] Steven Sondrup finds that "in the 'Psalm of Nephi,' just as in Hebrew poetry ... logical, formal or conceptual units are set parallel one to another.[37]

In addition to these overarching literary patterns, the Psalm of Nephi shares a surprisingly large amount of text with the Old Testament Psalms. It appears that Nephi (perhaps intentionally, or perhaps because of his familiarity with Psalmic material), drew on phrases of lament, praise, and worship from the Psalter as he composed his own words. Of the 660 words comprising the Psalm of Nephi, 127 (approximately 20 percent) are key words or phrases that are also found in the biblical Psalter. While some of these key words or phrases are used frequently throughout scripture, and thus did not qualify for inclusion in table 1,[38] others are significant, and appear only in these two pericopes. The concentration of references to Psalms may indicate intentionality on Nephi's part as he wrote these words. The Psalm of Nephi appears below, with potential allusions to Psalms in italics.

> Nevertheless, notwithstanding the great *goodness of the Lord* [Psalms 27:13; 33:5], in showing me his great and marvelous works, my heart exclaimeth: O wretched man that I am! Yea, my heart sorroweth because of my flesh; my soul grieveth *because of mine iniquities* [Psalm 31:10].

I am encompassed about, because of the temptations and the sins which do so easily beset me.

And when I desire to rejoice, my heart groaneth *because of my sins* [Psalm 38:3]; nevertheless, I know in whom *I have trusted* [Psalms 13:5; 26:1; 33:21].

My God hath been my support; he hath led me through mine afflictions in *the wilderness; and he* [Psalm 106:9] hath preserved me upon the waters of the great deep.

He hath filled me with his love, even unto the consuming of my flesh.

He hath confounded mine enemies, unto the causing of them to quake before me.

Behold, *he hath heard my* [Psalm 116:1] cry by day, and he hath given me knowledge by visions in the night-time.

And by day have I waxed bold in mighty prayer before him; yea, my voice have I sent up on high; and angels came down and ministered unto me.

And *upon the wings of* [Psalms 18:10; 104:3] his Spirit hath my body been carried away upon exceedingly high mountains. And mine eyes have beheld great things, yea, even too great for man; therefore I was bidden that I should not write them.

O then, if I have seen so great things, if the Lord in his condescension unto the children of men hath visited men in so much mercy, why should my heart weep and my soul linger in the valley of sorrow, and my flesh waste away, and my strength slacken, because of mine afflictions?

And why should I yield to sin, because of my flesh? Yea, why should I give way to temptations, that the evil one have place in my heart to destroy my peace and *afflict my soul* [Psalm 143:12]? Why am I angry *because of mine enemy* [Psalms 5:8; 8:2; 27:11; 69:18]?

Awake, my soul! No longer droop in sin. Rejoice, O my heart, and give place no more for the enemy of my soul.

Do not anger again *because of mine enemies* [Psalms 5:8; 8:2; 27:11; 69:18]. Do not slacken my strength because of mine afflictions.

Rejoice, O my heart, and *cry unto the Lord* [Psalm 107:19, 28], and say: O Lord, *I will praise thee forever* [Psalm 52:9]; yea, my soul will rejoice in thee [Psalms 9:2; 85:6], *my God, and the rock of my salvation* [Psalm 89:26].

O Lord, wilt thou *redeem my soul* [Psalm 49:15]? Wilt thou *deliver me out of the* [Psalm 69:14] *hands of mine enemies* [Psalm 31:15]? Wilt thou make me that I may shake at the appearance of sin?

May the gates of hell be shut *continually before me* [Psalms 38:17; 44:15; 50:8], because that my *heart is broken* and my *spirit is contrite* [Psalms 34:18; 51:17]! O Lord, wilt thou not shut the *gates of thy righteousness* [Psalm 118:19] before me, that *I may walk* [Psalm 56:13] *in the path of* [Psalms 23:3; 119:35] the low valley, that I may be strict in the plain road!

O Lord, wilt thou encircle me around in the robe of thy righteousness! O Lord, wilt thou make a way for mine escape before mine enemies! Wilt thou *make* my path *straight before* [Psalm 5:8] me! Wilt thou not place a stumbling block in my way—but that thou wouldst clear my way before me, and hedge not up my way, but the ways of mine enemy.

O Lord, *I have trusted in* [Psalms 13:5; 33:21] thee, and *I will trust in thee* [Psalms 55:23; 56:3] forever. I will not *put my trust in the* [Psalms 4:5; 73:28] arm of flesh; for I know that cursed is he that *putteth his trust in the* [Psalms 4:5; 73:28] arm of flesh. Yea, cursed is he that putteth his trust in man or maketh flesh his arm.

Yea, I know that God will give liberally to him that asketh. Yea, my God will give me, if I ask not amiss; therefore *I will lift up my* [Psalms 63:4; 121:1] voice unto thee; yea, *I will cry unto* [Psalm 57:2] thee, my God, *the rock of my* [Psalms 62:7; 89:26; 94:22; 95:1] righteousness. Behold, my voice shall forever ascend up unto thee, *my rock* [Psalms 18:2, 46; 28:1; 31:3; 42:9; 62:2, 6; 71:3; 78:35; 92:15] and mine everlasting God. Amen.

When the multiple connections to Psalms are added together, Nephi could have alluded to potentially forty-seven different Psalms in just eighteen verses.[39] It stretches one's imagination to believe that Joseph Smith could have been responsible for making all of these connections, particularly with the understanding that the Psalm of Nephi may have been translated in less than two hours.[40] While some sections of Nephi's soliloquy have relatively few allusions to Psalms, in other sections the number of connections is impressive. For example, 40 percent of the words in 2 Nephi 4:29–32 also appear in Old Testament Psalms (54 out of 135 words). I believe these allusions stem from Nephi's mediations on the Psalms and that the high concentration of psalmic references in this pericope indicates that Nephi had access to them (either from the plates or his own cultural experiences in Jerusalem).[41] Nephi's apparent familiarity and love of the psalms can provide motivation for Latter-day Saints to follow Nephi's example and become deeply familiar with the language of praise and worship as found in the Old Testament Psalms.

Conclusion

The Old Testament Psalms are beautiful, moving, and inspirational. They provide poetic praises in the Old Testament. They are also foundational in other books of scripture, such as the New Testament. In this paper I have demonstrated that the Psalms also influenced the ancient authors of the Book of Mormon. Nephi and Jacob in particular showed a propensity to provide textual allusions to the Psalms in their writings. I have proposed forty-three instances in which there may be textual allusions to the Psalms within the Book of Mormon. I have also explored some of the ramifications of these connections in the case of Jacob's use of Psalm 95 and Nephi's use of a variety of psalms when composing his own.

The Psalms provide powerful language of worship. With Nephi we can say, "O Lord, *I will praise thee forever,* yea, my soul will *rejoice in thee, my God, and the rock of my salvation* (2 Nephi 4:30; compare with Psalms 52:9; 9:2; 89:26). Hearing these echoes from the Psalter in the Book of Mormon should inspire in each of us the desire to drink more deeply from the moving, majestic Psalms of the Old Testament.

Notes

1. Jeffrey R. Holland, *For Times of Trouble* (Salt Lake City: Deseret Book, 2012), 7.

2. Franz Delitzsch, *Biblical Commentary on the Psalms,* trans. Francis Bolton (Grand Rapids, MI: William B. Eerdman's, 1959), 1:38.

3. Henry M. Shires, *Finding the Old Testament in the New* (Philadelphia: Westminster, 1974), 126.

4. Robert Alter, *The Book of Psalms: A Translation with Commentary* (New York: Norton, 2007), xiii.

5. The Book of Mormon contains several instances of textual allusions to material from the brass plates. Several of these allusions are explicit (for example, quotations from Isaiah). In addition, many textual connections are more subtle. For example, Julie M. Smith pointed out more subtle textual connections between Isaiah 55 and Alma 32; see "So Shall My Word Be: Reading Alma 32 through Isaiah 55," in *An Experiment on the Word: Reading Alma 32*, ed. Adam S. Miller (Salem, OR: Salt Press, 2011), 71–86. Reynolds examined textual connections between the Book of Mormon and the Book of Moses; see "The Brass Plates Version of Genesis," in *By Study and Also by Faith*, ed. John M. Lundquist and Stephen D. Ricks (Salt Lake City: Deseret Book, 1990), 2:138. For a broader discussion of intertextuality in the Book of Mormon, see John Hilton III, "Textual Similarities in the Words of Abinadi and Alma's Counsel to Corianton," *BYU Studies Quarterly* 52, no. 2 (2012): 39–60.

6. One issue that comes up regarding whether Psalms could have been a part of the brass plates is that some of what we have as Psalms may have been written after the time that Lehi left Jerusalem. Scholars disagree on which psalms are preexilic and which are postexilic. In the *Jewish Study Bible*, we find this statement: "Dating the psalms is notoriously difficult, partly because they contain few explicit references to specific historical events or personages . . . While many modern scholars believe that at least some, perhaps even many of the psalms are from the preexilic period (before 586 BCE), none can be dated on linguistic grounds to the tenth century BCE, the period of David. There is little consensus on the dating of preexilic psalms, or even on which psalms are preexilic." Michael Fishbane, Adele Berlin, and Marc Zvi Brettler, eds., *Jewish Study Bible* (New York: Oxford University Press, 2004), 1282. Nevertheless, because at least some of the psalms are preexilic, their presence on the brass plates is possible.

7. David J. Larsen, "Royal Themes in the Psalms and in the Dead Sea Scrolls" (PhD diss. currently in progress).

8. See Royal Skousen, "How Joseph Smith Translated the Book of Mormon: Evidence from the Original Manuscript," *Journal of Book of Mormon Studies* 7, no. 1 (1998): 22–31. Because we do not have original-language materials for the Book of Mormon, I compared the English translation of the Book of Mormon with the English translation of the Psalms as found in the King James Version. Comparisons with other versions of the Bible could yield different results.

9. For example, the psalmist Nephi could have both been referring to an unknown portion of the words of Zenos. Alternatively, a Book of Mormon author could have had a psalm in mind; however, the source of this psalm is a previous, unknown prophet.

10. Richard L. Schultz, *The Search for Quotation* (Sheffield, UK: Sheffield Academic, 1999), 18.

11. Sandmel referred to the propensity of some to find parallels that do not actually exist as "parallelomania," and said, "We might for our purposes define parallelomania as that extravagance among scholars which first overdoes the supposed similarity in passages and then proceeds to describe source and derivation as if implying literary connection flowing in an inevitable or predetermined direction." Samuel Sandmel, "Parallelomania,"

Journal of Biblical Literature 81 (March 1962): 1. Similarly, Lincoln Blumell points out, "With the aid of electronic databases and search engines where a word, root of a word, or even a short phrase, can be readily searched across a huge corpus, if one is willing to look hard enough, they can usually find numerous scriptural echoes and reminiscences. However, the obvious problem with this is that just because one can find a rare word or a distinct phrase . . . , it does not automatically guarantee the author . . . was necessarily echoing or reminiscing [another] passage"; Lincoln H. Blumell, *Lettered Christians: Christians, Letters, and Late Antique Oxyrhynchus* (Leiden: Brill, 2012), 220.

12. Robert Baker Girdlestone, *The Foundations of the Bible: Studies in Old Testament Criticism* (London: Eyre and Spottiswoode, 1890), 50.

13. One weakness of searching for textual allusions is missing potential conceptual allusions (for example Psalm 42:5, 11; compare 2 Nephi 4:26, 28, 30). Due to the length of the two texts, however, an exhaustive search for conceptual allusions was not practical for this study.

14. Available at http://wordcruncher.byu.edu.

15. In addition to acknowledging their efforts made by these research assistants, I also thank Jaclyn Nielson, who did significant work in preparing the final versions of tables 1 and 2.

16. Richard B. Hays, *Echoes of Scripture in the Letters of Paul* (New Haven, CT: Yale University Press, 1993), 29–31. These criteria are as follows: "(1) *Availability*. Was the proposed source of the echo available to the author and/or original readers? . . . (2) *Volume*. The volume of an echo is determined primarily by the degree of explicit repetition of words or syntactical patterns, but other factors may also be relevant [such as] how distinctive or prominent is the precursor text within Scripture. . . . (3) *Recurrence*. How often does [the author] elsewhere cite or allude to the same scriptural passage? . . . (4) *Thematic Coherence*. How well does the alleged echo fit into the line of argument that [the author] is developing? . . . (5) *Historical Plausibility*. Could [the author] have intended the alleged meaning effect? . . . (6) *History of Interpretation*. Have other readers, both critical and pre-critical, heard the same echoes? . . . (7) *Satisfaction*. With or without clear confirmation from the other criteria listed here, does the proposed reading make sense?" Noel B. Reynolds set forth similar criteria in "The Brass Plates Version of Genesis," in *By Study and Also by Faith: Essays in Honor of Hugh W. Nibley* (Provo, UT: FARMS; Salt Lake City: Deseret Book, 1990), 2:138. We referred to both sets of criteria in determining which phrases should be included in table 1.

17. While a discussion of each of these cases is beyond the scope of this article, I believe that based on Hays's criteria, a good argument for intertextual allusions could be made in each of these cases. In addition, I acknowledge that there are other potentially significant allusions not included here either because they were either shorter (for example, two or three words), inexact phrase matches (some words were transposed), or had conceptual (but not strong textual) connections. For example, Matthew L. Bowen finds impressive connections between Mosiah 5:7 and Psalm 2:7; see "Becoming Sons and Daughters at God's Right Hand," *Journal of the Book of Mormon and Other Restoration Scripture* 21, no. 2 (2012): 2–13. David Rolph Seely and John W. Welch find important conceptual conceptions between Psalm 52, Psalm 80, and Jacob 5; see "Zenos and the

Texts of the Old Testament," in *The Allegory of the Olive Tree: The Olive, the Bible, and Jacob 5*, ed. Stephen D. Ricks and John W. Welch (Salt Lake City: Deseret Book; Provo, UT: FARMS, 1994). In addition, there simply may have been allusions that were missed in the analysis process. I also note that allusions to Psalms that are present in Isaiah portions of the Book of Mormon were excluded from this analysis.

18. For example, consider case 7 in table 1: *because of my enemies*. Our search included variants of each of those words (while keeping the phrase intact). Thus, we would have counted the phrase *because of their enemy* as a match. The phrase *because of my enemies* seems like a common phrase, yet it appears only in Psalms and the Book of Mormon (even when including variant versions of each word). Each case has at least one *exact* phrase match between a Psalm and a Book of Mormon passage. When multiple verses are present in the "Book of Mormon," "Psalms," or "Appearances Elsewhere" columns, one or more of them may be a variant phrase match. Our purpose in including variants was to demonstrate that the phrases presented in table 1 are in fact relatively unique.

19. As noted previously, it is also possible that these phrases could be connected with another Old Testament text, an unknown prophetic phrase, or they could simply be part of the common language of the day.

20. In calculating this figure, I only included the first reference made to a specific phrase, based on the idea that later allusions to the phrase could have been the result of Nephi or Jacob's words. I also did not double count multiple references that Nephi or Jacob made to the same phrase.

21. Compare Psalm 34:18 with Ether 4:15. While the phrases "broken heart" and "contrite spirit" appear frequently in our vernacular, they appear together only once in the Bible. Furthermore, within the Bible, the four words *broken, heart, contrite*, and *spirit* only appear together in Psalms 34:18 and 51:17. Because Moroni, as the editor of the book of Ether, had access to the plates of brass, he could have inserted allusions to Psalms. It is also possible that Moroni drew these phrases from previous Nephite writings. The fact that textual allusions to Psalms do not appear in sections of Ether that most likely would have been drawn from the plates of Ether make for a neat apologetic argument, given that Ether would most likely not have had access to the book of Psalms.

22. These include Psalms 6, 7, 14, 18, 21, 23, 24, 25, 27, 30, 31, 33, 34, 35, 44, 47, 52, 53, 55, 56, 57, 62, 63, 69, 71, 89, 90, 95, 103, 104, 106, 111, 113, 115, 116, 119, 121, and 145.

23. Eight psalms (27, 34, 56, 69, 90, 106, 115, and 121) have two allusions, three psalms (5, 62, and 89) contain three, Psalm 95 has four allusions, and Psalm 145 has five. It should also be noted that there are five books that comprise the Psalms; apparent allusions appear from all five of these books.

24. Henry M. Shire, *Finding the Old Testament in the New* (Louisville, KY: Westminster Press, 1974), 129; spelling standardized. The Psalms he lists as having no direct relationship with the New Testament include 25, 43, 54, 58, 59, 60, 70, 85, 87, 100, 101, 108, 114, 120, 123, 127, 131, 133, and 142.

25. There are two minor exceptions. First, the phrase *put my trust in* is used in connection with the word *deliver* in Psalm 25:20 and five Book of Mormon passages. However, there are two other psalms from which this connection could have been drawn. Second,

the phrase *rejoice in thee* appears in Psalm 85:6 and 2 Nephi 4:30; however, it also appears in four other psalms.

26. After acknowledging a scholarly debate regarding the dating of Psalm 95 and considering a variety of factors, Howard states, "I conclude that the psalm is most likely preexilic and possibly goes back to the early monarchial period or earlier." David M. Howard Jr., "The Structure of Psalms 93–100," in *Biblical and Judaic Studies* (San Diego: Eisenbraus, 1997), 5:190. Jacob may also have alluded to Psalm 95 in 2 Nephi 9:45 (compare Psalm 95:1).

27. Grant Hardy provides footnotes to both of these connections to Psalm 95 in *The Book of Mormon: A Reader's Edition* (Urbana: University of Illinois Press, 2003), 140, 156. It should be noted that Hebrews chapters 3 and 4 and Alma 12:35 also contain extensive references to Psalm 95. An extended discussion of all of these texts is beyond the scope of this article. Peter E. Enns provides a discussion of the relationship between Psalm 95 and Hebrews 3:1–4:13; see "Creation and Re-Creation: Psalm 95 and its Interpretation in Hebrews 3:1–4:13," in *Westminster Theological Journal* (Philadelphia: Westminster Theological Seminary, 1993), 55:255–80.

28. While Jacob's record extends into chapter 7, it is clear that chapter 6 represents a conclusion of sorts (see Jacob 6:12–13).

29. This may be a literary form known as *inclusio*, which appears in the writings of Jeremiah and elsewhere in ancient scripture. See various examples in Jack R. Lundborn, *Jeremiah: A Study in Ancient Hebrew Rhetoric* (Winona Lake, IN: Eisenbrauns, 1997).

30. It is interesting to consider why Jacob quoted the second half of Psalms 95:7–8 before the first half. One possibility is that it is a manifestation of Seidel's law, which refers to instances when later authors quote from previous ones, and in doing so reverse the order of part of the quotation. Welch stated that "repetition in the opposite order of the original is thought by scholars to be a strong sign ... [of] a conscious form of quotation." John W. Welch, "Echoes from Sermon on the Mount," in *The Sermon on the Mount in Latter-day Scripture: The Thirty-Ninth Annual Brigham Young University Sidney B. Sperry Symposium*, ed. Gaye Strathearn, Thomas A. Wayment, and Daniel L. Belnap (Provo, UT: Religious Studies Center; Salt Lake City: Deseret Book, 2010), 315. See also Michael A. Lyons, "Marking Innerbiblical Allusion in the Book of Ezekiel," *Biblica* 88, no. 2 (2007), http://www.bsw.org/Biblica/Vol-88-2007/Marking-Innerbiblical-Allusion-In-The-Book-Of-Ezekiel/73/; and Pancratius C. Beentjes, "Discovering a New Path of Intertextuality: Inverted Quotations and their Dynamics," in *Literary Structure and Rhetorical Strategies in the Hebrew Bible*, ed. L. J. de Regt, J. de Waard, and J. P. Fokkelman (Assen, Netherlands: Van Gorcum, 1996). Thus Jacob's reversal may have been intended as a signal to readers that he using a quotation. While Jacob's inverted quotation of Psalm 95:7–8 does not match with the classical instance of Seidel's Law (given that the inverted quotations are separated by a significant amount of text), it is possible that this reverse order was Jacob's way of illustrating his intentionality in referencing these verses. Alternatively, Lyons demonstrates that allusions are sometimes marked "by the splitting and redistribution of elements in the borrowed locution" ("Marking Innerbiblical Allusion," 245). In either case Jacob could have been following conventions similar to Old Testament authors.

31. Beverly Roberts Gaventa and David Petersen, eds., *The New Interpreter's Bible: One-Volume Commentary* (Nashville: Abingdon, 2010), 336.

32. Catherine M. Thomas, "The Provocation in the Wilderness and the Rejection of Grace" in *Sperry Symposium Classics: The Old Testament*, ed. Paul Y. Hoskisson (Provo, UT: Religious Studies Center, Brigham Young University; Salt Lake City: Deseret Book, 2005), 165.

33. This phrase appears to have been coined by Sidney B. Sperry, *Our Book of Mormon* (Salt Lake City: Bookcraft, 1947), 110.

34. S. Kent Brown, "Nephi's Psalm," in *The Book of Mormon Reference Companion*, ed. Dennis Largey (Salt Lake City: Deseret Book, 2003), 602.

35. Matthew Nickerson, "Nephi's Psalm: 2 Nephi 4:16–35 in Light of Form-Critical Analysis," *Journal of Book of Mormon Studies* 6, no. 2 (1997): 26–42. Nickerson also notes textual similarities between 2 Nephi 4 and Psalms 6, 18, 27, and 51. See also the chapter by Kenneth L. Alford and D. Bryce Baker in this book.

36. S. Kent Brown, "Nephi's Psalm," 602.

37. Steven P. Sondrup, "The Psalm of Nephi: A Lyric Reading," in *BYU Studies* 21, no. 3 (1981): 359. While Sondrup's focus is not on textual connections to the Psalms, he does point out relationships between 2 Nephi 4 and both Psalm 51 and Psalm 84.

38. More common phrases (such as "cry unto the Lord") were not included in table 1, as their relative frequency throughout scripture made it difficult to determine whether a relationship exists between Psalms and the Book of Mormon. Nevertheless, given the high number of these phrases from Psalms concentrated in 2 Nephi 4, I included them in analyzing 2 Nephi 4. While some phrases may seem insignificant by themselves (for example "because of mine iniquities"), their similar contextual use in Psalms and the Book of Mormon may demonstrate important connections. Individually, some of these phrases may be insignificant, but collectively they are impressive.

39. Nephi makes multiple potential textual allusions to Psalms 27, 31, 33, 38, 56, 69, and 89.

40. See John W. Welch, "How Long Did It Take Joseph Smith to Translate the Book of Mormon?," *Ensign*, January 1988, 46.

41. It is also possible that these phrases came from personal revelation to Nephi or that they were part of a commonly held vocabulary with which he was familiar.

18

Parallels between Psalms 25–31 and the Psalm of Nephi

Kenneth L. Alford and D. Bryce Baker

The beautiful and carefully crafted Hebrew poetry found in the book of Psalms has comforted, inspired, admonished, and encouraged readers for millennia. According to R. Scott Burton, "Our English name 'Psalms' comes from the Septuagint . . . title of the book, *psalmoi*, plural of *psalmos*, meaning 'the twitching or twanging with fingers,' associated mostly with the strings of a musical instrument."[1] While there is some debate regarding the authorship of individual psalms, there is no dispute regarding their power and influence. Second only to the book of Isaiah, Psalms is the most frequently quoted book in the New Testament and was often quoted by the Savior.[2]

The Book of Mormon contains a variety of literary styles, and it should come as no surprise that the Psalms may have inspired the ancient prophet Nephi as he wrote upon the small plates. Nephi's soul-searching introspection found in 2 Nephi 4:16–35 is, "for many Latter-day Saints, one of the most cherished and moving passages in the Book of Mormon."[3] George Reynolds and Janne M. Sjodahl, in their 1955 *Commentary on the Book of Mormon*, titled that scriptural passage "A Song of Nephi" and called it "a remarkable piece of

---

Kenneth L. Alford is an associate professor of Church history and doctrine at Brigham Young University.
D. Bryce Baker is employed as a senior advisor in the US Office of Personnel Management.

poetry composed by Nephi."[4] Hugh Nibley called it "a thanksgiving hymn by Nephi, astonishingly like the Thanksgiving Hymn of the Dead Sea Scrolls."[5] The most popular name for those verses, the "Psalm of Nephi," was coined by Sidney B. Sperry in his 1947 book *Our Book of Mormon*, in which he argues that it is the only psalm in the Book of Mormon.[6] Latter-day Saint theologian Robert Millet has written, "The honest in heart could hardly read Nephi's psalm, taste its spirit, and then be critical of the Book of Mormon. Inspired poetry and music are especially attractive to the Spirit."[7]

We cannot determine with certainty the specific influences that affected Nephi as he drafted his psalm, but it is not unreasonable to entertain the possibility that Nephi may have turned to the brass plates for consolation and inspiration. The purpose of this essay is to suggest that Psalms 25–31 may have had a particular influence upon Nephi as he wrote his psalm.[8]

All seven of Psalms 25–31 are attributed to King David, although some questions remain regarding their provenance.[9] As the biblical scholar Konrad Schaefer notes, "Words and catch phrases do connect many psalms," and it appears that psalms "which share a common theme or genre were grouped" together anciently.[10] Scholars have proposed several ways to classify the psalms; Psalms 25–31 appear in what is often identified as the first of five "books" of the Psalter (Psalms 1–41).[11] In Psalm 25 the Psalmist "weaves together various attitudes which include trust in and longing for God's response (vv. 1–2, 5b, 15, 16, 20–21), guilt over past sin (vv. 7, 11, 18), the enemy threat (vv. 2, 15, 19)"—all topics addressed by Nephi in his psalm.[12] Psalms 26 and 27 discuss the Psalmist's love for the temple, which Nephi most certainly shared (see 2 Nephi 5:16, for example). Psalm 28 is a petition to the Lord to hear his prayers and an acknowledgement that God has answered those prayers. Psalm 29 declares the power of God, which is a frequent theme in the psalm of Nephi. Psalm 30 is a plea for God's mercy, and Psalm 31 is a declaration of rejoicing in the Lord. In Psalm 31 the Psalmist moves quickly "from complaint to rejoicing," as Nephi does in 2 Nephi 4:28.[13]

Why might Nephi have turned to those specific psalms for inspiration? In short, because he could have found in those few psalms most of the themes and emotions he was trying to express. Suggesting that the psalm of Nephi was written during an extremely challenging period in Nephi's life is an understatement. Even a cursory look at the opening chapters of 2 Nephi show that stresses and external pressures were building on Nephi from all sides.

In addition to the responsibilities Nephi had as a father and husband, Lehi, his beloved prophet-father, had recently died; Lehi's death is recorded only a few verses before Nephi's psalm (2 Nephi 4:12). Upon Lehi's death, Nephi became both the spiritual and political leader of his growing family kingdom. "Not many days" after the death of Lehi, Laman and Lemuel—the continually disgruntled and murmuring older brothers who were jealous of their younger brother's spiritual gifts and many talents—became angry with Nephi "because of the admonitions of the Lord" given for their benefit (2 Nephi 4:13). They became so incensed, in fact, that in the verses immediately following his psalm Nephi explains not just once, but twice, that Laman and Lemuel "did seek to take away" his life (2 Nephi 5:2 and 5:4). As a result, Nephi determined to "depart from them and flee into the wilderness" taking "all those who would go with" him (2 Nephi 5:5). After traveling "in the wilderness for the space of many days" (2 Nephi 5:7), Nephi and his followers began again in a new location.

The depth of Nephi's despair may be illustrated by the fact that Nephi seems to consciously omit the blessing he received from his dying father. Blessings for other family members are recorded in the opening chapters of 2 Nephi, but, as Grant Hardy has suggested, "It is possible that Nephi omitted his blessing because he did not want to appear as if he had let his father down."[14] Hardy suggests that Nephi deflects his readers' attention from his omission by including his psalm, which he declares is "a literary exercise in which he tries to work through some significant spiritual and psychological anxieties."[15]

We would expect a man of God like Nephi to turn to the scriptures on the brass plates for guidance. In fact, we find a number of scriptures that document his reliance on the brass plates—for example, see 1 Nephi 15:20; 1 Nephi 19:22–24; 1 Nephi 22:1, 30; 2 Nephi 11:8; and 2 Nephi 25:1–8. So we would expect Nephi to turn to the brass plates for inspiration and consolation during a period of great personal challenge following his father's death. And where in the scriptures might he have gone for help in dealing with discouragement and adversity? What better place is there to turn for consolation and encouragement in times of tribulation than the book of Psalms? Most telling of the role that the brass plates may have played in the writing of his psalm is that Nephi explicitly mentions them in the verse immediately preceding his psalm (2 Nephi 4:15). Nephi explains that on the small plates, where he would record his psalm, "I write the things of my soul, and many of the scriptures which are engraven upon the plates of brass" (2 Nephi 4:15). He further explains, "My soul delighteth in the scriptures, and my heart pondereth them, and writeth them for the learning and the profit of my children" (2 Nephi 4:15). The influence of the brass plates seems obvious. Clearly, Nephi was studying and pondering the scriptures on the brass plates, searching for inspiration to deal with his personal challenges, and then he proceeded to share what he had learned and experienced. Wouldn't this be a perfect application of Nephi's own admonition to "liken all scriptures unto us" (1 Nephi 19:23)?

If we assert that Nephi was inspired by the psalms on the brass plates, we must address the issue of whether the brass plates included the book of Psalms. While there are questions about the age and authorship of some of the later psalms, the earliest psalms are widely attributed to King David and are generally believed to have been composed in the eleventh century BC, almost half a millennium before Lehi left Jerusalem. It seems probable that Psalms would have been recorded on the brass plates. The earliest surviving manuscripts of Psalms, found among the Dead Sea Scrolls, show that the first eighty-nine psalms were nearly always arranged in the same sequence we have today.[16]

The best evidence that the book of Psalms was included on the brass plates is probably contextual—that is, evidence in the writings of the prophets in the Book of Mormon who had access to the brass plates showing that they were familiar with it. One example of a possible connection between Nephi and the book of Psalms, outside of Psalms 25–31, is found in a distinct metaphorical concept of diggers of a pit (wicked men) falling into the pit they dug. Compare 1 Nephi 14:3 and 22:14 with Psalms 7:15, 35:7–8, and 57:6. Another example is Nephi's reference to "pure hearts and clean hands" in 2 Nephi 25:16 which parallels the reference to "clean hands, and a pure heart" in Psalm 24:4—the only scripture in the Old Testament that uses this same terminology. As we demonstrate in this essay, we believe that the psalm of Nephi provides the strongest evidence of such familiarity.

The psalm of Nephi has received a good deal of attention from Book of Mormon scholars, and writers have analyzed the psalm of Nephi from a variety of viewpoints. The various analyses offer ample evidence that the psalm of Nephi was carefully and meticulously crafted. Richard Dilworth Rust has noted the "strength and lyricism" in the parallelism and chiasmus that are present in Nephi's psalm.[17] Latter-day Saint scriptorian John W. Welch observed that there was "an old liturgical requirement for showing respect and tenfold perfection in calling upon the divine name, especially when seeking atonement."[18] The name "Lord" appears exactly ten times in Psalm 25 and again in Psalm 30.[19] Interestingly, as Welch noticed, there are ten references to "Lord" within the psalm of Nephi (2 Nephi 4:16–17, 26, 30–34) showing the care with which Nephi constructed his psalm.[20]

Sandra and Dennis Packard looked closely at the historical setting of Nephi's psalm and provided verse-by-verse commentary.[21] Steven P. Sondrup analyzed the psalm as an excellent example of Hebrew poetry.[22] Sidney B. Sperry declared that the psalm of Nephi "is a true psalm in both form and ideas. Its rhythm is comparable to the notable cadence of David's poems. It not only praises God, but lays bare to us the very depths of Nephi's soul. A study of this psalm reveals how the scriptures delighted Nephi."[23] Steven Barton suggests that the psalm of Nephi exhibits several general characteristics of ancient Hebrew poetry: parallelism, a chiastic structure, and various Hebraisms.[24]

In 1926, the German theologian Hermann Gunkel outlined a method he labeled form-critical analysis to analyze psalms as a poetic art form.[25] Gunkel categorized four general types of psalms: hymns, thanksgiving songs, community laments, and individual laments. He identified Psalms 25–28 and 31 as individual laments, Psalm 29 as a hymn, and Psalm 30 as a thanksgiving psalm. Gunkel also listed five basic elements that appear in individual laments: an invocation, a complaint, a confession of trust, a petition, and a vow of praise. In 1997, Matthew Nickerson applied Hermann Gunkel's analysis method to 2 Nephi 4:16–35 to determine if it is "a psalm in the biblical sense of the term."[26] Nickerson methodically concluded that the psalm of Nephi is "a classic example of an ancient poetic form: the psalm of individual lament. . . . Clearly Nephi was participating in an ancient literary tradition when he wrote his psalm."[27]

We believe the specific connections between Nephi's psalm and Psalms 25–31 reviewed later in this essay provide further support for the conclusion that Nephi was writing in the ancient psalmist tradition. We concur with R. Scott Burton's observation that Nephi's psalm exhibits "a good deal of indebtedness to the Old Testament psalmic imagery and phraseology—Nephi seems, at times, to be quoting Old Testament psalms,"[28] but Burton did not attempt to identify specific psalms that may have provided Nephi's inspiration. If, indeed, Nephi read from Psalms for inspiration or used them as a model as he carefully composed his psalm, it is reasonable to assume that we might be able to find evidence in his psalm that he did so. In a 1981 essay in *BYU Studies*, Sondrup noticed some general similarities between Psalms 51 and 84 and the psalm of Nephi.[29] Nickerson, in his 1997 essay in the *Journal of Book of Mormon Studies*, identified possible influence from Psalms 6:6–7; 18:2, 6–7, 16, and 48; 25:1, 27:9, and 51:16–17 on Nephi's psalm. Like Sondrup, Nickerson, and others, we too feel that Nephi was clearly influenced by biblical psalms during the creation of his psalm. Our study of 2 Nephi 4:16–35 and the book of Psalms has caused us to consider that while many psalms may have affected and influenced Nephi, he appears to be most directly influenced by Psalms 25–31 based on an amazing concentration of shared feelings and phrases. In the text that follows, we will take phrases from Nephi's psalm and compare them with passages and phrases from Psalms 25–31 that may have influenced Nephi's writing.[30]

- One of the literary elements that makes Nephi's psalm appear so personal is his use of the phrase "my heart," which appears nine times (verses 16–17, 19, 26–28, 30, 32). Psalms 25–31 mention "my heart" six times (Psalms 25:17; 26:2; 27:3; 8; and 28:7). That phrase is used many times in other psalms, but Psalms 25–31 is the only place in the Psalter where four consecutive psalms use it.[31] Nephi also uses the phrase "my soul" five times (verses 15, 27, 28 [twice], 31); the phrase "my soul" is used frequently throughout the Psalter, including six times in Psalms 25–31 (Psalms 25:1; 25:20; 26:9; 30:3; 31:7, 9).

- Nephi speaks of the "great goodness of the Lord, in showing me his great and marvelous works" (2 Nephi 4:17). Psalm 31:19 similarly states, "Oh how great is thy goodness . . . which thou hast wrought for them that trust in thee." The only other place in the Psalms where the Lord's "great goodness" is mentioned is in Psalm 145:7. Also, in Psalm 26:7, the Psalmist cites the Lord's "wondrous works."

- Nephi despairs about his sins, saying "my soul grieveth because of mine iniquities" and "my heart groaneth because of my sins" (2 Nephi 4:17–19). These verses from Psalms sound similar in tone:

Psalm 25:11: "Pardon mine iniquity; for it is great."

Psalm 25:7: "Remember not the sins of my youth, nor my transgressions."

Psalm 25:17–18: "The troubles of my heart are enlarged. . . . Look upon mine affliction and my pain."

Psalm 31:9–10: "I am in trouble: mine eye is consumed with grief. . . . For my life is spent with grief, and my years with sighing: my strength faileth because of mine iniquity."

- Nephi cites God as "my support" (2 Nephi 4:20). Several verses in Psalms 27, 28, 29, and 31 speak of the Lord as a source of strength and support:

    Psalm 27:1: "The Lord is the strength of my life."

    Psalm 28:7: "The Lord is my strength and my shield."

    Psalm 28:8: "The Lord . . . is the saving strength of his anointed."

    Psalm 29:11: "The Lord will give strength unto his people."

    Psalm 30:1–2: "I will extol thee, O Lord; for thou hast lifted me up. . . . Thou hast healed me."

    Psalm 31:4: "Thou art my strength."

- Nephi declares that the Lord "hath heard my cry" (2 Nephi 4:23) and says, "I will lift up my voice unto thee; yea I will cry unto thee, my God" (2 Nephi 4:35). In commenting on Psalm 28, Schaefer observed that the use of the phrase "hath heard the voice of my supplications" probably meant that "either God has already intervened or the psalmist is so certain of his eventual intervention that he or she regards it as an already accomplished fact."[32] These verses from Psalms sound similar to Nephi's psalm:

    Psalm 28:6: "He hath heard the voice of my supplications."

Psalm 30:2: "O Lord my God, I cried unto thee, and thou hast healed me."

Psalm 30:8: "I cried to thee, O Lord; and unto the Lord I made supplication."

Psalm 31:22: "Thou heardest the voice of my supplications when I cried unto thee."

- Nephi speaks of God visiting men "in so much mercy" (2 Nephi 4:26). In his April 2005 conference address, Elder David A. Bednar cited "tender mercies" in 1 Nephi 1:20.[33] Other references to "tender mercies" can be found in 1 Nephi 8:8, in Ether 6:12, and in ten places in Psalms. Psalm 25:6, for example, states, "Remember, O Lord, thy tender mercies and thy loving kindnesses; for they have been ever of old." Nephi's effort to remember how the Lord had supported, blessed, and bestowed mercies upon him in 2 Nephi 4:20–26 invokes the same thought found in Psalm 26:3: "For thy lovingkindness is before mine eyes: and I have walked in thy truth."

- Nephi speaks of "mine afflictions" (2 Nephi 4:20, 29). Psalm 25 uses a similar phrase twice: "I am desolate and afflicted" (verse 16) and "Look upon mine affliction and my pain" (verse 18). In 2 Nephi 4:20, Nephi writes, "My God hath been my support; he hath led me through mine afflictions," which seems to echo the sentiment in Psalm 31:7—"Thou has known my soul in adversities."

- Nephi speaks of "mine enemies" and prays for God's help in dealing with them (2 Nephi 4:22, 27, 29–33). He asks, "Wilt thou deliver me out of the hands of mine enemies?" (2 Nephi 4:31) and, "Wilt thou make a way for mine escape before mine enemies?" (2 Nephi 4:31), and implores God to "hedge not up my way, but the ways of mine enemy" (2 Nephi 4:33). In 2 Nephi 4:29, Nephi additionally counsels himself to "not anger again because of mine enemies." Dealing with enemies is a common theme in Psalms. Here are similar references found in Psalms 25–31:

Psalm 25:2: "Let not mine enemies triumph over me."

Psalm 25:19: "Consider mine enemies; for they are many, and they hate me with cruel hatred."

Psalm 27:2: "Mine enemies . . . stumbled and fell."

Psalm 27:11–12: "Lead me in a plain path, because of mine enemies. Deliver me not over unto the will of mine enemies."

Psalm 31:15: "Deliver me from the hand of mine enemies."

- Nephi says, "Rejoice, O my heart" (2 Nephi 4:28). He also says, "My soul will rejoice in thee, my God" (2 Nephi 4:30). Psalms 27, 28, and 31 contain several similar references:

    Psalm 27:14: "Be of good courage, and he shall strengthen thine heart."

    Psalm 28:7: "My heart trusted in him, and I am helped; therefore my heart greatly rejoiceth."

    Psalm 31:7: "I will be glad and rejoice in thy mercy."

    Psalm 31:24: "Be of good courage, and he shall strengthen your heart, all ye that hope in the Lord."

- Nephi prays for strength and deliverance in 2 Nephi 4:28–34. (While the word "strength" is not used by Nephi, he is clearly praying for strength to overcome sin and his enemies.) Similar prayers are found in Psalms 25 and 30–31:

    Psalm 25:20: "O keep my soul, and deliver me."

    Psalm 30:10: "Hear, O Lord, and have mercy upon me: Lord, be thou my helper."

    Psalm 31:1: "Deliver me in thy righteousness."

Psalm 31:15: "Deliver me from the hand of mine enemies, and from them that persecute me."

- Nephi cries in his heart, "O Lord, I will praise thee forever" (2 Nephi 4:30). Similar expressions of praise and thanksgiving are found throughout the Psalter; here are examples from Psalms 26–28 and 30:

    Psalm 26:7: "That I may publish with the voice of thanksgiving, and tell of all thy wondrous works."

    Psalm 27:6: "I will sing praises unto the Lord."

    Psalm 28:7: "With my song will I praise him."

    Psalm 30:12: "O Lord my God, I will give thanks unto thee forever."

- Nephi speaks of "my God, and the rock of my salvation" (2 Nephi 4:30). He also speaks of God as "the rock of my righteousness" and "my rock" (2 Nephi 4:35), phrasing that is almost taken directly from Psalms.

    Psalm 27:1: "The Lord is my light and my salvation."

    Psalm 27:9: "O God of my salvation."

    Psalm 28:1: "O Lord my rock."

    Psalm 31:2–3: "Be thou my strong rock. . . . Thou art my rock."

- Nephi prays to God: "O Lord, wilt thou redeem my soul?" (2 Nephi 4:31). In like manner, the Psalmist pled:

    Psalm 25:20: "O keep my soul, and deliver me"

    Psalm 26:11: "Redeem me, and be merciful to me."

    Psalm 30:10: "Hear, O Lord, and have mercy upon me: Lord, be thou my helper."

> Psalm 31:1–2: "Deliver me in thy righteousness. . . . Deliver me speedily."
>
> Psalm 31:16: "Save me for thy mercies' sake."

- Nephi then prays, "O Lord, wilt thou not shut the gates of thy righteousness before me" (2 Nephi 4:32); in Psalm 27:9 the Psalmist likewise requests that the Lord "hide not thy face far from me; put not thy servant away in anger: . . . leave me not, neither forsake me." Both verses ask the Lord not to reject the person writing the psalm but to allow the Lord's presence or influence to abide with him.

- Nephi prays that he "may walk in the path of the low valley" and "be strict in the plain road" with the Lord making "my path straight before me" (2 Nephi 4:32–33).[34] The words "even" and "plain" found in the verses below are translated from the Hebrew noun *mîyshôwr*, which means a "level country" or "plain" and also denotes "uprightness."[35] Commenting on Nephi's request to "walk in the path of the low valley, that I may be strict in the plain road," Hugh Nibley wrote that "this prayer of Nephi, the desert traveler, sounds like stilted English until we take it in a literal sense. . . . In *our* civilization, the broadest roads are the safest; in the desert, they are the most confusing and dangerous."[36] Nephi's plea is similar to these verses from Psalms 25–31:

  > Psalm 25:4: "Shew me thy ways, O Lord, teach me thy paths."
  >
  > Psalm 26:12: "My foot standeth in an even place."
  >
  > Psalm 27:11: "Teach me thy way, O Lord, and lead me in a plain path."

- Nephi asks the Lord, "Encircle me around in the robe of thy righteousness" (2 Nephi 4:33). Nephi's desire to be surrounded and protected sounds similar to the request of the Psalmist that "in the time of trouble he [the Lord] shall hide me in his pavilion: in the secret of his tabernacle shall he hide me" (Psalm 27:5). The word "pavilion" is translated from the Hebrew noun *cok*, which is a "booth" or "covert";

the word "tabernacle" (*'ôhel*) commonly refers to a "nomad's tent," but specifically, and here more to the point, the portable tabernacle temple of Moses and the children of Israel.[37] (Several other scriptures in the book of Psalms describe the Lord's righteousness—"thy righteousness"—as having power to bless us. See Psalms 71:2; 89:16; 119:40.)

- Nephi prays, "O Lord, wilt thou make a way for mine escape" (2 Nephi 4:33). Psalms 25 and 31 use very similar wording:

    Psalm 25:17–20: "O bring thou me out of my distresses.... O keep my soul, and deliver me."

    Psalm 31:4: "Pull me out of the net that they have laid privily for me."

    Psalm 31:15: "Deliver me."

- Nephi prays that God would clear any "stumbling block" from his path and hedge up the ways of his enemies (2 Nephi 4:33). In Psalm 27:2, the Psalmist wrote "whom shall I fear? the Lord is the strength of my life: of whom shall I be afraid?" Thus, the context suggests that the Psalmist recognized that it was the Lord who caused his enemies to stumble.

- Nephi says, "O Lord, I have trusted in thee and I will trust in thee forever" (2 Nephi 4:34) and "I know in whom I have trusted. My God has been my support" (2 Nephi 4:19–20). The concept of trust in God is mentioned numerous times in Psalms 25–31:

    Psalm 25:2: "O my God, I trust in thee."

    Psalm 25:20: "I put my trust in thee."

    Psalm 26:1: "I have trusted also in the Lord."

    Psalm 28:7: "My heart trusted in him."

Psalm 31:1: "In thee, O Lord, do I put my trust."

Psalm 31:14: "But I trusted in thee, O Lord."

And there may be other influences from Psalms 25–31 on the psalm of Nephi that are yet to be discovered. This essay has relied primarily on the King James Version of the Bible; comparing the psalm of Nephi against other translations of Psalms, for example, may yield additional insights into the possible influences on Nephi.

To be clear, we are not claiming that Psalms 25–31 were the sole inspiration for Nephi as he wrote his inspiring psalm. References to enemies, for example, one of the most common subjects in Psalms, can be found in 56 of the 150 psalms. In 2 Nephi 4:32 Nephi states that "my heart is broken and my spirit is contrite"; a "broken heart" and a "contrite spirit" are mentioned twice in Psalms (34 and 51), but not within Psalms 25–31. Nephi's prayer to be encircled by the "robe of [the Lord's] righteousness" in 2 Nephi 4:33 seems likely to have been inspired by Isaiah 61:10, which speaks of the Lord covering a man with the "robe of righteousness." As Latter-day Saint scholar Noel B. Reynolds has noted, there may also be influences on the psalm of Nephi from scriptures that were present on the brass plates but that are not found in our current Old Testament canon. Reynolds suggests, for example, that Zenos's prayer quoted in Alma 3–11, "appears to have provided some of the inspiration for the so-called 'Psalm of Nephi.'"[38]

While we cannot tell what specifically influenced Nephi as he wrote, it appears quite possible that he composed his psalm after reading and pondering what we identify today as Psalms 25–31. Support for this hypothesis is found in the abundance of parallel expressions and sentiments found in both Nephi's psalm and Psalms 25–31, as outlined in this essay. Nephi knew the scriptures well enough to be influenced by them as he wrote for future generations. Nearly all of the major themes of Nephi's psalm can be found in Psalms 25–31 (under 5 percent of the entire book), and we are suggesting that those seven psalms appear to have influenced Nephi as he composed his psalm. In his psalm, Nephi integrated seamlessly the scriptures he loved with his own life experience, providing evidence that Nephi was a man who had searched the scriptures diligently and pondered them deeply, as he himself declared at the beginning of his psalm (1 Nephi 4:15). We believe that only a man who knew and loved the word of God intimately—who truly delighted in the scriptures—could merge his life experiences with the messages of the psalms in such a personal and powerful way.

Notes

1. R. Scott Burton, "The Hymnal of Ancient Israel (Psalms, Part 1)," in *Studies in Scripture*, vol. 4: *1 Kings to Malachi*, ed. Kent P. Jackson (Salt Lake City: Deseret Book, 1993), 413–14.

2. Bible Dictionary, "Quotations." It is worth noting that the Dead Sea Scrolls contain more copies of Psalms than any other book in the Bible. See Martin Abegg Jr., Peter Flint, and Eugene Ulrich, eds., *The Dead Sea Scrolls Bible* (San Francisco: HarperSanFrancisco, 1999), 505.

3. Burton, "Hymnal of Ancient Israel," 407–8.

4. George Reynolds and Janne M. Sjodahl, *Commentary on the Book of Mormon* (Salt Lake City: Deseret Book, 1955), 1:264–68. After providing commentary on many aspects of 2 Nephi 4:16–35, Reynolds and Sjodahl reformat those verses in a more poetical form and title it "A Song of Lamentation by Nephi, the Son of Lehi." Reynolds and Sjodahl, *Commentary on the Book of Mormon*, 1:269–71.

5. Hugh Nibley, *Since Cumorah* (Salt Lake City: Deseret Book, 1983), 140. Taking exception to calling this a psalm, Nibley commented, "Some have called this a psalm, but strictly speaking a psalm is a ritual hymn connected with the rites of the Temple."

6. Sidney B. Sperry, *Our Book of Mormon* (Salt Lake City: Stevens & Wallis, 1947), 110–11. As Rust notes, Sidney B. Sperry identified "the following literary types [within the Book of Mormon]: allegory, didactic exposition, editorial reflection or commentary, epistle, exhortation, genealogy, gospel, historical narrative, hortatory discourse, lamentation, memoir, oratory, patriarchal admonition, patriarchal blessing, prayer, prophecy of doom, prophetic dialogue, prophetic discourse, prophetic narrative, prophetic prediction, psalm, religious teaching, revelation, sermon, song of praise, symbolic prophecy, and war epistle. Additional types are aphorism, apocalyptic writing, judgment, and farewell speech." Richard Dilworth Rust, *Feasting on the Word: The Literary Testimony of the Book of Mormon* (Salt Lake City: Deseret Book, 1997), 253–54.

7. Robert L. Millet, *Doctrinal Commentary on the Book of Mormon*, vol. 1: *First and Second Nephi* (Salt Lake City: Bookcraft, 1987), 217.

8. During his work on the "New Translation," as the Joseph Smith Translation of the Bible was initially called, Joseph Smith made numerous changes to the book of Psalms. As R. Scott Burton noted, "Around two hundred verses in some fifty different psalms saw revision at the hands of Joseph Smith." "Hymnal of Ancient Israel," 408. A close comparison of the King James Version and Joseph Smith Translation of Psalms 25–31 shows that most of the changes made "to the Psalter are of various types and of varying significance. Some, for example, are as mundane as changing 'hath' to 'has,' 'an' to 'a,' 'mine' to 'my,' 'shew' to 'show,' 'that' to 'who,' 'as' to 'like,' 'thine' to 'thy,' etc." "Hymnal of Ancient Israel," 409.

9. Victor L. Ludlow, *Unlocking the Old Testament* (Salt Lake City: Deseret Book, 1981), 126–27. Ludlow notes that the "phrase 'psalm of David' could also be translated as 'psalm *to* David' (that is, dedicated to David), 'psalm *about* David' (written about an event in his life), or even 'psalm *like* David' (in the style or pattern of David's psalms)" (127).

10. Konrad Schaefer, "Psalms," in *Berit Olam: Studies in Hebrew Narrative & Poetry*, ed. David W. Cotter (Collegeville, MN: Liturgical Press, 2001), xxi.

11. See Schaefer, "Psalms," xx; Hermann Gunkel, *The Psalms: A Form-Critical Introduction*, trans. Thomas M. Horner (Philadelphia: Fortress, 1967), 19; and Mitchell Dahood, *Psalms 1: 1–50*, Anchor Bible 16 (New York: Doubleday, 1965), xxx–xxxi.

12. Schaefer, "Psalms," 62. Psalm 25 is also a Hebrew alphabet acrostic (the first words of each line begin with the letters of the Hebrew alphabet). See Dahood, *Psalms 1*, 155.

13. Schaefer, "Psalms," xxiii. As Schaefer notes, "More often the brusque transition from complaint to assurance has no apparent cause. . . . Psalm 31 is a fine example" (xxiii).

14. Grant Hardy, *Understanding the Book of Mormon: A Reader's Guide* (New York: Oxford University, 2010), 52.

15. Hardy, *Understanding the Book of Mormon*, 52.

16. We are uncertain in what order the psalms appeared on the brass plates, but it is probable that Psalms 25–31 appeared contiguously as they do in the Masoretic Psalter. Peter W. Flint, director of the Dead Sea Scrolls Institute at Trinity Western University in British Columbia, has noted that "the [Dead Sea] Psalms scrolls bear witness to an early collection of psalms whose arrangement was virtually stabilized well before the second century B.C.E." "Psalms and Psalters in the Dead Sea Scrolls," in *The Bible and the Dead Sea Scrolls*, ed. James H. Charlesworth (Waco, TX: Baylor University, 2006), 243. Out of thirty-six Psalm scrolls found at Qumran, Psalms 1–89 appear in the familiar Masoretic order in all but seven. Esther Chazon, "Hymns and Prayers in the Dead Sea Scrolls," in *The Dead Sea Scrolls after Fifty Years: A Comprehensive Assessment*, ed. Peter W. Flint and James C. VanderKam (Leiden: Brill, 1998), 1:264. There is some indication that the prophet Jeremiah, a contemporary of Lehi, was familiar with the book of Psalms. For example, in Lamentations, Jeremiah refers to Jerusalem using the words "perfection of beauty" and "joy of the whole earth." In Psalm 48: 1–2, the city of God, mount Zion, is called the "joy of the whole earth" and, in Psalm 50:2, Zion is called "the perfection of beauty." Also compare Jeremiah 15:16–17 with Psalm 1:1–2 and Jeremiah 17:8 with Psalm 1:3.

17. Richard Dilworth Rust, "Poetry in the Book of Mormon," in *Rediscovering the Book of Mormon: Insights You May Have Missed Before*, ed. John L. Sorensen and Melvin J. Thorne (Salt Lake City: Deseret Book, 1991), 100–103.

18. John W. Welch, "A Steady Stream of Significant Recognitions" in *Echoes and Evidences of the Book of Mormon*, ed. Donald W. Parry, Daniel C. Peterson, and Jack W. Welch (Provo, UT: FARMS, 2002), 332.

19. Some psalms (43, 49, 52, 53, 60, 61, 63, 65, 67, and 82) do not include the name "Lord."

20. Welch, "Steady Stream," 332.

21. Sandra Packard and Dennis Packard, *Feasting upon the Word* (Salt Lake City: Deseret Book, 1981), 92–107.

22. Steven P. Sondrup, "The Psalm of Nephi: A Lyric Reading," *BYU Studies* 21, no. 3 (1981): 1–16.

23. Sperry, *Our Book of Mormon*, 111.

24. Steven Barton, "The Psalm of Nephi and Biblical Poetry," http://home.comcast.net/~openskyvisions/PsalmOfNephiEssay.html.

25. Hermann Gunkel, *The Psalms: A Form-Critical Introduction*, trans. Thomas M. Horner (Philadelphia: Fortress, 1967). Gunkel's original work is entitled *Die Psalmen: Handkommentar zum Alten Testament* (Gottingen: Vandenhoeck & Ruprecht, 1926).

26. Sondrup, "Psalm of Nephi," 358, quoted in Matthew Nickerson, "Nephi's Psalm: 2 Nephi 4:16–35 in the Light of Form-Critical Analysis," *Journal of Book of Mormon Studies* 6, no. 2 (1997): 41.

27. Nickerson, "Nephi's Psalm," 41.

28. Burton, "Hymnal of Ancient Israel," 408.

29. Sondrup, "Psalm of Nephi," 11.

30. We recognize that we are comparing the King James English translation of the Hebrew Old Testament to the English translation of the Book of Mormon. Thus we would not always expect parallelism in exact wording; we are looking for parallelism of concepts. We acknowledge that some connections are stronger than others and are not claiming that Nephi deliberately relied on a concept in Psalms for each concept in his psalm. However, we believe the large number of parallel concepts supports the idea that Nephi was familiar with these particular psalms, Psalms 25–31. We also acknowledge that psalms outside Psalms 25–31 include parallel concepts too, but, based on our study, the connections to Psalms 25–31 are particularly numerous and compelling and warrant special focus.

31. In addition to four instances in Psalms 25–31 (appearing in 57 percent of those psalms), the phrase "my heart" is found in twenty-seven (19 percent) of the remaining psalms.

32. Schaefer, "Psalms," 70.

33. David A. Bednar, in Conference Report, April 2005, 104–8.

34. See John W. Welch and Daniel McKinlay, "Getting Things Strai[gh]t" in *Reexploring the Book of Mormon*, ed. John W. Welch (Salt Lake City: Deseret Book; and Provo, UT: Foundation for Ancient Research and Mormon Studies, 1992), 260–62. The authors note that "going back to the 1829 manuscripts of the Book of Mormon, one finds that the word *strait* appears over twenty times in the Printer's Manuscript" (including 2 Nephi 4:33). The strait path may be thought of as narrow, straight, or smooth or level. Welch and McKinlay cite both Psalms 26:12 and 2 Nephi 4:32.

35. James Strong, *The Exhaustive Concordance of the Bible* (New York: Abingdon Press, 1965), "mîyshôwr."

36. Hugh Nibley, *Temple and Cosmos: Beyond This Ignorant Present* (Salt Lake City: Deseret Book, 1992), 219; italics in original.

37. Strong, *Exhaustive Concordance of the Bible*, "cok," "'ôhel."

38. In Reynold's view, "Nephi appears to have applied the sentiments and language of [Zenos's] prayer to his own trying circumstances, finding in Zenos's words a source of encouragement and faith in the face of hostility and affliction. Nephi ends his psalm

with a prayer of approximately the same length and in a style similar to Zenos's prayer text. In their respective texts, Zenos uses the invocation 'O God' or 'O Lord' five times; Nephi six. Nephi begins his psalm by recognizing the Lord's great goodness in showing him 'his great and marvelous works' (2 Nephi 4:17) in answer to Nephi's prayer (see 1 Nephi 11). . . . Zenos ends by emphasizing that because the Lord did hear him in his afflictions, he will continue to cry to him 'in all mine afflictions' (Alma 33:11); furthermore, Zenos asserts generally that God is 'merciful unto [his] children when they cry unto [him]' (Alma 33:8); Nephi knows that 'God will give liberally to him that asketh' (2 Nephi 4:35)." Noel B. Reynolds, "Nephite Uses and Interpretations of Zenos," in *Allegory of the Olive Tree: The Olive, the Bible, and Jacob 5*, ed. Stephen D. Ricks and John W. Welch (Salt Lake City: Deseret Book, 1994), 34. As it is unknown when the prophet Zenos lived and wrote, it seems entirely possible that Zenos could also have been influenced by Psalms—further confusing the relationship between an original influence and the results of that influence.

19

The Psalms Sung: The Power of Music in Sacred Worship

Shon D. Hopkin and J. Arden Hopkin

There are two main ways in which Latter-day Saints might understand the formation of the Psalms in the Hebrew Bible and, particularly, those that contain pointed prophecies of Christ, such as Psalm 22. The first is that they were developed by a prophetic figure such as David, who was inspired to speak true doctrines that foretold precisely and clearly of Jesus Christ, such as in Psalm 22:16, "They pierced my hands and my feet."[1] The second, held by many biblical scholars, is that the Psalms were originally written by inspired authors to reflect the yearnings, experiences, and understanding of Israelites in their time. When the Gospel authors gave their accounts of Jesus' life and death, they saw in his life the culmination of all the experiences of Israel as expressed in the Psalms and organized their account in such a way as to show that he was the fulfillment of those yearnings and that profound understanding.[2] In other words, the experiences of Israel expressed beautifully the future experiences of their Messiah and became a foreshadowing of his life that was understood by the Gospel authors as representing him.

Shon D. Hopkin is an assistant professor of ancient scripture at Brigham Young University. J. Arden Hopkin is a professor of voice at Brigham Young University.

For Latter-day Saints, these two viewpoints need not be seen as mutually exclusive. Since Christ is "the way, the truth, and the life" (John 14:6), writings that prophesy pointedly of Christ's life also reflect a pattern for the experiences of God's covenant people who seek to follow him. As indicated in the Beatitudes, it is not only Christ who is called upon to be reviled and persecuted (see Matthew 5:10–12). His followers should also expect similar persecution in their own lives. This combined understanding of the Psalms see them as prophesying of Christ in a way that also reflects the experiences of his people, and allows a more complete view of their potential meaning and usefulness in the lives of the early Israelites, who often did not clearly understand the prophecies of the suffering Messiah (see D&C 84:26–27). Without a clear concept of their future fulfillment in Christ, the Psalms would have disappeared if the Israelites did not find in them an expression of their own trials, longings, and religious desires.[3]

Although the Psalms teach important spiritual truths and many of these psalms prophesy of a future Messiah, this paper will demonstrate that psalms were often used in early Israelite practice and throughout time in the context of liturgical worship (what Latter-day Saints would understand as worship services centered on ordinances, such as the sacrament or temple ordinances). More specifically, we will show that psalms were set to music in order to enhance worship and will also show the various forms psalms have taken that would have functioned to teach lessons through music and to help draw the worshipper into a state in which she or he was prepared to commune with God. In order to demonstrate this, we will first discuss the various types of psalms, how most of these could have connected to worship in the ancient temple, and the evidence showing the importance of music in Old Testament times. We will show textually how psalms were designed to mirror important functions of the sacrificial ritual. Next, we will show some of the most widespread forms psalms have taken in music over time, and how those musical forms were designed to teach and mirror the progress of the soul into a state of communion. Finally, we will briefly discuss the use of psalms in Latter-day Saint worship and how an understanding of the temple tradition of psalms could enhance sacrament and temple worship in that community.

Psalms as Forms of Worship in Ancient Temples

Numerous biblical scholars see the existence and use of many of the psalms as connected to worship in the Temple of Solomon or later in the Second Temple that was built after the Jewish return from exile in Babylon.[4] First and Second Chronicles—likely written by a temple Levite around 350 BC during the time of the Second Temple—connect Israelite music directly to the office of the Levites and a temple setting. Although scholars disagree whether these accounts reflect an accurate understanding of the use of psalms in David's day or if they instead are more indicative of temple usage during the Second Temple, the connection with temple worship is not under debate.[5] First Chronicles 15 shows David leading a procession in song and dance as they brought the ark of the covenant, the most central symbol of God's presence in Israel, back among the Israelites to reside in the tabernacle. As the Levites made holy sacrifices and entered into the tabernacle or temple, David delivered a psalm of thanksgiving (see 1 Chronicles 16:4–36), and urged his people to "sing unto [the Lord], sing psalms unto him. . . . Glory ye in his holy name. . . . Seek the Lord and his strength, seek his face continually" (1 Chronicles 16:9–11). David thus connected music with the temple activity of seeking the face of the Lord, as found symbolically at the ark. The backdrop for David's psalm includes the music of the Levitical priests, who had been appointed "to minister before the ark of the Lord" (1 Chronicles 16:37), "with psalteries and with harps, . . . with cymbals, . . . with trumpets continually before the ark of the covenant of God" (1 Chronicles 16:5–6). Asaph, whose name is recorded at the beginning of many of the psalms, was specifically mentioned as a musician there.

In 2 Chronicles 5:12–13, similar behaviors at the dedication of Solomon's Temple, when the Lord actually entered his temple, are recorded. The text makes clear that the Levites had been sanctified and were dressed in sacred temple robes of white. A number of them, including Asaph, played "cymbals and psalteries and harps," standing at the east end of the altar with one hundred and twenty priests playing trumpets. The "trumpeters and singers were as one, to make one sound to be heard in praising and thanking the Lord . . . when they lifted up their voice . . . that then the house was filled with a cloud, even the house of the Lord" (2 Chronicles 5:12–14). This passage points to the music and singing itself as the behavior that directly led to the presence of God entering into the temple.

Although they may have been added later, subtitles such as those found in Psalms 83 and 84 connected various psalms to figures such as Asaph or the sons of Korah (see Exodus 6:24). These were Levitical priest-figures who served in the temple of God, again demonstrating the biblical connection between the psalms and the temple.[6] Many psalms also give directions for how to perform the music as the words are being sung, showing that the psalms were given in the context of musical performance. For example, although modern scholars cannot agree on the translation of the word *selah*, almost all are in accord that it indicated some type of instruction to the performers with the largest group believing that it indicated a pause in the music (see Psalm 3:2, 4, 8).[7]

Although written many centuries later, the Talmud supports the view that one of the most important roles of the Levites was to sing in the temple during the performance of sacred ordinances, as can be seen in the description of the Day of Atonement:

> They gave him the wine for the drink offering, and the high priest stood by each horn of the altar with a towel in his hand, and two priests stood at the table of the fat pieces with two silver trumpets in their hands. . . .When he stooped and poured out the drink-offering the lead priest waved the towel and Ben Arza clashed the cymbals and the Levites broke forth into singing. When they reached a break in the singing they blew upon the trumpet and at every blowing of the trumpet a prostration. This was the rite of the Daily Whole-offering. . . .This was the singing which the Levites used to sing in the temple.[8]

The Talmud even indicated that certain psalms were sung on each day of the week: Sunday, Psalm 24; Monday, Psalm 48; Tuesday, Psalm 82; Wednesday, Psalm 94; Thursday, Psalm 81; Friday, Psalm 93; and Saturday (the Sabbath), Psalm 92.[9]

The themes expressed by the psalms as mentioned below connect closely with the purposes of temple worship and animal sacrifice under the law of Moses: forgiveness, prayers of thanksgiving, pleas for aid in trials, holy festivals, the anointing and support of kings, songs to prepare for temple worship, and religious instruction.[10] These themes are also familiar to Latter-day Saints, who know the temple as a place for prayers of thanksgiving and requests for divine help, a place where they can contemplate and celebrate the mercy and might of God over the history of his interactions with mankind, a place of gospel instruction, a place where they enter into covenants of holiness, and a place strengthening and upholding the royal priesthood of God. The poetic temple prayers set to music were designed to express the feelings of a wide range of the people, so that they could be sung alone or together and heighten the mood of worship in various circumstances. The psalms can be divided into seven groups, which will be described here in order to show how they connect with temple worship in various situations:[11]

1. *Psalms of lament or prayer.* These likely arose from times of national or personal crisis, when the community gathered (at the temple, if possible) in order to offer sacrifice and pray for deliverance: 12, 22, 23, 44, 60, 74, 79, 80, 83, 85, 90, 94, 108, 123, 129, and 137. Saul's desire to sacrifice before going to war (1 Samuel 13:8–10) is an example of the type of circumstance in which these psalms could have been performed. Many of these psalms exhibit a three-part division. After addressing themselves to God, the supplicants, first, describe their trial; second, plea for help; and third, express their complete confidence that God will deliver them. Sometimes they speak of God's help as if he has already saved them. This three-part division likely connects with the ritual of sacrifice and will be discussed further below.

2. *Psalms of praise.* These psalms often begin with a command or call to Israel to gather as a community (most importantly, at the temple) and praise the Lord: 8, 19, 29, 33, 47, 65, 66, 78, 93, 95–100, 103–6, 11, 113, 114, 117, 134, 135, 136, and 145–50. After the call to praise, the hymns describe the power and the mercy of the Lord, often describing what he has done for Israel in the past and emphasizing his role as the creator and his divine reign as king of Israel. These psalms, once thought of as synagogue hymns, are now thought to mark times of national festival gatherings, such as the festival at Rosh Hashanah, which commemorated God's creation of the earth, and the anointing of God as king (and the mirrored anointing of the king of Judah/Israel) at the temple.

3. *Songs of thanksgiving.* These psalms reflect the gratitude of an individual or community after they have been delivered from a trial by God: 18, 30, 34, 40, 66, 92, 116, 118, and 138. This gratitude typically would have been demonstrated with a sacrifice at the temple, and accompanied by the singing of a hymn or psalm. Although it predates the creation of the temple, Noah's

sacrifice after leaving the ark (Genesis 8:20–21) shows the connection between the offering of thanks and the sacrificial ordinances of the temple.

4. *Royal psalms.* These psalms celebrated important events in the lives of royalty, which for Christian readers often reflected the royal life and reign of the Messiah: 2, 18, 20, 21, 45, 72, 89, 101, 110, 132, and 144. These often combine the previous two categories—pleas for aid and psalms of thanksgiving—but are expressed in terms of royal favor and desire. Psalm 18, for example, could fit in category 3 in that it provides thanksgiving after a successful battle, while Psalm 20 could fit in category 1 in that it is a royal prayer for aid in war. Again, these types of prayers would frequently have been made in connection with some type of sacrifice at the temple. The example cited above, in which King Solomon dedicated the Temple to the accompaniment of psalms, demonstrates the connection between the temple and royal psalms.

5. *Songs of Zion.* These psalms celebrate the location of the temple at Mount Zion, rejoice that the Lord's presence is there, and express a longing to visit the temple that could have acted also as a call to worship: 46, 48, 76, 84, 87, and 122.

6. *Liturgies.* These psalms are clearly designed for antiphonal dialogue in a way that worshippers could respond to the call of a priest, or the Levites could perform a song in a call and response fashion, thereby strengthening the message of the psalm: 15, 24, 50, 68, 81, 82, 95, 115, and 132. Psalm 15, for example, appears to have functioned as a call and response that would allow the worshipper to enter into the temple.[12] The worshipper (or priest) would ask, "Lord, who shall abide in thy tabernacle?" and the priest (or worshipper) would respond with the qualifications for temple service, "He that walketh uprightly and worketh righteousness." Psalm 24 functions in a similar way, with the worshipper (or the priest) asking, "Who shall ascend into the hill of the Lord?" (3). The priest (or the worshipper) would then respond, "He that hath clean hands and a pure heart" (4). Some Latter-day Saints consider this format to be similar to the temple recommend question demonstrating that there were worthiness requirements in order to enter into the temple.[13] Whether or not this is a valid connection, the call and response format of the psalm would have caused thoughtful reflection among the temple worshippers and helped lift their souls to higher levels of devotion. Psalm 50 appears to be appropriate in the context of the reinitiation of a covenant, including a reference to a list of covenant requirements in verse 16. Psalm 121 likely was

used as a liturgical hymn for the use of pilgrims on their way to the temple in Jerusalem.

7. *Wisdom and Torah psalms.* These psalms seem to function differently than the others, not serving as a prayerful petition to God, but rather discussing religious truths and providing advice on how to successfully live a godly life, similar to the advice found in Proverbs or Ecclesiastes: 37, 49, 73, 112, 127, 128, and 133. As such they do not connect inherently to the temple or worship in the same way as the other psalms, but they may indicate the importance of teaching groups that are gathered at the temple to be instructed by the Mosaic priesthood or similar gatherings at the home.

There is no way to know beyond educated guesses what form temple music would have taken. The form of some of the psalms themselves, however, such as the call and response feature discussed in connection with Psalm 24 above (known as *anah* or "reply" in Hebrew[14]), indicates that some of the music was likely responsorial or antiphonal (forms which will be discussed below). As it has been mentioned, other psalms show a type of three-part division. Biblical scholars describe these divisions as leading from one stage to another—from a lament to a plea for help and finally to an expression of triumph or a statement of trust.[15] Using different titles, modern anthropologists have also recognized the commonality of a threefold division in behaviors during rituals.[16] The connection made below between the threefold division of many psalms, the threefold nature of ritual suggested by anthropologists, and the threefold division in the ritual of sacrifice is in many respects unique to this paper. The tentative nature, however, of these proposed connections—meant to demonstrate one way in which the psalms could have assisted in temple worship—should not call into question the following: first, that a threefold division in many of the psalms exists; second, that the threefold division would have been reflected musically; and third, that many psalms were clearly connected with temple ritual.[17]

Using the wording of modern ritual theory to describe the threefold progression in the psalm and the sacrifice, many behaviors in rituals begin with a separation stage—the lament stage—that is designed to disconnect the worshipper from previous worldly associations, attitudes, and behaviors. The stage would be symbolized by the worshipper's entrance into the sacred precincts of the temple and movement towards the altar, where the sacrifice brought from the world would have hands laid upon its head to indicate its status as a proxy for the worldly sinner. The animal would then be sacrificed in an ultimate symbol of separation (see Leviticus 1:3–4). The ritual then proceeds to a liminal (from Latin *limen* meaning "threshold") stage—the plea stage—in which the worshipper is moving from one state of being to another and is often characterized by new behaviors, orientations, and attitudes. This stage is reflected in the middle phases of the animal sacrifice, in which the blood of the animal is spilt with some of the blood sprinkled upon specific corners or horns of the altar. The animal is then skinned and divided into appropriate portions with the entrails removed and appropriately handled (see Leviticus 1:5–7). Finally, the ritual concludes in an aggregation stage—the triumph stage—in which the worshipper is brought into a state of holier communion with God and with his people. The connection with God is symbolized by placing various parts of the sacrifice upon the altar where God's priesthood accepts the sacrifice, and the smoke from the sacrifice ascends up into heaven and becomes a pleasing savor unto the Lord (see Leviticus 1:7–9). Worshippers are thereby forgiven of their sins or receive confidence that the Lord will help them to pass through their trials. They are separated from the world, and they and God become one in newly formed, sacred communion.

As has been stated, a similar threefold ritual process is reflected in many of the psalms and may indicate that the words and music of these psalms were designed to be sung by the Levites at each stage of the ritual process, indicating cues to move to the next stage. In this way, the worshipper would be carried emotionally from the distressing state of separation—the lament stage—through the liminal state in which he has not yet been accepted by God—the plea stage—and triumphantly into the new relationship of holiness—the triumph stage. The music and words act as an emotional and intellectual conduit throughout, strengthening the meaning of the behaviors in the ritual and solidifying the results in the heart of the participant. Psalm 22 demonstrates this type of three-part division. Verses 1–18 describe the challenging condition in the separation or lament stage in which the worshipper finds himself. He questions, "Why hast thou forsaken me?" (1) and states that he is "despised of the people" (6); "trouble is near" (11); his "strength is dried up like a potsherd" (15). Although it is unknown how the music would have been performed during the ritual, it is possible to imagine a sorrowful tune accompanying the above words as the lamb was being brought to the temple and then killed as a symbol of difficulty and separation. For Christian readers, the images cited most powerfully portray the separation experiences of the atoning Christ that would lead up to his death, similar to the death of the innocent lamb. The second stage of the psalm is characterized by pleas for help, found in verses 19–21. The worshipper asks the Lord to "be not thou far from me" and "haste thee to help me" (19) and cries to the Lord to "save [him] from the lion's mouth" (21). During this liminal stage in which the worshipper is not yet defeated but has not yet been delivered from his affliction, it is possible to imagine the music of the psalm tending upwards or increasing in volume, reflecting the soul yearning for help and bringing the worshippers to be emotionally in tune with the ritual being performed as the blood of the lamb is being sprinkled upon the altar and the parts of the lamb are being washed and placed upon the altar. Finally the psalm enters the aggregation stage found in verses 22–31, in which the final success of the plea is anticipated as if it had already occurred. The Psalmist declares that God "hath not despised nor abhorred the affliction of the afflicted; neither hath he hid his face from him but ... he heard" (24). The Psalmist states that his "praise shall be of [God] in the great congregation" (25), promising that he will continue to praise God for his successful deliverance as he is praising him now in singing the hymn. The music of the psalm would likely have reflected the triumphant conclusion of the sacrifice, in which God had accepted the offering, and the worshippers were rejoicing in the assurance of their deliverance, feeling the reality of deliverance as they participated in the sacred music of the psalm. For Christians who read this psalm, the effect that Christ's death had upon the temple, at which the veil was rent in two (Matthew 27:51), demonstrates that Christ's sacrifice was seen by Gospel writers as connected to the temple, granting eventual access to all—the successful conclusion of the aggregation stage—back into the presence of God.[18]

The Use of the Psalms by Jews and Christians after the Temple

As has been mentioned, performances of the psalms did not find their way immediately into Jewish synagogue services.[19] This was likely because of the sharp distinction that was seen between the temple, in which worshippers attended under the direction of priesthood authority to participate in ritual ordinances, and the synagogue, where priesthood authority did not officiate.[20] The Jews, who had participated in both forms of worship simultaneously,[21] may have been slow to adopt temple forms directly into synagogue worship. This reluctance in the synagogues seems to have been directed more at the singing of the psalms rather than their reading, since reading scripture was one of the primary purposes of synagogue worship. Over time the synagogue adopted many psalms into their synagogue services, using them particularly during the *shacharit* or morning service,[22] likely reflecting the ancient temple practice of the morning sacrifice.[23] Many additional psalms are recited on the Sabbath,[24] and they also form an important part of other weekly services, such as the Friday evening service that begins the Sabbath, and many festivals, including Passover, Shavuot, Sukkot, Simhat Torah, and Hanukkah.[25] Additionally, certain psalms are recited as a tradition when someone is ill or when a certain blessing is desired. Further personalizing the use of the psalms, some Jews will recite a verse from the psalms during *Amidah*—the most central prayer of the Jewish faith—that begins with the first letter of the worshipper's Hebrew name, thereby connecting the worshipper's name with the sacred, temple-centered text.[26] Ancient temple practices from the Second Temple are mirrored in all of these usages (with the possible exception of the Amidah).

The Christian churches appear to have begun their use of the psalms in their worship services soon after the establishment of Christianity. Paul directed Christians to worship by "speaking to [them]selves in psalms and hymns and spiritual songs, singing and making melody in [their] heart[s] to the Lord" (Ephesians 5:19). Eventually in both the Eastern Orthodox Church and in the Roman Catholic Church, a cycle of psalm singing was designed that would allow all 150 psalms to be repeated every week, such as in the Eastern Orthodox *Kathismata*[27] or the *Roman Catholic Liturgy of Hours or Divine Office*.[28] In fact, in early centuries of Christian worship, a candidate for bishop was expected to recite all 150 psalms from memory.[29] Some Protestant churches continue to imitate this use of the psalms, reciting one psalm each day of the month. The Eastern Orthodox Church uses psalms in its rites of consecration and ordination, and the Eucharist and the Roman Catholic Churches use various psalms in rites of baptism, confirmation, Holy Communion, matrimony, funeral services, ordination, and consecration of churches. With their decreased emphasis on liturgy, Protestants often sing psalms in their worship services but do not always connect the psalms directly with specific ordinances. Some Protestant churches, such as the Reformed Presbyterian Church of North America, the Westminster Presbyterian Church in the United States, and the Free Church of Scotland, only allow biblical psalms to be sung during their worship services. Individual uses of the psalms have always been important in Christianity, with favorite psalms being used as prayers during illness or times of trial, and other psalms used to express gratitude.[30] For example, Augustine designated Psalm 23 as the "Psalm for Martyrs," and it was often sung or recited by early Christians as they were being put to death.[31]

Early Forms of Psalm Performance: Chanting, Plainchant or Plainsong, Responses, and Antiphonal Music

Possibly because of Jews' reluctance to adopt temple practices into the synagogue, early reading of psalms in the synagogue would have simply used the cantillation marks—known as *te'amim*—currently found in the Hebrew text, which guides the reading of the scriptures in a heightened style of voice that resembled chanting or simple song forms, using pauses, lengthening certain syllables, and changing the pitch of the voice to emphasize the scriptural message.[32] This type of reading has many of the benefits of musical forms that use a wider variety of tones. The vibrancy of the voice tends to engage new parts of the brain to reading the words and aids in attention and memory while also signifying an entrance into sacred time.[33] The reading or chanting of texts, still practiced today and in which Jewish youth receive training before their *bar* or *bat mitzvah*, shows that the word of God should be treated differently than the mundane speech of every day. The use of this style of speech also emphasizes—by pauses, increased stress, raised and lowered pitch of the voice, and lengthened words—the message of the scriptures in a way that affects not just the mind but also the emotions.

This type of reading resembles the chant regularly used until the present day in Eastern Orthodox religions, which have preserved very early Christian adaptations of Jewish practices, and which in the Roman Catholic Church would develop into Plainsong chanting and later (in the eighth century) into Gregorian chant. The Plainsong chant, or Plainchant, uses different tones to emphasize certain words and syllables, typically by a higher tone and a longer note. Its rhythm is completely dictated by the needs of the text.[34] This form of singing without any type of meter—which would continue as the primary method of singing the psalms until the sixteenth century when metered forms were introduced during the Reformation—reflects the nature of Hebrew poetry, which exhibits a type of meter in the rhythmic rise and fall of the Hebrew words but has no form as rigidly metered as poetry such as iambic pentameter.

The chant was sung, at least for the first few centuries, in unison, although later developments witnessed the introduction of simple harmonies known as *organum*. The effects of this type of chanting, which sounds even more musical than the reading from cantillation discussed above, has similar advantages that move the congregation into a spiritual time and space in which the word of God is spoken with greater resonance than regular speech.[35] Additionally, the movement in Plainsong from one note to another, coupled with the emphasis on the absolute unity of the singers, emphasizes the unifying power of the word of God. As the worshippers listen, their bodies practically reverberating with the power of unified singing, the congregation is lifted into unity with the singers and the power of the word of God. They are separated from their worldly existence and are prepared for communion with God in an emotionally altered, heightened state.

There is early evidence in Jewish and Christian usage for both responsorial singing and antiphonal singing, two related forms of music, although both seem to have been used first in Christian worship.[36] In responsorial singing, the leader, cantor, or priest sings a phrase of scripture and then the phrase is repeated by the congregation, with the leader guiding the congregation through entire scriptural texts.[37] Responsorial singing can also contain a question from the cantor or leader and an appropriate response from the congregation. As mentioned above, some psalms such as Psalm 24 function well not with simple repetition, but in this question and answer format. The cantor calls out a phrase of the psalm such as, "Who shall ascend into the hill of the Lord?" and the congregation then responds, "He that hath clean hands, and a pure heart" (Psalm 24:3–4). In Psalm 24 the question and answer format continues throughout the psalm, allowing for call and response, although certain verses would have been sung in unison or sung only by the cantor in order to emphasize the message. The responsorial mode of singing not only allows the congregation to learn and participate in the singing of scriptural texts by repetition, but also brings disparate units—the priest, the worshipper, and the word of God—into unity as they sing the same words. Seen in a symbolic sense, the leader brings the worshipper through song into a higher level of holiness signified by the sanctified priest and his words. The repetition also emphasizes the authority of the priest and scriptural text, while it engages the congregation and allows them to reaffirm codes of morality or scriptural truths with their own mouths. The cantor (or the scriptures) is solidified in his role as teacher, and the congregation acknowledges its role as disciple learners; each plays a part in the sacred enactment of God's word. The portions of unison singing allow the congregation to progress from a symbolic disunity, as indicated by the separate singing, into a state of oneness.

The call and response mentioned above is also found in antiphonal singing, a more complex form of responsorial singing that is typically sung by a choir while the audience listens.[38] With the ability to practice and prepare, the choir can develop many more intricate melodies with memorized lines that either mirror or contrast beautifully with each other, leading to eventual unity (whether in unison or in harmony). Psalm 124 offers another type of poetry that functions well with antiphonal singing, since it progresses by repeating portions of the preceding phrase. Verse 1 states, "If it had not been the Lord who was on our side, now may Israel say," and verse 2 continues, using the same phrase but modifying the ending: "If it had not been the Lord who was on our side, when men rose up against us." Verse 3 then gives a new phrase stating, "Then they had swallowed us up quick," and verse 5 modifies the phrase, affirming, "Then the proud waters had gone over our soul." It is possible to imagine the effectiveness of these modified phrases being sung by opposite sides of a choir: progressing through the psalm, often taking turns, but then beginning to sing the various parts at the same time, and finally ending in unison. Indeed, the very parallel nature of Hebrew poetry allows antiphonal singing to work effectively with almost any psalm. Psalm 23:2 demonstrates the balanced, repeated messages that are constantly employed in the poetically parallel portions of the Old Testament. "He maketh me to lie down in green pastures" opens the verse and is followed by a parallel concept, but using different imagery: "He leadeth me beside the still waters." Antiphonal singing serves to emphasize the repetition but with unique imagery that exists throughout the Psalms. It should also be noted that antiphonal singing can be used similarly to responsorial singing, in which the two sides of the choir repeat the same phrases, at first singing at different times then at the same time (or in close succession) and eventually building to unity. This practice was developed extensively later in what is known as the fugues, in which one portion of the choir musically chases the other portion through a series of harmonized, repeated lines until eventually evolving into unity at the end.[39]

Singing in the antiphonal mode exhibits the same advantages of responsorial singing with repetition and unification of the choir or the congregation with the cantor. In the Catholic tradition, the beauty of this antiphonal singing is emphasized aurally and visually with the choir sometimes positioned in the two opposite transepts that form the arms of the cathedral's cross-shaped formation (although the choir is stationed often at the end of the nave in clear view of the worshippers). Additionally, some forms of antiphonal singing also provide a three-part division that can mirror the ritual process found at Solomon's temple and in some of the psalms. The choir's parts are divided and separated. This singing evolves into a liminal stage in which the choir sings similar parts, but the parts overlap each other in ways that are not completely unified. The singing ends in an aggregation stage in which the choir comes together in a beautiful unity of sound and timing. The congregation follows the pattern as they are listening. At first, they are confronted with feelings of isolation and then moved through a tense and exciting liminal stage before being brought, now emotionally prepared, into a state of union.

The Development of Meters; Harmonizing; Other Modern Adaptations

Since the psalms come from Hebrew poetry, which does not demonstrate strict meter, music that adhered faithfully to the text could not be metrical in the modern sense (such as the meter of iambic pentameter). For this reason, the music of the psalms continued without meter until the sixteenth century. At this point, influenced by the Reformation, it began slowly to adopt more popular, metered forms (although the traditional forms continued as well). A departure from long-held traditions with relation to the psalms began during the Reformation in connection with the translation of the scriptures into languages understandable to the laity and a growing distaste for the strict, liturgical, and ritual styles employed by the Roman Catholic Church. The popular, metered, and religious tunes that had previously been used for other hymns were now adopted for the psalms, and eventually tunes that had been used for nonreligious singing were even connected with psalms.[40] This, of course, necessitated a change in the words of the psalms, because they were adapted to the tune, rather than the tune adapted to the words. After the words were being altered to fit the meter of the tune, further alteration to create rhyme began, which had not formally existed previously since rhyme is not found in Hebrew poetry of the Bible. These types of tunes can be found in the popular book *The Bay Psalms Book*, which rendered all 150 psalms into metered tunes with rhyming words.[41]

Two additional trends were reinforced in this shift. First, although harmonies had already been in use for hundreds of years in singing the psalms, the versification of the psalms allowed for greater creativity and diversity in harmonizing by a lay audience rather than just by the choir, because it made the psalms into recognizable tunes that were often repeated several times. Thus harmony in psalm singing became the norm for many Protestant churches while unison singing dropped into greater obscurity. Second, while dynamics had previously been employed to emphasize the meaning of specific words in the text, the importance of dynamics increased in order to focus on beautifully moving music. The usefulness of dynamics in order to understand the meaning of the psalm was not lost, but this understanding now was focused more on the general concepts rather than specific words since the overall message, rather than the individual words, was seen as sacred.[42]

Although there may have been some losses in meaning with these alterations, the memorability of the tunes enhanced the congregation's understanding of the overall meaning of the psalms and allowed these scriptural prayers to be called to mind more readily in times of personal need. Because the tunes were easy to learn, the congregation was able to participate more readily in the unifying process of worship through singing.[43] With the greater liveliness of some of the tunes, the body was inclined to respond with the heart and mind in an emotional, physical response. In this sense, the tunes helped prepare the congregation for connection with the divine. These forms differed from typical forms of speech in regards to the meter, rhythm, and rhyme of the psalms, yet they retained and possibly even enhanced the sense that the singers had entered into sacred time and space and that they were worshipping in orderly forms pleasing to God. The order and organization of a metered hymn mirrored the order and organization found in heaven. In other words, the harmonies bore witness of the natural order that had been restored and was made possible to Christians through the power of the Atonement. The beautiful harmonies gave the sense that the singers were each contributing in their own ways that, in the composite, became a unified plea or witness of God's love and power.[44] The audible wavelengths created by harmony compared with those of voices in unison emphasized the power of unity with God. The increased use of minor keys that resolved at the end of the hymn and leading notes that reached completion at the end of the hymn mirrored the ritual feeling of a soul in a liminal state moving into a state of aggregation. The dynamics helped raise the soul of the singer into ecstatic or reverent communion with the divine, whichever the setting required. Thus sacred time was still marked by singing psalms, although it was in a different form than had been engaged in previously.

Further adaptations of the psalms have occurred in modern times, as their use outside of liturgical purposes has encouraged their presence outside of traditionally religious settings. Psalms have been adapted for use in the music of both religious and almost completely secular rock groups. A survey of modern usage of Psalm 23 includes such groups and singers as Kanye West ("Jesus Walks"), Coolio ("Gansta's Paradise"), Good Charlotte ("The River"), Notorious B.I.G. and Puff Daddy ("You're Nobody 'til Somebody Kills You"), Alice in Chains ("Sickman"), U2 ("Love Rescue Me"), Pink Floyd ("Sheep"), The Grateful Dead ("Ripple"), Megadeth ("Shadow of Death"), and Peter Tosh ("Jah Guide").[45] While ancient and modern worshippers might be shocked by the broad use in which the psalms are now placed, in another sense the truths taught by the psalms can be dispersed and also function to lift the spirits of those who are not completely prepared to worship in liturgical settings.

Latter-day Saint Use of the Psalms

Although Latter-day Saints often use unmetered, traditional versions of the psalms sung as interludes during their sacrament meetings, their organized use of the psalms in their weekly worship clearly follows the Protestant pattern of metered, rhymed, and altered versions of the Psalms that makes them more accessible to the congregation. The psalms that have been either put to music in the current Latter-day Saint hymnal or are somewhat reflected in the hymns are Psalms 5, 8, 16, 23, 25–33, 36, 37, 43, 47, 48, 55, 62, 68, 69, 73, 82, 84, 86, 87, 90–92, 95, 97–100, 104, 107, 119, 121, 126, 138, 143, and 145–50. Some of these psalmic hymns are traditionally used to open or close the weekly sacrament meeting, such as "We Love Thy House, O God,"[46] "For the Beauty of the Earth,"[47] or "Rejoice, the Lord Is King."[48] Other psalms are connected more closely with the sacred ordinance of the sacrament, such as "Father in Heaven,"[49] or "Precious Savior, Dear Redeemer."[50] The purposes of the psalms and of music is to create a sacred time and space and to bring the soul into communion with God. This can heighten the effectiveness of the hymns in sacrament meeting connecting with the ordinance of the sacrament. Understanding that the psalms were sung and used anciently for this purpose of connection can increase the likelihood that those who participate can obtain the same goals now.

When Joseph Smith restored the practice of ancient temple worship, weekly Latter-day Saint worship services retained a feeling similar to Protestant worship, focused on preaching the word, singing, and celebrating the sacrament. More involved ritual ordinances were reserved for the holy precincts of the temple, which left behind Protestant practices to restore the temple practices to their proper place. Although temple practices do not include singing psalms today (besides temple dedications, where music is common), the nature of instruction might be considered as similar to singing in many ways: the call and response used in the temple, the physical engagement of the body in the temple ordinances, and the prescribed, orderly nature of these ritual behaviors all serve to mark the entrance into sacred space and time, with the actions marking the movement through the ritual stages of separation, liminality, and aggregation. If Latter-day Saint worshippers were to envision the teaching, actions, and covenant making of temple ordinances as a type of a song of worship that allows them to return to the divine presence and engage in a divine conversation with God, their worship in the setting of the temple could only be enhanced. This was the ancient purpose of the psalms, and it was the ancient purpose of temple worship as well.

Notes

I offer thanks for the excellent research assistance provided by Quinten Barney that made the writing of this article possible.

1. Although this Christ-centered meaning of Psalm 22:16 does not exist in the Masoretic text, it is a correct translation of the Septuagint, and is also found in the Dead Sea Scrolls. See Peter W. Flint, *The Dead Sea Psalms Scrolls and the Book of Psalms*, ed. F. Garcia Martinez and A. S. Van Der Woude, Studies on the Texts of the Desert of Judah 17 (New York: Brill, 1997), 88; Shon D. Hopkin, "The Psalm 22:16 Controversy: New Evidence from the Dead Sea Scrolls," *BYU Studies* 44, no. 3 (2005): 168.

2. For this viewpoint, which reflects the direction of much modern biblical scholarship, see Stephen P. Ahearne-Kroll, *The Psalms of Lament in Mark's Passion : Jesus' Davidic Suffering*, Society for New Testament Studies Monograph Series (Cambridge: Cambridge University Press, 2007). 3–9.

3. William L. Holladay, *The Psalms Through Three Thousand Years* (Minneapolis: Augsburg Fortress, 1993), 37–39.

4. See, for a few examples, Sigmund Mowinckel, *The Psalms in Israel's Worship*, trans. D. R. Ap-Thomas (Oxford: Basil Blackwell, 1962), 2:29–31; Svend Holm-Nielsen, "The Importance of Late Jewish Psalmody for the Understanding of the Psalmodic Tradition," *Studia Theologica* 14, no. 1 (1960): 1–53; Erhard S. Gerstenberger, *Psalms Part I: With an Introduction to Cultic Poetry* (Grand Rapids, MI: William B. Eerdmans, 1988), 108–13; Claus Westermann, *Praise and Lament in the Psalms* (Edinburgh: T. & T. Clark, 1981), 64–79; Margaret Barker, *Temple Themes in Christian Worship* (London: Bloomsbury T&T Clark, 2008); Laurence Paul Hemming, "With the Voice Together Shall They Sing," *BYU Studies* 50, no. 1 (2011): 25–45; Andrew Wilson-Dickson, *The Story of Christian Music: From Gregorian Chant to Black Gospel*, 1st ed. (Oxford, England: Lion Book, 1992). 20; Holladay, *The Psalms Through Three Thousand Years*: 17–18.

5. Holm-Nielsen, "The Importance of Late Jewish Psalmody for the Understanding of the Psalmodic Tradition," 1–53.

6. The Book of Mormon also indicates a connection between worship and music. Abinadi places singing in the realm of the prophetic office—with imagery that symbolizes union among the community of the prophets—in Mosiah 15:29: "Yea, Lord, thy watchmen shall lift up their voice; with the voice together shall they sing; for they shall see eye to eye, when the Lord shall bring again Zion." Alma the Younger connects music with forgiveness of sin that, in a Law of Moses setting, would have connected with sacrifices at the temple: "Their souls did expand, and they did sing redeeming love" (Alma 5:9). Mormon connected music with covenant making at the sacred space of the waters of Mormon: "How blessed are they, for they shall sing to his praise forever" (Mosiah 18:30). Moroni demonstrated the importance of music in settings of worship: "For as the power of the Holy Ghost led them whether to preach, or to exhort, or to pray, or to supplicate, or to sing, even so it was done" (Moroni 6:9). In the modern day, the revelations of Joseph Smith have connected prayers with singing, reminiscent of the great Psalm prayers of the Old Testament: "Yea, the song of the righteous is a prayer unto me" (D&C 25:12). Finally, in the Doctrine and Covenants, Abinadi's statement quoted above is connected to the prophetic ability shed forth upon all of God's people in the last days, creating a great community of the righteous: all "shall be filled with the knowledge of the Lord, and shall see eye to eye, and shall lift up their voice, and with the voice together sing this new song" (D&C 84:98).

7. James Limburg, "Psalms, Book of," in *The Anchor Bible Dictionary*, ed. David Noel Freedman (New York: Doubleday, 1992), 5:527.

8. Talmud 7:3.

9. Talmud 7:4.

10. Baruch A. Levine, "Leviticus, Book of," in *Anchor Bible Dictionary*, ed. David Noel Freedman (New York: Doubleday, 1992), 4:311–21.

11. In the creation of these categories, we have adapted information from Limburg, "Psalms, Book of," 531–34.

12. Wilson-Dickson, *The Story of Christian Music*: 21.

13. See, for example, Donald Parry, "Temple Worship and a Possible Reference to a Prayer Circle in Psalm 24," *BYU Studies* 32, no. 4 (1992), 57–62.

14. Wilson-Dickson, *The Story of Christian Music*: 21.

15. See *Praise and Lament in the Psalms*, 64–79.

16. For a description of this three-stage ritual process, see Victor Witter Turner, *The Ritual Process: Structure and Anti-Structure* (Chicago: Aldine, 1969), 94–96.

17. For the ritual nature of the Psalms, see J.M. Powis Smith, "Law and Ritual in the Psalms," *The Journal of Religion* 2, no. 1 (1922): 59–60.

18. Interestingly, the same threefold division can be seen in what is traditionally known as Nephi's psalm. 2 Nephi 4:17–19 details a separation stage, in which Nephi talks of his weaknesses and trials. Verses 20–33, the liminal stage, describe Nephi's memories of how God has helped him in the past, his commitments to increased obedience, and his pleas to the Lord for help. Finally, in the aggregation stage found in verses 34–35, Nephi rejoices in his assurance that God will help him and commits to praise him forever. This threefold separation of Nephi's psalm is reflective of many biblical Psalms and could suggest a temple or sacrificial setting for Nephi's prayer.

19. "Psalm-singing, or more specifically the singing of the daily psalms once used in the Temple, was one of the last elements of Temple worship to be taken up in the synagogue, to judge by its absence from documents of Jewish religious teaching before the sixth century." David Hiley, *Western Plainchant: A Handbook* (Oxford: Clarendon, 1993), 485. See also note 3.

20. Wilson-Dickson, *The Story of Christian Music*: 22.

21. See Eric Werner, *The Sacred Bridge: Liturgical Parallels Between Synagogue and Early Church* (London: Schocken Books, 1970), 24–25.

22. During the morning service, Psalms 30, 100, and 145–50 are all recited (with some variations in different Jewish congregations, such as Reform or Conservative, Sephardic or Ashkenazi), and the Psalm designated by the Talmud for each day of the week (listed above) is also added.

23. For the information in this paragraph, see Holladay, *The Psalms Through Three Thousand Years*, 134–49.

24. Including Psalms 19, 33, 90–93, 98, 103, 121–24, 135, and 136.

25. The Hallel, a group of praise psalms including Psalms 113–18, is said on many of these occasions.

26. For Jewish usage of the Psalms, see Holladay, *The Psalms Through Three Thousand Years*, 48–52.

27. For the information regarding the Eastern Orthodox use of the Psalms found in this paragraph, see John Alexander Lamb, *The Psalms in Christian Worship* (London: Faith Press, 1962), 47–69.

28. For the information regarding the Roman Catholic use of the Psalms found in this paragraph, see Lamb, *The Psalms in Christian Worship*, 80–127.

29. Lamb, *The Psalms in Christian Worship*, 24.

30. Lamb, *The Psalms in Christian Worship*, 139–42.

31. Rowland E. Prothero, *The Psalms in Human Life* (London: Thomas Nelson & Sons, 1903), 22.

32. David C. Mitchell, "Resinging the Temple Psalmody," *Journal for the Study of the Old Testament* 36, no. 3 (2012): 355–78. In this fascinating study, Mitchell reviews

the traditional understanding of the *te'amim* in the Masoretic text but proposes that these markings have been completely misunderstood, and they actually reflect an early Jewish notation system for singing the scriptures. Although Mitchell makes interesting arguments in support of his position, he currently stands almost completely alone in this viewpoint.

33. As Thomas Carlyle noted, "All passionate language does of itself become musical—with a finer music than the mere accent; the speech of a man even in zealous anger becomes a chant, a song." Quoted in Bruce Chatwin, *The Songlines* (New York: Penguin Books, 1988), 302. For discussions on the mental and emotional impact of music discussed here and other places in this paper, see Mantle Hood, *The Ethnomusicologist* (Kent, OH: Kent State University Press, 1982), xviii–xiv; Peter Michael Hamel, *Through Music to the Self* (Shaftesbury: Element Books, Ltd., 1986), 89–90; John Ortiz, *The Tao of Music: Music Psychology* (York Beach: Weiser Books, 1997); Suzanne Hanser, *The Music Therapist's Handbook* (St. Louis: Warren H. Green, 1988), 1–12.

34. Wilson-Dickson, *The Story of Christian Music*: 29–34.

35. See note 25.

36. Wilson-Dickson, *The Story of Christian Music*: 30, 35.

37. Winfred Douglas, *Church Music in History and Practice: Studies in the Praise of God*, Hale lectures (New York: C. Scribner's, 1937), 86.

38. Douglas, *Church Music in History and Practice*, 87–89.

39. Karl Kroeger, "Dynamics in Early American Psalmody," *College Music Symposium* 26 (1986): 103.

40. Walterus Truron, "The Rhythm of Metrical-Psalm Tunes," *Music and Letters* 9, no. 1 (1928): 29–33. See also Charles P. St-Onge, "Music, Worship and Martin Luther," (working paper, Concordia Theological Seminary, Fort Wayne, IN, 2003).

41. Henry Wilder Foote, *Three Centuries of American Hymnody* (Hamden, CT: Archon Books, 1968), 51–54.

42. Kroeger, "Dynamics in Early American Psalmody," 100–03.

43. Kroeger, "Dynamics in Early American Psalmody," 105.

44. Kroeger, "Dynamics in Early American Psalmody," 105.

45. Karl Jacobson, "Through the Pistol Smoke Dimly: Psalm 23 in Contemporary Film and Song," *Society of Biblical Literature Forum*. http://www.sbl-site.org/publications/article.aspx?articleId=796.

46. William Bullock, "We Love Thy House, O God," *Hymns* (Salt Lake City: The Church of Jesus Christ of Latter-day Saints, 1985), no. 247.

47. Folliott S. Pierpoint, "For the Beauty of the Earth," no. 92.

48. Charles Wesley, "Rejoice, the Lord Is King!" *Hymns*, no. 66.

49. Angus S. Hibbard, "Father in Heaven," *Hymns*, no. 133.

50. H. R. Palmer, "Precious Savior, Dear Redeemer," *Hymns*, no. 103.

20

"Give Me Right Word, O Lord": The JST Changes in the Psalms

David A. LeFevre

Joseph Smith's translation of the Bible (referred to in the Church today as the Joseph Smith Translation and abbreviated as JST) was a revelatory and educational experience that played an important role in tutoring, preparing, and training the young prophet for his mission.[1] This paper takes the position that Joseph Smith's translation of the Psalmist's words through the inspiration of the Holy Ghost was the most personal part of the entire effort, reflecting his own experiences, situation, and feelings. It is easy to hear the pleas and prayers of a man learning the truths of God through revelation in these inspired revisions.

The biblical psalms are individual and communal expressions of faith, pleading, worship, or praise. Many of the JST changes to the Psalms turned those sacred writings into autobiographical expressions of the Prophet's own feelings and reflect his own circumstances, including the First Vision, instruction for the temple, the establishment of Zion, and the persecutions he had already experienced in his ministry. The changes also hinted at the future challenges for the Saints. In these changes, we are given an intimate

---

David A. LeFevre is a BYU Adult Religion teacher in Redmond, Washington.

window into the deep passion that drove Joseph Smith's understanding of his own sense of destiny and his profound commitment to his calling.

A careful exegesis of the changes, correlated against the events of Church history and Joseph's life during and after the translation period, show that as the Psalms were translated by the Prophet, they

- became more eschatological—focused on the last days, the Second Coming, and the final triumph of the Lord, as well as the role of the temple in preparing Saints for those events;

- offered encouragement to Joseph Smith against enemies and criticism;

- gave hope that the Lord would contend against the forces of darkness in his behalf;

- were reflective of his own revelations and visions;

- echoed the young prophet's commitment to both hear and speak the word of the Lord; and

- expressed Joseph Smith's great but still developing desire for the success of Zion.

The Date of the Translation Work on the Psalms

Because the JST manuscripts of Psalms are undated and no other records mention translating them, the translation work on Psalms cannot be dated precisely. However, several related sources can narrow the timeframe. The translation of the New Testament was completed in July 1832, and the Prophet then returned to the Old Testament, picking up in Genesis 24 where he had left off in April 1831.[2] He continued to work on the Old Testament (and review the New Testament translation, which was completed on February 2, 1833)[3] through the fall and winter of 1832–33, though no work was done on the translation from October 5, 1832, to November 6, 1832, while the Prophet traveled to Boston and Albany.[4] It appears that he had progressed to at least Isaiah by March 8, 1833, for the Lord made reference to his current focus in section 90 of the Doctrine and Covenants: "And when you have finished the translation of the prophets" (v. 13). Thus it is likely that he finished working on Psalms just prior to the reception of section 90.

All of these considerations combine to give us an approximate date for the translation of Psalms of January and February 1833. Understanding the timing of this work helps position these inspired changes in the context of Joseph Smith's life and tie them to events in Church history, and this context helps us understand the meaning of the changes to Joseph Smith, the young Church, and us today.

Increased Eschatology

The translation of the Bible provided substantial insights to Joseph Smith about the last days, the Second Coming, and the ultimate triumph of the Lord. The most striking example of this is Joseph Smith—Matthew and Doctrine and Covenants section 45, which preceded this translation of Matthew 24 and prepared the Prophet for it.[5] But a number of changes in the psalms also shifted some of their messages from a present-tense, Old Testament focus to one looking forward to the Second Coming and the events preceding it.

One pervasive trend in the JST psalms is that verses were shifted to future tense,[6] bringing their message forward to the last days and the Lord's Coming—topics Joseph and many of the early Saints were anxious about. R. Scott Burton states, "While reading the JST, . . . one gets the feeling that it is a prophetic insight on the part of the Psalmist concerning some far-distant occurrence. . . . What this means is that the Prophet read some psalms as prophetic oracles concerning the latter days which the KJV read as historical occurrences within ancient Israel."[7] For example, Psalm 10:16 reads: "**And** the Lord ~~is~~ **shall be** King for ever and ever **over his people: for** the ~~heathen~~ **wicked** ~~are perished~~ **shall perish** out of his land."[8] The original verse declared that the Lord was King and caused the heathen to be removed from the land of Israel. The JST puts the Psalmist's plea in an eschatological perspective, focused on the future coming of the Lord and how the Lord will judge the wicked and care for his own people. Instead of a plea for help, this translated psalm is a prophetic statement of faith in the future grace and power of the Lord.

Another example of a change to future tense is found in Psalm 46: "The heathen ~~raged~~ **shall be enraged**, ~~the~~ **and their** kingdoms ~~were~~ **shall be** moved: ~~he uttered~~ **and the Lord shall utter** his voice, **and** the earth **shall be** melted.

The Lord of hosts, *is* **who shall be** with us; the God of Jacob *is* our refuge. Selah. Come, behold the works of the Lord, what desolations he ~~hath made~~ **shall make** in the earth **in the latter days**" (vv. 6–8).

This entire psalm is therefore put into a future context, a dramatic shift from the past tense of the original. The events become prophetic, set not in the Psalmist's lifetime but "in the latter days" (v. 8). The psalm concludes, "**And saith unto the nations,** Be still, and know that I *am* God: I will be exalted among the heathen, I will be exalted in the earth. The Lord of hosts *is* **shall be** with us; the God of Jacob *is* our refuge. Se~~lah~~" (vv. 10–11).

The prophecy here is that in the last days, God will speak these words to the nations (the Gentiles). That, in effect, was fulfilled in December 1833, shortly after the work on the JST was completed, through D&C 101:16. Like this psalm, section 101 has Zion as its subject: "Therefore, let your hearts be comforted concerning Zion; for all flesh is in mine hands; be still and know that I am God."

In the JST, both Psalms 11:1 and 12:1 start with the phrase "In that day," a clear reference to the future day of God's judgment, retribution, and triumph.[9] "In that day" the Lord "shalt come" to his temple (Psalm 11:1) or "shalt help" the poor and the meek (Psalm 12:1). In 11:1, the Lord's people will also hear his voice calling to them: "**Thou shalt say unto thy people, for my ear hath heard thy voice:** ~~How~~ **thou shalt** say ~~ye to my~~ **unto** every soul, Flee ~~as a bird to your~~ **unto my** mountain?**, and the righteous shall flee like a bird that is let go from the snare of the fowler**" (Psalm 11:1). The phrase "my mountain" in this verse parallels "his holy temple" (Psalm 11:4), as the image of a mountain does in other Old Testament scriptures, such as Isaiah 2:2–3. God's people are commanded to flee from the wickedness of the world to his mountain/temple, even as a bird miraculously freed from its snare. Variations on the phrase "snare of the fowler" are repeated in other psalms (91:3 and 124:7) and in Hosea 9:8, so this JST change adds a fourth occurrence of the image. "Fowler" can be seen as a metaphor for the devil and his evil powers and influences. (Compare 1 Timothy 3:7; 6:9; and 2 Timothy 2:26, all of which associate a snare, or bird's trap, with the devil.) The uniqueness of this verse is that the righteous are called to flee the satanic snare with great haste in order to get to the safety of God's holy mountain.

Prior to translating the psalms, Joseph Smith received section 88 of the Doctrine and Covenants (dated December 27, 1832), which includes "a commandment that you assemble yourselves together, and organize yourselves, and prepare yourselves, and sanctify yourselves; yea, purify your hearts, and cleanse your hands and your feet before me, that I may make you clean" (D&C 88:74). After recounting great events of the last days leading up to the Second Coming, the revelation continues: "Therefore, verily I say unto you, my friends, call your solemn assembly, as I have commanded you. . . . Organize yourselves; prepare every needful thing; and establish a house, even a house of prayer, a house of fasting, a house of faith, a house of learning, a house of glory, a house of order, a house of God" (D&C 88:117, 119). This is the first revelation in the Doctrine and Covenants that directed the Saints to build a temple in this dispensation. The translation of Psalm 11 came chronologically just after section 88, so the psalm's "mountain" and "holy temple" can be interpreted through that revelation. These phrases then refer not only to a place to worship but to a sanctuary from Satan's power, an additional and powerful motivation to construct the house of God called for in section 88.

Protecting the righteous by the Lord's power is an important theme of the last days. Psalm 24 in the JST reflects this emphasis:

> ~~Who is this King of glory?~~ **And** the Lord strong and mighty, the Lord mighty in battle, **who is the king of glory, shall establish you forever. And he will roll away the heavens, and will come down to redeem his people; to make you an everlasting name; to establish you upon his everlasting rock.** Lift up your heads, O ye gates **generations of Jacob**; even lift *them* up **your heads**, ye everlasting doors **generations**; and **the Lord of hosts, the King of Kings; even** the King of glory shall come in **unto you; and shall redeem his people, and shall establish them in righteousness.** (Psalm 24:8–9)

Thus the heavens are rolled away so that the Lord in his power is revealed. Isaiah used similar language when he said, "The heavens shall be rolled together as a scroll" (Isaiah 34:4). This image is also used in Revelation 6:14 and in Doctrine and Covenants 88:95, which was revealed to Joseph Smith in late December 1832 and early January 1833, just prior to his work on this psalm.

Another eschatological sense of these psalms is one of judgment, captured in many verses but illustrated particularly in one verse: "**Therefore, thus saith** the Lord, I will arise in that day, I will stand upon the earth, and I will judge the earth for the oppression of the poor, for the sighing of the needy; ~~now will I arise, saith~~ and their cry hath entered into mine ear, therefore the Lord; shall sit in judgment, upon all those who say in their hearts, We all sit ~~I will set him~~ in safety ~~from him that~~ and puffeth at him" (Psalm 12:5).

The expression added by the Prophet at the beginning of Psalm 12:5, "Thus saith the Lord," is common in scripture—used over five hundred times—when a prophet is declaring the words of God, but it is never employed in Psalms in the KJV. In the Doctrine and Covenants, the phrase appears sixty-two times, many of those prior to the time the Prophet labored on the psalms. Joseph Smith understood well what it meant to say "thus saith the Lord." This phrase's addition to Psalm 12 in the JST makes this psalm prophetic, highlighting the direct revelation to the Psalmist. This thought continues in the next verse where it is confirmed that "**these are** the words of the Lord, ~~are~~ **yea** pure words" (Psalm 12:6).

The inserted phrase toward the end of JST Psalm 12:5, "the Lord shall sit in judgment," applies to those who oppress the poor and ignore their sighing. Other scriptures speak of the Lord judging the poor (see Psalm 72:2, 4; Isaiah 11:4; Jeremiah 22:16; 2 Nephi 30:9), but not to their condemnation. Rather, in Psalms, judgment "refers to the activity of a third party who sits over two parties at odds with one another. This third party hears their cases against one another and decides where right is and what do to about it."[10] This image of judgment fits perfectly with the JST changes to the Lord judging between the poor and their oppressors and coming down on the side of his covenant people: "Thou shalt ~~keep them~~ **save thy people**, O Lord, **thou shalt keep them;** thou shalt preserve them from **the wickedness of** ~~this generation~~ **these generations** for ever" (Psalm 12:7). The Lord provides his people with a temporal and spiritual preservation because they made and kept covenants. It is through covenants that God will preserve his people from the wickedness of the world around them in the latter days. The JST addition of "save" in this verse brings into focus the ultimate goal of that preservation—to bring the people to the salvation of God, for which they worship the Lord Jehovah.

Encouragement against Enemies

By early 1833, Joseph Smith had already experienced much persecution, starting with his early accounts of the First Vision being rejected by a local minister (Joseph Smith—History 1:21). Some enemies came from outside the Church—in June 1830, while the Prophet was preparing to baptize some people in Colesville, New York, a mob spurred on by a local minister attempted to prevent the activity.[11] Other enemies were actually Church members who turned against the Prophet, such as Ezra Booth, who decided that Joseph Smith was "Mormonism's signal weakness,"[12] or Symonds Ryder, who left the Church in anger when his name was misspelled.[13] In early 1832, the Prophet was tarred and feathered by an angry group of which Ryder was a member and which was stirred on by Booth's hatred. Additionally, in the summer of that year, Joseph labored to establish credibility with some Missouri Saints who were anxious to point out flaws they perceived in Joseph's behavior.[14] All of this opposition left the Prophet sensitive to the words and efforts of those he perceived to be his enemies, whether in or out of the Church. Revelation about how the Lord views the enemies of his people and kingdom would have been highly comforting, such as that included in Psalm 10:

> ~~Wherefore doth~~ The wicked contemn God, **wherefore** he ~~hath said~~ **doth say** in his heart, Thou wilt not require *it* **iniquity at my hand. Oh Lord,** thou hast seen it **all this**; for thou beholdest mischief and spite, to requite *it* with thy hand: the poor committeth himself unto thee; thou art the helper of the fatherless. **Oh Lord, thou wilt** break thou the arm of the wicked and **of** the evil *man*: **and** seek out his wickedness ~~till~~ **until** thou find none **that remain. And** the Lord *is* **shall be** King for ever and ever **over his people: for** the ~~heathen~~ **wicked** ~~are perished~~ **shall perish** out of his land. (Psalm 10:13–16)

The opening question in verse 13 is changed to a statement, declaring that the wicked not only condemn God but deny that God will judge them for their iniquities. In verses 14 and 15, the Psalmist pleads with the Lord that this will not be the case, with the JST addition of "Oh Lord" at the beginning of both verses to confirm to whom the prayerful words are addressed or to add emphasis and pathos to the pleading to the Lord. The entire section is changed to future tense to anticipate God's judgment on the wicked, and it seems to foresee more potential persecutions.

Verse 16 presents the first psalm change that anticipates teachings about Zion, which become more clear and direct in subsequent changes (see "The Desire for Zion" below).[15]

Another passage promises that enemies will be held accountable for their crimes: "The wicked walk on every side, ~~when~~ **and** the vilest men are exalted~~.~~**;** **but in the day of their pride thou shalt visit them**" (Psalm 12:8). "Visit" in the Old Testament is typically translated from *pāqad* (in the Qal form), meaning to "exercise oversight over a subordinate, either in the form of inspecting or of taking action to cause a considerable change."[16] The change can either be a promised reward (as in Genesis 50:24, where Joseph promised his family the Lord would take them back to the land of Abraham) or a punishment (as in Exodus 32:34, where the Lord punished the people for making the golden calf). In the JST of Psalm 12:8, the sense is clearly one of punishment of the wicked and is in stark contrast to the promised preservation and salvation of the righteous in the preceding verse. This change completes the eschatological reversal of the JST changes elsewhere in this psalm—in the JST, the wicked will be punished; in the KJV, the wicked are left in their positions of power and authority.

While many of these changes emphasize the judgment that will come upon the wicked, some also provide comfort to those suffering under their hands: "~~I had fainted,~~ Unless I had believed to see the goodness of the Lord in the land of the living, **thou wouldest deliver my soul into hell. Thou didst say unto me,** Wait on the Lord: be of good courage, and he shall strengthen ~~thine~~ **thy** heart: wait, I say, on the Lord" (Psalm 27:13–14).

The Psalmist elsewhere shows gratitude to God for delivering his soul from the lowest hell (Psalm 86:13; see also Proverbs 23:14). Alma also exhorts members of the Church to remember how the Lord delivered the souls of their fathers from hell (Alma 5:6). This addition to Psalm 27:13 presents that concept from another perspective—without belief in the Lord, he *would be* delivered into hell—at the same time poetically paralleling verse 12, where the Psalmist asks to be delivered from the will of his enemies.

In a remarkable turn in verse 14, the Psalmist's words become the Lord's direction, emphasizing the revelatory nature of the counsel and giving courage and strength to Joseph and the fledgling Church against their enemies.

Another change confirming the Lord's support is found in Psalm 138: "The Lord will perfect ~~that which~~ ~~concerneth~~ me **in knowledge, concerning his kingdom.~~:~~** ~~thy mercy~~ **I will praise thee**, O Lord, ~~endureth~~ for ever: **for thou art merciful, and wilt not** forsake ~~not~~ the works of thine own hands" (Psalm 138:8).

Many psalms are doxologies, meaning they are focused on praise. The Prophet changed Psalm 138 from a plea for God to remember his children to a doxology—a bold and positive declaration that the merciful Lord will not forsake them, giving greater reason to praise and worship the Lord.

Reflective of Revelations and Visions

Joseph Smith received many revelations, visitations, and visions prior to 1833. The most significant had to be the First Vision. In the summer of 1832, Joseph Smith was working on the first recorded history we have from him. In that history, he paraphrased Psalm 14:1 as a concept that struck him before the vision: "My heart exclaimed well hath the wise man said the <it is a> fool <that> saith in his heart there is my God."[17] During the account of the vision itself, he quoted Psalm 14:3 as part of what the Lord said to him: "None doeth good no not one."[18] Both of these uses of Psalm 14 are nearly identical to how they appear in the KJV, so it would seem reasonable not to expect any later JST changes. But during the translation work, the Prophet dramatically transformed the first four verses of Psalm 14 to become almost "another account of the First Vision":[19]

> The fool hath said in his heart, **There is no man that hath seen God, because he sheweth himself not unto us, therefore,** *there is* no God. **Behold,** they are corrupt, they have done abominable works, ~~there is~~ **and** none ~~that~~ **of them** doeth good. **For** the Lord ~~looked~~ **look** down from heaven upon the children of men, **and by his voice said unto his servant, seek ye among the children of men,** to see if there ~~were~~ **are** any that ~~did~~ **do** understand~~, and seek~~ God. **And he opened his mouth unto the Lord, and said, behold, all these who say they are thine.** **The Lord answered and said,** They are all gone aside, they are ~~all~~ together become filthy: ~~there is~~ **thou canst behold** none **of these** that ~~doeth~~ **are doing** good, no, not one. **All they** have **for their teachers** ~~all the~~ **are** workers of iniquity **and there is** no knowledge **in them?.** **They are** ~~they~~ who eat up my people; ~~as~~ they eat bread, and call not upon the Lord. (Psalm 14:1–4)

There is a subtle and appropriate shift in theology in these verses. In the KJV, the Lord is the one looking down and seeking to know the current state of things, while in the Prophet's revised psalm, the Lord is instructing his servant about what is happening.[20]

The Prophet made other inspired changes in the Bible to teach that man does indeed see God under certain conditions,[21] and the Prophet referred to this revealed truth in the psalm's message: not only does the fool say there is no God, but his reason for saying this is that he believes no one can see God. Of course, Joseph saw God and was persecuted by such "fools" for saying so (Joseph Smith—History 1:21–22).

Even with Joseph's multiple accounts of the First Vision, we do not have all the details of his conversation with the Lord.[22] In verses 2–4 of JST Psalm 14, we perhaps get a sense of that extended conversation. First, the Lord asks his servant to consider if anyone around him understands God. The servant's reply is that they all claim to speak for God, but it is a response of confusion and uncertainty, just as Joseph felt prior to his vision. Then the Lord states his position on these people: as Joseph can readily see ("thou canst behold"), they live in apostasy, work iniquity, and lack the knowledge of the truth. After the First Vision, Joseph Smith noted in his history that his "soul was filled with love and for many days I could rejoice with great Joy and the Lord was with me."[23] The translation of Psalm 14 could well have renewed such feelings of joy for the young Prophet.

Hear and Speak the Word of the Lord

Other psalms appear to address the struggle Joseph Smith expressed in his histories to be forgiven of sins and thus be ready to receive the word of the Lord. In some of his early letters, written just prior to or during the translation of Psalms, Joseph Smith wrote about "an awful struggle with satan"[24] and how he was "left to morn w <and> Shed tears of sorrow for my folly in Sufering the adversary of my Soul to have so much power over me."[25] He lamented, "I often times wandered alone in the lonely places seeking consolation of him who is <alone> able to console me."[26] In all of this, he sought to hear and speak the word of the Lord that he might better fulfill his calling. He longed to "stand together and gase upon Eternal wisdom engraven upon the hevens," praying that God would "deliver us in thy due time from the little narrow prison almost as it were totel darkness of paper pen and ink and a crooked broken scattered and imperfect language."[27] Inspired changes in the psalms reflect these same desires and concerns.

Joseph Smith's translation of Psalm 13 starts, "*How* long ~~wilt thou forget me,~~ O Lord, **wilt thou withdraw thyself from me?** ~~for ever?~~ how long wilt thou hide thy face from me **that I may not see thee? wilt thou forget me, and cast me off from thy presence forever?**" (Psalm 13:1). The JST expansion of verse 1 greatly deepens the feeling of despondency in this psalm, which already expresses a "deep sense of abandonment."[28] The author feels distanced from God, for the Lord has withdrawn himself and hidden his face from him. The author no longer experiences divine visitations, and he wonders how long (a phrase repeated four times in the first two verses) until he will see the Lord again. Most importantly, he fears God will forget him (*shākah*, which has the sense of intentional neglect or ceasing to care),[29] causing him to be driven out of the Lord's presence forever.

His concern for this outcome is because of his sins: "Consider **me, O Lord,** *and* hear ~~me~~ **my cry**, O ~~Lord~~ my God: **and** lighten mine eyes, lest I sleep the ~~sleep of~~ death **of the ungodly**" (Psalm 13:3). He fears his sins might bring him "the death of the ungodly." But he is sorrowing and praying for forgiveness ("Consider me, O Lord, and hear my cry"), similar to the plea in Nephi's psalm (2 Nephi 4:16–35), in which the Nephite prophet sought to be delivered out of the hands of his enemies but also recognized that sin was "the enemy of my soul" (2 Nephi 4:28).

Changes to Psalm 17 extend the developing plea in the KJV to a worshipful commitment to act when the author's prayer is answered: "~~Hear the~~ **Give me** right **word**, O Lord, **speak and thy servant shall hear thee;** attend unto my cry, **and** give ear unto my prayer,. ~~that goeth~~ **I come** not **unto thee** out of feigned lips" (v. 1). The phrase "right word" (from the Hebrew word *yōšer*) is used elsewhere only in Job 6:25, where the term refers to words of "uprightness" (in the ASV and JPS translations of the Bible) or "honesty" (NASB and NIV). The most important addition is the commitment to hear the Lord's teachings, implying both hearing the words and obeying them. To show his readiness to do this, the writer declared that God had "proved ~~mine~~ **my** heart" (Psalm 17:3), meaning the writer had passed the Lord's test and enjoyed visits from him in the past. Continuing to expound his qualifications, the author told God that "**thou** shalt find nothing **evil in me**"[30] and that his own "mouth shall not transgress" (v. 3). So Joseph Smith, after the First Vision, felt concerned about his own sins, but he also clarified that he was not "guilty of any great or malignant sins" and had "full confidence in obtaining a divine manifestation" (Joseph Smith—History 1:28–29).

In Psalm 22, it is easy to hear the concern of the young Prophet as he struggles to be directed by the Lord in establishing Zion in Missouri and building a temple in Kirtland but feels alone in these great responsibilities: "My God, my God, why hast thou forsaken me? **My God, hear the words of my roaring. why art Thou so art** far from helping me, and from the words of my roaring?. O my God, I cry in the daytime, but thou hearest **answerest** not; and in the night season, and am not silent" (Psalm 22:1–2). Such words are also reminiscent of a later prayer from the depths of Liberty Jail (D&C 121:1–6).

Joseph Smith's burden of declaring God's word to so many people comes through in one psalm: "When I kept silence, **my spirit failed within me. When I opened my mouth,** my bones waxed old through my roaring **speaking** all the day long. For day and night thy hand **spirit** was heavy upon me: my moisture is turned into the drought of summer. Selah" (Psalm 32:3–4). These verses naturally draw the reader to Jeremiah 20:8–9, where that prophet, though tired of speaking the Lord's message, felt God's word like a burning fire in his bones and could not keep from speaking it to the people even though it brought him great persecution. Joseph Smith expressed a similar sentiment in one of his letters: "my bowels is filled with compassion towards them and I am determined to lift up my voice . . . [though] I prefer reading and praying and holding comuneion with the holy spirit and writing to <you> then walking the streets."[31]

Joseph Smith greatly desired to commune with the Lord. In fact, one of the main goals of the School of the Prophets, organized in January 1833—the same time as the translation of Psalms was beginning—was to allow all its members to see the Lord: "The Lord helping us we will obey, as on conditions of our obedience, he has promised <us> great things, yea <even> a visit from the heavens to honor us with his own presence." But the Prophet also feared that they "should fail of this great honor which our master proposes to confer on us."[32] This desire is captured beautifully in Psalm 42, along with a sense of the writer's vulnerability to the criticism of his enemies: "My soul thirsteth for **to see** God, for **to see** the living God: when shall I come and appear before **thee, O** God? My tears have been my meat **poured out unto thee** day and night, while they **mine enemies** continually say unto me, Where *is* thy God?" (Psalm 42:2–3).

The Prophet's rendering of the KJV expression—"My tears have been my meat **poured out unto thee** day and night"—is marvelously literal, interpreting the symbolic meaning that tears have been the Psalmist's only food (KJV "meat") to reflect his constant prayers for the desired blessings. Finally, it is not clear in the KJV what the antecedent for "they" is in the last part of verse 3. The inspired change to "mine enemies" has support from modern translations, one of which (NLT) indeed uses the word "enemies" in verse 3.

The Desire for Zion

The concept of Zion was prominent in the minds of Church members in early 1833. Through the translation of Genesis, Joseph Smith had learned of Enoch's Zion, where the people "were of one heart and one mind, and dwelt in righteousness; and there was no poor among them" (Moses 7:18). Additional revelations followed in 1831 that mentioned Enoch and Zion and commanded the Saints to "be one" and care for the poor (D&C 38:4, 25, 27, 35); promised that with faith they would receive God's law (D&C 41:3); revealed the law of consecration (D&C 42); and established Independence as the center of Zion (D&C 57:1–3). In 1831, Saints had started moving to Missouri to build up Zion there, and Joseph Smith traveled to Missouri in the summer of 1831 and spring of 1832 to dedicate a temple location, hold conferences, and keep the work moving forward.

Thus it is not surprising that the JST changes four of the psalms to focus them on the establishment of Zion, a word already appearing thirty-seven times in the KJV psalms. On the surface, the addition of four more references to Zion in the JST (Psalms 14:7; 15:1; 46:5; 53:6) might seem a small change, but each addition adds a significant dimension to the biblical picture of Zion.

In the JST, Psalm 15:1 reads, "Lord, who shall abide in thy tabernacle? who shall dwell in thy holy hill **of Zion**?" The phrase "holy hill of Zion" is found uniquely in Psalm 2:6 in the KJV, though the place called Zion (often a mount or hill) is mentioned in other scriptures, such as Psalms 48:2, 11; 74:2; 125:1; Isaiah 4:5; 8:18; 10:32; 18:7; 24:23; and 31:4. The poetic parallelism between the two phrases ending with "tabernacle" and "holy hill" is enhanced by the JST addition "of Zion," since *Zion* also refers to the temple or the dwelling place of God (Psalms 9:11; 76:2; Joel 3:17).

The JST of Psalm 46:5 reads, "**For Zion shall come, and** God *is* **shall be** in the midst of her; she shall not be moved: God shall help her, *and that* right early." While other psalms plead for Zion to come down, this translation is a prophetically sure statement—Zion *will* come and God *shall* be in her midst (compare Moses 7:64).

The next addition of *Zion* in the JST appears in Psalm 53:6: "Oh that **Zion were come,** the salvation of Israel, ~~were come~~ **for** out of Zion **shall they be judged,**! when God bringeth back the captivity of his people, **and** Jacob shall rejoice, ~~and~~ Israel shall be glad." The Lord judging the people is a common theme in Psalms (e.g., 96:13) and other scriptures (e.g., Jeremiah 11:20), but this is the only reference in all scripture to judgment issuing from Zion.[33]

The most significant JST changes relating to Zion are found in the last three verses of Psalm 14, the same psalm that starts as an account of the First Vision, linking the beginning of and the major reason for the Restoration. In 1833, achieving Zion was "the most important subject which then engrossed the attention of the saints"[34] and "one of the main objects of Joseph Smith's ministry."[35] These last three verses read, "~~There were~~ They **are** in great fear: for God is **dwells** in the generation of the righteous. **He is the counsel of the poor, because they are ashamed of the wicked, and flee unto the Lord for their refuge.** ~~Ye have shamed~~ **They are ashamed of** the counsel of the poor, because the Lord *is* his refuge. Oh that **Zion were established out of heaven,** the salvation of Israel. ~~were come out of~~ **O Lord, when wilt thou establish** Zion!? When the Lord bringeth back the captivity of his people, Jacob shall rejoice, ~~and~~ Israel shall be glad" (Psalm 14:5–7).

As in the Book of Moses, Zion in Psalm 14 is where "God dwells"; his presence brings fear to the city's enemies. Zion is where the poor "flee unto the Lord for their refuge." A refuge is "a shelter where vulnerable animals or vulnerable human beings hide from attack or storm or sun. . . . It thus comes to be a figure for Yhwh's [Jehovah's] relationship with vulnerable people."[36] Because the Church needed that refuge in 1833, the Prophet's inspired prayer that "Zion were established out of heaven" was an impassioned call for Enoch's city to return and join the fledgling New Jerusalem in Jackson County (Moses 7:62–63). The plea immediately following, "O Lord, when wilt thou establish Zion?" implies, like Doctrine and Covenants 58:3–4, that it may not be soon. In January 1833—the likely time he was translating the psalms—Joseph Smith wrote with prophetic optimism to N. C. Saxton, the editor of the *American Revivalist, and Rochester Observer,* "The City, of Zion, spoke of by David in the 102 Psalm will be built upon the Land of America and the ransomed of the Lord shall return and come to it with songs and everlasting joy upon their heads, and then they will be delivered from the overflowing scourge that shall pass through the Land."[37] But four years later, after the Saints were persecuted in Missouri and had their homes and lands seized, Joseph wrote another letter with a different tone, referring to language in Psalm 137:1–4:

> When the children of Zion are stranger[s] in a strange land their harps must be hung upon the willows: and they cannot sing the songs of Zion: but should mourn and not dance. Therefore brethren, it remains for all such to be exercised with prayer, and continual supplication, until Zion is redeemed. We realize the situation that all the brethren and sisters must be in, being deprived of their spiritual privileges, which are enjoyed by those who set in heavenly places in Christ Jesus; where there are no mobs to rise up and bind their consciences. Nevertheless, it is wisdom that the church should make but little or no stir in that region, and cause as little excitement as possible and endure their afflictions patiently until the time appointed.[38]

The tension between seeking to establish Zion and patiently waiting for the Lord to fully reveal his hand was the story of the Church for many years to come.

Conclusion

The songs of prayer, lament, praise, and worship that are the psalms have played an important role in Jewish synagogues and Christian churches for more than two thousand years, teaching millions about God and how to communicate with him at the deepest, most personal level. Joseph Smith was clearly a student of the Psalter before he began his translation, for he saw in them his own struggle prior to the First Vision.[39] Even before he completed the translation of the psalms in early 1833, the Prophet's personal feelings were often expressed in psalm-like language, and this kind of language only increased after the translation.[40] This work also pushed Joseph Smith to a new understanding of many psalms. Like Nephi with Isaiah (2 Nephi 11:2–8), the Prophet directly applied the words of the psalms to himself and the young Church, and he delighted in what he discovered. The result was an intensely personal and prophetic experience that reflected Joseph Smith's focus on the last days, Zion, and the struggles of the Church, and that provided echoes and insights into his own visions, revelations, and individual experiences with the Almighty. With the authors of the psalms, he sought to worship God and understand, teach, and live his commandments: "Give me right word, O Lord; speak and thy servant shall hear" (JST, Psalm 17:1).

Notes

1. See Robert J. Matthews, *"A Plainer Translation": Joseph Smith's Translation of the Bible, a History and Commentary* (Provo, UT: Brigham Young University Press, 1975), 264–65; Robert J. Matthews, moderator, "The JST: Retrospect and Prospect—A Panel," in *The Joseph Smith Translation: The Restoration of Plain and Precious Things*, ed. Monte S. Nyman and Robert L. Millet, Religious Studies Monograph Series 12 (Provo, UT: Religious Studies Center, Brigham Young University, 1985), 292.

2. Joseph Smith to William W. Phelps, in *The Personal Writings of Joseph Smith*, comp. and ed. Dean C. Jessee, rev. ed. (Provo, UT: Religious Studies Center, Brigham Young University; Salt Lake City: Deseret Book, 2002), 274.

3. *History of the Church of Jesus Christ of Latter-day Saints*, ed. B. H. Roberts, 2nd ed. rev. (Salt Lake City: Deseret Book, 1980), 1:324.

4. *History of the Church*, 1:295, 322.

5. Matthew 24 was probably translated in late May or early June 1831, but no later than June 19, 1831, the day Joseph Smith and his scribe, Sidney Rigdon, left for Missouri. This departure concluded the work on the New Testament at Matthew 26:71 until they returned in October and resumed translating; see *History of the Church*, 1:188; and Scott H. Faulring, Kent P. Jackson, and Robert J. Matthews, eds., *Joseph Smith's New Translation of the Bible: Original Manuscripts* (Provo, UT: Religious Studies Center, Brigham Young University, 2004), 58.

6. Although some contest that the English language does not really have a future tense, these examples and others throughout the paper inarguably indicate futurity and will be referred to as future tense for the sake of simplicity.

7. R. Scott Burton, "The Hymnal of Ancient Israel," in *Studies in Scripture*, vol. 4, *1 Kings to Malachi*, ed. Kent P. Jackson (Salt Lake City: Deseret Book, 1993), 409.

8. Unless otherwise specified, passages from the Bible are presented with the King James Version as the base text and with JST deletions indicated by strikeout and additions by **bold**, following the text as presented in *The Complete Joseph Smith Translation of the Old Testament*, ed. Thomas A. Wayment (Salt Lake City: Deseret Book, 2009). Italicized words, which frequently attracted the Prophet's attention because they represent words not in the original languages, are presented as they appear in the KJV.

9. For example, see Isaiah 2:11; 4:2; 7:18, 23; 11:11; 22:12; 24:21; 26:1; Jeremiah 3:16; 30:8; Ezekiel 24:26–27; Hosea 2:18; Joel 3:18; Zechariah 14:4–21.

10. W. E. Vine, Merrill F. Unger, and William White Jr., *Vine's Complete Expository Dictionary of Old and New Testament Words* (Nashville: Thomas Nelson Publishers, 1996), 125.

11. Karen Lynn Davidson, David J. Whittaker, Mark Ashurst-McGee, and Richard L. Jensen, eds., *Histories, Volume 1: Joseph Smith Histories, 1832–1844*, vol. 1 of the Histories series of *The Joseph Smith Papers*, ed. Dean C. Jessee, Ronald K. Esplin, and Richard Lyman Bushman (Salt Lake City: Church Historian's Press, 2012), 390–97; hereafter *H1*.

12. Richard Lyman Bushman, *Joseph Smith: Rough Stone Rolling* (New York: Alfred A. Knopf, 2005), 169.

13. See Bushman, *Rough Stone Rolling*, 170.

14. See Bushman, *Rough Stone Rolling*, 186–87.

15. It is significant with these verses that though the Hebrew is consistently translated in the present tense in all translations, including the KJV, the change to the future tense in the JST is matched in the Greek Septuagint (LXX) version, providing a supportive text.

16. R. Laird Harris, Gleason L. Archer, and Bruce K. Waltke, *Theological Wordbook of the Old Testament* (Chicago: Moody Publishers, 1980), 731.

17. *H1*, 12.

18. *H1*, 13.

19. Joseph F. McConkie, "Joseph Smith and the Poetic Writings," in *The Joseph Smith Translation*, 111.

20. Burton, "Hymnal of Ancient Israel," in *1 Kings to Malachi*, 410.

21. See the JST versions of Exodus 33:20, 23; John 1:18; 1 Timothy 6:15–16; 1 John 4:12.

22. As illustrated by this comment: "He again forbade me to join with any of them; and many other things did he say unto me, which I cannot write at this time" (Joseph Smith—History 1:20).

23. *H1*, 13.

24. *Personal Writings of Joseph Smith*, 257.

25. *Personal Writings of Joseph Smith*, 264.

26. *Personal Writings of Joseph Smith*, 272.

27. *Personal Writings of Joseph Smith*, 287.

28. John Goldingay, *Psalms*, vol. 1, *Psalms 1–41* (Grand Rapids, MI: Baker Academic, 2006), 204.

29. Francis Brown, S. R. Driver, and Charles A. Briggs, *The Brown-Driver-Briggs Hebrew and English Lexicon* (Peabody, MA: Hendrickson Publishers, 2001), 1013; *Theological Wordbook of the Old Testament*, 922.

30. While "evil in me" is not in the KJV, the JST addition agrees with the LXX version of this verse, which reads, "Thou hast tried me as with fire, and unrighteousness (*adikia*) has not been found in me." *Adikia* is also used in New Testament scriptures, including John 7:18 ("unrighteousness") and 1 Corinthians 13:6 ("iniquity").

31. *Personal Writings of Joseph Smith*, 279.

32. *Personal Writings of Joseph Smith*, 293.

33. Other scriptures do relate that in the millennial day "out of Zion shall go forth the law" (Isaiah 2:3; see also Micah 4:2), perhaps implying judgment by the standard of that law.

34. Quoted in Bushman, *Rough Stone Rolling*, 161.

35. Burton, "Hymnal of Ancient Israel," in Jackson, *Studies in Scriptures* 4, 409.
36. Goldingay, *Psalms 1–41*, 216.
37. *Personal Writings of Joseph Smith*, 297.
38. *Personal Writings of Joseph Smith*, 365–66.
39. See *H*1, 12.
40. Joseph Smith's journal entries are often laced with short prayers that have the ring of the psalms, such as "oh may God grant that I may be directed in all my thoughts Oh bless thy Servant" and "Oh how marvellous are thy works Oh Lord and I thank thee for thy me[r]cy unto me thy servent Oh Lord save me in thy kingdom for Christ sake Amen" (18). Dean C. Jessee, Mark Ashurst-McGee, and Richard L. Jensen, eds., *Journals, Volume 1: 1832–1839*, vol. 1 of the Journals series of *The Joseph Smith Papers*, ed. Dean C. Jessee, Ronald K. Esplin, and Richard Lyman Bushman (Salt Lake City: Church Historian's Press, 2008), 9, 18. Scores of similar pleas are found in the 1832–34 journal in the same volume.

21

The Great Jerusalem Temple Prophecy: Latter-day Context and Likening unto Us

Jeffrey R. Chadwick

The great Jerusalem temple prophecy, found in Isaiah 2:1–3, is one of the most remarkable passages in the Hebrew Bible, or indeed, in all of ancient scripture. It is reliably translated into English in the King James Version of the Bible as follows:

> The word that Isaiah the son of Amoz saw concerning Judah and Jerusalem.
>
> And it shall come to pass in the last days, *that* the mountain of the Lord's house shall be established in the top of the mountains, and shall be exalted above the hills; and all nations shall flow unto it.
>
> And many people shall go and say, Come ye, and let us go up to the mountain of the Lord, to the house of the God of Jacob; and he will teach us of his ways, and we will walk in his paths: for out of Zion shall go forth the law, and the word of the Lord from Jerusalem.[1]

This triumphant passage heralding the Jerusalem temple of the last days serves as the lead prophecy for the entire collection of Isaiah's writings and

---

Jeffrey R. Chadwick is an associate professor of Religious Education and Jerusalem Center professor of archaeology and Near Eastern studies.

as the actual beginning of his ancient book. In this paper, I shall first explain why this is so and then clarify the latter-day context of the passage, which is set in Judah and in Jerusalem—subjects which are largely unrecognized and rarely discussed in Latter-day Saint circles. Why this passage actually refers, in its latter-day context, to the great temple yet to be built in Jerusalem will be made clear. Finally, I will comment on how it is both legitimate and instructive for Latter-day Saints to liken the Isaiah 2 passage to themselves and their own temples, the Jerusalem context of the prophecy notwithstanding.

Isaiah's Lead Prophecy

The great Jerusalem temple prophecy of Isaiah 2 stands as the lead passage for the entire book of Isaiah; it is first in the chronological order of Isaiah's oracles.[2] It must be remembered that the content of Isaiah chapter 1 was not the earliest of Isaiah's writings. Chapter 1 is actually a series of admonitions which would chronologically come right after the narrative of Isaiah 36–39.[3] That narrative reports the destruction of Judah by the Assyrian forces of Sennacherib in 701 BC and describes the miraculous salvation of Jerusalem at that time. The content of Isaiah 1 reflects the situation in 700 BC, in the aftermath of Judah's destruction, when all that was left of the Israelite nation was the single city of Jerusalem.[4] If placed in chronological order, the material of Isaiah 1 would probably appear between Isaiah 39 and Isaiah 40.

Isaiah 1 acts much like section 1 of the Doctrine and Covenants. A chronological placement of D&C 1 would actually put it between D&C 66 and D&C 67, as suggested in the heading to section 67. Section 1 was placed at the beginning of the Doctrine and Covenants not because it was the first section given or recorded but because it was specifically delivered as "the Lord's preface" for the whole collection of Joseph Smith's published revelations. Likewise, a strict chronological ordering of the chapters in Isaiah would place Isaiah 1 directly after the report of the Assyrian attack in chapters 36–39 and probably before or alongside chapter 40, where Isaiah addresses the aftermath of the destruction of all the kingdom of Judah but Jerusalem.[5] This was the conclusion of a disaster that had started with the total destruction of the kingdom of Israel two decades earlier.

Thus, the true commencement of Isaiah's writings was not any part of Isaiah 1 but the lead passage of Isaiah 2—the great Jerusalem temple prophecy. At some point in early Jewish history, perhaps around 620 BC, during the reign of King Josiah, the admonitions that now constitute Isaiah 1 were placed in their current position as "the Lord's preface" to the entire book of Isaiah. That preface notwithstanding, the nature of Isaiah 2:1–3 as the beginning oracle of all that Isaiah wrote was, and is, still obvious. It is interesting, then, that Nephi, in his lengthy quotation of Isaiah chapters in 2 Nephi, began not with what we now call Isaiah 1, but with Isaiah 2 (see 2 Nephi 12).

As the lead passage of Isaiah's writings, the Jerusalem temple prophecy also serves as the beginning of what may profitably be called "Isaiah Part One," Isaiah 2–35. This will require a bit of background to appreciate in a Latter-day Saint setting. Biblical scholars have long recognized that the thematic trends in Isaiah 1–39 are quite different from the themes which appear in Isaiah 40–66. Isaiah 1–39 is referred to as "First Isaiah" by much of the world of biblical scholarship, and Isaiah 40–66 is generally known as "Second Isaiah,"[6] although some subdivide it into "Second Isaiah" and "Third Isaiah." The general consensus of non-LDS biblical scholarship is that First Isaiah was penned by Isaiah himself, in the years up to 700 BC, but that Second Isaiah (including Third Isaiah in some models) was written by one or more authors who lived as much as two centuries later (about 520 to 500 BC) following the Jewish return to Jerusalem from Babylonian captivity. The widely different themes of Isaiah 1–39 and Isaiah 40–66 convince the consensus that the two general sections of Isaiah could not have been written by one person and that Second Isaiah does not fit contextually with the setting in Judah prior to 700 BC.

It is also generally recognized that Isaiah 36–39 was not authored by Isaiah himself, but by biblical writers in the late seventh century BC, who compiled and crafted the historical record of Israel and Judah found in Joshua through 2 Kings. The material in Isaiah 36–39 is more or less directly quoted from 2 Kings 18:13–20:19, as may be easily seen by comparing the two passages. Chapters 18–20 of 2 Kings were composed around 620 BC, during the reign of Josiah, and its narrative can only have been added to the compilation of Isaiah's writings at that date or afterward.[7]

Most Latter-day Saint commentators on the Bible reject the various two-Isaiah models, due largely to the fact that extensive passages of both the earlier and later chapters of Isaiah appear or are alluded to in the writings of Nephi and the teachings of Jacob and Abinadi (see 1 Nephi 20–21; 2 Nephi 7–8; 12–24; Mosiah 14). That passages from all parts of Isaiah—early, middle, and late chapters—appear in the Book of Mormon would seem to indicate that the whole book of Isaiah existed in Nephi's day (ca. 600 BC) in more or less the same state as the present book of Isaiah. This would render the various two-Isaiah theories impossible models for understanding the thematic differences between the earlier and later parts of the book.[8]

The fact remains that Isaiah 2–35 is thematically very different from Isaiah 40–66, but the reason why is not so difficult to ascertain. The earlier chapters, with their thematic emphasis on the threats and destruction ancient Israel and Judah faced if they did not repent, were addressed to pre-701 BC audiences that had not yet been attacked, destroyed, or deported by the Assyrians. The later chapters, however, with their emphasis on comforting wounded Israel and looking forward to a regeneration and gathering of Israel in a distant future period, were addressed to a post–701 BC audience, essentially the small community of Israel in Jerusalem, which was the only remnant of all Israel that had not been destroyed or deported in the Assyrian attacks. The early chapters of Isaiah are thematically so different from the later chapters because their audiences were so different—the predestruction, predispersion Israel and Judah in the decades prior to 701 BC as contrasted with remnant of Judah in Jerusalem after everything and everyone else had been annihilated or carried away.[9]

With this in mind, it would not be inaccurate—in fact, it would probably be quite helpful—for Latter-day Saint teachers and students to refer to Isaiah 2–35 as "Isaiah Part 1," and to Isaiah 40–66 as "Isaiah Part 2." This distinction would not only reflect the contextual and thematic reality of the two different parts of the book of Isaiah, but would also assure Latter-day Saint students that recognizing the division does not obligate us to accept the two-Isaiah theory of authorship. It might even serve as a beginning point for conversation between Latter-day Saint students of Isaiah and those of other religious or scholarly backgrounds who subscribe to the notion of two or more different "Isaiahs." The actual structure of the book of Isaiah, as we now have it, may thus be displayed in these terms, ordered chronologically:

A. Isaiah 2–35 ("Isaiah Part 1")—composed by Isaiah prior to 701 BC

B. Isaiah 36–39 (historical bridge)—excerpted from 2 Kings 18–20

C. Isaiah 1—a post-701 BC oracle, later placed as a preface for all of Isaiah's writings

D. Isaiah 40–66 ("Isaiah Part Two")—composed by Isaiah after 700 BC

As seen in this diagram, the chapter we now refer to as Isaiah 2 was the first of all Isaiah's writings. The great Jerusalem temple prophecy of Isaiah 2:1–3 seems deliberately placed in its position at the very beginning of Isaiah's works as the grand opening oracle of the his entire composition. So what is it that makes this temple prophecy great?

The Context of Isaiah 2

In exploring the Bible, it is valuable to know the actual historical context behind the writings. The actual name of the man we call (in English) Isaiah was ישעיהו—pronounced *Yeshayahu*. He is called (in English) the son of Amoz, which is the Hebrew name אמוץ—pronounced *Amotz*. *Yeshayahu ben Amotz* lived in the kingdom of Judah from approximately 760 to 685 BC and presumably spent all or most of his life residing at Jerusalem. His calling as a prophet, at a young age, came in a vision he dated to "the year that King Uzziah died" (Isaiah 6:1), which can be calculated to 742 BC. His relationship with the kings of Judah was mixed: he was mostly ignored by Ahaz but was a valued counselor of Ahaz's son, Hezekiah, who became the sole monarch of Judah in 715 BC. In his lifetime, Isaiah witnessed the destruction of Judah's northern neighbor, the kingdom of Israel, and the deportation of many thousands of its survivors to captivity in the northern and eastern regions of the Assyrian empire. In 701 BC, Isaiah also witnessed the near-complete destruction of the kingdom of Judah and the deportation of over two hundred thousand more people into Assyrian captivity. Isaiah's final years, after 700 BC, were spent in the only surviving city of Judah—Jerusalem was essentially a lone city-state for two generations. Upon Hezekiah's death in 687 BC, Isaiah became *persona non grata* in the city and according to Jewish tradition was torturously executed by Hezekiah's son, Manasseh.[10]

Isaiah's great Jerusalem temple prophecy appears to have been written at the outset of his prophetic ministry; when he was a young man, reporting a vision in which he "saw" the word of God "concerning *Judah and Jerusalem*"

(Isaiah 2:1; emphasis added). In terms of interpretation, it is vital here to emphasize that the context of this revelation was "Judah and Jerusalem," *not* Ephraim and Salt Lake City, *not* Joseph and Jackson County, and *not* America and the Mormons. Though this will seem shocking to Latter-day Saints, Isaiah, in context, was *not* speaking of the Mormons and their temples throughout the world. (How these figure into Isaiah's prophecy will be discussed below.) The context of this oracle is very clearly stated at the outset—Isaiah's revelation was about Judah and Jerusalem, and the time context of the prophecy is set in the last days. I mention this rather obvious fact only because commentaries occasionally attempt to confine Isaiah's sayings to his own era. And it is true that many of Isaiah's references have a context in his own time and locale. But the Jerusalem temple prophecy was separated from Isaiah's own era with deliberate contextual phrasing: "it shall come to pass in the last days" (Isaiah 2:2).

The specific location context of the prophecy, within Jerusalem, is "the mountain of the Lord's house" (Isaiah 2:2). The apostrophe possessive in the King James Version phrasing slightly obscures the exact wording of Isaiah's original Hebrew, which reads הר בית־יהוה—*har beyt-Yahuweh*.[11] Literally, this means "mountain of the house of Jehovah." But holding to the ancient Jewish tradition that limits pronunciation of the Divine Name (compare D&C 107:4), and as adapted by the King James translators, we express the phrase in English as "mountain of the house of the Lord."[12] This mountain is a very specific place, not merely a metaphoric reference to any holy location in general. It is the hilltop also known in the Hebrew Bible as Mount Moriah (2 Chronicles 3:1), the well-known Temple Mount in Jerusalem. The Temple of Solomon, which stood on Mount Moriah, was commonly called "the house of the Lord" (בית־יהוה—*beyt Yahuweh*) from the time of its construction around 950 BC (1 Kings 6:1) until the day of its destruction in 586 BC (2 Kings 25:9). Therefore, the phrase "mountain of the house of the Lord," as used by Isaiah, is a clear and specific reference to one place, and one place only: the Temple Mount in Jerusalem—the site of Solomon's Temple.

But it was not Solomon's Temple of which Isaiah was speaking in his great temple prophecy. The edifice built by Solomon would be destroyed by the Babylonians in 586 BC, just a century after Isaiah's death. By contrast, the "last days" mentioned in the prophecy would be more than twenty-seven centuries in Isaiah's future. The only possible contextual meaning of Isaiah's oracle is that the "house of the Lord" of which he spoke is a temple of the people of Judah to be built in Jerusalem, upon Mount Moriah, in the last days.

It is instructive to consider the title by which Jews have referred to Mount Moriah for more than two millennia. Many years before the birth of Christ, Jewish custom, as mentioned, came to require refraining from pronouncing the Hebrew divine name *Yahuweh*. By the time of Jesus, Mount Moriah was no longer publicly referred to as "the mountain of the house of Yahuweh" but simply as "the mountain of the house"—*har habayit* (הר הבית) in Hebrew—leaving the name of "the Lord" unspoken. This is the title by which it is still known among all Jews in the State of Israel and throughout the world: *har habayit*, "the mountain of the house." It is the place where Jews who had returned to Jerusalem built the temple of Zerubbabel in 520 BC and where the temple of Herod was subsequently constructed in 20 BC to replace Zerubbabel's five-hundred-year-old edifice. Both the temple of Zerubbabel and the temple of Herod are referred to in Jewish conversation as the Second Temple. It was the temple of Herod which Jesus knew and revered and which was destroyed by the Romans when they obliterated Jerusalem in AD 70, ending the Second Temple Period. Jewish tradition recognizes Isaiah's great temple prophecy as predicting a latter-day Jewish temple on *har habayit*, a future temple which is referred to in Jewish conversation as the Third Temple.

That the "Third Temple" would be a temple of the people of Israel is clear from the wording of Isaiah 2:3: "Come ye, and let us go up to the mountain of the Lord, to the house of the God of Jacob." Jacob, of course, was also known as Israel (see Genesis 32:28); therefore, the house of the God of Jacob is the house of the God of Israel—the house of the Lord. But it is also of note that the latter-day Jerusalem temple is predicted to be a place to which "all nations shall flow" (v. 3). The Hebrew term translated as "nations" in Isaiah 2:3 is *hagoyim* (הגוים), which literally means "the Gentiles." This passage could legitimately be rendered "to it shall flow all the Gentiles," meaning that the latter-day Jerusalem temple would attract all people, its administration by the people of Judah notwithstanding. The divine judgment and peace which would prevail at the time of that temple, as described in Isaiah 2:4, would be conducive to a worldwide appreciation of the latter-day Jewish temple in Jerusalem.

At this juncture, it is important to emphasize that this study does not attempt to predict how or when the latter-day Jerusalem temple referred to in Isaiah 2 will be built upon "the mountain of the house." Nor does this study take any position on religious, cultural, or political issues concerning present-day Jerusalem. It is common knowledge that the Jewish Temple Mount in Jerusalem is presently occupied by an Islamic shrine built in AD 687 known as the Dome of the Rock. The entire Temple Mount is referred to in Islamic conversation as *Haram al-Sharif* (the Noble Sanctuary), and conversely as *al-Aqsa*, in reference to the *al-Aqsa* mosque, built in AD 710 just south of the Dome of the Rock. It is generally agreed that the Dome of the Rock stands on the very site of the ancient temples on Mount Moriah. Only time will tell just how the plot on which the Muslim shrine is now located could come to be the site of a temple built by the people of Judah. All that this study aims to do is to clarify that this is the implication of the temple prophecy in Isaiah 2, which cannot be changed or ignored.

Out of Zion Shall Go Forth the Law

The final component of Isaiah 2:3 is a well-known couplet: "for out of Zion shall go forth the law, and the word of the LORD from Jerusalem." This type of couplet is called a synonymous parallel, and employs two synonymous elements within a single parallel couplet: (1) Zion, a synonym and alternative name for Jerusalem, and (2) law, an alternative expression for the word of the Lord. Let us examine these two terms more closely.

The name Zion (Hebrew ציון, pronounced *tziyon*) is another name for Jerusalem. It first appears in the Hebrew Bible in 2 Samuel 5:7, where it is a clear reference to the city of Jerusalem at the time of David's conquest. And every other time (I emphasize *every other time*) that Zion appears in the Bible, it is a direct and contextual reference to Jerusalem. Latter-day Saints have a variety of ways in which they understand the term Zion (and these are perfectly legitimate), so it generally comes as a surprise to them to learn that in the Bible, Zion always means Jerusalem, in every primary context where the name is found, including all references to Zion in the writings of Isaiah.

The word translated into English as "law" in Isaiah 2:3 is the Hebrew term *torah* (תורה). The term *torah* refers to the law of Moses in most passages where it appears in the Hebrew Bible text. The full expression is *Torat Moshe*—literally the "Torah of Moses"—but even though the term appears frequently without the accompanying name of Moses, it is still generally understood as referring to the Mosaic law. Sometimes the term *torah* appears in the Bible describing not the whole law of Moses, but a component part of the law (such as a sacrifice or other ordinance), and sometimes the word *torah* is personalized to reflect an individual's commitment to the law from Sinai.[13] Contextually, Isaiah 2:3 is predicting that, in the last days, "out of Zion shall go forth the law of Moses," although it is possible that *torah* could have additional meaning in a latter-day context to come.

A contextual understanding of "out of Zion shall go forth the law" can be a bewildering issue for Latter-day Saints, since they have generally been led to think that this phrase is describing something entirely different than Jerusalem and the law of Moses (a topic I will address shortly). Yet, it is contextually the case that to say "out of Zion shall go forth the law" is simply another way of saying "out of Jerusalem shall go forth the word of the Lord." The two phrases of Isaiah's final couplet in this synonymous parallel are expressing the same thing, identifying the same city, and indicating the same divine law. To say "out of Zion shall go forth the law" is also to say "the word of the LORD (will go out) from Jerusalem." Isaiah's great temple prophecy is indicating that when a latter-day temple is built in Jerusalem, it will be the location from which God's word and sacred law will go forth to the people of Israel.

Latter-day Saint Commentaries on Isaiah 2

Having established the contextual meaning and understanding of Isaiah 2:1–3, it is interesting to explore what Latter-day Saint commentaries on the passage have to say. Of all the Latter-day Saint commentaries on Isaiah or the Old Testament currently in print, none identifies this passage as having its primary context in Jerusalem or as primarily referring to a latter-day temple in Jerusalem.[14] A brief survey of the most respected of these commentaries is instructive. The only Church-correlated commentary on Isaiah is the *Old Testament Student Manual: 1 Kings–Malachi, Religion 302*. It is widely and heavily used by both professional and lay teachers of Old Testament courses, college religion courses, and Church classes. The manual's segment explanation (13–10) of Isaiah 2:1–5 does not mention Jerusalem at all. "The establishment of the Church headquarters in Salt Lake City" is described as "only a beginning of the fulfillment of that inspired declaration," although the entry notes that "other world centers will be included." The Salt Lake Temple is referred to, but no mention is made about a temple in Jerusalem.[15] The specific explanation (13–11) for Isaiah 2:3 quotes President Joseph Fielding Smith, who identified "Jerusalem of old" as a holy city for the Jews, whereas "on this continent [North America], the city of Zion, New Jerusalem, shall be built, and from it the law of God shall also go forth."[16] A 1945 statement by Elder Harold B. Lee is also quoted to suggest that the "law" of Isaiah 2:3, which should go forth from Zion would be the principles of the United States Constitution, which would be used by other modern governmental systems.[17] No mention of the Judah/Jerusalem context, the Jerusalem temple, *Zion* as a name for Jerusalem, the "law" as the law of Moses, or any other attempt at contextual explanation for the Isaiah temple prophecy appears anywhere in this Old Testament manual.

The very highly respected book *Understanding Isaiah* does make reference to Jerusalem, but only after identifying the temple of Isaiah's prophecy in other terms: "Isaiah 2:2 is a prophecy with multiple applications; it refers to the Salt Lake Temple, nestled in the hills and mountains; to the future temple of Jerusalem, established in the mountains of Judea; and to other temples."[18] This brief sentence is all that appears on the subject. There is no reference to the Judah/Jerusalem context, nor is context referred to—only Latter-day Saint applications of the passage are offered. Specifics on the location of the Jerusalem temple are not discussed. Regarding "out of Zion shall go forth the law," there is no explanation of the phrase as part of a synonymous parallel couplet, and Independence, Missouri, is paired with "old Jerusalem" in an explanation that "both centers will be called Zion and Jerusalem." Although Donald W. Parry, the lead author, is an excellent and accomplished Hebrew scholar, no mention is made of the fact that "law" is translated from *torah*. Rather, the "law" is identified as modern governmental systems inspired by the United States Constitution, based on the same 1945 statement by Elder Harold B. Lee that appears in the Old Testament student manual.[19]

Another highly respected book, *Isaiah: Prophet, Seer, and Poet* by Victor L. Ludlow, also makes only passing reference to Jerusalem. Ludlow's first focus in discussing Isaiah 2:3 is the Salt Late Temple, followed by the Kirtland Temple, and then a "last great temple to be built in Jackson County, Missouri." He follows up with the idea that "temples to be built in the last days in both Old and New Jerusalem will serve as the Lord's 'holy mountains.'" Ludlow describes how "numerous prophets and apostles of this dispensation have quoted verses 2–4 of Isaiah and related how the prophecy has been fulfilled by the Latter-day Saints going to the Rocky Mountains, building temples, sending out missionaries, gathering converts, conducting general conference sessions, and presiding over the Lord's kingdom." He then allows that "Jewish readers of these verses will, of course, find ready application of the ideas to themselves."[20] There is, however, no reference to the Judah/Jerusalem context, the location of the Jerusalem temple, or its status as the chief subject of the prophecy. Ludlow's approach to the synonymous parallel couplet in verse 3 is instructive but equivocal. He recognizes that "a Latter-day Saint might consider both 'Zion' and 'Jerusalem' to mean 'America,' while a Jew would believe both terms to mean 'Israel,'" but he suggests that readers "consider the phrases to be a composite and consider that 'Zion' and 'Jerusalem' could have a broad range of possible applications."[21] Ludlow's main approach seems to be application. There is no specific explanation of the term *Zion* as a synonym for Jerusalem throughout the Bible, nor of the "law" as a translation of *torah*.

The utilitarian commentary by W. Cleon Skousen, *Isaiah Speaks to Modern Times*, makes only the most passing of references to Jerusalem in its commentary on Isaiah 2. Skousen does not discuss the Judah/Jerusalem context of verse 1. He maintains that Zion is America, specifically the Latter-day Saint center in America, and does not discuss the notion that Zion is a synonym for Jerusalem. With regard to the latter-day temple of verse 2, Skousen's first focus is on the Latter-day Saints: "This great prophecy has already been literally fulfilled in Zion and will be duplicated in its fulfillment when the Lord's temple is finally built in Jerusalem." He quotes from verse 3 with a definitive parenthetical identifier when he explains, "Isaiah makes an interesting comment that 'out of Zion' (America) would 'go forth the law,' and the 'word of the Lord from Jerusalem.'"[22] Skousen clearly does not see Zion as a synonym for Jerusalem, nor does he see the passage in which the term occurs as a synonymous parallel couplet, and there is no hint of the fact that "law" is translated from *torah*. But, like those who wrote after him, Skousen sees that "law" as a reference to the effect of the United States Constitution, and he quotes from the Idaho Falls Temple dedicatory prayer by President George Albert Smith to that effect.[23]

Two other popular Isaiah commentaries, the simple but instructive book "*Great Are the Words of Isaiah*" by Monte Nyman[24] and the idiosyncratic translation and narrative by Avraham Gileadi,[25] make no mention whatsoever of the Jerusalem Temple in their treatments of Isaiah 2, focusing strictly on Latter-day Saint temples and issues. And none of the shorter, more holistic, or populist books on Isaiah themes, such as *Making Sense of Isaiah* by Terry B. Ball and Nathan Winn[26] or *Isaiah for Airheads* by John Bytheway,[27] contains any reference to the Jerusalem Temple, the Judah/Jerusalem context, or the biblical identity of Zion as Jerusalem.

From the sources above, and numerous others which are not specifically Isaiah commentaries,[28] it seems clear that standard Latter-day Saint interpretations of Isaiah 2:1–3 do not focus on Judah, Jerusalem, the Jerusalem Temple, the *torah* (law of Moses) that should come forth from Zion, or the fact that Zion is Jerusalem. Instead, Latter-day Saint understandings of the passage feature these themes: (1) the Salt Lake Temple, and other Latter-day Saint temples, as the "house of the Lord" spoken of, (2) Church headquarters in Salt Lake City as "established in the tops of the mountains," (3) general conference as the entity to which all nations flow, (4) Church headquarters, either in Salt Lake City or eventually in Independence, Missouri, as Zion and therefore the site from which the law should go forth, (5) the law as the gospel teachings of the restored Church, (6) the law alternatively as modern government inspired by the United States Constitution, and finally (7) Jerusalem as the site from which the word of the Lord would come in the millennial day.

The question that may be legitimately posed at this point is whether this is a proper and credible course of interpretation. The issue of actual context aside, may we as Latter-day Saints approach Isaiah 2 in this manner and consider it a worthy and truly instructive understanding of the passage? The answer to this, in my opinion, comes in two parts.

"Ye May Liken Them unto You"

The first part of the answer is, of course, that we ought to be teaching the actual context of Isaiah 2, as outlined above in this presentation. In addition to all of our usual Latter-day Saint interpretations, we have a duty to faithfully represent the original meaning and context of all ancient scripture. The Judah/Jerusalem context and meaning of Isaiah 2, and of the rest of the book of Isaiah, should be among the first components of any lesson or commentary we deliver on the writings of the great prophet. Providing an overview of actual context *before* offering traditional Latter-day Stain interpretations should be considered a requirement of good teaching. In the spirit of Jesus' instruction given at Jerusalem's very Temple Mount—"These ought ye to have done, and not to leave the other undone" (Matthew 23:23)—context should be offered first. And, in fact, by explaining context first, any Latter-day Saint teacher will actually strengthen the impact of additional interpretations and applications.[29]

The second part of the answer, however, is very clearly given in the Book of Mormon: we are to liken all scriptures unto ourselves, especially Isaiah! Nephi emphasized how much we can benefit from the gift of having holy scriptures. Explaining how he taught his own brothers, and speaking of scripture in general but of Isaiah in particular, Nephi said the following: "I did read many things unto them which were written in the books of Moses; but that I might more fully persuade them to believe in the Lord their Redeemer I did read unto them that which was written by the prophet Isaiah; for I did liken all scriptures unto us, that it might be for our profit and learning" (1 Nephi 19:23). Nephi also told his brothers: "Hear ye the words of the prophet . . . and liken them unto yourselves" (1 Nephi 19:24).

When we liken scriptures unto ourselves, such as the Isaiah 2 prophecy explored in this presentation, we do not necessarily dwell at great length on the original context of the passages we examine. The context of those passages is not affected by our creative attempts to apply the scriptures to our own situations in modern life. That we have a clear obligation to understand and teach the actual context of scripture should be obvious. But the instructions of Nephi also make it clear that we are allowed, and even specifically instructed, to take scripture passages out of their original context and interpret them in new and even unique ways that help us understand our own position and potential in the plans of God.

When preparing to copy lengthy selections from the writings of Isaiah into his own record on metal plates, Nephi emphasized how important it would be for latter-day readers to apply the Isaiah passages to themselves. In the very last verse that appears before the Isaiah 2:1–3 prophecy in 2 Nephi, Nephi once again exhorted us with these explicit instructions: "And now I write some of the words of Isaiah, that whoso of my people shall see these words may lift up their hearts and rejoice for all men. Now these are the words, and ye may liken them unto you and unto all men" (2 Nephi 11:8).

In light of Nephi's remarks, it seems most appropriate that we, in our teaching and commentary, would creatively liken Isaiah 2:1–3 to our own temples, cities, conference gatherings, proselyting, gospel teachings, civil jurisprudence, and even political aspirations. And the words of the Lord himself in Doctrine and Covenants 133:12–13 represent perhaps the most appropriate example of how Isaiah's great temple prophecy may be applied to our own Latter-day Saint context: "Let them, therefore, who are among the Gentiles flee unto Zion. And let them who be of Judah flee unto Jerusalem, unto the mountains of the Lord's house." In conclusion, it is clearly proper, and even vital, that having considered the contextual reality of the great Jerusalem Temple prophecy, we move beyond that context to apply the passage to ourselves in ways that enlighten and inspire us to carry forth the great works of the Restoration with which we have been charged.[30]

Notes

1. In this passage the font devices of the King James Version are retained, including the use of italics for words added that do not appear in the Hebrew original (such as *"that"* in verse 2), and the use of all capital letters for the term "Lord" when it is rendered from the divine name יהוה (*Yahuweh*, or Jehovah). It is noteworthy that there is no difference of any substance in the way this passage appears in the Book of Mormon (2 Nephi 12:1–3) as compared to the King James Version. The only differences are that the italicized word *"that"* appears as *"when"* in the 2 Nephi version, and that the term "Lord" does not appear in capital letters. There is likewise no difference of any substance in the Joseph Smith Translation version of Isaiah 2:1–3.

2. Chronologically, the book of Isaiah begins with chapter 2. Isaiah 2–4 constitutes the first unified literary block in the collection of Isaiah's writings, an oracle contrasting the ideal of a righteous latter-day Israel with the corrupt ancient Israel of Isaiah's own day. Isaiah 5, by itself, constitutes the second distinct literary block, a declaration of divine judgment upon that wicked Israelite nation. Isaiah 6, the third literary unit of the book, flashes back to the calling received by young Isaiah to be a prophet of warning to his people, and even though it comes after the first two literary blocks (2–4 and 5), chapter 6 appears to be in its original placement. Isaiah 7–12 then relates the historical-prophetic narrative beginning with the Syro-Ephaimite war with Judah.

3. That Isaiah chapter 1 serves as a forward to the collection of Isaiah's writings, whereas the actual beginning of Isaiah's prophecies begin with the second chapter, is acknowledged by Young, who notes that "Chapter 1 is an introduction to the entire prophecy, whereas with chapter 2 the prophetic messages proper begin." Edward J. Young, *The Book of Isaiah: The English Text, With Introduction, Exposition, and Notes*, vol. 1, chapters 1–18 (Grand Rapids, MI: Eerdmans, 1965), 94ff. See also the view of Blenkinsopp, "As it stands . . . this first superscription introduces the entire book of Isaiah. The poem in the first chapter was prefixed at some point to the passage (Chapter 2) predicting the restoration of Jerusalem." Joseph Blenkinsopp, *Isaiah 1–39, A New Translation with Introduction and Commentary*, The Anchor Bible 19 (New York: Doubleday, 2000), 175ff.

4. The first chapter of Isaiah alludes to events in the aftermath of the 701 BC attack on Judah by the Assyrian armies of Sennacherib, as well as the earlier attacks upon and deportations from Judah's northern neighbor, the kingdom of Israel, in the years between 733 and 720 BC: "Your country is desolate, your cities are burned with fire: your land, strangers devour it in your presence, and it is desolate, as overthrown by strangers"

(Isaiah 1:7). The reference to "strangers" alludes to the Assyrians having resettled areas of Samaria and the Galilee (in territory of the defunct kingdom of Israel) with Gentiles brought from other regions in the ancient Near East which Assyria had conquered (see 2 Kings 17:24; see also Isaiah 9:1's "Galilee of the nations," which refers to residents from gentile nations, cf. Matthew 4:15 "Galilee of the Gentiles"). Much of the depopulated territory of Hezekiah's kingdom of Judah was occupied, in the aftermath of the 701 BC attack, by Philistines, whom Sennacherib charged to move there from their coastal state. The Prism of Sennacherib reports: "As for his (Hezekiah's) towns which I plundered, I detached from his country and gave them to Mitinti, king of Ashdod, to Padî, king of Ekron, and to Sil-Baal, king of Gaza"—English translation by Rainey in Anson F. Rainey and R. Steven Notley, *The Sacred Bridge: Carta's Atlas of the Biblical World* (Jerusalem: Carta, 2006), 245. That Jerusalem, alone, of all the cities of Judah, avoided conquest, destruction, and deportation in 701 BC is alluded to in Isaiah 1:8–9: "And the daughter of Zion is left as a cottage in a vineyard, as a lodge in a garden of cucumbers, as a besieged city. Except the LORD of hosts had left unto us a very small remnant, we should have been as Sodom, and we should have been like unto Gomorrah." In other words, had Jerusalem (Zion) not avoided conquest and deportation, the entire people of Israel would have become extinct. Because Jerusalem was spared, however, the kingdom of Judah was able to recover and grow again in the century after 700 BC.

5. The lead verses of Isaiah 1 serve not as a heading for that chapter itself but for the entire book of Isaiah. For a discussion of this point and the suggestion that Isaiah 1 was composed around the same time as Isaiah 40–66, see Young, *Book of Isaiah*, 1:27–28, 28n3.

6. For non-LDS scholarly perspectives of the two-Isaiah model, prepared for a general audience, see the introductions in Blenkinsopp, *Isaiah 1–39*, and John L. McKenzie, *Second Isaiah*, The Anchor Bible 20 (New York: Doubleday, 1968).

7. For a discussion of the dating and authorship of 2 Kings (as well as the rest of the Deuteronomic history found in the Old Testament), see chapters 5 and 6 in Richard Elliott Friedman, *Who Wrote the Bible?* (New York: Summit Books, 1987).

8. For a scholarly Latter-day Saint perspective on the theory of multiple authorship in Isaiah, see Richard Neitzel Holzapfel, Dana M. Pike, and David Rolph Seely, *Jehovah and the World of the Old Testament* (Salt Lake City: Deseret Book, 2009), 295.

9. For a scholarly Latter-day Saint perspective on ancient Israel and Judah under Assyrian control, as well as the devastation of both kingdoms by Assyrian invasions and deportations, see Jeffrey R. Chadwick, "Lehi's House at Jerusalem and the Land of His Inheritance," in *Glimpses of Lehi's Jerusalem*, ed. John W. Welch, David Rolph Seely, and Jo Ann H. Seely (Provo UT: FARMS, 2004), 87–105.

10. It can be inferred from two Hebrew Bible references that Isaiah died during Manasseh's reign, and his death is mentioned specifically in two early Jewish sources and two early Christian sources. Isaiah 1:1 mentions that the prophet's visions dated to the reigns of kings Uzziah, Jotham, Ahaz, and Hezekiah, but it omits Manasseh. The reference that "Manasseh shed innocent blood very much" (2 Kings 21:16) is generally viewed as including his execution of Isaiah. The Babylonian Talmud (TB Yevamot 49b) and the Jerusalem Talmud (TJ Sanhedrin 10) say that the aged Isaiah found refuge from Manasseh inside a tree but that Manasseh had the tree sawed through, thus killing

the prophet. The Christian pseudepigraphic *Ascension of Isaiah* reports the prophet's death in the same general manner. The Epistle to the Hebrews in the New Testament makes reference to the fate of ancient prophets, mentioning one who was "sawn asunder" (Hebrews 11:37), which is generally thought to be a reference to Isaiah and the Talmudic tradition of his death.

11. The divine name יהוה is usually rendered in English as *Yahweh*; however, I prefer the longer *Yahuweh*, with the middle *u* preserving a lengthened *oo* sound evident in the theophoric *yahu* element of many Israelite proper names from the Hebrew Bible. See Jeffrey R. Chadwick, "Sariah in the Elephantine Papyri," *Journal of Book of Mormon Studies* 2, no. 2 (Fall 1993): 197n7.

12. The English phrase "mountain of the house of the Lord" was actually used by the King James translators in their rendition of *har beyt-Yahuweh* from Micah 4:1. The passage in Micah 4:1–2 is a nearly complete parallel of Isaiah's great Jerusalem temple prophecy. "Micah the Morasthite" (Micah 1:1) was a contemporary of Isaiah who lived in the low hills (*Shfelah*) of Judah. He was either a native of Moresheth-gath (Micah 1:14), to the view of most commentaries, or a native of Mareshah (Micah 1:15), according to my own reading of the Hebrew text. The notion that Micah is the original source of the Jerusalem temple prophecy should, in my opinion, be disregarded. Micah seems clearly to be repeating the chief oracle of his more famous prophet contemporary, Isaiah.

13. The Hebrew Bible term *torah* literally means "direction" or "instruction." See תורה in Ludwig Koehler and Walter Baumgartner, *The Hebrew and Aramaic Lexicon of the Old Testament*, trans. and ed. M. E. J. Richardson (Leiden: Brill, 1999), 4:1710. In the context of the Hebrew Bible, the term generally refers explicitly or implicitly to the law given to Moses on Mount Sinai, although there are a few exceptions. For example, in the passage "this is the law of the burnt offering" (Leviticus 6:9), *torah* refers to a specific sacrificial ordinance in the law of Moses, and the admonition "My son, forget not my law" (Proverbs 3:1) shows the speaker (traditionally Solomon) personalizing the *torah* as his own, though it is clear from the chapter's context that the law is that of God.

14. In researching this issue I examined every available book and commentary on Isaiah produced by Latter-day Saint authors over the last forty years, both in and out of print, as well as every available Old Testament commentary that might contain a section on Isaiah.

15. *Old Testament Student Manual: 1 Kings–Malachi, Religion 302*, 3rd ed. (Salt Lake City: The Church of Jesus Christ of Latter-day Saints, 1982), 138.

16. *Old Testament Student Manual*, 138–39.

17. *Old Testament Student Manual*, 139. See also Joseph Fielding Smith, *Doctrines of Salvation* (Salt Lake City: Bookcraft, 1956), 3:69–71.

18. Donald W. Parry, Jay A. Parry, and Tina M. Peterson, *Understanding Isaiah* (Salt Lake City: Deseret Book, 1998), 26.

19. Parry, Parry, and Peterson, *Understanding Isaiah*, 27.

20. Victor L. Ludlow, *Isaiah: Prophet, Seer, and Poet* (Salt Lake City: Deseret Book, 1982), 87.

21. Ludlow, *Isaiah*, 88.

22. W. Cleon Skousen, *Isaiah Speaks to Modern Times* (Salt Lake City: Ensign Publishing, 1984), 153.

23. Skousen, *Isaiah Speaks to Modern Times*, 154.

24. Monte S. Nyman, *"Great Are the Words of Isaiah"* (Salt Lake City: Bookcraft, 1980).

25. Avraham Gileadi, *The Book of Isaiah: A New Translation with Interpretive Keys from the Book of Mormon* (Salt Lake City: Deseret Book, 1988).

26. Terry B. Ball and Nathan Winn, *Making Sense of Isaiah: Insights and Modern Applications* (Salt Lake City: Deseret Book, 2009).

27. John Bytheway, *Isaiah for Airheads* (Salt Lake City: Deseret Book, 2006).

28. See, for example, LeGrand Richards, *A Marvelous Work and a Wonder*, rev. ed. (Salt Lake City: Deseret Book, 1972), 235.

29. Eric D. Huntsman, "Teaching through Exegesis: Helping Students Ask Questions of the Text," in *Religious Educator* 6, no. 1 (2005): 107–26.

30. I wish to thank Professors David Rolph Seely and Dana M. Pike for their helpful suggestions for this paper, which clarified and simplified a number of key issues. I emphasize that I am alone responsible for the ideas and conclusions arrived at in this study.

22

What Old Testament Temples Can Teach Us about Our Own Temple Activity

Richard O. Cowan

Temple worship is not unique to the present dispensation. The Lord directed his people in Old Testament times to construct these holy structures, and even from the beginning of this earth's history, mortals have felt the need of establishing sacred sanctuaries where they can get away from worldly concerns and receive instruction pertaining to the eternities. Elder John A. Widtsoe believed that "all people of all ages have had temples in one form or another." There is ample evidence, he was convinced, that from the days of Adam "there was the equivalent of temples," that in patriarchal times "temple worship was in operation," and that even after the Flood "in sacred places, the ordinances of the temple were given to those entitled to receive them."[1] Elder Joseph Fielding Smith likewise explained that the Lord taught the fullness of the gospel to Adam and his posterity and gave them the law of sacrifice as a means of pointing their attention forward to his own infinite Atonement. An understanding of temple worship in Old Testament times can broaden our perspective and thus help us appreciate our own temple service even more.

Richard O. Cowan is a professor of Church history and doctrine at Brigham Young University.

Specifically, temples have two essential functions: "A temple . . . is characterized not alone as the place where God reveals Himself to man, but also as the House wherein prescribed ordinances of the Priesthood are solemnized."[2]

The Lord Revealed Detailed Specifications for His Sacred Sanctuaries

Moses' tabernacle. In all ages the Savior has revealed the patterns according to which his sacred houses were to be built. Exodus chapters 25–27 contain the divine revelation of the tabernacle's design and functions. The Lord specifically instructed Moses to construct the tabernacle and its furnishings "after the pattern" he would show him (Exodus 25:9).

The tabernacle itself was to be a tent measuring ten by thirty cubits, or about fifteen by forty-five feet. Inside the tabernacle's entrance, which faced the east, was the main room measuring twenty cubits, or about thirty feet, in length. This room was known as the "holy place" (Exodus 26: 33).

The innermost room of the tabernacle, the *Most* Holy Place (Exodus 26:34) or "Holy of Holies," was a perfect cube which measured approximately fifteen feet in height, width, and depth. It was separated from the Holy Place by a veil of "fine twined linen" adorned with cherubim, which were "traditional guardians of kings and thrones elsewhere in the ancient Near East,"[3] embroidered in blue, purple, and scarlet (Exodus 26:1).[4] A latter-day revelation (D&C 132:19) speaks of angels as guardians along the way to exaltation in the kingdom of God. Hence the veil may have symbolized the division between God and humans.

Into this most sacred room was placed the ark of the covenant, a chest of acacia wood overlaid with gold, which measured about three feet nine inches in length and two feet three inches in height and width (see Exodus 25:10). It contained the tablets of the law given to Moses on Mount Sinai and so was a tangible reminder of God's covenant with his people. It also held a pot of manna as well as Aaron's rod that had bloomed miraculously—two other reminders of God's special blessings.

Solomon's Temple. When the children of Israel ended their wanderings and settled in the promised land, they were in a position to build a permanent temple. Eventually, after Israel had grown in strength, King David's thoughts turned to building a temple to the Lord: "I dwell in an house of cedar," the king lamented, "but the ark of God dwelleth [only] within curtains" (2 Samuel 7:2). The Lord, however, declined David's offer: "Thou shalt not build a house for my name, because thou hast been a man of war, and hast shed blood" (1 Chronicles 28:3). Thus, as Elder Talmage pointed out, "it was not enough that the gift be appropriate, but that the giver must also be worthy."[5] Nevertheless, the Lord assured David that his son, Solomon, who would succeed him as king, would be permitted to build the temple (see 1 Chronicles 28:6).

Solomon commenced building the temple in the fourth year of his reign (see 1 Kings 6:1). As had been the case with Moses building the tabernacle, the Lord gave Solomon specific instructions: "And the word of the Lord came to Solomon, saying, concerning this house which thou art in building, if thou wilt walk in my statutes, and execute my judgments, and keep all my commandments to walk in them; then will I perform my word with thee, which I spake unto David thy father" (1 Kings 6:11–12).

Solomon's Temple was twice as large as the tabernacle (see 1 Kings 6:2). President Brigham Young insisted that "the pattern of this Temple, the length, and breadth, and height of the inner and outer courts, with all the fixtures thereunto appertaining, were given to Solomon by revelation, through the proper source. And why was this *revelation-pattern* necessary? Because that Solomon had never built a Temple, and did not know what was necessary in the arrangement of the different apartments, any better than Moses did what was needed in the Tabernacle."[6] The record in 1 Kings is very precise in giving the dimensions of the temple's various features, suggesting that these facts were significant.

The temple itself consisted of two main rooms, as had the tabernacle—the main hall and the inner sanctuary (1 Kings 6:16–20). Surrounding the temple on three sides was a series of small "chambers" on three levels (1 Kings 6:5–6).

Ezekiel's temple vision. Ezekiel chapters 40–44 record a vision of the gathering of Israel and of another great temple which would be built at Jerusalem in the future. Sidney B. Sperry, after whom this symposium is named, spent much of his career studying the prophets of the Old Testament and concluded the following concerning Ezekiel's vision of the latter-day temple: "It would appear to me after studying all of the chapters which in any way give clues to the use of the sacred structure, that no provision is made in it for any but the most simple rites, and these are not those of the sacred endowments as we know them."[7] Still, there are concepts Ezekiel emphasized that can enhance Latter-day Saints' temple worship.

In this vision, a measuring rod was provided so Ezekiel could know the temple's precise dimensions (see Ezekiel 40:5). He was also shown a temple similar to the one built by Solomon. This new structure was to be surrounded by an outer court and an inner court, with the sacrificial altar at the center of the latter. Each court was to be a perfect square: the symmetry of these concentric courts may have reflected divine order. These two courts and the ten-foot-thick walls that surrounded them emphasized that the temple was removed from the outside world and worldliness.

Ezekiel also saw "waters" flowing out from under the temple. He noticed that the further they flowed, the deeper they became, until they entered and "healed" the Dead Sea (see Ezekiel 47:1–12). Likewise in our lives, the impact of temple blessings increases as we return again and again to the Lord's house. *The Interpreter's Bible* links Ezekiel's description with the Arabic tradition that "the sacred rock at the sanctuary at Jerusalem" is thought of "to be from paradise, and it is affirmed that all sweet waters issue from the rock, there to divide and flow to all parts of the world."[8] This vision may also be linked with the "pure river of water of life" that John the Revelator saw flowing from the throne of God (Revelation 22:1).

Kirtland Temple. The Lord has also been involved in designing his holy houses in the present dispensation. In the spring of 1833, the Lord gave information about the house to be built at Kirtland in which he would "endow [his Saints] with power from on high" (D&C 95:8). The temple was not to be built "after the manner of the world" (D&C 95:13) but after the pattern he would reveal. It would have two large rooms, one above the other in the inner court or main body of the temple. Notice how the phrase *inner court* echoes descriptions of Old Testament temples. The Lord promised to reveal the design to three appointed brethren (see D&C 95:13–17). Truman O. Angell, one of the supervisors of temple construction, later testified that the Lord's promise to show the building's design was literally fulfilled. On an occasion when Joseph Smith invited his counselors in the First Presidency to kneel with him in prayer, the building appeared before them in vision. "After we had taken a good look at the exterior, the building seemed to come right over us," testified second counselor Frederick G. Williams. Later, while speaking in the completed temple, he affirmed that the hall in which they were convened coincided in every detail with the vision given to the Prophet.[9]

Nauvoo Temple. A few years later, the Prophet Joseph Smith invited interested individuals to submit designs for a second temple at Nauvoo.[10] Several designs were received, but none suited him. When William Weeks, a recent convert who was an architect and builder from New England, came in with his plans, "Joseph Smith grabbed him, hugged him and said, 'you are the man I want.'"[11] As had been the case with the Kirtland Temple, the Prophet testified that the basic plan for the Nauvoo Temple had been given to him by revelation. On a later occasion, for example, Weeks questioned the appropriateness of placing round windows on the side of the building. Joseph Smith, however, explained that the small rooms in the temple could be illuminated with one light at the center of each of these windows, and that "when the whole building was thus illuminated, the effect would be remarkably grand. 'I wish you to carry out *my* designs,'" the Prophet insisted. "'I have seen in vision the splendid appearance of that building illuminated, and will have it built according to the pattern shown me.'"[12] The Nauvoo Temple followed the general plan of the earlier temple in Kirtland, with two large meeting halls (one above the other) with arched ceilings. The temple would also include a baptismal font in the basement and facilities for other sacred ordinances on the attic level.

Salt Lake Temple. Concerning the Salt Lake Temple, President Brigham Young declared:

> I scarcely ever say much about revelations, or visions, but suffice it to say, five years ago last July [1847] I was here, and saw in the Spirit the Temple not ten feet from where we have laid the Chief Corner Stone. I have not inquired what kind of a Temple we should build. Why? Because it was represented before me. I have never looked upon that ground, but the vision of it was there. I see it as plainly as if it was in reality before me. Wait until it is done. I will say, however, that it will have six towers, to begin with, instead of one. Now do not any of you apostatize because it will have six towers, and Joseph only built one. It is easier for us to build sixteen, than it was for him to build one.[13]

President Young described his vision to the temple's architect, Truman O. Angell. Drawing on a slate in the architect's office, President Young explained: "There will be three towers on the east, representing the President and his two Counselors; also three similar towers on the west representing the Presiding Bishop and his two Counselors; the towers on the east the Melchisedek [sic] Priesthood, those on the west the Aaronic preisthood [sic]. The center towers will be higher than those on the sides, and the west towers a little lower than those on the east end. The body of the building will be between these."[14]

After describing his vision of the six-towered temple, President Young continued, "The time will come when there will be one [tower] in the centre of Temples we shall build, and, on the top, groves and fish ponds. But we shall not see them here, at present."[15] Some temples built in the twentieth century, including Hawaii, Los Angeles, and Oakland, would represent a fulfillment of this prophecy, as would the Conference Center across the street from Temple Square.

Los Angeles Temple. Just as the tabernacle and Solomon's Temple had their entrances toward the east, that is also the preferred direction for latter-day temples to face. In October 1954 the statue of the angel Moroni was hoisted to the roof of the Los Angeles Temple and coated with twenty-three-karat gold. President David O. McKay, who frequently visited the temple and followed "with avid interest each phase of the work," made it a point to be present when the statue was placed on the temple's tower.[16] According to the architectural plan, the angel was placed to face the front of the temple, which was toward the southeast. President McKay, however, asked the temple architect to have the statue turned so that it faced due east.[17] While in ancient times, temple doors often opened toward the sunrise and may have reflected the Garden of Eden, which was entered from the east,[18] in the latter days the temple entrance is symbolic of watching for the Lord's Second Coming, which has been compared to the dawning in the east of a new day (see Matthew 24:27; Joseph Smith—Matthew 1:26).

Ogden and Provo Temples. In 1967, plans were announced to build the Ogden and Provo Temples, and Emil B. Fetzer was named as the architect. A few days later, he and Fred Baker of the Building Committee flew to Europe on Church business. In New York, they boarded a plane for the overnight trans-Atlantic flight. After the midnight dinner, they proceeded to discuss the great assignment to design the two temples. Brother Fetzer recalled: "All of a sudden it was in my mind as if I were walking through a building, and I started to describe to Brother Baker what I was seeing—the recommend desk, the inner foyer, the locker room, and then on the upper floor the sealing rooms. But the most important thing was on the floor above the sealing rooms. There was a central room surrounded by a cluster of six ordinance rooms."[19] Before they knew it, it was daylight, and the plane was landing in Frankfurt; they had been discussing the temple all night long. Fetzer later testified that this "unique and fundamental modification of Temple design concept was more than my own thinking. It was a direct inspiration given to me by the Holy Spirit."[20]

Only the Finest Materials and Workmanship Were to Be Employed

Even though the tabernacle of Moses was to be portable, it was nevertheless to be made of the finest materials available. It was to be the house of the Lord, comparable to our modern temples. To this end, the Lord directed Moses to call on the people for an offering of such materials as gold and silver, fine linens, and precious stones (see Exodus 25:1–7).

The tabernacle's framework was of the most precious wood available, overlaid with gold and covered by fine linens and costly skins. Gold was used in the innermost chamber to enhance the feeling of reverence, in contrast to the silver and bronze employed in the outer room and outside court. Nevertheless, President Boyd K. Packer reminded us, "It is not the building itself but the visitations of the Spirit that sanctify. When the people stray from the Spirit their sanctuary ceases to be the house of the Lord."[21]

Like the portable tabernacle in the wilderness, the permanent temple that Solomon built in the promised land was made with the finest possible materials and craftsmanship. Because the Israelites lacked experience in erecting such a magnificent structure as the temple was to be, Solomon turned to King Hiram of Tyre, who supplied architects, artisans, and cedar wood. Unusual steps were taken to preserve the spirit of reverence surrounding the temple, even during its construction: for example, the limestone was prepared far away at the quarry so that no sound of hammers or other iron tools would be heard at the building site (see 1 Kings 6:7). This specific precaution may hark back to the Lord's earlier instructions that Moses should make an altar of unhewn stones (see Exodus 20:24–25). Interestingly, however, Solomon's altar would not be made of stone.

With the aid of Hiram's craftsmen, several large objects of bronze were prepared for the area immediately in front of the temple. One was the altar, which was twenty feet high and more than thirty feet square at its base (see 2 Chronicles 4:1). Another was the "molten sea" or large font of bronze, which measured over thirty feet in diameter, weighed over twenty-five tons, and had a capacity of at least twelve thousand gallons. It was mounted on the backs of twelve oxen, three facing toward each of the cardinal points of the compass (1 Kings 7:23–26).[22] These twelve oxen were symbolic of the twelve tribes of Israel.[23]

In his discussion about Solomon's Temple, James E. Talmage noted that "the temple workmen numbered scores of thousands, and every department was in charge of master craftsmen. To serve on the great structure in any capacity was an honor; and labor acquired a dignity never before recognized." He concluded that "the erection of the Temple of Solomon was an epoch-making event, not alone in the history of Israel, but in that of the world."[24]

Similarly, in the present dispensation, God's people must be willing to sacrifice in order to provide these holy sanctuaries. For example, the dedicatory prayer of the Kirtland Temple acknowledged, "We have done this work through great tribulation; and out of our poverty we have given of our substance to build a house to thy name" (D&C 109:5). Later, the revelation directing construction of the Nauvoo Temple invited, "Come ye, with all your gold, and your silver, and your precious stones, and with all your antiquities; and with all who have knowledge of antiquities, that will come, may come, and bring the box tree, and the fir tree, and the pine tree, together with all the precious trees of the earth; and with iron, with copper, and with brass, and with zinc, and with all your precious things of the earth; and build a house to my name, for the Most High to dwell therein" (D&C 124:26–27). Among Latter-day Saint architects and contractors, the phrase *temple quality* has come to represent the highest standards for materials and workmanship.

Temple Dedications Were Times of Rejoicing

After seven and a half years, Solomon's Temple was completed. Its dedication was a milestone in the history of Israel and a spiritual feast for the people. King Solomon, the leaders of all the tribes, and a throng of people representing "all the congregation of Israel" gathered in the court directly in front of the temple (see 1 Kings 8:1–5). As the ark of the covenant was taken into the Most Holy Place, God's glory filled the house like a cloud, and after the people offered sacrifices, the king dedicated the temple to the Lord: "I have surely built thee an house to dwell in," he prayed, "a settled place for thee to abide in for ever" (1 Kings 8:13). King Solomon concluded his dedicatory prayer by petitioning: "The Lord our God be with us, as he was with our fathers: let him not leave us, nor forsake us: that he may incline our hearts unto him, to walk in all his ways, and to keep his commandments" (1 Kings 8: 57–58). At the conclusion of the days of dedication, the people left in a similar manner to that of the faithful in later dispensations, "joyful and glad of heart for all the goodness that the Lord had done" for them (1 Kings 8:66).

In the present dispensation, the dedication of the Kirtland Temple was likewise a joyous occasion climaxing a season of remarkable spiritual outpourings.[25] The dedicatory prayer, given by revelation (D&C 109), set the pattern for prayers at subsequent temple dedications. It was written out and then read by the Prophet, perhaps so that it would be delivered word for word in each of the two dedicatory services. The prayer covered a variety of concerns. The Prophet prayed that "thy glory may rest down upon thy people, and upon this thy house, which we now dedicate to thee, that it may be sanctified and consecrated to be holy, and that thy holy presence may be continually in this house" (D&C 109:12). He also prayed for "the nations of the earth" and their leaders and for the gathering of Israel (D&C 109:54, 61). The Prophet concluded his prayer of dedication by asking the Lord to bless the General Authorities and their families and to help his work roll forth in preparation for the glorious Second Coming (see D&C 109:68–76).

Subsequent temple dedicatory prayers have included ideas similar to those revealed by the Lord at Kirtland. Supplications for protection were typical, but several of the prayers reflected unique local circumstances. For example, Provo's dedicatory prayer petitioned, "Let that great temple of learning—the Brigham Young University . . .—be prospered to the full. Let Thy enlightening power rest upon those who teach and those who are taught."[26]

Dedicatory prayers have been followed by the sacred Hosanna Shout, which is an expression of joyous praise. The word *hosanna* literally means "save now."[27] In ancient times, this shout was typically given out of doors and included the waving of leafy tree branches. In modern times, white handkerchiefs have been substituted, as the Hosanna Shout has generally been given indoors. It has been a regular part of every temple dedication and has been rendered on a few other occasions, including the 1892 placing of the Salt Lake Temple capstone, the 1930 centennial general conference, and the

2000 dedication of the Conference Center adjacent to Temple Square. The shout is also reflected in the chorus of "The Spirit of God." This hymn has been sung at the dedication of every temple, often in conjunction with a choir singing the "Hosanna Anthem" composed for the Salt Lake Temple's dedication.[28]

Preparation Essential for Serving in the Temple

Old Testament scriptures emphasized that those who participated in temple worship needed to be prepared. Specifically, the priests who officiated had to be ordained or consecrated. Each time they entered the temple they were washed with water and clothed in "holy garments." On certain occasions they were also anointed with pure olive oil. The Lord directed, "And thou shalt bring Aaron and his sons unto the door of the tabernacle of the congregation, and wash them with water. And thou shalt put upon Aaron the holy garments, and anoint him, and sanctify him; that he may minister unto me in the priest's office" (Exodus 40:12–13; compare Exodus 29:4–7). This anointing had special meaning because ancient people attributed life-giving powers to olive oil: "[it] was associated with prosperity, wealth, cleansing, healing, and purity and symbolized the Spirit."[29] It was used as an ingredient in cooking, as a source of heat and light, and as a medicine.[30] Some ancient people even identified the olive tree with the tree of life.[31] Furthermore, kings and queens were customarily anointed with olive oil as part of their coronation. Hence the anointing with this oil in the temple could have reminded the worshipper of his or her potential to become a king or queen in the kingdom of God.

The "holy garments" worn by the priests included white linen breeches or trousers, a "coat" and a "girdle" (translated as "tunic" and "sash" in many modern English versions), and "bonnets" ("hats" or "caps" in Hebrew) (Exodus 28:40–42). Their whiteness suggested cleanliness, purity, or heavenliness. In addition, the high priest wore other garments with colored embroidery, including an *ephod* (a long, intricately woven apron), a robe, and a *mitre* (a crown or turban); the ephod supported the breastplate containing the Urim and Thummim (see Exodus 28:4–7, 22–30, 39).

The high priest's hat also had a pure gold plate just above the forehead bearing the inscription "Holiness to the Lord" (Exodus 28:36–38).[32] This phrase is also inscribed on all Latter-day Saint temples, suggesting the purpose and spirit of the holy work done there. President James E. Faust admired how this phrase not only appeared on the facade of the Salt Lake Temple but also adorned even its doorknobs. For him, this meant that "the days of our lives will be greatly blessed as we frequent the temples to learn the transcending spiritual relations we have with Deity. We need to try harder to be found standing in holy places."[33]

Sacred Ordinances in Old Testament Times

From the beginning of scriptural history, God instructed his people to sacrifice the "firstlings of their flocks." An angel informed Adam that these offerings were a "similitude of the sacrifice of the Only Begotten of the Father" (Moses 5:5–7). Other Old Testament patriarchs, including Noah, Abraham, Isaac, and Jacob, continued the practice of erecting altars and offering sacrifices (see Genesis 8:20; 12:7–8; 13:18; 26:25; 33:20; and 35:7). After Jacob saw his dream of the ladder reaching into heaven and received great promises from the Lord, he named the place where he received this vision *Bethel* (which in Hebrew literally means "the house of God"), and he referred to it as "the gate of heaven" (Genesis 28:17). Commenting on this, Marion G. Romney wrote, "Temples are to us all what Bethel was to Jacob. Even more, they are also the gates to heaven for all of our unendowed kindred dead. We should all do our duty in bringing our loved ones through them."[34]

The Lord specified to Moses that such altars should be constructed of stones in their natural state—not shaped by human tools (see Exodus 20:24–25). Because these altars were thought of as being places between heaven and earth, they may appropriately be regarded as forerunners of the holy houses in which the Lord promised to communicate with his people.

The Old Testament describes in detail the sacrifices and other performances associated with the lesser or Aaronic Priesthood and with the Mosaic "law of carnal commandments," but it says nothing about any higher ordinances. Still, the tabernacle's furnishings and ordinances taught the children of Israel how they must prepare in order to return to the presence of God. The altar of sacrifice was the most prominent object in the tabernacle's courtyard; constructed of acacia wood and overlaid with bronze, it stood nearly five feet tall and measured nearly eight feet square at the base. It was here that the people complied with the Lord's commands to make animal sacrifices and other offerings, which served as a reminder of his great future atoning sacrifice and reemphasized the vital principles of obedience and sacrifice. Between the altar and the tabernacle was the *laver*, or large bronze water basin, in which the priests washed their hands and feet before entering the tabernacle or before officiating at the altar (see Exodus 30:18–21). In this ritual we see the symbolism of becoming clean in order to progress back to God's presence.

Elder Mark. E. Petersen believed that these sacred rites helped define the hallowed nature of the tabernacle: "The tabernacle was but a forerunner of the temple," he explained, because "sacred ordinances were performed therein."[35]

By the time of Solomon's Temple, these rites had experienced further development. As Old Testament scholars William J. Hamblin and David R. Seely put it, "Temple worship focused on a complex series of animal sacrifices for thanksgiving, atonement, and purification from sin." During the three major feasts of the year—Passover, Pentecost, and Tabernacles—"the people celebrated and renewed their covenantal relationship with God."[36]

Modern revelation affirms that both the tabernacle of Moses and the Temple of Solomon were built so that "those ordinances might be revealed which had been hid from before the world was" (D&C 124:38). Even though Moses and the higher priesthood had been taken from the Israelites as a whole (see D&C 84:24–27), Latter-day Saint writers have offered the opinion that the Lord's people in Old Testament times nevertheless had access to ordinances linked to the Melchizedek Priesthood, probably even including some temple ordinances. "One has only to read the scriptures carefully, particularly the modern scriptures," stated Sidney B. Sperry, a respected Latter-day Saint scholar of the scriptures, "to discover that temples [or other holy sanctuaries] must have been built and used in great antiquity even in the days of the antediluvian patriarchs."[37] He reasoned that the Lord's requirements for exaltation, and therefore the need for temples, were the same then as they are now.

Speaking at the opening of the St. George Temple, Brigham Young declared that Solomon had built his temple "for the purpose of giving endowments," but President Young then acknowledged that "few if any" of these ordinances were actually received at that time.[38] Additionally, a revelation given through Joseph Smith indicates that the ancient patriarchs and prophets held the sealing power (D&C 132:39). He taught that Elijah was the last to hold these keys before the coming of the Savior.[39]

The nature and extent of these ancient ordinances as well as the exact location inside the temple buildings where they were performed have been the subject of much conjecture. For example, the purpose of the small chambers surrounding Solomon's Temple is not specified, but there have been suggestions that they could have been used for various sacred purposes as well as for storage of clothing and other items used in temple service. W. Cleon Skousen offered particularly specific opinions, which many scholars consider speculative, on where he believed the endowment was received in the tabernacle of Moses and Temple of Solomon.[40]

"Such ordinances are sacred and not for the world," Elder Joseph Fielding Smith concluded; therefore, no detailed account of them has been made available. "There are, however, in the Old Testament references to covenants and obligations under which the members of the Church in those days were placed, although the meaning is generally obscure."[41]

Although vicarious service for the dead was not inaugurated until New Testament times, Latter-day Saints believe that ordinances for the living were available during earlier dispensations. The verb *wash* is used in reference to sacred rituals performed anciently (see, for example, Exodus 29:4, 30:18, 40:12). Elder Joseph Fielding Smith was convinced that Old Testament washings included baptisms (the word *baptism* was introduced in New Testament times from Greek roots).[42] Even though these Old Testament baptisms were only for the living, latter-day temple fonts used in baptisms for the dead have been patterned after the sea in Solomon's Temple.[43]

The Temple as a Place of Revelation

Dr. Hugh Nibley, a noted Latter-day Saint scholar, spent years researching what various ancient religions understood temples to be. That which makes a temple different from other buildings is not just its sacredness, he concluded, but rather its unique function. The earliest temples were regarded as "meeting-places at which men at specific times attempted to make contact with the powers above."[44] In this respect they resembled sacred mountains, which originally had been similar places of "contact between this and the upper world."[45] These ancient peoples thought of the temple as being the highest point in the human world, the best place to observe and learn the ways of the heavens. Consequently, many ancient temples were built atop mountains, but even if they were physically in the valley, they were still regarded as spiritual peaks where one could be closest to God. In a very real sense the temple represented a halfway place between heaven and earth.[46]

Ziggurats in Mesopotamia, as well as Mayan pyramids in ancient America, had the function of supporting the temples built on top of them and elevating them closer to heaven. Consequently, the prominent stairways up their sides came to symbolize the pathway leading from the human to the divine world. Perhaps the best known of these Mesopotamian ziggurats was the Tower of Babel (see Genesis 11:1–9). Although the builders' motives were materialistic and selfish, the name of this tower does reflect a true function of temples. In the ancient Babylonian language (as well as in modern Arabic), the syllable *Bab-* meant "gate," while the suffix *-el* was a widely recognized reference to "deity." Hence the name *Babel* literally means "the gate of the god."[47]

The tabernacle that the Lord commanded Moses to build was to serve both purposes mentioned by Elder Talmage: in addition to being a place for ordinances, it was also to be a place of revelation. The Lord directed his people to "make me a sanctuary; that I may dwell among them" (Exodus 25:8). He specifically promised to appear above the ark of the covenant, whose solid-gold lid was topped with two cherubim (see Exodus 25:18–22). The Hebrew name of this lid, *kappōret*, is related to the verb *kappar*, meaning to cover, expiate, atone, or forgive, and it is translated as "mercy seat" in the King James Bible. The Greek Old Testament calls this object the *hilasterion*, which is the same word used to refer to Christ's Atonement. This is also the word used in the New Testament to refer to Christ as the "propitiation" (or reconciliation) for sin (see Romans 3:25).[48] Appropriately, the author of the Atonement promised to reveal himself above the object bearing that very title. Hence the ark with its mercy seat powerfully represented God's atoning love. Jesus subsequently fulfilled the promise to manifest himself: "And it came to pass, as Moses entered into the tabernacle, the cloudy pillar descended, and stood at the door of the tabernacle, and the Lord talked with Moses . . . face to face, as a man speaketh unto his friend" (Exodus 33:9–11).

As had been the case with the tabernacle of Moses, the innermost room of Solomon's Temple was the most sacred area. Its Hebrew name *debhîr* may shed light on the nature of this holiest place. Some Bible commentators have associated *debhîr* with a Semitic root referring to the back or rear part, hence the translation "inner sanctuary" in the revised Standard and New International Versions.[49] Others have linked this name with the Hebrew word *dābhar*, meaning "to speak," perhaps referring to the fact that this was the place in the temple where the Lord would speak to his people. This may be why the King James translators called this room the "oracle" (meaning place of revelation).

Worthiness and Admission

People sometimes ask why Mormon temples are not open to just anybody. The Old Testament provides a key to answer this question. As the Israelites pitched their camp, the twelve tribes were arranged around the tabernacle as if to provide a protective shield from the outside world. This layout of the ancient tabernacle grounds emphasized its sacredness and separation from the world. At the innermost was located the tribe of Levi, which included those with priestly authority (see Numbers 2–3). The open "court" surrounding the tabernacle, measuring approximately 75 by 150 feet, was enclosed by a wall of fabric panels approximately eight feet high, and it represented an additional protection (see Exodus 38:9–12).

Admission to these holy precincts was progressively more restricted as one approached the ark. While all worthy Israelites could enter the open courtyard, only the priests were allowed in the tabernacle's outer room. Only one man, the high priest, was permitted to enter the inner Most Holy Place, and he could do so only once each year—on the Day of Atonement, or *Yom Kippur* (see Leviticus 16:29–34). The Apostle Paul later explained that this foreshadowed the Savior's atoning sacrifice: just as the ancient high priest entered the earthly tabernacle once each year and offered a blood sacrifice "for himself, and for the errors of the people," even so Christ, the great "high priest of good things to come," entered into the heavenly tabernacle and "by his own blood . . . obtained eternal redemption for us" (Hebrews 9:7, 11–12, 24).

Interestingly, the phrase *Holy of Holies* does not occur anywhere in the Latter-day Saint standard works. The King James Bible's Most Holy Place is translated from the Hebrew *qōdesh haqqŏdāshīm*, which is related to the verb *qadash*, meaning "to separate, reserve, or set apart for sacred purposes." Hence *qōdesh haqqŏdāshīm* is a Hebrew phrase literally referring to "that which is holy among all things that are holy." This type of construction implies the superlative as in Christ's title "King of Kings, and Lord of Lords" (Revelation 19:16). Wycliffe's 1382 Bible used the phrase "holi of halowes," while the King James Bible employed the phrase "most holy place." Milton was first to use the present wording "Holy of holies" in 1641, thirty years after the King James Bible had been published.[50] In recent years the New English Bible and the Jewish Publication Society's Old Testament have also used the term "Holy of Holies."

The Temple of Solomon was similarly set apart from the outside world by a "great court" and by an "inner court of the house of the Lord" (1 Kings 7:12). At least one passage (2 Kings 20:4) also mentions a "middle court." We are specifically told that this temple's innermost room was the *qodesh ha-qadashim*, or Holy of Holies (see 1 Kings 6:16).

As has been seen, Ezekiel's vision was of a temple separated from the world by two courts and a thick wall. A similar plan for a future ideal temple is found in the Temple Scroll, which is the longest of the Dead Sea Scrolls and which dated from just before the time of Christ.[51] Though this scroll is not to be regarded as inspired scripture, it does to some degree reflect concepts revealed in earlier centuries concerning temples. The Temple Scroll's plan provided for an even greater separation of the temple from the wicked world. It was to be surrounded by a protective low fence or balustrade, an inner court, a middle court, an outer court (nearly a half-mile square), and finally a 150-foot-wide moat. The scroll's greatest emphasis is on the need for personal purity on the part of all who would enter the temple. Elaborate laws of purification governed the temple and its surroundings. Even the whole city where the temple was located was to be kept holy and pure.[52] This was consistent with the Lord's desire that his people should be "a kingdom of priests, and an holy nation" (Exodus 19:6).

The Psalmist referred to the need to be worthy to enter the temple: "Who shall ascend into the hill of the Lord? or who shall stand in his holy place? He that hath clean hands, and a pure heart; who hath not lifted up his soul unto vanity, nor sworn deceitfully" (Psalm 24:3–4). Elder Robert D. Hales likened these questions to a temple recommend interview. He concluded that "worthiness to hold a temple recommend gives us the strength to keep our temple covenants."[53]

Conclusion

A study of Old Testament temples confirms that the Lord has been involved in designing these holy structures and that they should be built of the finest materials available. This practice has remained in place in modern times. The precise extent of temple ordinances and where they were performed in Old Testament times is not fully known, but the Bible makes clear that those who served in the temple needed to prepare for this sacred experience. Similarly, we prepare for temple activity by keeping the commandments and praying for the Spirit, looking forward to being in the Lord's house. Because the temple was to be a place of communication between God and man, it had to be kept pure; this brought certain restrictions on who would be considered worthy to enter these holy precincts. In like spirit, we respond to searching questions during our temple recommend interviews to assure our own spiritual preparedness. Even though parallels between present and ancient practices are not always exact, a study of Old Testament temples does enhance our understanding of our own temple service.

Notes

1. John A. Widtsoe, "Temple Worship," *Utah Genealogical and Historical Magazine*, April 1921, 52.

2. James E. Talmage, *The House of the Lord* (Salt Lake City: Bookcraft, 1962), 17.

3. Richard Neitzel Holzapfel, Dana M. Pike, and David Rolph Seely, *Jehovah and the World of the Old Testament* (Salt Lake City: Deseret Book, 2009), 106.

4. See Bible Dictionary, "tabernacle," 778–80.

5. Talmage, *The House of the Lord*, 6.

6. Brigham Young, in *Journal of Discourses* (London: Latter-day Saints' Book Depot, 1854–86), 2:30; emphasis in original.

7. Sidney B. Sperry, *The Voice of Israel's Prophets: A Latter-day Saint Interpretation of the Major and Minor Prophets of the Old Testament* (Salt Lake City: Deseret Book, 1961), 231.

8. George Arthur Buttrick and others, *The Interpreter's Bible* (New York: Abingdon Press, 1956), 6:326.

9. Truman O. Angell, autobiographical sketch, MS 3, Harold B. Lee Library, Brigham Young University, Provo, UT, quoted in Marvin E. Smith, "The Builder," *Improvement Era*, October 1942, 630.

10. For an excellent discussion of the Nauvoo Temple and its construction, see Don F. Colvin, *Nauvoo Temple: A Story of Faith* (American Fork, UT: Covenant Communications, 2002).

11. F. M. Weeks to J. Earl Arrington, March 7, 1932, quoted in J. Earl Arrington, "William Weeks, Architect of the Nauvoo Temple," *BYU Studies* 19, no. 3 (Spring 1979): 340.

12. Joseph Smith, *History of the Church of Jesus Christ of Latter-day Saints*, ed. B. H. Roberts, 2nd ed. rev. (Salt Lake City: Deseret Book, 1957), 6:196–97; emphasis in original.

13. Brigham Young, in *Journal of Discourses*, 1:133.

14. "Who Designed the Temple?" *Deseret News Weekly*, April 23, 1892, 578.
15. Brigham Young, in *Journal of Discourses*, 1:133.
16. Francis M. Gibbons, *David O. McKay: Apostle to the World, Prophet of God* (Salt Lake City: Deseret Book, 1986), 342–43, 357–58; see also Joseph Lundstrom, "Angel Moroni Statue Lifted to Top of LA Temple Steeple," *Church News*, October 23, 1954, 4.
17. "Now Faces East," *Church News*, February 5, 1955, 13.
18. Holzapfel, Pike, and Seely, *Jehovah and the World of the Old Testament*, 224.
19. Gregory A. Prince and Wm. Robert Wright, *David O. McKay and the Rise of Modern Mormonism* (Salt Lake City: University of Utah Press, 2005), 270.
20. Emil Baer Fetzer, "The Sacred Twin Temples: Ogden Temple Provo Temple," in *Completed Writings of Emil Baer Fetzer*, by Emil Baer Fetzer and June Seyfarth Fetzer (n.p.: published by the authors, 2003), 4.
21. Boyd K. Packer, *The Holy Temple* (Salt Lake City: Bookcraft, 1980), 94.
22. Bible Dictionary, "Temple of Solomon," 782–83.
23. Bruce R. McConkie, *Mormon Doctrine*, 2nd ed. (Salt Lake City: Bookcraft, 1966), 103–4.
24. Talmage, *The House of the Lord*, 6–7.
25. See Richard O. Cowan, *Temples to Dot the Earth* (Springville, UT: Cedar Fort, 2011), 33–45.
26. "Provo Temple Dedicatory Prayer," *Church News*, February 12, 1972, 5.
27. Bible Dictionary, "Hosanna."
28. Lael J. Woodbury, "The Origin and Uses of the Sacred Hosanna Shout," *Sperry Lecture Series* (Provo, UT: Brigham Young University Press, 1975), 18–22.
29. Holzapfel, Pike, and Seely, *Jehovah and the World of the Old Testament*, 197.
30. Holzapfel, Pike, and Seely, *Jehovah and the World of the Old Testament*, 152.
31. Truman G. Madsen, "The Olive Press," *Ensign*, December 1982, 57–58.
32. See *Encyclopedia Judaica* 13 (Jerusalem, Israel: Keter Publishing House), s.v. "priestly vestments," 1063; see also Moshe Levine, *The Tabernacle: Its Structure and Utensils* (Tel Aviv: Soncino Press, 1969), 124–140.
33. James E. Faust, "Standing in Holy Places," *Ensign*, May 2005, 67.
34. Marion G. Romney, "Temples—the Gates to Heaven," *Ensign*, March 1971, 16.
35. Mark E. Petersen, *Moses, Man of Miracles*, (Salt Lake City: Deseret Book, 1977), 96.
36. William J. Hamblin and David Rolph Seely, *Solomon's Temple* (London: Thames & Hudson, 2007), 27–28.
37. Sidney B. Sperry, "Some Thoughts Concerning Ancient Temples and Their Functions," *Improvement Era*, November 1955, 814.
38. Brigham Young, in *Journal of Discourses*, 18:303.
39. Joseph Smith, *History of the Church of Jesus Christ of Latter-day Saints*, ed. B. H. Roberts, 2nd ed., rev. (Salt Lake City: Deseret Book, 1960), 4:211.
40. W. Cleon Skousen, *The Third Thousand Years* (Salt Lake City: Bookcraft, 1964), 302–3; W Cleon Skousen, *The Fourth Thousand Years* (Salt Lake City: Bookcraft, 1966), 222–25.

41. Joseph Fielding Smith, "Was Temple Work Done in the Days of the Old Prophets?" *Improvement Era*, November 1955, 794.

42. Smith, "Was Temple Work Done in the Days of the Old Prophets?," 794.

43. McConkie, *Mormon Doctrine*, 103–4.

44. Hugh Nibley, "The Idea of the Temple in History," *Millennial Star* 120, no. 8 (August 1958): 231; this article was republished in pamphlet form by BYU Press in 1963 under the title "What Is a Temple?"

45. G. Contenau, *Le Deluge Babylonien* (n.p., 1952) 246, quoted in Nibley, "The Idea of the Temple in History," 231.

46. Nibley, "The Idea of the Temple in History," 231.

47. *Oxford English Dictionary*, s.v. "Babel," accessed January 30, 2013, http://www.oed.com/view/Entry/14210?redirectedFrom=babel#eid.

48. *Oxford English Dictionary*, "mercy-seat," accessed March 18, 2013, http://www.oed.com/view/Entry/116715?redirectedFrom=mercy-seat#eid.

49. George Arthur Buttrick, ed., *The Interpreter's Dictionary of the Bible* (New York: Abingdon Press, 1962), 4:540.

50. *Oxford English Dictionary*, s.v. "holy of holies," accessed March 18, 2013, http://www.oed.com/view/Entry/87833?redirectedFrom=holy+of+holies#eid1477026.

51. For background information on the Dead Sea Scrolls and the Temple Scroll in particular, see James VanderKam, *The Dead Sea Scrolls Today*, rev. ed. (Grand Rapids, MI: William B. Eerdmans, 2010); see also Donald W. Parry, "The Dead Sea Scrolls Bible," *Studies in the Bible and Antiquity* 2 (2010): 1–27.

52. See Yigael Yadin, "The Temple Scroll," in David Noel Freedman, ed., *New Directions in Biblical Archaeology* (Garden City, NY: Doubleday, 1969), 156–66; Jacob Milgrom, "The Temple Scroll," *Biblical Archaeologist* 41, no. 13 (1978): 105–120.

53. Elder Robert D. Hales, "Coming to Ourselves: The Sacrament, the Temple, and Sacrifice in Service," *Ensign*, May 2012, 35.

Index

Aaron: anointing of, 26–27; rod of, 33, 222, 385; typifies Christ, 86; objects to Moses's power, 240; sees God, 272;
Aaronic high priest. *See* High priests
Abel, 158
Abihu, 126, 238, 272
Abinadi, 24
Abraham: bows down, 124; offers up Isaac, 126, 187; receives God's blessing, 136, 159; invokes blessing on God, 137; servant of, 142; speaks with God, 233
Abram, 140, 233
Adam: as priest, 41–43, 209; as God's representative, 44; transgression of, 54–56; blessing of, 136; as recipient of Abrahamic covenant-like promises, 158; expulsion of, 209
Adamgirkʻ, 58
Adnah, 145
Ahaz, 68, 371
Alma, 71, 128, 299
Altar: of incense, 15, 21; of burnt offering, 21; three levels of, 215n18; as representation of Yahweh, 226; construction of, 394
Alter, Robert, 291
Amidah, 338
Ammon, 296, 299
Ammonihah, 71
Amos, 31–32n19, 247, 272
Amoz, 371
Amun-Ra, 237
Angell, Truman O., 387, 388
Anna, 265

Anointing, 24–28, 259–60, 393
Antionah, 71
Aphek, 189
Aramaki, Alyssa, 293
Ark, of covenant: description of, 17–18, 385; law regarding, 57; absence of, 69; and cherubim, 72–73; as Israel's graven God, 190–91; as representation of Jesus' love, 397
Ark, of testimony. *See* Ark, of covenant
Asaph, 332
Asherah, 188
Atonement: spiritual rituals of, 20–21, 23, 28; of Jesus Christ, 71, 95, 398
Atonement, Day of: as day of access to Holy of Holies by high priest, 69–70, 398; priest garments on, 88; censing occurring on, 175; description of, 332
Axis mundi, 50

Baal, 111, 133, 187
Babel, Tower of, 160–61, 397
Babylon, 203–4, 210
Baker, Fred, 389
Balaam, 139
Balak, 139
Ball, Terry B., 377–78
Belial, 261
Baluʻah, 114
Barker, Margaret, 57, 271
Barton, Steven, 316
Basilica of the Agony, 5
Bednar, David A., 319
Begrich, J., 281–82

Ben Azra, 332
Benson, Ezra Taft, 133
Bethany, 2
Bethel, 394
Bethphage, 2
Blessing: nature of, 136; definition of, 137; given to God, 137, 141–47; etymology of, 138; by God in Old Testament, 138–39; on behalf of God, 140–41; modern English translations regarding, 147–48; as expression of praise, 148–50
Block, Daniel, 204, 206
Blood: in atonement rituals, 21–22, 23; in anointment rituals, 25–27
Boaz, 141
Booth, Ezra, 355
Bowing down: in Old Testament, 123–26; in temple context, 126–30
Breastplate, of judgment, 92, 94–96, 393
Brown, Matthew B., 92, 118
Brown, S. Kent, 51, 55, 303
Burton, R. Scott, 312, 351
Bush, burning, 51–52, 220, 235
Bushman, Richard Lyman, 285
Bytheway, John, 377–78

Caiaphas, 5
Cain, 160, 186
Calf, molten, 126
Canaan, 227, 231, 234
Candles, bundle of, 7
Center, sacred, 50–52
Chanting, 339–40
Chebar, 73
Cherubim: images of, in tabernacle, 15, 16, 71–72; as guardians, 16, 40, 71–73; as chariots of God, 16, 83n24; in Ezekiel's temple vision, 209; as personification of thundercloud, 252–53n30; nature of, 253–54n39
Church, St. Anne's, 2
Church of All Nations, 5
Church of St. Peter, 5
Church of the Holy Sepulcher, 7
Church of the Resurrection, 7
Clothing. *See* Garments, holy
Colors, significance of, 14–15, 93

Commandments, Ten, 123, 124–25, 225
Commentary on the Book of Mormon, 312–13
Covenant, Mosaic: establishment of, 223–26; renewal of, 227–29. *See also* Moses, law of
Cowdery, Oliver, 133
Craigie, Peter C., 283
Credentials, 76, 77

Dagon, 190
Damascus, 68
Daniel, 137
Darkness: symbolic meaning of, 6; in Exodus and Deuteronomy, 234–40; in Samuel, Psalms, and Kings, 240–41; in Isaiah, 241–44; in Ezekiel, 244–47; in Amos, 247; as indirect divine manifestation, 247–48
David: blesses God, 146; song of, 264; prepares place for temple, 273; psalms attributed to, 315; connects music with temple activity, 331; wishes to build a temple to God, 385–86
Day, John, 77
Dead Sea, 387
Dead Sea Scrolls: on Hannah's words, 258; textual connection of, to Psalms, 292; Thanksgiving Hymn of, 313; longest of, 399
Deity: as perceived in Mesopotamia, 33n26, 203; as perceived in ancient Egypt, 33n26, 222; response to coming into presence of, 116, 118; as object of blessing, 145, 153n19. *See also* God
Delitzsch, Franz, 278, 291
Donkey, 2, 4
Draper, Richard D., 55
Durham, John, 221–21, 226
Dynasty, Davidic, 264

Easter, and Old Testament, 1–11
Eden, Garden of: and temple, 39–41, 43, 45–46; expulsion from, 45, 209; layout of, 50–52; Alma's interpretation of, 71; stones found in, 95; as first temple, 158; allusions to, in Ezekiel's vision, 208–10

Egypt: attitude toward deity in, 33n26; ritual entry and credentials in, 76, 283–84; art of, 114–16; slavery in, 125; temple rituals of, 157–78; wealth and power of, 222
El, 111
Eli: blessing offered by, 140; role of temple in life of, 255, 260; contrast between Hannah and, 256, 260–63, 266–67; fall of, 190, 260–63
Elijah: contest of, with priests of Baal, 133, 249; as true worshipper, 188; as last holder of sealing power, 395
Elisabeth, 264–65
Elkanah: as recipient of blessing, 140; attitude of, toward Hannah's barrenness, 256; on Lord's word, 257; attitude of, toward children, 260
Emmaus, 9, 10
Enoch, 60, 158, 233
Entry, 75–76
Ephraim, 140
Ephrem, the Syrian, 53–54
Esarhaddon, 206
Eschatology, 350, 351–54
Ethiopia, 9
Euphrates, 41
Evangelists, 8
Eve, 54–56, 136
Eyring, Henry B., 226
Ezekiel: on cherubim, 16, 73, 83n24; prophesy of, 42; on Eden, 50; becomes a prophet, 176; temple vision of, 203–4; 386–90; on temple entry, 281

Faith, 10
Faithfulness, 130–32
Faust, James E., 393–94
Feast(s): of Unleavened Bread, 142, 276, 277; of Harvest, 276, 277; of Ingathering, 277
Fetzer, Emil B., 389–90
Fire, 219, 225, 235–49
First Temple. *See* Solomon's temple
Fishbane, Michael A., 50, 205, 209–10
Flame, 7, 7–8

Forgiveness: at the heart of temple sacrifice, 10; through Christ's sacrifice, 24; as part of God's nature, 228; as theme of psalms, 332–33
Freedman, David Noel, 221
Fretheim, Terence, 223, 228
Fruit, forbidden, 45, 55, 56–59

Gallicantu, 5
Galling, K., 281–82
Garden of Eden. *See* Eden, Garden of
Garments, holy: symbolism of, 86–87; linen coat, 87–89, 393; breeches, 89, 393; girdle; 89–90, 393; robe of ephod, 90–92; ephod, 92–93, 393; curious girdle of ephod, 93–94; breastplate of judgment and the Urim and Thummim, 92, 94–96, 393; miter and holy crown, 96–97
Gate, St. Stephen's, 2
Gatekeepers, 75–76, 79–80. *See also* Guardians
Gates, 76–79
Gee, John, 76, 284
Genesis: on Creation, 43; naming in, 43–44; divine presence in, 233–34
Genesis Rabbah, 42
Gesture(s), of praise: raising both hands in prayer as, 106–11; in ancient inscriptions, 111–12; in ancient Levantine art, 112–16; meaning of, 116–19
Gethsemane, Garden of, 4–6
Gideon, 248
Gihon, 41
Gileadi, Avraham, 377
Girdlestone, Robert, 292
Glory: as divine presence, 73, 232; Israel's loss of, 190; three degrees of, 215n18; as nature of God, 218; described as fire, 219; being too high to be revealed, 239; as having many connotations, 235, 242–47, 249
Go-Between, The, x, xi
God: presence of, in temple, ix, 270–90; associated with light, 8; nature of, 12–13, 228; physical presence of, 233–47;

indirect presence of, 247–48; temple as house of, 274–75. See also Deity; Jehovah; Light; Darkness
Goodness, 228
"Great Are the Words of Isaiah," 377
Gruber, Mayer, 110, 116
Guardians, 67, 70, 73–75. See also Gatekeepers
Gunkel, Hermann, 281–82, 316

Habakkuk, 106, 194
Hales, Robert D., 399
Hallo, William W., 156
Hallstrom, Donald L., 199
Hamath, 111
Hamblin, William J., 395
Hamilton, Victor P., 223
Hand, placement of, 19–22
Hands, laying on of, 20
Hannah: as seeker of God's blessing, 139; as recipient of Eli's blessing, 140; role of temple in life of, 255, 266; sorrow of, 256–57; joy of, 257–60; contrast between Eli and, 260–63, 266–67; long shadow of, 264–65
Hanukkhah, 338
Hapi, 222
Hardy, Grant, 314
Harmony, 343–44
Hartley, L. P., ix
Hays, Richard, 293
Herod, temple of, 229, 373. See also Second Temple
Hezekiah, 139, 142, 371
Hiram, 390
Holland, Jeffrey R., 291
Holy: terminology of, 22–23, levels of, 69, 70
Holy City. See Jerusalem
Holy Fire, 7
Holy garments. See Garments, holy
Holy of Holies: as tree of life, 16, 53; separated from Holy Place, 17; cloth surrounding, 17; access to, 69; as center of temple, 69, 70; in Ezekiel's vision, 208
Holy Place: contents of, 68–69; access to, 69
Holy Saturday, 7

Holy Thursday, 5
Holy Week, 2
Homily, 1, 86–98
Hophni, 189–90
Hosea, 197
Hosanna, 3, 392–93
Hospitality, 15–16, 31–32n19, 32n20

Idaho Falls (Idaho) Temple, 377
Inclusion, rite of. See Anointing
Independence, Missouri, 362, 376, 378
Induction, rite of. See Anointing
Interpreter's Bible, The, 387
Isaac, 126, 142, 159
Isaiah (book of): allusion to ritual renaming in, 38, 39; on false worship, 191, 192–94; on falsity of outward appearances, 195; on internal vs. external worship, 197–98; context of chapter 2 of, 371–74, 378–80; Latter-day Saint commentaries on chapter 2 of, 375–78
Isaiah (prophet): role of light in prophecy of, 8; Suffering Servant prophecy of, 9; importance of inner commitment in prophecy of, 199; absolving of, 176; Jerusalem temple prophecy of, 367–68; brief overview of life of, 371
Isaiah for Airheads, 377–78
Isaiah: Prophet, Seer, and Poet, 376–77
Isaiah Speaks to Modern Times, 377
Israel, ancient: Jehovah as God of, 4, 8; light in temples of, 6; temple rituals of, 18, 21; spiritual deliverance of, 10; place of worship for, 13; relationship between God and, 17–18, 23–24; significance of ark for, 189–90, 190–91; tendency of, to forget God, 194; attitude of, toward worship, 195–96; destruction of, 371
Israel (Jacob). See Jacob

Jacob: blesses other people, 140; receives temple covenant promises, 159–60; dreams of ladder reaching heaven, 234, 394; sees God, 234, 272; uses Psalm 95, 300–03
James, 137

Jared, 161
Jared, brother of, 194–95
Jehovah: as ancient Israel's God, 4, 8; nature of, 10; as represented to Moses, 52; as source of blessings and curses, 139; as both hidden and filled with light, 237, 238–39. *See also* God
Jeremiah: on repentance, 175; God puts words into mouth of, 176; prophesy of, 186, 199; on externality of worship, 191–92, 194, 196–97
Jerusalem: as only location of Holy Fire celebration, 7; during Babylonian captivity, 38; destruction of, 192; Isaiah's prophecy regarding great temple in, 367–68; salvation of, 368; Zion as alternative name for, 374
Jerusalem, temple in: orientation of, x; function of, 43; as symbol of center, 50; God's rejection of, 73; as place of God's dwelling, 274–75; pilgrimage to, 276–78
Jesus Christ: Second Coming of, 4; life of, 9; suffering of, 9; resurrection of, 9; message of, 10; character of, 10; atonement of, 71, 95, 398; as final gatekeeper, 80; on worship, 129. *See also* Light of Life; Triumphal Entry
Jethro, 146, 219
Joab, 141
Job, 139
John, Gospel of, 3–4
John, the Baptist, 10–11, 133
John, the Revelator, 199, 387
Jordan, 114
Joseph, 265
Josephus, 89, 90
Joshua, 177
Judah, 196–97, 368
Judgment: breastplate of, 92, 94–96, 393; not to be replaced by compassion, 228–29; in psalms, 353–55

Keel, Othmar, 116
Kirta, 111, 116–17, 118
Kirtland Temple: models for, ix; dedication of, ix, 391, 392; revelation on completion of, 284; God's instructions regarding building of, 285, 387
Korah, family of, 74, 332
Korihor, 129
Kraus, Hans-Joachim, 282
Kuntillet Ajrud, 145
Kuraszkiewicz, Kamil O., 174

Laban, 142
Laman, 187, 188–89, 314
Lamassu, 210–13
Lane, William L., 221
Larsen, David, 292
Laver, 26, 40, 394–95
Law: letter of, 18; spirit of, 18. *See also* Moses, law of
Lee, Harold B., 376
Lehi, 24, 314
Lemuel, 187, 188–89, 314
Levant, art of, 110, 112–16
Levenson, Jon, 207, 210
Levine, Baruch, 89
Levites: role of, in tabernacle, 19–20, 127, 332; seal a written covenant, 178; at dedication of Solomon's temple, 331
Life of Adam and Eve, 43
Light: symbolic meaning of, 6, 8; in Genesis, 233–34; in Exodus and Deuteronomy, 234–40; in Samuel, Psalms, and Kings, 240–41; in Isaiah, 241–44; in Ezekiel, 244–47; in Amos, 247; as indirect divine manifestation, 247–48
Light of Life, 6–8
Liminality: in ritual of worship, 14–18, 70; and movement between levels of holiness, 70, 336
Liturgy, 75–79; 184, 334–35
Los Angeles (California) Temple, 389
Lowenthal, David, xi
Ludlow, Victor L., 376–77
Luke, Gospel of: on Triumphal Entry, 2–3; on events in Gethsemane, 6; allusion to Hannah in, 264–65
Lundquist, John, 229

Maeser, Karl G., 229
Making Sense of Isaiah, 377–78
Malachi, 189
Mamre, 124
Manasseh, 140
Manna, 17–18, 301, 385
Mark, Gospel of: on Triumphal Entry, 3; on events in Gethsemane, 5–6
Mary, 265
Matthew, Gospel of: on Triumphal Entry, 3–4; on events in Gethsemane, 6
Maxwell, Neal A., 186, 198
McConkie, Bruce R., 97
McConkie, Joseph Fielding, 91
McKay, David O., 389
Mehu, 169
Melchizedek, 140, 159
Menkheperresonb, 114–15, 118
Menorah: function of, 15; as symbol of tree, 15, 40; as representation of burning bush, 51–52
Mercy: availability of God's, 10, 228; in psalms, 150, 286, 333; measure of, 195; atypical for ancient religious milieu, 227; cannot replace justice, 228
Mercy seat, 17, 72–73, 263–64, 397
Meribah, 301
Mesopotamia: iconography of, 31–32n19; perception of deity in, 33n26, 204; temple gateposts in, 63n30; protective spirits in, 71; art of, 106, 115–16; statues of, 119n3, 211–12; temples of, 203–4, 206, 207; ziggurats in, 397
Messiah: as Israel's God, 4, 10; signified by clothing, 88; anticipation for, 265; experiences of, revealed in Psalms, 329–30. *See also* Jehovah; Jesus Christ
Meter, 342–43
Meyers, Carol, 220
Micah, 197
Midrash Tanhuma, 50
Millet, Robert, 313
Milton, John, 398–399
Miracle: of Holy Fire, 7; power of Moses to perform, 222–23, 301; of forgiveness, 228; salvation of Jerusalem as, 368
Miriam, 240, 265

Mizpeh, 175
Moab, 108
Mordecai, 124
Moriah, Mount, 187, 274, 373
Mormon, 194
Moroni, 389
Moses: tabernacle of, 40, 391; vision of, 51; as recipient of Urim and Thummim, 94; gestures of, during prayer, 107; at Mount Sinai, 128; blesses God, 137; revelation of, on temple building and rituals, 160, 277; on externality of worship, 196; commission of, 219–23; rod of, 222
Moses, Book of: on Adam and Eve, 43, 60, 233; on Christ's divine nature, 98; on Zion as God's dwelling, 362
Moses, law of: rituals of, 18–24, 67; reception of, 25; slavery under, 125; worship practices of, 127; as determiner of worship patterns, 185–86; referred to as *torah*, 374–75. *See also* Covenant, Mosaic
Mount of Olives, 2, 4, 5
Mowinckel, Sigmund, 271, 278, 281–82

Nachmanides, 94
Nadab, 126, 238, 272
Naming, 43–45. *See also* Renaming
Naomi, 141, 146
Nature, of God, 13–14
Nauvoo Temple, ix–x, 388
Nebuchadnezzar, 68
Nehemiah, 109
Nephi (son of Helaman), 187
Nephi (son of Lehi): on law of Moses, 24; on serpent in Eden, 55; on all things as typifications of Jesus, 97; Psalm of, 303–4, 312–28; on application of Isaiah passages, 379
Nibley, Hugh W.: on capturing the essence of eternity, 57; on Satan's revealing of secrets, 59; on Nephi's thanksgiving hymn, 313; on Nephi's request to "walk in the path of the low valley," 322; on function of temple, 396
Nickerson, Matthew, 303, 316

Nile, 222
Nimrud, 114
Noah: ark of, 53–54; righteousness of, 54, 60; as recipient of God's blessing, 136; as son of God, 159; sacrifice of, 333–34
Numbers: on worship rites, 9–20, 22, 23; allusion to ritual renaming in, 38–39; on priests' role as temple guardians, 42–43; on Aaronic priestly blessing, 140
Nyman, Monte, 377

Obadyaw (Obadiah), 145
Odell, Margaret, 207
Offering: burnt, 19, 225; sin, 21, 24; peace, 25, 34n36, 225
Ogden (Utah) Temple, 389–90
Oil, 26, 393
Olah, 19
Old City, 2, 7
Old Kingdom, Egyptian, 157, 161
Old Testament: and Easter, 1–11; message of, 9
Olives, Mount of, 2, 4, 5
Opening of the Mouth, 162–65
Ordinances, sacred, 394–96
Otto, E., 163
Our Book of Mormon, 313

Packard, Dennis, 316
Packard, Sandra, 316
Packer, Boyd K., 198, 390
Palm Sunday, 2, 4
Paradise, 53
Parry, Donald W., 77, 376
Passover, 142, 276, 277
Past Is a Foreign Country, The, ix
Patriarch, of Jerusalem: Latin, 2; Greek Orthodox, 7–8
Patriarchs: earlier, 157, 158–60, 177–78; later, 159; preparations of, in temple, 176; worship rituals of, 394; held sealing power, 395
Paul: on developing the attributes of God, 98; on lifting both hands in prayer, 109–10; on serving, 125, 126; on tabernacle entry, 398
Peninnah, 256, 260

Pentateuch, 59–60
Pentecost, 265
Peter, 265
Petersen, Mark E., 395
Petition, 286–87
Pharaoh: in Egyptian art, 114–15, 118; God's instructions to Moses regarding, 128; blessed by Jacob, 140; first, 157, 161; headdress of, 222
Pharisees, 197
Phelps, W. W., 285
Philip, 9
Philistines, 34n38, 190–91
Phinehas, 189–90
Pilgrimage, 276–78. *See also* Holy Fire; Palm Sunday
Pison, 41
Plainchant, 339–40
Plainsong, 339, 340
Plates, of brass, 292, 296, 315
Porter, Bruce H., 43–44
Praise: symbolism in, 8; gestures of, 105–19; and petition, 286–87. *See also* Holy Fire; Triumphal Entry
Prayer: definition of, 105; Muslim, 117. *See also* Gesture(s), of praise
Presence, table of, 15
Preuss, Horst Dietrich, 124
Priest(s): as mediators, 41–42, 140–41; Adam as, 41–42, 210; as guardians of sanctuary, 42–43, 281–82; garments of, 86–98, 393–94; Malachi's accusations against, 189; prerogative of, 224
Prince of Peace, 4, 159
Pritchard, James, 106, 156
Prophecy: of Zechariah, 4; of Isaiah, 9, 367–68; of Ezekiel, 42; of Jeremiah, 186, 199; of Brigham Young, 389
Propp, William: on God's name, 221; on temporary celibacy, 224; on sound of ram's horn, 225; on repetition of God's name, 227
Provo (Utah) Temple, 389–90
Psalms: on importance of gatekeepers, 74; gates in book of, 76–79; on lifting both hands in prayer, 106, 108; on worship, 127; on people blessing God, 142–43,

148–49, 150; on seeing God in temple, 271–72, 275, 279–80; singing of Hallel, 277; and prerequisites for worship, 278–80, 282–83; New Testament allusions to, 291–92; Book of Mormon allusions to, 292–299; Jacob's use of Psalm 95, 300–03; of Old Testament and "Psalm of Nephi," 303–6, 312–28; formation of, 329–30; as forms of worship, 331–37; types of, 333–35; use of, in synagogues, 337–38, 339; in Christian churches, 338–39; early forms of performance of, 339–42; modern adaptations of, 342–44; Latter-day Saint use of, 344–45; JST changes in, 349–66

Pyramid Texts, Egyptian, 76, 157, 161–74

Qadosh, 22
Qidron, 2
Qidron Valley, 2, 5
Qodesh, 22

Rachel, 159
Reade, Julian, 211
Rebekah, 141
Red Sea, 223
Renaming, 36–37, 38–39, 46
Repentance, 10
Restoration: desired by Jews, 3; for Latter-day Saints, 18, 284; major reason for, 362
Resurrection, celebration of, 2, 7
Reynolds, George, 312–13
Reynolds, Noel B., 324
Rhodes, Michael D., 55
Ricks, Stephen D., 43–44
Ringgren, Helmer, 130–31
Ritual(s): pilgrimage as, ix; of hospitality, 15–16, 31–32n19; spiritual value of, 18–19; of burnt offering, 19; of atonement, 20–24; of anointing, 24–28; renaming as, 36–37, 38–39, 46; of entry in temple, 75–76, 76–77; overview of, in Egyptian temple, 157–58; sequence of, in earliest Egyptian temple, 161–74; Opening of the Mouth, 162–65; Egyptian vs. Old Testament temple, 174–78; cleansing, 281; threefold nature of, 335–36; of washing before service, 394–95

Rock, Dome of, 374
Rod: of Aaron, 33, 222, 385; of Moses, 222; of iron, 294, 297
Romney, Marion G., 394
Rosh Hashanah, 333
Rust, Richard Dilworth, 315–16
Ruth, 141
Ryder, Symonds, 355

Sabbath, 338
Sacrifice: temple, 10, 67, 394, 395; of Jesus Christ, 24, 398; willingness in, 200n5; ritual of, 335–36; law of, 384. *See also* Atonement; Offering
Salt Lake City, 378
Salt Lake Temple, 376, 378, 388–89
Salvation, 10
Samson, 248
Samuel, 191, 261–62; 263–64
Sanctuary: architecture and contents of, 15–16, 30–31n14; Eden as, 41, 50; veil of, 52–54; in Ezekiel's vision, 207–8; Mount Sinai as, 218; function of, 384; detailed specifications for, 385–90
Sarah, 124, 136, 15
Satan: as woman, 55; as serpent, 58; strategy of, 56; condemnation of, 58; as fowler, 352
Saul, 145, 333
Saxton, N. C., 362
Schaefer, Konrad, 313, 318
Schneider, H. W., 194
Seat, mercy. *See* Mercy seat
Second Coming, 4, 389
Second Temple (building): characteristics of, 68, 69; construction of, 331; in Jewish conversation, 373. *See also* Herod, temple of
Second Temple (period): late, 141, 152n15; priestly clothing in, 177; end of, 373
Seely, David R., 395
Sennacherib, 368
Sentinels. *See* Guardians

Septuagint: on values of temple and world, 75; worship gesture in, 109; on purpose of going to temple, 280
Seraphim: as guardian, 55; nature of, 55, 242, 252–53n30
Sermon. *See* Homily
Sermon on the Mount, 280–81
Serpent: as representation of Christ, 34n38, 55; in temple, 40, 45; multiple meanings of, 47n10; as Satan, 58; as symbol, 186–87; as sign, 222
Serving: in Old Testament, 123–26; in temple context, 126–30; preparation for, 393–94
Seth, 158
Sethe, Kurt Heinrich, 172
Shavuot, 338
Shiloh, 192, 263
Shires, Henry, 291
Simhat Torah, 338
Sin: as greatest enemy, 10; origins of, 60
Sinai: demarcations on, 53–54; as holy space, 70; God's appearance at, 70, 128, 218–31
Singing: antiphonal, 340, 341–42; responsorial, 340–41
Sjodahl, Janne M., 312–13
Skousen, W. Cleon, 377
Smith, Emma, 265
Smith, George Albert, 377
Smith, Joseph: and dedication of Kirtland Temple, ix, 392; reveals previously unknown doctrine, 36; on punishment, 59; on dispute, 86; John the Baptist's address to, 133; on entering Melchizedek order, 179n7; regarding seeing God in temple, 284–85; temple worship practices restored by, 345; translation of Psalms by, 349–66; encouragement against enemies in translation of Psalms by, 354–57; visions and revelations of, reflected in translation of Psalms, 357–58; desires and concerns of, reflected in translation of Psalms, 358–61; Kirtland Temple vision of, 387; Nauvoo Temple vision of, 388, 391; revelation of, regarding possession of sealing power, 395
Smith, Joseph Fielding, 375–76, 384, 396
Smith, Mark, 271, 287
Smoke. *See* Darkness
Solomon: gestures of, during prayer, 107; blesses God, 137, 146; receives instruction regarding building of temple, 386
Solomon's temple: architecture of, 30n6; interior of, 39; construction of, 41, 372, 385–86; dedication of, 41, 331, 391–92; materials and craftsmanship used for, 67, 390–91; compared with Second Temple, 68; cherubim in, 72; as realization of the Sinai experience, 229; as house of Lord, 372; destruction of, 372; function of chambers surrounding, 396; courts surrounding, 399
Son of David, 3
Sondrup, Steven P., 303, 316, 317
Space, sacred: borders of, 66; guardians of, 67, 70, division of, 69–70; vertical conceptualization of, 204–7; horizontal conceptualization of, 207–10
Sperry, Sidney B.: on Psalm of Nephi, 313, 316; on Ezekiel's vision, 386; on need for temples, 395
Statue, 210–11
St. George (Utah) Temple, 395
Stone, tablets of, 17–18, 25, 385
Stuart, Douglas K., 268n13
Suffering Servant, 132
Sukkot, 338
Sweeney, Marvin, 209
Symbolism: in worship, 8, 18, 395; in sacrificial acts, 23–24, 336; in anointing rituals, 25; of sacred center, 50–52; of temple and its officers, 75; of holy garments, 86–87, 97–98; of linen coat, 88; of girdle, 89–90; of robe of ephod, 90–92; of ephod, 92–93; of curious girdle of ephod, 94; of breastplate of judgment and the Urim and Thummim, 95–96; of miter and holy crown, 96–97
Synagogue, 337–38

Tabernacle: meaning of, ix; light in, 8; characteristics of, 13–14; symbolism of, 13–18; as liminal space, 14–16; of Moses, 385; layout of area surrounding, 398
Tablet. *See* Stone, tablets of
Talmage, James E., 386, 391, 397
Talmud, 332
Temple: significance of, 66; Kirtland, ix, 285, 387; Nauvoo, ix–x, 388; characteristics of, 13–14; as liminal space, 14; of ancient times, 37–38; and Garden of Eden, 39–41, 43, 45–46; in Jerusalem, 43, 73; heavenly vs. earthly, 57; architecture of, 67–69; Second, 68, 69; of Zerubbabel, 67; Egyptian, 157–78; Mesopotamian, 206, 207; as realization of the Sinai experience, 229; function of, 267n3, 332–33, 385; encounters of God in, 271–74; as place of God's dwelling, 274–75; pilgrimages to, 276–78; Third, 373; Salt Lake, 376, 378, 388–89; Idaho Falls (Idaho), 377; Los Angeles (California), 389; Ogden (Utah), 389–90; Provo (Utah), 389–90; dedications of, 391–93; preparation for serving in, 393–94; as place of revelation, 396–98. *See also* Jerusalem, temple in; Solomon's temple; admission in, 398–399
Temple Scroll, 399
Thebes, 114
Theophany: at Mount Sinai, 218–31; in Genesis, 233–34, 272; in Exodus and Deuteronomy, 234–40, 272; in Samuel, Psalms, and Kings, 240–41, 273; in Isaiah, 241–44, 272; in Ezekiel, 244–47; in Amos, 247, 272; in tabernacle, 270–71
Third Temple, 373
Thomas, Catherine, 56, 301
Tigris, 41
Tjy, 174
Torah, 335, 374–75
Tree of knowledge: location of, 49–50; as veil of the sanctuary, 52–54; partaking of, 56

Tree of life: guarded by cherubim, 16, 71; location of, 49–50, 52–53; partaking of, 56
Triumphal Entry, 2–4
Tuell, Steven, 205
Turner, Victor, 30n12, 70
Tyndale, William, 20
Tyre: king of, 42, 390; as Eden, 209

Ugarit, 111
Unas, 165
Understanding Isaiah, 376
Urim and Thummim, 94, 95

van Gennep, Arnold, 30n12, 70
Veil: in temple, 16–17, 72; passage through, 56–58
Vision: of Zechariah, 40; of Moses, 51–52; of Ezekiel, 203–4, 386–90; of Jacob, 394

Walters, Stanley D., 259
Washing: of Aaron and his sons, 26; as hospitality rite, 31–32n19; in Egyptian temple rituals, 162, 167, 171; in Israelite temple rituals, 176, 393; of clothes, 224; baptisms included in ancient rituals of, 396
Weeks, William, 388
Welch, John W., 316
Well, Samaritan woman at, 185
Wenham, Gordon J., 57
Widtsoe, John A., 384
Williams, Frederick G., 387
Woodall, Sam, 293
Worship: symbolism in, 8, 18; in temple context, 10, 126–30; aim of, 11, 184; definition of, 12; etymology of, 122; in Old Testament, 123–26; as way of life in terms of covenant faithfulness, 130–32; as way of life in example of servants, 132–34; ancient Egyptian rites of, 156–83; true, 158–60, 185–87; false, 160–61, 188–92; exteriority of, 192–96; inner-oriented type of, 196–98; of Saints, 198–99; requirements for, 278–84; Latter-day Saints requirements for, 284–85; power of music in,

330; psalms as forms of, 331–37; in synagogue, 337–38. *See also* Holy Fire; Triumphal Entry

Wycliffe, 398

Yahweh, 225

Yom Kippur. *See* Atonement, Day of

Young, Brigham: on splendor of God, 13; on temple entry, 80; on gathering up of all truths, 216–17n41; on Solomon's temple, 386; on Salt Lake Temple, 388–89; on temple ordinances of Old Testament times, 395

Younger, K. Lawson, 156

Zakkur, 111–12, 116–17

Zechariah: prophecy of, 4; vision of, 40

Zenos, 324, 327–28n38

Zerubbabel, temple of, 373. *See also* Second Temple (building)

Ziggurat, 203, 397

Zimmerly, Walter, 204, 208

Zion: Enoch's, 186, 361; as place or as people, 198; songs of, 334; as subject of psalms, 349, 352, 361–63; as alternative name for Jerusalem, 374

Zohar, The, 52